PROFESSIONAL WEB DESIGN
TECHNIQUES AND TEMPLATES
(CSS AND XHTML)
THIRD EDITION

CLINT ECCHER

Charles River Media
A part of Course Technology, Cengage Learning

COURSE TECHNOLOGY
CENGAGE Learning

Australia • Brazil • Japan • Korea • Mexico • Singapore • Spain • United Kingdom • United States

![COURSE TECHNOLOGY CENGAGE Learning]

**Professional Web Design
Techniques and Templates
(CSS and XHTML)
Third Edition**

Clint Eccher

**Publisher and General Manager,
Course Technology PTR:** Stacy L. Hiquet

Associate Director of Marketing:
Sarah Panella

Manager of Editorial Services:
Heather Talbot

Marketing Manager: Mark Hughes

Acquisitions Editor: Mitzi Koontz

Project Editor: Kim Benbow

Technical Reviewer: Eric Hunley

CRM Editorial Services Coordinator:
Jennifer Blaney

Copy Editor: Kim Benbow

Interior Layout Tech: Judith Littlefield

Cover Designer: Tyler Creative Services

CD-ROM Producer: Brandon Penticuff

Indexer: Katherine Stimson

Proofreader: Sandy Doell

For product information and technology assistance, contact us at
Cengage Learning Customer & Sales Support, 1-800-354-9706

For permission to use material from this text or product, submit all requests online at **cengage.com/permissions**
Further permissions questions can be emailed to
permissionrequest@cengage.com

Library of Congress Control Number: 2007939376
ISBN-13: 978-1-58450-567-9
ISBN-10: 1-58450-567-2

Course Technology
25 Thomson Place
Boston, MA 02210
USA

Cengage Learning is a leading provider of customized learning solutions with office locations around the globe, including Singapore, the United Kingdom, Australia, Mexico, Brazil, and Japan. Locate your local office at **international.cengage.com/region**

Cengage Learning products are represented in Canada by Nelson Education, Ltd.

For your lifelong learning solutions, visit **courseptr.com**
Visit our corporate website at **cengage.com**

Printed in Canada
3 4 5 6 7 11 10 09

Beanie,
You are filled with an incredibly high amount of ability
that becomes increasingly apparent every day.
I couldn't be prouder of the person you are and whom you're becoming.

CONTENTS

INTRODUCTION   **XV**

CHAPTER 1   **OVERVIEW OF WEB DEVELOPMENT TODAY**   **1**

Defining Web Design   2
Knowing the Seven Rules of Web Design   5
Understanding Three Web-Design Philosophies   7
Summary   15

CHAPTER 2   **DESIGNING FOR THE PAST, PRESENT, AND FUTURE**   **17**

Feeling Browser Pains   18
Incorporating Usage Statistics   20
Branching Pages   22
Understanding Bandwidth   23
Building on Previous Design Weaknesses   25
Summary   35

CHAPTER 3   **THINGS TO CONSIDER BEFORE BEGINNING**   **37**

Using Requirements   38
Knowing Bandwidth Requirements   43
Deciding on Resolution   45
Deciding on Color Depth   51
Designing for Scalability   54
Summary   58

CHAPTER 4	ENHANCING USABILITY	**59**
	Simplifying Architecture	60
	Creating Layout	63
	Developing Navigation	65
	Designing for Accessibility	70
	Designing for Content	70
	Summary	72
CHAPTER 5	GATHERING REQUIREMENTS AND CREATING A COMP	**73**
	Gathering and Basing a Site on Requirements	75
	Creating a Comp for the Client	78
	Receiving a Decision on the Chosen Comp and Making Edits	87
	Summary	88
CHAPTER 6	WHAT IS NEEDED TO BUILD MORTISED SITES	**89**
	Understanding the Concept of Mortising Images	90
	Understanding XHTML	99
	Understanding Graphics	101
	Understanding CSS	101
	Block- and Inline-Level Tags	105
	Understanding Include Files	109
	Summary	109
CHAPTER 7	UNDERSTANDING GRAPHICS	**111**
	Learning about Vector and Bitmap Images	112
	Learning about JPGs and GIFs	114
	Misusing Image Formats	126
	Understanding Graphics/Compression Software	132
	Summary	133
CHAPTER 8	UNDERSTANDING THE BASICS OF CREATING MORTISED CSS DESIGNS	**135**
	CSS-Based Design versus XHTML Table Design	136
	Understanding the Box Model	149
	When to Use Tables	154
	Validating Code	154
	Testing Designs in Various Browsers	155
	Summary	156

CHAPTER 9   **CASE STUDY: LOW-CONTENT CSS DESIGN**   **157**

Understanding the Design's Structure   158
Building the Structure   163
Constructing Second-Level Pages   182
Summary   196

CHAPTER 10   **CASE STUDY: MEDIUM-CONTENT CSS DESIGN**   **197**

Understanding the Design's Structure   198
Building the Structure   201
Constructing Second-Level Pages   224
Constructing a Second-Level Page with Two Columns   230
Summary   235

CHAPTER 11   **CASE STUDY: HIGH-CONTENT CSS DESIGN**   **237**

Understanding the Design's Structure   238
Building the Structure   242
Constructing Second-Level Pages   267
Summary   286

CHAPTER 12   **CASE STUDY: FULL-HEIGHT THREE-COLUMN LAYOUT**   **287**

Understanding the Design's Structure   288
Building the Structure   292
Constructing Second-Level Pages   307
Summary   307

CHAPTER 13   **CASE STUDY: BACKGROUND-BASED DESIGN**   **309**

Understanding the Design's Structure   310
Building the Structure   314
Constructing Second-Level Pages   331
Summary   332

CHAPTER 14   **CASE STUDY: A CSS FORM**   **333**

Understanding the Form's Structure   334
Explaining the Style Sheet Used for the Form   336
Building the Form Row by Row   338
Summary   349

CHAPTER 15   **CASE STUDY: LOW-CONTENT XHTML TEMPLATE**   **351**

Creating the Design for a Low Amount of Content   352
Understanding the Strengths and Weaknesses of the Chosen Design   352
Adding Guides and Slices   354
Creating the Parent Table   355
Creating and Linking the Style Sheet   357
Creating the Menu Table   357
Adding an Image to the Center Column   360
Creating the Content (Right-Area) Table   361
Creating the Footer Information   365
Summary   367

CHAPTER 16   **TIPS AND TECHNIQUES**   **369**

Tantek or Box Model Hack   370
Naming Rules and Properties Correctly   374
Removing Body Margins and Padding   378
Creating the Framework for a Fixed-Width CSS Design   379
Taking Into Account Increasing and Decreasing Column Heights   388
Centering a Fixed-Width Design   390
Creating a Liquid Design   394
Rendering the <HR /> Tag Consistently   395
Creating a Line Without the <HR /> Tag   397
Using Background Images as Design Elements   398
Coding CSS Mouseovers   399
Using JavaScript Dropdown Menus   400
Remembering the Order of Margin and Padding Shortcuts   401
Using the Border and Background Properties for Troubleshooting   402
Commenting Out Code for Troubleshooting   405
Using Unique Naming Conventions   406
Controlling the Margins in <FORM> Tags   406
Avoiding Horizontal Scrollbars   409
Using CSS Shortcuts   409
Understanding Font Units   409
Using Globally Driven <SPAN> and <DIV> Tags for Printing Purposes   410
Using Non-graphical Elements When Designing Rebrandable Sites   410
Including Hidden <DIV> Tags for Future Use   412
Positioning the line-height Property Correctly   413
Testing Continually and Consistently   413
Creating Source Image Files That Can Be Easily Customized and Resaved 414
Breaking Out Sections of Source Image Files   414

	Creating Smart Navigation	416
	Reusing Images	417
	Indenting and Commenting Code	420
	Removing Spaces and Comments	420
	Summary	421
CHAPTER 17	**CUSTOMIZING THE DESIGNS INCLUDED IN THIS BOOK**	**423**
	Steps to Customizing a Template	424
	Photoshop Tutorials	430
	Summary	443
APPENDIX	**TEMPLATES INCLUDED ON THE CD**	**445**
	Designs – Third Edition Folder	447
	Designs – First Edition Folder	657
	Summary	726

ACKNOWLEDGMENTS

Joe and Nancy Eccher—For all the editing, photography, and support that is necessary to make such a book possible.

Lori and Justin Discoe—For all the truly creative ways to look at life, especially through the lens.

Ron Stern—For all the high-caliber professional photography that makes my job so much easier.

Daniel Yu—To the guy who started me down the Web road so many years ago. It's hard to believe this journey all started with the Lynx browser. :-)

Kim Benbow—For your amazingly attentive and critical editing eyes. Your ability to question the big picture all the way down to the minutia has been incredibly impressive and appreciated.

For all those who helped contribute to this book—Chelsea Miller, Brian Shaver, Donna Sue Mastalka, Chris Manguso, Gary Hixon, Sarah Bashore, Mike Renfro, Stu Nicholls, Brett Tatman, and Jon Mullett.

For all those at the Pulse who make working out so easy and enjoyable—Laury, Michelle, Derrick and Tara, Sonja, Karen, Lindsey, Michael, Tim and Kathy, Courtney, Megan, Mike, Jim, Stacey, Ruthie, Rick, Jerry, Sarah, Afton, Natalie, Tyson, Paul, Dominick, Jay, Mark, Kevin, Kaili, Maako, and Noriko.

For all those at Catalyst and La Dolce Vita who provide the right amount of chai and energy—Fade and Ben, Izzy, Jamison, Patrick, Shannon and Brian, Yonky, Molly, G, Frank, Sue, Rita, Sara, Paolo, Brina, and Lee.

For all of A5design's clients over the years—without you, none of this would have occurred.

ABOUT THE AUTHOR

Clint Eccher is an award-winning Web designer with more than 13 years of experience designing and developing professional Web sites. He is the owner of A5design, a Web design company that not only subcontracts to various marketing, advertising, and IT organizations, but also is commissioned by Fortune 500 companies, local and national nonprofit organizations, and small businesses for Web design and/or development. In addition to authoring *Professional Web Design: Techniques and Templates (CSS and XHTML), Third Edition*, which has been published in five different languages, he is also the author of *Advanced Professional Web Design: Techniques and Templates (CSS and XHTML)*. Eccher lives and works in Fort Collins, Colorado.

INTRODUCTION

The methods and processes in which professional Web sites are created have not changed much since the first edition of this book. Designers still need to understand requirements, realize the technical pros and cons of layouts, create comps, save images using the correct file types, and test sites similarly to how it's been done for more than a decade. Some of the technical ways in which these processes are accomplished, however, has changed.

Probably the most significant change that has occurred during this time is how the framework of sites is built. Table-based HTML designs (Hypertext Markup Language), now XHTML (Extensible Hypertext Markup Language) designs, have been the staple for laying out Web sites for many years. This method, however, has changed, in favor of Cascading Style Sheet (CSS)-based designs. In other words, the content is primarily laid out using style sheets, which provides more overall control using less code. This change in coding was the driving force behind replacing a large portion of this book with new methods, tips, case studies, and templates that were included in the first two editions.

The goal of *Professional Web Design: Techniques and Templates (CSS and XHTML), Third Edition* is still to educate beginning-to-intermediate Web designers on the various issues involved with Web design. This is accomplished through general discussion, case studies, and specific tips and techniques. There are many ways in which designers today create sites. What is included in this book is how A5design, the company owned by the author, has satisfied its clients since the late 1990s.

This book is written in the least technical terms possible. While some technical terminology is always going to be necessary, a lot of it has been simplified, or even excluded, to help the reader more quickly understand the general concepts and then apply them in an effective, quick manner. The premise that learning is much easier once the reader gets some momentum going is accomplished by less tripping over technical terminology.

That's not to say this book doesn't deal with specific issues designers will most likely run into—it does. Many of the tips and techniques included in the book will eventually be experienced by the reader if he or she does enough Web design.

The tips and techniques included in this book come from many years of troubleshooting, pitfalls, and flat-out stupid mistakes. They have been fine-tuned, however, through creative solutions and technical common sense. After having read through this book, the reader will have a strong understanding of how and what it takes to create a highly professional Web site.

OVERVIEW OF WEB DEVELOPMENT TODAY

In This Chapter

- Defining Web Design
- Knowing the Seven Rules of Web Design
- Understanding Three Web-Design Philosophies

Web design is still relatively new compared to many other industries. While it may be considerably more technologically advanced than it was more than a decade ago, the industry still has issues to address, such as browser functionality and consistency, high-bandwidth availability, search-engine compatibility, and site aesthetics. Depending on which designer you ask, the industry will have reached Nirvana either when Web sites for all users are loaded with multimedia functionality or when they are stripped of all "excess" graphics and functionality.

It's hard to know where the industry is headed. However, one thing's certain: the majority of Web designers will still have to work with currently available technologies, rather than those that are overly progressive, as well as methods of Web design to best communicate the intended information. Oddly enough, as the industry has evolved, the benchmark for aesthetic designs has not always taken steps forward. While there have been some fads that have required designers to create more aesthetically appealing designs, some of the latest have not pushed the abilities of many designers. The quality of Web design, in many cases, has actually taken a step backward. There are two main reasons for this. One, whether it's because of the designer's drive or the client's wishes, there is a mentality of playing it safe and designing sites exactly as most of the other sites are designed, which makes everything look the same. And, two, with the advent of CSS-driven design, many designer's coding skills have regressed because of the change from table-driven layout to CSS-driven layout. While it is up to the designers and clients to address the former, this book addresses the latter, showing designers how to create sites using CSS that are just as visually advanced as they used to be with table-driven layouts. One of the main reasons for this is because this book offers a simple, unique way of creating a three-column full-height design, which is fully explained later in the book.

For the designer who produces highly professional, creative work, the market still provides many many opportunities. To be able to produce such sites, though, a Web designer needs to have a thorough understanding of the basics of Web design.

DEFINING WEB DESIGN

Web design is an ambiguous term. Web professionals define it differently all the time. While one might define it as programming the back-end functionality of a site, another might define design as the development of the front-end look and feel that gives a sense of the company or individual it represents. The truth of the matter is, both of these definitions are correct.

In the "older" days of graphical Web development (circa 1995), Web design meant creating static HTML (Hypertext Markup Language) pages with linked text and graphics. All content and functionality was hard coded in each page. Today's environment, however, involves creating dynamic Web sites that use other programming languages, for example, .NET, JSP (JavaServer Pages), and ColdFusion, to interact with databases and browsers, along with XHTML (Extensible Hypertext Markup Language) pages, graphics, and CSS (Cascading Style Sheets).

A well-rounded Web designer, therefore, needs to understand many of the technical and artistic aspects of Web design, though not necessarily needing to specialize in both. Today's technical standards, in many instances, involve creating dynamic database-driven sites that are versatile, scalable, efficient, and search-engine friendly. However, if such sites consist only of unformatted pages with black text on white screens, they will not communicate as effectively to the majority of their audiences. On the other hand, if a site uses the latest graphic design methods but consists of static pages that are difficult to update, or that do not enhance or simplify the user's experience, then the site is going to be more inflexible and, depending on the site's requirements, impractical.

Many of the technical and artistic issues that Web designers should consider are discussed throughout this book. However, here are a few examples and explanations of what a Web designer must consider before commencing.

Figure 1.1 is an example of a design that uses back-end programming. It is easy to update. Unfortunately, it employs little artistic design to make the site attractive to most users.

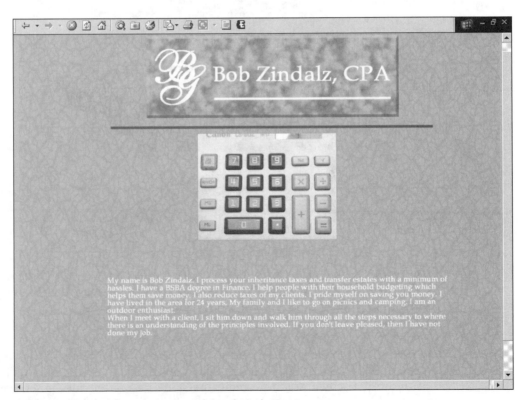

FIGURE 1.1   Site that focuses more on the technical aspects.

Figure 1.2 is an example of the opposite situation. It is graphically appealing, but this design cannot be easily maintained or expanded because the page is almost entirely made up of graphics. Such a design not only requires the designer to rework the code but also do much more graphics work.

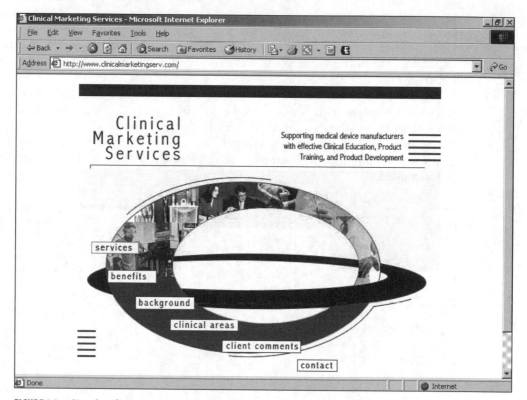

FIGURE 1.2   Site that focuses more on aesthetic aspects.

Figure 1.3, though, is an example of a nice blending of the two disciplines. Not only is it graphically appealing, but it is also a database-driven site that allows for large amounts of text to be added without compromising the layout of the design when extended vertically.

For example, in Figure 1.3, the color below the cow on the left and the colors below the photos on the right repeat themselves no matter how long the page runs, while the photos stay in their respective positions. This allows the original look and feel of the initial screen area to remain the same no matter how much content is added. The site also makes use of images in their most optimal formats and compression, which keeps the file sizes small and the download times fast.

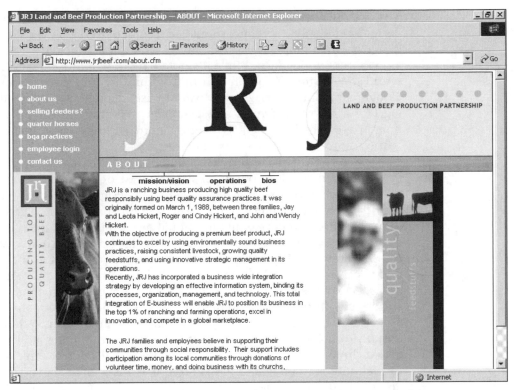

FIGURE 1.3 Web site that brings together both aesthetic and technical aspects of design. Copyright © 2002 by JRJ Land and Beef Production Partnership. All rights reserved.

KNOWING THE SEVEN RULES OF WEB DESIGN

There are seven basic rules that, if followed, will help a beginning or intermediate designer become a professional:

1. **Just because you can does not mean you should**—Web technology offers many options and tools to build Web sites; however, just because the technology is there does not mean a designer should use that technology just for the sake of using it. Many times, adding technology can impede the performance of a site and/or irritate users into leaving the site. An example of this is using Flash to animate a logo of a site. While the company may want to show its new logo, the user, most likely, does not care or want to see it move every time she hits a page. When using a new technology, the important question a designer should ask is, "Does the technology add value to the site or is it being added strictly as a novelty?"

2. **There is almost always an exception**—There rarely are absolutes in Web design. A designer, therefore, should be careful of ruling out a technology or design method simply because it did not work for another site. Take, for example, the rotating logo. While it's not going to work for 99 percent of the world's Web sites, a corporation that is running an extremely expensive global rebranding campaign may want to use animation to show off its new logo for a month or two. It may even elect to show the animation on the home page, which probably is a better approach to showing the new image without forcing it on the user too frequently.

3. **Users are the ultimate judge**—Opinions are never lacking when a site is in the design process. While an experienced designer may think a site should function or appear a certain way, the designer's boss may think differently. The bottom line is that the users are the bottom line. The site needs to make sense to them, so the site should be designed with them in mind.

4. **Crossover experience is something a designer needs to always strive for**—Professional Web design requires understanding of the user's needs, regardless of how the designer personally believes the aesthetic and technical aspects of the site should be designed. Whatever the issue may be, a designer benefits from a comprehensive understanding of the many technical aspects of the site's design. A perfect example is that of forms. While it is important to make a form easy to use and attractive, the designer must also take technical considerations into mind. One pitfall a non-technical designer can fall into is creating a form field that may be layered above a JavaScript down menu when expanded.

5. **Humility is the best approach**—Because there are so many intricacies of Web design, there are always going to be designers with more attractive sites or newer technology or who use technology in a more creative way. If a designer does not let pride get in his way, learning from others can strengthen his skills.

6. **It is impossible to please everyone**—Whether it is the estimated 1.1 billion Web users around the world or three people in the office, a design is never going to make everyone happy. Everyone has an opinion. However, there is a fine line between making the majority happy and attempting to create a site that will actually be effective in properly communicating. A designer sometimes should take a stand to maintain certain functional and aesthetic aspects of a design.

7. **Try to stay on top of specifications and standards**—Web specifications and standards are constantly changing and will continue to do so. The designer, however, should have a basic understanding of the latest techniques, which will affect future work. CSS-driven Web design, is one such example, which is what the revision of this book explains. While the first edition explained how to create table-driven Web designs, this edition now focuses on creating sites that enable CSS position and style elements.

UNDERSTANDING THREE WEB-DESIGN PHILOSOPHIES

One helpful way of understanding the more than 100 million Web sites in the world today is to divide them into three distinct philosophies: usability, multimedia, and mortised. Depending on the designer, any of the three philosophies does the best job of satisfying the goal of a Web site, which is to communicate to the user in the most effective manner. While multimedia and usability represent the proverbial argument between form and function, respectively, mortising represents the coming together of these two philosophies.

When considering the pros and cons of each philosophy, a designer should take into account how each philosophy addresses the following three factors of any site:

1. **Aesthetics**—How professional is the look and feel of the site? Is it is consistent with the desired branding of the business or individual?
2. **Usability**—How quickly and easily can a user find and process information while being able to perform necessary tasks?
3. **Functionality**—Programming should enable the functional aspects of the site, such as forms and database-driven content.

Because of the vast array of hardware, software, and users on the Internet, no one philosophy is the perfect answer for everyone. However, by understanding each philosophy and its strengths and weaknesses, a designer can have a clear understanding of which one will best address the requirements of a particular site.

Usability Philosophy

Usability is a universal term that can be used when describing any site. It represents the ease with which the user can find and process information, as well as perform certain tasks.

The philosophy of usability takes this term to its most far-reaching scope. It attempts to make sites easily usable for all members of their Internet audience.

One method used to accomplish this goal is to strip down a site to its bare essentials, which includes the majority, if not all, of its images. Some followers of the usability philosophy consider graphics a complication rather than facilitation of the communication process. They also believe in designing sites that all browsers can view.

To better illustrate the philosophy of usability, Figure 1.4 is an example of such a site. Notice that there is only HTML-generated color and no images. There is very little on this site that can be misconstrued by different browsers.

Pros and Cons

As with any issue in life, there are always people with divergent views. Web design is no exception. The philosophy of usability is at the most conservative side of the design spectrum, which, obviously, is going to have its detractors. Not all designers agree with the philosophy because of the simplicity of the designs, which resemble

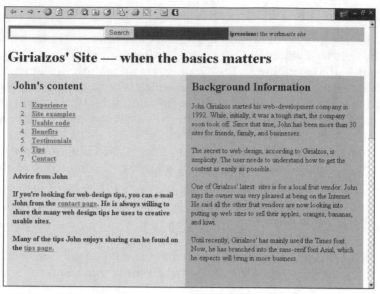

FIGURE 1.4   Site based on the usability philosophy.

sites created in the 1990s. Visual usability, however, is only one area that this philosophy addresses. There are also other technical and non-technical aspects that the usability philosophy takes into account. In accordance with the fourth rule of Web design, there are several practical points designers can and should take into consideration when designing:

1. Download time should always be as minimal as possible.
2. Navigation should be intuitive.
3. Consistent Web terminology and metaphors, such as the shopping cart system, should be used (unless there is a valid reason for an exception).
4. Writing should be clear and concise to expedite use.
5. Sites should always be tested by a variety of users in a variety of browser environments.
6. Accessibility for users with disabilities should be accounted for.

Anyone who has surfed the Internet would agree that finding information should be as easy as possible. No one likes to spend valuable time clicking all over a site to find a phone number or waste time with hyperlinks that do not go anywhere. This basis of the usability philosophy cannot be disputed for 99.9 percent of the world's sites.

One of the perceptions of usability, however, is to appeal to everyone. This is simply not true. The sixth rule of Web design is that it is impossible to please everyone. As the number of users increases, a design quickly becomes "too complicated," "too simple," "too colorful," "too short," "too long," "too wild," or "too conservative," depending on the user.

The philosophy advocates limiting graphics to increase mass appeal. Graphics, however, many times increase the usability of a site in four ways:

1. **The impression of a site, thus the identity of a business or individual, is first judged visually**—Most people form an immediate opinion when first coming to a site, if nothing more than at the subconscious level. If the site appears to be a five-minute design by an amateur, a user is going to question the professionalism and credibility of the business or individual and will very likely leave the site. The designer in Figure 1.5 valued aesthetics more than the designer of the site in Figure 1.4. Granted, the concept behind the site in Figure 1.4 is simplicity; however, the designer could have been more creative and used at least a couple of small 5-KB to 10-KB images to drastically improve the look of the site without noticeably increasing the download time.

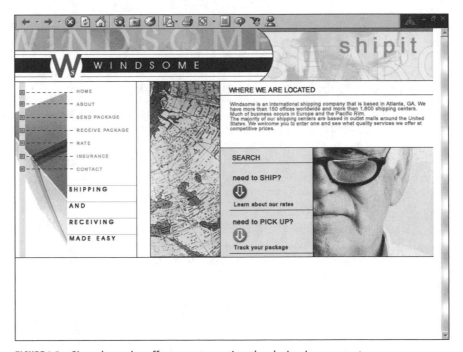

FIGURE 1.5   Site where the effort spent creating the design is apparent.

2. **The brain processes images more quickly than it does text**—Many traffic signs, called *ideograms*, are designed for quick, initial recognition of motor vehicle warnings, laws, and conditions. The reason is that the brain can process a sign, such as that in Figure 1.6, exponentially faster than if the sign were to read, "It is illegal to make a left-hand turn at this intersection."

FIGURE 1.6   Ideogram that is more quickly processed by the brain than text.

Web images work in the same way; they reduce the frustration of a user who is forced to read when a simple image will do. When a user looks at Figure 1.5, it is fairly obvious the site has something to do with shipping or a related industry. Whereas with Figure 1.4 there are no images cluing the user into the design's meaning. The user, therefore, has to spend time reading the page.

3. **Graphics, along with color, help lead a person's eye**—Similar to using an image to help a user quickly understand a concept, graphics and colors can be used to help lead a user's eye to where the designer intended. This is useful when a designer has prioritized content that the user should see first. The site in Figure 1.5 uses colored buttons to catch the viewer's eye. The buttons are shortcuts to areas of the site that the two target audiences most likely come for: to ship or to pick up a shipment. The site in Figure 1.4 is split into two sides with no dominant color or images, leaving the user's eyes floating.

 When designing for accessibility, a designer should not rely solely on color because of color blindness.

4. **Graphic technology can enhance functionality**—Immersive imagery (360-degree photos) is one example of technology that designers can use in certain instances to improve a user's experience and cognition. If a user were looking to spend $5,000 on a vacation to Mexico and wanted to view the rooms of hotels, would it be better to read about the rooms or look completely around them? If a picture is worth a thousand words, the entire page of Figure 1.4 would come up short when describing one room; the homepage, which stretches considerably farther than the figure depicts, has fewer than 900 words. It should be noted that in this example, immersive photos do require a longer download time. To make the site applicable to users with slow Internet connections, a designer should also provide traditional photographs as an alternative.

Multimedia Philosophy

On the other end of the design spectrum from the usability philosophy is the multimedia philosophy. Multimedia sites use animation, audio, and video to create more interactive sites, such as the one shown in Figure 1.7, which changes the image with different breeds of dogs, while the site plays an upbeat tempo in the background. Many use vector-based graphics, which can be compressed smaller than bitmap images and generally resized without much degradation of the images, unlike bitmap images.

Many of these multimedia sites are called Flash sites; they are created with Adobe's Flash animation software. Depending on the increasing prevalence of broadband and where technology heads in the future, such sites could play a more dominant role on the Internet.

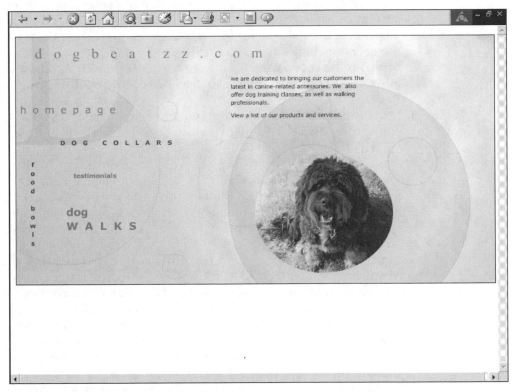

FIGURE 1.7   Site based on the multimedia philosophy.

Pros and Cons

While many multimedia designers are still learning how to effectively design using this type of functionality, it is certainly an effective way to communicate via the Web. Some of the advantages of multimedia design include the following:

1. Much of the technology is vector- and mathematics-based image technology, which allows for higher compression and the ability to resize images without much loss of image quality.
2. It has a similar learning curve to XHTML and CSS. Much basic layout of simple content on a page can be reasonably easy to learn with programs like Flash. However, advanced capabilities of these programs can, in fact, be a challenge.
3. It communicates multidimensionally with graphics, animation, and audio.

The technology for multimedia sites, unfortunately, is not only a strength but also a weakness. Multimedia sites are still not practical for the majority of Internet users for several reasons:

1. **Browsers must have a plug-in for the user to view the graphics or site**—Over the past several years, this issue has become increasingly unimportant to almost non-existent with the ease of adding and updating such plug-ins. It still should be at least a consideration whether the user will have the necessary plug-in or none at all.
2. **Multimedia software still does not integrate with databases as easily as existing Web technology, such as .NET, Cold Fusion, and JavaServer Pages.**
3. **Multimedia sites work well with vector-based images, but they sometimes do not add many compression benefits for bitmap images, such as GIFs.**
4. **Multimedia sites are usually more cost-prohibitive to the designer and to the client**—In addition to graphics software, a designer needs animation and, possibly, audio editing software to create a multimedia site, depending on the site's requirements. Because Flash sites generally aren't as easy to update as XHTML sites, it usually takes more time and costs more to do so.
5. **Many designers have yet to learn discretion when using the power of multimedia software**—Although vector-based images compress well, the file sizes found on many multimedia sites are still considerably larger compared to traditional Web sites. This is because designers often use too much animation, graphics, and audio, which increases the download time of a page and which isn't always apparent when a user has broadband access. This goes back to Rule 1: just because you can does not mean you should. The issue is not only with the download time of a page. It is also frustrating, for example, for users to come to a site where they have to see the same intro animation every time they visit. It should not be required to have to click past an intro to get into the site.

 Because users may view a site at work, it is usually prudent to default with the sound off in an animation.

Mortised Philosophy

David Siegel, in his best-selling book *Creating Killer Web Sites* (Hayden Books, 1997), describes *mortising* as piecing two images together using a table. Mortising, however, can be a much broader term, which represents the philosophy of piecing together graphics, text, and functionality, such as forms, to build striking, graphically appealing sites that are fast, highly usable, and flexible.

Such sites bring together the best of both usability and multimedia worlds, combining them into professional designs that can be viewed by nearly all of today's Web users (see Figure 1.8). Mortising not only complements the functionality of a site, but it also enables designers to use techniques that the graphic design industry has spent decades perfecting without sacrificing download time.

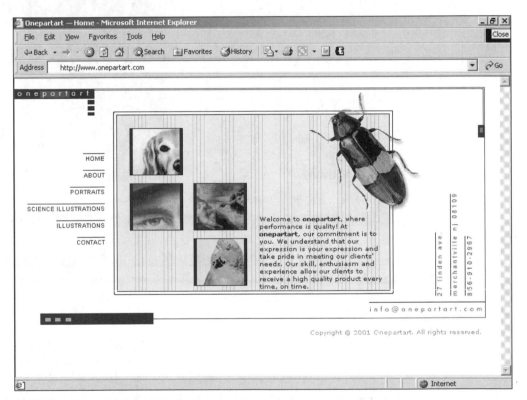

FIGURE 1.8   Example of a mortised site. Copyright © 2002 by Onepartart. All rights reserved.

Just because a site looks appealing does not necessarily make it a mortised site. Mortised sites are about more than aesthetics. Many WYSIWYG (What You See Is What You Get) HTML editors, such as Microsoft's Office SharePoint Designer (which has replaced FrontPage) and Adobe's Dreamweaver, allow a novice to create very appealing sites. Mortised sites, however, are knowledge-driven rather than purely software-driven. This difference enables a designer to use XHTML, CSS, and images in creative ways that many times produce faster, more customized designs with less code. If, for example, Figure 1.9 were created in a WYSIWYG editor, the download file size could be as large as 70 to 80 KB. Using XHTML and images creatively, the entire home page is reduced to under 35 KB.

FIGURE 1.9   Site based on the mortised philosophy. Copyright © 2007 colo-insurance.com. All rights reserved.

Pros and Cons

While there is no "perfect" type of Web design, mortised sites are, for many designers, the best current solution for effectively communicating to the largest possible audience on the Web. Following are some of the pros of the philosophy:

1. **Per Andre Agassi, "Image is everything"**—Mortised sites can be striking, fast, and highly usable, allowing clients to create powerful and lasting first impressions on their users.
2. **Because they can use more graphics and less text, the user can more quickly understand concepts, ideas, and emotions used in designs**— The use of graphics also allows designers to better take advantage of traditional, time-tested graphic design aspects, including layout, color theory, and typography.

3. **Mortised sites not only work with static Web pages but also with dynamic database-driven sites**—Because they use existing XHTML and CSS technology, such sites can be easily customized to work with Microsoft .NET, Adobe ColdFusion technology, PHP technology, or Java technology, specifically JavaServer Pages.

4. **The learning curve to build such sites is extremely low for experienced Web designers because the technology is not new**—Methods used in this book employ simple, creative, and practical ways to use XHTML and CSS in exciting, useful ways.

5. **While they do not have to be, mortised sites can be easily designed to be scalable, database-driven sites**—If a client or business wants to add three sections to a Web site, a well-designed mortised site can be easily expanded.

6. **Mortised sites are modular**—This enables a designer to take advantage of various design options, such as Flash, in selected portions of a page. For example, a designer may not want to create an entire site in Flash but only want an advertisement of a new product in the center of the page. With a mortised site, adding such an element is easy when the site is designed with such flexibility in mind.

While mortised sites satisfy the site requirements of the majority of the world's Web sites, they are not the complete answer. They still face the same issues that usability and multimedia sites must contend with:

1. Similar to multimedia sites, mortised sites require plug-ins to use some of their elements, such as animation and, in some cases, audio.

2. Mortised sites are limited by the knowledge of the designer. A designer can create a similar-looking site in a WYSIWYG editor, but such software is always going to limit the designer's work in one way or the other if he doesn't fully understand what goes on "under the hood."

SUMMARY

There are seven rules of Web design that help a beginner to develop into a professional designer: just because you can does not mean you should, there is almost always an exception, users are the ultimate judge, crossover experience is something a designer should always strive for, humility is the best approach, it is impossible to please everyone, and try to stay on top of specifications and standards. Each of these rules is applicable in certain instances when building a site.

The goal of a Web site is to most effectively communicate to the largest audience possible. Any of these three design philosophies can be used to accomplish this goal: usability, multimedia, and mortised. Mortised sites, however, typically offer the best of both worlds, which is why they are continually sought after by clients.

2

DESIGNING FOR THE PAST, PRESENT, AND FUTURE

In This Chapter

- Feeling Browser Pains
- Incorporating Usage Statistics
- Branching Pages
- Understanding Bandwidth
- Building on Previous Design Weaknesses

A common struggle for a Web designer is designing for the largest audience possible without sacrificing the desired graphical and functional aspects that might be desired or required for a site. Since the 1990s, and probably earlier, this struggle has been a common issue with designers; unfortunately, it will continue to be an issue as long as new technology and design methods are introduced.

While a designer might want to take advantage of the latest technology, there should also be concern that the audience will think usability implications were not taken into consideration if newer technology is employed that is not fully supported by all hardware and/or software. When designing for the past, present, and future, a professional designer designs for the needs of the site. When creating sites for the largest possible audience, one should become resolved to the fact, in most cases, that it is not always possible to use the latest technology. The designer must focus on making the best use of the most practical technology that is available. Fortunately, as the Web industry has progressed since the 1990s, it is no longer difficult to build highly usable, fast, graphical sites with existing technology.

FEELING BROWSER PAINS

As previously discussed, the issue of various browser platforms continues to be, and will continue to be, an issue for Web designers. In the 1990s, a Web designer needed to decide whether to design for a graphical browser, such as Mosaic or Netscape, or a text browser, such as Lynx. As users slowly updated their hardware and software, the decisions gradually evolved into new ones that designers must now address. Today, the number of users who have text browsers is extremely low; but now a designer must decide whether to use JavaScript, Java, or Flash in certain situations while keeping in mind that not all users' browsers support these functionalities. Plus, with the addition of cell phones and Personal Digital Assistants (PDAs) capable of viewing Web pages flooding the marketplace, new design considerations are always going to be a concern.

One of the most important issues a designer faces is which browsers will a site support? While there are many available browsers, Internet Explorer (IE) still dominates market share (more than 55 percent); other browsers, such as Firefox (more than 30 percent), are continually chipping away at Microsoft's majority.

With the advent of CSS-based design and coding standards set forth by the World Wide Web Consortium (W3C), browsers have done an increasingly better job of displaying Web sites more consistently across the board. The problem, however, is if a designer isn't aware of certain coding issues, the mistakes can now be much more pronounced than they were when sites were made by nesting XHTML tables. Figure 2.1 is a site in Firefox 1.5.0.6. Figure 2.2 is the same site in IE 6.0.

FIGURE 2.1   Site viewed in Firefox 1.5.0.6.

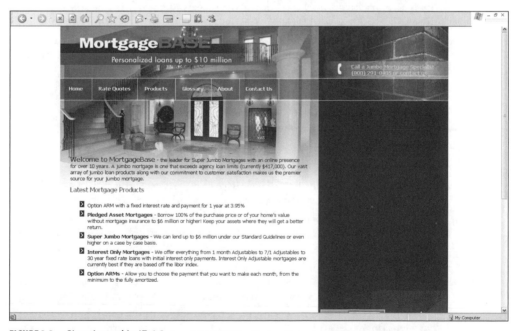

FIGURE 2.2   Site viewed in IE 6.0.

Unlike past browser issues, which were a result of XHTML table-based design, today's issues can be much more pronounced. Figure 2.2 shows how a bug in IE 6.0 drastically displays floated containers nested in floated containers. In other words, all the content in the right column is placed below that in the left column. As the content in the left column grows vertically, so will the content in the right column be dropped, correspondingly. Fortunately, there are ways to avert this and other issues—many of which are explained in Chapter 16.

INCORPORATING USAGE STATISTICS

Because there is a growing discrepancy in the number of browser versions, as well as monitors with varying resolutions and bandwidth issues, the Web user with the most outdated hardware and software continually lags behind. Therefore, it is nearly impossible to keep a user with the latest hardware and software satisfied while designing for those who might still be downloading sites with a dial-up modem, using IE 5.0, and viewing on a monitor with 800 × 600 resolution. This is why it is wise to base most Web design decisions on global usage statistics.

Global usage statistics give the designer useful information about the general population of Web users. This allows the designer to create a site that will best suit as many users as possible. The previous section illustrated screenshots in Figure 2.1 and Figure 2.2 that were taken using Firefox and IE, respectively. These two browsers were used because, according to usage statistics at the time of publication (www.w3schools.com/browsers/browsers_stats.asp), Firefox and IE, and their various versions, were used by approximately 93 percent of the Internet population. Browser version, of course, is just one type of statistic available to the designer. Following are other usage statistics a designer can use:

- Which version of JavaScript does the browser support, and does the user have JavaScript turned on in the browser?
- What is the operating system of the user?
- What is the resolution of the user's monitor?

Basing a site's design on general usage statistics is always a smart way to begin a site design. Once the site is created, however, the designer can then also use statistics specific to that site. How this works on a Windows server, for example, is that a log file is collected every day. It collects data that includes everything from what browser the user was using to each individual page the user visited (see Figure 2.3).

Once the log information has been saved, Web analysis software is then required to analyze the data and display it in an understandable format. One of the most commonly analyzed statistics is page visits. Figure 2.4 outputs such data from the log file in Figure 2.3, which was collected for August 13, 2007.

Another commonly used statistic is which search engines are hitting a site. This allows the designer to tweak the site so it ranks better among the various search engines (see Figure 2.5).

FIGURE 2.3   Log file created on a Windows server.

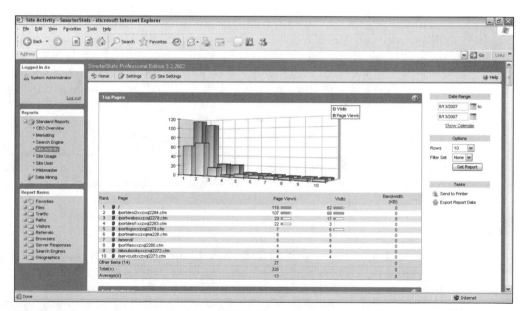

FIGURE 2.4   Page statistics captured for a Web site for one day.

There are many different software packages used to analyze Web logs. Web-Trends, which was discussed in the first edition of this book, has been a commonly used program since the 1990s. The software used to output the data in Figures 2.4 and 2.5 is SmarterStats.

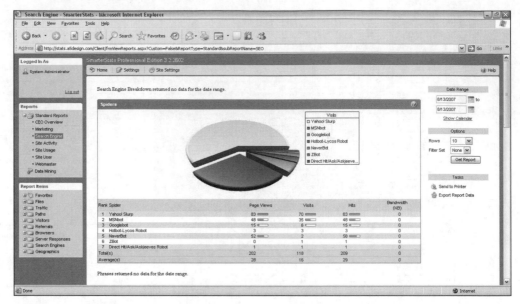

FIGURE 2.5 Browser statistics based on the log file in Figure 2.3.

Another option for capturing usage statistics is to use free or fee-based online applications. The way it works is a site, such as www.extremetracking.com, provides JavaScript code that is added to the bottom of one or more pages in a site. When that page is hit, data is then sent to the tracking site, where the designer can then log in and view the statistics. Not only does this require less technical knowledge, but it also doesn't take nearly as long to set up. The downside is the code needs to be added on any page the designer wants to track.

Once all this information is collected and analyzed, the designer can use the results to best modify a site for its users based on the highest usage times and days of a site, which search engines the users came from, which pages are most frequently entered into and exited from, and the most and least popular pages of a site.

BRANCHING PAGES

The inconsistent support of XHTML, JavaScript, and CSS by IE and Netscape has made some developers resort to *branching* their pages. In other words, once a user hits a page, a basic JavaScript code is used to determine a user's software information, such as which browser is being used and what version of JavaScript, if any, it supports. Once the browser version, for example, is determined, one piece of script can be used for Netscape while another is used for IE.

Branching is advantageous for techniques like drop-down menus that only work with Netscape's DOM (Document Object Model) or IE's DOM. Such scripts, however, not only increase the download time of a page, but, more importantly, they increase the amount of work necessary to maintain a site.

If a designer treats IE and Netscape with equal significance, using branching scripts for style sheets is unnecessary. If the style sheets are written correctly, the way the text and images are displayed should not be significantly different. All of the style sheets used in the designs for this book support both browsers; this not only decreases download time, but it also eliminates the headache of maintaining two different pieces of code.

Understanding Bandwidth

Bandwidth is the amount of data that is either uploaded or downloaded over a specified time. In other words, for designers, how quickly can a site can be downloaded without losing the user? Studies in the past have shown that the number-one complaint of users is that a site is too slow, which makes speed a high priority when designing.

For someone who began designing in the 1990s, today's bandwidth standards are more than adequate for creating fast, striking sites. When the Internet first started becoming popular, the typical user usually had something comparable to a 9600-bps (bits per second) modem.

As years passed, 14.4Kbps (kilobits per second) modems appeared, and then the 28.8Kbps modems and 56Kbps modems. Today, while there are still people using 14.4Kbps, 28.8Kbps, and 56Kbps modems, an increasing number have high-bandwidth connections, such as DSL (Digital Subscriber Line, approximately 256 Kbps and higher), cable modems (approximately 10 Mbps, or 10 million bits per second, depending on various factors), wireless, and satellite services with varying speeds that are comparable to DSL, commonly referred to as *broadband*, although the term itself generally refers to a connection faster than 256 Kbps, barring extremely large "pipes," such as T1s.

The Internet is all about speed. While designing download-intensive multimedia sites is fun and a powerful way to communicate, one of the quickest ways to lose a user (or more importantly, a customer) is to design a slow-loading site.

Unfortunately, while high bandwidth will eventually become a reality for the masses, most users still have 28.8Kbps and 56Kbps modems. So unless the target audience has high-bandwidth connections, or designers are developing a site where it can be assumed that users have high-bandwidth requirements, such as for downloading MP3s, it is still not practical to create sites with excessively large page downloads that will bog down slower modems.

What is a large page download for a site? Some designers like to determine the speed of a site by the time it takes to download. The problem with this type of measurement is that it is relative. The same site that might take 10 seconds to load using one modem might take 30 seconds for someone else who has the same modem, depending on the user's Internet connection, the total usage of the Internet at that time, or the usage of the site's server(s) at that time, among other factors.

A more accurate method of determining the speed of a site is by the *weight* of a page (the amount of kilobytes). The standard for many years was to keep the site under 35 KB. With the growth of CSS-based sites and Flash, this standard ranges from 20 KB to anywhere around 300 KB, depending on the type of site, the purpose of the site, and its users' connections. These sites include CSS, graphics, possible multimedia components, and the output XHTML. (Output HTML is the eventual XHTML a database-driven site returns to the browser. The actual page on the server with all the programming code can be considerably larger.)

Some designers believe it is impossible to build graphical sites and keep them fast. This is simply not true. Many of the sites that require a large download are designed incorrectly. One way to correctly design a site for a small download is to properly compress its images. Take, for example, Figures 2.6 and 2.7. Figure 2.6 was taken with a digital camera using no compression.

FIGURE 2.6   Uncompressed JPG photo that is 76 KB.

Figure 2.7 is the same image after being compressed. When resized to 250×214 pixels, it is possible to compress it more than 66 percent from its original 76.0 KB to 14.5 KB with very little visible difference.

Compressing images allows a designer to get a site well under 50 KB; however, without compression, the same site could easily be larger than 125 KB.

Once a designer knows the tricks of keeping a site small, it is important to keep the download goal in mind when designing a site. Whenever designing, it is a good practice for a designer to keep the download calculator going in his or her head and constantly keep track of how big the site will eventually be. Once the goal of, say, 50 KB is met, the designer should stop to make sure that all necessary content has been added. If it has not, the designer should try to take away or reduce in size a design element to make up for the additional download size of required content.

FIGURE 2.7   Compressed JPG photo that is 14.5 KB.

BUILDING ON PREVIOUS DESIGN WEAKNESSES

A designer should continually strive toward making sites technically and aesthetically superior to previous designs. Looking at Figure 2.8, it is fairly easy to find room for improvement—the color choice is too simple, the presentation of the artwork could be improved, and the layout does not make good use of space.

This era is one a Web designer should cherish. Not only are there millions of sites that need to be redesigned, but, as more businesses and individuals decide to put up new sites, there are more opportunities to create sites that communicate more effectively.

Building more effective sites involves improving on past design weaknesses. The first step in accomplishing this is to understand and avoid such weaknesses. Following are some examples a designer should try to avoid.

IFrames and Frames

Framed sites, for the most part, have gone the way of the dinosaur. IFrames, however, can still be beneficial to a designer. An *IFrame* is an individual frame that can be placed anywhere in a page, controlling how long a page could be. In other words, the designer can output a large amount of data, such as 150 countries with associated data for each, within 500 pixels of vertical space, without requiring the user to scroll down the screen many pages if the same data were output in a non-framed environment.

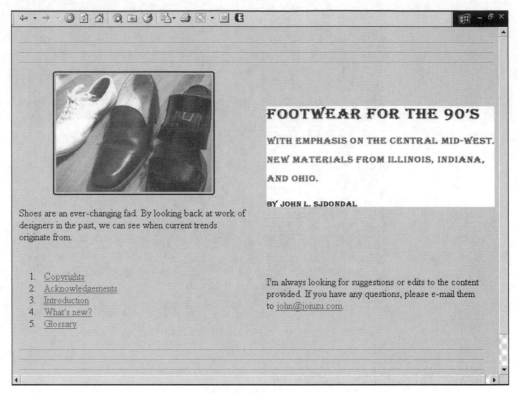

FIGURE 2.8   Site that could be designed to appear more professional.

As for frames, although they are almost entirely extinct, clients may still occasionally ask about or request them. Following are several reasons a designer could give a client as to why traditional framed sites should not be used:

1. Allowing a user to bookmark a site is impossible unless JavaScript is used. The problem is that when a user bookmarks a page, only one frame is bookmarked (usually, it is the last frame that was clicked in) rather than all the frames. As mentioned previously, though, this can be a benefit in some circumstances.
2. Targeting frames and passing programming variables is considerably more complicated than when using Include files (that is, SSI, or Server Side Includes).
3. Increasing the number of scrollbars decreases the amount of space a designer has to work with (see Figure 2.9).
4. Search engines do not like frames. Therefore the site will suffer in search-engine rankings, if it's ranked at all.

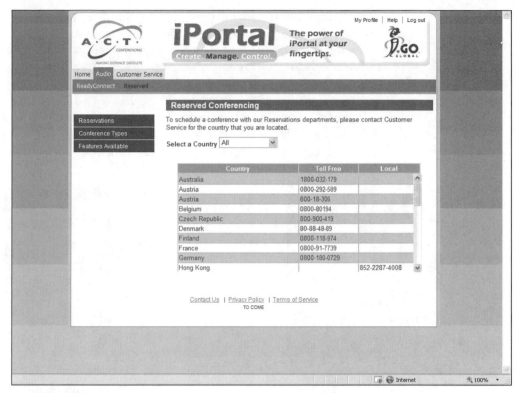

FIGURE 2.9   Site that uses an IFrame to control how much space a large amount of data takes up.

Image Buttons

Creating menu items as images, rather than text, can be attractive. However, simply for the advantage of a mouseover image, they are not necessary or practical for four reasons:

1. **Download time**—A designer can drastically increase the download time of a site when using mouseover images as menu items. This is because the user has to download the images for both the On and Off states. In Figure 2.10, for example, the user has to download the eight images in the Off state, and the eight images in the On state, which is shown in Figure 2.11.

   The entire download size of the images for the menu in Figure 2.10 is 20 KB. This is already nearly half of the goal for the entire homepage.

2. **Maintenance**—Creating, editing, and adding such buttons to a site is time-consuming.

3. **Dynamic functionality**—The advantage of database-driven sites is their ability to create pages on the fly. This functionality allows menus to be created

dynamically, as well. When a designer creates menu items as static images, it defeats the purpose of being able to dynamically create such items.

4. **Search engines**—When text is saved as an image, search engines don't read it, although they can read the Alt tags. It's almost always a wise idea to make your site as search-engine friendly as possible.

CSS menus can use background images in menu items. Using such a method also allows the designer to lay text over the image, allowing for the best of both worlds. Such usage of background images is incorporated in many designs included with this book.

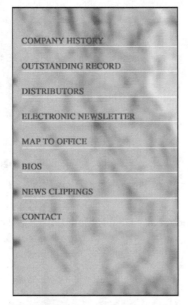

FIGURE 2.10   Menu items saved as images in the Off state.

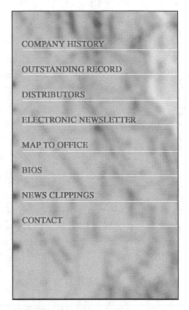

FIGURE 2.11   Menu items saved as images in the On state (a white glow around the text).

Background Images

Background images can enhance a Web site to give it mood and depth. While the use of background images has changed slightly over the years, the concepts are fairly similar. There are several uses of background images that the designer can be creative with. The first is using a background image to serve as the majority or entire backdrop of a Web site while layering the HTML and graphics on top of it. While this wasn't advisable in the past, it now is much more acceptable with increased bandwidth and CSS-driven layouts, which require less download time. Figure 2.12 illustrates a site that uses one image to serve as the entire background.

Figure 2.13 is the background image that was used.

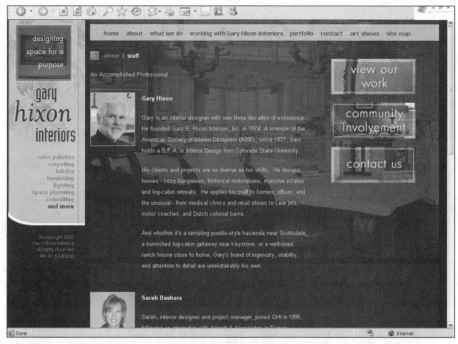

FIGURE 2.12   Site that uses a large image for its background.   Copyright © 2007 by Gary Hixon Interiors. All rights reserved.

FIGURE 2.13   Image that was used for the entire background of the site in Figure 2.12. Copyright © 2007 by Gary Hixon Interiors. All rights reserved.

Another creative use of background images is giving the impression that a design has colors running down both sides of it indefinitely. Although this used to be an easy process with XHTML table sites, it now takes a little trickery to accomplish the same result. Such a technique is explained in Chapter 12; however, Figure 2.14 illustrates the concept.

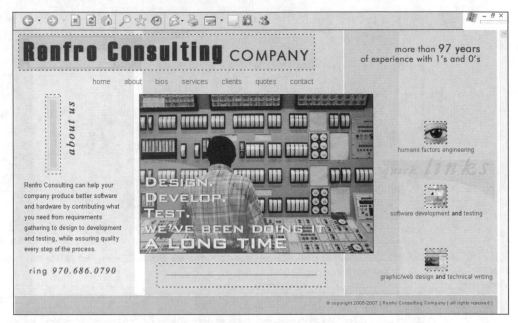

FIGURE 2.14   Site that uses background images to run colors down both sides of a design indefinitely, similar to how XHTML table designs work. Copyright © 2007 by Renfro Consulting Company. All rights reserved.

A third use of background images, as mentioned in the previous section, is using the images for menus. Using CSS, a designer can use an image for, say, a menu item, while not having to include the text with the image itself. In other words, the text is layered over the image. Figure 2.15 shows a site that does just that.

Although many clients don't like the width of their sites changing because the content shifts around, a background image, depending on the resolution, can be repeated to allow for such expansion while maintaining a similar look and feel. The designer has to be careful to make sure that the background image is designed correctly for higher resolutions, though. While the design in Figure 2.16 doesn't expand horizontally, the background image does. Unfortunately, it does not look professional because the designer did not remove the lines on the right side of the image.

One instance that designers should probably stay away from is using a repeating background image endlessly both horizontally and vertically. While it can work in certain situations, for the most part, it is amateurish looking. This is probably because it was so easy to do since the dawning of graphical Web browsers that millions

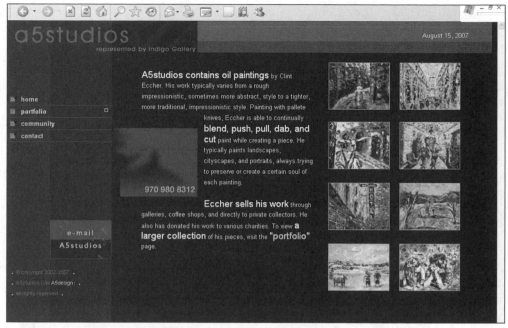

FIGURE 2.15   Background images that are used in a menu to show Over and Off states.

FIGURE 2.16   Page repeating an awkward looking background image in a resolution higher than the design was created for.

of sites used the technique, similar to glowing text. These days, sites, such as the one shown in Figure 2.17, aren't designed very often.

FIGURE 2.17   Site that infinitely repeats the background image of a cloud both horizontally and vertically.

This is a good time to review the basics covered in Chapter 1. Rule 1 should be repeated: just because you can does not mean you should.

FIGURE 2.18   Background image that is repeated in Figure 2.17.

Uncontrolled Color

Color can make or break a Web site. Not only should the colors be appropriate and appealing to the target audience, but they should also be used with intention and discretion. One of the strengths of using color is that a designer can help lead the user's eye. If a designer, on the other hand, uses too many colors, the user can quickly become confused as to what the most important information is. The user then has to start reading all of the hyperlinks to find the desired content.

Uncompressed Images

The easiest way to drive away a user from a site is to make it slow, and one of the easiest ways to make a site slow is to use uncompressed images. Figure 2.19 shows a Web site in which the central image (the image of the neighborhood) is 33 KB. Compressed, this image could easily be reduced to 13 KB, drastically increasing the speed of the download without a visible loss in the quality of the image.

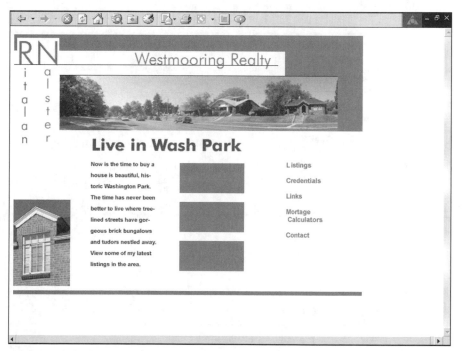

FIGURE 2.19   Site that does not use compressed images.

In the early to 1990s, the closest a designer could come to compressing an image was reducing the bit depth (2, 4, 8, 16, 32, 64, 128, or 256 colors) of a GIF or reducing the JPG compression percentage in increments of 10. Today, because of the vast improvement in graphics software, GIFs can not only be compressed one color at a time, but a designer can even select which colors to use, and JPGs can now be compressed one percentage point at a time. Image editing software, such as Adobe Photoshop, is also doing a better job of compressing images to the same level but with less degradation.

Thumbnails

A thumbnail is a smaller version of an image, which allows the user to preview the larger version without having to actually download the image until it is clicked. A mistake Web designers occasionally make is in resizing images to appear as thumbnail images. Figure 2.20 illustrates a Web page that includes many thumbnails of larger photos.

FIGURE 2.20   Site that makes use of thumbnail images.

When the user clicks on a thumbnail, an enlarged copy of the image is displayed (see Figure 2.21).

When a designer places an image in HTML, the height and width attributes can be changed to tell the browser to resize the viewable size of the image. For example, the designer could tell the browser to resize an image from 500×500 pixels to 20×20 pixels. This is a mistake designers often make.

FIGURE 2.21   Larger version of a thumbnail image.

While it is possible to tell the browser to forcibly change the visual size of the image, it does not physically change the file size or download size of the image. In other words, if the 500 × 500 image is 60 KB, it will remain 60 KB when resized to 20 × 20. If all 14 photos in Figure 2.20 were only 20 KB, the download of the entire page would be nearly 300 KB.

To create thumbnails correctly, a designer needs to make two images: the original photo and the original photo resized smaller. While it is more work, the user will appreciate the increased speed of the download.

SUMMARY

Designers have been dealing with browser issues since the 1990s, and today is no exception. Many times, a designer should determine design requirements based on usage statistics that not only provide browser information but also information on monitor color depth, resolution, and JavaScript support, among other issues.

It is always smart to learn from the past. There are several mistakes designers have made over the years that today's designers can learn from and improve on: frames, image buttons, background images, uncontrolled color, uncompressed images, and thumbnails.

THINGS TO CONSIDER BEFORE BEGINNING

In This Chapter

- Using Requirements
- Knowing Bandwidth Requirements
- Deciding on Resolution
- Deciding on Color Depth
- Designing for Scalability

Working in a logical, practical manner is one of the keys to becoming a professional Web designer. It is particularly important to be logical and practical when working on the technical aspects of a site, such as collecting requirements, taking the client's concerns into mind, and designing for scalability and flexibility. While contemplating the design in depth beforehand requires more initial time and forethought, doing so can save many hours, if not days, addressing future problems.

USING REQUIREMENTS

Site requirements can best be compared to a recipe that tells a designer what needs to be included in the site, the steps required to complete each task, plus additional information, such as how to present the site and the types of people it will serve. Although every designer's and/or company's requirements are different, they all share a common goal—an agreed upon document that helps serve as a road map, as best as possible, to the completed site.

When constructing a site, some of the most important information a designer needs to document includes the following:

1. **Look and feel requirements**—These include content placement, how the site conveys the company's message, the color palette, and font and image concepts to be presented.
2. **Bandwidth requirements**—The way a site is designed will determine how large of a download the site will require. By understanding the bandwidth (download size) requirements, a designer can determine the balance between graphics and text to be used.
3. **Resolution requirements**—A site with improper resolution can hinder its usability and/or credibility.
4. **Scalability requirements**—Because nearly all sites are in continual evolution, it is important for the designer to consider how the site can be expanded and/or changed in the future.
5. **Content requirements**—The content volume of a site will influence nearly all other requirements, including the look and feel, and the bandwidth, resolution, and scalability.

Depending on the size of a Web site, different levels of documentation are necessary. Many small sites (around 5 to 15 pages) only require the designer and client to e-mail or call each other during the development process. Larger sites (more than 15 pages), many times require more thorough documentation, which includes an official requirements document. Without such documentation, the designer could have a site nearly completed when the client says, "Oh, that's not what I meant. You actually need to do it this way." At that point, changes are not only time-consuming and painful, but the designer is left in the awkward position of whether to make the corrections pro bono or charge the client an additional fee. This mode of edits continually coming in with no foreseeable end is referred to as *scope creep*.

Because of documentation time, site requirements might increase the cost of the site. However, while initially taking more time and money, requirements can save considerable expense when the designer has everything planned prior to development.

Take, for example, a 20-field form. Without requirements, the form might start out at 20 fields. The client, though, after seeing the first draft, says, "Oh, I forgot a few items we need to add." They probably do not know that this involves making changes to not only the form, but also to the database and additional server-side scripted pages that complete the functionality. And that is just the first draft. The client might then run the form by a peer or boss who will have additional changes that the designer will have to incorporate. Before long, the same form could include 35 fields.

This may seem like a small-scale issue. However, it can become quite problematic resulting in larger-scale meltdowns, such as major design problems. The designer might create a site with a horizontal navigation menu at the top. Then the client comes back with five additional sections to add to the site after weeks or months of development. What then? The initial solution would be to add the items to the menu. What if the menu already takes up the full width of the screen? One possibility would be to add another row of menu items. But this might look awkward or impede the usability of the site; or the design simply might not support a vertical stretch of the header area. Taking a very long step backward, the designer then realizes that the lacking requirements have drastically changed the scope of the project. A lot of the site is now going to need redesigning.

Collecting the Requirements

Requirements lacking detail can be just as detrimental as not having requirements. There are many different areas that should be addressed when documenting requirements. While many answers to questions are collected to help in the marketing and back-end (programming) development of the site, many can also be used by a designer to ensure that the design best supports current and future demands. Getting a feel for the areas that need to be addressed comes with experience; however, following is a minimal list of areas that will probably need to be documented. An in-depth requirements document should probably cover the following:

1. **Site/Client name**—Not all sites have the same name as the company they are designed for. Therefore, this is important to know before beginning a design.
2. **Prepared by**—It is always helpful for your client to know who prepared the document and how to get in touch with that person.
3. **Date**—While it might seem obvious, knowing the date helps the designer write future summary reports and/or track site-design efficiency.
4. **Client contact(s)**—The more contacts the better. A designer can never have too many people to call when various questions arise during development.

5. **Version**—While the version of the requirements document should also be covered with the naming convention of the document (for example, requirements_v3.doc), it is also wise to include it in the document itself. Sometimes the version number will remind the designer to save the current document as a new document.

6. **Executive summary**—This summary gives the designer and/or design team the gist of the site. Half the battle of designing a site is getting "the big picture." An executive summary helps make more sense of the specifics.

7. **Assumptions**—Many times the designer and client do not share the same assumptions. For example, the designer might not know that an intranet site also needs to serve as an extranet site, which could change the technical requirements. The fewer the presumptions, the more effective and efficient the development will be.

8. **Dependencies**—While not all sites have dependencies, it is important to know if any exist. An example of one possible dependency could be if the site must rely on another company or site for live content, such as an RSS (Really Simple Syndication) feed.

9. **Objectives**—It is easy for a designer to lose focus when getting into a project. Being able to revisit the objectives of a site can be helpful in regaining and clarifying that focus.

10. **Action items**—Action items provide more detailed information on what specific steps need to be taken to accomplish various tasks.

11. **Detailed requirements (includes front-end questions, functional requirements, and a site map/flowchart)**—These are the heart of a requirements document, at least for a designer. They give the specific details on design, content, and functionality that a designer needs to include when creating the site. An example of such a requirement might read, "Include login form area on the homepage that includes the User ID and Password fields, along with a Submit button."

12. **Proposed solution(s)**—Talking about and documenting solutions are two different things. While the client may think one thing after a phone conversation, the solution actually written out may present another picture. Such documentation helps to prevent misunderstandings.

13. **Possible future site considerations**—Because sites are in continual evolution, it is important to create a scalable design that can handle future additions. In other words, the client may say, "We need only 15 pages for this phase; however, the design will need to accommodate another 20 pages in phase 2."

14. **Sign-off section**—Signing off on a document provides closure for the client and assurance for the designer, signifying that both sides are in agreement on the road map of a site.

Front-end requirements and flowcharts are usually most beneficial when designing comps for a site. It is from these two documents that a designer bases the design, site architecture, and navigation.

When collecting requirements, there are three rules a designer would be wise to follow:

1. **Document everything**—One of the best methods for documenting things is for the designer to Cc or Bcc himself or herself on all e-mails. It's surprising how many of these e-mails are eventually referenced again.
2. **Save each document as a different version**—Not only is it wise to back up all files in case of hard-drive failure, it is also wise to back up all files in case of human failure. Whether human failure means accidentally deleting a file or having to clarify a point of confusion by going back to previous versions of a document, it is wise to save all files, whether graphics or text, as new versions. The first round of writing requirements, for instance, could possibly be saved as requirements_v1.doc, with the "v1" representing "version 1." When that document is revised, it should then be saved as requirements_v2.doc for version 2. It is just as important to save versions of graphics files. Many times a client will request changes, realize they do not work well, and then come back and say, "Well, I think we liked the first version better." At that point, it is much easier to open the original version of the file than to have to recreate it.
3. **Receive a sign-off on the requirements before beginning work**—Until a designer receives the sign-off to begin work, whether it be with an e-mail or a deposit check, nothing is set in stone. One minute a client may say, "Yes, that is exactly what we want," and the next the response may be, "Well, we just met, and we have some more changes we want to add before you start." At that point, precious time has not been spent working on a *comp* (or composite) that will need to satisfy completely different requirements.

A comp is a layered art file that shows what the homepage will look like in terms of layout, color, images, text, functionality, and typography. Comps are generally created and edited in Adobe Photoshop (as PSD files) before being broken up into XHTML, graphics, and CSS.

Obtaining Front-End Requirements

If the designer does not have the time or resources to collect in-depth requirements, a shorter version of a requirements document can be used to collect information. Such a document should provide the designer with enough information to enable him to create a design that supports the look and feel, architecture, and future possibilities of a site. Following are 13 questions a designer should try to have answered before beginning a site's comp:

1. Who is the audience, and what is the purpose of the site?
2. What is the feeling you want to convey to your audience with your Web site?

3. Will the site need to be expandable, in terms of sections, in the future?
4. What browser platform and resolution (for example, Internet Explorer/Firefox or 1024 × 768 or higher) do you require?
5. How many levels, or "clicks," can the deepest information be?
6. What is the most important information that should be put on the home page?
7. When can text and graphics (logo) samples be supplied for designing the comp?
8. Do the images and colors on the site need to be consistent with any existing branding?
9. Does it matter if the site scrolls vertically?
10. What kind of functionality (for example, forms, dynamic text, or multimedia elements) does your site need to have?
11. What is the desired download size of the home page?
12. Does your company have a tagline?
13. What is the proposed deadline(s)?

The designer can send the document to the client to fill out or fill out the document himself over initial meetings, phone calls, and/or e-mails. Usually, having the designer fill out the document is the best choice simply because the client may not have enough design experience or savvy to answer all the questions. Once completed, the designer should reiterate and confirm the answers, as well as receive a sign-off before beginning the site's comp.

Creating a Flowchart

Smaller sites do not necessarily require a flowchart simply because it is not difficult to visualize a site with About Us, Services, Products, Testimonials, and Contact sections. Larger sites, especially application sites with 10 or more pages, though, are considerably easier to create when the designer has a flowchart. Not only is it easier to visualize the site, but it also saves a lot of time clarifying questions.

Figure 3.1 illustrates the possible complexity of an application site. When initially looking at the site, the user would see only six items on the menu, including a link back to the homepage. Surfing through the site, though, it quickly becomes apparent that the site contains more than 30 different pages.

The flowchart *in Figure 3.1 was created using Microsoft Visio. While flowcharts can be created in other programs, such as Microsoft PowerPoint, Visio contains functionality that not only easily creates but also easily edits documents. With Visio, a designer could select all the items under the Client Info section on the left, move them wherever desired, and have all the flow lines move with the boxes while automatically skipping over other, stationary flow lines. This can save innumerable hours when working with a client that continually makes changes.*

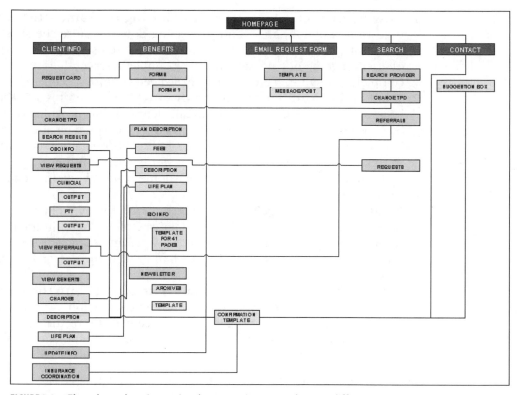

FIGURE 3.1   Flowchart showing a site that contains more than 30 different pages.

Another advantage to creating a flowchart is that it can be used to create a site map by taking out workflow lines, explanations, and back-end items. While it may not be necessary to include all sections in a sitemap, doing so only helps to increase the site usability.

KNOWING BANDWIDTH REQUIREMENTS

The amount of bandwidth a user can download determines how many graphical elements should be incorporated into a design. If the anticipated audience's bandwidth limitations are strict, the homepage design may possibly have to fit under 30 KB. On the other hand, if the bandwidth limitations are liberal, the limit for the homepage design could be anywhere from 50 KB to 250 KB or even higher.

As previously mentioned, user bandwidth is a relative term. No matter what the supposed connection speed is, many factors influence what that bandwidth really is. Some of those factors include the following:

1. **How many users are concurrently hitting the same site?** The media used to occasionally report on sites going down because the sites' servers were not equipped to handle so many immediate users. While the problem of a server going down is an extreme example, a server does not need to go completely down to have its download speed compromised.

2. **What is the overall usage of the Internet?** Whether it is a 56K modem, DSL, or cable access, every user can fall victim to slow downloads as a result of a bogged down Internet. One hour the Internet could be pumping the bits like wildfire and the next it could be spitting bits one at a time. A common example of slowing down of data transfer is when, during the school year and around 3 p.m. to 4 p.m., kids get home from school and log on to the Internet *en masse*.

3. **What is the ISP usage?** ISP usage is similar to the overall usage of the Internet, but in more specific circles. America Online (AOL) in the mid-1990s received widespread criticism for its slow serving of sites. The company's infrastructure was not equipped to handle the success of its marketing department.

4. **What is the condition of the phone line coming into the computer?** A phone line can also slow down an Internet connection. A user could have a 56K modem but only receive 36K service because of the incoming line. Distance also can play into this problem, and DSL technology is limited to a certain distance it can pump bits.

Understanding various factors that affect the data transfer of a site is why it does not make sense to design a site totally on the basis of the actual time it takes to download. There are too many factors that may change the download time from minute to minute. It is better to build sites that meet a goal of so many kilobytes. This number includes everything—the Web page(s) used to build the homepage, the homepage itself, and the graphics used. It is generally wise for a designer to create a site that is no larger than 50 KB, although with many site requirements anymore, this is no longer always feasible.

There are three general instances when a larger site might be designed without any bandwidth issues:

1. **Intranet versus Internet site**—Intranet sites, which are internal business networks to businesses, usually offer a considerably higher bandwidth than the external Internet, which is subject to many more variables.

2. **Corporate versus a more general audience**—Sometimes a more advanced corporation, such as Cisco, will have an audience with higher bandwidth capability than a site designed for a more general audience, such as a mom-and-pop shop that sells homemade gift baskets.

3. **High-bandwidth functionality versus purely content-driven**—Sometimes the purpose of a site also allows for higher bandwidth flexibility. For instance, an online music store is going to have users with higher bandwidth than a site that is designed to offer pure text content.

Moderation is the secret in Web design. The three examples above are not necessarily excuses for a designer to create a site with a larger download. If there are technical reasons, for example, to have a higher download for an intranet site, then that is all right. If the higher download, on the other hand, is the result of a designer's adding unnecessary elements because it's possible, then it is not all right. Rather than think, "Wow. This is an intranet, so I can build a site with a high download," the designer should think, "If this site is optimized to be as fast as possible for a slow connection, it is going to be that much faster over an intranet."

The designer should take increasing server and network usage into consideration. As more people use a site, the usage will take more of a toll on the server. The smaller a site, the less effect the overall usage will have on the speed of the site. Play it safe; the designer should always strive to cut as many bits from a site as possible. This has traditionally been the case, and will continue to be the case for years to come because of various technologies, such as PDAs.

DECIDING ON RESOLUTION

One of the biggest problems with Web design is designing for resolution. Web sites are designed for a certain monitor resolution. Monitors, however, have varying resolutions that are set independently of the site.

If the user's monitor resolution does not match the resolution the site was designed for, the site will appear differently than was originally intended. In other words, the way a monitor resizes a screen is similar to that of a television set. Whether a monitor screen size is 17 inches or 30 inches, the content will be dynamically resized to fill the entire screen the same way. However, the problem is that computer monitors, unlike television sets, allow the user different resolutions. If the resolution of a monitor, for example, is set at 800×640 pixels, a site that is designed for 1024×768 resolution will appear too wide. If the resolution of the monitor is 1024×768, the same site will appear either too narrow and short or it will be stretched horizontally.

Figures 3.2, 3.3, and 3.4 show how A5design's site, which was designed for 1024×768 resolution, appears on monitor resolutions of 800×600, 1024×768, and 1280×800, respectively.

The Web design industry for years designed sites for 640×480 resolution. Then around 1999, more sites began to be designed for 800×600 resolution. Over the past year or two, nearly all sites have been designed for 1024×768 resolution.

It is difficult to say when the next expansion will occur. Most likely, it will take longer to reach that level because more and more baby boomers, who make up a growing segment of the Internet, are tired of not being able to read smaller text, which is usually a result of higher resolution monitors. Although there are workarounds, people, by nature, don't like change. This is only theory, though. Many times it's difficult to truly know where the Web world will end up.

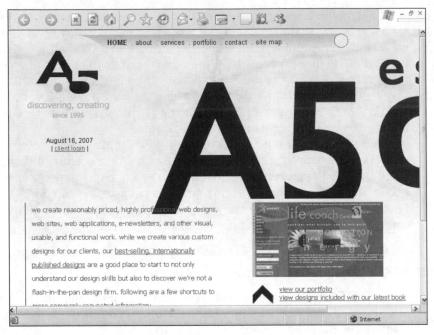

FIGURE 3.2   Site at 800 × 600 resolution.

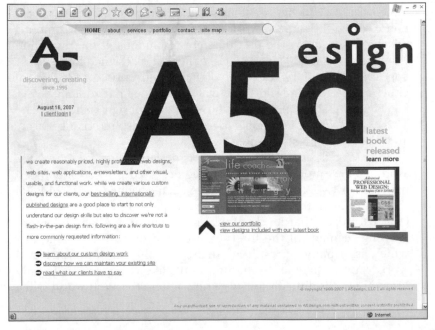

FIGURE 3.3   Site at 1024 × 768 resolution.

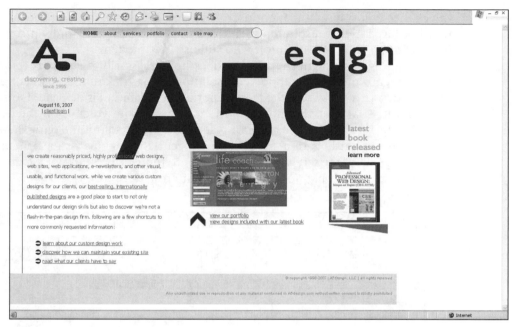

FIGURE 3.4   Site at 1280 × 800 resolution.

The real question a designer needs to ask is "What is critical mass?" This ultimately helps determine whether the newer resolution should be designed for. This is a call that, many times, a designer can leave to the client. Some people would say 75 percent of all users is critical mass. Others, though, might say 95 percent, claiming that taking the risk of losing 25 percent of a user base is not worth the benefit of going to a higher resolution. Making such a decision cannot be based solely on general statistics. It should also be based on the type of audience a site is geared toward. If the audience is high-tech, a site will likely be designed for the highest acceptable resolution much sooner than if the site were geared toward a more general audience, such as a search-engine site intended to satisfy the largest audience possible. It is the job of the designer to know the statistics, understand the implications of the various resolutions, and, if need be, make the call on the resolution if the client "doesn't care."

One aspect of going to a higher resolution that a designer must consider is the quantity and ratio of content. As resolution increases, so does the screen real estate. Jumping from a resolution of 800 × 600 to 1024 × 768 increases the available screen area by nearly 40 percent. When designing for a content-intensive page, this extra space can be advantageous. The designer can either add more content or make current content look less busy by reworking the layout.

This extra real estate is not as advantageous, however, for a site with limited content. Sites that have less content usually are supplemented with more graphics. Considering that this can and probably will increase the download, it also increases the chance of losing an impatient user. Also, do not assume that just because a user's monitor has a higher resolution then the user also has higher bandwidth. There are users with 1024×768 resolution who still use 56K modems.

Designing for a higher resolution does not necessarily mean that the designer need disregard monitors with lower resolutions. One trick that designers frequently use is to design a site where the least important information is delegated to a column to the right. That way, the most important information, which is on the left, is still viewable by a user when the monitor is set to a lower resolution. Figure 3.5 and Figure 3.6 are screenshots of a site designed specifically for this issue. Looking at the right-hand side of the screen shot in Figure 3.5, there is a column of advertisements that the user is probably not going to be as interested in.

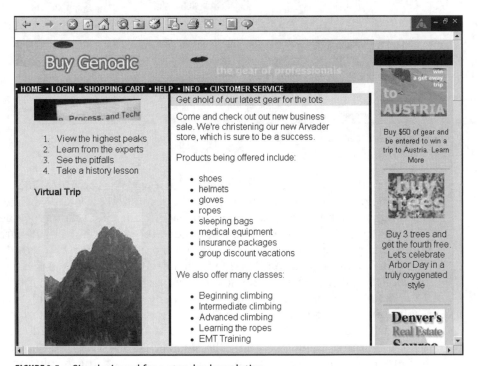

FIGURE 3.5   Site designed for a standard resolution.

When dropped down to a lower resolution, the column to the right is no longer visible. The main content to the left, however, is still viewable.

Designing a site in this manner is a smart and easy way to address monitors with lower resolutions. It is generally good practice to show a little of the right-hand column so that the low-resolution user knows that there is more information available by scrolling to the right.

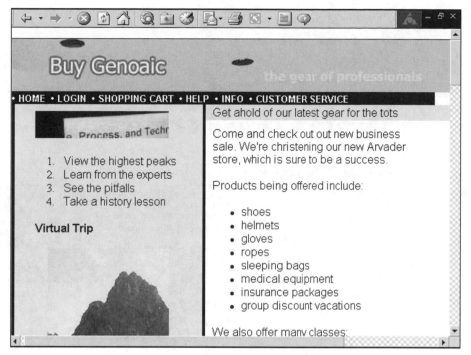

FIGURE 3.6   Same site as in Figure 3.5, but in a lower resolution.

Designing Fixed versus Relative Sites

A site designed for a lower resolution will not dynamically resize to fit the screen of a monitor with a larger resolution. It can, however, stretch horizontally to at least fill the full width. These kinds of pages, which use this relative resizing to fit a screen, are called *relative* pages. Figures 3.7 through 3.9 are the same site viewed at the resolutions of 640 × 480, 800 × 600, and 1024 × 768.

The advantage of these sites is that they fill up the full width of the higher-resolution screen. It can be distracting to some users if the site does not at least fill the screen horizontally.

The disadvantage of relative sites is that the layout can be compromised, which can hurt the site's usability. As it stretches across the screen, the site will reposition certain text and images horizontally. Research has shown that after the text reaches a certain point in terms of width, the user will be less likely to continue reading it. Also, if the design was created to lead a user's eye to certain areas, those areas will not necessarily be in the same position at a higher resolution.

Most designers like to have control over the layout, which relative pages do not allow for. Many designers spend time strategically, and sometimes artistically, placing text and images to be visually most effective. Relative pages, however, might distort the intended layout at different resolutions. Special care must be taken when designing a page with fixed sizes on the tables to allow for expansion.

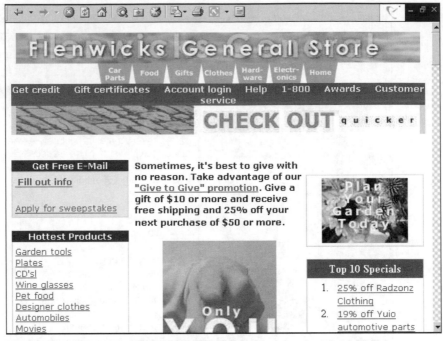

FIGURE 3.7 Relative site at 640 × 480 resolution.

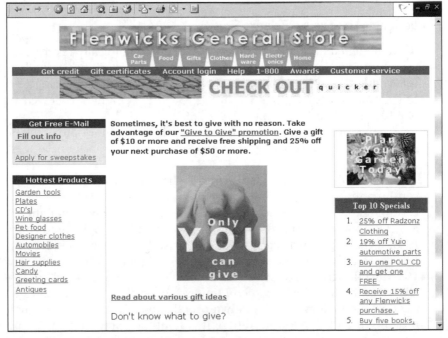

FIGURE 3.8 Relative site at 800 × 600 resolution.

FIGURE 3.9   Relative site at 1024 × 768 resolution.

In order to tackle some of the resolution issues, designers can either force the width of the site or choose which columns will not expand by specifying a width in CSS for specific containers.

Creating Versions of a Site to Satisfy Differing Resolutions

If controlling the look and feel of a site for different resolutions is important enough, a designer can develop different versions of the same site for different resolutions. Branching JavaScript can be used to automatically detect a user's resolution and serve up the right code for a specific resolution. Such a solution involves much more time in creating and maintaining the site, but it also ensures a controlled look and feel for differing resolutions. Using database-driven technology can also drastically reduce the time spent maintaining such a site.

DECIDING ON COLOR DEPTH

Color depth is not nearly as complicated an issue as is resolution. *Color depth* refers to the number of colors a monitor can display. Similar to GIFs, the numbers increase exponentially, beginning with 2 (that is, 2, 4, 8, 16, 32, 64, 128, 256, and so on). After a certain bit depth, however, the human eye cannot detect a difference.

Several years ago, there was a considerable break-point in the number of colors a monitor provided. The difference was between 8-bit (256 colors) and 16-bit (65,536 colors) depth. While saving an image as a GIF with 256 colors makes it look very much like a normal photo, monitors do not offer the same quality. Figures 3.10 through 3.12 are the same JPG photo with the monitor resolution set to 8-bit, 16-bit, and 32-bit.

FIGURE 3.10   Monitor color depth set to 8-bit (256 colors).

Using 16-bit resolution to view images is more than adequate. Today's monitors, however, offer 32-bit color, which can display 16.7 million colors. But because the human eye can only detect approximately 2 million colors, 32-bit is somewhat overkill, as seen with Figures 3.11 and 3.12, which show no "visible" difference.

Why does this all matter? Some designers still design for monitors with 256 colors, thus the color-safe palette, which is used to guarantee that browsers display colors the same, rather than providing their own versions of a "light blue." This, however, is no longer necessary. Monitors have supported at least 16-bit color depth since 1996. Usage statistics confirm the fact that the majority of users have at least 16-bit color depth. A designer should still understand the issue because it occasionally comes up with other design jobs, such as creating icons.

FIGURE 3.11   Monitor color depth set to 16-bit (65,536 colors).

FIGURE 3.12   Monitor color depth set to 32-bit (16.7 million colors).

DESIGNING FOR SCALABILITY

Back in the mid-1990s there were very few extremely large sites (hundreds or thousands of pages). The majority of sites were small by today's standards and built with only static content. Because revising these small sites was so easy, it was common practice to redesign them every six months to a year. Today, however, sites are exponentially larger, more technically complicated, and more in tune with brand recognition. It is no longer easy or cost-effective to redesign a large site.

More importantly for some designers, a site must be easily maintainable. The fun part of Web design is creating a site. The real work begins when the client requests maintenance. This is why it is important that designers build sites that are scalable in two possible ways:

1. **Editable sites**—A designer should be able to edit pages and sections of a site without any major rework of the design.
2. **Modular sites**—A homepage, for example, should be comprised of several files, or pieces put together, that can be easily replaced or edited. An analogy would be that of changing the oil in a car: if it were not possible to easily drain and refill the oil via a plug on the bottom and cap on the top, a mechanic would have to remove the engine, take it apart, drain and refill the oil, and then put the engine back into the vehicle.

Scalable sites are not difficult to create. They simply require a little more forethought by both the designer and client. In addition to the forethought that goes into creating a flexible design, two aspects are used to create scalable sites—nested containers and include files.

 CSS will also play a significant role in making a site expandable. It offers the ability to change multiple pages with one document.

Using Include Files

Include files are used by developers to call code that is used repeatedly throughout a site. In other words, a single file could be reused by 10 different pages. Include files are commonly used to contain the footer information of the site, which would, very likely, be used on every single page. Such files are a blessing to designers. They reduce development and maintenance time, which, depending on the size of a site, can be considerable. Another advantage of include files is that they make a site modular. In other words, they allow for one page, such as the homepage, to be built with various individual pages. Those same pieces can then be used to build other pages.

Figure 3.13, which is a second-level page of a site, is a good example of modular functionality. The area on the right containing the oval circle is an include file. This file not only serves a functional purpose, but it also reduces the amount of space of the body if the content is not as long as other pages.

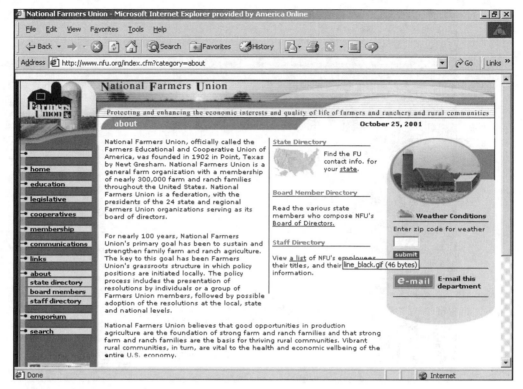

FIGURE 3.13   Modular site that uses an include file in the right section of the body. Copyright © 2002 by National Farmers Union. All rights reserved.

Figure 3.14 is a third-level page of the same site that requires the full width of the body for the map. To accommodate this space, the designer simply removed the include file on the right.

Creating a Flexible Design

The look and feel of a site is obviously a determining factor for its shelf life. If the site looks outdated, it will make the company or individual that the site represents appear outdated. Another factor that plays into the shelf life of a site is flexibility—a designer's ability to add and delete pages and portions of pages.

If a designer needs to spend hours changing the layout of a site because the client wants to add two sections, but the menu will not support it, then the site has a poor, inflexible design. If the designer simply needs to add only a few rows of content in a nested container, then that is a flexible design.

Figure 3.15 is an example of an inflexible design. Notice the menu at the bottom center of the page. Not only are the items in an area that does not allow much vertical expansion, but the menu items are also images, which are easy to create but

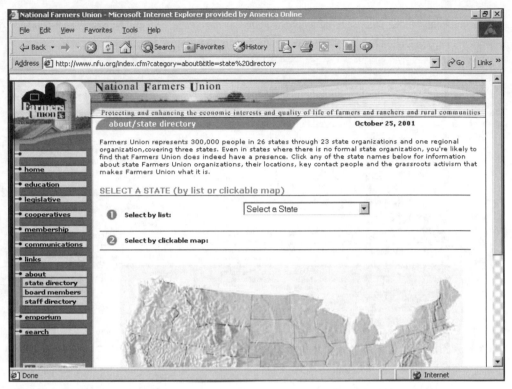

FIGURE 3.14   Third-level page of the site in Figure 3.13 where the right section was removed.

more difficult to maintain. Another weakness of this design is that the menu items have to be repositioned for subsequent pages, usually at the top or left of the main body.

There are three areas of a site that should be designed to be flexible:

1. **Menu navigation**—This is probably the most common flexibility problem of designs. If a site undergoes edits, many times the client is going to add or delete menu items. While deleting is not as much of a problem, adding items is. The menu, therefore, needs to be able to have items added to it without requiring a redesign.

   Another flexibility problem is in making the menu too narrow, whether it is a vertical or horizontal menu. (Navigation and developing menus are discussed in Chapter 4.)

2. **Content layout**—Whether a site has a low or high amount of content, there is almost always the possibility that new text or graphics will be added; therefore, the layout of the site should be able to accommodate such changes without being compromised. The site in Figure 3.15 would not be

able to handle growth in the content area unless the font sizes were reduced, which might not be a wise decision because the entire site is very graphic-intensive. If the amount of text was increased, it would flow over the images to the right and to the bottom.

3. **Title areas**—It is necessary for a user to be able to identify second- and third-level pages. One way to identify pages past the homepage is to include a text description, such as in Figure 3.16. It is wise to build an area that can handle some of the longer section names. The site in Figure 3.16 allows plentiful room to add even the longest of titles. As wide as "Application Development" is, it could be longer and still be supported by the design.

FIGURE 3.15   Example of an inflexible design.

Per the seven rules of Web design (see Chapter 1), there is nearly always an exception. So is the case for flexibility. The downside to flexibility is that it limits a designer in what can be done with the layout of a site. Many sites that do not require much, if any, maintenance are perfect candidates for designing flowing graphical designs that are comprised of minimal text. A perfect example would be a short-term site, such as a site of an upcoming movie that might be in existence for only six

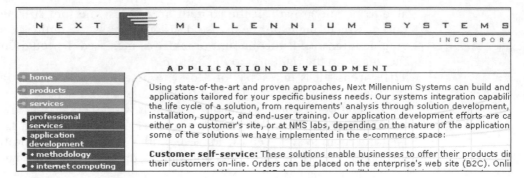

FIGURE 3.16   Design that supports long second- and third-level titles. Copyright © 2002 by Next Millennium
Systems, Inc. All rights reserved.

months, after which it probably would be taken down or left unmaintained. In a rare
case like this, the designer does not need to worry as much about creating a site that
can be easily managed.

SUMMARY

A well-designed site is a well-thought-out site. Much of the work that goes into a
design begins with collecting requirements so the designer understands the needs of
the site. Such efforts can drastically reduce future time spent making corrections or
redesigning.

A designer should take many requirements, such as bandwidth concerns, resolution, and color depth, into consideration before beginning the design. Once this information is collected, the designer should create flexible, scalable sites using include
files.

4

ENHANCING USABILITY

In This Chapter

- Simplifying Architecture
- Creating Layout
- Developing Navigation
- Designing for Accessibility
- Designing for Content

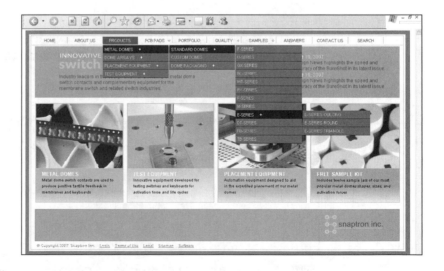

Thee are not many users who like being confused or having to wait when they come to a site. Studies have shown that visitors spend no longer than 10 to 20 seconds on the homepage, alone. This is not a lot of time to communicate a message. Usability, therefore, is king when trying to keep a user at the site—not only on the homepage, but also on subsequent pages.

Download time, resolution, and browser compatibility are three previously discussed areas that can make or break the usability of a site. There are, though, three areas that have not yet been discussed that are just as, if not more, important: site architecture, layout, and navigation.

SIMPLIFYING ARCHITECTURE

Architecture is the way a site is constructed and flows in terms of sections and pages. A site map is a visual representation of the site's architecture. As shown in Figure 4.1, a user can discover how this site is laid out by reading the Contents site map page. It is easy to see that the Sol-O-Matic page is in the Additional Products section, which in turn falls under the Coin-Op Equipment heading.

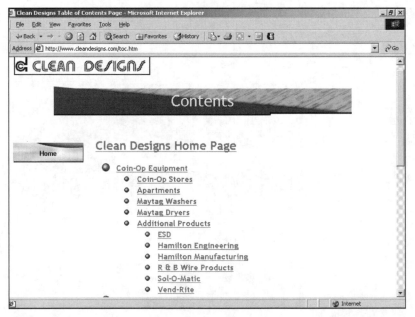

FIGURE 4.1   Site map of a site. Copyright © 2002 by Clean Designs, Inc. All rights reserved.

The designer, however, should never rely solely on providing the user a site map for their understanding of how a site is constructed. Rather, the site should be intuitive in the way it is designed. Following are several aspects a designer should consider when creating the architecture of a site.

Use a Consistent Naming Convention

A designer typically should not try to get creative when naming sections and pages, unless they are unique to only that site. While it was more acceptable to be creative in the mid-1990s, this is no longer the case because certain usability standards have been set. In other words, users expect to see one thing, so why run the risk of losing them if they cannot find what they are expecting?

The company contact section in most sites is a perfect example; it is common practice to put contact information in a Contact, Contact Us, or Customer Service link on the site. This is an easily understandable, general, catchall term that can include the postal address, e-mail address(es), and phone and fax numbers. If the designer, on the other hand, were to name the link Communications Center, the user might not make the initial association.

One instance where it is slightly more acceptable to be creative with naming conventions is when a site has a metaphorical theme, such as a town theme, for its sections. Naming the Contact Us section the Post Office is going to be fairly intuitive as long as every section falls under a similar naming convention, such as Library, General Store, and Town Hall. Using metaphorical themes, though, can be risky. The designer is taking the chance that the majority of users will understand the theme and meanings of the sections. When designing a site for an international audience, the risk of confusion becomes even higher.

Limit the Clicking

Back in the mid-1990s, the standard number of clicks to get to any page from the homepage was as high as five or six. Today, however, it is generally wise to try to design a site so that a user can reach the majority of information within three clicks, although there are always exceptions to the rule. Limiting the number of clicks simply allows the user to get to the content more quickly, thus limiting the frustration of having to deal with numerous hyperlinks and waiting to download additional pages. There are certainly exceptions to this rule, such as forms and application sites with large amounts of content that require more clicks, but three clicks should always be the goal of a designer. Figure 4.1 demonstrates the value of limiting the number of clicks a user must make. Note that all of the sections are within three clicks of the homepage.

Avoid Linking the User Out of the Section

Linking a user out of a section means that when a user clicks into, for example, the About Us section, then clicks on a subnavigation item E-mail Us, they end up in the Contact Us section. It can be confusing to the user if the subnavigation of a site suddenly changes because the hyperlink is connected to another section.

 While using the bread crumbs technique (showing the page path in the title, About Us/History/ Early Years) can be helpful, it does not eliminate the confusion of unexpectedly ending up in a new section of a site.

While this particular example is not overly confusing, it becomes more so when the flow becomes circular. Take Figure 4.2 for an example. If a user came to this site and clicked the Professional Services bullet on the menu to the left, the hyperlink would take that user to the subpage displayed in the right-hand section of the figure.

The subnavigation on that page, however, is where the confusing circular navigation begins. If the user were to click on RIZNA Consulting, the hyperlink would go to the RIZNA Consulting section, which also is in the left-hand menu area. If the user were to click on Running Consulting in the subnavigation menu, they would return to Professional Services, completely making a loop back to where the trip started. To confuse the issue even more, the subnavigation items Virtual Consulting and Technologies Used, which are on both of those pages, take the user to entirely different pages in entirely different sections.

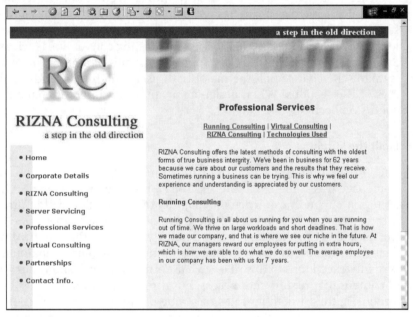

FIGURE 4.2   Site that confuses the user with its circular flow.

The problem of circular flow usually occurs when a client wants the site to appear to have more pages than it really has. Ultimately though, this problem makes the site appear disorganized and should be avoided at all costs for the sake of usability.

Create Cascading Architecture versus Flat Architecture

Flat architecture has long been a staple of many sites. Flat architecture involves putting as much information on the homepage as possible so that the user need only click once or twice to find the desired page. The problem with a flat-architecture site, such as the one in Figure 4.3, is that the user becomes overwhelmed, confused, and frustrated with the difficult navigation. The site offers so much information that it is difficult for the user to find items without having to slowly search the entire page.

FIGURE 4.3   Site that uses flat architecture to place as many links as possible on one page.

Cascading architecture, on the other hand, eliminates a lot of the confusion by organizing similar types of content in their own intuitive subsections of a site. Then when the user clicks, for example, on a link entitled Finance, similar items, such as tips, news, portfolio information, a stock ticker, and other financial areas, are all bundled on the same, concise Finance page. By combining consistent information on one "mini-homepage," the user does not have to drudge through all the sub-menus, lists, and shortcuts that are randomly included all over the homepage of a flat-architecture site.

CREATING LAYOUT

A good layout is essential for the presentation of a professional image of a site. It also is important for the usability of a site. A user should be able to locate information with complete ease. Much of this is accomplished with the layout. Layout, in this instance, refers more to the positioning of elements, rather than the site's look and feel. Two areas a designer must consider when creating a layout are scrolling and positioning.

Scrolling versus Nonscrolling

Everyone and every study on usability has an opinion on whether a site should scroll or not. It is one of those design issues that will never have a resolution, only trends advocating or opposing it. Because scrolling is always up for debate, it is smart for the designer to make it one of the required front-end questions for the client. Following are some pros and cons of scrolling.

Pros of Scrolling

1. The design can fit more content on one page.
2. The user does not have to click and wait for another page to load. This not only takes time, but the user must also refocus her eyes on a new area, most likely at or near the top of the screen.
3. It is easy to quickly navigate if the user has a mouse with a scroller wheel or a stylus, which also allows for easy cursor movement.

Cons of Scrolling

1. It takes less effort to click on a link that opens a new page than to mouse over to the scrollbar, click on it, and drag it up or down.
2. Because scrollable pages are longer, their download is typically larger.

One instance where scrolling is absolutely unacceptable is when the designer creates wide pages that force the user to scroll horizontally. Not only does it contradict accepted usability standards, but it also requires more motion than vertical scrolling because the Web page width is wider than its height.

Positioning Content

Probably, the most important component of a professional, intuitive design is the positioning of content. The user should not have to go searching for the most relevant information of the site. Rather, it should be positioned where it is easy to find.

Probably the first item a designer must address is the positioning of the menu. Since the mid-1990s, designers have experimented with placing the menu on the left, right, top, center, or bottom of the page—anywhere a designer can imagine, a menu has been placed there.

Over the years, placing the menu to the left or on the top of the page has become the more traditional standard. There are technical reasons for this, which are explained in the next section.

The second area a designer should address is the header. This area typically includes any of the following items:

1. Company logo
2. Advertisements
3. Links, such as Today's Date, for globally used functionality

4. Company tagline
5. Hyperlinks that do not necessarily belong in the menu
6. Content

When designing the header section of a site, a smart strategy is to use as much content that can be cached by the browser as possible. This decreases the download time of subsequent pages that use the same header file because content is already cached in the computer's memory. While it is tempting to create a unique header for every section of a site, the designer should ask the question, "Does it improve or hinder communication?" There is a difference between being creative to improve communication and being creative just to be different. Associating a color with a specific section might be beneficial, or it might just confuse the user, depending on the execution of the design elements.

When creating the header, a designer can take advantage of existing Web-usability standards. It is very common, for example, for a logo to be placed in the upper-left corner of a site. Because so many sites use this same design structure, users are accustomed to looking up there for the logo. What a designer can do is place content in the upper-left corner that is deemed by the client to be more important than the logo. That way, the designer takes advantage of Web usability to increase the usability of that particular site.

The final area to consider when positioning is the body. Because designs can be shifted and shaped however desired, the best positioning location is not an easy call. Typically, the prime real estate of a site is the upper-center to upper-left section of the page(s). Users who come in at lower resolutions are going to lose the right side and bottom of a design before anywhere else; this, by default, makes the right and bottom areas less effective for communicating. This is not to say that these areas cannot be effectively used in a design. If the designer leads the user's eye with graphics or color, any section of the initial screen can be used.

The bottom line is that there are exceptions to every rule, and a designer should experiment with positioning. No site is perfect, and nearly all sites are in constant evolution. If Web designs became too similar and predictable, the user's eye would become lazy and less controllable.

Users, of course, are the ultimate judges. If a site does not compel them to stay, then the designer has not done a good job of communicating.

DEVELOPING NAVIGATION

Both usability and maintenance are issues when creating the navigation, or menu(s) of a site. As mentioned previously, the menu is a key component of effective Web design. It should intuitively help a user find any item. If not, the designer runs the risk of losing the user who becomes frustrated and leaves the site. There also are technical reasons for designing a smart menu. Maintaining a site is not always easy or convenient. Therefore, a menu should be designed so that items can be easily added, edited, or deleted.

Creating Consistency

To confuse is to lose a user. Following an inconsistent menu is the same as using a map that constantly changes from minute to minute. There are three flaws a designer should avoid when creating the menu:

1. **Moving the menu**—When inside the site, it is considered poor design to move the menu vertically or horizontally to accommodate other content that is added to the area. The user should be able to always look in the same area(s) for the same menu(s). A secondary menu is sometimes necessary for certain pages when the global menu (main menu included on all pages) will not support them. These menus should be placed in the same place on every page, rather than being placed wherever or whenever they may fit.
2. **Changing the menu**—Once a menu is past the homepage, it should be set in stone. A designer should not be adding items unless there are pages and/or subcategories being added below parent sections that existed in the original menu on the homepage. The designer, for example, can confuse the user by adding a section of an existing menu on one or two pages and then eliminating it from the menu on all other pages. The user is not always going to follow such changes.
3. **Limiting the number of menus**—A menu serves as a convenient, concise listing of sections or pages of a site that a user can quickly locate. Once a designer begins adding mini-menus to other areas of a design, intuitive navigation is decreased. An example of such menus is shown in Figure 4.4. One menu is to the right of the global menu, which is in the upper-left corner of the page; the other menu is in the row below the World Tradeshow content.

Portal sites, which offer many resources and services, are usually the most common abusers of multiple-menu design. While there may be a menu for larger sections of the site, there may also be two or three other mini-menus that the user has to find. A well-designed site should rarely use more than two menus on any given page. Often, links or sections in mini-menus can be included in the global menu. Sometimes they may fit very well in existing sections, or sometimes they need to have a special subsection created.

Using Text for Menu Items

Creating images for menu items can sometimes add to the look of a site, but most of the time they require a lot more work on the designer's part to add or edit them in the future. Often, text with a simple mouseover image that can be repeated can be used in place of individual images for each item. Not only does this solution decrease the download size of a site, but it also makes a menu very easy to create and edit.

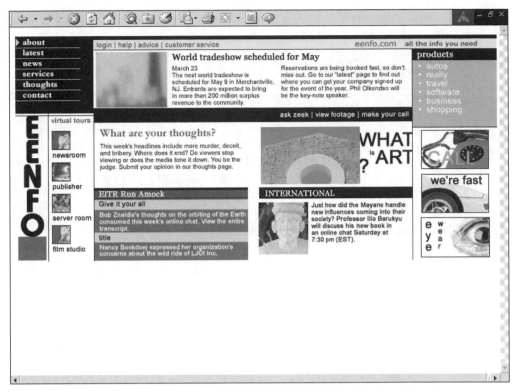

FIGURE 4.4   Site that includes two mini-menus in addition to a global menu.

Deciding Whether to Use a Horizontal or Vertical Structure

Both horizontally and vertically structured menus have advantages and disadvantages. A horizontal menu structure allows the designer to use the full width of the screen for content. This is particularly useful for application sites that display large amounts of information in columns. Using a horizontal menu, though, has a drawback. There is only so much room to expand sideways. Therefore, if a design exceeds the width of the page, the designer will need to add another row for the menu, which can be awkward, or the site will require a redesign. Another problem is that the menu can easily exceed the viewable area of monitors with lesser resolution. If, for example, the site is designed for 1024 × 768 resolution, a monitor with 800 × 600 resolution will lose 224 pixels on the right side of the screen. The advantages and disadvantages of a vertical menu are exactly opposite to those of a horizontal menu. An advantage is that vertical menus can easily be expanded because they stretch the page downward, which requires the user to simply scroll down. Because they take up horizontal space, vertical menus naturally minimize the amount of horizontal room the designer needs to work with. Of course, while this can be a disadvantage for an application site, it can actually be considered an advantage for a site that is lacking in content. A designer can use a wider vertical menu to take up the overall space of a low-content site.

Allowing Enough Width

Whether using a horizontal or vertical menu structure, the designer should always take the length of menu items into account before designing. If many of the items are long, then the menu might not even initially fit the width of the screen. Vertical menus also fall prey to this problem, though not as badly. If a menu item is too long in a vertical menu, it will either stretch the menu too wide or wrap around to the next line. Many times the client will need to rename the menu items so they fit in a specified space.

Understanding the Different Types of Menus

There are five main types of menus that are used in Web sites, and each has its pros and cons. Many of the considerations for deciding which menu type to use are the same as those faced when designing an entire site: download time, browser support, and maintenance. Following are the various menus:

1. **JavaScript or Java applets**—These menus can expand and contract when items are clicked. The advantages of these menus are that they allow the user to view the entire site by quickly scanning the navigation on one page, and they can be cached. The disadvantages are that they are more difficult to maintain (unless dynamically built on the fly using data from the database), they may need to be programmed for the two different DOMs, and they generally have a sizable initial download.

2. **Macromedia Flash**—If the designer wants to build more creative menus, Flash is the way to go. It not only allows a designer with limited programming experience to build graphically animated menus, but Flash also allows MP3 and WAV audio to be added when a user mouses over or clicks on menu items. The disadvantages are that the user must have the Flash plug-in, these menus are more difficult to maintain, and they can annoy the user if not designed correctly. This last reason is similar to one of the overriding problems with multimedia sites—form precedes function. Users, for example, do not always want to see a round ball spin, shrink, expand, or change to a rectangle when each menu item is activated. The wow factor is great the first time, but quickly loses its appeal thereafter.

3. **Image-mapped graphic**—By adding image mapping to a graphic, a designer can make any section of an image clickable. This allows more creativity with menus. Image-mapping functionality is also well-supported by older browsers, and such menus can be cached. The problems with image-mapped menus are that they have a higher download because of the image, additional code is necessary, and both the image and code must be maintained, which is considerably more time-consuming. For the most part, these types of menus are no longer used.

4. **HTML text with mouseover**—These menus, which use text along with a couple of small mouseover images, are supported by all browsers, require only a small download, and can be dynamic. They still let the user know when an item has been selected, and they are extremely easy to maintain. A disadvantage is that while the designer can be creative with the mouseover images, the font types are limited to Web text unless embedded fonts are used, which requires a plug-in and the download of the font. Another disadvantage is that while they can be dynamically created with a database-driven site, each time a new menu is created, the user's browser cannot take advantage of caching the menu.

5. **CSS**—One of the most simple menu options is CSS menus. There are several different versions included with the designs in this book that run either horizontally or vertically. More importantly, though, there are CSS drop-down menus that are easy to update, while also being search-engine friendly, not to mention that they also don't require JavaScript code that can be more complicated and code-intensive. Stuart Nicholls with CSSplay (www.cssplay.co.uk/menus/simple_vertical.html) has come up with an incredibly flexible and easy-to-use system that is well supported. Figure 4.5 shows a site that uses CSSplay's menu system.

This CSS menu system is included on the CD for the designer to use.

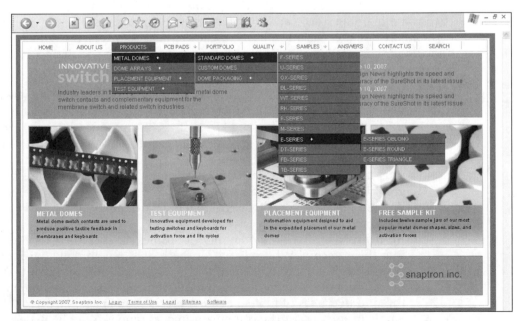

FIGURE 4.5   A simple yet powerful CSS menu provided for free by www.cssplay.co.uk. Copyright © 2007 by Stu Nicholls. All rights reserved.

Because menus are so important to the usability of a site, it is important that the designer uses the right type of menu. If the audience is more advanced, Java, JavaScript, or Flash menus may be the way to go. If the audience contains both advanced and novice users, then XHTML or CSS menus should probably be used, depending on how they're created. Most of the designs included with this book use XHTML or CSS menus because of their limited download and ease of adding, editing, and deleting.

DESIGNING FOR ACCESSIBILITY

There are some Internet users who consider usability as much of a technical issue as a visual, navigational, or comprehensibility issue. In other words, can the content of a site actually be obtained and used—that is, is it accessible?

When planning a site, the designer needs to consider different issues, such as, will the content need to be obtained by a voice browser? If a user has a slow connection, is it possible to read what an image is about before seeing it? Or is it wise to use server-side processing when client-side processing will suffice?

DESIGNING FOR CONTENT

The amount of content in a site usually determines how a site will be designed. Some clients simply need a couple of pages put up, while others need full-blown database-driven sites that include thousands of pages. Therefore, the designer needs to understand the site's requirements before beginning. If a site has little content, then the remaining space can be supplemented with images. If a site requires more content, the designer will, most likely, use fewer images to keep the download smaller and the design less busy. Following are three types of sites a designer can create, based on content (they are templates that are included in this book):

1. **Low content**—These sites are usually designed for the client who only wants to have an "online brochure." Such sites generally include the basic information a user is looking for, such as information about the client, services and products offered, and contact information. Because these sites have a limited amount of content, they require more graphics to fill a page. This does not mean, however, that the entire page has to be filled with graphics. Much of it can also be white space, such as is shown in Figure 4.6. The ratio of content to images is generally around 20 percent to 80 percent, respectively.

2. **Medium content**—The majority of business sites created for the Web fall into this category. While clients for these sites may initially have a medium amount of content, they could be holding back on larger content so that they do not overwhelm the user on the homepage; such sites generally have three to five areas of limited content on the homepage. Figure 4.7 is an example of such a site. The content-to-images ratio is roughly 50 percent to 50 percent, respectively.

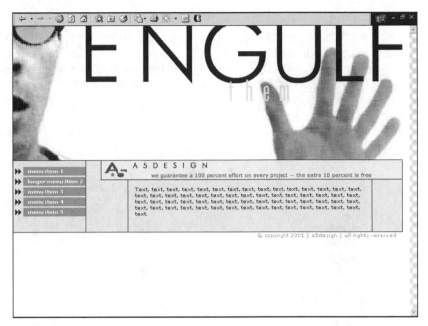

FIGURE 4.6   Low-content design that uses graphics to supplement the limited amount of content.

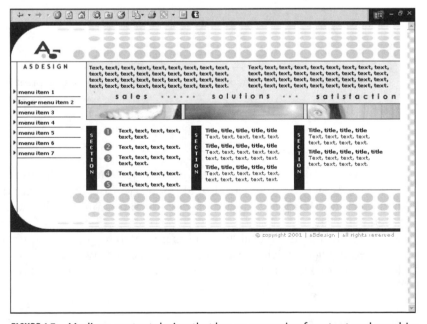

FIGURE 4.7   Medium-content design that has an even mix of content and graphics.

3. **High content**—These sites are all about disseminating information and/or selling a product. Because they have so much content, the amount of images is limited, particularly large-size images. In other words, while images are used, they are generally smaller, such as the blurred images in the center of the site shown in Figure 4.8. These sites typically have more than five areas of content.

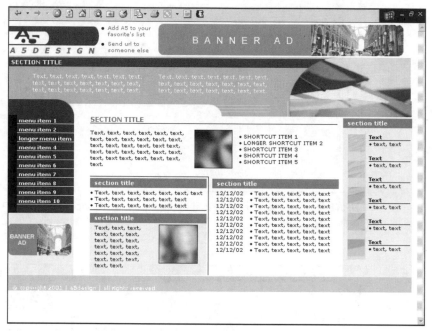

FIGURE 4.8 High-content design that offers a large amount of content and limited graphics.

SUMMARY

No matter what the design philosophy is, usability should always be considered when creating a site. The user should not be confused by the naming of menu items or hyperlinks that go to unrelated sections; nor should he be overwhelmed by too much content.

A key factor in the usability and maintainability of a site is its navigation. Well-designed navigation will have items that can be easily added, edited, or deleted; that download quickly; and that are supported by the target users' browsers.

GATHERING REQUIREMENTS AND CREATING A COMP

In This Chapter

- Gathering and Basing a Site on Requirements
- Creating a Comp for the Client
- Receiving a Decision on the Chosen Comp and Making Edits

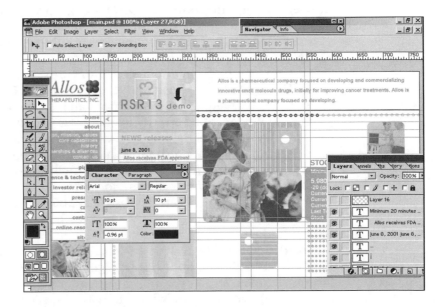

Once a designer understands the fundamentals of building a mortised site, then the fun begins—actually building the site. There are 10 general steps a designer should follow when building a mortised site:

1. **Gathering and basing a site on requirements**—Requirements determine, among other things, how many graphics the designer will use, what colors will be used, how fast the site must be, what future growth or changes the design must accommodate, and what content and functionality will be included on the homepage and subsequent pages.

2. **Creating comp(s) for the client**—It's simpler and more efficient to build the look and feel of the site (that is, a comp) in Photoshop than to build the actual homepage piece by piece. Comps are also important because they can define many of the styles that are cascaded throughout the site.

3. **Receiving a decision on the chosen comp and making edits**—Once a comp is decided upon, the client may very well request that a few changes be made to the design, such as "lighten the blue and replace the orange with yellow," or "replace this section of text with that one," or "use another photo in the upper-right corner." Once the edits are received, the changes are made, and the selected comp is then resubmitted for approval. Sometimes this process can take several iterations before the final comp is approved.

4. **Breaking up the comp into XHTML, graphics, and CSS**—At this point, the selected comp is sliced into different images and saved as compressed images. XHTML and CSS are then used to bring together the images, text, and possible functionality.

5. **Testing the page in most commonly used browsers**—The designer should usually test a page in IE (versions 6 and 7), Firefox, Opera, and Safari as elements are added to it. Otherwise, after spending hours building a page, it might not function correctly in a browser that was not used during development. Sometimes the browsers that need to be tested will change due to site requirements or which browsers are most commonly used.

6. **Saving components of the page as include files and testing again**—To decrease the download time for subsequent pages and make maintenance considerably easier, the designer should save individual components, such as the menu, header, and footer, as separate include files. The design should then be tested again.

7. **Building second- and third-level pages from the homepage template**—Usually, the homepage design can be taken and reused as the general template structure for subsequent pages if it makes use of cached images and include files, which decrease download time. The designer then enters content into the body of each page of the site.

8. **Working with the client as the site is built**—The designer should have the client view the pages as they are built. Otherwise, if the requirements were misunderstood by either party, corrections could still be made before

considerable time is wasted working on a site that will likely need redesign-ing. Another common issue with requirements is that while they may sometimes look good on paper, better ideas come about when the site is built.

9. **Testing the entire site**—On larger sites where the budget allows, the de-signer can hire a professional tester(s) to test a site. However, on sites with limited budgets, it is usually the designer and client who test the site.

10. **Implementing the site**—The designer uploads the site to the live server, whether it be an internal or external Web server.

While not every step is needed, they all are used to some degree for the majority of sites.

GATHERING AND BASING A SITE ON REQUIREMENTS

Requirements are the roadmap for the designer to build upon. Misunderstandings between the client and designer are considerably less likely when requirements exist.

Requirements can be included in a couple of informal e-mails or phone calls, or they can be included in more involved documents that can be many pages long. Although requirements are not always gathered the same way, the designer should always try to document as much as possible before beginning work.

While there is no set way to collect requirements, an example of how and what to collect is shown in the redesign of the Allos Therapeutics, Inc. site shown in Figure 5.1.

Under the guidance of the director of corporate communications, the company wanted to redesign its site to have a fresh, upbeat, professional look and be database-driven. The director wanted to incorporate Allos' new branding, as well as create a contemporary site that uses updated, relevant information.

The director and designer initially spoke together on the phone several times be-fore scheduling a meeting. The director had a good idea of what she wanted. She had the entire site map laid out, along with several sentences describing the requirements for each page. She also knew the general look and feel that she was interested in. Having worked on many sites, the director knew the requirements would need input, revisions, and consensual agreement from her staff before beginning work on the site. Following a meeting with her peers, she and the designer discussed the various options and implications that the new site should address. At this point, the designer collected what is known as the *front-end requirements*.

Using the answers to those questions and specific requests made by the director about the site's database functionality, the designer created and delivered three comps. Incorporating some of the aspects from the other two designs, Figure 5.2 illustrates the look, feel, and functionality that was decided upon.

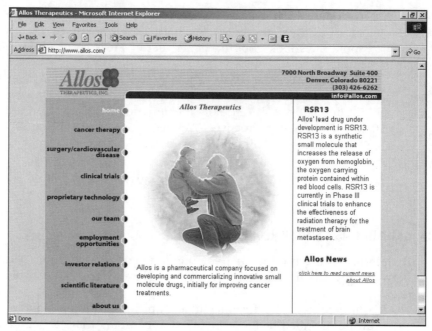

FIGURE 5.1   Allos Therapeutics, Inc.'s old design. Copyright © 2002 by Allos Therapeutics, Inc. All rights reserved.

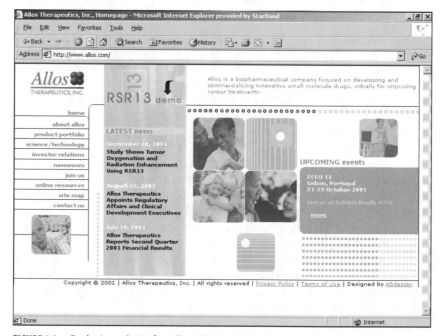

FIGURE 5.2   Redesigned site for Allos Therapeutics, Inc. Copyright © 2002 by Allos Therapeutics, Inc. All rights reserved.

Following are some of the various attributes of the new design:

1. There was a dominance of yellow, which gave the site the fresh, upbeat, professional look desired. However, because yellow is a color that can become overwhelming for some people, the majority of it was removed on subsequent pages.
2. Since the client wanted the content to be dynamically generated from a database, each section was designed to be expandable without disrupting the design. This is why content containers were nested in each column.
3. Because the second- and third-level pages had varying amounts of content, a nested container was designed into the right side of the page (see Figure 5.3). If a page had limited content, the area could be included to make the content area look fuller. If, on the other hand, a page had a lot of content, the container, which created an additional column, could be removed.
4. To provide consistent navigation, the same expandable menu was saved as an include file in the left column for all pages. This also made future maintenance simple, enabling the designer to edit the entire site by changing only one file.
5. The header was also saved as an include file to simplify maintenance.

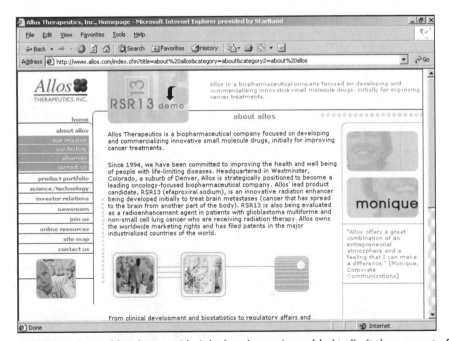

FIGURE 5.3   Second-level page with right-hand container added to limit the amount of content that is necessary to fill a page. Copyright © 2002 by Allos Therapeutics, Inc. All rights reserved.

The requirements process does not always end after a requirements document is approved. Throughout the building process, the director and designer added, deleted, and edited pages, as well as adjusted the functionality of the site. Fortunately, because many of the major requirements (such as the site's look and feel and site table structure) were finalized at the beginning of the project, future changes were minimal.

Many times with smaller sites, clients do not have the time, experience, or interest in discussing requirements. They simply want a site. In these cases, the client prefers to leave the decisions to the designer. The designer should still try, nonetheless, to provide options, explain the pros and cons of those options, and let the client make the decisions whenever possible. One example of such a decision is resolution. If a client recently purchased a computer with default resolution that is greater than the standard resolution of the average user's monitor, the designer should explain the situation to the client. By explaining the issue at hand, the client knows that if the site were created for her computer, it would probably be too wide for the majority of users with the standard resolution.

CREATING A COMP FOR THE CLIENT

Designing a comp is where the majority of the creative aspects of building a site occurs. It is where the designer lays out the text, images, possible functionality, and colors in a composition that will closely resemble the final product. The comp is then delivered to the client for possible editing and ultimate approval.

When creating a comp, the designer should take the technical as well as aesthetic aspects of a site into consideration. One thought process, for example, might be, "If I place this content in the header, will it remain there for the rest of the site, or will it be replaced by another element? If it is replaced by other content, what will that content be? Will it be text, or will it be a text-field box for testimonials?" In other words, at this point the designer considers what kind of programming will be required to get the page or site to function properly.

As previously mentioned, a comp is created in image editing software. For the purposes of this book, all examples use Adobe Photoshop (see Figure 5.4).

There are several advantages to creating a comp with Photoshop:

1. A design can be created more quickly than when built as an actual Web page using XHTML, graphics, and CSS.
2. Changes can quickly be made to a design during the comp process or in the future, once the site is live and the client requests a change.
3. Because Photoshop uses layers, the design is extremely flexible. If a designer needs to replace one image that is on its own layer, only that layer needs to be changed.
4. The slicing technology included with Photoshop allows for the designer to add slices (boxes) on the file and then create and save many individual images from the one file. For example, if an older version of a logo is used in the comp while a newer one is being created, the designer can eventually switch out the logo, save the new slice that creates the newer image, and then just upload that one particular file to the server.

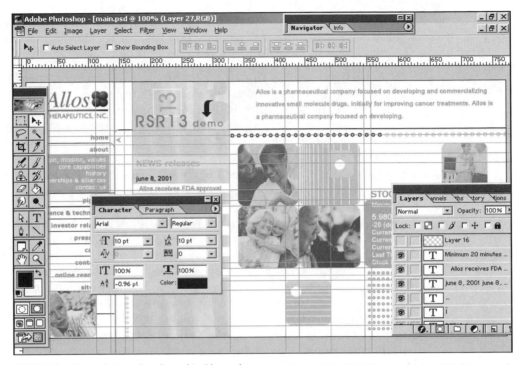

FIGURE 5.4   Comp being developed in Photoshop.

Because the look, feel, and styles included in the comp will be cascaded down throughout the entire site, it is important to make sure the feeling and appearance they project is correct. This is why the designer, depending on the client's budget, should provide at least three different comps. It not only gives the client a choice of designs, but it also gives her the ability to mix and match certain pieces of the various designs. The client, for example, might say, "I like the black-and-white treatment you did to the photos in the first design. Can you add those to the third design?" Much of the designing of a comp is left to the creativity of the designer.

The way in which a designer delivers comps can vary. Sometimes a lot of them will be delivered at once, or each one could be delivered after feedback is provided on the previous comps. Many times, the latter method works better because the designer can more efficiently and effectively incorporate the latest edits, along with earlier ones that remain pertinent.

Creating a Source Directory

There are many types of files (Web files, images, and source files) that go into creating a mortised site. If all files were saved together in one directory, individual files would be difficult to find. This is why a designer should use a consistent filing and naming system.

Creating a basic folder system before beginning a site takes at most a minute, but it saves the designer time and headaches when looking for files in the future. Following is one filing system method that requires four directories:

1. **Web project name**—This folder is usually named after a specific project. After years of creating and archiving many sites, it is easy to forget the specific URL of the site, which is why it is sometimes wise to name the folder after the site itself. This is particularly helpful if the site URL doesn't match that of the company, or if the designer can't remember if the site is ".com" or ".net."

2. **Images**—This is where all the images used in the site are located. It is generally common practice to separate Web files from image files of Web sites.

3. **Sources**—Because a designer may often have to refer back to the original PSD file(s), it is wise to keep them in a consistent area. A good place to store this folder is in a subdirectory under the Images folder. Some developers save the source files in a completely different area so the files are not accidentally copied over to a live server. Not only does a designer not want to allow access to such files, but they also can be an extremely large upload.

4. **Stock**—While stock photos can be saved in the Sources folder, it is a good practice to save them in their own folder. Otherwise, if there are only three or four PSD files included in the Sources folder, they could be difficult to find if they are among all the stock photo images.

In addition to using an organized folder system, a designer should also try to be consistent with the naming of files. This is particularly important for the Images folder. Because a mortised site can contain images used for spacing, backgrounds, and photos, it is generally helpful to use a naming convention that keeps such images in their respective families. One good method is to include the family of the image first in the name, and then include the text that identifies that specific image in the second half of the file name. For example, if the image is a background for the menu, the name could be bg_menu.gif. The "bg_" classifies the image as a background image, and the "menu" identifies the image as the background behind the menu.

The advantage to this naming convention is that it is easy to find one file among many, especially if the designer knows what family the image is in. Figure 5.5 shows the Images folder for a site that has 35 images. Notice that all the background images are identified as "bg_," all the bullets as "bullet_," and all the photos as "photo_."

If the designer uses an image for second- or third-level pages that has the same name as an image for the first level or homepage, an "_sl" (standing for "second level") can be added to the end of the image name. If the background image for a menu is different on the second level, for example, it could be named bg_menu_sl.gif.

Collecting and Documenting Stock Images

Using stock images is one way to make a site appear professional. Fortunately for the Web designer, stock photos can be much less expensive than for print designers. A

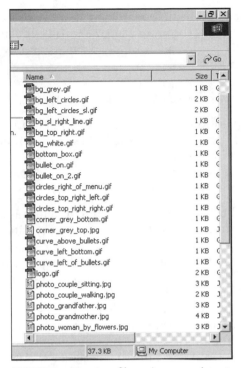

FIGURE 5.5   Directory files using a consistent naming convention that identifies them in families.

high-resolution, print-ready image that costs $600 can cost around $150 for the low-resolution version (72 dpi)—exactly what is needed for Web design.

Prices generally range from $1 to more than $1,000, depending on which company the designer purchases from and whether the image is royalty-free. Generally, and depending on the company, royalty-free means that the image's number of uses and applications is unlimited by the designer once the image is purchased—as long as the image is not used in pornographic or defamatory ways. It is important to check the usage agreement before purchasing a photo because not all agreements are the same.

Images can usually be purchased either individually or bundled together with other images on a CD-ROM. They also can be collectively downloaded, depending on the stock photo company. Buying an individual image is less expensive, and the image's subject matter (for example, the Amazon River dolphin) might be one that the designer will never need additional photos of. On the other hand, if the designer is going to be creating many high-tech Web sites, a bundled CD-ROM of unique, high-tech images might be the way to go. Bundled stock collections are more expensive, but they contain many similar images for a subject, which dramatically drops the cost of each individual photo. One photo, for example, that costs $30 individually could be included on a CD-ROM of 100 similar images for $400, which drops the price to $4 per image. It simply depends on how much the designer anticipates using such photos.

 Listed here are some popular stock image sources that can be found on the Web:

- www.istockphoto.com (At time of publication, this was one of the most reasonably priced stock imagery sites on the internet.)
- www.corbis.com
- www.getty-images.com
- www.comstock.com

When collecting stock images for a design, it is a good practice to document all the images—that is, what the image is, which site it was found on, how much it costs, and the photo ID. (Most sites give a specific identifier or stock number for each image, such as #IE55648.) The designer can store this information in a text file in the Sources folder. That way, it is easy to know where to go when the image needs to be officially purchased for a site.

Because nearly all stock image companies allow the designer to download and temporarily use comp versions of images in their comp designs, the designer should not purchase the official image(s) until final approval and payment for the site has been received. Until that time, the designer should leave the watermarked (comp) version or thumbnail of the image(s) in the site—all the more incentive for the client to pay its bill.

Selecting Colors

Color plays an integral part in any Web site, which is why a professional Web designer should have a sound understanding of color theory. Color not only helps set the look and feel of a site, but it also can be used to increase the usability of a site by leading the user's eye and helping to prioritize content.

Many color schemes are possible when designing a site. The designer can use a black-and-white scheme with one or two spot colors, a monochromatic scheme (different shades of one color), complementary schemes (colors that complement each other), or split-complementary schemes (two colors that are "one off" of a color that complements a color on the other side of a color wheel).

One of the questions a designer should ask a client before designing a site is what type of mood or feel the site should convey. The answer to this question can then be translated into the choice of colors used in a site, if the branding for the company hasn't already been determined. If, for instance, the client wanted a secure, conservative look, probably the best color to start with would be blue. It is a cool color that is used in many instances to convey a safe, reserved feeling.

The audience also comes into play when using color. Colors do not represent the same emotions in various countries. While white, for example, is used in weddings in the United States, it is used in funerals in China. The designer, therefore, might want to research colors when designing international sites. Another audience issue the designer must consider is color blindness. The most common form is red/green color blindness; red and green look similar to someone with this blindness.

 Sites can also be run through www.vischeck.com to determine how they will appear to color blind people. It also gives definitions and examples of the different types of color blindness.

Following are a couple of references that will give the designer a foundation for color theory:

- *Color Harmony: A Guide to Creative Color Combinations* by Hideako Chijiiwa (Rockport Publishers, 1987)
- *Color Bytes: Blending the Art and Science of Color* by Jean Bourges (Specialty Marketing Group, 1997)
- **Color wheel**—A good color wheel will show the designer different combinations, such as complementary and split-complementary colors. Color wheels can generally be found in art stores and online.

Deciding Layout

While there are obvious aesthetic considerations to the layout of a site, there are technical aspects as well. If the site is not designed correctly for the technical aspects, many repercussions can arise in the future for both the designer and, possibly, the programmer. Depending on the design and site requirements, following are four aspects of layout that should be taken into consideration:

1. **Vertical versus horizontal space**—A designer needs to consider the amount and type of content a site needs to support before designing the framework for the site. If the body requires a lot of room for content, then a wider design will be necessary. If the content is limited, then the designer is going to want to keep the body area narrow to avoid the appearance that it lacks substance. A good way to control the space of the content area is by using either a vertical or horizontal menu. When placed in the header, a horizontal menu allows the designer to use the full area below it for space-intensive sites, such as Web applications that may include many columns of content. Vertical menus, on the other hand, can take up horizontal space and help supplement sites that lack content.

   If the screen simply does not offer enough room for content, the only other option, other than reducing font sizes, is to increase the required resolution of a site. A site with 1280×800 resolution has nearly 25 percent more screen space than a site with 1024×768 resolution.

   If the screen offers too much room, the designer has an alternative to using vertical menus—he can fill the space with fixed content. A designated space, such as that shown in the right side of Figure 5.3, can be used on any pages that do not have enough content. This space can either include photos or other content that has less priority.

2. **Menu width**—If possible, a vertical menu should be wide enough so that menu items do not have to be carried over to a second line. Sometimes this involves renaming menu items to be shorter, and sometimes it requires making the menu area wider. If the designer needs to make the menu area wider, it should not take away valuable space in the body of the site. If it does take away valuable space, adding a <br /> tag to have the longer menu item(s) take up two lines instead of one is probably wiser.

3. **Height of header**—The header area of a site generally remains the same throughout all pages of a site. If it is too high vertically, then valuable space is lost on pages that require large amounts of content. On the other hand, some sites have very limited content, which justifies using a header with more height. A good practice is to take the requirements of all the pages into consideration before building spatial areas, such as the header.

4. **Placement of rounded edges and corners**—Many sites use rounded edges and corners. The advantage to rounded edges is that they soften the look of a site. Figure 5.6 uses a rounded corner just to the left of the upper part of the body of the page.

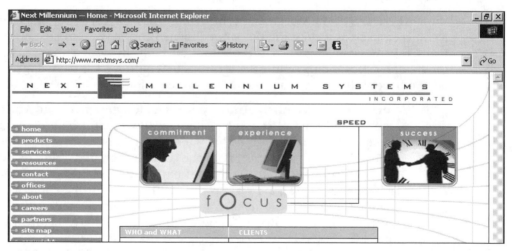

FIGURE 5.6 Design that uses a rounded edge for the upper-left corner of the page body. Copyright © 2002 by Next Millennium Systems, Inc. All rights reserved.

Developing Layers

As previously mentioned, using layers in Photoshop saves a designer an inordinate amount of time when creating and editing a comp. Any item, whether text, shapes, or photos, can be saved on its own layer. That way, items cannot only be moved individually, but they can also be replaced individually without disrupting content on other layers.

Figure 5.7, for example, is an image that consists of six layers, including the white background. The Photoshop Layers panel is shown in Figure 5.8.

FIGURE 5.7   Image that is made up of layers.

FIGURE 5.8   Layers panel in Photoshop.

If the client requested the text to be changed to "yo!," all the designer would need to do is open the file in Photoshop, click on the layer that says "hey," select the Text tool, click on the text in the file, and retype "hey" to read as "yo!"

While making this change, the designer could also move the lines or the "ARE YOU GOING LEFT OR RIGHT?" text, and reposition the newly retyped "yo!" text (see Figure 5.9). When creating comps for homepages, it is not unusual to create as many as 60 to 80 layers, which, additionally, can be nested within parent layers—in other words, a layer can serve as a folder for additional layers.

FIGURE 5.9   Same image as Figure 5.7 but with layers edited.

Another advantage of layers is that they can be easily turned off so that if the client wanted to see the image in Figure 5.9 without the word "yo!," the designer could simply shut off that layer and save a new version of the Photoshop PSD file.

Layers can also be merged together for further editing. The "yo!" in Figure 5.9 could be merged with the elevator lights image. The two could then, for instance, have a motion blur added. When all the layers are merged together, the PSD file is *flattened* (the selected layers are merged to make one layer). Rarely will the designer ever want to flatten an image. If Figure 5.7 had been flattened, it would require considerable time and effort to cut "hey" out of the image, recreate the elevator image behind the word that was also cut out, and retype the word "yo!" Unfortunately, Photoshop PSD files can be flattened accidentally, which is why it is wise for a designer to back up all files. It usually takes only one accident and one experience with recreating 70 layers of a comp for the designer to learn this lesson.

When merging several layers together at a time in Photoshop, the designer may want to make copies of the layers and turn them off before merging. This allows the designer to come back and more easily edit pieces of the merged layer in the future, if necessary.

Using Masks

Masks are extremely useful when a designer wants to control the shape or placement of an image. According to Adobe, a mask enables a designer to "isolate and protect areas of an image as you apply color changes, filters, or other effects to the rest of the image."

If a designer wanted to set an image inside the word "yo!" from Figure 5.9, the text could be *rasterized* (converted to a bitmapped image, which will not allow textual editing) and used as a mask. In Figure 5.10, the letters are used as a mask for an image of water. In other words, the water image is placed inside the letters. This can be advantageous when there is a photo or shape included in a design that cannot be moved, but the designer needs to replace it with another image. All the designer need do is use the original image as a mask, which the new image is then inserted into. Because the mask will initially be created as its own layer, the old layer can then be turned off or deleted to ensure that the edges of the image are smooth.

FIGURE 5.10   Image that uses the letters "yo!" as a mask for an image of water.

RECEIVING A DECISION ON THE CHOSEN COMP AND MAKING EDITS

Web sites are in continual evolution. They especially evolve during the comp process. A design that works for a designer may not work for the person leading the project or that person's boss or peers. Frequently, the person in charge of the project will say, "It looks great to me. Let me just run it by so-and-so real quickly, and we'll be ready to go." While this sounds positive, there is usually a good chance that the next person will suggest additional changes.

The varying steps in the approval process make it wise for the designer to await approval on a comp before breaking it up into XHTML, graphics, and CSS. Because the breaking-up process can be time consuming and difficult to subsequently change, it is best to wait rather than begin, stop, and start all over again. Even though a design should be flexible, it can only be flexible for certain changes. If the client says, "My boss really wants you to move the menu from the left to the center," this edit will usually call for reworking the entire design.

Each site will go through its own unique process of approval. One site might require only one person's approval, while another site might require committee approval. There are several rules that the designer should follow when attempting to get approval:

1. **Be patient**—There is a fine line between calling the client every day and showing the proper follow-through. Most companies, especially in corporate America, move slowly. While a client with few people involved in approving a comp may quickly do so on the phone, it could take days to weeks for a corporate client to approve a certain desired look and feel.

2. **Attempt to document all communications**—If the designer has the choice between calling or e-mailing a client, the wiser choice, many times, is to e-mail. Not only is an e-mail less intrusive, but it is also a good way of documenting communications. Whenever a client requests a change, the designer should ask for the change(s) to be submitted via e-mail. That way, it protects both parties. Most disagreements or misunderstandings can be resolved by looking back at previous e-mails.

3. **Offer alternatives**—Not all clients are going to be as technically or artistically minded as their designer. They may simply not know the various options a site can offer. Offering alternatives also lets the client know that the designer is keeping its best interests in mind. Color alternatives can be a good thing to offer a client if there is not a set palette. Because the slightest disproportion of a color can change the entire look and feel of a site, it is difficult to imagine changes without testing.

4. **Do not get attached to the work**—For every client who trusts the judgment of the designer, there are two who would prefer that a design look the way they desire. It is always amazing how quickly a design can change for the worse, at least to the designer's viewpoint. It is important, therefore, that the designer not become attached to a design. The paying client has the final say. If there is an affinity to a specific design look, the designer can always ask for permission to use the preferred version in a portfolio.

5. **Limit the number of changes from the outset**—Many times the approval process can get out of control. What once was one design can turn into three or four versions without the client's paying for the extra changes. This is why the designer should explain the approval process before beginning work on the designs. That way, there are no surprises when additional charges for excessive changes are incurred.

SUMMARY

There are 10 general steps to building a mortised site. One of the first and most important steps is gathering requirements and basing the site on those requirements. While requirements involve more work up front, defining requirements can make the development of a site considerably more time- and cost-efficient, as well as more effective.

Once the requirements are collected, the designer creates the comp(s) in Photoshop. There are several procedures a designer should follow to ensure that the comping process goes smoothly: create a source directory, collect and document stock images, and select colors.

After the first draft of a comp is completed, the designer then works with the client to edit and finalize the site's functionality, appearance, and usability.

CHAPTER

6

WHAT IS NEEDED TO BUILD MORTISED SITES

In This Chapter

- Understanding the Concept of Mortising Images
- Understanding XHTML
- Understanding Graphics
- Understanding CSS
- Block- and Inline-Level Tags
- Understanding Include Files

As an accomplished artist once said, "Everyone has the same tools. The only difference is how each person uses them." This statement epitomizes mortised sites. Building such sites is not difficult, especially for the experienced Web designer. There is, in fact, a very low learning curve for such designers because mortised sites do not introduce any new Web development technologies. Other than learning a graphics software program, such as Adobe Photoshop, the designer need only learn creative methods of using XHTML, graphics, and CSS—common tools of today's Web designer. Of course, using JavaScript, Flash, programming languages, and other tools can also enhance a mortised site.

The difference in the quality of a site is determined by a designer's knowledge of building sites and how the designer uses that knowledge. Two of the most important aspects to building such sites is using CSS to position the majority of content, rather than XHTML tables, and properly compressing and saving images. While CSS allows the designer to create nearly any layout possible, which may include additional programming, properly compressed and saved graphics make the site attractive and more usable. Together, they give the designer the means to build a homogenous site.

Before beginning to fully grasp these and other concepts, the designer should have an understanding of the big picture—that is, knowing the various steps that go into building a mortised site from conception to production. Following are 10 steps in the typical building of a mortised site:

1. Gathering and basing a site on requirements
2. Creating comp(s) for the client
3. Receiving a decision on the chosen comp and making edits
4. Breaking up the comp into XHTML, graphics, and CSS
5. Testing the page in the most widely used browsers
6. Saving components of the page as include files and testing again
7. Building second-level pages from the homepage template
8. Working with the client as the site is built
9. Testing the entire site
10. Implementing or uploading the site

This general overview helps a designer understand the entire process, which helps to make sense of the many specifics included in this book.

UNDERSTANDING THE CONCEPT OF MORTISING IMAGES

Building a mortised site is similar to piecing a puzzle together. The designer pieces images, content, and functionality together in a manner that allows form and function to complement each other rather than compete against each other.

Mortising can be accomplished at different levels. At the basic level, a designer can mortise just two images together. At the more advanced level, the designer can nest mortised containers (usually content in <SPAN> and <DIV> tags) inside mortised containers to accomplish complex designs. It all, however, begins with a basic understanding of how to piece together two or more images.

Figure 6.1 is an example of three images seamlessly pieced together. All of the images are compressed and saved in their best possible image format.

FIGURE 6.1   Three images mortised together.

While they appear to be one image, when spaces are added in between the images, it becomes apparent that there are three separate images (see Figure 6.2).

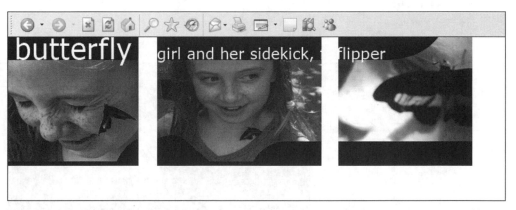

FIGURE 6.2   Mortised images with borders set to 1 to show they are three separate images, unlike how they appear in Figure 6.1.

Following is the code for this example. While there are more involved mortising examples throughout the book, this particular code can be reused in many different ways. It is especially important to note that all the spaces have been removed so the images aren't incorrectly output in some browsers, such as shown in Figure 6.3.

```
<div style="width:692px;"><span style="float:right;"><img src="images/photo-bottom-
center.jpg" width="266" height="209" alt="" border="0" /><img src="images/photo-
bottom-right.jpg" width="213" height="209" alt="" border="0" /></span><span
style="float:left;"><img src="images/photo-bottom-left.jpg" width="213" height="209"
alt="" border="0" /></span></div>
```

Notice how the first two images are nested together in a <SPAN> tag and then floated to the right of the left image. If the designer were to simply add all three images together or try floating them nearly any other way, they would not piece together seamlessly. It should also be noted that for this code to work, as well as other occasional CSS, it cannot have spaces in between it. Following is an example of how the code should not look:

```
<div style="width:692px;">
  <span style="float:right;">
  <img src="images/photo-bottom-center.jpg" width="266" height="209" alt=""
border="0" />
  <img src="images/photo-bottom-right.jpg" width="213" height="209" alt=""
border="0" /></span>
  <span style="float:left;">
  <img src="images/photo-bottom-left.jpg" width="213" height="209" alt=""
border="0" />
  </span>
</div>
```

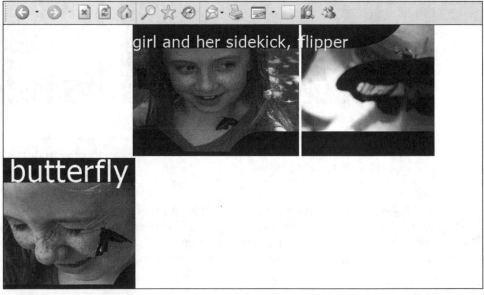

FIGURE 6.3 An example of how the images in Figure 6.2 will "fall apart" when normal spacing is added between the elements.

There are several advantages to mortising:

- The designer can save parts of images in their best respective image formats. For instance, in Figure 6.2, any of the three images could be saved as a GIF and placed among the other two JPG images, if the designer needed such flexibility. Or that image could be saved as a background image of a container that could have text layered over it.
- The designer can have more freedom with layouts. Although everything is saved and structured in rigid, linear shapes in CSS Web design, the design does not have to appear that way. Instead, text, colors, and images can flow through a page, leading the user's eyes and creating a sense of motion and/or emotion with the design (see Figure 6.4).
- The designer can be guaranteed of content and image placement because positioning is fixed.

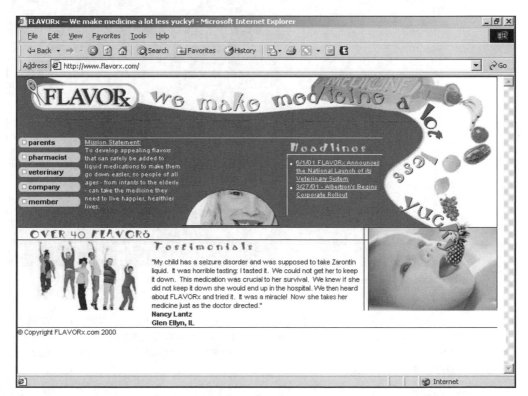

FIGURE 6.4   Site that uses images to create a sense of motion. Copyright © 2002 by FLAVORx.com.

Figure 6.5 represents another way to mortise three images together. It shows how to place images together with absolute and/or relative positioning. The designer can control placement of an image by wrapping a container around it and assigning the position, top, left, and right properties to it. Figure 6.5 shows how the first of three images is positioned in a container with the ID of a5-header. It is assigned absolute positioning, placing it 0 pixels from the top and 0 pixels from the left side.

The 627-pixel-wide container is assigned a black background to differentiate it from the white background of the page.

FIGURE 6.5   The first of three images positioned in the container.

After the first image has a <DIV> wrapped around it and is placed in the parent container, a second image is added. It also has a container wrapped around it. This image, however, is placed 247 pixels from the left, which positions the two images together (see Figure 6.6).

The third image is positioned 304 pixels from the left, which is the sum total width of the first two images (247 + 57 = 304 pixels). Depending on the instance of mortising, the right property can be used in place of the left property. Listing 6.1 is the code to build the completed mortised images in Figure 6.7.

FIGURE 6.6   The second of three images positioned in the container.

LISTING 6.1   Code for Figure 6.7

```
<!DOCTYPE html PUBLIC "-//W3C//DTD XHTML 1.0 Transitional//EN"
    "DTD/xhtml1-transitional.dtd">
<html><head><title>Mortised Images</title>
<style>
    #a5-header {
        position:relative;
        top:0px;
        left:0px;
        width:627px;
        height:400px;
        background:black;
    }
    #a5-photo-left {
        position:absolute;
        top:0px;
        left:0px;
    }
    #a5-photo-center {
        position:absolute;
```

```
        top:0px;
        left:247px;
    }
    #a5-photo-right {
        position:absolute;
        top:0px;
        left:304px;
    }
</style>
</head>
<body>
<div id="a5-header">
    <div id="a5-photo-left"><img src="images/photo-left.jpg"
        width="247" height="400" alt="" border="0" /></div>
    <div id="a5-photo-center"><img src="images/photo-center.jpg"
        width="57" height="400" alt="" border="0" /></div>
    <div id="a5-photo-right"><img src="images/photo-right.jpg"
        width="323" height="400" alt="" border="0" /></div>
</div>
</body>
</html>
```

FIGURE 6.7   All three images positioned in the container.

Placing background images in a container is another way to mortise images together. One reason a designer may want to do so is to place text over the image. Figure 6.8 shows how the left image of a container is added.

 The 1000-pixel-wide container is assigned a black background to differentiate it from the white background of the page.

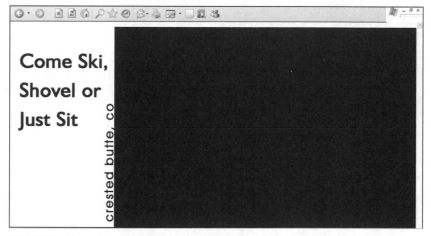

FIGURE 6.8   The left image added to the container.

Once the first image has been added, the second is inserted (see Figure 6.9). In this example, the left text is saved as an image, so the process of mortising the two images together is the same as the previous example.

FIGURE 6.9   The center image added to the container.

Adding the right container is where this example becomes more complex. The designer is going to size and position the `a5-text-right` <DIV>; however, the text is going to be added to another <DIV> that is nested inside. This allows for padding and line-height properties and values to be added at a local level. Listing 6.2 is the code used to create the final layout (see Figure 6.10).

LISTING 6.2   Code for Figure 6.10

```
<!DOCTYPE html PUBLIC "-//W3C//DTD XHTML 1.0 Transitional//EN"
    "DTD/xhtml1-transitional.dtd">
<html><head><title>Mortised Images</title>
<style>
    #a5-container {
        position:relative;
        top:0px;
        left:0px;
        width:1000px;
        height:500px;
        background:black;
    }
    #a5-image-left {
        position:absolute;
        top:0px;
        left:0px;
    }
    #a5-photo-center {
        position:absolute;
        top:0px;
        left:251px;
    }
    #a5-text-right {
        position:absolute;
        bottom:0px;
        right:0px;
        width:333px;
        height:500px;
        background:url("images/bg-right.jpg") no-repeat;
    }
</style>
</head>
<body>
<div id="a5-container">
    <div id="a5-image-left"><a href="x.htm"><img src="images/
        image-left.gif" width="251" height="500" alt="" border="0"
        /></a></div>
```

```
<div id="a5-photo-center"><a href="x.htm"><img src="images/photo-
    center.jpg" width="416" height="500" alt="" border="0"
    /></a></div>
<div id="a5-text-right">
    <div style="padding:250px 10px 10px 10px;line-height:60px;">
        This is sample text that can be added over the background
        image. While the background image cannot be hyperlinked,
        the <a href="x.htm">text can</a>.</div>
    </div>
</div>
</body>
</html>
```

FIGURE 6.10   Background image and text added to the right column.

When using background images, it is important that the designer consider whether a user is going to think it is clickable, because background images cannot be clicked. While this seems obvious, it is an easy mistake to make because when mortising images, using at least one background image can sometimes be tempting.

UNDERSTANDING XHTML

XHTML can be compared to the game of chess—it is easy to learn but difficult to become good at. This, at least, is how it used to be when creating table-based designs when they had to be nested within each other to mortise Web page elements together. Today, XHTML plays a much smaller role in creating professional-looking sites.

In CSS-driven designs, XHTML mainly provides the framework for the page, which includes the <HTML>, <HEAD>, <TITLE>, and <BODY> tags; the structure of containers, which include <SPAN> and <DIV> tags; and the general tags for page elements to be built, such as forms and embedded elements like hyperlinks and images.

The majority of positioning and layout is now controlled with CSS. This is not to devalue XHTML code. Its tags are still crucial in creating code that can be read by search engines and text readers, among other things. The good thing for the designer is that the <TABLE>, <TR>, and <TD> tags are now used mainly for displaying table data, such as in a spreadsheet.

Using a Limited Number of Tags

Out of more than 110 XHTML tags, a designer only needs to know a small number of them to build mortised sites with basic form functionality. Rather than spending time learning more tags, the designer can spend time logically and creatively manipulating this limited number of tags with CSS, rather than hundreds of lines of <TABLE> code. Included in Table 6.1 is a list of popular tags, along with some of their possible attributes and uses.

TABLE 6.1   Basic Tags for Building Mortised Sites

TAG	DESCRIPTION
<html>	Standard tag used in all pages, except include files. Closed at end of page with </html>.
<head>	Standard tag used in all pages, except include files. Closed at the end of the header information with </head>.
<title>	Standard tag used in all pages, except include files. Closed with </title>.
<meta name="" content="">	Standard tag used on pages. This tag provides information, determined by the designer, to be indexed by search engines. It is usually placed between the <head> and </head> tags.
<body>	Standard tag used in all pages. All content seen by the user falls within this tag set. Closed at the end of the page with </body>.
<p>, 	Essential for breaking lines in page layout. The <p> tag also can be used when applying a style to a block of text and/or images. The <p> tag is closed with a </p>, and the is simply closed within itself.
<table>	Essential tag for building tables. Closed at the end of the table with </table>.
<tr>	Essential tag for building table rows. Closed with </tr>.

$\rightarrow$

TAG	DESCRIPTION
`<td>`	Essential tag for creating table cells. Closed with a `</td>`.
`<img src="" width="" height="" alt="" border="" name="" />`	Essential for adding images to a page. The forward slash (/) is included in the tag so that it closes itself.
`<a href="" class="" target="">`	Essential for linking to pages, documents, and images. Closed with `</a>`.
`<div class="" style="">`	Used with CSS usually to control font size and color, images, multiple block-level elements, and content positioning. Closed with `</div>`.
`<span class="" style ="">`	Used to add styles to content. Closed with `</span>`.
`<strong>`	Used to bold text when it is not controlled using a style that is associated with text. Closed with `</strong>`.
`<!– comment –>`	Used to comment code. Used for all comments—single and multiple lines.
`<form id="" name="" action="" method="">`	Used to create forms in XHMTL. Closed with `</form>`.
`<input type="" id="" name="" value="" />`	Input is used to create form fields, such as "text," "radio," and "checkbox." The tag closes itself with a forward slash (/).
`<label for="" id="">`	Used for positioning elements with fields in a form.
`<textarea>`	Used for large text input entries. Closed with `</textarea>`.
`<select id="" name="" multiple="multiple">`	Used for dropdown form elements. Closed with `</select>`.
`<option selected="selected" value="" label="">`	Used to delineate individual items in a dropdown form field. Closed with `</option>`.

UNDERSTANDING GRAPHICS

Creating, using, saving, and compressing images in their best possible formats is essential to professional Web design. Because it is so important, the issue is addressed in depth in Chapter 7.

UNDERSTANDING CSS

Unlike in the past where CSS (Cascading Style Sheet) was used mainly to style text, it now plays a much more involved role in positioning and styling content, whether at the global, local, and/or inline level. Used to its greatest potential, one CSS document controls the styles of the entire site, similar to the concept of an include file (discussed later in this chapter). This book has been considerably rewritten to explain this new use of CSS and how it can be used to create highly professional Web sites. While chapters 8 through 14 and 16 go into more specifics about this subject, the following sections are an overview a designer needs for a general understanding.

Understanding CSS Terminology

It is assumed that the designer has a working, if limited, knowledge of CSS. Recalling terminology, however, is not always the easiest thing to do, which is why Figure 6.11 was created. It provides a basic visual example of CSS elements and their terminology in a CSS style sheet.

FIGURE 6.11   A visual reference of CSS terminology, including an example of the Tantek Celik Hack.

Following are the various items to note about the code in Figure 6.11:

- **Selectors**—These are used when declaring and calling a particular rule. Figure 6.11 identifies two types of selectors, an ID selector and a Class selector, both of which can be used with XHTML tags, such as <DIV> or <SPAN>.

- **Properties**—Various aspects of a selector that can be used for different styles.
- **Values**—The specific qualities of properties.
- **Shorthand Properties**—A method of combining multiple related values for a property under one general property. An example would be combining `padding-top: 10px; padding-right:15px; padding-bottom:25px; padding-left:30px` into one property that looks like `padding:10px 15px 25px 30px;`.
- **Rule**—The entire grouping of a selector, a property (or properties), and value(s).
- **Tantek Celik Hack**—While this is not necessarily considered CSS terminology, it is used enough by many designers that it is worth noting in a visual example.

 It's important to understand that the Tantek hack is not standard CSS and can throw errors in some validators. Fortunately, as designers stop designing for IE 5.0 and 5.5, this hack is no longer necessary. The hack is explained further in Chapter 16.

CSS Used in This Book

The CSS coding philosophy used in this book is to be creative with a limited number of CSS properties and values, rather than use those that do not necessarily function under all conditions. In other words, the goal is to be the most flexible with the smallest number of properties and values that are proven to work in the widest range of browsers and their versions. While there is a much wider array of possibilities for a designer, it is left to the designer to expand upon what is discussed in this book. Table 6.2 lists many properties that are used in this book. Many of them are shorthand examples, meaning one property is used to set the various values that could be broken up into other properties.

TABLE 6.2   Some of the CSS Properties Used in this Book

EXAMPLE PROPERTY	USAGE
`margin:0px 0px 0px 0px;`	Used for setting the distance between the outside border of a container and what is nested inside of it.
`padding:0px 0px 0px 0px;`	Used for setting the distance between the outside border of a container and what is nested inside it.
`font:13px Arial, Helvetica, sans-serif;font-weight:bold;`	Used to set the size, face, and weight of a font. The bold value, however, does not work in all situations, which is why it is sometimes separated out as `font-weight:bold;` or included in the XHTML code.
`color:#000000;`	Used to set the text color.

$\rightarrow$

EXAMPLE PROPERTY	USAGE
`a:link { color:#FF7800; }`	Used to set a hyperlink color.
`a:visited { color:#FF5A00; }`	Used to set the hyperlink color of a visited or previously clicked link.
`a:active { color:#FFC600; }`	Used for defining the color of a link while it is being clicked and has not yet been released.
`a:hover { color:#000000; }`	Used for changing the color of a hyperlink when it is moused over but has yet to be clicked.
`a.linklist:link { text-decoration: none;color:#308DAE;}`	Used for setting the color of a link with an assigned class (e.g., `class="linklist"`).
`a.linklist:visited { text-decoration: none;color:#308DAE;}`	Used for setting the visited color of a link with an assigned class (e.g., `class="linklist"`).
`a.linklist:active { text-decoration: none;color:#308DAE;}`	Used for setting the active color of a link with an assigned class (e.g., `class="linklist"`).
`a.linklist:hover { text-decoration: underline;color:#FF7800;}`	Used for setting the hover color of a link with an assigned class (e.g., `class="linklist"`).
`border: 1px solid #000000;`	Used for setting the border of a CSS element to 1, with a specified color.
`text-align:left;` `text-align:right;` `text-align:center;`	Used to control the horizontal placement of content, whether the value `left`, `right`, or `center` is used.
`position:relative;` `position:absolute;`	Used to define whether a box, or container, in the box model will be assigned relative or absolute positioning.
`float:right;` `float:left;` `float:center;`	Used to position elements to the left or right in content.
`clear:both;`	Used to remove floating elements from the left and right sides of a container.
`width:100%;`	Used to set the width of an element, such as a box.
`margin-left:auto;` `margin-right:auto;`	Used when centering a fixed-width Web page.
`left:0px;` `right:0px;`	Used for setting how many pixels an element is placed from the left or right side of the body or a parent box.

$\rightarrow$

EXAMPLE PROPERTY	USAGE
`top:0px;` `bottom:0px;`	Used for setting how many pixels an element is placed from the top or bottom of the body or a parent box.
`height:78px;`	Used for forcing the height of an element.

`width:88px;`
`voice-family:"\"}\"";`
`voice-family:inherit;`
`width:78px;`
`}`
`html>body #a5-header {`
`    width: 78px;`
`}`
	Used for setting various properties and values for different browsers. It is called the Tantek Celik hack, or Tantek hack.

`line-height:42px;` `vertical-align:30%;`	Used for forcing the vertical positioning of text in an element. The line-height property needs to be included for the vertical-align property to be interpreted by the browser. It also should appear after the font property to work for the various browsers.

`background:#000000`
`url(images/bg-menu.gif)`
`repeat-x 0px 0px;`
	Used for determining what background image is used, where it is placed, and how it is repeated. The HEX value sets what the background color of an element will be if the background does not fill the entire space.

BLOCK- AND INLINE-LEVEL TAGS

Block- and inline-level tags are at the core of positioning and styling content in a Web site. The most common block-level element is the <DIV> tag. The most common inline-level tag is the <SPAN> tag. Together, they are used, similarly to how XHTML tables were used to create mortised sites. The <DIV> tag is used as a "box" to place content in, position and style, similar to a table. The <SPAN> tag is used to style individual elements inside a block-level tag, although a <DIV> tag can be, and frequently is, used to do the same. Chapter 8 provides a basic understanding of how these tags are used, while Chapters 9, 10, 11, 12, 13, and 14 provide actual case studies on how to do so. A more technical explanation of these types of tags can be found on the World Wide Web Consortium (W3C) site at www.w3.org/TR/REC-CSS2/visuren.html#q5.

Understanding the DocType Declaration

A DocType Declaration (DTD) is a line of code that should be included in the first line of every Web page, barring include files. The most basic explanation of a DTD is that it defines the rules of how a browser should render a Web page, based on W3C's standards. Various types of declarations can be used, depending on how the designer wants a Web page to be interpreted by a browser and validated by the W3C. In other words, pages can be interpreted on their HTML, XHTML, or XML coding. The latest designs in this book are created using the following XHTML 1.0 transitional declaration:

```
<!DOCTYPE XHTML PUBLIC "-//W3C//DTD XHTML 1.0 Transitional//EN"
    "DTD/xhtml1-transitional.dtd">
```

Linking to CSS Style Sheets

While there are different ways to include a style sheet, such as linking, embedding, and including inline, imported style sheets offer one thing the others do not: they prevent older browsers, which do not fully support CSS, from crashing. In the past, style sheets were imported to keep browsers, such as Netscape 4.7, from choking on the CSS. Listing 6.3 provides the code to import a style sheet:

LISTING 6.3   Code Used to Import a Style Sheet

```
<style type="text/css" media="all">
    @import "mainstyle.css";
</style>
```

Including Print Style Sheets

A designer no longer has to create separate pages that are used specifically for printing a page. The following stylesheet link simply needs to be added to the page's code.

```
<link rel="stylesheet" href="print.css" type="text/css"
    media="print" />
```

Once this link has been added, the browser will call a separate style sheet that it will use for printing purposes. Usually, the style sheet is a copied version of the main style sheet, which is then modified to display the page as the designer desires. If the header, for example, does not need to be printed, the designer can change the style sheet to hide that element of the page. Following are several things a designer should consider changing to make a page more printer-friendly:

- The font size could be changed to points for printing purposes. Otherwise, the page may not print sizes, such as pixels, clearly.
- Any section can be turned off by replacing all navigation rules in a `<DIV>` or `<SPAN>` tag with the rule `display:none;`. For example, the following style could have all of its rules removed:

```
#a5-header {
    position:relative;
    top:0px;
    height:73px;
    background-image: url(images/bg-header.gif);
    voice-family: "\"}\""; voice-family:inherit;
    height:73px;
    }
    XHTML>body #a5-header {
    height:73px;
    }
```

The `display:none;` rule could then be added to make the style look like:

```
#a5-header {
    display:none;
    }
```

By making this change, anything in the container with the `id` value of `a5-header` would be hidden from the printer. To test what the page will look like, the designer can select Print Preview in the browser rather than actually having to print it.

- The text to be printed can be easily resized to fit the screen however the designer chooses.
- Colors that may not print very well in grayscale, such as a yellow, can be changed to a darker color.

Figure 6.12 shows how a site is displayed in a browser. Figure 6.13 illustrates how drastically the same page can appear when reading a print style sheet. Many of the elements of the page, including the header, menu, and content columns, were removed so that only the necessary information would be printed.

By simply selecting Print Preview in Internet Explorer, the browser will give the designer an idea of how the page will appear when it is printed. The great thing about this functionality is that the designer can test a page without actually having to print it.

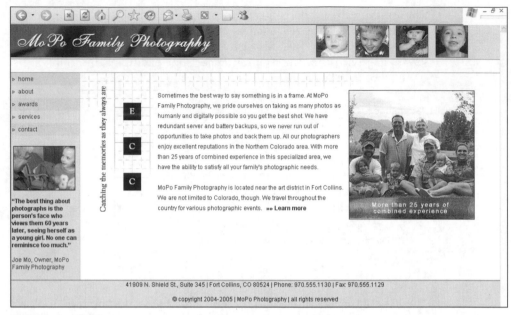

FIGURE 6.12   A Web page as it appears with a nonprinting style sheet.

FIGURE 6.13   The same Web page as in Figure 6.12 but in Print Preview mode, which uses a print style sheet to determine what is printed.

UNDERSTANDING INCLUDE FILES

Include files are individual files that can be repeatedly called into different pages (for example, ColdFusion, PHP, .NET, or JSP pages). A blessing to Web designers, include files not only allow a site to be modular (various easily interchangeable pieces), but more importantly, they also reduce maintenance time. An example of an include file might be the footer text of a site. Instead of placing the text in every page, a designer might include one line of code in every page that calls that footer text, which is in only one file. Then, when the footer needs to be edited, the designer edits only one page.

To use include files, all a designer needs is to host a site on a server that offers server-side processing, such as Microsoft (.NET pages), Apache HTTP Server (SHTML pages), Adobe ColdFusion server (CFM pages), JSP server (JSP pages), or a open-source server that runs PHP pages. Following are examples of code that are used to include files into other files:

Code to call include file in a .NET page:
```
<!- #include file="menu.txt" ->
```

Code to call include file in an SHTML page:
```
<!-#include file="filename.shtml" ->
```

Code to call include file in a ColdFusion page:
```
<cfinclude template="menu.cfm">
```

Code to call include file in a PHP page:
```
<?php include("pagename.php"); ?>
```

Code to call include file in a JSP page:
```
<%@ include file="menu.jsp" %>
```

SUMMARY

The three components of building mortised sites are XHTML, CSS, and graphics. A designer, however, should also understand several concepts, such as mortising images, using block- and inline-level tags, and taking advantage of include files.

Mortised sites have a low learning curve because they do not require a Web designer to learn any new technologies—just a different coding methodology. Building such sites also requires a limited amount of XHTML and CSS. The designer, rather, needs to use existing tools and methods in new, creative ways to build fast, highly usable, professional sites.

7

UNDERSTANDING GRAPHICS

In This Chapter

- Learning about Vector and Bitmap Images
- Learning about JPGs and GIFs
- Misusing Image Formats
- Understanding Graphics/Compression Software

One of the most important aspects of building mortised sites is properly saved and compressed graphics. Unlike working with XHTML, saving and compressing graphics leaves less to the imagination of the designer. Rather, the nature of the image will usually dictate how it should be saved, though there are times when the designer can be creative. This does not necessarily mean, however, that the image will be saved as it should. The designer must understand how to best create, use, save, and compress images; and the first place to start is by understanding the two types of images used on the Web.

LEARNING ABOUT VECTOR AND BITMAP IMAGES

There are two general types of graphics used on the Web: vector and bitmap. Bitmap images, which are mainly comprised of JPGs and GIFs, continue to be the most commonly used type of image on the Internet. The second type of graphics are vector images. These use mathematically based lines and curves to display images, as opposed to bitmap images, which use pixels to display images. The best way to understand the difference between the two types of images is to view an example. Figure 7.1 is an image of a circle.

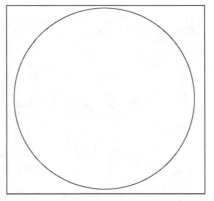

FIGURE 7.1   Circle that could be created as both a vector or bitmap image.

A designer could create the same exact image in both a vector-based program, such as Adobe Illustrator, or a bitmap-based program, such as Adobe Photoshop. (More recent versions of Photoshop now also support vector-based images.) When zooming in on the bottom-left corner of the circle in both programs, the difference between vector and bitmap images is apparent. Figure 7.2 is the vector image, and Figure 7.3 is the bitmap image. The vector image is smooth, while the bitmap image is jagged.

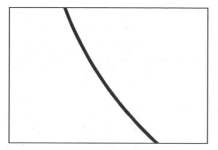

FIGURE 7.2   Corner of a circle that was saved as a vector image.

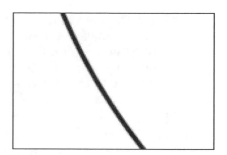

FIGURE 7.3   Corner of a circle that was saved as a bitmap image.

When viewing each image at 100 percent in Photoshop, the two images look fairly similar. This is because individual pixels make up the different shades of black used in the bitmap image. Shades of gray soften the edges (called *anti-aliasing*) to give the illusion of one color. Despite anti-aliasing, vector images still appear sharper.

Not only are lines in vector images crisper, but they also have smaller file sizes than bitmap images. Vector images are also more easily resized with less degradation to the image. There are, however, two advantages of bitmap images over vector images:

- Bitmap images compress and display images with millions of colors much better than vector images.
- Bitmap images are supported by all browsers, while most types of vector images still require a browser plug-in to view.

Many multimedia sites are vector-based. One example of vector-based graphics is Scalable Vector Graphics (SVG). This is a language that allows a designer to create vector-based images, vector shapes, and text. In other words, instead of a designer having to create Figure 7.4 as a traditional image, ASCII text can actually be used for text. This not only makes maintenance easier, but it also allows search engines to be able to index the text. Unfortunately, SVG graphics also require a plug-in.

FIGURE 7.4   Text saved as an image.

Once again, however, when considering the differences between bitmap and vector images, a designer must consider Rule 1 of Web design—just because you can does not mean you should. Bitmap images continue to be the images of choice for Web developers. This is not something that will change soon; it will be difficult to get the critical mass of more than 1 billion Web users to either upgrade to a browser that supports vector images or download plug-ins that support the images.

This makes it important for a designer to understand and use currently supported image formats. Once a designer has a full understanding of bitmap images, it is possible to use them to create striking, fast, usable sites. Fortunately, there are only two bitmap formats that are necessary to learn in order to build or customize mortised sites—GIFs and JPGs.

 Another image format is PNG (Portable Network Graphic). Pronounced ping, the format was created to replace GIFs. In many respects, the PNG format is preferable to the GIF format. Unfortunately, despite the wishes of some designers, the format has been slow to catch on.

LEARNING ABOUT JPGS AND GIFS

With as much incompatibility as there is with Web software and hardware, it is refreshing to know that JPGs and GIFs are fully supported by all significant graphical browsers. It is important, though, that a designer learn the strengths and weaknesses of both formats. Otherwise, image quality and size can be drastically compromised.

Using GIFs

GIFs support up to 256 colors. Although that does not seem like a lot compared to the JPG format, which supports millions of colors, GIFs, nonetheless, have their benefits. Following are five advantages of using GIFs over JPGs:

1. **GIFs do a better job of compressing large areas of solid color**—GIFs not only compress such images smaller, but the images also appear crisper.
2. **GIFs support animation**—Although animated GIFs have been overused and misused in the past and have been replaced mainly by Flash animation, there are still occasional, more obscure uses for them. One example would be using a "loading" image for an application site that doesn't use Flash. Without motion, users may believe that the site, their connection, or their systems are locked up.
3. **GIFs allow for one color in an image to be transparent**—This is beneficial for a designer when layering an image over various background images, such as in Figure 7.5 and Figure 7.6, where the text "bob's floral specials" is layered over the different floral JPGs.

    However, there is a disadvantage to using transparent images. Because GIFs allow only one color to be transparent, they do not display anti-aliased images very well. In other words, the images appear jagged. This is an instance where the designer might want to consider using a PNG.
4. **GIFs allow resizable color palettes**—Pulling colors out of the color palette the image is using can reduce GIF file sizes further. If the colors are not in the actual image, they are unnecessary data and can be tossed without any loss of quality.

5. **GIFs maintain original color better**—Unlike JPGs, GIFs maintain the original colors of an image better than JPGs. A good example of this is a JPG that is compressed too far. The white turns a pinkish tint on different monitors, many times disrupting the consistent flow of white in a design. This, at least, was the case with older versions of Photoshop. It does not occur that often anymore.

FIGURE 7.5   Image where the black strip and text on top is layered over a background image.

FIGURE 7.6   Image that uses the same layered black strip and text as in Figure 7.5.

Although a designer can save a GIF with up to 256 colors, it is not always the wise move. If that many colors are necessary to make a photo acceptable, then it is probably best to save the image as a JPG. Generally, it is good practice to save GIFs with a limited number of colors, anywhere from 2 to 64, depending on the physical size of the image. A designer should probably save an image as a GIF when the following situations occur:

1. **The image has a limited number of solid colors**—The smaller the physical size of the image, the more colors a designer can use while maintaining an acceptable file size (see Figure 7.7).

FIGURE 7.7   Image that should most likely be saved as a GIF because of its limited colors.

While larger images, such the one in Figure 7.8, can be saved as GIFs, they usually should not have too many colors. Of course, you must remember Rule 2 of Web design: there nearly always is an exception to a rule.

When saving images as GIFs, a designer should be aware of the fact that gradations, such as drop shadows, will increase the file size or not be displayed with strong enough quality. Due to the fact that there are a fewer number of colors available, an effect called *banding* can occur. This causes the gradations to be represented by solid bands of color instead of flowing into one another. There is a process called *dithering*, which causes the bands to be broken into different patterns of tiny dots to imitate shades of color by placing certain colors beside one another. Unfortunately, it increases file size significantly. Figure 7.9 is a zoomed-in view of the curved edge of Figure 7.8. It takes many shades of gray to make the image appear to be raised. While it is still possible to adequately compress Figure 7.8, the additional colors will increase the file size of the image.

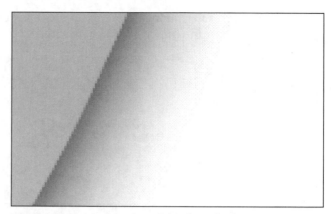

FIGURE 7.8   Image that uses a drop shadow to give the illusion of being raised.

FIGURE 7.9   Zoomed-in view of the drop shadow in Figure 7.8.

2. **The image is a line drawing**—Although this technically falls into the previous category, it is differentiated for one reason—when saving an image as a GIF, the white is guaranteed to stay white, unlike a JPG. Figure 7.10 is a cartoon that is sharper and whiter when saved as a GIF, as opposed to a JPG.

FIGURE 7.10   Line drawing that should be saved as a GIF.

3. **Text is saved as an image if it is not on a complex background, such as a photo**—Generally, to make a site smaller, a designer should try to save text separately from images like photographs, which should be saved as JPGs. If the text is separate, it should be saved as a GIF, such as in Figure

7.11. Saving the image as a GIF keeps the text nearly as crisp as when it was in the image-editing software.

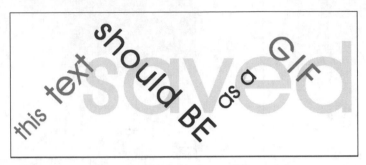

FIGURE 7.11   Text that should be saved as a GIF image.

4. **The image is a thumbnail photo**—Depending on the physical size of the image and how many colors it uses, a GIF will make a thumbnail appear sharper for about the same file size. If the number of colors is limited, such as in the photo of the house in Florence, Italy, shown in Figure 7.12, the image should be saved as a GIF. If saved as a JPG at the same file size, the body of the house could become splotchy. Of course, this is not a hard and fast rule, especially with how the compression functionality of Photoshop has improved over the years.

FIGURE 7.12   Thumbnail that should be saved as a GIF because of the solid colors.

In contrast, the photo of the Dover Cliffs shown in Figure 7.13 uses many gradations throughout the sky, cliffs, and channel, which makes it a better candidate to be saved as a JPG.

FIGURE 7.13 Thumbnail that should be saved as a JPG because of the many gradations.

5. **Small graphics are used**—One way to keep a Web site small is to use and reuse small graphics, whether in the layout of the page or as a mouseover. Strictly because of their size, such images, including buttons, bullets, and mouseovers, should generally be saved as GIFs (see Figure 7.14). The reason is that GIF compression handles a small number of colors much better than does JPG compression.

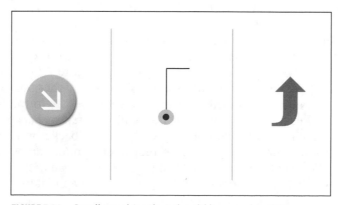

FIGURE 7.14 Small graphics that should be saved as GIFs.

Knowing How GIF Compression Works

It is helpful for a designer to understand how GIF compression works. By creating and saving images a certain way, the designer can drastically reduce the download size of images, thus speeding up the site. The secret of the GIF format is that it compresses so many pixels of one solid color at a time while running horizontally. In other words, if a designer creates an image where areas of one color run horizontally rather than vertically, the image will be compressed significantly smaller. Figure 7.15 is the exact same image as Figure 7.16; however, by merely rotating Figure 7.15 90 degrees and saving it so that the lines are horizontal, the image in Figure 7.16 can be compressed by more than 50 percent.

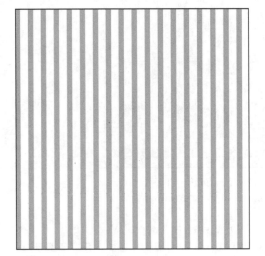

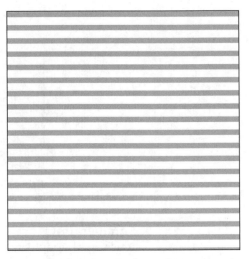

FIGURE 7.15   File size of image with vertical lines is 1 KB.

FIGURE 7.16   File size of image with horizontal lines is .457 KB.

This, of course, is a very specific example because not all images have lines. It does illustrate, however, that the more solid colors that run horizontally, the more the image can be compressed.

Unfortunately, if the image is already created, there is not much the designer can do. When starting a design from scratch, however, this can be helpful to know if the download size of the site is extremely critical. Figure 7.17 is a design that was created especially to benefit from GIF compression. Notice that nearly all the lines run horizontally. Not only does this take advantage of the GIF format's best compression, but it also takes advantage of using the ability to repeat background images. In other words, each line that cannot be saved just as a background color can be saved as a background image, which can be repeated infinitely across the x axis (horizontal) using CSS. That way, the design requires a download of only a few images. It is then up to the browser to repeat the images, rather than making it necessary to download larger images.

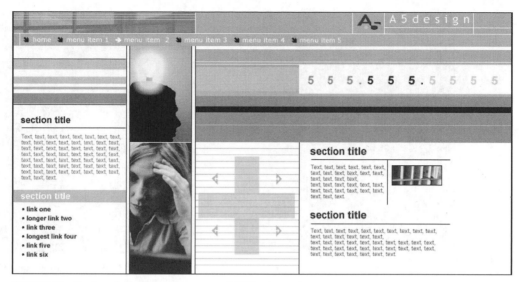

FIGURE 7.17   Design that takes advantage of GIF horizontal compression.

Using JPGs

While the GIF format is useful for saving images with limited colors, the JPG format is just as powerful when saving images with hundreds, thousands, or millions of colors. Unlike multiple benefits from the GIF format, this one advantage of the JPG format makes it remarkably valuable when building mortised sites.

A designer should typically save an image as a JPG in the following situations.

Saving a Photograph

Other than in certain instances when saving thumbnails or dealing with flat planes of color, as outlined in the "Using GIFs" section, photographs should almost always be saved as JPGs. The image in Figure 7.18 was saved as a GIF with 128 colors. The same image was saved as a JPG in Figure 7.19 with the quality (compression) level set to 41 in Photoshop. There is no visible difference in the two photos. The JPG photo, however, is compressed to be more than 80 percent smaller.

Saving an Image That Has Gradations

Although this is not an absolute rule, in most cases, the JPG format will compress images with gradations considerably better than the GIF format. This is because gradations contain many colors. Depending on the area, gradations can range from a few colors to millions of colors. Figure 7.20 is an image of a tulip that is mainly comprised of gradations throughout the photo. Figure 7.21 is a zoomed-in view of the rectangle section shown in Figure 7.20.

FIGURE 7.18 GIF photo saved at 25 KB.

FIGURE 7.19 JPG photo used at 5 KB.

FIGURE 7.20 Photo of tulip that is made up of many gradations.

The human eye cannot physically detect that there are 167 colors used to create the area. A computer, however, can detect those colors, and, unless otherwise directed when saving the image, will try to save each of those colors, considerably increasing the file size.

Some gradations, of course, can also be saved as GIFs. The rectangle that makes up Figure 7.21 is an example of this situation. When saved with the entire photo, the rectangle would need to be saved as a JPG. However, if the rectangle were to be

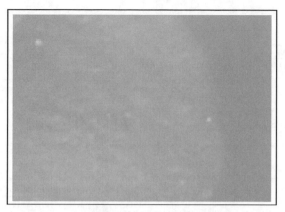

FIGURE 7.21 Zoomed-in view of the rectangle area in Figure 7.20.

cropped and saved on its own, it could be saved as a GIF with only 16 colors, as opposed to 167. Once again, this is because the human eye cannot physically detect that many colors in that small of an area. Viewing the image at 100 percent, it is difficult to detect more than a handful of colors. Thus when a color is subtracted from the image, it is replaced with a color that is still present in the image. Therefore, using 16 colors would be more than adequate.

Figure 7.22 is an example of a gradated design. The gradated circles (see Figure 7.23) at the top and bottom of the design are saved as GIFs rather than JPGs for two reasons:

1. Because they are small, fewer colors are needed, which keeps the file size small.
2. If they were saved as JPGs, the circles could lose their exact hue and the white in the image could have a pinkish tint, which would disrupt the design. This, though, is not that much of problem anymore with the improvement of Adobe's compression functionality in Photoshop.

Saving Text on Top of a Photo

When creating a mortised site, the goal is to make it as fast as possible. This usually means creating designs where elements can be saved in their best possible formats. In other words, generally save text as GIFs and photographs as JPGs. This, however, is not always possible. One instance is when a designer saves an image with text on top of a background, such as a photo (see Figure 7.24). The problem the designer runs into with this example is that if the photo is saved as a GIF to keep the text crisp, it could be as large as 70 KB. However, if the entire image were compressed as a JPG with a smaller size, the text would probably be blurred and splotchy. There are only two solutions. The first is to save the text as a separate image with a transparent color and layer it over the church, which would be used as a background image.

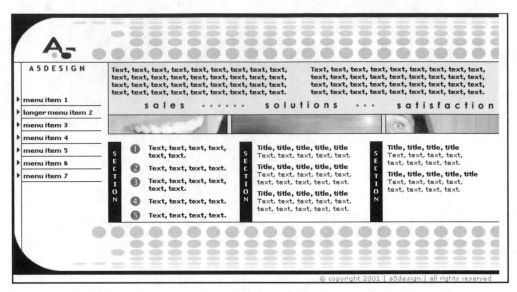

FIGURE 7.22   Design that uses gradated circles across the top and bottom of the image.

FIGURE 7.23   A zoomed-in view of some of the gradated circles in Figure 7.22.

The other would be to simply save the image as a higher quality JPG, which is usually the best decision. Saving it this way, the designer can compress the image to around 15 KB without compromising the quality of the text too much.

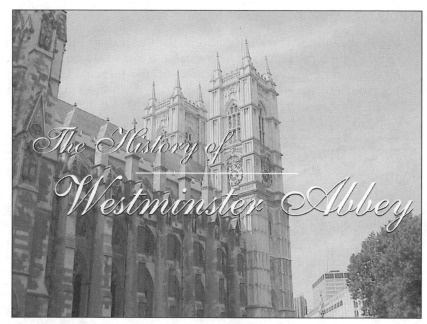

FIGURE 7.24 Photo with text layered on top that should be saved as a JPG.

Using the JPG file format considerably broadens a designer's ability to build striking graphical sites. Figure 7.25 is a graphical site that has a total download of 35 KB.

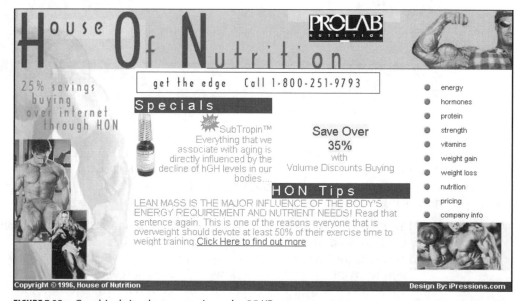

FIGURE 7.25 Graphical site that comes in under 35 KB.

MISUSING IMAGE FORMATS

Properly creating, saving, and compressing images can make or break a site. Figure 7.25 was a perfect example of how small the download can be of a largely graphical site when properly using the JPG and GIF file formats. Figure 7.26, on the other hand, is at the other end of the spectrum. The site misuses images in enough instances to make the entire site download larger than 300 KB.

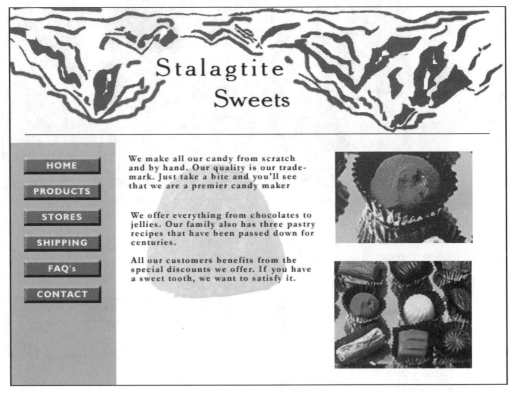

FIGURE 7.26   Site that misuses graphics; the entire page download is larger than 300 KB.

With today's software and coding techniques, it is no longer necessary, in most instances, to have a site come in at more than 50 KB. Following are seven instances where a designer can compromise the quality of a site by incorrectly saving and/or compressing an image.

1. **Saving an uncompressed image**—This is the most common mistake made by designers. Just saving an image with the correct file format is not enough. The designer still needs to compress the image. Figure 7.27, for example, when saved at the absolute lowest JPG compression setting in Photoshop, comes in at 65 KB, while saving it with the absolute highest compression, the

file size is reduced to 5 KB. This allows a lot of room for variation. While the quality would be severely compromised at 5 KB, saving the image at 65 KB, too, is a mistake. Most JPGs need only be saved with so much compression. After a certain quality has been met, decreasing the compression only creates a larger file size; it does not improve the quality of the image.

GIFs, too, can many times be compressed. Because each color that is eliminated from a GIF during compression is replaced by another color, images that are saved as GIFs can be drastically reduced many times.

2. **Photo saved as GIF**—While this was more of an issue in years past, designers still save photos as GIFs. Figure 7.28 is a photo that, when saved as a GIF, is 54 KB. If the image were saved as a JPG, a file size of 14 KB would provide acceptable image quality.

FIGURE 7.27   Photo after being compressed.

FIGURE 7.28   Image that should be saved as a JPG rather than a GIF.

3. **Solid colors saved as a JPG**—The JPG format is ironic. Because it can compress millions of colors so easily, it is easy for a designer to believe it can do the same for limited colors. This, however, is not the case. Figure 7.29 is an image that was saved as a GIF.

Figure 7.30 is the same image saved as a JPG. Following are three problems with the latter image:

• Although compressed nearly 80 percent, Figure 7.30 is still 4 KB, as opposed to Figure 7.29, which is 2 KB.
• The lines on the right in Figure 7.30 are completely splotchy, unlike the lines in Figure 7.29, which are crisp.
• The level at which the JPG is compressed slightly changes the background color.

FIGURE 7.29   Image saved as a GIF.

FIGURE 7.30   Image from Figure 7.29 saved as a JPG.

4. **Mixing JPG and GIF formats to maintain one color**—When compressing an image as a JPG, the image sometimes loses its color accuracy. In other words, the colors do not always remain the same after being compressed. In Figure 7.31, a clock with a colored border was saved on a background with the same color as the border. The clock with the border was saved as a JPG, while the background was saved as a GIF.

FIGURE 7.31   Example of color loss between a GIF and a JPG.

Taking a closer look at the seam where the two images were mortised together (Figure 7.32), it is apparent the smoothness and clarity of the clock's border becomes splotchy.

FIGURE 7.32   Zoomed-in view of splotchiness in Figure 7.31.

5. **Over compressing an image**—While compressing an image is not overly complicated, obtaining an eye for a properly compressed image takes a little experience. What initially may look good to a designer one day, may look overly compressed the next. When a JPG is overly compressed (see Figure 7.34) from its original state (Figure 7.33), the image loses its crispness.

FIGURE 7.33   Image saved as a JPG with proper compression.

One of the first places to show degradation is in solid colors, such as people's faces. All three faces and the lines on the floor in Figure 7.34 have lost their clarity.

FIGURE 7.34   Same image as Figure 7.33 saved as a JPG with too much compression.

When a GIF is overly compressed, the image becomes pixilated in areas with more colors. Figure 7.35 is the original image, while Figure 7.36 is an overly compressed version.

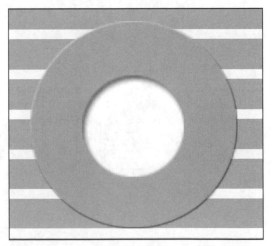

FIGURE 7.35   Image saved as a GIF with the correct number of colors.

Notice how spotty the drop shadow within the inner white circle becomes in Figure 7.36.

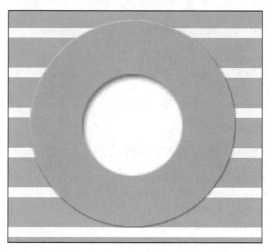

FIGURE 7.36   Image saved as a GIF with too few colors.

6. **Not saving images as GIFs or JPGs**—As previously mentioned, the two main image file formats used with the Internet today are GIFs and JPGs. However, a Web page can also use BMP files, and the browser will display them. The header image of Figure 7.26 was saved as a BMP. It is 159 KB; if it had been saved as a GIF, it could have been saved at around 14 KB.

Figure 7.37 is a photo saved as a JPG that is 4 KB, while the same image saved as a BMP file (Figure 7.38) is 166 KB.

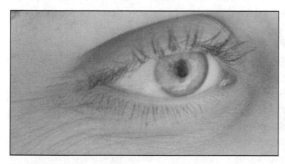

FIGURE 7.37   Image saved as a JPG (4 KB).

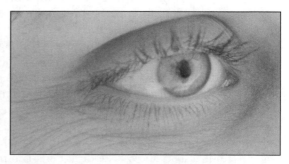

FIGURE 7.38   Image saved as a BMP (166 KB).

7. **Saving large, animated GIFs**—The GIF format is versatile in that a designer can not only create a regular GIF and a GIF with a transparent color, but he can also save a GIF that is animated. Unfortunately, just because a designer can save an animated GIF does not necessarily mean it should be done (Web design Rule 1).

Using an animated GIF can, at times, increase the usability of a site if the file is typically under 10 KB. However, when animated GIFs are used to display several photos, a designer is not only incorrectly saving the photos as GIFs, but two, three, or four of them are being saved into one animated GIF, amplifying the mistake.

UNDERSTANDING GRAPHICS/COMPRESSION SOFTWARE

Prior to the considerable growth of the Internet in the early to mid-1990s, the goal of graphics software was to create high-quality images, such as TIF, BMP, and EPS files. The reason was that the graphics created by the programs were mainly used for printers. Unfortunately, this created a problem for Web designers. Because a minimum of 300 dpi (dots per inch) to 600 dpi was required by printers, designers had to try to compress images to work with monitors, which mostly show only 72 dpi. Anything in excess of 72 dpi for images increases the file size without improving the quality of the image.

Large images coupled with slow modems severely handcuffed designers because it was difficult to create fast-downloading sites. Although the software allowed the designer the ability to compress images, opportunities were limited. To compress a GIF, the designer could assign only a certain bit depth to an image. In other words, the designer had the choice of saving the image with only 2, 4, 8, 16, 32, 64, 128, or 256 colors. To compress a JPG, the designer could assign compression only in increments of 10. In other words, the designer had the choice to save an image only at a level of 0, 1, 2, 3, 4, 5, 6, 7, 8, 9, 10.

Fortunately, software companies have made great strides in offering designers more flexibility in compressing images. Today, not only have these companies created and improved their own image-compression software, but they also have included this functionality in their image-editing programs.

Compressing images has never been more flexible. Now, instead of determining the compression of a GIF in groups of numbers, a designer can select the specific number of colors to include in an image. For even more control, the designer can even select certain colors that must remain in an image as the total number of colors is reduced. Figure 7.39 illustrates the compression component included with Photoshop. It not only shows a designer which colors are selected for the particular image, but it also allows the designer to compare the original version with the compressed version as changes are made.

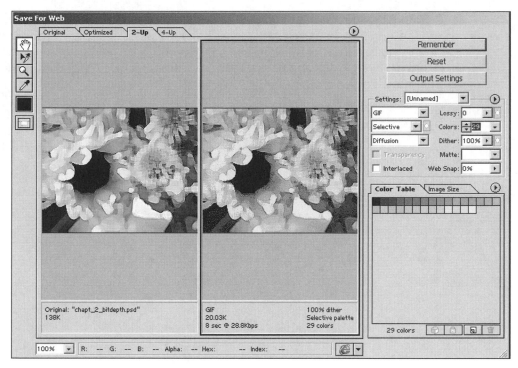

FIGURE 7.39   Image-compression window in Photoshop.

When choosing to compress an image with the JPG format, the designer now has the flexibility of increasing or decreasing compression by 1 percent instead of 10 percent at a time. This is incredibly useful because it allows the designer to take advantage of a unique characteristic of the JPG format. Sometimes when increasing the compression from, say, a quality level of 46 to 45, the quality of the image decreases. However, then when quality is dropped one more percent to 44, the image quality will shift enough to where it appears sharper than the lesser compression level of 45. This allows a designer the ability to trim the excess file size down to the bare-bones minimum.

SUMMARY

Much of the speed and quality of a site is determined by its graphics. This is why it is important for a designer to understand how to create, use, save, and compress images. While vector-based images are the newest technology available, traditional bitmap images, such as GIFs and JPGs, are the most widely and consistently supported.

Both GIFs and JPGs can do a good job of compressing images if the correct format is used. A designer, however, can also use the formats incorrectly, which can compromise the quality of a site. If the designer, however, understands how and when to use the formats along with compression software, sites can be highly graphical and yet fast at the same time.

CHAPTER

8

UNDERSTANDING THE BASICS OF CREATING MORTISED CSS DESIGNS

In This Chapter

- CSS-Based Design versus XHTML Table Design
- Understanding the Box Model
- When to Use Tables
- Validating Code
- Testing Designs in Various Browsers

Since the inception of the Internet, the front-end design of Web sites has been built primarily using HTML. While back-end development, such as database-driven programming and e-commerce functionality, has made large strides over the years, so has the front-end design of sites. In the past, to create a Web site that had the look and feel of traditional graphic design, the designer had to resort to using nested HTML (now XHTML) tables for the majority of content placement. The tables not only allowed the designer to mortise images together, but they also allowed for the layout of XHTML text that was styled using CSS. With the evolution of browsers over the past several years, nearly all layouts can now be accomplished using CSS. While Chapter 6 outlined essential basic information about CSS, this chapter explains the basics of how to use that code to create such sites. The chapter also explains the differences between XHTML table-based design and CSS-driven design.

CSS-BASED DESIGN VERSUS XHTML TABLE DESIGN

The first question a designer usually asks when it comes to creating CSS designs is, "If HTML has worked well for so many years, why is it not good enough now?" Unfortunately, there is not one answer to this question. Yes, HTML sites have been the main staple of designers since the mid-1990s. Yes, they are logical in the way they work. Yes, XHTML code, having replaced HTML as the standard, is compact enough, allowing for fast downloads, depending on included images and any extra code. The bottom line, though, is that nearly everything can be improved, and XHTML's table-based design is no exception. There are several advantages to creating CSS-based designs:

- The output Web page, barring the style sheet, is much cleaner and easier to follow because it takes considerably less code to accomplish the same look and feel. This makes it easier for the designer to understand nested elements and how they relate to other content and containers. While nesting is still necessary to accomplish the same look and feel as XHTML-table design, the amount of code needed to do so is drastically reduced.
- The combined download size, or weight, of the XHTML and CSS files is considerably smaller. Whether a user has a low- or high-speed connection, faster sites are always appreciated.
- The structure and styling of the site can be easily added, edited, and deleted. Although this concept is not new to those who create database-driven sites, CSS allows for changes made to one page to cascade through an entire site.
- Pages can be printed with much more control and consistency than can XHTML pages.

This is not to say that CSS is the perfect solution to coding Web sites. As with any Internet technology, there are going to be some disadvantages. However, it can be argued that the advantages outweigh the disadvantages, but the designer needs to be aware of these shortcomings:

- There is a learning curve. Even if a designer is familiar with CSS, using the language to lay out an entire site takes longer to learn than just styling text. The main reason is that there are idiosyncrasies with how CSS and its various elements interact in different browsers. The workarounds or hacks to solve many of these idiosyncrasies are explained in the following chapters.

- CSS is not supported as consistently in browsers as XHTML tables are, so it requires more testing by the designer. Not only are there compliant and noncompliant browsers that handle CSS differently, but there also are different versions of such browsers. This means there are more bugs and thus more workarounds and hacks that a designer must be familiar with to fix the bugs.

Web design always seems to be evolving. An increasing number of Web sites are being programmed with CSS as the main layout method. It is just a matter of time before the industry, and thus clients, demand that sites be coded this way. While it is not a perfect solution, CSS design is much more powerful and efficient than XHTML table-based design. One of the goals of this book is to decrease the learning curve by explaining how the process works and how to avoid and correct issues when they arise.

The Basics of CSS-Based Design Works versus XHTML Table-Based Design

With traditional Web design, the content of a homepage is mortised, or pieced, together using XHTML tables. This content may include text, images, or both. No matter what is included in the design, a minimum of one table is typically used to position the elements. CSS is then generally used to format the text. Figure 8.1 is an

FIGURE 8.1   Mortised XHTML homepage, with the border's value set to 3, that uses one table to display both text and images. © 2006 Onepartart.com. Used with permission.

example of a site that uses one table to display the content. The table border is set to 3 to help show how the page is constructed.

Unfortunately, most XHTML sites that employ more visually and technically advanced design usually cannot be created with one table. The designer therefore must nest tables inside of tables to position the various elements of the site. Figure 8.2 is the combination of nested tables used to place all the elements together in a design.

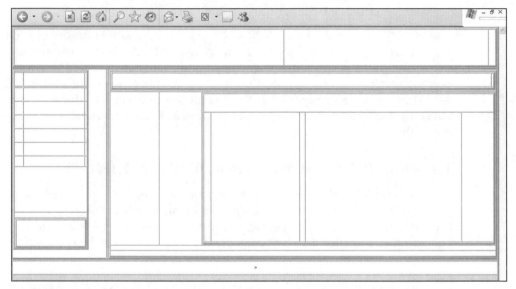

FIGURE 8.2   Table structure of a more complex table-based design, with the nested tables' borders set to 3 to display the framework.

Notice in Figure 8.2 that tables are nested inside one another. The purpose of this method is to place the content in various positions, down to the specific pixel in some cases. This design is created to be a "liquid" design, which means it can flex to wider resolutions. Figure 8.3 shows what the design looks like when the images and text, along with the basic CSS formatting, are added.

As complex as this design is, CSS can also be used to lay out the content. With relatively basic coding, a designer can make most sites look close, if not exact, to their table-based counterparts. Figure 8.4 is the same design as Figure 8.3 but laid out using a limited amount of CSS.

In general, CSS sites work by using block- and line-level tags, such as <DIV> and <SPAN> tags, in addition to a few other XHTML tags, such as <BR /> and <H1>, to format and position the content. The <DIV> and <SPAN> tags are wrapped around individual elements of content and then assigned rules in a style sheet to position and style them. While the design in Figure 8.4 does not have tables that can have their borders set to 3 to show the layout, the borders or backgrounds of the tags can be set to 3 to differentiate them. Figure 8.5 shows the design with the borders "turned on" and the images and content removed.

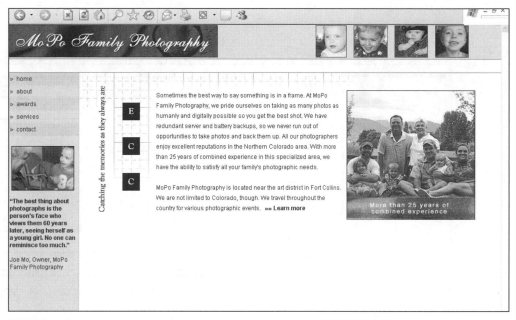

FIGURE 8.3   Design with table borders set to 0, and images, text, and CSS added to populate the table cells.

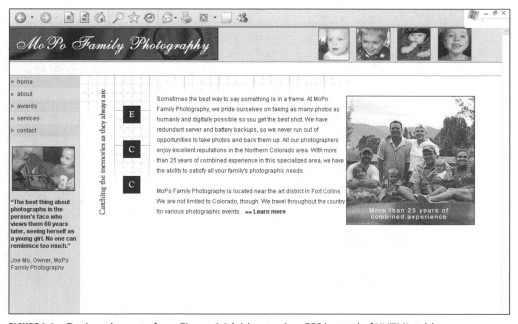

FIGURE 8.4   Design elements from Figure 8.3 laid out using CSS instead of XHTML tables.

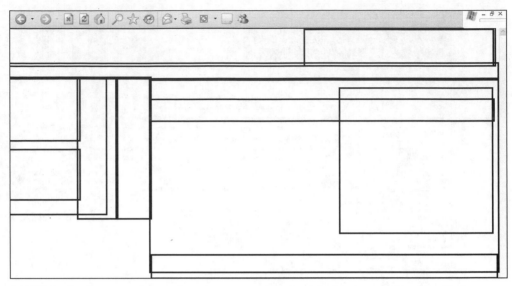

FIGURE 8.5   Borders turned on and content removed to show the basic structure of the site.

One thing to note about CSS-based sites is that they require considerably less coding. Listing 8.1 is the XHTML code that is used to lay out the design in Figure 8.3.

LISTING 8.1   XHTML Code for Figure 8.3

```
<!DOCTYPE html PUBLIC "-//W3C//DTD XHTML 1.0 Transitional//EN"
    "http://www.w3.org/TR/xhtml1/DTD/xhtml1-transitional.dtd">
<html xmlns="http://www.w3.org/1999/xhtml" xml:lang="en" lang="en">
<head>
    <title>MoPo Photography</title>
— enter meta data here for search engines, such as the following example —>
    <meta HTTP-EQUIV="Content-Type" CONTENT="text/html; charset=iso-8859-1" />
    <meta content="" name="keywords" />
    <meta content="" name="description" />
<!— link to javascript that enables any mouseovers on the page —>
<script src="mouseovers.js" type="text/javascript"></script>
<!— link to main stylesheet that controls text sizes and colors,
    among other things —>
<link rel="stylesheet" href="mainstyle.css" type="text/css" />
</head>
<body style="background-color: #ffffff; margin: 0px">
<!— Note: To make this page stretch to resolutions higher than
    800x600 or remain fixed at 800 x 600, change the width of the
    below table tag from "770" to "100%" and vice versa —>
<table width="100%" cellspacing="0" cellpadding="0" border="0">
```

```html
<tr>
<!- ###### header start ###### ->
    <td colspan="3" align="left" valign="top" style="background-image:
        url(images/bg_header.gif); background-repeat: repeat-x">
        <table width="100%" cellspacing="0" cellpadding="0" border="0">
        <tr>
            <td align="left" valign="top"><img src="images/
                header_left.jpg" width="431" height="73" alt=""
                border="0" /></td>
            <td align="center" valign="top"><img src="images/
                header_right.jpg" width="329" height="73" alt=""
                border="0" /></td>
            <td><img src="images/spacer.gif" width="10" height="1"
                alt="" border="0" /></td>
        </tr>
        </table>
    </td>
<!- ###### header end ###### ->
</tr>
<tr>
    <td colspan="3" bgcolor="#919191"><img src="images/spacer.gif"
        width="1" height="1" alt="" border="0" /></td>
</tr>
<tr>
<!- ###### menu column start ###### ->
    <td align="left" valign="top" bgcolor="#EDEAD1">
        <table width="144" cellspacing="0" cellpadding="0" border="0">
        <tr>
            <td colspan="3" bgcolor="#ffffff"><img src="images/
                spacer.gif" width="1" height="1" alt="" border="0"
                /></td>
        </tr>
        <tr>
            <td bgcolor="#ffffff"><img src="images/spacer.gif"
                width="1" height="1" alt="" border="0" /></td>
            <td align="left" valign="middle" bgcolor="#ffffff">
                 </td>
            <td bgcolor="#ffffff"><img src="images/spacer.gif" name="menu_item_1"
                width="3" height="26" alt="" border="0" /></td>
        </tr>
        <tr>
            <td colspan="3" bgcolor="#909290"><img src="images/
                spacer.gif" width="1" height="1" alt="" border="0"
                /></td>
```

```
        </tr>
        <tr>
            <td align="left" valign="middle" bgcolor="#E4E1C6"><img
                src="images/bullet_menu_1_off.gif" name="homepage"
                width="17" height="24" alt="" border="0" /></td>
            <td align="left" valign="middle" bgcolor="#E4E1C6"><a
                href="index.htm" onmouseover="document.homepage.src=
                bullet_menu_1_on.src;"
onmouseout="document.homepage.src=bullet_menu_1_off.src" style=
                "text-decoration: none; color: #003366">home</a></td>

            <td bgcolor="#E4E1C6"><img src="images/spacer.gif"
                width="3" height="26" alt="" border="0" /></td>
        </tr>
    <tr>
            <td align="left" valign="middle" bgcolor="#EDEAD1"><img
                src="images/bullet_menu_2_off.gif" name="about"
                width="17" height="24" alt="" border="0" /></td>
            <td align="left" valign="middle" bgcolor="#EDEAD1"><a
                href="about.htm" onmouseover="document.about.src=
                bullet_menu_2_on.src;"
            onmouseout="document.about.src=bullet_menu_2_off.src"
                style="text-decoration: none; color: #003366">about
                </a></td>
            <td bgcolor="#EDEAD1"><img src="images/spacer.gif"
                width="3" height="26" alt="" border="0" /></td>
        </tr>
        <tr>
            <td align="left" valign="middle" bgcolor="#E4E1C6"><img
                src="images/bullet_menu_1_off.gif" name="bios"
                width="17" height="24" alt="" border="0" /></td>
            <td align="left" valign="middle" bgcolor="#E4E1C6"><a
                href="awards.htm" onmouseover="document.bios.src=
                bullet_menu_1_on.src;"
            onmouseout="document.bios.src=bullet_menu_1_off.src"
                style="text-decoration: none; color: #003366">awards
                </a></td>
            <td bgcolor="#E4E1C6"><img src="images/spacer.gif"
                width="3" height="26" alt="" border="0" /></td>
        </tr>
        <tr>
            <td align="left" valign="middle" bgcolor="#EDEAD1"><img
                src="images/bullet_menu_2_off.gif" name="services"
                width="17" height="24" alt="" border="0" /></td>
```

```
        <td align="left" valign="middle" bgcolor="#EDEAD1"><a
            href="services.htm" onmouseover="document.services.src=
            bullet_menu_2_on.src;"
onmouseout="document.services.src=bullet_menu_2_off.src"
    style="text-decoration: none; color: #003366">services</a></td>
        <td bgcolor="#EDEAD1"><img src="images/spacer.gif"
            width="3" height="26" alt="" border="0" /></td>
    </tr>
    <tr>
        <td align="left" valign="middle" bgcolor="#E4E1C6"><img
            src="images/bullet_menu_1_off.gif" name="contact"
            width="17" height="24" alt="" border="0" /></td>
        <td align="left" valign="middle" bgcolor="#E4E1C6"><a
            href="contact.htm" onmouseover="document.contact.src=
            bullet_menu_1_on.src;"
            onmouseout="document.contact.src=bullet_menu_1_off.src"
            style="text-decoration: none; color: #003366">contact
            </a></td>
        <td bgcolor="#E4E1C6"><img src="images/spacer.gif"
            width="3" height="26" alt="" border="0" /></td>
    </tr>
    <tr>
        <td><img src="images/spacer.gif" width="17" height="20"
            alt="" border="0" /></td>
        <td><img src="images/spacer.gif" width="124" height="1"
            alt="" border="0" /></td>
        <td><img src="images/spacer.gif" width="3" height="1"
            alt="" border="0" /></td>
    </tr>
    <tr>
        <td colspan="3"><a href="index.htm"><img src="images/
            photo_bottom_left.jpg" width="144" height="92" alt=""
            border="0" /></a></td>
    </tr>
    <tr>
        <td><img src="images/spacer.gif" width="1" height="10"
            alt="" border="0" /></td>
    </tr>
    <tr>
        <td colspan="3" align="left" valign="top">
            <table width="100%" cellspacing="0" cellpadding="4"
            border="0">
            <tr>
            <td align="left" valign="top"><b>"The best thing about
```

```
                        photographs is the person's face who views them 60
                        years later, seeing herself as a young girl. No one
                        can reminisce too much."</b><br /><br />Joe Mo, Owner,
                        MoPo Family Photography
    <br /><br /></td>
                    </tr>
                    </table>
                </td>
            </tr>
            </table>
        </td>
<!- ###### menu column end ###### ->
<!- ###### forces minimum height of body start ###### ->
        <td align="left" valign="top" bgcolor="#CAC9CA"><img src="images/
            spacer_white.gif" width="1" height="26" alt="" border="0"
            /></td>
<!- ###### forces minimum height of body end ###### ->
<!- ###### main content start ###### ->
        <td align="left" valign="top">
            <table width="100%" cellspacing="0" cellpadding="0" border="0">
            <tr>
<!- ###### top center links start ###### ->
                <td colspan="3">
                    <table width="100%" cellspacing="0" cellpadding="0"
                        border="0">
                    <tr>
                        <td align="left"> </td>
                        <td><img src="images/spacer.gif" width="1"
                        height="26" alt="" border="0" /></td>
                    </tr>
                    <tr>
                        <td><img src="images/spacer.gif" width="500" height="1"
                            alt="" border="0" /></td>
                        <td><img src="images/spacer.gif" width="1"
                            height="1" alt="" border="0" /></td>
                    </tr>
                    </table>
                </td>
<!- ###### top center links end ###### ->
            </tr>
            <tr>
                <td colspan="3" bgcolor="#909290"><img src="images/
                spacer.gif" width="1" height="1" alt="" border="0" /></td>
```

```
            </tr>
            <tr>
                <td align="left" valign="top"><img src="images/tagline.gif"
                    width="80" height="285" alt="" border="0" /></td>
                <td align="left" valign="top"><img src="images/image_left_
                    of_text.gif" width="69" height="285" alt="" border="0"
                    /></td>
<!-- ###### main text column start ###### -->
                <td align="left" valign="top">
                    <table width="100%" cellspacing="0" cellpadding="0"
                        border="0">
                    <tr>
                        <td colspan="5" align="left" valign="top"><img
                            src="images/image_above_text.gif" width="476"
                            height="36" alt="" border="0" /></td>
                    </tr>
                    <tr>
                        <td><img src="images/spacer.gif" width="1"
                            height="1" alt="" border="0" /></td>
                        <td align="left" valign="top" style="line-height:
                            16pt">
Sometimes the best way to say something is in a frame. At MoPo Family
    Photography, we pride ourselves on taking as many photos as humanly
    and digitally possible so you get the best shot. We have redundant
    server and battery backups, so we never run out of opportunities to
    take photos and back them up. All our photographers enjoy excellent
    reputations in the Northern Colorado area.  With more than 25 years
    of combined experience in this specialized area, we have the
    ability to satisfy all your family's photographic needs.
<br /><br />
MoPo Family Photography is located near the art district in Fort
    Collins. We are not limited to Colorado, though. We travel
    throughout the country for various photographic events.
      <a href="x.htm" style="text-decoration:none"><b>&raquo;
    &raquo; Learn more</b></a></td>
                        <td><img src="images/spacer.gif" width="1"
                            height="1" alt="" border="0" /></td>
                        <td align="left" valign="top"><a href="x.htm"><img
                            src="images/photo_middle_right.jpg" width="260"
                            height="265" alt="" border="0" /></a></td>
<!-- ###### forces minimum height of body start ###### -->
                        <td><img src="images/spacer.gif" width="1"
                            height="257" alt="" border="0" /></td>
```

```
<!- ###### forces minimum height of body end ###### ->
                    </tr>
                    <tr>
                        <td><img src="images/spacer.gif" width="10"
                            height="1" alt="" border="0" /></td>
                        <td><img src="images/spacer.gif" width="146"
                            height="1" alt="" border="0" /></td>
                        <td><img src="images/spacer.gif" width="8"
                            height="1" alt="" border="0" /></td>
                        <td><img src="images/spacer.gif" width="260"
                            height="1" alt="" border="0" /></td>
                        <td><img src="images/spacer.gif" width="52"
                            height="1" alt="" border="0" /></td>
                    </tr>
                    </table>
                </td>
<!- ###### main text column end ###### ->
        </tr>
        <tr>
            <td colspan="3" style="background-image: url(images/
                bg_bottom_line.gif); background-repeat: repeat-x"><img
                src="images/bottom_left_square.gif" width="80"
                height="9" alt="" border="0" /></td>
        </tr>
        <tr>
            <td colspan="3"><img src="images/spacer.gif" width="1"
                height="10" alt="" border="0" /></td>
        </tr>
        </table>
    </td>
<!- ###### main content end ###### ->
</tr>
<tr>
    <td bgcolor="#7D7D7D"><img src="images/spacer.gif" width="144"
        height="1" alt="" border="0" /></td>
    <td bgcolor="#7D7D7D"><img src="images/spacer.gif" width="1"
        height="1" alt="" border="0" /></td>
    <td bgcolor="#7D7D7D"><img src="images/spacer.gif" width="625"
        height="1" alt="" border="0" /></td>
</tr>
<!- ###### footer start ###### ->
<tr>
<td colspan="3" style="background-color: #CAC9CA;"><img src="images/
    spacer.gif" width="1" height="1" alt="" border="0" /></td>
```

```
    </tr>
    <tr>
        <td colspan="3" style="background-color: #EDEAD1;"><img
            src="images/spacer.gif" width="1" height="10" alt=""
            border="0" /></td>
    </tr>
    <!- ###### footer end ###### ->
    </table>
    </body>
        </html>
```

The preceding code contains seven tables and 185 lines of code to lay out the elements of the page. CSS-based design has much cleaner XHTML code, reducing the weight, or download file size, of a page. The page contains only 67 lines of code. Listing 8.2 displays the code to produce the design in Figure 8.4.

LISTING 8.2   CSS Code for Figure 8.4

```
<!DOCTYPE html PUBLIC "-//W3C//DTD XHTML 1.0 Transitional//EN"
    "DTD/xhtml1-transitional.dtd">
<html xmlns="http://www.w3.org/1999/xhtml" xml:lang="en" lang="en">
<head>
<title>MoPo Photography</title>
<!-- link to main stylesheet that controls text sizes and colors,
    among other things -->
<link rel="stylesheet" href="mainstyle.css" type="text/css" />
</head>
<body>
<div id="a5-header">
    <span class="toprightimage"><img src="images/header-right.jpg"
        width="329" height="73" alt="" border="0" id="toprightimage"
        /></span>
    <img src="images/header-left.jpg" width="431" height="73" alt=""
        border="0" />
</div>
<div id="a5-title">
     
</div>
<!- ###### left column start ###### ->
<div id="a5-column-left">
<!- ###### menu start ###### ->
    <div id="a5-menu">
        <div class="a5-menu-odd">
            <a href="index.htm">home</a>
        </div>
```

```
        <div class ="a5-menu-even">
            <a href="about.htm">about</a>
        </div>
        <div class ="a5-menu-odd">
            <a href="awards.htm">awards</a>
        </div>
        <div class ="a5-menu-even">
            <a href="services.htm">services</a>
        </div>
        <div class ="a5-menu-odd">
            <a href="contact.htm">contact</a>
        </div>
    </div>
<!- ###### menu end ###### ->
    <br />
    <div id="photo_bottom_left">
        <a href="index.htm"><img src="images/photo_bottom_left.jpg"
            width="144" height="92" alt="" border="0" /></a>
    </div>
    <div style="padding:12px 5px 0px 5px;"><b>"The best thing about
        photographs is the person's face who views them 60 years
        later, seeing herself as a young girl. No one can reminisce
        too much."</b><br /><br />Joe Mo, Owner, MoPo Family
        Photography</div>
</div>
<!- ###### left column end ###### ->
<div id="a5-column-left-center">
    <img src="images/tagline.gif" width="80" height="285" alt=""
        border="0" />
</div>
<div id="a5-column-right-center">
    <img src="images/image-left-of-text.gif" width="69" height="285"
        alt="" border="0" />
</div>
<!- ###### right column start ###### ->
<div id="a5-column-right">
    <img src="images/image-above-text.gif" width="476" height="36"
        alt="" border="0" />
    <div id="a5-column-right-bottom">
        <span class="photo"><img src="images/photo-middle-right.jpg"
            width="260" height="265" alt="" border="0" /></span>
Sometimes the best way to say something is in a frame. At MoPo Family
    Photography, we pride ourselves on taking as many photos as
    humanly and digitally possible so you get the best shot. We have
```

```
        redundant server and battery backups, so we never run out of
        opportunities to take photos and back them up. All our
        photographers enjoy excellent reputations in the Northern Colorado
        area.  With more than 25 years of combined experience in this
        specialized area, we have the ability to satisfy all your family's
        photographic needs.
<br /><br />
MoPo Family Photography is located near the art district in Fort
        Collins. We are not limited to Colorado, though. We travel
        throughout the country for various photographic events.
          <a href="x.htm" style="text-decoration:none"><b>&raquo;
        &raquo; Learn more</b></a>
        </div>
        <div id="copyright">
            41909 N. Shield St., Suite 345  |  Fort Collins, CO 80524  |
                Phone: 970.555.1130 | Fax: 970.555.1129
        </div>
    </div>
    <!- ###### right column end ###### -->
    </body>
        </html>
```

Not only is the code much cleaner in Listing 8.2, but the file size is dramatically reduced, coming in at approximately 3.2 KB versus 11.2 KB for the table-based design in Listing 8.1. Because there is more CSS added to a style sheet to create such a design, the style sheet is going to be larger, but not by much. The style sheet weight for Listing 8.1 is approximately 0.70 KB, while the weight for Listing 8.2 comes in at around 3.6 KB. When the entire coding weight of each design is added up, the table-based design comes in at around 12 KB, while the CSS-based design comes in at 6.8 KB, making a difference of nearly 50 percent. And this is only for one page. When the reduced file size for additional pages on the site is compounded, the reduction becomes much greater.

UNDERSTANDING THE BOX MODEL

To design a CSS-based design, such as in Figure 8.4, the designer needs to use the *box model* method. This method involves wrapping <DIV> and <SPAN> tags (at least with the style used in this book) around page elements to position and place them. These tags are commonly referred to as containers because they are used to style elements that are contained within them.

When thinking in terms of a table-based design, the box model's containers are analogous to individual tables being nested inside one another. Positioning with CSS-based design is different than with table-based design. The latter uses table elements, such as table rows, columns, and cells, many times in association with spacer.gifs, to determine where items are placed. The former uses CSS's absolute or relative positioning to tell the boxes exactly where they will be in terms of any corner, usually at the top left or top right of the browser or in relation to a box or container in which it is nested.

The code in Listing 8.3 displays a Web page with a style sheet that tells the box with the id value of photo_bottom_left where it needs to be positioned in relation to the top-left corner of the page, where the x,y coordinates are 0,0.

LISTING 8.3   Code for a Web Site That Uses the Box Model

```
<!DOCTYPE html PUBLIC "-//W3C//DTD XHTML 1.0 Transitional//EN"
    "DTD/xhtml1-transitional.dtd">
<html xmlns="http://www.w3.org/1999/xhtml" xml:lang="en" lang="en">
<head>
    <title>A5design</title>
    <style>
        body {
            margin:0px;
            padding:0px;
            background:#ffffff;
            }
        #logo {
            position:absolute;
            top:245px;
            left:160px;
border:1px solid #000000;
            }
    </style>
</head>
<body>
    <div id="logo"><a href="index.htm"><img src="images/logo.jpg"
        width="144" height="92" alt="" border="0" /></a></div>
</body>
    </html>
```

Figure 8.6 illustrates how the image is placed 245 pixels from the top and 160 pixels from the left. The property border has been added with a value of 1 and a color of #000000. This turns on the border to allow the designer to better see the size of the box.

When two other <DIV> tags are added, for example, they also can have either absolute or relative positioning assigned to them. In Listing 8.4, the <DIV> tag with the id of box2 is given absolute positioning outside the photo_bottom_left box (shown in Figure 8.7). The <DIV> tag with the id of box3 is given relative positioning inside the <DIV> tag with the id of box2.

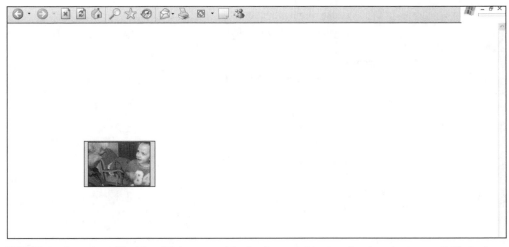

FIGURE 8.6   Box placed inside a Web page with absolute positioning, forcing the image 245 pixels from the top and 160 pixels from the left.

LISTING 8.4   Two Additional Boxes Added, One with Relative Positioning and the Other with Absolute Positioning

```
<!DOCTYPE html PUBLIC "-//W3C//DTD XHTML 1.0 Transitional//EN"
    "DTD/xhtml1-transitional.dtd">
<html xmlns="http://www.w3.org/1999/xhtml" xml:lang="en" lang="en">
<head>
    <title>A5design</title>
    <style>
        body {
            margin:0px;
            padding:0px;
            background:#ffffff;
            }
        #photo_bottom_left {
            position:absolute;
            top:245px;
            left:160px;
            border:1px solid #000000;
            }
        #box2 {
            position:absolute;
            top:400px;
            left:350px;
            width:100px;
            color:#ffffff;
```

```
            background:#000000;
            border:1px solid #000000;
            }
        #box3 {
            position:relative;
            top:0px;
            left:50px;
            height:100px;
            background:#D5C012;
            border:1px solid #000000;
            }
    </style>
</head>
<body>
    <div id="photo_bottom_left"><a href="index.htm"><img src="images/
        photo_bottom_left.jpg" width="144" height="92" alt=""
        border="0" /></a></div>
    <div id="box2">
        This is box 2
        <div id="box3">This is box 3</div>
    </div>
</body>
</html>
```

 The margin:0px; and padding:0px properties and values are added to the <BODY> tag in the stylesheet to ensure that the content is positioned in the top-left corner of the browser. If these attributes are not added, content will not always begin at the x,y attributes of 0,0 in a browser. Depending on the browser, this distance can change. Similar to XHTML table-based designs, it is necessary to declare background page colors when creating CSS-based designs, which is why the background property is added. This is included to ensure that all browsers use the same background color, not leaving the option to be declared by their default values.

When the page is displayed, box2 is located 100 pixels from the top and 350 pixels from the left. Box3 is then placed inside the box2 tag and positioned 50 pixels from the left. Both boxes are assigned background colors and have their borders turned on to better illustrate their shapes and positions (see Figure 8.7).

Because box3 is positioned inside box2 using relative positioning, the latter stretches to the full height of both boxes. If, however, box3 is assigned absolute, instead of relative, positioning in the style sheet (see Listing 8.4), it will react differently (see Figure 8.8).

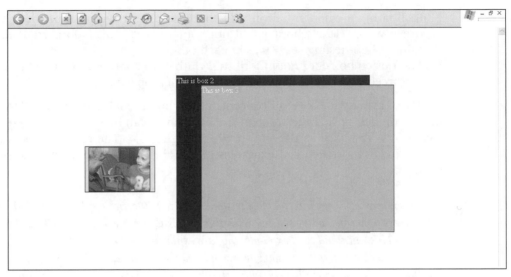

FIGURE 8.7   A box with relative positioning placed inside a box with absolute positioning.

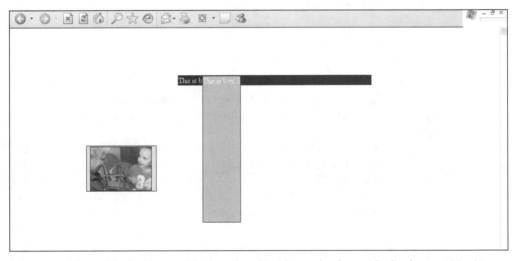

FIGURE 8.8   A box with absolute positioning placed inside another box with absolute positioning.

Following are three things to notice about how the relationship between the two boxes changes:

- Rather than position itself relative to box2, box3 positions itself from the top-left corner of box2.
- Box2 will not recognize the combined height of the two boxes. Rather, it will recognize only its own height. This is because absolute-positioned elements, similar

to floating elements, fall outside the flow of relative-positioned elements. In other words, `box2`'s border will not contain `box3`. This is important to keep in mind when nesting `<DIV>` tags in each other.

- The nested box does not inherit the width of the parent box. It will now need to be forced in the style sheet, using the `width` property.

These are just the overall concepts of the box model. Similar to XHTML tables, the box model, once understood at the basic level, can be used in more creative and advanced ways, such as the site shown in Figure 8.4. The case studies later in the book provide more detailed examples of building more advanced sites, such as in this figure.

The box model is not interpreted the same between Internet Explorer (IE) 5.0 and IE 5.5 browsers. One method of dealing with this bug is to use the Tantek Celik hack in the style sheet). This hack and the box model bug are explained in Chapter 16.

   Adding elements with various properties and values can alter the way containers interact with each other, especially depending on the browser version and operating system. This requires the designer to always test a site in different browsers and sometimes even on different operating systems.

WHEN TO USE TABLES

Some CSS purists believe CSS Web designs should include very little, if any, XHTML tables. While there are more advantages than disadvantages to creating CSS-based sites over table-based designs, this does not mean that there is no longer a need for tables.

   Tables serve a practical purpose in Web design: handling columns and rows of data. While there are ways to handle such content using CSS, there is no reason XHTML cannot and should not be used in such circumstances, such as in Figure 8.9. In this example, 77 cells are used in the table. CSS would, in many cases, be too time-consuming to create and maintain.

VALIDATING CODE

The W3C is the governing body when it comes to the creation of Web standards that help the Web "reach its true potential," according to the consortium. Over the years, an increasing number of designers and developers have begun adhering to such standards.

First Name	Last Name	City	State	Zip	Phone	Fax
Mikayla	Missun	Wellington	CO	80550	555.555.5555	970.555.5555
Charlie	Joseph	Eaton	CO	80524	555.555.5555	970.555.5555
Kata	Anne	Fort Collins	CO	80524	555.555.5555	970.555.5555
Josh	Dogin	Phoenix	AZ	68798	555.555.5555	970.555.55555
Daniel	Yu	San Francisco	CA	89787	555.555.5555	970.555.5555
Susan	Jones	Boulder	CO	80540	555.555.5555	970.555.5555
William	Anderson	Denver	CO	80234	555.555.5555	970.555.5555
Josephie	Kuehl	Longmont	CO	80524	555.555.5555	970.555.5555
Jen	Marie	Crested Butte	CO	80113	555.555.5555	970.555.55555
Melissa	York	New York	NY	89747	555.555.5555	970.555.5555

FIGURE 8.9   Example Web page where using an XHTML table is more practical than using CSS to position 77 cells of data.

During Web page design, both XTHML and CSS should be validated using the W3C's free online validating services. They not only help a developer understand what code is not compliant, but they now provide explanations and examples of correctly written code. Following are the URLs for each validating service:

XHTML Markup Validation Service (http://validator.w3.org/)

CSS Validation Service (http://jigsaw.w3.org/css-validator/)—At the time of publication, some properties are validated differently if a URL, as opposed to an uploaded file, is submitted to the validator. Because the URL version of the software is used more often, it is probably wise for the designer to validate pages on servers beforehand.

The W3C also offers a downloadable version of its CSS Validator. The software can be found at http://dev.w3.org/cvsweb/2002/css-validator/.

 Once a page is validated, the W3C provides and encourages designers and developers to include a W3C validation image on the page, which verifies that the page has been validated for either XHTML or CSS or both.

TESTING DESIGNS IN VARIOUS BROWSERS

Because CSS is not interpreted as consistently as XHTML, it requires more testing. Because there are so many designs included with this book, the browsers for which they were tested have changed from edition to edition. The latest designs have been tested using the following browsers:

- Internet Explorer (IE) 6.029 and 7
- Firefox 1.5.0.6
- Opera 8.5
- Safari

Based on Web usage statistics by W3C Schools (www.w3schools.com/browsers/browsers_stats.asp), these browsers represent more than 95 percent of the users on the Web. Obviously, such statistics fluctuate, depending on whose statistics are considered and what their target audience is; however, it is safe to assume that these six browsers will represent the majority of users in the near future.

 Downloading versions of non-Microsoft browsers can be accomplished by visiting their respective sites. Downloading older versions of IE is not so easy. A useful site for downloading various browsers is http://browsers.evolt.org/. The site offers various versions of IE, in addition to many other browsers. Because IE 6 has been fully integrated into Microsoft operating systems, it is sometimes necessary to load modified versions of IE 5.5 and IE 5.0. It is important to note that this book's author and its publisher are not to be held accountable for any adverse effects of loading such software. The designer or developer does so at his or her own risk. IE 7, fortunately, can be easily added and, if necessary, removed from systems that may still have IE 6 on them.

SUMMARY

While there is a learning curve that comes with changing a coding style from creating XHTML table-based designs to CSS-based designs, this chapter gives a basic understanding of the benefits of the CSS method and how it works. (Chapters 9 through 14 will then put these principles to use.) The box model is explained, including how absolute and relative positioning are used to position block elements. Reasons also are given for why tables should not be entirely shunned. As with all development, testing is encouraged. W3C validation services are included to give the designer a place to validate both the XHTML and CSS of a site.

CASE STUDY: LOW-CONTENT CSS DESIGN

In This Chapter

- Understanding the Design's Structure
- Building the Structure
- Constructing Second-Level Pages

S ince the introduction of CSS-based design, Web designs have started taking a more simple look, similar to how they used to look before designers used more complex layouts, using nested XHTML tables. This look could be simply a design fad, which the industry experiences every few years, or it may be that designers simply do not know how to create the complex designs that give a site a more professional, unique look and feel. This chapter shows a designer how easy it is to create a more complex look by using CSS in a more creative way by breaking the "visual" confines of linear (rectangular and square) containers. In other words, this chapter explains how to make designs look as if the designer wants them to look, rather than having to make a design look like images were merely placed in columns because that is all that could technically be done. The design in this chapter was created for 800 × 600 resolution; however, no matter the resolution, the same techniques apply to creating larger designs.

The design explained in this chapter is design 121 on the accompanying CD-ROM (photo credits: www.idlerphotography.com).

UNDERSTANDING THE DESIGN'S STRUCTURE

Before beginning to build a design, it is important that the designer understand the page's infrastructure. The design shown in Figure 9.1 is a simple layout that uses a header and two columns below it to mortise the images together and therein place the content.

FIGURE 9.1   The low-content design explained in this chapter.

The Reasoning Behind Guides and Creating Slices in Photoshop Files

When building a design, one should usually create it in image editing software, such as Photoshop, rather than spending time coding the actual design. While creating a *comp*, or sample design, is time-consuming, it will save time because most of the technical considerations are worked out during this phase of the process. It is also time-saving because the client is usually going to want to make changes to the design, and it is easier to make these changes when first creating the entire page. Then, once the design is approved, the designer simply needs to code it to appear as it does in the Photoshop file.

After a design is created in Photoshop, the designer is going to want to *break up*, or code, the design in XHTML and CSS. To begin this process, guides are placed to ensure that the elements are lined up in their correct positions. Slices, which are used to save areas of the design as images, can then be easily fashioned once everything is correctly positioned.

Figure 9.2 shows how the guides and slices are positioned. The numbers added to the design are used to point out the 10 most important guides and slices.

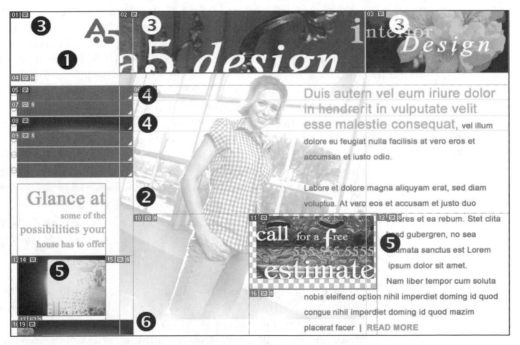

FIGURE 9.2   Guides and slices strategically placed within the design.

There are several things to note about the guides and slices in Figure 9.2:

- The horizontal guide just below number 1 is added to separate the header row from the lower part of the design.
- The vertical guide to the left of number 2 separates the left column, which includes the menu, from the right column, which contains the main content for the page.
- The three number 3s represent the slices that are used in the header area.

 A slice is indicated by the small numbered rectangle in the top-left corner of each outlined rectangle or square.

- The two number 4s indicate, to the left of them, the background images that are used in each menu item. The top number 4 represents the menu item when the user has not selected that item. The lower number 4 represents the background when the hyperlinked menu item is in hover mode.
- The two number 5s represent slices used to save images for the design that are not mortised together with any others. The right image, which says, "call for a free estimate," has the background image removed from it. This is accomplished by cropping out the background, and any other images, below the slice. When saving the Photoshop file, the designer can designate the checkered background, which is the background of the file, as a transparent background. This allows the image to be easily layered over any background in the file so that background can appear through the area that is checkered. The advantage of this technique is that the image can then be moved anywhere over the background image of the woman, without the "estimate" image containing remnants of her checkered shirt. It is a coincidence that the Photoshop background and the woman's shirt are both checkered. If the image contained the woman's shirt, rather than that area being transparent, and was positioned differently, the image and background images would appear disjointed.

 If the image had a curve and that image was saved with a transparent background, the curve would have a jagged edge because of anti-aliasing, which blends colors to give the perception of one color being curved.

- The slice to the left of number 6 represents the background image that is used for the page title row for second-level pages (see Figure 9.3). Often it is easier to save images that are not necessarily used on the homepage with the source file that is used for the homepage. This often eliminates the need to save a completely new PSD (Photoshop) file for just one image.

Because multiple images are layered and saved over the background image of the woman, it is helpful to duplicate the source PSD file and save it independently so the background can be saved. When the file has been duplicated, the extra images, all slices, and most guides can be removed, leaving only the background image. The

FIGURE 9.3   The page title area on second-level pages that uses a background image saved from the Photoshop file created for the homepage.

designer then adds a slice around the portion of the file that will be saved as an individual image.

One advantage of duplicating the existing homepage file and deleting excess images is that the background image's placement remains the same. Because the main slice, represented by number 2 in Figure 9.2, is not removed, the designer knows exactly where to place the new slice. Figure 9.4 shows the homepage saved as a separate source file with all the original slices and excess images removed.

FIGURE 9.4   Homepage source file that is duplicated and saved as a separate file so the background image of the woman can be saved independently from the images layered over it.

Understanding the Placement of CSS Containers

More than 10 <DIV> tags are used to lay out the images saved from the Photoshop file and XHTML content. Figure 9.5 shows the <DIV> tags with all the images and content removed and their borders "turned on" by setting them to 1px.

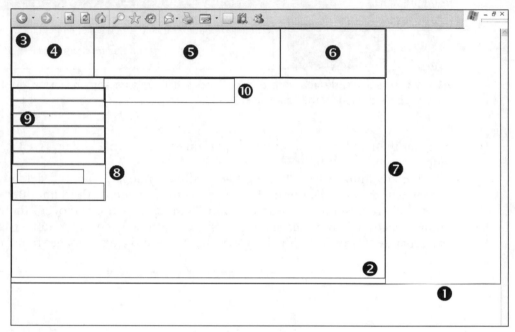

FIGURE 9.5   Design with images and content removed and various <DIV> tags turned on.

The <DIV> tags are used for different functions in the design, such as setting up its basic infrastructure, providing containers to position content within, and styling the content. Following are explanations of the 10 most useful <DIV> tags in Figure 9.4:

- The <DIV> tag above number 1 is used for centering the design in IE 5 and 5.5 if it is to have a fixed width. The container starts at the very top-left corner of the browser window.
- The <DIV> tag below number 2 determines whether the design has a fixed width or is a liquid layout. It also begins in the top-left corner of the browser window.
- The <DIV> tag to the left of number 3 contains the images that are used in the header area.
- Numbers 4, 5, and 6 are images in the header area that are assigned absolute positioning.
- The <DIV> tag to the left of number 7 contains both the left and right columns of the body.

- Number 8 defines the left column, which contains, among other things, the menu.
- Number 9 represents the container that styles and positions the menu.
- Number 10 is the <DIV> that contains the content in the right column. It expands to the full width of the design when enough content is included to force the full width.

BUILDING THE STRUCTURE

Following are the steps for constructing the design, step by step. It is assumed that the Photoshop file has already been created or customized and the designer need only position the images and text.

Creating the XHTML and CSS Framework

The first step to building the design is to create the XHTML framework and initial CSS containers. Listing 9.1 is the code that is used to output the page in Figure 9.6.

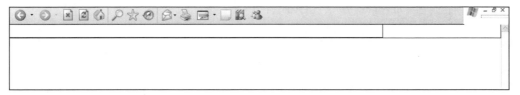

FIGURE 9.6   Basic XHTML and CSS framework for the design.

LISTING 9.1   Code for Figure 9.6

```
<!DOCTYPE html PUBLIC "-//W3C//DTD XHTML 1.0 Transitional//EN"
    "DTD/xhtml1-transitional.dtd">
<html xmlns="http://www.w3.org/1999/xhtml" xml:lang="en"
lang="en"><head><title>Design 121</title>
<meta http-equiv="Content-Type" content="text/html;
    charset=iso-8859-1" />
<style type="text/css">
/* ++++++++++ global general styles start ++++++++++*/
html, body {
    margin:0px;
    padding:0px;
    font: 13px Arial, Helvetica, sans-serif;
    color:#766D6D;
    background:#ffffff;
}
```

```
/* ++++++++++ global general styles end ++++++++++*/

/* ++++++++++ global structure styles start ++++++++++*/
#a5-body-center {
    text-align:left;
    border:1px solid #000000;
    }
#a5-body {
    position: relative;
    width: 770px; /* change this to a specific amount for a fixed
        design or a relative amount if the design should expand to a percentage
of the screen. E.g., 770px or 100%, respectively. */
    /* remove these comment tags if the page is to be centered. The 'text-
        align' property in the 'a5-body-center' rule must also be changed
        from 'left' to 'center'
    margin-left: auto;
    margin-right: auto;*/
    text-align:left;
    padding-bottom:10px;
    border:1px solid #000000;
    }
/* ++++++++++ global structure styles end ++++++++++*/
</style>
</head>
<body>
<div id="a5-body-center">
    <div id="a5-body">
        Enter text here.
    </div>
</div>
</body>
</html>
```

There are several things to note about the code in Listing 9.1:

- The CSS style sheet is commented into a couple of different sections. The global general styles comment tags contain the general styles, such as the formatting of the <HTML> and <BODY> tags, hyperlinks, and fonts. The global structure styles comment tags include the styles used to define the structure of the design and elements included in that structure.
- Several rules define the <HTML> and <BODY> tags. The margin and padding properties are used to ensure that the design is placed in the very top-left corner of the browser, with no space between the design and the edges of the viewable area. The default font style for the site is set using the shorthand FONT property. The default font color is defined with the COLOR property. The background color also

is assigned, even if it is only white (that is, #ffffff). This guarantees that all browsers display the site with the same background color because the default color is not always the same among browsers.

- The a5-body-center and a5-body rules are used to force the design to the left side of the browser screen with a fixed width of 770 pixels. If the designer wanted the design to fill the full width of the screen, the value of 770px would need to be changed to 100%. If, however, the designer wanted to center the design, the value of the text-align property in the a5-body-center rule would need to be changed from left to center. The margin-left and margin-right properties in the a5-body rule would only need to have the comment tags around them removed. This system allows the designer flexibility when more than one site is going to be built using this same default code. By adding this code to every design, it does not take much effort to quickly change a design to fit a client's needs.

- Both the a5-body-center and a5-body rules have their borders turned on using the following code: border:1px solid #000000;. For demonstration purposes, the code was added to both rules to show what the structure of the <DIV> tags looks like with no content added. Turning on the borders also helps when building a site because it is not always apparent where elements are placed or expanding to. Rather than remove these rules, it is easier to change the value of 1px to 0px, turning the borders off, rather than removing them. Troubleshooting often involves turning the borders back on, thereby saving time and taking up very little download size by keeping them in the style sheet.

- Because the <div id="a5-body"> is nested inside the <div id="a5-body-center"> tag, it is indented. This allows for quicker recognition of nested tags, which becomes a useful technique when the page has more code added to it later.

Adding the Header Content

Once the XHTML and basic CSS framework have been added, the header area is then added into the code. Listing 9.2 is the code that is used to output the page in Figure 9.7.

FIGURE 9.7   Design with all three header images added.

The newly added code is bold to differentiate it from the existing code that is being built upon in this case study.

LISTING 9.2   Code for Figure 9.7

```
<!DOCTYPE html PUBLIC "-//W3C//DTD XHTML 1.0 Transitional//EN"
    "DTD/xhtml1-transitional.dtd">
<html xmlns="http://www.w3.org/1999/xhtml" xml:lang="en"
lang="en"><head><title>Design 121</title>
<meta http-equiv="Content-Type" content="text/html;
    charset=iso-8859-1" />
<style type="text/css">
/* ++++++++++ global general styles start ++++++++++*/
html, body {
    margin:0px;
    padding:0px;
    font: 13px Arial, Helvetica, sans-serif;
    color:#766D6D;
    background:#ffffff;
    }
/* ++++++++++ global general styles end ++++++++++*/
/* ++++++++++ global structure styles start ++++++++++*/
#a5-body-center {
    text-align:left;
    border:0px solid #000000;
    }
#a5-body {
    position: relative;
    width: 770px; /* change this to a specific amount for a fixed
        design or a relative amount if the design should expand to a percentage
of the screen. E.g., 770px or 100%, respectively. */
    /* remove these comment tags if the page is to be centered. The 'text-
        align' property in the 'a5-body-center' rule must also be changed
        from 'left' to 'center'
    margin-left: auto;
    margin-right: auto;*/
    text-align:left;
    padding-bottom:10px;
    border:0px solid #000000;
    }
/* ++++++++++ global structure styles end ++++++++++*/
#a5-header {
    position:relative;
    left:0px;
    top:0px;
    height:98px;
    border:0px solid #000000;
    }
```

```
    #a5-header-center {
        position:absolute;
        left:169px;
        top:0px;
        }
    #a5-header-right {
        position:absolute;
        left:553px;
        top:0px;
        }
</style>
</head>
<body>
<div id="a5-body-center">
    <div id="a5-body">
<!-- ###### header start ###### -->
        <div id="a5-header">
            <div><a href="index.htm"><img src="images/header-left.gif"
                width="169" height="98" alt="" border="0" /></a></div>
            <div id="a5-header-center"><img src="images/
                header-center.jpg" width="384" height="98" alt=""
                border="0" /></div>
            <div id="a5-header-right"><img src="images/
                header-right.jpg" width="217" height="98" alt=""
                border="0" /></div>
        </div>
<!-- ###### header end ###### -->
    </div>
</div>
</body>
</html>
```

There are several things to note about the code in Listing 9.2:

- Three images are being mortised together in the header area, rather than just one (see Figure 9.8).
- The a5-header rule is created to contain the three header images inside it. This container also allows the designer to easily move all those elements included inside it as one entity because their positioning is based off its top-left corner.
- Because it is assigned relative positioning, with the left and top properties set to 0px, the a5-header container begins at the very top-left corner of the Web browsers because the <DIV> tags it is nested inside also begin at the x,y (0,0) coordinates of the page. The relative positioning also ensures that the <DIV> tag will stretch to the full width of the area it is occupying, which is 770 pixels. The height property of the rule, which is set to 98px, is added to ensure that the con-

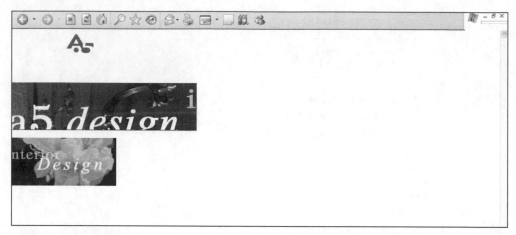

FIGURE 9.8   Three images that are mortised together in the header area.

tainer collapses perfectly around the three images. Otherwise, browsers may not structure the container similarly.

- `<DIV>` tags are wrapped around the `header-left.gif` image, which is the first image in the header area. This is to ensure that no additional space is added around the image, stretching the `a5-header` container too high, such as in Figure 9.9, which is a result of an entirely different cause, as noted.

 Sometimes, spaces or carriage returns in XHTML code can alter the way `<DIV>` tags are interpreted. The image located in the first `<DIV>` tag nested inside the `a5-header` `<DIV>` is a perfect example of this. If a space or carriage return is added after the closing `</a>` tag, the `a5-header` container will add extra space below the image(s) in IE 6 (see Figure 9.9). The background color of the container was set as black to show the difference in the image. It should be noted that one space in XHTML code will render one space in a design, if that space is in the content area. A space usually doesn't make a difference between lines of code. This note is one exception to this rule.

FIGURE 9.9   Extra space added below the header area because of a carriage return in the XHTML code.

To ensure that no space appears between the image and the container's border around the image, the code must look like the following:

```
<div><a href="index.htm"><img src="images/header-left.gif" width="169"
    height="98" alt="" border="0" /></a></div>
```

Rather than like this:

```
<div><a href="index.htm"><img src="images/header-left.gif" width="169"
    height="98" alt="" border="0" /></a>
</div>
```

- Both the `a5-header-center` and `a5-header-right` rules are added to the style sheet to position the other two images in the header area. Both of these rules use absolute positioning. This makes the `left` and `top` properties particularly important because they assign where the top-left corner of the container will be positioned. Because the first image is 169 pixels wide, the `a5-header-center` tag must start 169 pixels from the left—thus the `169px` value. Because the center image is 384 pixels wide, that width added to the width of the first image determines that the third image must start 553 pixels from the left (384 + 169 = 553 pixels). This positioning, however, works only if the borders are turned off, so they are not entered into the equation in some browsers. To guarantee that both images begin at the top of the `a5-header` container, the `top` property, with a value of `0px`, is added to both rules.

Adding <DIV> in Which to Nest Left and Right Columns

Before the left and right columns of the design can be added, a `<DIV>` must be added that can contain the columns. In this case, the `a5-body-content` container serves two functions:

- Once the left and right columns are nested inside the `<DIV>`, the entire area can be easily moved in relation to the header area. If, for example, the design is customized to be 150 pixels high, the `top` property of the `a5-body-center` container would need to be changed to `150px`.
- A background image can be applied specifically to this section. In this case, it is the image of the woman.

 The background image can also be applied to the HTML, BODY *rule and have its location controlled by the shorthand background rule:* background: #ffffff url(images/ bg-body-content.jpg) no-repeat 0px 98px;. *The* left *(0px) and* top *(98px) properties at the end of the rule tell the background image where it should be displayed in relation to the top-left corner of the browser window.*

Figure 9.10 shows what the image looks like when the `<DIV>` is added. Without content in the `<DIV>`, it would normally collapse and not show the background. The `a5-body-content` rule, however, has been assigned a height of `410px`, which will guarantee that the entire image always shows, whether or not there is enough content included in the `<DIV>` to make it expand to its full height.

FIGURE 9.10   The page with the `a5-body-content` container added, which will not only contain the left and right columns, but will also display a background image.

 This rule is also assigned a `margin-right` *property with the value of* `15px`. *This is to ensure that eventually, when text is added to the center column, it will not touch the right side and make its readability more difficult.*

Creating the Left Column

After the `a5-body-content` container has been added, the left column can be created. This column will contain the menu, the Glance At box, and the copyright areas. Listing 9.3 shows what the code looks like, which then displays the design, as shown in Figure 9.11.

 The newly added code is bold to differentiate it from the existing code that is being built upon in this case study.

FIGURE 9.11   The design with the left column added to the a5-body-content container.

LISTING 9.3   Code for Figure 9.11

```
<!DOCTYPE html PUBLIC "-//W3C//DTD XHTML 1.0 Transitional//EN"
    "DTD/xhtml1-transitional.dtd">
<html xmlns="http://www.w3.org/1999/xhtml" xml:lang="en"
lang="en"><head><title>Design 121</title>
<meta http-equiv="Content-Type" content="text/html;
    charset=iso-8859-1" />
<style type="text/css">
/* ++++++++++ global general styles start ++++++++++*/
html, body {
    margin:0px;
    padding:0px;
    font: 13px Arial, Helvetica, sans-serif;
    color:#766D6D;
    background:#ffffff;
    }
/* ++++++++++ global general styles end ++++++++++*/
/* ++++++++++ global structure styles start ++++++++++*/
#a5-body-center {
    text-align:left;
    border:0px solid #000000;
    }
```

```
#a5-body {
    position: relative;
    width: 770px; /* change this to a specific amount for a fixed
        design or a relative amount if the design should expand to a percentage
of the screen. E.g., 770px or 100%, respectively. */
    /* remove these comment tags if the page is to be centered. The 'text-
        align' property in the 'a5-body-center' rule must also be changed
        from 'left' to 'center'
    margin-left: auto;
    margin-right: auto;*/
    text-align:left;
    padding-bottom:10px;
    border:0px solid #000000;
    }
/* ++++++++++ global structure styles end ++++++++++*/
#a5-header {
    position:relative;
    left:0px;
    top:0px;
    height:98px;
    background:#000000;
    }
    #a5-header-left {
        width:169px;
        }
    #a5-header-center {
        position:absolute;
        left:169px;
        top:0px;
        }
    #a5-header-right {
        position:absolute;
        left:553px;
        top:0px;
        }
  #a5-body-content {
      position:relative;
      background: #ffffff url(images/bg-body-content.jpg) no-repeat;
      height:410px;
margin-right:15px;
      border:0px solid #000000;
      }
      #a5-column-left {
          position:absolute;
          left:0px;
```

```
        top:19px;
        width:190px;
        }
    #a5-menu {
    font:bold 13px Arial, Helvetica, sans-serif;
        }
    #a5-menu a {
        display:block;
        text-align:left;
        line-height:23px;
        vertical-align:50%;
        padding-left:15px;
        margin-bottom:1px;
        text-decoration:none;
        background: url(images/bg-menu-off.gif) no-repeat 0px 0px;
        color:#E9F92C;
        }
    #a5-menu a:hover {
        background: url(images/bg-menu-on.jpg) no-repeat 0px 0px;
        margin-bottom:1px;
        color:#E9F92C;
        }
    #a5-bottom-left-content {
        width:136px;
        font:bold 12pt times, garamond, serif;
        line-height:26px;
        text-align:right;
        margin:9px 0px 0px 10px;
        color:#DF9B05;
        border:1px solid #999A8D;
        }
    #a5-copyright {
        font-size:8pt;
        padding:10px 50px 10px 10px;
        color:#766D6D;
        }
</style>
</head>
<body>
<div id="a5-body-center">
    <div id="a5-body">
<!-- ###### header start ###### -->
        <div id="a5-header">
            <div><a href="index.htm"><img src="images/header-left.gif"
                width="169" height="98" alt="" border="0" /></a></div>
```

```
                    <div id="a5-header-center"><img src="images/
                        header-center.jpg" width="384" height="98" alt=""
                        border="0" /></div>
                    <div id="a5-header-right"><img src="images/
                        header-right.jpg" width="217" height="98" alt=""
                        border="0" /></div>
            </div>
    <!- ###### header end ###### ->

    <!- ###### body content start ###### ->
        <div id="a5-body-content">
            <div id="a5-column-left">
                <div id="a5-menu">
                    <a href="index.htm">menu item 1</a>
                    <a href="menu-item-2.htm">longer menu item 2</a>
                    <a href="menu-item-3.htm">menu item 3</a>
                    <a href="index.htm">menu item 4</a>
                    <a href="index.htm">menu item 5</a>
                    <a href="index.htm">menu item 6</a>
                </div>

                <div id="a5-bottom-left-content">
                    <span style="font:bold 24pt times, garamond, serif;
                        ">Glance at</span><br />
                    some of the<br />
                    <span style="font:bold 13pt times, garamond, serif;
                        ">possibilities your</span><br />
                    house has to offer    <div style="padding-top:10px;">
                        <a href="index.htm"><img src="images/
                        photo-bottom-left.jpg" width="136"
                        height="93" alt="" border="0" /></a></div>
                </div>
                <div id="a5-copyright">
                    |  &copy; copyright 2006  
                        |<br />|  your company  |
                        <br />|  all rights reserved 
                         |
                </div>
            </div>
        </div>
    <!- ###### body content start ###### ->
        </div>
    </div>
    </body>
    </html>
```

There are several things to note about the code in Listing 9.3:

- The `a5-column-left` container is assigned absolute positioning. This guarantees that it will always be in the same location. The one disadvantage to absolute positioning is that the `a5-column-left` container will fall outside the flow of the document, meaning it can end up vertically longer than the `a5-column-left` container. Fortunately, for this design, this would not be visible if it were the case because the column does not have a background color or image the content needs to remain over.

- The `a5-menu` container contains the menu items that are styled to enable easy mouseovers. The column is given a specific width to guarantee that the first element is positioned correctly in all browsers.

- The `a5-menu a` descendant rule is used to display and style each menu item. The display property with the `block` value will output each item in the `<DIV>` in its own row. The text is then left justified, assigning the `text-align` property a value of `left`. The `line-height` and `vertical-align` properties, which need to be used together for the `vertical-align` property to be interpreted, force the height of the menu item and how the text will be vertically aligned. The `padding-left:15px;` rule forces the menu items 15 pixels from the left so they do not fall on the circular image at the very left of the row. Because the menu is layered over the `a5-body-content` background image to the right, the `margin-bottom:1px;` rule is added to ensure that there is transparent spacing between the menu items so the layering effect is noticeable (see Figure 9.12).

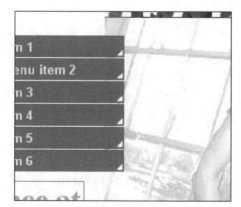

FIGURE 9.12 The menu items are assigned a `margin-bottom` value of 1px to ensure it is apparent that the menu is layered over the background image in the `a5-body-content` rule.

One of the most important properties of this rule is the shorthand `background` property, which assigns a background image to a hyperlink and thus an item in the menu. This property works in conjunction with the `a5-menu a:hover` rule, which changes the background image when the user mouses over a menu item, avoiding the need for JavaScript (see Figure 9.13).

- The `a5-bottom-left-content` rule is added to create a separate text section below the menu. It employs many of the properties already discussed in this chapter. What gives it a different appearance is that the border is turned on and given a different color. While default font styling is included in the rule, additional styling is used at a local level in the `<DIV>` tag to resize text, such as "Glance at." The image in the container also is given local styling so that it has 10 pixels of padding between it and the text above it. If `<DIV>` tags are not added around the image, the border will not collapse around the image in IE 5, 5.5, and 6 browsers (see Figure 9.14).

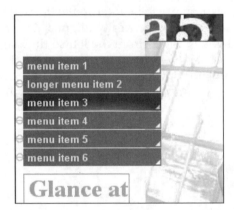

FIGURE 9.13 Background image that is switched using the code `background: url(images/bg-menu-on.jpg) no-repeat 0px 0px;`.

FIGURE 9.14 An image in a container that will not allow the border to collapse around the bottom, in all browsers, unless additional `<DIV>` tags are added.

- The only unique thing to note about the `a5-copyright` rule is where it is placed. If either the left or right columns, or `<DIV>` tags nested in them, are assigned absolute positioning, then the copyright should probably not be included in a footer row across the bottom of the entire site; this is because if the text runs too long in these absolute-positioned `<DIV>` tags, they can extend below the footer, either over or under it.

Adding the Center (Right) Column

At this stage most of the coding has been accomplished for the homepage. The designer needs to add only a column to the right. Because this design could always be turned into a three-column design, the column to the right is called `a5-column-center`, leaving the possibility of naming a right column `a5-column-right`. Listing 9.4 shows the completed code for the homepage design, which is shown in Figure 9.15.

The newly added code is bold to differentiate it from the existing code that is being built upon in this case study.

FIGURE 9.15   The completed design once the `a5-column-right` rule and content have been added.

LISTING 9.4   Code for Figure 9.15

```
<!DOCTYPE html PUBLIC "-//W3C//DTD XHTML 1.0 Transitional//EN"
    "DTD/xhtml1-transitional.dtd">
<html xmlns="http://www.w3.org/1999/xhtml" xml:lang="en"
lang="en"><head><title>Design 121</title>
<meta http-equiv="Content-Type" content="text/html;
    charset=iso-8859-1" />
<style type="text/css">
/* ++++++++++ global general styles start ++++++++++*/
html, body {
    margin:0px;
```

```
        padding:0px;
        font: 13px Arial, Helvetica, sans-serif;
        color:#766D6D;
        background:#ffffff;
        }
    /* ++++++++++ global general styles end ++++++++++*/
    /* ++++++++++ global structure styles start ++++++++++*/
    #a5-body-center {
        text-align:left;
        border:0px solid #000000;
        }
    #a5-body {
        position: relative;
        width: 770px; /* change this to a specific amount for a fixed
            design or a relative amount if the design should expand to a percentage
 of the screen. E.g., 770px or 100%, respectively. */
    /* remove these comment tags if the page is to be centered. The
        'text-align' property in the 'a5-body-center' rule must also be
        changed from 'left' to 'center'
        margin-left: auto;
        margin-right: auto;*/
        text-align:left;
        padding-bottom:10px;
        border:0px solid #000000;
        }
    /* ++++++++++ global structure styles end ++++++++++*/
    #a5-header {
        position:relative;
        left:0px;
        top:0px;
        height:98px;
        background:#000000;
        }
        #a5-header-left {
            width:169px;
            }
        #a5-header-center {
            position:absolute;
            left:169px;
            top:0px;
            }
        #a5-header-right {
            position:absolute;
            left:553px;
```

```
          top:0px;
          }
#a5-body-content {
    position:relative;
    background: #ffffff url(images/bg-body-content.jpg) no-repeat;
    height:410px;
    margin-right:15px;
    border:0px solid #000000;
    }
    #a5-column-left {
        position:absolute;
        left:0px;
        top:19px;
        width:190px;
        }
        #a5-menu {
            font:bold 13px Arial, Helvetica, sans-serif;
            }
        #a5-menu a {
            display:block;
            text-align:left;
            line-height:23px;
            vertical-align: 50%;
            padding-left:15px;
            margin-bottom:1px;
            text-decoration:none;
            background: url(images/bg-menu-off.gif) no-repeat 0px 0px;
            color:#E9F92C;
            }
        #a5-menu a:hover {
            background: url(images/bg-menu-on.jpg) no-repeat 0px 0px;
            margin-bottom:1px;
            color:#E9F92C;
            }
        #a5-bottom-left-content {
            width:136px;
            font:bold 12pt times, garamond, serif;
            line-height:26px;
            text-align:right;
            margin:9px 0px 0px 10px;
            color:#DF9B05;
            border:1px solid #999A8D;
            }
            #a5-copyright {
```

```
                    font-size: 8pt;
                    padding:10px 50px 10px 10px;
                    color:#766D6D;
                    }
        #a5-column-center {
            position:absolute;
            left:190px;
            top:0px;
            line-height:18pt;
            padding:24px 0px 0px 268px;
            }
</style>
</head>
<body>
<div id="a5-body-center">
    <div id="a5-body">
<!- ###### header start ###### ->
        <div id="a5-header">
            <div><a href="index.htm"><img src="images/header-left.gif"
                width="169" height="98" alt="" border="0" /></a></div>
            <div id="a5-header-center"><img src="images/
                header-center.jpg" width="384" height="98" alt=""
                border="0" /></div>
            <div id="a5-header-right"><img src="images/
                header-right.jpg" width="217" height="98" alt=""
                border="0" /></div>
        </div>
<!- ###### header end ###### ->

<!- ###### body content start ###### ->
        <div id="a5-body-content">
            <div id="a5-column-left">
                <div id="a5-menu">
                    <a href="index.htm">menu item 1</a>
                    <a href="menu-item-2.htm">longer menu item 2</a>
                    <a href="menu-item-3.htm">menu item 3</a>
                    <a href="index.htm">menu item 4</a>
                    <a href="index.htm">menu item 5</a>
                    <a href="index.htm">menu item 6</a>
                </div>

                <div id="a5-bottom-left-content">
                    <span style="font:bold 24pt times, garamond,
                        serif;">Glance at</span><br />
```

```
                    some of the<br />
                    <span style="font:bold 13pt times, garamond,
serif;">possibilities your</span><br />
                    house has to offer
                    <div style="padding-top:10px;"><a href="index.htm">
                        <img src="images/photo-bottom-left.jpg"
                        width="136" height="93" alt="" border="0" /></a></div>
                </div>
                <div id="a5-copyright">
                |  &copy; copyright 2006  |<br />|
                      your company  |<br />|
                      all rights reserved  |
                </div>
            </div>
            <div id="a5-column-center">
                <span class="color1text18">Duis autem vel eum iriure
                    dolor in hendrerit in vulputate velit esse
                    malestie consequat,</span> vel illum dolore eu
                    feugiat nulla facilisis at vero eros et
                    accumsan et iusto odio.<br /><br />
    Labore et dolore magna aliquyam erat, sed diam voluptua. At vero eos et
        accusam et justo duo dolores et ea rebum. <span style="float:left;
        padding:10px; margin-left:-86px;"><a href="index.htm"><img src=
        "images/photo-center-middle.gif" width="199" height="117" alt=""
        border="0" /></a></span>Stet clita kasd gubergren, no sea takimata
        sanctus est Lorem ipsum dolor sit amet. Nam liber tempor cum
        soluta nobis eleifend option nihil imperdiet doming id quod congue
        nihil imperdiet doming id quod mazim placerat facer   |   <a href=
        "index.htm">READ MORE</a>
            </div>
        </div>
<!- ###### body content start ###### ->
    </div>
</div>
</body>
</html>
```

There are several things to note about the code in Listing 9.4:

- Only one rule is added to style the right column: a5-column-center. It is given absolute positioning to ensure that the content does not fill the full width of the remaining screen. If the design were a liquid design, relative positioning would be the desired value.
- The <DIV> tag uses the left property to position the text 190 pixels from the left.

- The "call for a free estimate" image included in the container's text is assigned a local style that floats it to the left. The image is then assigned a `margin-left` property with the value of `-86px`. This forces the image to the left, partially outside the text flow (see Figure 9.16).

FIGURE 9.16   The design with the "call for a free estimate" image forced to the left, outside the main content flow.

This is where the transparency of the image between the border and the main part of the image becomes useful. This image can be added wherever the designer chooses within the content area. This is possible because the area between the border and the main part of the image will show the actual area over which it is layered.

CONSTRUCTING SECOND-LEVEL PAGES

A portion of the homepage design can be reused many times with other pages to maintain consistency and to limit the additional download necessary for second-level pages (that is, the user's browser can cache certain images so they do not have to be downloaded again, making the page load faster). When developing CSS sites, this process is much cleaner than with XHTML tables that can include many nested tables. Listing 9.5 shows the code used to create a second-level page after it has been customized from the homepage (see Figure 9.17).

 The newly added code is bold to differentiate it from the existing code that is being built upon in this case study.

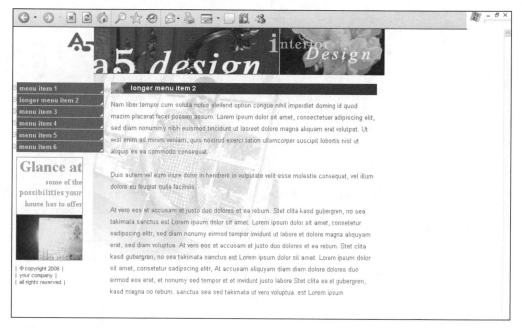

FIGURE 9.17   A second-level page of the site constructed from the homepage design and code.

LISTING 9.5   Code for Figure 9.17

```
<!DOCTYPE html PUBLIC "-//W3C//DTD XHTML 1.0 Transitional//EN"
    "DTD/xhtml1-transitional.dtd">
<html xmlns="http://www.w3.org/1999/xhtml" xml:lang="en"
lang="en"><head><title>Design 121</title>
<meta http-equiv="Content-Type" content="text/html;
    charset=iso-8859-1" />
<style type="text/css">
/* ++++++++++ global general styles start ++++++++++*/
html, body {
    margin:0px;
    padding:0px;
    font: 13px Arial, Helvetica, sans-serif;
    color:#766D6D;
    background:#ffffff;
    }
a:link { color:#CB951D; }
a:visited { color:#A8B32D; }
a:active { color:#A8B32D; }
a:hover { color:#000000; }
.color1text18 {
```

```css
        font-family: arial, geneva, sans-serif;
        font-size: 18pt;
        color: #A8B32D;
        }
/* ++++++++++ global general styles end ++++++++++*/
/* ++++++++++ global structure styles start ++++++++++*/
#a5-body-center {
    text-align:left;
    }
#a5-body {
    position: relative;
    width: 770px; /* change this to a specific amount for a fixed
        design or a relative amount if the design should expand to a percentage
of the screen. E.g., 770px or 100%, respectively. */
    /* remove these comment tags if the page is to be centered. The
        'text-align' property in the 'a5-body-center' rule must also be
        changed from 'left' to 'center'
        margin-left: auto;
        margin-right: auto;*/
    text-align:left;
    padding-bottom:10px;
    border:0px solid #000000;
    }
#a5-header {
    position:relative;
    left:0px;
    top:0px;
    height:98px;
    border:0px solid #000000;
    }
    #a5-header-center {
        position:absolute;
        left:169px;
        top:0px;
        }
    #a5-header-right {
        position:absolute;
        left:553px;
        top:0px;
        }
#a5-body-content {
    position:relative;
    background: #ffffff url(images/bg-body-content.jpg) no-repeat;
    height:410px;
```

```css
    margin-right:15px;
    border:0px solid #000000;
    }
#a5-column-left {
    position:absolute;
    left:0px;
    top:19px;
    width:190px;
    }
    #a5-menu {
        font:bold 13px Arial, Helvetica, sans-serif;
        }
    #a5-menu a {
        display:block;
        text-align:left;
        line-height:23px;
        vertical-align:50%;
        padding-left:15px;
        margin-bottom:1px;
        text-decoration:none;
        background: url(images/bg-menu-off.gif) no-repeat 0px 0px;
        color:#E9F92C;
        }
    #a5-menu a:hover {
        background: url(images/bg-menu-on.jpg) no-repeat 0px 0px;
        margin-bottom:1px;
        color:#E9F92C;
        }
    #a5-bottom-left-content {
        width:136px;
        font:bold 12pt times, garamond, serif;
        line-height:26px;
        text-align:right;
        margin:9px 0px 0px 10px;
        color:#DF9B05;
        border:1px solid #999A8D;
        }
    #a5-copyright {
        font-size: 8pt;
        padding:10px 50px 10px 10px;
        color:#766D6D;
        }
#a5-column-center {
    position:absolute;
```

```
                    left:190px;
                    top:0px;
                    line-height:18pt;
                    padding:24px 0px 0px 268px;
                    }
/* ++++++++++ global structure styles end ++++++++++*/
/* ++++++++++ second level start ++++++++++*/
#a5-body-content-sl {
    position:relative;
    background: #ffffff url(images/bg-body-content-sl.jpg) no-repeat;
    height:410px;
    margin-right:15px;
    border:0px solid #000000;
    }
    #a5-column-center-sl {
        position:absolute;
        left:190px;
        top:0px;
        line-height:18pt;
        padding:18px 0px 0px 18px;
        }
        #a5-sl-title {
            height:24px;
            font:bold 14px Arial, Helvetica, sans-serif;
            background:#4E2124 url(images/bg-title.jpg) no-repeat
                left top;
            color:#ffffff;
            padding:3px 0px 0px 40px;
            margin-bottom:10px;
            border:0px solid #000000;
            voice-family:"\"}\"";
            voice-family:inherit;
                height:20px;
            }
            html>body #a5-sl-title {
                height:20px;
            }
/* ++++++++++ second level end ++++++++++*/
</style>
</head>
<body>
<div id="a5-body-center">
    <div id="a5-body">
<!-- ###### header start ###### -->
        <div id="a5-header">
```

```
            <div><a href="index.htm"><img src="images/header-left.gif"
                width="169" height="98" alt="" border="0" /></a></div>
            <div id="a5-header-center"><img src="images/
                header-center.jpg" width="384" height="98" alt=""
                border="0" /></div>
            <div id="a5-header-right"><img src="images/
                header-right.jpg" width="217" height="98" alt=""
                border="0" /></div>
        </div>
<!— ###### header end ###### —>
<!— ###### body content start ###### —>
        <div id="a5-body-content-sl">
            <div id="a5-column-left">
                <div id="a5-menu">
                    <a href="index.htm">menu item 1</a>
                    <a href="menu-item-2.htm">longer menu item 2</a>
                    <a href="menu-item-3.htm">menu item 3</a>
                    <a href="index.htm">menu item 4</a>
                    <a href="index.htm">menu item 5</a>
                    <a href="index.htm">menu item 6</a>
                </div>
                <div id="a5-bottom-left-content">
                    <span style="font:bold 24pt times, garamond,
                        serif;">Glance at</span><br />
                    some of the<br />
                    <span style="font:bold 13pt times, garamond,
                        serif;">possibilities your</span><br />
                    house has to offer
                    <div style="padding-top:10px;"><a href="index.htm">
                        <img src="images/photo-bottom-left.jpg"
                        width="136" height="93" alt="" border="0"
                        /></a></div>
                </div>
                <div id="a5-copyright">
                    |  &copy; copyright 2006  
                        |<br />|  your company  |
                        <br />|  all rights reserved 
                         |
                </div>
            </div>
            <div id="a5-column-center-sl">
<!— ###### title start ###### —>
                <div id="a5-sl-title">longer menu item 2</div>
<!— ###### title end ###### —>
```

```
                        Nam liber tempor cum soluta nobis eleifend option
                        congue nihil imperdiet doming id quod mazim
                        placerat facer possim assum. Lorem ipsum dolor sit
                        amet, consectetuer adipiscing elit, sed diam
                        nonummy nibh euismod tincidunt ut laoreet dolore
                        magna aliquam erat volutpat. Ut wisi enim ad minim
                        veniam, quis nostrud exerci tation ullamcorper
                        suscipit lobortis nisl ut aliquip ex ea commodo
                        consequat.
        <br /><br />
Duis autem vel eum iriure dolor in hendrerit in vulputate velit esse molestie
consequat, vel illum dolore eu feugiat nulla facilisis.
        <br /><br />
At vero eos et accusam et justo duo dolores et ea rebum. Stet clita kasd gubergren,
no sea takimata sanctus est Lorem ipsum dolor sit amet. Lorem ipsum dolor sit amet,
consetetur sadipscing elitr, sed diam nonumy eirmod tempor invidunt ut labore et
dolore magna aliquyam erat, sed diam voluptua. At vero eos et accusam et justo duo
dolores et ea rebum. Stet clita kasd gubergren, no sea takimata sanctus est Lorem
ipsum dolor sit amet. Lorem ipsum dolor sit amet, consetetur sadipscing elitr, At
accusam aliquyam diam diam dolore dolores duo eirmod eos erat, et nonumy sed tempor
et et invidunt justo labore Stet clita ea et gubergren, kasd magna no rebum. Sanctus
sea sed takimata ut vero voluptua. est Lorem ipsum
                    </div>
                </div>
        <!-- ###### body content end ###### -->
            </div>
        </div>
        </body>
        </html>
```

There are several things to note about the code in Listing 9.5:

- The `a5-body-content` container is renamed `a5-body-content-sl` because it uses a different background image for the second-level pages that is lightened to help make the text more visible on the pages where it is layered over the woman. The `a5-body-content-sl` rule then calls this new image.
- The `margin-right:15px;` code, as on the homepage, ensures that the text will never touch the right side of the browser window if it is a liquid design that expands to the full width of the screen.
- The `a5-sl-title` rule is added to allow the designer to place a title on every page so the user knows which page is selected. The main thing to note about this code is that because the container is given padding, the Tantek hack is used so the height of the row is the same in the tested browsers, which included IE 5 and 5.5 for this design. A `margin-bottom` value of `10px` is also added to provide space between the title area and the text for that page.

Adding a Floating Container for Additional Content

In the case study designs in Chapters 10, 11, 12 and 13, a third column is added to allow for more layout options. In this design, however, a new <DIV> is merely added and floated to the right side of the text to allow for similar functionality. Figure 9.18 illustrates what the new code (outlined in Listing 9.6) will look like.

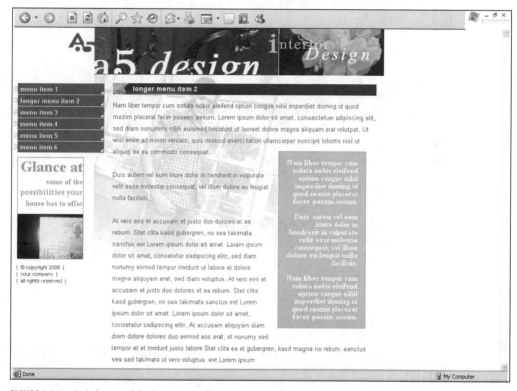

FIGURE 9.18   A right text block area is added to second-level pages to allow for more layout possibilities.

The newly added code is bold to differentiate it from the existing code that is being built upon in this case study.

LISTING 9.6   Code for Figure 9.18

```
<!DOCTYPE html PUBLIC "-//W3C//DTD XHTML 1.0 Transitional//EN"
    "DTD/xhtml1-transitional.dtd">
<html xmlns="http://www.w3.org/1999/xhtml" xml:lang="en"
lang="en"><head><title>Design 121</title>
```

```
<meta http-equiv="Content-Type" content="text/html;
    charset=iso-8859-1" />
<style type="text/css">
/* ++++++++++ global general styles start ++++++++++*/
html, body {
    margin:0px;
    padding:0px;
    font: 13px Arial, Helvetica, sans-serif;
    color:#766D6D;
    background:#ffffff;
    }
a:link { color:#CB951D; }
a:visited { color:#A8B32D; }
a:active { color:#A8B32D; }
a:hover { color:#000000; }
.color1text18 {
    font-family: arial, geneva, sans-serif;
    font-size: 18pt;
    color: #A8B32D;
    }
/* ++++++++++ global general styles end ++++++++++*/
/* ++++++++++ global structure styles start ++++++++++*/
#a5-body-center {
    text-align:left;
    }
#a5-body {
    position: relative;
    width: 770px; /* change this to a specific amount for a fixed
        design or a relative amount if the design should expand to a percentage
of the screen. E.g., 770px or 100%, respectively. */
    /* remove these comment tags if the page is to be centered. The
        'text-align' property in the 'a5-body-center' rule must also be
        changed from 'left' to 'center'
    margin-left: auto;
    margin-right: auto;*/
    text-align:left;
    padding-bottom:10px;
    border:0px solid #000000;
    }
#a5-header {
    position:relative;
    left:0px;
    top:0px;
    height:98px;
```

```
        border:0px solid #000000;
        }
    #a5-header-center {
        position:absolute;
        left:169px;
        top:0px;
        }
    #a5-header-right {
        position:absolute;
        left:553px;
        top:0px;
        }
#a5-body-content {
    position:relative;
    background: #ffffff url(images/bg-body-content.jpg) no-repeat;
    height:410px;
    margin-right:15px;
    border:0px solid #000000;
    }
    #a5-column-left {
        position:absolute;
        left:0px;
        top:19px;
        width:190px;
        }
        #a5-menu {
            font:bold 13px Arial, Helvetica, sans-serif;
            }
        #a5-menu a {
            display:block;
            text-align:left;
            line-height:23px;
            vertical-align:50%;
            padding-left:15px;
            margin-bottom:1px;
            text-decoration:none;
            background: url(images/bg-menu-off.gif) no-repeat 0px 0px;
            color:#E9F92C;
            }
        #a5-menu a:hover {
            background: url(images/bg-menu-on.jpg) no-repeat 0px 0px;
            margin-bottom:1px;
            color:#E9F92C;
            }
```

```css
            #a5-bottom-left-content {
                width:136px;
                font:bold 12pt times, garamond, serif;
                line-height:26px;
                text-align:right;
                margin:9px 0px 0px 10px;
                color:#DF9B05;
                border:1px solid #999A8D;
                }
            #a5-copyright {
                font-size: 8pt;
                padding:10px 50px 10px 10px;
                color:#766D6D;
                }
        #a5-column-center {
            position:absolute;
            left:190px;
            top:0px;
            line-height:18pt;
            padding:24px 0px 0px 268px;
            }
/* ++++++++++ global structure styles end ++++++++++*/
/* ++++++++++ second level start ++++++++++*/
#a5-body-content-sl {
    position:relative;
    background: #ffffff url(images/bg-body-content-sl.jpg) no-repeat;
    height:410px;
    margin-right:15px;
    border:0px solid #000000;
    }
    #a5-column-center-sl {
        position:absolute;
        left:190px;
        top:0px;
        line-height:18pt;
        padding:18px 0px 0px 18px;
        }
        #a5-sl-title {
            height:24px;
            font:bold 14px Arial, Helvetica, sans-serif;
            background:#4E2124 url(images/bg-title.jpg) no-repeat
                left top;
            color:#ffffff;
            padding:3px 0px 0px 40px;
```

```
            margin-bottom:10px;
            border:0px solid #000000;
            voice-family:"\"}\"";
            voice-family:inherit;
                height:20px;
            }
            html>body #a5-sl-title {
                height:20px;
            }
    #a5-content-right-sl {
        float:right;
        width:182px;
        font:bold 12pt times, garamond, serif;
        line-height:16px;
        text-align:right;
        padding:15px;
        margin:10px 10px 10px 15px;
        color:#ffffff;
        border:1px solid #999A8D;
        background:#C1C96A;
        voice-family:"\"}\"";
        voice-family:inherit;
            width:150px;
        }
        html>body #a5-content-right-sl {
            width:150px;
        }
/* ++++++++++ second level end ++++++++++*/
</style>
</head>
<body>
<div id="a5-body-center">
    <div id="a5-body">
<!– ###### header start ###### –>
        <div id="a5-header">
            <div><a href="index.htm"><img src="images/header-left.gif"
                width="169" height="98" alt="" border="0" /></a></div>
            <div id="a5-header-center"><img src="images/
                header-center.jpg" width="384" height="98" alt=""
                border="0" /></div>
            <div id="a5-header-right"><img src="images/
                header-right.jpg" width="217" height="98" alt=""
                border="0" /></div>
        </div>
```

```
<!- ###### header end ###### ->
<!- ###### body content start ###### ->
        <div id="a5-body-content-sl">
            <div id="a5-column-left">
                <div id="a5-menu">
                    <a href="index.htm">menu item 1</a>
                    <a href="menu-item-2.htm">longer menu item 2</a>
                    <a href="menu-item-3.htm">menu item 3</a>
                    <a href="index.htm">menu item 4</a>
                    <a href="index.htm">menu item 5</a>
                    <a href="index.htm">menu item 6</a>
                </div>
                <div id="a5-bottom-left-content">
                    <span style="font:bold 24pt times, garamond,
                        serif;">Glance at</span><br />
                    some of the<br />
                    <span style="font:bold 13pt times, garamond,
                        serif;">possibilities your</span><br />
                    house has to offer
                    <div style="padding-top:10px;"><a href="index.htm">
                        <img src="images/photo-bottom-left.jpg"
                        width="136" height="93" alt="" border="0"
                        /></a></div>
                </div>
                <div id="a5-copyright">
                    |  &copy; copyright 2006  |
                        <br />|  your company  |
                        <br />|  all rights reserved 
                         |
                </div>
            </div>
            <div id="a5-column-center-sl">
<!- ###### title start ###### ->
                <div id="a5-sl-title">longer menu item 2</div>
<!- ###### title end ###### ->
                Nam liber tempor cum soluta nobis eleifend option
                    congue nihil imperdiet doming id quod mazim
                    placerat facer possim assum. Lorem ipsum dolor sit
                    amet, consectetuer adipiscing elit, sed diam
                    nonummy nibh euismod tincidunt ut laoreet dolore
                    magna aliquam erat volutpat. Ut wisi enim ad minim
                    <div id="a5-content-right-sl">Nam liber tempor cum
                    soluta nobis eleifend option congue nihil imperdiet
                    doming id quod mazim placerat facer possim assum.
```

```
          <br /><br />Duis autem vel eum iriure dolor in
          hendrerit in vulputate velit esse molestie
          consequat, vel illum dolore eu feugiat nulla
          facilisis.<br /><br />Nam liber tempor cum soluta
          nobis eleifend option congue nihil imperdiet doming
          id quod mazim placerat facer possim assum.</div>
          veniam, quis nostrud exerci tation ullamcorper
          suscipit lobortis nisl ut aliquip ex ea commodo
          consequat.
    <br /><br />
Duis autem vel eum iriure dolor in hendrerit in vulputate velit esse molestie
consequat, vel illum dolore eu feugiat nulla facilisis.
    <br /><br />
At vero eos et accusam et justo duo dolores et ea rebum. Stet clita kasd gubergren,
no sea takimata sanctus est Lorem ipsum dolor sit amet. Lorem ipsum dolor sit amet,
consetetur sadipscing elitr, sed diam nonumy eirmod tempor invidunt ut labore et
dolore magna aliquyam erat, sed diam voluptua. At vero eos et accusam et justo duo
dolores et ea rebum. Stet clita kasd gubergren, no sea takimata sanctus est Lorem
ipsum dolor sit amet. Lorem ipsum dolor sit amet, consetetur sadipscing elitr, At
accusam aliquyam diam diam dolore dolores duo eirmod eos erat, et nonumy sed tempor et
et invidunt justo labore Stet clita ea et gubergren, kasd magna no rebum. Sanctus sea
sed takimata ut vero voluptua. est Lorem ipsum
               </div>
          </div>
    <!– ###### body content end ###### –>
       </div>
  </div>
  </body>
  </html>
```

There are several things to note about the code in Listing 9.6:

- The `a5-content-right-sl` rule uses the Tantek hack to ensure that the width is the same among all tested browsers. While none of the CSS is new at this point in the design, floating a `<DIV>` in the text can have varied results. Depending on where the container is included in the text, various browsers will render the line wraps and the line height (at least for one or two lines) differently. The designer should definitely test pages that use this layout technique.

 Barring varied rendering issues, there are several noted bugs associated with floating various designed `<DIV>` tags in content. Rather than use more complex floats, it is recommended that the designer use structured columns. If floats are used and the designer runs into problems, the Holly hack and Peek-a-boo bug are two places to begin researching a solution.

SUMMARY

The design built in this chapter is a two-column layout that allows for including a floating <DIV> area on second-level pages. The chapter explains how the design could work as a liquid design or as a fixed design. Other techniques, such as using switching background images for mouseovers, mortising images, and using transparent GIFs in a layout are discussed. While a designer may not follow this exact coding method, all the techniques can be applied independently when creating other designs.

10

CASE STUDY: MEDIUM-CONTENT CSS DESIGN

In This Chapter

- Understanding the Design's Structure
- Building the Structure
- Constructing Second-Level Pages
- Constructing a Second-Level Page with Two Columns

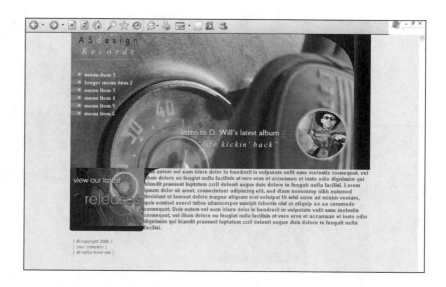

T he complexity of a Web design can be deceptive. A design that looks simple can require more complex CSS coding, while a visually complex design may merely involve simple coding to achieve the proper mortising of images and content placement. The design in this chapter, while its look and feel appears similar to the design in Chapter 9, is more complex because it uses a three- rather than two-column design. Also, it is centered in the browser and uses mortised images on the top half of the homepage so the user can not only view the images but also click on them. The second level uses a screened version as the background image. This allows the design to add content freely over the image.

The design explained in this chapter is design 122 on the accompanying CD-ROM (photo credits: www.idlerphotography.com).

UNDERSTANDING THE DESIGN'S STRUCTURE

Figure 10.1 shows the design that is explained in this chapter. It involves two basic overall columns, one for the left side, which includes the menu, and one for the right, which includes additional nested `<DIV>` tags to position and style the content on the right. This includes the In the News and Purchase Online text areas.

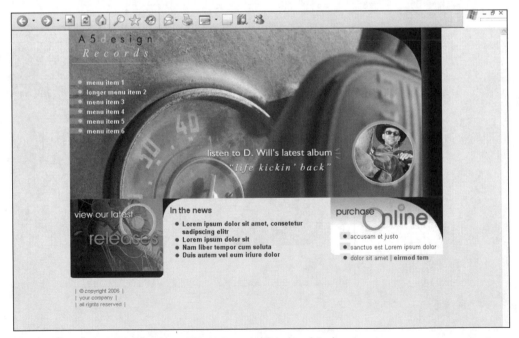

FIGURE 10.1   The medium-content CSS design explained in this chapter.

Reasoning Behind Guides and Creating Slices in a Photoshop File

There are 11 slices included in this design, all deriving their positioning from the numerous guides that were added. Understanding these is the first step to better visualizing how to efficiently structure and style the various containers.

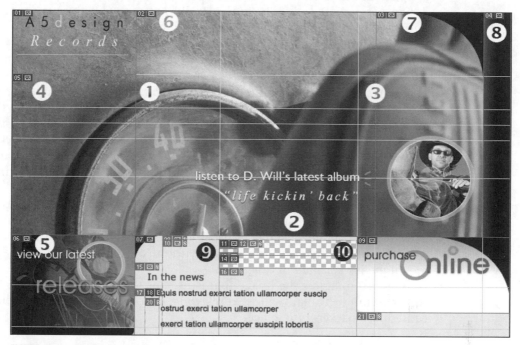

FIGURE 10.2   Guides and slices strategically placed within the design.

Figure 10.2 outlines 10 of the most important slices and guides the designer needs to understand. While some are used similarly in the design in Chapter 9, others offer additional ways to build mortised CSS sites.

- The guide to the left of number 1 is used to separate the design into left and right columns. The left column includes the menu, and the right column is a parent column that will have two columns, the center and right columns, nested inside it.
- The guide below number 2 represents the guide that is used to not only outline the bottom of the background image in the menu, but also to separate the main graphical area on the right from the XHTML text, In the News and Purchase Online content, that is included below.
- The guide to the left of number 3 is used to separate the center and right columns, both of which are nested inside the parent right column.

- The slice indicated by number 4 is the background image that is used for the menu area of the design. One consideration in this type of design is that the background does not repeat vertically because it is not designed to do so. This forces the designer to work within a specified height, which includes any height taken up by submenu items. By using a nonrepeatable background image, the designer can mortise it with the slice illustrated by number 5. If, however, the design were altered visually so that it did not matter if the two images were mortised together, the menu could be changed structurally to stretch down as far as the designer wanted.
- Number 5 shows the slice that creates an image placed below the menu in the left column.
- The images represented by numbers 6, 7, and 8 are mortised together to form the large image area of the right column. All three images are saved, so they can be hyperlinked or, for example, replaced by a Flash movie. Because they are nested in a fixed <DIV>, if the design were changed to be liquid, the background color on the right, which is black, would extend to the right of the images. The extension would be seamless because the right image is gradated into solid black.
- The slices to the right of number 9 are used for the background images of each menu item in Normal and Hover modes. The images are cut from them so their backgrounds can be saved as transparent. This enables the items to be moved over the menu's background image without containing the top image. This technique is explained in Chapter 9.
- Number 10 indicates the image that is used as the background of the bottom-right column text area. While text is layered over it, it cannot be hyperlinked because it is a background image.

Understanding the Placement of CSS Containers

The number of <DIV> tags used in this design is similar to the design in Chapter 9. The main difference is in how they are used. Figure 10.3 shows the structure of the designs with the borders of the <DIV> tags turned on.

The <DIV> tags are used for different functions in the design, such as setting up the basic infrastructure of the design, providing containers to position content within the infrastructure, and styling the content within the containers. Following are explanations for the 10 most useful containers in Figure 10.3:

- The <DIV> tag to the left of number 1 is used for centering the design in IE 5 and 5.5. It extends the full width of the screen.
- The <DIV> tag above number 2 determines whether the design has a fixed width or is a liquid layout.
- The <DIV> tag to the left of number 3 contains both the left and right parent columns of the body. They are considered parent columns because the right column contains the code for the visual center and right columns of the design. This container extends to the right edges of the <DIV> outlined by number 2.

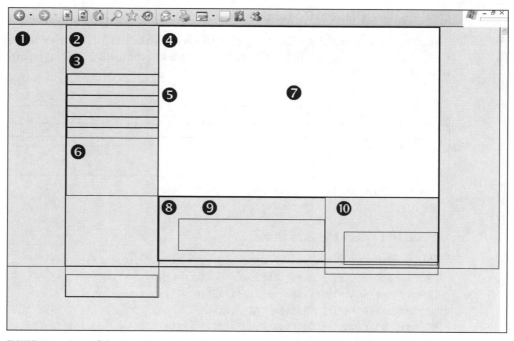

FIGURE 10.3   Ten of the most important containers used to build the design in this chapter.

- The <DIV> to the left of number 4 defines the right column. This contains everything to the right of the left column, which in this example, is for the sake of visual simplicity.
- The menu column lies to the left of number 5, which is included in the left column.
- Number 6 represents a <DIV> that contains the "view our latest releases" image in the left column below the menu.
- Number 7 identifies the <DIV> that contains the top nested images in the right column.
- The <DIV> to the left of number 8 is used to contain the center and right content columns that begin below the <DIV> that includes numbers 8, 9, and 10.
- Number 9 shows the bottom-center content column that is nested inside number 8.
- Number 10 represents the bottom-right content column nested inside number 8.

BUILDING THE STRUCTURE

Following are step-by-step instructions to building the design. It is assumed that the Photoshop file has already been created or customized and the designer only needs to position the images and text.

Creating the XHTML and CSS Framework

The first step to building the design is to create the XHTML framework and initial CSS containers. Listing 10.1 is the code that is used to output the page shown in Figure 10.4.

FIGURE 10.4   Basic XHTML and CSS framework for the design.

LISTING 10.1   Code for Figure 10.4

```
<!DOCTYPE html PUBLIC "-//W3C//DTD XHTML 1.0 Transitional//EN"
    "DTD/xhtml1-transitional.dtd">
<html xmlns="http://www.w3.org/1999/xhtml" xml:lang="en"
lang="en"><head><title>Design 122</title>
<meta http-equiv="Content-Type" content="text/html; charset=iso-8859-1" />
<style type="text/css">
/* ++++++++++ global general styles start ++++++++++*/
html, body {
    margin:0px;
    padding:0px;
    font: 13px Arial, Helvetica, sans-serif;
    color:#766D6D;
    background:#F8F4EB;
    }
/* ++++++++++ global general styles end ++++++++++*/
/* ++++++++++ global structure styles start ++++++++++*/
#a5-body-center {
    text-align:center;
    border:1px solid #000000;
    }
#a5-body {
    position: relative;
    width: 770px; /* change this to a specific amount for a fixed
        design or a relative amount if the design should expand to a percentage
of the screen. E.g., 770px or 100%, respectively. */
    margin-left: auto;
    margin-right: auto;
    text-align:left;
    padding-bottom:10px;
```

```
    border:1px solid #000000;
    }
/* ++++++++++ global structure styles end ++++++++++*/
</style>
</head>
<body>
<div id="a5-body-center">
    <div id="a5-body">
     
    </div>
</div>
</body>
</html>
```

There are several things to note about the code in Listing 10.1:

- The CSS style sheet is commented into a couple of different sections. The `global general styles` comment tags contain the general styles, such as the formatting of the `<HTML>` and `<BODY>` tags, hyperlinks, and fonts.
- Several rules define the `<HTML>` and `<BODY>` tags. The `margin` and `padding` properties are used to ensure that the design is placed in the very top-left corner of the browser, with no space between the design and the edges of the viewable area. The default font style is set using the shorthand `FONT` property. The default font color is defined with the `COLOR` property. The background color also is assigned (that is, #F8F4EB). This guarantees that all browsers display the site with the same background color because they would not otherwise always necessarily be the same.
- The `a5-body-center` and `a5-body` rules are used to force the design to the left side of the browser screen with a fixed width of 770 pixels. If the designer wanted to fill the full width of the screen, the value of `770px` would need to be changed to 100%. If, however, the designer wanted to simply justify the design to the left, the value of the `text-align` property in the `a5-body-center` rule would need to be adjusted from `center` to `left`. The `margin-left` and `margin-right` properties in the `a5-body` rule ensure that the extra white space is evenly split on both sides. This system allows more than one site to be built with ease and flexibility, using the same default code, allowing the designer to quickly adjust to a client's needs.
- Both the `a5-body-center` and `a5-body` rules have their borders turned on using the following code: `border:1px solid #000000;`. For demonstration purposes, the code was added to both rules to show what the structure of the `<DIV>` tags look like with no content added in them. Turning on the borders also helps a designer when building a site because it is not always apparent where elements are placed or to where they are expanding. Rather than remove these rules, it is easier to change the value of `1px` to `0px`, turning the borders off. Troubleshooting often involves turning the borders back on because it saves time and takes up little download size to keep them in the style sheet.

- Because the `<div id="a5-body">` tag is nested inside the `<div id="a5-body-cen-ter">` tag, it is indented. This allows for quicker recognition of tags that are nested inside each other, which becomes useful when the page has more code added later.

Adding the Left Column

After the framework has been built, the left column needs to be added. This section includes the logo, menu, and bottom-left image of the design. Figure 10.5 shows what the design looks like after the code in Listing 10.2 has been added.

 The newly added code is bold to differentiate it from the existing code that is being built upon in this case study.

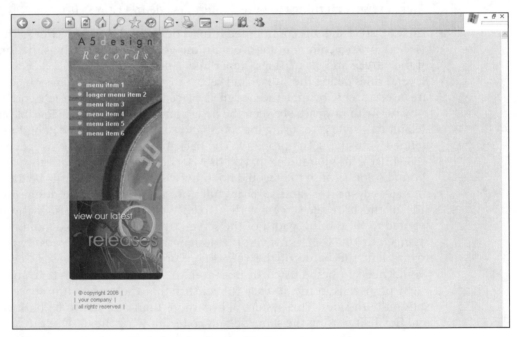

FIGURE 10.5 The design with the left column added.

LISTING 10.2 Code for Figure 10.5

```
<!DOCTYPE html PUBLIC "-//W3C//DTD XHTML 1.0 Transitional//EN"
    "DTD/xhtml1-transitional.dtd">
<html xmlns="http://www.w3.org/1999/xhtml" xml:lang="en"
lang="en"><head><title>Design 122</title>
    <meta http-equiv="Content-Type" content="text/html;
        charset=iso-8859-1" />
```

```css
<style type="text/css">
/* ++++++++++ global general styles start ++++++++++*/
html, body {
    margin:0px;
    padding:0px;
    font: 13px Arial, Helvetica, sans-serif;
    color:#766D6D;
    background:#F8F4EB;
    }
/* ++++++++++ global general styles end ++++++++++*/
/* ++++++++++ global structure styles start ++++++++++*/
#a5-body-center {
    text-align:center;
    }
#a5-body {
    position: relative;
    width: 770px; /* change this to a specific amount for a fixed
        design or a relative amount if the design should expand to a percentage
of the screen. E.g., 770px or 100%, respectively. */
    margin-left: auto;
    margin-right: auto;
    text-align:left;
    padding-bottom:10px;
    border:0px solid #000000;
    }
#a5-column-left {
    position:absolute;
    left:0px;
    top:0px;
    width:191px;
    border:0px solid #000000;
    }
#a5-menu {
    font:bold 13px Arial, Helvetica, sans-serif;
    height:249px;
    background:url(images/bg-left-column.jpg) no-repeat;
    }
#a5-menu a {
    display: block;
    text-align:left;
    line-height:20px;
    vertical-align: 30%;
    height:20px;
    padding-left:35px;
```

```css
        text-decoration:none;
        background: url(images/bg-menu-off.gif) no-repeat 0px 0px;
        color:#ffffff;
        }
    #a5-menu a:hover {
        background: url(images/bg-menu-on.gif) no-repeat 0px 0px;
        color:#F9F68C;
        }
        #a5-menu-sl {
            width:191px;
            color:#000000;
            font:bold 12px Arial, Helvetica, sans-serif;
            text-align:left;
            }
        #a5-menu-sl a {
            display: block;
            text-align:left;
            line-height:18px;
            vertical-align: 50%;
            height:18px;
            padding-left:40px;
            font-weight:normal;
            text-decoration:none;
            background: url(images/bg-menu-off-sl.gif) no-repeat
                0px 0px;
            color:#000000;
            }
        #a5-menu-sl a:hover {
            background: url(images/bg-menu-on-sl.gif) no-repeat
                0px 0px;
            color:#4C5C6B;
            }
    #a5-copyright {
        font-size: 11px;
        padding:20px 50px 10px 10px;
        color:#978872;
        }
/* ++++++++++ global structure styles end ++++++++++*/
</style>
</head>
<body>
<div id="a5-body-center">
    <div id="a5-body">
```

```
<!— ###### left column start ###### —>
        <div id="a5-column-left">
            <div><a href="index.htm"><img src="images/header-left.jpg"
                width="191" height="100" alt="" border="0" /></a></div>
            <div id="a5-menu">
                <a href="index.htm">menu item 1</a>
                <a href="menu-item-2.htm">longer menu item 2</a>
                <a href="menu-item-3.htm">menu item 3</a>
                <a href="index.htm">menu item 4</a>
                <a href="index.htm">menu item 5</a>
                <a href="index.htm">menu item 6</a>
            </div>
            <div><a href="index.htm"><img src="images/image-bottom-
                    left.jpg" width="191" height="162" alt=""
                    border="0" /></a></div>
            <div id="a5-copyright">
                |  &copy; copyright 2006  |<br />
                |  your company  |<br />
                |  all rights reserved  |
            </div>
        </div>
<!— ###### left column end ###### —>
    </div>
</div>
</body>
</html>
```

There are several things to note about the code in Listing 10.2:

- The a5-column-left rule has absolute positioning assigned to it. Its left and top properties are both assigned 0px to force the <DIV> into the top-left corner of the a5-body container it is nested within. The width of the column is fixed at 191 pixels, using the width property. This ensures that the column's width will not change, no matter what other content is included in the right column. It also forces the width of the left column so the menu items fill its full width.
- When the logo is added as the first item in the a5-column-left container, it needs to have <DIV> tags wrapped around it to eliminate extra space between it and the menu area below in some browsers, such as IE 5, 5.5, and 6 (see Figure 10.6).
- The a5-menu rule is assigned the height of 249 pixels, which forces it to be the full height of the background image, which also is 249 pixels. To call the background image, a version of the shorthand property for backgrounds is used: background:url(images/bg-left-column.jpg) no-repeat;. Font size, bolding, and family also are assigned to this <DIV>, which will then cascade down to any nested or child containers.

FIGURE 10.6   Space that is added between the logo and the menu area in IE 5, 5.5, and 6 because <DIV> tags were not wrapped around the image.

- The a5-menu a descendant rule is used to display and style each menu item. The display property with the block value will output each item in the <DIV> in its own row. The line-height is set to 20 pixels. Unlike the design in Chapter 9, the vertical-align property is not assigned here because it will move the text in relation to the background image, which is declared using the following shorthand code: background: url(images/bg-menu-off.gif) no-repeat 0px 0px;.
- The a5-menu a:hover rule is used to reassign the background image from bg-menu-off.gif to bg-menu-on.gif and the color of the text from #ffffff to #F9F68C when the user mouses over the text.

 There is a case difference between the color of the a link and the hover link (that is, #ffffff and #F9F68C). The reason for this is that #ffffff was entered manually while building the site, and #F9F68C was copied from the Color Picker in Photoshop when grabbing the exact HEX color (see Figure 10.7).

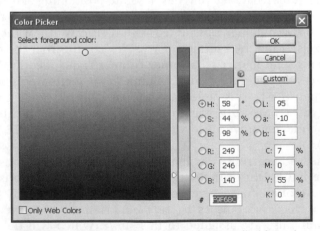

FIGURE 10.7   HEX color #F9F68C, which was pulled from the Color Picker in Photoshop.

- The `image-bottom-left.jpg` image below the menu is added after the `a5-menu` `<DIV>` in the code. It has no styling added to it other than `<DIV>` tags wrapped around it.
- The `a5-copyright` rule positions the copyright text below the `image-bottom-left.jpg` image, using padding around the text. The `padding:20px 50px 10px 10px;` code adds 20 pixels of padding to the top of the text, 50 pixels to the right, 10 pixels to the bottom, and 10 pixels to the left.

Adding `<DIV>` to Nest Center and Inside-Right Columns

An `a5-body-content` `<DIV>` is added to create a right column inside which the top-right images, bottom-left content area, and bottom-right content area will be nested. Figure 10.8 shows what the design looks like with the `a5-body-content` `<DIV>` border turned on.

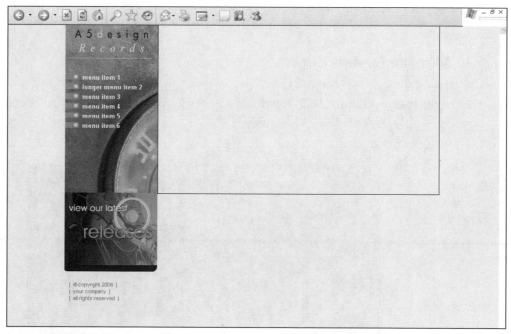

FIGURE 10.8   Page with the `a5-body-content` `<DIV>` added to form the right column.

This container is added because it will contain a background image in the second-level pages. By building the design around it in the homepage, the second-level pages, which are built from the homepage, are easier to construct because the base foundation of the code is already incorporated into the code. Following is the rule once it is added to the style sheet:

```
#a5-body-content {
    position:relative;
    margin-left:191px;
    height:349px;
    border:1px solid #000000;
    }
```

There are three things to note about the preceding code:

- The code has relative positioning so that it will flex to the full width of the a5-body container within which it is nested. This helps ensure that the design can also serve as a liquid design if the width of the a5-body rule is changed to 100%.
- The container is assigned a value of 191px to its margin-left property. This forces its left side 191 pixels from the left side of the design, so it is placed just past the left column.
- The height property is added to ensure the container is 349 pixels high, which is the height of the background image that is added.

Adding the Top-Right Images

The first stage in adding the content in the right parent column is to add the top-right images. Figure 10.9 illustrates the design once the images are added into the code, which is included in Listing 10.3.

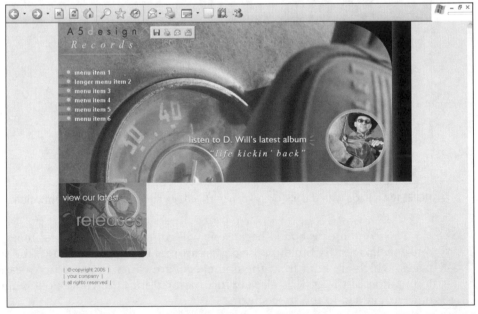

FIGURE 10.9   The first step to adding content to the right parent column is to add the mortised images.

The newly added code is bold to differentiate it from the existing code that is being built upon in this case study.

LISTING 10.3   Code for Figure 10.9

```
<!DOCTYPE html PUBLIC "-//W3C//DTD XHTML 1.0 Transitional//EN"
    "DTD/xhtml1-transitional.dtd">
<html xmlns="http://www.w3.org/1999/xhtml" xml:lang="en"
lang="en"><head><title>Design 122</title>
<meta http-equiv="Content-Type" content="text/html; charset=iso-8859-1" />
<style type="text/css">
/* ++++++++++ global general styles start ++++++++++*/
html, body {
    margin:0px;
    padding:0px;
    font: 13px Arial, Helvetica, sans-serif;
    color:#766D6D;
    background:#F8F4EB;
    }
/* ++++++++++ global general styles end ++++++++++*/
/* ++++++++++ global structure styles start ++++++++++*/
#a5-body-center {
    text-align:center;
    }
#a5-body {
    position: relative;
    width: 770px; /* change this to a specific amount for a fixed
        design or a relative amount if the design should expand to a percentage
of the screen. E.g., 770px or 100%, respectively. */
    margin-left: auto;
    margin-right: auto;
    text-align:left;
    padding-bottom:10px;
    border:0px solid #000000;
    }
#a5-column-left {
    position:absolute;
    left:0px;
    top:0px;
    width:191px;
    border:0px solid #000000;
    }
    #a5-menu {
        font:bold 13px Arial, Helvetica, sans-serif;
        height:249px;
```

```
        background:url(images/bg-left-column.jpg) no-repeat;
        }
#a5-menu a {
    display: block;
    text-align:left;
    line-height:20px;
    vertical-align: 30%;
    height:20px;
    padding-left:35px;
    text-decoration:none;
    background: url(images/bg-menu-off.gif) no-repeat 0px 0px;
    color:#ffffff;
    }
#a5-menu a:hover {
    background: url(images/bg-menu-on.gif) no-repeat 0px 0px;
    color:#F9F68C;
    }
    #a5-menu-sl {
        width:191px;
        color:#000000;
        font:bold 12px Arial, Helvetica, sans-serif;
        text-align:left;
        }
        #a5-menu-sl a {
        display: block;
        text-align:left;
        line-height:18px;
        vertical-align: 50%;
        height:18px;
        padding-left:40px;
        font-weight:normal;
        text-decoration:none;
        background: url(images/bg-menu-off-sl.gif) no-repeat
            0px 0px;
        color:#000000;
        }
    #a5-menu-sl a:hover {
        background: url(images/bg-menu-on-sl.gif) no-repeat
            0px 0px;
color:#4C5C6B;
        }
#a5-copyright {
    font-size: 11px;
    padding:20px 50px 10px 10px;
    color:#978872;
```

```
        }
#a5-body-content {
    position:relative;
    margin-left:191px;
    border:0px solid #000000;
    }
#a5-top-row {
    position:relative;
    left:0px;
    top:0px;
    background:#000000;
    border:0px solid #000000;
    }
/* ++++++++++ global structure styles end ++++++++++*/
</style>
</head>
<body>
<div id="a5-body-center">
    <div id="a5-body">
<!- ###### left column start ###### ->
        <div id="a5-column-left">
            <div><a href="index.htm"><img src="images/header-left.jpg"
                width="191" height="100" alt="" border="0" /></a></div>
            <div id="a5-menu">
            <a href="index.htm">menu item 1</a>
                <a href="menu-item-2.htm">longer menu item 2</a>
                <a href="menu-item-3.htm">menu item 3</a>
                <a href="index.htm">menu item 4</a>
                <a href="index.htm">menu item 5</a>
                <a href="index.htm">menu item 6</a>
            </div>
            <div><a href="index.htm"><img src="images/image-bottom-
                left.jpg" width="191" height="162" alt="" border="0"
                /></a></div>
            <div id="a5-copyright">
                |  &copy; copyright 2006  |<br />
                    |  your company  |<br />| 
                     all rights reserved  |
            </div>
        </div>
<!- ###### left column end ###### ->
<!- ###### body content start ###### ->
        <div id="a5-body-content">
            <div id="a5-top-row">
                <div><a href="x.htm"><img src="images/photo-center-
```

```
                        top.jpg" width="373" height="349" alt=""
                        border="0" /></a></div>
                    <div style="position:absolute;left:373px;top:0px">
                        <a href="x.htm"><img src="images/photo-right-
                        top.jpg" width="164" height="349" alt=""
                        border="0" /></a></div>
                    <div style="position:absolute;left:537px;top:0px;">
                        <a href="x.htm"><img src="images/image-right-
                        top.gif" width="42" height="349" alt="" border="0"
                        /></a></div>
                </div>
            </div>
    <!-- ###### body content end ###### -->
            </div>
        </div>
    </body>
</html>
```

There are several things to note about the code in Listing 10.3:

- The only rule that is added to the page-level style sheet is a5-top-row. This rule, however, provides a container for the three images to be nested inside it. Because it is assigned relative positioning and a background value of #000000, a black background will expand to the right if the page is turned into a liquid design (see Figure 10.10).

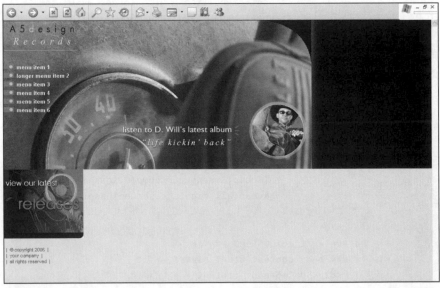

FIGURE 10.10   The a5-top-row rule can be expanded to the full width of the page if the design is changed to a liquid format.

- Most of the styling in the a5-top-row container occurs at the local level. The first image is wrapped with <DIV> tags to ensure that no additional space is added to the bottom of the container in IE 5, 5.5, and 6, such as in Figure 10.11.

FIGURE 10.11   Additional space added to the bottom of the container in IE 5, 5.5., and 6 when <DIV> tags are not wrapped around the first image when it is added.

The other two images, however, are given absolute positioning, so they are mortised together. The first image is positioned 373 pixels from the left by adding the following style in the local <DIV> tag: style="position:absolute;left:373px;top:0px". This is 373 pixels because the coordinates of all images are based off the top-left corner of the a5-top-row <DIV> in which they are nested. Since the first image is 373 pixels wide, the second image must begin 373 pixels from the left (see Figure 10.12).

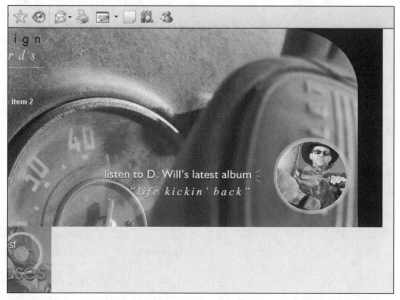

FIGURE 10.12   The top-right area after the second image is added 373 pixels from the left side of the container.

The third image is given absolute positioning that forces it 537 pixels from the left, which is the total width of the left image and center image: 373 pixels + 164 pixels = 537 pixels. Figure 10.9 shows what the design looks like with the addition of the third image, which, as with the other two images, is positioned 0 pixels from the top so that they all touch the top of the browser window.

Adding the Bottom, Center, and Right Content Areas

The final step in creating the homepage is to add the a5-bottom-row container and its contents. Figure 10.13 shows what the design looks like when the final code is added to the page (see Listing 10.4).

The newly added code is bold to differentiate it from the existing code that is being built upon in this case study.

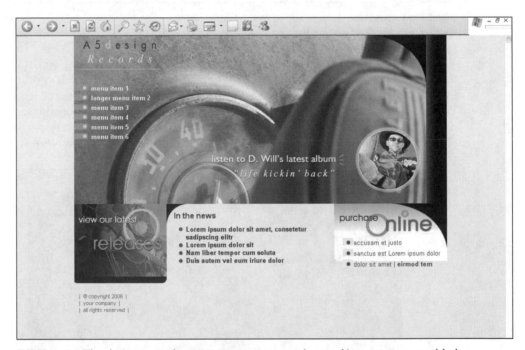

FIGURE 10.13   The design once the a5-bottom-row container and its contents are added.

LISTING 10.4   Code for Figure 10.13

```
<!DOCTYPE html PUBLIC "-//W3C//DTD XHTML 1.0 Transitional//EN"
"DTD/xhtml1-transitional.dtd">
<html xmlns="http://www.w3.org/1999/xhtml" xml:lang="en"
lang="en"><head><title>Design 122</title>
```

```
<meta http-equiv="Content-Type" content="text/html;
    charset=iso-8859-1" />
<style type="text/css">
/* ++++++++++ global general styles start ++++++++++*/
html, body {
    margin:0px;
    padding:0px;
    font: 13px Arial, Helvetica, sans-serif;
    color:#766D6D;
    background:#F8F4EB;
    }
a:link { color:#CB951D; }
a:visited { color:#A8B32D; }
a:active { color:#A8B32D; }
a:hover { color:#000000; }

a.linklist1:link { text-decoration:none;color:#191718;}
a.linklist1:visited { text-decoration:none;color:#064791;}
a.linklist1:active { text-decoration:none;color:#064791;}
a.linklist1:hover { text-decoration:underline;color:#0781E1;}

a.linklist2:link { text-decoration:none;color:#0762AD;}
a.linklist2:visited { text-decoration:none;color:#064791;}
a.linklist2:active { text-decoration:none;color:#064791;}
a.linklist2:hover { text-decoration:underline;color:#191718;}

.color-1-text-12 {
    font-family: arial, geneva, sans-serif;
    font-size: 12pt;
    color: #044465;
    }
/* ++++++++++ global general styles end ++++++++++*/
/* ++++++++++ global structure styles start ++++++++++*/
#a5-body-center {
    text-align:center;
    }
#a5-body {
    position: relative;
    width: 770px; /* change this to a specific amount for a fixed
        design or a relative amount if the design should expand to a percentage
of the screen. E.g., 770px or 100%, respectively. */
    margin-left: auto;
    margin-right: auto;
    text-align:left;
```

```
        padding-bottom:10px;
        border:0px solid #000000;
        }
#a5-column-left {
    position:absolute;
    left:0px;
    top:0px;
    width:191px;
    border:0px solid #000000;
    }
#a5-menu {
    font:bold 13px Arial, Helvetica, sans-serif;
    height:249px;
    background:url(images/bg-left-column.jpg) no-repeat;
    }
#a5-menu a {
    display: block;
    text-align:left;
    line-height:20px;
    vertical-align: 30%;
    height:20px;
    padding-left:35px;
    text-decoration:none;
    background: url(images/bg-menu-off.gif) no-repeat 0px 0px;
    color:#ffffff;
    }
#a5-menu a:hover {
    background: url(images/bg-menu-on.gif) no-repeat 0px 0px;
    color:#F9F68C;
    }
    #a5-menu-sl {
        width:191px;
        color:#000000;
        font:bold 12px Arial, Helvetica, sans-serif;
        text-align:left;
        }
    #a5-menu-sl a {
        display: block;
        text-align:left;
        line-height:18px;
        vertical-align: 50%;
        height:18px;
        padding-left:40px;
        font-weight:normal;
```

```
            text-decoration:none;
            background: url(images/bg-menu-off-sl.gif) no-repeat
                0px 0px;
            color:#000000;
            }
        #a5-menu-sl a:hover {
            background: url(images/bg-menu-on-sl.gif) no-repeat 0px 0px;
            color:#4C5C6B;
            }
    #a5-copyright {
        font-size: 11px;
        padding:20px 50px 10px 10px;
        color:#978872;
        }
#a5-body-content {
    position:relative;
    margin-left:191px;
    border:0px solid #000000;
    }
#a5-top-row {
    position:relative;
    left:0px;
    top:0px;
    background:#000000;
    border:0px solid #000000;
    }
#a5-bottom-row {
    position:relative;
    left:0px;
    top:0px;
    height:100%;
    border:0px solid #000000;
    }
#a5-column-middle {
    position:relative;
    left:0px;
    top:0px;
    margin:0px 230px 0px 0px;
    font-weight:bold;
    background: url(images/bg-curve-bottom-middle.gif) no-repeat
        top left;
    border:0px solid #000000;
    }
    #list-1 {
```

```
                margin-top:1Opx;
                line-height:16px;
                vertical-align:top;
                list-style-image: url(images/bullet.gif);
                }
        #a5-column-right {
            position:absolute;
            right:-1px;/*explain this is a bug with IE */
            top:Opx;
            width:23Opx;
            background: url(images/bg-right-column.jpg) no-repeat Opx Opx;
            border:Opx solid #OOOOOO;
            voice-family:"\"}\"";
            voice-family:inherit;
                right:-1px;
                width:23Opx;
            }
            html>body #a5-column-right {
                right:Opx;
                width:23Opx;
            }
            #list-2 {
                line-height:22px;
                vertical-align:top;
                list-style-image: url(images/bullet.gif);
                }
/* ++++++++++ global structure styles end ++++++++++*/
</style>
</head>
<body>
<div id="a5-body-center">
    <div id="a5-body">
<!- ###### left column start ###### ->
        <div id="a5-column-left">
            <div><a href="index.htm"><img src="images/header-left.jpg"
                width="191" height="100" alt="" border="0" /></a></div>
            <div id="a5-menu">
                <a href="index.htm">menu item 1</a>
                <a href="menu-item-2.htm">longer menu item 2</a>
                <a href="menu-item-3.htm">menu item 3</a>
                <a href="index.htm">menu item 4</a>
                <a href="index.htm">menu item 5</a>
                <a href="index.htm">menu item 6</a>
            </div>
```

```
        <div><a href="index.htm"><img src="images/image-bottom-
            left.jpg" width="191" height="162" alt="" border="0"
            /></a></div>
        <div id="a5-copyright">
            |  &copy; copyright 2006  |<br />
                |  your company  |<br />| 
                 all rights reserved  |
        </div>
    </div>
<!- ###### left column end ###### ->
<!- ###### body content start ###### ->
    <div id="a5-body-content">
        <div id="a5-top-row">
            <div><a href="x.htm"><img src="images/photo-center-
                top.jpg" width="373" height="349" alt=""
                border="0" /></a></div>
            <div style="position:absolute;left:373px;top:0px">
                <a href="x.htm"><img src="images/photo-right-
                top.jpg" width="164" height="349" alt="" border="0"
                /></a></div>
            <div style="position:absolute;left:537px;top:0px;">
                <a href="x.htm"><img src="images/image-right-
                top.gif" width="42" height="349" alt=""
                border="0" /></a></div>
        </div>
        <div id="a5-bottom-row">
            <div id="a5-column-middle">
                <div class="color-1-text-12" style="padding:15px
                0px 0px 15px;"><b>In the news</b></div>
                <ul id="list-1">
                    <li><a href="x.htm" class="linklist1">Lorem
                        ipsum dolor sit amet, consetetur sadipscing
                        elitr</a></li>
                    <li><a href="x.htm" class="linklist1">Lorem
                        ipsum dolor sit</a></li>
                    <li><a href="x.htm" class="linklist1">Nam
                        liber tempor cum soluta</a></li>
                    <li><a href="x.htm" class="linklist1">Duis
                        autem vel eum iriure dolor</a></li>
                </ul>
            </div>
            <div id="a5-column-right">
                <ul id="list-2" style="margin-top:70px;">
                    <li><a href="x.htm" class="linklist2">accusam
```

```
                                    et justo </a></li>
                        <li><a href="x.htm" class="linklist2">sanctus
                            est Lorem ipsum dolor</a></li>
                        <li><a href="x.htm" class="linklist2">dolor sit
                            amet</a>  |  <a href="x.htm" class=
                            "linklist2"><b>eirmod tem</b></a></li>
                    </ul>
                </div>
            </div>
        </div>
    <!- ###### body content end ###### ->
        </div>
    </div>
    </body>
    </html>
```

There are several things to note about the code in Listing 10.4:

- Rules are added between the `global general styles` comment tags for three types of links: the default links, the list in the bottom-center content area, and the list in the bottom-right content area. The default link style is added for all links without a specific class assigned to them. The `a.linklist1:link` rule is applied to the bottom-left list links, and the `a.linklist2:link` is assigned to the bottom-right list links. Both custom link rules were given general naming conventions so they could be assigned to lists that may be added elsewhere in the site.

- The `color-1-text-12` rule is added between the `global general styles` comment tags. It is used to style the In the News headline of the bottom-center content area.

- The `a5-bottom-row` rule and container are added to position the bottom-center and bottom-right content areas. They are assigned relative positioning with both the left and right properties set to `0px`. This positions the container below the `a5-top-row` `<DIV>`. It is assigned the `height` property with a value of `100%` so larger amounts of content can be added to the column. Otherwise, the text will be cut off in IE 5, 5.5, and 6.

- The `a5-column-middle` rule provides the container for the bottom-center content area. Because it is assigned relative positioning, it will stretch to the far right edge of the design. A larger body of text is included in the area for Figure 10.14 to show how the text could fill the design without any padding or margin values set.

The advantage of this structure is that the center column can stretch if the design is changed to a liquid design. Because the bottom-right column is 233 pixels wide, the `a5-column-middle` rule is assigned 240 pixels of margin to the right. This guarantees that the text in the center column will not only stop before it reaches the right column's area, but it will have 7 pixels of space between the two containers.

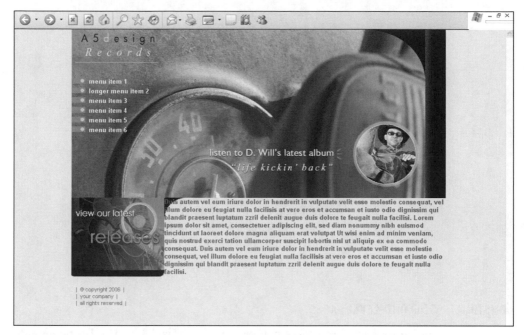

FIGURE 10.14   If given no constraints, the `a5-column-middle` rule would allow content to stretch the full width of the design, such as in this example, which includes a larger amount of dummied content.

The `a5-column-middle` rule also has a background image declared in it, which provides the black curve in the top-left corner of the design.

- The `list-1` rule provides styling to the list that is included in the `a5-column-middle` container. The `list-style-image` is used in conjunction with the `line-height` rule and `vertical-align` rule to position the bullets in somewhat similar positions among the various tested browsers.
- Adding the `a5-column-right` rule and content is the final step in completing the design. The container is assigned the Purchase Online background image. Because of a positioning bug in IE, the Tantek hack must be used to position the container 1 pixel to the right of its default location so the entire container, and thus the background image, lines up with the image in the top row. If the hack is not used, the page will be positioned incorrectly, as shown in Figure 10.15.
- To prevent the list in the `a5-column-right` container from covering the text portion of the background image (that is, the Purchase Online image), the `list-2` rule is assigned a local style. This style sets the top margin to 70 pixels. The `margin-top` rule is separated from the `list-2` rule in the page-level style sheet to enable the designer to control the positioning of the list if the rule is reused elsewhere in the site. If the two rules were combined, this list would always be forced down 70 pixels from the top wherever it was included.

FIGURE 10.15 The Tantek hack must be used to position the bottom-right content area 1 pixel to the right or else there will be a 1-pixel difference between it and the image above.

CONSTRUCTING SECOND-LEVEL PAGES

As with most sites, the second-level pages are based on the homepage design. This allows images from the homepage to be reused for subsequent pages, not only to provide visual consistency in the design, which improves usability, but also to allow browsers to cache the original images, making the page download quicker. In this design, two second-level templates are created: one that contains three columns and one that contains two columns.

Constructing a Second-Level Page with Three Columns

The first second-level template that is created is the page that appears when the designer clicks on the menu item titled Longer Menu Item 2. This page contains three columns. Such a design offers the ability to supplement pages with less content with a right column that could contain repetitive information, such as photos, announcements, and specials. Of course, this is not the only reason for a three-column design. The purpose, for example, could also be to provide a more advanced visual layout by adding another element, which, in turn, could have more elements added to it. Figure 10.16 shows what the design looks like when the final code (see Listing 10.5) is added to the page.

The newly added code is bold to differentiate it from the existing code that is being built upon in this case study.

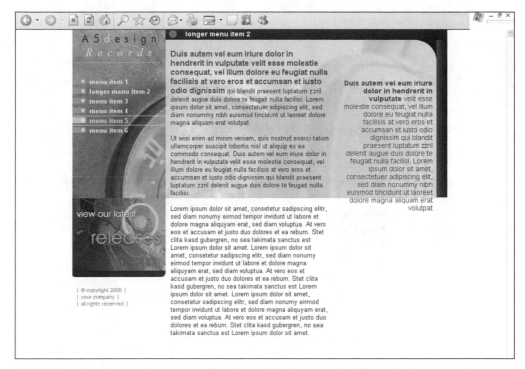

FIGURE 10.16   The three-column second-level template that is derived from the homepage design.

LISTING 10.5   Code for Figure 10.16

```
<!DOCTYPE html PUBLIC "-//W3C//DTD XHTML 1.0 Transitional//EN"
    "DTD/xhtml1-transitional.dtd">
<html xmlns="http://www.w3.org/1999/xhtml" xml:lang="en"
lang="en"><head><title>Design 122</title>
<meta http-equiv="Content-Type" content="text/html;
    charset=iso-8859-1" />
<!- link to main stylesheet that control text sizes and colors, among
    other things ->
<link rel="stylesheet" href="mainstyle.css" type="text/css" />
<style>
/* +++++++++ global sl structure styles start +++++++++*/
#a5-body-content-sl {
    position:relative;
    margin-left:191px;
    height:100%;
    background: url(images/bg-body-content-sl.jpg) no-repeat 0px 0px;
    border:0px solid #000000;
    }
```

```css
#a5-top-row-sl {
    position:relative;
    left:0px;
    top:0px;
    height:100%;
    border:0px solid #000000;
    }
#a5-sl-title {
    height:24px;
    font:bold 14px italic Arial, Helvetica, sans-serif;
    background: #000000 url(images/bg-title.gif) no-repeat 0px 0px;
    color:#ffffff;
    padding:4px 0px 0px 40px;
    margin-bottom:10px;
    border:0px solid #000000;
    voice-family:"\"}\"";
    voice-family:inherit;
        height:20px;
    }
html>body #a5-sl-title {
        height:20px;
    }
#a5-column-middle-sl {
    position:relative;
    left:0px;
    top:10px;
    margin:0px 230px 0px 10px;
    padding-right:10pt;
    border:0px solid #000000;
    }
#a5-column-right-sl {
    position:absolute;
    right:-1px;
    top:11px;
    width:230px;
    height:800px;
    text-align:right;
    background: url(images/bg-right-column-sl.gif) repeat-y
        0px 0px;
    border:0px solid #000000;
    voice-family:"\"}\"";
    voice-family:inherit;
        right:-1px;
        top:10px;
```

```
            width:230px;
        }
        html>body #a5-column-right-sl {
            right:0px;
            top:10px;
            width:230px;
        }
        #a5-column-right-content-sl {
            position:relative;
            right:0px;
            top:15px;
            width:230px;
            font: 14px italic Arial, Helvetica, sans-serif;
            color:#044465;
            padding:80px 30px 10px 20px;
            border:0px solid #000000;
            voice-family:"\"}\"";
            voice-family:inherit;
                width:180px;
            }
            html>body #a5-column-right-content-sl {
                width:180px;
            }
/* ++++++++++ global sl structure styles end ++++++++++*/
</style>
</head>
<body>
<div id="a5-body-center">
    <div id="a5-body">
<!- ###### left column start ###### ->
        <div id="a5-column-left">
            <div><a href="index.htm"><img src="images/header-left.jpg"
                width="191" height="100" alt="" border="0" /></a></div>
            <div id="a5-menu">
                <a href="index.htm">menu item 1</a>
                <a href="menu-item-2.htm">longer menu item 2</a>
                <a href="menu-item-3.htm">menu item 3</a>
                <a href="index.htm">menu item 4</a>
                <a href="index.htm">menu item 5</a>
                <a href="index.htm">menu item 6</a>
            </div>
            <div><a href="index.htm"><img src="images/image-bottom-
                left.jpg" width="191" height="162" alt="" border="0"
                /></a></div>
```

```
        <div id="a5-copyright">
            |  &copy; copyright 2006  |<br />
                |  your company  |<br />| 
                 all rights reserved  |
        </div>
    </div>
<!- ###### left column end ###### ->
<!- ###### body content start ###### ->
    <div id="a5-body-content-sl">
        <div id="a5-top-row-sl">
            <div id="a5-sl-title">longer menu item 2</div>
            <div id="a5-column-middle-sl">
<span class="color-1-text-12"><b>Duis autem vel eum iriure dolor in
    hendrerit in vulputate velit esse molestie consequat, vel illum
    dolore eu feugiat nulla facilisis at vero eros et accumsan et iusto
    odio dignissim</b></span> qui blandit praesent luptatum zzril
    delenit augue duis dolore te feugait nulla facilisi. Lorem ipsum
    dolor sit amet, consectetuer adipiscing elit, sed diam nonummy nibh
    euismod tincidunt ut laoreet dolore magna aliquam erat volutpat
<br /><br />
Ut wisi enim ad minim veniam, quis nostrud exerci tation ullamcorper
    suscipit lobortis nisl ut aliquip ex ea commodo consequat. Duis
    autem vel eum iriure dolor in hendrerit in vulputate velit esse
    molestie consequat, vel illum dolore eu feugiat nulla facilisis at
    vero eros et accumsan et iusto odio dignissim qui blandit praesent
    luptatum zzril delenit augue duis dolore te feugait nulla facilisi.
<br /><br />
Lorem ipsum dolor sit amet, consetetur sadipscing elitr, sed diam
    nonumy eirmod tempor invidunt ut labore et dolore magna aliquyam
    erat, sed diam voluptua. At vero eos et accusam et justo duo
    dolores et ea rebum. Stet clita kasd gubergren, no sea takimata
    sanctus est Lorem ipsum dolor sit amet. Lorem ipsum dolor sit amet,
    consetetur sadipscing elitr, sed diam nonumy eirmod tempor invidunt
    ut labore et dolore magna aliquyam erat, sed diam voluptua. At vero
    eos et accusam et justo duo dolores et ea rebum. Stet clita kasd
    gubergren, no sea takimata sanctus est Lorem ipsum dolor sit amet.
    Lorem ipsum dolor sit amet, consetetur sadipscing elitr, sed diam
    nonumy eirmod tempor invidunt ut labore et dolore magna aliquyam
    erat, sed diam voluptua. At vero eos et accusam et justo duo
    dolores et ea rebum. Stet clita kasd gubergren, no sea takimata
    sanctus est Lorem ipsum dolor sit amet.
            </div>
            <div id="a5-column-right-sl">
                <div id="a5-column-right-content-sl">
```

```
<b>Duis autem vel eum iriure dolor in hendrerit in vulputate</b> velit
    esse molestie consequat, vel illum dolore eu feugiat nulla
    facilisis at vero eros et accumsan et iusto odio dignissim qui
    blandit praesent luptatum zzril delenit augue duis dolore te
    feugait nulla facilisi. Lorem ipsum dolor sit amet, consectetuer
    adipiscing elit, sed diam nonummy nibh euismod tincidunt ut laoreet
    dolore magna aliquam erat volutpat
                    </div>
                </div>
            </div>
        </div>
<!- ###### body content end ###### ->
    </div>
</div>
</body>
</html>
```

There are several things to note about the code in Listing 10.5:

- A second style sheet has been added for the second-level pages. For demonstration, the style sheet for the homepage has been saved as `mainstyle.css` and includes a link to the page. The style sheet for the second-level pages has been included as a page-level style sheet, which will be interpreted after the first style sheet.
- The `a5-body-content` rule has been renamed as the `a5-body-content-sl` rule. This enables the designer to include the background image `bg-body-content-sl.jpg` for the container. While the container was initially built into the homepage design, it is not assigned a background image until this page because the top-right images in the homepage need to be hyperlinked but do not need to have text flow over them. Saving the images together as one image and using it as a background image for this page maintains the look and feel of the top-right area of the homepage. It is assigned 100% height to ensure that the text will fill its full height. Otherwise, it could get cut off in IE 5, 5.5, and 6.

The rules added in the second-level template have –sl appended to their names to signify that they are to be used for secondary pages. Otherwise, if the rules contain the same name in both the `mainstyle.css` *and* `mainstyle-sl.css` *files, a browser may use the incorrect style for that page.*

- Because the content is now nested inside what was the `a5-top-row` container, it has to be renamed `a5-top-row-sl` and have its background color of #000000 removed. The background image is now more transparent, so this `<DIV>` does not necessarily need to have a background color if it is changed to a liquid format.

- The `a5-sl-title` rule is added to include the page title for secondary pages at the top of the page. The height of the `<DIV>` is set at 24 pixels to guarantee that it expands to the specified height of the background image. Padding is used to position the title vertically in the container and 40 pixels from the left, which is taken up by the background image `bg-title.gif`. To ensure that the color of the `bg-title.gif` is continued across the screen, the shorthand background property is assigned a background color value of #000000. Because padding is used to position the text within the container, the Tantek hack is added to ensure that the height of the container is the same for both compliant and noncompliant browsers.

- Similar to the bottom two nested containers that were used in the homepage (`a5-column-middle` and `a5-column-right`), the `a5-column-middle-sl` and `a5-column-right-sl` `<DIV>` tags were added to provide the two right columns of the design. Because the `a5-column-right-sl` container is assigned an absolute positioning value, it also is assigned a height of 800 pixels to ensure that the text does not run beyond the container—not that there would be a visible difference because there is no repeating background image or color the text would run beyond. If the text were to run farther down the page than 800 pixels and the column were to include a background color, for example, the designer might want to change the forced height of the column so that the text did not pass the color.

- The content included in the `a5-column-right-sl` container is nested inside the `a5-column-right-content-sl` `<DIV>` tag. The main thing to note about this rule is that it is assigned padding that forces it 80 pixels from the top, which guarantees that the text will not be placed over the background image `bg-right-column-sl.gif` in the `a5-column-right-sl` column. This is done to avoid black text running over the black background of the image, which would make it appear invisible.

CONSTRUCTING A SECOND-LEVEL PAGE WITH TWO COLUMNS

The full-width second-level template included with this design is the page the designer comes to when clicking on the Menu Item 3 link in the menu. The purpose of this template is to provide a page where more content can be added. The designer, of course, may also choose to use the extra space to include a more customized layout on the page. Whatever the reason for using this template, the page allows more visual real estate with which to work. Figure 10.17 shows what the design looks like when the final code is added to the page (see Listing 10.6).

 The newly added code is bold to differentiate it from the existing code that is being built upon in this case study.

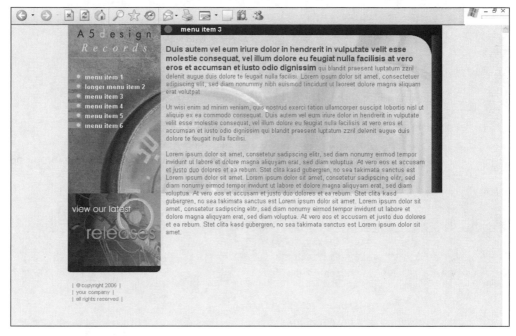

FIGURE 10.17   The two-column second-level template that is based on the homepage design.

LISTING 10.6   Code for Figure 10.17

```
<!DOCTYPE html PUBLIC "-//W3C//DTD XHTML 1.0 Transitional//EN"
    "DTD/xhtml1-transitional.dtd">
<html xmlns="http://www.w3.org/1999/xhtml" xml:lang="en"
lang="en"><head><title>Design 122</title>
<meta http-equiv="Content-Type" content="text/html;
    charset=iso-8859-1" />
<!- link to main stylesheet that control text sizes and colors, among
    other things ->
<link rel="stylesheet" href="mainstyle.css" type="text/css" />
<style>
/* ++++++++++ global sl structure styles start ++++++++++*/
#a5-body-content-sl {
    position:relative;
    margin-left:191px;
    height:100%;
    background: url(images/bg-body-content-sl.jpg) no-repeat 0px 0px;
    border:0px solid #000000;
    }
```

```
#a5-top-row-sl {
    position:relative;
    left:0px;
    top:0px;
    border:0px solid #000000;
    }
#a5-sl-title {
    height:24px;
    font:bold 14px italic Arial, Helvetica, sans-serif;
    background: #000000 url(images/bg-title.gif) no-repeat 0px 0px;
    color:#ffffff;
    padding:4px 0px 0px 40px;
    margin-bottom:10px;
    border:0px solid #000000;
    voice-family:"\"}\"";
    voice-family:inherit;
        height:20px;
    }
html>body #a5-sl-title {
        height:20px;
    }
#a5-column-middle-sl {
    position:relative;
    left:0px;
    top:10px;
    margin:0px 230px 50px 10px;
    padding-right:10pt;
    padding-bottom:20px;
    border:0px solid #000000;
    }
#a5-column-right-sl {
    position:absolute;
    right:-1px;
    top:11px;
    width:230px;
    height:800px;
    text-align:right;
    background: url(images/bg-right-column-sl.gif) repeat-y
        0px 0px;
    border:0px solid #000000;
    voice-family:"\"}\"";
    voice-family:inherit;
        right:-1px;
        top:10px;
```

```
                    width:230px;
            }
            html>body #a5-column-right-sl {
                right:0px;
                top:10px;
                width:230px;
            }
            #a5-column-right-content-sl {
                position:relative;
                right:0px;
                top:15px;
                width:230px;
                font: 14px italic Arial, Helvetica, sans-serif;
                color:#044465;
                padding:80px 30px 10px 20px;
                border:0px solid #000000;
                voice-family:"\"}\"";
                voice-family:inherit;
                    width:180px;
            }
            html>body #a5-column-right-content-sl {
                    width:180px;
            }
        #a5-column-full-sl {
            position:relative;
            left:0px;
            top:10px;
            margin:0px 20px 0px 10px;
            padding-right:10pt;
            border:0px solid #000000;
            }
/* ++++++++++ global sl structure styles end ++++++++++*/
</style>
</head>
<body>
<div id="a5-body-center">
    <div id="a5-body">
<!-- ###### left column start ###### -->
        <div id="a5-column-left">
            <div><a href="index.htm"><img src="images/header-left.jpg"
                width="191" height="100" alt="" border="0" /></a></div>
            <div id="a5-menu">
                <a href="index.htm">menu item 1</a>
                <a href="menu-item-2.htm">longer menu item 2</a>
```

```
                                <a href="menu-item-3.htm">menu item 3</a>
                                <a href="index.htm">menu item 4</a>
                                <a href="index.htm">menu item 5</a>
                                <a href="index.htm">menu item 6</a>
                            </div>
                            <div><a href="index.htm"><img src="images/image-bottom-
                                left.jpg" width="191" height="162" alt="" border="0"
                                /></a></div>
                            <div id="a5-copyright">
                                |  &copy; copyright 2006  |<br />
                                    |  your company  |<br />| 
                                     all rights reserved  |
                            </div>
                        </div>
            <!-- ###### left column end ###### -->
            <!-- ###### body content start ###### -->
                    <div id="a5-body-content-sl">
                        <div id="a5-top-row-sl">
                            <div id="a5-sl-title">menu item 3</div>
                            <div id="a5-column-full-sl">
<span class="color-1-text-12"><b>Duis autem vel eum iriure dolor in
    hendrerit in vulputate velit esse molestie consequat, vel illum
    dolore eu feugiat nulla facilisis at vero eros et accumsan et
    iusto odio dignissim</b></span> qui blandit praesent luptatum
    zzril delenit augue duis dolore te feugait nulla facilisi. Lorem
    ipsum dolor sit amet, consectetuer adipiscing elit, sed diam
    nonummy nibh euismod tincidunt ut laoreet dolore magna aliquam
    erat volutpat
<br /><br />
Ut wisi enim ad minim veniam, quis nostrud exerci tation ullamcorper
    suscipit lobortis nisl ut aliquip ex ea commodo consequat. Duis
    autem vel eum iriure dolor in hendrerit in vulputate velit esse
    molestie consequat, vel illum dolore eu feugiat nulla facilisis at
    vero eros et accumsan et iusto odio dignissim qui blandit praesent
    luptatum zzril delenit augue duis dolore te feugait nulla facilisi.
<br /><br />
Lorem ipsum dolor sit amet, consetetur sadipscing elitr, sed diam
    nonumy eirmod tempor invidunt ut labore et dolore magna aliquyam
    erat, sed diam voluptua. At vero eos et accusam et justo duo
    dolores et ea rebum. Stet clita kasd gubergren, no sea takimata
    sanctus est Lorem ipsum dolor sit amet. Lorem ipsum dolor sit
    amet, consetetur sadipscing elitr, sed diam nonumy eirmod tempor
    invidunt ut labore et dolore magna aliquyam erat, sed diam
    voluptua. At vero eos et accusam et justo duo dolores et ea rebum.
```

```
         Stet clita kasd gubergren, no sea takimata sanctus est Lorem ipsum
         dolor sit amet. Lorem ipsum dolor sit amet, consetetur sadipscing
         elitr, sed diam nonumy eirmod tempor invidunt ut labore et dolore
         magna aliquyam erat, sed diam voluptua. At vero eos et accusam et
         justo duo dolores et ea rebum. Stet clita kasd gubergren, no sea
         takimata sanctus est Lorem ipsum dolor sit amet.
               </div>
            </div>
         </div>
<!- ###### body content end ###### ->
      </div>
</div>
</body>
</html>
```

There are several things to note about the code in Listing 10.6:

- The only rule added to the second-level style sheet is `a5-column-full-sl`. This rule forces the container to fill the full width of the page, barring the assigned padding and margin values.
- After the rule is added, the actual container replaces the `a5-column-middle-sl` and `a5-column-right-sl` `<DIV>` tags in the code. Because it is assigned margin and padding settings, the text does not touch the right image.

SUMMARY

The design in this chapter is very different from the one in Chapter 9. It not only contains three columns in the homepage, but it also uses mortised images in the top-right section of the page. These images are then saved as one lighter background image that is included in the second-level pages. These pages use a second style sheet that is assigned specifically to them. To avoid any interpretation issues between the two style sheets, the rules in the second-level style sheet have `-sl` appended to the end. The two- and three-column structures in the second-level pages offer the designer more content layout flexibility, depending on the amount of content included in the design.

11

CASE STUDY:
HIGH-CONTENT CSS DESIGN

In This Chapter

- Understanding the Design's Structure
- Building the Structure
- Constructing Second-Level Pages

The design explained in this chapter uses many of the same techniques as the layouts in Chapters 9 and 10; the key difference is that it contains more content. The technical structure is a hybrid of the two designs in that it uses a header <DIV> across the top, as in Chapter 9, and incorporates a three-column layout below, as does the design in Chapter 10. It is designed to display more content than many sites, whether the purpose is to sell product, provide large amounts of content, or even a combination of the two.

The design explained in this chapter is design 123 in the accompanying CD-ROM (photo credits: www.idlerphotography.com).

UNDERSTANDING THE DESIGN'S STRUCTURE

Figure 11.1 illustrates the design explained in this chapter. It is designed to easily work as either a fixed or liquid design. Because the header area stretches across the entire design, elements can be added, edited, or removed without having to modify other areas of the site.

FIGURE 11.1   The high-content CSS design explained in this chapter.

This design, along with those in Chapters 9 and 10, was written at a time when the resolution for which designers created sites was 800 × 600. This is no longer the case. At the time of publication, the percentage of users who viewed sites at 800 × 600 resolution was only about 15 percent, while more than 80 percent of users viewed sites at 1024 × 768 resolution or higher. The principles of this design are still very applicable, no matter the resolution. The designer would merely need to widen any or all of the columns and/or even add another column.

Reasoning Behind Guides and Creating Slices in Photoshop Files

There are 15 slices used in the main Photoshop file and one in a secondary file to create the images for the homepage design. Figure 11.2 shows all the slices used in the homepage file and outlines the 10 most important guides and slices necessary in constructing the design with XHTML and CSS.

FIGURE 11.2   Ten of the most important guides and slices used to build the design in this chapter.

Following are explanations of the 10 most important guides and slices used in Figure 11.2:

- The guide above number 1 is used to separate the header row from the bottom portion of the design, which includes the left, center, and right columns.
- The guide to the left of number 2 is used to separate the left column, which includes the menu, from the right column, which includes the nested center and right columns.
- The guide above number 3, which is difficult to differentiate from the black line it abuts, is used to separate the menu area from the content below.
- The slice to the top left of number 4 is used to save the `header-left` image, which includes the company's logo.
- The two images in the header row to the far right of number 5 are mortised together, along with their text. The first image found to the right of number 5 is the background image that is repeated horizontally across the header file. This works even if the design is changed to a liquid format.
- Number 6 does not represent a slice in the homepage file shown in Figure 11.2 but highlights the image behind the form that is saved as a background image in a separate file (see Figure 11.3). Similar to the Chapter 9 and 10 designs, a separate Photoshop file is used to save such an image. Although a slice could be created to save this background image in the main Photoshop file, a designer may want the image to run down the left column behind content other than the form. For this reason the image was created in a separate Photoshop file. Number 1 represents this slice in Figure 11.3.
- The slice to the top left of number 7 is used to save the Search button. If the designer were to continue building this e-commerce site, it would require additional buttons that would, most likely, be consistent with this image. Therefore, the designer might want to crop and save the button in a separate Photoshop file, which would make saving separate files easier.
- The slice to the top left of number 8 represents a banner ad saved from the homepage file. The important thing to note about this image is that it is saved with extra space to the left and right sides, which gives the designer room to be flexible if the image needs to be moved to the left or right down the road or if a larger image needs to be added.
- Number 9 represents a product used in the homepage design. Although each of the four products are saved individually in this homepage file, they could be saved as their own separate Photoshop files for the same reason the button image could be saved individually.
- Number 10 represents two slices. The slice to the top left of the number is used to provide a line at the bottom of the right column to give it a sense of closure. Because the column is assigned absolute positioning, it will not automatically maintain the same height as the center column. This line could also be created by simply adding a bottom border to the area with CSS. The slice to the bottom left of number 10 is used as the background image of the title area for the second-level pages.

FIGURE 11.3   A Photoshop file that includes the background image behind the form, saved separately from the homepage file.

Understanding the Placement of CSS Containers

Slightly more <DIV> tags are used in this design than in the designs explained in Chapters 9 and 10 because more individual content elements are used here. Structurally, all three designs require the same number of <DIV> tags to build their infrastructures. They are merely placed differently. As mentioned earlier, this design, as shown in Figure 11.4, is a hybrid of those two designs in that it uses a horizontal header container and a three-column format below the header.

Following are explanations for 10 of the most useful containers in Figure 11.4:

- The <DIV> tag to the right of number 1 is used for centering the design in IE 5 and 5.5.
- Number 2 represents the header <DIV>, which contains the nested content to the right of the number.
- The <DIV> tag to the top left of number 3 represents the left column's container.
- Number 4 represents the banner ad that is saved for the left column. It also shows how the left column, which is assigned absolute positioning, extends past the boundaries of the containers within which it is nested.

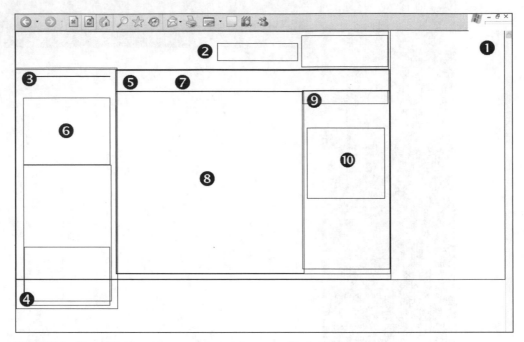

FIGURE 11.4   Ten of the most important containers used to build the design.

- The `<DIV>` to the top left of number 5 is the `a5-column-right` container, which includes the menu row and center and right columns.
- Number 6 points out the `<DIV>` in the left column that contains the search form.
- Number 7 represents the container within which the menu is nested.
- The center column of content is nested inside the container indicated by number 8.
- The right column container begins at the top-left corner of number 9.
- Number 10 represents a `<DIV>` tag that is used to nest additional content in the right column.

BUILDING THE STRUCTURE

Following are the step-by-step instructions for building the design. It is assumed that the Photoshop file has already been created or customized and that the designer only needs to position the images and text.

Creating the XHTML and CSS Framework

The first step to building the design is to create the XHTML framework and initial CSS containers. Listing 11.1 is the code that is used to output the page in Figure 11.5.

FIGURE 11.5   Basic XHTML and CSS framework for the design.

LISTING 11.1   Code for Figure 11.5

```
<!DOCTYPE html PUBLIC "-//W3C//DTD XHTML 1.0 Transitional//EN"
    "DTD/xhtml1-transitional.dtd">
<html xmlns="http://www.w3.org/1999/xhtml" xml:lang="en"
lang="en"><head><title>Design 123</title>
<meta http-equiv="Content-Type" content="text/html;
    charset=iso-8859-1" />
<style type="text/css">
/* ++++++++++ global general styles start ++++++++++*/
html, body {
    margin:0px;
    padding:0px;
    font: 13px Arial, Helvetica, sans-serif;
    color:#000000;
    background:#ffffff;
    }
/* ++++++++++ global general styles end ++++++++++*/
/* ++++++++++ global structure styles start ++++++++++*/
#a5-body-center {
    text-align:left;
    border:1px solid #000000;
    }
#a5-body {
    position: relative;
    width: 770px; /* change this to a specific amount for a fixed
        design or a relative amount if the design should expand to
a percentage of the screen. E.g., 770px or 100%, respectively. */

    /* remove these comment tags if the page is to be centered
    margin-left: auto;
    margin-right: auto;*/
    text-align:left;
    padding-bottom:10px;
    border:1px solid #000000;
    }
    /* ++++++++++ global structure styles end ++++++++++*/
```

```
</style>
</head>
<body>
<div id="a5-body-center">
    <div id="a5-body">
         
    </div>
</div>
</body>
</html>
```

There are several things to note about the code in Listing 11.1:

- The CSS style sheet is commented into a couple of different sections. The global general styles comment tags contain the general styles, such as the formatting of the <HTML> and <BODY> tags, hyperlinks, and fonts. The global structure styles comment tags include the styles used to define the structure of the design and elements included in that structure.
- Several rules define the <HTML> and <BODY> tags. The margin and padding properties are used to ensure that the design is placed in the very top-left corner of the browser, with no space between the design and the edges. The default font style for the site is set using the shorthand FONT property. Defining the default font color is accomplished with the COLOR property. The background color is assigned to ensure that all browsers display the same color because not all browsers show the same color.
- The a5-body-center and a5-body rules are used to force the design to the left side of the browser screen with a fixed width of 770 pixels. If the designer wanted to fill the full width of the screen, the value of 770px would need to be changed to 100%. If, however, the designer wanted to simply justify the design to the left, the value of the text-align property in the a5-body-center rule would need to be changed from center to left. The margin-left and margin-right properties in the a5-body rule ensure that the extra white space is split evenly on both sides. While this system tends to be more complex, it allows the designer flexibility when more than one site is going to be built. By adding this code to every design, it does not take much work to quickly modify a design to fit a client's needs.
- Both the a5-body-center and a5-body rules have their borders turned on using the following code: border:1px solid #000000;. For demonstration purposes, the code was added to both rules to show what the structure of the <DIV> tags looks like without content added. Turning on the borders helps a designer when building a site because it is not always apparent where elements are placed or expanding. Rather than remove these rules, it is easier to change the value of 1px to 0px, turning the borders off rather than removing them. Troubleshooting often involves turning the borders back on, so it saves time and takes up very little download size to keep them in the style sheet.

- Because the `<div id="a5-body">` is nested inside the `<div id="a5-body-center">` tag, it is indented. This allows for quicker recognition of tags that are nested inside each other, which becomes a useful technique when the page has more code added to it.

Adding the Header Row

Once the XHTML and basic CSS framework have been added, the header area is then added into the code. Listing 11.2 is the code that is used to create the updated page in Figure 11.6.

 The newly added code is bold to differentiate it from the existing code that is being built upon in this case study.

FIGURE 11.6   The header row that is added to the design.

LISTING 11.2   Code for Figure 11.6

```
<!DOCTYPE html PUBLIC "-//W3C//DTD XHTML 1.0 Transitional//EN"
    "DTD/xhtml1-transitional.dtd">
<html xmlns="http://www.w3.org/1999/xhtml" xml:lang="en"
lang="en"><head><title>Design 123</title>
<meta http-equiv="Content-Type" content=vtext/html;
    charset=iso-8859-1" />
<style type="text/css">
/* ++++++++++ global general styles start ++++++++++*/
html, body {
    margin:0px;
    padding:0px;
    font: 13px Arial, Helvetica, sans-serif;
    color:#000000;
    background:#ffffff;
    }
a:link { color:#FF7800; }
a:visited { color:#FF5A00; }
a:active { color:#FFC600; }
a:hover { color:#000000; }
```

```
a.linklist1:link { text-decoration:none;color:#0ECOFF;}
a.linklist1:visited { text-decoration:none;color:#0ECOFF;}
a.linklist1:active { text-decoration:none;color:#0ECOFF;}
a.linklist1:hover { text-decoration:none;color:#D5EE03;}


/* ++++++++++ global general styles end ++++++++++*/
/* ++++++++++ global structure styles start ++++++++++*/
#a5-body-center {
    text-align:left;
    }
#a5-body {
    position: relative;
    width: 770px; /* change this to a specific amount for a fixed
        design or a relative amount if the design should expand to
a percentage of the screen. E.g., 770px or 100%, respectively. */
    /* remove these comment tags if the page is to be centered
    margin-left: auto;
    margin-right: auto;*/
vvtext-align:left;
    padding-bottom:10px;
    border:0px solid #000000;
    }
#a5-header {
    position:relative;
    left:0px;
    top:0px;
    height:78px;
    background: #000000 url(images/bg-header.gif) repeat-x;
    border:0px solid #000000;
    }
    #a5-login {
        position:absolute;
        top:24px;
        right:186px;
        width:165px;
        font: 15px Arial, Helvetica, sans-serif;
        border:0px solid #ffffff;
        }
    #a5-call {
        position:absolute;
        top:8px;
        right:0px;
        width:177px;
        font: 13px Arial, Helvetica, sans-serif;
```

```
        color:#ffffff;
        border:0px solid #000000;
        }
/* ++++++++++ global structure styles end ++++++++++*/
</style>
</head>
<body>
<div id="a5-body-center">
    <div id="a5-body">
<!- ###### header start ###### ->
        <div id="a5-header">
            <div><a href="index.htm"><img src="images/logo.gif"
                width="357" height="78" alt="" border="0" /></a></div>
            <div id="a5-login">
                <span style="float:left;"><a href="x.htm"><img
                    src="images/reseller-button.gif" width="33"
                    height="23" alt="" border="0" /></a></span>
                <a href="x.htm" class="linklist1"><b>Reseller Login
                    </b><br />
                Forgot Password?</a>
            </div>
            <div id="a5-call">
                <span style="float:left;padding-right:6px;"><a href=
                    "x.htm"><img src="images/photo-header-right.jpg"
                    width="58" height="64" alt="" border="0"
                    /></a></span>
                <div style="margin-top:8px;">
                    <span style="font: 14px Arial, Helvetica, sans-
                        serif;"><b>Need Help?</b></span><br />
                    Call us at<br />
                    1-800-555-5555
                </div>
            </div>
        </div>
<!- ###### header end ###### ->
    </div>
</div>
</body>
</html>
```

There are several things to note about the code in Listing 11.2:

- Both the default link colors and linklist1 link rules are added. While the default colors are added before they will actually be used, the linklist1 style is used for the Reseller Login link.

- The `a5-header` rule and code are added to provide a container for the nested elements. The rule has relative positioning assigned to it, so it expands to the full width of the screen. It is assigned a height of 78 pixels, which is the height of the images in the header. Using the background property, the `bg-header.gif` is repeated horizontally across the header.
- The `logo.gif` file is included in a `<DIV>` tag. This ensures that the image will appear at the top-left corner of the header with no additional space around it in some browsers, such as IE 5, 5.5, and 6 (see Figure 11.7).

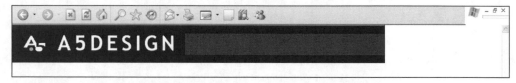

FIGURE 11.7   Header after the `logo.gif` image is added to the left side of the container.

- The `a5-login` container is added after the `logo.gif` image in the header. The rule is given absolute positioning, locating the container 186 pixels from the right. This allows space for the final `<DIV>` to be added within those 186 pixels between it and the right side (see Figure 11.8).

FIGURE 11.8   The header after the `a5-login` container has been added to the right of the `logo.gif` image.

The `reseller-button.gif` image is floated to the left of the "Reseller Login. Forgot Password?" text. In this instance, the `float` property is assigned to the image using a `<SPAN>` tag at the local level in the code. Because the button image does not take up the full height of the header, the container is positioned 24 pixels from the top of the header, using the `top` property.

- The final container in the header is included using the `a5-call` rule (see Figure 11.9). This rule is assigned absolute positioning, similarly to the `a5-login` container. The former, however, is located 0 pixels from the right, with a width of 177 pixels. This not only guarantees that the `<DIV>` will abut the right side of the container, but it will also have 9 pixels of padding between it and the `a5-login` container because the `a5-login` `<DIV>` is located 186 pixels from the right (186 – 177 = 9 pixels).

The layout of this content is a bit more involved than the previous containers in the `a5-header` row. It has two nested elements: the `photo-header-right.jpg` (which

FIGURE 11.9   After the final container `a5-call` is added, the header has all the elements added to it.

is floated to the left of the text, including 6 pixels of padding to the right) and a `<DIV>` that contains the text (which also has a `<SPAN>` tag styling the "Need Help" text). Barring the default font color and size, the majority of styling is completed at the local level.

Creating the Left Column

After the `a5-header` container has been added, the left column needs to be added. This column includes a search form, content area, and the image used as a banner ad. Figure 11.10 shows what the design looks like after the code in Listing 11.3 has been added.

 The newly added code is bold to differentiate it from the existing code that is being built upon in this case study.

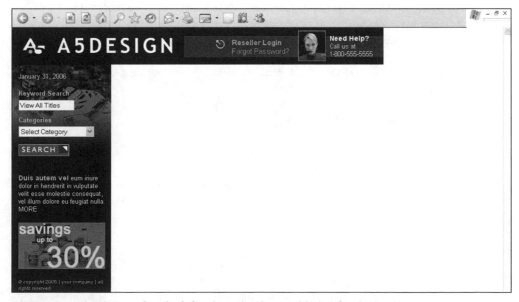

FIGURE 11.10   The design after the left column has been added under the header row.

LISTING 11.3   Code for Figure 11.10

```
<!DOCTYPE html PUBLIC "-//W3C//DTD XHTML 1.0 Transitional//EN"
"DTD/xhtml1-transitional.dtd">
<html xmlns="http://www.w3.org/1999/xhtml" xml:lang="en"
lang="en"><head><title>Design 123</title>
<meta http-equiv="Content-Type" content="text/html;
    charset=iso-8859-1" />
<style type="text/css">
/* ++++++++++ global general styles start ++++++++++*/
html, body {
    margin:0px;
    padding:0px;
    font: 13px Arial, Helvetica, sans-serif;
    color:#000000;
    background:#ffffff;
    }
a:link { color:#FF7800; }
a:visited { color:#FF5A00; }
a:active { color:#FFC600; }
a:hover { color:#000000; }

a.linklist1:link { text-decoration:none;color:#0ECOFF;}
a.linklist1:visited { text-decoration:none;color:#0ECOFF;}
a.linklist1:active { text-decoration:none;color:#0ECOFF;}
a.linklist1:hover { text-decoration:none;color:#D5EE03;}

.color-1-text-13 { font-family: arial, geneva, sans-serif; font-size:
    13px; color: #FFAE00;}
.color-1-text-14 { font-family: arial, geneva, sans-serif; font-size:
    14px; color: #FFAE00;}

.color-2-text-14 { font-family: arial, geneva, sans-serif; font-size:
    14px; color: #000000;}
/* ++++++++++ global general styles end ++++++++++*/
/* ++++++++++ global structure styles start ++++++++++*/
#a5-body-center {
    text-align:left;
    }
#a5-body {
    position: relative;
    width: 770px; /* change this to a specific amount for a fixed
        design or a relative amount if the design should expand to
a percentage of the screen. E.g., 770px or 100%, respectively. */
```

```
/* remove these comment tags if the page is to be centered
    margin-left: auto;
    margin-right: auto;*/
    text-align:left;
    padding-bottom:10px;
    border:0px solid #000000;
    }
#a5-header {
    position:relative;
    left:0px;
    top:0px;
    height:78px;
    background: #000000 url(images/bg-header.gif) repeat-x;
    border:0px solid #000000;
    }
    #a5-login {
        position:absolute;
        top:24px;
        right:186px;
        width:165px;
        font: 15px Arial, Helvetica, sans-serif;
        border:0px solid #ffffff;
        }
    #a5-call {
        position:absolute;
        top:8px;
        right:0px;
        width:177px;
        font: 13px Arial, Helvetica, sans-serif;
        color:#ffffff;
        border:0px solid #000000;
        }
#a5-column-left {
    position:absolute;
    left:0px;
    top:78px;
    width:207px;
    color:#ffffff;
    padding:0px 12px 50px 15px;
    background: #000000 url(images/bg-left-column.jpg) no-repeat;
    border:0px solid yellow;
    voice-family:"\"}\"";
    voice-family:inherit;
        width:180px;
```

```
        }
html>body #a5-column-left {
    width:180px;
}
#date {
    position:relative;
    top:16px;
    left:0px;
    color:#ffffff;
    border:0px solid #ffffff;
    }
#formsearch {
    position:relative;
    top:35px;
    left:0px;
    border:0px solid yellow;
    }
#a5-column-left-content {
    position:relative;
    left:0px;
    top:35px;
    color:#ffffff;
    border:0px solid #ffffff;
    }
    #a5-copyright {
        position:relative;
        left:0px;
        top:10px;
        bottom:5px;
        font: 10px Arial, Helvetica, sans-serif;
        color:#9D9D9D;
        text-align:left;
        border:0px solid #000000;
        }
/* ++++++++++ global structure styles end ++++++++++*/
</style>
</head>
<body>
<div id="a5-body-center">
    <div id="a5-body">
<!-- ###### header start ###### -->
        <div id="a5-header">
            <div><a href="index.htm"><img src="images/logo.gif"
                width="357" height="78" alt="" border="0" /></a></div>
```

```
        <div id="a5-login">
            <span style="float:left;"><a href="x.htm"><img src=
                "images/reseller-button.gif" width="33"
                height="23" alt="" border="0" /></a></span>
            <a href="x.htm" class="linklist1"><b>Reseller Login
                </b><br />
            Forgot Password?</a>
        </div>
        <div id="a5-call">
            <span style="float:left;padding-right:6px;"><a href=
                "x.htm"><img src="images/photo-header-right.jpg"
                width="58" height="64" alt="" border="0" /></a>
                </span>
            <div style="margin-top:8px;">
                <span style="font: 14px Arial, Helvetica,
                    sans-serif;"><b>Need Help?</b></span><br />
                Call us at<br />
                1-800-555-5555
            </div>
        </div>
    </div>
<!-- ###### header end ###### -->
<!-- ###### left column start ###### -->
        <div id="a5-column-left">
            <div id="date">
                January 31, 2006
            </div>
            <div id="formsearch" class="color-1-text-13">
                <form method="post" action="x.htm" name="search"
                    style="margin-top:0px;">
                    <b>Keyword Search</b>
                    <div style="padding:5px 0px 10px 0px;"><input
                        type="text" size="15" name="keywords"
                        value="View All Titles" /></div>
                    <b>Categories</b>
                    <div style="padding:5px 0px 15px 0px;">
                    <select name="categories" size="1">
                        <option value="All">Select Category</
                            option>
                        <option value="sample">This is a sample
                            entry</option>
                    </select>
                    </div>
                    <input type="image" src="images/button-
```

```
                                     search.gif" />
                        </form>
              </div>
                  <div id="a5-column-left-content">
                      <div style="padding:15px 0px 10px 0px;color:
                          #ffffff;"><span class="color-1-text-14"><b>
                          Duis autem vel</b></span> eum iriure dolor in
                          hendrerit in vulputate velit esse molestie
                          consequat, vel illum dolore eu feugiat nulla.
                          MORE</div>
                      <div style="padding:10px 0px 10px 0px;color:
                          #ffffff;"><a href="x.htm"><img src="images/
                          banner-left-bottom.jpg" width="180"
                          height="96" alt="" border="0" /></a></div>
                      <div id="a5-copyright">
                          &copy; copyright 2006 | your company | all
                              rights reserved
                      </div>
                  </div>
              </div>
          </div>
<!- ###### left column end ###### ->
      </div>
  </div>
  </body>
  </html>
```

There are several things to note about the code in Listing 11.3:

- The `a5-column-left` container, which contains all the content in the left column, is assigned absolute positioning. It remains on the left side of the design and begins 78 pixels from the top of the page, exactly below the header. It is assigned a width of 207 pixels. Using the `padding` property, the entire column is given padding on the left and right sides. Because of the box model bug, the Tantek hack must be used so that the left and right padding is properly interpreted similarly by both compliant and noncompliant browsers. This is why the width is changed to 180 pixels for compliant browsers—because 17 pixels need to be subtracted from the original specified width.
- The date container is the first content added. Although in this design the date is static text, scripts to output the date using JavaScript or a database-driven programming language can be easily added. Two more things to note about this container are that it is assigned relative positioning, which makes it take up the entire width of the column, and it is positioned 16 pixels from the top of the column using the `top` property.

- After the date container has been added, the `formsearch <DIV>` is added. It contains all the form elements, such as the "Keyword Search" text and input field, "Categories" text and drop-down menu, and the Search button. The positioning of the elements in the form occur at the local level. One style to note is `style="margin-top:0px;"`, which is included in the parent `<FORM>` tag. This helps override the default margin settings of some browsers so the form is positioned similarly among browsers. The `color-1-text-13` rule is added to style the text in the `formsearch <DIV>`.

- The `a5-column-left-content <DIV>` is added after the `formsearch <DIV>`. The first three words are not only styled with the `color-1-text-14` rule that was added to the style sheet, but the container is assigned local padding to the top and bottom.

- Finally, the `a5-copyright` rule is added to the style sheet to position and style the copyright statement at the bottom of the column.

Adding the Center Column

After the left column is completed, the right column is added to the design, completing it. Figure 11.11 shows what the design looks like after it has been completed (see Listing 11.4).

The newly added code is bold to differentiate it from the existing code that is being built upon in this case study.

FIGURE 11.11   The design after the entire right column has been added.

LISTING 11.4   Code for Figure 11.11

```
<!DOCTYPE html PUBLIC "-//W3C//DTD XHTML 1.0 Transitional//EN"
    "DTD/xhtml1-transitional.dtd">
<html xmlns="http://www.w3.org/1999/xhtml" xml:lang="en"
lang="en"><head><title>Design 123</title>
<meta http-equiv="Content-Type" content="text/html;
    charset=iso-8859-1" />
<style type="text/css">
/* ++++++++++ global general styles start ++++++++++*/
html, body {
    margin:0px;
    padding:0px;
    font: 13px Arial, Helvetica, sans-serif;
    color:#000000;
    background:#ffffff;
    }
a:link { color:#FF7800; }
a:visited { color:#FF5A00; }
a:active { color:#FFC600; }
a:hover { color:#000000; }

a.linklist1:link { text-decoration:none;color:#0EC0FF;}
a.linklist1:visited { text-decoration:none;color:#0EC0FF;}
a.linklist1:active { text-decoration:none;color:#0EC0FF;}
a.linklist1:hover { text-decoration:none;color:#D5EE03;}

.color-1-text-13 { font-family: arial, geneva, sans-serif; font-size:
    13px; color: #FFAE00;}
.color-1-text-14 { font-family: arial, geneva, sans-serif; font-size:
    14px; color: #FFAE00;}

.color-2-text-14 { font-family: arial, geneva, sans-serif; font-size:
    14px; color: #000000;}
/* ++++++++++ global general styles end ++++++++++*/
/* ++++++++++ global structure styles start ++++++++++*/
#a5-body-center {
    text-align:left;
    }
#a5-body {
    position: relative;
    width: 770px; /* change this to a specific amount for a fixed
        design or a relative amount if the design should expand to
a percentage of the screen. E.g., 770px or 100%, respectively. */
```

```
    /* remove these comment tags if the page is to be centered
        margin-left: auto;
        margin-right: auto;*/
        text-align:left;
        padding-bottom:10px;
        border:0px solid #000000;
        }
#a5-header {
        position:relative;
        left:0px;
        top:0px;
        height:78px;
        background: #000000 url(images/bg-header.gif) repeat-x;
        border:0px solid #000000;
        }
        #a5-login {
            position:absolute;
            top:24px;
            right:186px;
            width:165px;
            font: 15px Arial, Helvetica, sans-serif;
            border:0px solid #ffffff;
            }
        #a5-call {
            position:absolute;
            top:8px;
            right:0px;
            width:177px;
            font: 13px Arial, Helvetica, sans-serif;
            color:#ffffff;
            border:0px solid #000000;
            }
#a5-column-left {
        position:absolute;
        left:0px;
        top:78px;
        width:207px;
        color:#ffffff;
        padding:0px 12px 50px 15px;
        background: #000000 url(images/bg-left-column.jpg) no-repeat;
        border:0px solid yellow;
        voice-family:"\"}\"";
        voice-family:inherit;
            width:180px;
```

```
            }
        html>body #a5-column-left {
            width:180px;
        }
        #date {
            position:relative;
            top:16px;
            left:0px;
            color:#ffffff;
            border:0px solid #ffffff;
            }
        #formsearch {
            position:relative;
            top:35px;
            left:0px;
            border:0px solid yellow;
            }
        #a5-column-left-content {
            position:relative;
            left:0px;
            top:35px;
            color:#ffffff;
            border:0px solid #ffffff;
            }
            #a5-copyright {
                position:relative;
                left:0px;
                top:10px;
                bottom:5px;
                font: 10px Arial, Helvetica, sans-serif;
                color:#9D9D9D;
                text-align:left;
                border:0px solid #000000;
                }
    #a5-column-right {
        position:relative;
        right:0px;
        top:0px;
        margin-left:207px;
        border:0px solid #000000;
        }
        #a5-menu-box {
            position:relative;
            top:0px;
```

```
        left:0px;
        height:42px;
        width:100%;
        color:#ffffff;
        line-height:42px;
        vertical-align:30%;
        background:url(images/bg-menu.gif) repeat-x 0px 0px;
        border:0px solid #000000;
        }
        #a5-menu a {
            display:inline;
            text-decoration:none;
            color:#94CCDE;
            font-weight:normal;
            }
        #a5-menu a:hover {
            font-weight:normal;
            color:#ffffff;
            }
    #a5-column-right-left {
        position:relative;
        left:0px;
        top:0px;
        padding:10px 10px 10px 10px;
        margin-right:177px;
        border:0px solid #000000;
        }
        .a5-products {
        height:300px;
        border: 0px solid #000000;
        }
        .a5-individual-product {
        float: left;
        margin:0px 2px 0px 2px;
        border:0px solid #000000;
        }
        .a5-individual-product p {
        border-top:1px solid #BFBFBF;
        width:170px;
        text-align: center;
        }

#a5-column-right-right {
        position:absolute;
```

```
        right:0px;
        top:42px;
        width:177px;
        height:365px;
        color:#ffffff;
        padding:0px 9px 0px 9px;
        background:#215F5F url(images/bg-bottom-line-right-column.gif)
            no-repeat left bottom;
        border:0px solid red;
        voice-family:"\"}\"";
        voice-family:inherit;
            width:159px;
        }
        html>body #a5-column-right-right {
            width:159px;
        }
        .a5-title-right {
            font-family: arial, geneva, sans-serif;
            font-size: 13px;
            color: #D5EE03;
            line-height:25px;
            font-weight:bold;
            margin:0px -9px 0px -9px;
            padding-left:5px;
            margin-bottom:10px;
            background:#000000;
            border:0px solid #000000;
            }
        #a5-right-nested-box {
            position:relative;
            right:0px;
            top:23px;
            width:159px;
            padding:10px 10px 0px 10px;
            background:#000000;
            color:#ffffff;
            border:1px solid #0ECOFF;
            voice-family:"\"}\"";
            voice-family:inherit;
                width:139px;
            }
            html>body #a5-right-nested-box {
            width:139px;
            }
```

```
/* ++++++++++ global structure styles end ++++++++++*/
</style>
</head>
<body>
<div id="a5-body-center">
    <div id="a5-body">
<!- ###### header start ###### ->
        <div id="a5-header">
            <div><a href="index.htm"><img src="images/logo.gif" width=
                "357" height="78" alt="" border="0" /></a></div>
            <div id="a5-login">
                <span style="float:left;"><a href="x.htm"><img
                    src="images/reseller-button.gif" width="33"
                    height="23" alt="" border="0" /></a></span>
                <a href="x.htm" class="linklist1"><b>Reseller Login
                    </b><br />
                Forgot Password?</a>
            </div>
            <div id="a5-call">
                <span style="float:left;padding-right:6px;"><a
                    href="x.htm"><img src="images/photo-header-
                    right.jpg" width="58" height="64" alt=""
                    border="0" /></a></span>
                <div style="margin-top:8px;">
                    <span style="font: 14px Arial, Helvetica,
                        sans-serif;"><b>Need Help?</b></span><br />
                    Call us at<br />
                    1-800-555-5555
                </div>
            </div>
        </div>
<!- ###### header end ###### ->
<!- ###### left column start ###### ->
            <div id="a5-column-left">
                <div id="date">
                    January 31, 2006
                </div>
                <div id="formsearch" class="color-1-text-13">
                    <form method="post" action="x.htm" name="search"
                        style="margin-top:0px;">
                        <b>Keyword Search</b>
                        <div style="padding:5px 0px 10px 0px;"><input
                            type="text" size="15" name="keywords"
                            value="View All Titles" /></div>
```

```
                                <b>Categories</b>
                                <div style="padding:5px 0px 15px 0px;">
                                <select name="categories" size="1">
                                    <option value="All">Select Category
                                        </option>
                                    <option value="sample">This is a sample
                                        entry</option>
                                </select>
                                </div>
                                <input type="image" src="images/
                                    button-search.gif" />
                            </form>
                    </div>
                    <div id="a5-column-left-content">
                        <div style="padding:15px 0px 10px 0px;color:
                            #ffffff;"><span class="color-1-text-14"><b>
                            Duis autem vel</b></span> eum iriure dolor in
                            hendrerit in vulputate velit esse molestie
                            consequat, vel illum dolore eu feugiat nulla.
                            MORE</div>
                        <div style="padding:10px 0px 10px 0px;color:
                            #ffffff;"><a href="x.htm"><img src="images/
                            banner-left-bottom.jpg" width="180"
                            height="96" alt="" border="0" /></a></div>
                        <div id="a5-copyright">
                            &copy; copyright 2006 | your company | all
                                rights reserved
                        </div>
                    </div>
                </div>
    <!- ###### left column end ###### ->
    <!- ###### right column start ###### ->
                <div id="a5-column-right">
                    <div id="a5-menu-box">
                        <div id="a5-menu">
                               
                            <a href="index.htm">menu item 1</a>  
                                .  
                            <a href="menu-item-2.htm">longer menu item 2
                                </a>  .  
                            <a href="menu-item-3.htm">menu item 3</a> 
                                 .  
                            <a href="index.htm">menu item 4</a>  
                                .  
```

```
                              <a href="index.htm">menu item 5</a>  
                                  .  
                          </div>
                      </div>
<!-- ###### column right left start ###### -->
                      <div id="a5-column-right-left">
                          <span class="color-2-text-14" style="padding-
                              bottom:5px;"><b>View Our Latest Products</b></span>
                          <br /><br />
                          <div class="a5-products">
                              <div class="a5-individual-product">
                                  <a href="x.htm"><img src="images/
                                      product-1.jpg" width="175" height="95"
                                      alt="" border="0" /></a><br />
                                  <p><a href="x.htm">Product 1 title</a></p>
                              </div>
                              <div class="a5-individual-product">
                                  <a href="x.htm"><img src="images/
                                      product-2.jpg" width="175" height="95"
                                      alt="" border="0" /></a><br />
                                  <p><a href="x.htm">Product 2 title</a></p>
                              </div>
                              <div class="a5-individual-product">
                                  <a href="x.htm"><img src="images/
                                      product-3.jpg" width="175" height="95"
                                      alt="" border="0" /></a><br />
                                  <p><a href="x.htm">Product 3 title</a></p>
                              </div>
                              <div class="a5-individual-product">
                                  <a href="x.htm"><img src="images/
                                      product-4.jpg" width="175" height="95"
                                      alt="" border="0" /></a><br />
                                  <p><a href="x.htm">Product 4 title</a></p>
                      </div>
                          </div>
                          <br />

                          <div class="color-2-text-14"><b>Learn About Our
                              Technical Classes</b></div>
                          Duis autem vel eum iriure dolor in hendrerit in
                              vulputate velit esse molestie consequat, vel
                              illum dolore eu feugiat nulla ... <a href=
                              "x.htm">MORE</a>
```

```
                    </div>
    <!- ###### column right left end ###### ->
    <!- ###### column right right start ###### ->
                    <div id="a5-column-right-right">
                        <div class="a5-title-right">
                            <b>View Our Specials</b>
                        </div>
                        <div>Duis autem vel eum iriure dolor in hendrerit
                            in vulputate velit esse molestie consequat.
                        </div>
                        <div id="a5-right-nested-box"><span class="color-1-
                            text-14"><b>Duis autem vel</b></span> eum
                            iriure dolor in hendrerit in vulputate velit
                            esse molestie consequat, vel illum dolore eu
                            feugiat nulla.
                            <div style="margin:24px 0px 20px 0px;"><img
                                src="images/banner-right-middle.jpg"
                                width="136" height="73" alt="" border="0"
                                /></div>
                        </div>
                    </div>
    <!- ###### column right right end ###### ->
            </div>
    <!- ###### right column end ###### ->
        </div>
    </div>
    </body>
    </html>
```

There are several things to note about the code in Listing 11.4:

- All the content in the right column, including the menu, the center column (which includes the products) and the right column, are nested inside the a5-column-right container. It is assigned relative positioning, with a margin-left value of 207 pixels. This guarantees that the container will be positioned 207 pixels from the left, which is the width of the left column.
- To ensure that the menu occurs consistently on every page, including the different second-level pages, the a5-menu-box container is added with relative positioning above the rest of the content in the <DIV>. Figure 11.12 shows what the design looks like with just the menu added.

One thing to consider about such a menu is that it is limited in the number of items that can be added because of limited horizontal space. This is where drop-down CSS, JavaScript, or Flash menus can become useful because more menu items can be added when the user mouses over a menu item. The menu in this instance works fine because the site is created to be driven by the search form on the left,

FIGURE 11.12   The menu is the first element to be added to the right column.

which can be used to navigate hundreds or thousands of pages. The menu itself is designed more for general sections, such as About, Customer Service, and Specials.

While the menu code looks the same as that in the designs in Chapters 9 and 10, it is styled slightly differently. The display property in the `a5-menu` rule in this design is assigned a value of `inline` instead of `block`, meaning the items will be output horizontally across a line, as opposed to vertically.

- The `a5-column-right-left` rule is used to output the content in the center column of the design. It is assigned relative positioning, with a `margin-right` value of 177 pixels, which keeps it from crossing over into the right column. One unique aspect of this container, compared to any others in this design or in Chapters 9 or 10, is that it includes repeated floating `<DIV>` tags, which contain each product. Normally handled with an XHTML table, these products wrap around to form separate columns and rows. If the width of the design were expanded to fill 1024 × 768 resolution, three products would appear in the first row, as opposed to two in the 800 × 600 version. While they do not have to expand, by doing so, they fill the extra white space of the design that would normally exist because only two products are used to fill it. This function is accomplished by adding a container that is assigned the `a5-products` rule. The one thing to note about this rule is that it is assigned a height of 300 pixels. If this height is not set, the text below the images will randomly reposition itself in different browsers at 1024 × 768 resolution. Because the height value is assigned, the developer cannot output more products than the height will allow, which is four in this example. Each product is positioned and styled inside the `a5-products` container, using the `a5-individual-product` and `a5-individual-product p` rules. Figure 11.13 shows the design with the center column added with the border of the products table turned on to show the space it takes up.

Using comment tags to separate code makes finding particular sections much easier. Using an intuitive system is important for designers to understand their code. In this section of code the "right column" is the parent column, while "column right left" represents the left column of the right section. Visually, though, in the design, this column is the center column. A designer could also name this section the "center column," or name the "right column" the "parent right column," signifying that there will be a child right column.

FIGURE 11.13   The center column added to the design with the border of the products table turned on.

- The content in the right column is nested inside the `a5-column-right` container. Because it is assigned absolute positioning, it is placed 42 pixels from the top of the container. These 42 pixels force the column down past the menu area. Otherwise, the column would begin in the area across which the menu runs (see Figure 11.14).

FIGURE 11.14   An image of how the right column would look if it were not positioned 42 pixels from the top.

Because the container is assigned absolute positioning, it is given a height value of 365 pixels to ensure that the nested content inside it does not run below the container. The `<DIV>` is assigned the `bg-bottom-line-right-column.gif` background image, which is the black line at the bottom of the column. No matter the height of the column, the background image will automatically place itself at the bottom because of the bottom value included in the shorthand `background` property.

- The a5-title-right <DIV>, which is the first item nested in the right column, is placed at the top of the column. One of the most useful properties assigned to the rule is margin-bottom, which has a value of 10 pixels. This creates some visual space between the title area and the text below it.
- The a5-right-nested-box rule is added to create the nested <DIV> in the column, which contains the text and image. Because padding is added to the container, the width of the <DIV> needs to be adjusted for various browsers, using the Tantek hack. The image is positioned using a local style that is included in the <DIV> tags wrapped around it.

Constructing Second-Level Pages

As with the designs in Chapters 9 and 10, the homepage is duplicated and modified for second-level templates. This design includes both three- and two-column versions to provide the design layout more flexibility.

Constructing a Second-Level Page with Three Columns

The first second-level template created is the page that appears when the designer clicks on the menu item titled Longer Menu Item 2. This page contains three columns. Such a design offers the designer the ability to supplement content with a right column that could contain information that could be included on more than one page, such as photos and descriptions. Figure 11.15 shows what the design looks like when the final code is added to the page (see Listing 11.5).

FIGURE 11.15   A three-column second-level template created from a customized version of the homepage design.

The newly added code is bold to differentiate it from the existing code that is being built upon in this case study.

LISTING 11.5   Code for Figure 11.15

```
<!DOCTYPE html PUBLIC "-//W3C//DTD XHTML 1.0 Transitional//EN"
    "DTD/xhtml1-transitional.dtd">
<html xmlns="http://www.w3.org/1999/xhtml" xml:lang="en"
lang="en"><head><title>Design 123</title>
<meta http-equiv="Content-Type" content="text/html;
    charset=iso-8859-1" />
<style type="text/css">
/* ++++++++++ global general styles start ++++++++++*/
html, body {
    margin:0px;
    padding:0px;
    font: 13px Arial, Helvetica, sans-serif;
    color:#000000;
    background:#ffffff;
    }
a:link { color:#FF7800; }
a:visited { color:#FF5A00; }
a:active { color:#FFC600; }
a:hover { color:#000000; }

a.linklist1:link { text-decoration:none;color:#0EC0FF;}
a.linklist1:visited { text-decoration:none;color:#0EC0FF;}
a.linklist1:active { text-decoration:none;color:#0EC0FF;}
a.linklist1:hover { text-decoration:none;color:#D5EE03;}

.color-1-text-13 { font-family: arial, geneva, sans-serif; font-size:
    13px; color: #FFAE00;}
.color-1-text-14 { font-family: arial, geneva, sans-serif; font-size:
    14px; color: #FFAE00;}

.color-2-text-14 { font-family: arial, geneva, sans-serif; font-size:
    14px; color: #000000;}
/* ++++++++++ global general styles end ++++++++++*/
/* ++++++++++ global structure styles start ++++++++++*/
#a5-body-center {
    text-align:left;
    }
```

```
#a5-body {
    position: relative;
    width: 770px; /* change this to a specific amount for a fixed
        design or a relative amount if the design should expand to
a percentage of the screen. E.g., 770px or 100%, respectively. */
    /* remove these comment tags if the page is to be centered
    margin-left: auto;
    margin-right: auto;*/
    text-align:left;
    padding-bottom:10px;
    border:0px solid #000000;
    }
#a5-header {
    position:relative;
    left:0px;
    top:0px;
    height:78px;
    background: #000000 url(images/bg-header.gif) repeat-x;
    border:0px solid #000000;
    }
    #a5-login {
        position:absolute;
        top:24px;
        right:186px;
        width:165px;
        font: 15px Arial, Helvetica, sans-serif;
        border:0px solid #ffffff;
        }
    #a5-call {
        position:absolute;
        top:8px;
        right:0px;
        width:177px;
        font: 13px Arial, Helvetica, sans-serif;
        color:#ffffff;
        border:0px solid #000000;
        }
#a5-column-left {
    position:absolute;
    left:0px;
    top:78px;
    width:207px;
    color:#ffffff;
    padding:0px 12px 50px 15px;
```

```css
        background: #000000 url(images/bg-left-column.jpg) no-repeat;
        border:0px solid yellow;
        voice-family:"\"}\"";
        voice-family:inherit;
            width:180px;
        }
        html>body #a5-column-left {
            width:180px;
        }
        #date {
            position:relative;
            top:16px;
            left:0px;
            color:#ffffff;
            border:0px solid #ffffff;
            }
        #formsearch {
            position:relative;
            top:35px;
            left:0px;
            border:0px solid yellow;
            }
        #a5-column-left-content {
            position:relative;
            left:0px;
            top:35px;
            color:#ffffff;
            border:0px solid #ffffff;
            }
            #a5-copyright {
                position:relative;
                left:0px;
                top:10px;
                bottom:5px;
                font: 10px Arial, Helvetica, sans-serif;
                color:#9D9D9D;
                text-align:left;
                border:0px solid #000000;
                }
    #a5-column-right {
        position:relative;
        right:0px;
        top:0px;
        margin-left:207px;
```

```
border:0px solid #000000;
}
#a5-menu-box {
    position:relative;
    top:0px;
    left:0px;
    height:42px;
    width:100%;
    color:#ffffff;
    line-height:42px;
    vertical-align:30%;
    background:url(images/bg-menu.gif) repeat-x 0px 0px;
    border:0px solid #000000;
    }
    #a5-menu a {
        display:inline;
        text-decoration:none;
        color:#94CCDE;
        font-weight:normal;
        }
    #a5-menu a:hover {
        font-weight:normal;
        color:#ffffff;
        }
#a5-column-right-left {
    position:relative;
    left:0px;
    top:0px;
    padding:10px 10px 10px 10px;
    margin-right:177px;
    border:0px solid #000000;
    }
    .a5-products {
    height:300px;
    border: 0px solid #000000;
    }
    .a5-individual-product {
    float: left;
    margin:0px 2px 0px 2px;
    border:0px solid #000000;
    }
    .a5-individual-product p {
    border-top:1px solid #BFBFBF;
    width:170px;
```

```
        text-align: center;
        }


#a5-column-right-right {
        position:absolute;
        right:0px;
        top:42px;
        width:177px;
        height:365px;
        color:#ffffff;
        padding:0px 9px 0px 9px;
        background:#215F5F url(images/bg-bottom-line-right-column.gif)
            no-repeat left bottom;
        border:0px solid red;
        voice-family:"\"}\"";
        voice-family:inherit;
            width:159px;
        }
        html>body #a5-column-right-right {
            width:159px;
        }
        .a5-title-right {
            font-family: arial, geneva, sans-serif;
            font-size: 13px;
            color: #D5EE03;
            line-height:25px;
            font-weight:bold;
            margin:0px -9px 0px -9px;
            padding-left:5px;
            margin-bottom:10px;
            background:#000000;
            border:0px solid #000000;
            }
        #a5-right-nested-box {
            position:relative;
            right:0px;
            top:23px;
            width:159px;
            padding:10px 10px 0px 10px;
            background:#000000;
            color:#ffffff;
            border:1px solid #0EC0FF;
            voice-family:"\"}\"";
            voice-family:inherit;
```

```
                width:139px;
        }
        html>body #a5-right-nested-box {
                width:139px;
        }
/* ++++++++++ global structure styles end ++++++++++*/
/* ++++++++++ second level start ++++++++++*/
#a5-column-right-left-sl {
    position:relative;
    left:0px;
    top:0px;
    padding:0px 10px 0px 10px;
    margin-right:177px;
    border:0px solid #000000;
    }
#a5-sl-title {
    margin:0px -10px 10px -10px;
    padding:5px 0px 0px 40px;
    height:25px;
    color:#000000;
    background:#DBDBDB url(images/bg-sl-title.gif) no-repeat left top;
    border:0px solid #000000;
    font:bold 14px italic Arial, Helvetica, sans-serif;
    voice-family:"\"}\"";
    voice-family:inherit;
        height:20px;
    }
    html>body #a5-sl-title {
        height:20px;
    }
#a5-column-left-full {
    position:relative;
    left:0px;
    top:1px;
    color:#000000;
    padding:0px 10px 0px 10px;
    }
/* ++++++++++ second level end ++++++++++*/
</style>
</head>
<body>
<div id="a5-body-center">
    <div id="a5-body">
<!-- ###### header start ###### -->
```

```
<div id="a5-header">
    <div><a href="index.htm"><img src="images/logo.gif"
        width="357" height="78" alt="" border="0" /></a></div>
    <div id="a5-login">
        <span style="float:left;"><a href="x.htm"><img
            src="images/reseller-button.gif" width="33"
            height="23" alt="" border="0" /></a></span>
        <a href="x.htm" class="linklist1"><b>Reseller Login
            </b><br />
        Forgot Password?</a>
    </div>
    <div id="a5-call">
        <span style="float:left;padding-right:6px;"><a href=
            "x.htm"><img src="images/photo-header-right.jpg"
            width="58" height="64" alt="" border="0" /></a>
            </span>
        <div style="margin-top:8px;">
            <span style="font: 14px Arial, Helvetica,
                sans-serif;"><b>Need Help?</b></span><br />
            Call us at<br />
            1-800-555-5555
        </div>
    </div>
</div>
<!-- ###### header end ###### -->
<!-- ###### left column start ###### -->
    <div id="a5-column-left">
    <div id="date">
        January 31, 2006
        </div>
        <div id="formsearch" class="color-1-text-13">
            <form method="post" action="x.htm" name="search"
                style="margin-top:0px;">
                <b>Keyword Search</b>
                <div style="padding:5px 0px 10px 0px;"><input
                    type="text" size="15" name="keywords"
                    value="View All Titles" /></div>
                <b>Categories</b>
                <div style="padding:5px 0px 15px 0px;">
                <select name="categories" size="1">
                    <option value="All">Select Category
                        </option>
                    <option value="sample">This is a sample
                        entry</option>
```

```
                            </select>
                            </div>
                            <input type="image" src="images/
                                    button-search.gif" />
                        </form>
                    </div>
                    <div id="a5-column-left-content">
                        <div style="padding:15px 0px 10px 0px;color:
                            #ffffff;"><span class="color-1-text-14"><b>
                            Duis autem vel</b></span> eum iriure dolor in
                            hendrerit in vulputate velit esse molestie
                            consequat, vel illum dolore eu feugiat nulla.
                            MORE</div>
                        <div style="padding:10px 0px 10px 0px;color:
                            #ffffff;"><a href="x.htm"><img src="images/
                            banner-left-bottom.jpg" width="180"
                            height="96" alt="" border="0" /></a></div>
                        <div id="a5-copyright">
                            &copy; copyright 2006 | your company | all
                                rights reserved
                        </div>
                    </div>
                </div>
<!-- ###### left column end ###### -->
<!-- ###### right column start ###### -->
                <div id="a5-column-right">
                    <div id="a5-menu-box">
                        <div id="a5-menu">
                               
                            <a href="index.htm">menu item 1</a> 
                                 .  
                            <a href="menu-item-2.htm">longer menu item 2
                                </a>  .  
                            <a href="menu-item-3.htm">menu item 3</a> 
                                 .  
                            <a href="index.htm">menu item 4</a>  
                                .  
                            <a href="index.htm">menu item 5</a>  
                                .  
                        </div>
                    </div>
<!-- ###### column right left start ###### -->
                    <div id="a5-column-right-left-sl">
                        <div id="a5-sl-title">
```

```
                              longer menu item 2
                          </div>
                          Enter text here.
                      </div>
      <!– ###### column right left end ###### –>
      <!– ###### column right right start ###### –>
                      <div id="a5-column-right-right">
                          <div class="a5-title-right">
                              <b>View Our Specials</b>
                          </div>
                          <div>Duis autem vel eum iriure dolor in hendrerit
                          in vulputate velit esse molestie consequat.</div>
                          <div id="a5-right-nested-box"><span class="color-
                              1-text-14"><b>Duis autem vel</b></span> eum
                              iriure dolor in hendrerit in vulputate velit
                              esse molestie consequat, vel illum dolore eu
                              feugiat nulla.
                          <div style="margin:24px 0px 20px 0px;"><img
                              src="images/banner-right-middle.jpg"
                              width="136" height="73" alt="" border="0"
                              /></div>
                          </div>
                      </div>
      <!– ###### column right right end ###### –>
              </div>
      <!– ###### right column end ###### –>
          </div>
      </div>
      </body>
      </html>
```

There are several things to note about the code in Listing 11.5:

- The second level start and second level end comment tags are added to separate the rules specifically added for the second-level area from the rest of the style sheet. Unlike the design in Chapter 9, the two style sheets are included as one in this chapter, which is more an issue of preference. Sometimes a designer may include everything in one style sheet to keep all the code together or want to break it up into separate style sheets for more of a distinct separation.

 The rules added in the second-level template have –sl appended to their names to signify that they are to be used for secondary pages.

- The `a5-column-right-left-sl` rule is added to the style sheet for the second-level template. It replaces the `a5-column-right-left` rule, which is the container for the center column on the homepage. The only difference between the two styles is that the content on the second-level page, which is styled by the `a5-column-right-left-sl` rule, adds 10 pixels of padding to the top and bottom of the container to position itself with the menu and to add extra spacing on the bottom.
- The `a5-sl-title` rule is added to include the page title for secondary pages at the top of the page. This rule sets the height of the `<DIV>` at 25 pixels, using the `height` property. Padding also is used to position the title from the top and left sides in the container. To ensure that the color of the `bg-title.gif` is continued across the screen, the shorthand `background` property is assigned a background color value of `#DBDBDB`. Because padding is used to position the text within the container, the Tantek hack is added to ensure the height of the container is the same for both compliant and noncompliant browsers.

Constructing a Second-Level Page with Two Columns

The full-width second-level template included with this design is the page the designer comes to when clicking on the Menu Item 3 link in the menu. The purpose of this template is to provide a page with more white space for the designer to work with. Figure 11.16 shows what the design looks like when the final code is added to the page and the right column is removed from the design in Figure 11.16 (see Listing 11.6).

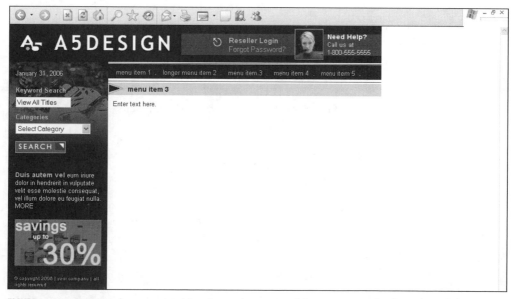

FIGURE 11.16   A two-column second-level template created from a customized version of the homepage design.

The newly added code is bold to differentiate it from the existing code that is being built upon in this case study.

LISTING 11.6   Code for Figure 11.16

```
<!DOCTYPE html PUBLIC "-//W3C//DTD XHTML 1.0 Transitional//EN"
    "DTD/xhtml1-transitional.dtd">
<html xmlns="http://www.w3.org/1999/xhtml" xml:lang="en"
lang="en"><head><title>Design 123</title>
<meta http-equiv="Content-Type" content="text/html;
    charset=iso-8859-1" />
<style type="text/css">
/* ++++++++++ global general styles start ++++++++++*/
    html, body {
    margin:0px;
    padding:0px;
    font: 13px Arial, Helvetica, sans-serif;
    color:#000000;
    background:#ffffff;
    }
a:link { color:#FF7800; }
a:visited { color:#FF5A00; }
a:active { color:#FFC600; }
a:hover { color:#000000; }

a.linklist1:link { text-decoration:none;color:#0EC0FF;}
a.linklist1:visited { text-decoration:none;color:#0EC0FF;}
a.linklist1:active { text-decoration:none;color:#0EC0FF;}
a.linklist1:hover { text-decoration:none;color:#D5EE03;}

.color-1-text-13 { font-family: arial, geneva, sans-serif; font-size:
    13px; color: #FFAE00;}
.color-1-text-14 { font-family: arial, geneva, sans-serif; font-size:
    14px; color: #FFAE00;}

.color-2-text-14 { font-family: arial, geneva, sans-serif; font-size:
    14px; color: #000000;}
/* ++++++++++ global general styles end ++++++++++*/
/* ++++++++++ global structure styles start ++++++++++*/
#a5-body-center {
    text-align:left;
    }
#a5-body {
    position: relative;
```

```
        width: 770px; /* change this to a specific amount for a fixed
               design or a relative amount if the design should expand to
   a percentage of the screen. E.g., 770px or 100%, respectively. */

       /* remove these comment tags if the page is to be centered
           margin-left: auto;
           margin-right: auto;*/
           text-align:left;
           padding-bottom:10px;
           border:0px solid #000000;
           }
       #a5-header {
           position:relative;
           left:0px;
           top:0px;
           height:78px;
           background: #000000 url(images/bg-header.gif) repeat-x;
           border:0px solid #000000;
           }
           #a5-login {
               position:absolute;
               top:24px;
               right:186px;
               width:165px;
               font: 15px Arial, Helvetica, sans-serif;
               border:0px solid #ffffff;
               }
           #a5-call {
               position:absolute;
               top:8px;
               right:0px;
               width:177px;
               font: 13px Arial, Helvetica, sans-serif;
               color:#ffffff;
               border:0px solid #000000;
               }
       #a5-column-left {
           position:absolute;
           left:0px;
           top:78px;
           width:207px;
           color:#ffffff;
           padding:0px 12px 50px 15px;
           background: #000000 url(images/bg-left-column.jpg) no-repeat;
```

```
        border:0px solid yellow;
        voice-family:"\"}\"";
        voice-family:inherit;
            width:180px;
        }
        html>body #a5-column-left {
            width:180px;
        }
        #date {
            position:relative;
            top:16px;
            left:0px;
            color:#ffffff;
            border:0px solid #ffffff;
            }
        #formsearch {
            position:relative;
            top:35px;
            left:0px;
            border:0px solid yellow;
            }
        #a5-column-left-content {
            position:relative;
            left:0px;
            top:35px;
            color:#ffffff;
            border:0px solid #ffffff;
            }
            #a5-copyright {
                position:relative;
                left:0px;
                top:10px;
                bottom:5px;
                font: 10px Arial, Helvetica, sans-serif;
                color:#9D9D9D;
                text-align:left;
                border:0px solid #000000;
                }
    #a5-column-right {
        position:relative;
        right:0px;
        top:0px;
        margin-left:207px;
        border:0px solid #000000;
```

```
}
#a5-menu-box {
    position:relative;
    top:0px;
    left:0px;
    height:42px;
    width:100%;
    color:#ffffff;
    line-height:42px;
    vertical-align:30%;
    background:url(images/bg-menu.gif) repeat-x 0px 0px;
    border:0px solid #000000;
    }
    #a5-menu a {
        display:inline;
        text-decoration:none;
        color:#94CCDE;
        font-weight:normal;
        }
    #a5-menu a:hover {
        font-weight:normal;
        color:#ffffff;
        }
#a5-column-right-left {
    position:relative;
    left:0px;
    top:0px;
    padding:10px 10px 10px 10px;
    margin-right:177px;
    border:0px solid #000000;
    }
    .a5-products {
    height:300px;
    border: 0px solid #000000;
    }
    .a5-individual-product {
    float: left;
    margin:0px 2px 0px 2px;
    border:0px solid #000000;
    }
    .a5-individual-product p {
    border-top:1px solid #BFBFBF;
    width:170px;
    text-align: center;
    }
```

```
#a5-column-right-right {
    position:absolute;
    right:0px;
    top:42px;
    width:177px;
    height:365px;
    color:#ffffff;
    padding:0px 9px 0px 9px;
    background:#215F5F url(images/bg-bottom-line-right-column.gif)
        no-repeat left bottom;
    border:0px solid red;
    voice-family:"\"}\"";
    voice-family:inherit;
        width:159px;
}
html>body #a5-column-right-right {
    width:159px;
}
.a5-title-right {
    font-family: arial, geneva, sans-serif;
    font-size: 13px;
    color: #D5EE03;
    line-height:25px;
    font-weight:bold;
    margin:0px -9px 0px -9px;
    padding-left:5px;
    margin-bottom:10px;
    background:#000000;
    border:0px solid #000000;
    }
#a5-right-nested-box {
    position:relative;
    right:0px;
    top:23px;
    width:159px;
    padding:10px 10px 0px 10px;
    background:#000000;
    color:#ffffff;
    border:1px solid #0EC0FF;
    voice-family:"\"}\"";
    voice-family:inherit;
        width:139px;
    }
    html>body #a5-right-nested-box {
```

```
                        width:139px;
                }
/* ++++++++++ global structure styles end ++++++++++*/
/* ++++++++++ second level start ++++++++++*/
#a5-column-right-left-sl {
    position:relative;
    left:0px;
    top:0px;
    padding:0px 10px 0px 10px;
    margin-right:177px;
    border:0px solid #000000;
    }
#a5-sl-title {
    margin:0px -10px 10px -10px;
    padding:5px 0px 0px 40px;
    height:25px;
    color:#000000;
    background:#DBDBDB url(images/bg-sl-title.gif) no-repeat left top;
    border:0px solid #000000;
    font:bold 14px italic Arial, Helvetica, sans-serif;
    voice-family:"\"}\"";
    voice-family:inherit;
        height:20px;
    }
    html>body #a5-sl-title {
        height:20px;
    }
#a5-column-left-full {
    position:relative;
    left:0px;
    top:1px;
    color:#000000;
    padding:0px 10px 0px 10px;
    }
/* ++++++++++ second level end ++++++++++*/
</style>
</head>
<body>
<div id="a5-body-center">
    <div id="a5-body">
<!- ###### header start ###### ->
    <div id="a5-header">
            <div><a href="index.htm"><img src="images/logo.gif"
                width="357" height="78" alt="" border="0" /></a></div>
```

```
                    <div id="a5-login">
                        <span style="float:left;"><a href="x.htm"><img src=
                            "images/reseller-button.gif" width="33"
                            height="23" alt="" border="0" /></a></span>
                        <a href="x.htm" class="linklist1"><b>Reseller Login
                            </b><br />
                        Forgot Password?</a>
                    </div>
                    <div id="a5-call">
                        <span style="float:left;padding-right:6px;"><a
                            href="x.htm"><img src="images/photo-header-
                            right.jpg" width="58" height="64" alt=""
                            border="0" /></a></span>
                        <div style="margin-top:8px;">
                            <span style="font: 14px Arial, Helvetica,
                                sans-serif;"><b>Need Help?</b></span><br />
                            Call us at<br />
                            1-800-555-5555
                        </div>
                    </div>
                </div>
        </div>
    <!- ###### header end ###### ->
    <!- ###### left column start ###### ->
            <div id="a5-column-left">
                <div id="date">
                    January 31, 2006
                </div>
                <div id="formsearch" class="color-1-text-13">
                    <form method="post" action="x.htm" name="search"
                        style="margin-top:0px;">
                        <b>Keyword Search</b>
                        <div style="padding:5px 0px 10px 0px;"><input
                            type="text" size="15" name="keywords"
                            value="View All Titles" /></div>
                        <b>Categories</b>
                        <div style="padding:5px 0px 15px 0px;">
                        <select name="categories" size="1">
                            <option value="All">Select Category
                                </option>
                            <option value="sample">This is a sample
                                entry</option>
                        </select>
                        </div>
                        <input type="image" src="images/
```

```
                            button-search.gif" />
            </form>
        </div>
        <div id="a5-column-left-content">
            <div style="padding:15px 0px 10px 0px;color:
                #ffffff;"><span class="color-1-text-14"><b>
                Duis autem vel</b></span> eum iriure dolor in
                hendrerit in vulputate velit esse molestie
                consequat, vel illum dolore eu feugiat nulla.
                MORE</div>
            <div style="padding:10px 0px 10px 0px;color:
                #ffffff;"><a href="x.htm"><img src="images/
                banner-left-bottom.jpg" width="180"
                height="96" alt="" border="0" /></a></div>
            <div id="a5-copyright">
                &copy; copyright 2006 | your company | all
                    rights reserved
            </div>
        </div>
    </div>
<!- ###### left column end ###### ->
<!- ###### right column start ###### ->
        <div id="a5-column-right">
            <div id="a5-menu-box">
                <div id="a5-menu">
                       
                    <a href="index.htm">menu item 1</a>  
                        .  
                    <a href="menu-item-2.htm">longer menu item 2
                        </a>  .  
                    <a href="menu-item-3.htm">menu item 3</a> 
                         .  
                    <a href="index.htm">menu item 4</a>  
                        .  
                    <a href="index.htm">menu item 5</a>  
                        .  
                </div>
            </div>
<!- ###### column right left start ###### ->
            <div id="a5-column-left-full">
                <div id="a5-sl-title">
                    menu item 3
                </div>
                    Enter text here.
            </div>
```

```
<!- ###### column right left end ###### ->
        </div>
<!- ###### right column end ###### ->
    </div>
</div>
</body>
</html>
```

There are two things to note about the code in Listing 11.6:

- The right column is removed by eliminating all the code between the `column right right start` and `column right right end` comment tags.
- Once the right column is removed, the center column can expand to the full width of the screen. Before it can do this, though, the `a5-column-right-left-s1` container needs to be duplicated and named `a5-column-left-full`. The style then needs to be changed by removing the `margin-right` property so the new container can expand all the way to the right edge of the screen. The left and right padding properties and values need to remain in the rule so the text in the container does not touch the left and right edges.

SUMMARY

Overall, the structure and CSS used in this design is a hybrid of the designs explained in Chapters 9 and 10. Several characteristics make it unique, though. Because it contains considerably more content, this design requires more rules to be created. Another difference is that the homepage outputs products, which uses a wrapping `<DIV>` technique that can be used in various sites and circumstances to output content in a similar "portfolio" manner. The final major difference of this design from the other chapters is that the menu is given a limited amount of space and is aligned horizontally rather than vertically. Therefore, the design relies on the search form in the left column to drive the majority of content. While not all sites will look and function similarly to the one in this chapter, elements of it can always be copied and modified to work in another design.

CASE STUDY: FULL-HEIGHT THREE-COLUMN LAYOUT

In This Chapter

- Understanding the Design's Structure
- Building the Structure
- Constructing Second-Level Pages

Since the mid-1990s, creating a three-column table-based layout in XHTML, where all three columns can each have their own background colors, has been an easily accomplished, widely used, technique. As one column is increased in height, the other two change accordingly, maintaining the same colors. In CSS, however, it takes some maneuvering to modify the code because elements that are assigned absolute positioning or are floated fall outside the normal document flow, meaning they are not controlled by parent elements. Fortunately, there is a solution to this problem.

This chapter outlines the design structure A5design has created for its clients. It is a simple, clean, hack-free solution that is used in many of the CSS designs included in this book. Following are some of the requirements it satisfies:

- The design can be easily changed from a fixed to liquid design and vice versa. The design explained in this chapter was created for 1024 × 768 resolution.
- A footer is included at the bottom of the three columns.
- No matter the height of any column, the colors of all three columns will run from the top of the page down to the footer.

As with all CSS design, it does not take much to break the code, so it does not function similarly within all browsers. Therefore, the challenge is to modify the main structure of this design so it will continue to work. Several designs included with this book use a modified version of this design.

ON THE CD

The design explained in this chapter is design 131 on the CD-ROM (photos credits: www.idlerphotography.com and www.gooligoo.com).

UNDERSTANDING THE DESIGN'S STRUCTURE

Figure 12.1 illustrates the design explained in this chapter. As with the previous three case studies, it is created to function as a fixed or liquid design. Basic fundamental differences, however, allow it to work unlike many other CSS templates. These differences, which include a couple more <DIV> containers and a new core framework, are explained later in this chapter.

Reasoning Behind Guides and the Creating of Slices in Photoshop File

There are 13 slices used from the Photoshop file to create the images for the homepage design. Figure 12.2 shows all the slices used in the file. It also outlines the 10 most important guides and slices necessary in constructing the design with XHTML and CSS.

FIGURE 12.1   The full-height three-column design explained in this chapter.

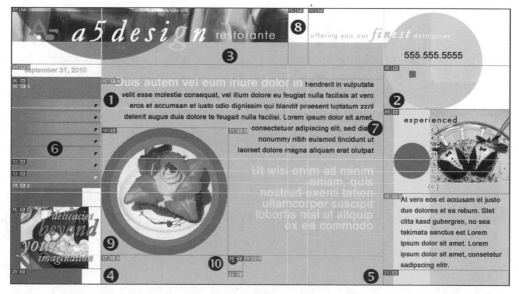

FIGURE 12.2   Ten of the most important guides and slices used to build the design in this chapter.

Following are explanations of the guides and slices illustrated in Figure 12.2:

- The guide to the left of number 1 is used to separate the left column from the center column.
- The guide to the left of number 2 is used to separate the center column from the right column.
- The guide below number 3 is used to differentiate the header from the content below it.
- The slice to the left of number 4 is very important in understanding this new design technique because it will be repeated as a background image for the entire height of the left column.
- The slice to the right of number 5 is similar to the slice represented in number 4. It will be repeated on the right side from the top of the design, all the way to the footer. It illustrates the flexibility of this design technique because the background color does not necessarily have to extend the full column width, which is represented by number 2. This technique allows for the text to appear as though it is layered over the center column's color, even though, technically, it is included in the right column.
- The two slices below number 6 are used as the background images of the On and Off states of the menu items.
- The slice to the right of number 7 creates an image that is included in the right column. This image is noteworthy because it includes the background image, so when the image is layered over the background, the change between the two is seamless.
- The slice represented by number 8 is used to save a background image for the header. It repeats horizontally in the design for both fixed and liquid formats.
- The slice to the left of number 9 is similar to the slice to the right of number 7 in that it includes the background image, which is repeated for the full height of the left column.
- The slice to the right of number 10 is used as the background image in the title area for the second-level pages (see Figure 12.3).

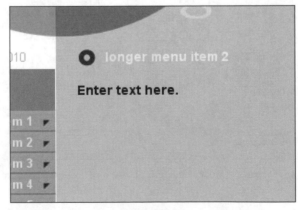

FIGURE 12.3 The background image of second-level titles that is saved from the homepage design.

Understanding the Placement of CSS Containers

There are 20 <DIV> tags used in this design. The number is higher than in the previous case studies in this book, mainly because this design structure requires a few more to accomplish its flexibility and functionality.

Following are explanations of the 10 most useful containers, shown in Figure 12.4:

- The <DIV> tag to the top left of number 1 is used for centering the design in IE 5 and 5.5.
- The <DIV> nested inside number 1, represented by number 2, illustrates the a5-body container that is used to control, among other things, the width of the design.
- Number 3 illustrates the a5-bg-left <DIV> that is nested inside the a5-body <DIV>. This container is used to run a background image down the left side of the entire design, no matter what element is layered over it.
- Number 4 represents the a5-bg-right container that runs a background image down the right side of the entire design.
- The <DIV> that contains number 5 represents the header row that is positioned across the top of the design.
- Number 6 illustrates the left column of the design.
- Number 7 points out the <DIV> that is used for the entire area to the right of the left column. This area contains both the center and right columns.
- Number 8 is the right column that is nested inside the number 7 container. It is then floated to the right.
- The container represented by number 9 is used as the footer area.
- Number 10 represents a <DIV> tag that is used for the most complex nested container, which is used for the menu.

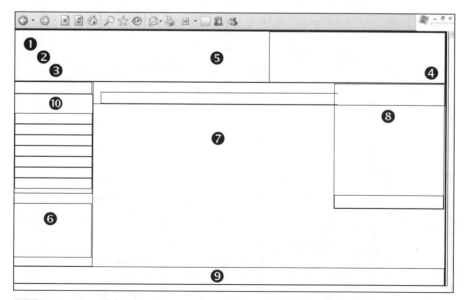

FIGURE 12.4   Ten of the most important containers used to build the design.

BUILDING THE STRUCTURE

Following are the steps to building the design. It is assumed that the Photoshop file has already been created or customized and the designer needs only to position the images and text.

Creating the XHTML and CSS Framework

The first step in building the design is to create the XHTML framework and initial CSS containers. Listing 12.1 is the code that is used to output the page shown in Figure 12.5.

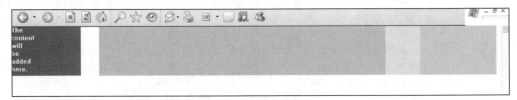

FIGURE 12.5   Basic XHTML and CSS framework for the design.

LISTING 12.1   Code for Figure 12.5

```
<!DOCTYPE html PUBLIC "-//W3C//DTD XHTML 1.0 Transitional//EN"
    "DTD/xhtml1-transitional.dtd">
<html xmlns="http://www.w3.org/1999/xhtml" xml:lang="en"
lang="en"><head><title>Design 131</title>
<meta http-equiv="Content-Type" content="text/html;
    charset=iso-8859-1" />
<style type="text/css">
/* ++++++++++ global general styles start ++++++++++*/
html, body {
    margin:0px;
    padding:0px;
    font: 12.8pt arial, helvetica, sans-serif;
    color:#000000;
    }
/* ++++++++++ global general styles end ++++++++++*/
/* ++++++++++ global structure styles start ++++++++++*/
.a5-bg-left {
    width:100%;
    margin-bottom:-10px;
background:url(images/bg-left-column.gif) repeat-y left top;
    }
```

```css
.a5-bg-right {
    width:100%;
    background:url(images/bg-right-column.gif) repeat-y right top;
    }
#a5-body-center {
    text-align:left;
    }
#a5-body {
    position: relative;
    width: 1000px; /* change this to a specific amount for a fixed
    design. E.g., 1000px. Or, it can be changed to a percentage, which
    will allow the design to be liquid */

/* remove these comment tags if the page is to be centered
    margin-left: auto;
    margin-right: auto;*/
    text-align:left;
    background:#7ED0D4 url(images/bg-right-column.gif) repeat-y right
        top;
    border:0px solid #000000;
    }
/* ++++++++++ global structure styles end ++++++++++*/
</style>
</head>
<body>
<div id="a5-body-centerv>
    <div id="a5-body">
        <div class="a5-bg-left">
        <div class="a5-bg-right">
            <b><span style="color:#ffffff;">The<br />
            content<br />
            will<br />
            be<br />
            added<br />
            here.</b><br /> </span>
        </div>
    </div>
</div>
</body>
</html>
```

There are several things to note about the code in Listing 12.1:

- The CSS style sheet is commented into two sections. The `global general styles` comment tags contain the general styles, such as the formatting of the `<HTML>` and `<BODY>` tags, hyperlinks, and fonts. The `global structure styles` comment tags include the styles used to define the structure of the design and elements included in that structure.
- Several rules define the `<HTML>` and `<BODY>` tags. The `margin` and `padding` properties are used to ensure that the design is placed in the very top-left corner of the browser with no space between the design and the edges. The default font style for the site is set using the shorthand `FONT` property. Defining the default font color is accomplished with the `COLOR` property. The background color also is assigned to ensure that all browsers display the same color, which is not always the case.
- The `a5-body-center` and `a5-body` rules are used to force the design to the left side of the browser screen with a fixed width of 1000 pixels. If the designer wants to fill the full width of the screen, the value of `1000px` needs to be changed to `100%`. If, however, the designer wants to simply justify the design to the left, the value of the `text-align` property in the `a5-body-center` rule needs to be changed from `center` to `left`. The `margin-left` and `margin-right` properties in the `a5-body` rule ensure that the extra white space is split evenly on both sides.
- The big difference at this stage, compared to the previous case studies in Chapters 9, 10, and 11, is the addition of the `a5-bg-left` and `a5-bg-right` classes and `<DIV>` containers. These provide relatively positioned containers for the entire site to be nested within. The `a5-bg-left` `<DIV>` runs its background image down the left side, while the `a5-bg-right` runs its background image down the right side. Thus, rather than using browser-generated colors, the background images, which are found at the bottom-left and bottom-right corners (see Figure 12.6) of the Photoshop design, are repeated.
- A background color is added to the `a5-body` container to give the center column color.

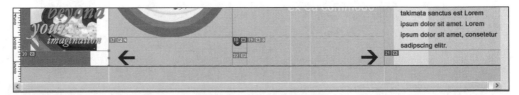

FIGURE 12.6   Slices, indicated by the left and right arrows, that are used to create the left and right background images that repeat down the design.

The `a5-bg-left` rule has the `margin-bottom` property added with a value of `-10px`. This ensures that the background images will not extend past the footer in some browsers. When the content is added to the core area, without any columns or positioning, it shows that the background images repeat vertically (refer to Figure 12.5).

If the length of the content is increased, the background images repeat accordingly (see Figure 12.7).

FIGURE 12.7   Text added to the design to illustrate how both background images will repeat vertically.

Adding the Rows and Columns to the Framework

Unlike in the previous case studies, the row and column framework of this design is explained upfront because it all works together to create a flexible design. Once understood, the content just needs to be added into these containers. Listing 12.2 is the code that is added to create the updated page in Figure 12.8.

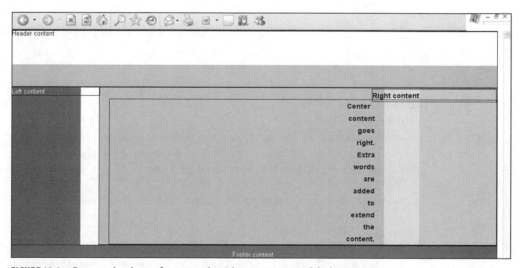

FIGURE 12.8   Row and column framework without content added to it.

The newly added code is bold to differentiate it from the existing code that is being built upon in this example

LISTING 12.2   Code for Figure 12.8

```
<!DOCTYPE html PUBLIC "-//W3C//DTD XHTML 1.0 Transitional//EN"
    "DTD/xhtml1-transitional.dtd">
<html xmlns="http://www.w3.org/1999/xhtml" xml:lang="en"
lang="en"><head><title>Design 131</title>
<meta http-equiv="Content-Type" content="text/html;
    charset=iso-8859-1" />
<style type="text/css">
/* ++++++++++ global general styles start ++++++++++*/
html, body {
    margin:0px;
    padding:0px;
    font: 12.8pt arial, helvetica, sans-serif;
    color:#000000;
    }
/* ++++++++++ global general styles end ++++++++++*/
/* ++++++++++ global structure styles start ++++++++++*/
.a5-bg-left {
    width:100%;
    margin-bottom:-10px;
    background:url(images/bg-left-column.gif) repeat-y left top;
    }
.a5-bg-right {
    width:100%;
    background:url(images/bg-right-column.gif) repeat-y right top;
    }
#a5-body-center {
    text-align:left;
    }
#a5-body {
    position: relative;
    width: 1000px; /* change this to a specific amount for a fixed
        design. E.g., 1000px. Or, it can be changed to a percentage,
        which will allow the design to be liquid */

/* remove these comment tags if the page is to be centered
    margin-left: auto;
    margin-right: auto;*/
    text-align:left;
    background:#7ED0D4 url(images/bg-right-column.gif) repeat-y right
```

```css
        top;
    border:0px solid #000000;
    }
#a5-header {
    position:relative;
    left:0px;
    top:0px;
    height:117px;
    background: url(images/bg-header.gif) repeat-x;
    border:1px solid #000000;
    }
#a5-column-left {
    float:left;
    width:181px;
    height:auto;
    border:1px solid #000000;
    }
#a5-body-content {
    position:relative;
    margin-left:181px;
    border:1px solid #000000;
    }
    #a5-column-center {
        position:relative;
        left:0px;
        top:0px;
        margin:23px 0px 0px 20px;
        font: bold 10.8pt arial, helvetica, sans-serif;
        line-height:19pt;
        border:1px solid #000000;
        }
    #a5-column-right {
        float:right;
        width:250px;
        margin-top:-23px;
        text-align:left;
        border:1px solid #000000;
        }
#a5-footer {
    clear:both;
    text-align:center;
    line-height:35px;
    background:#4A7A7D;
    border:1px solid #000000;
    }
```

```
/* ++++++++++ global structure styles end ++++++++++*/
</style>
</head>
<body>
<div id="a5-body-center">
    <div id="a5-body">
        <div class="a5-bg-left">
        <div class="a5-bg-right">
<!- ###### header start ###### ->
            <div id="a5-header">
            Header content
            </div>
<!- ###### header end ###### ->
<!- ###### left column start ###### ->
            <div id="a5-column-left">
                <span style="color:#ffffff;">Left content</span>
            </div>
<!- ###### left column end ###### ->
<!- ###### body content start ###### ->
            <div id="a5-body-content">
                <div id="a5-column-center">
                    <div id="a5-column-right">
                        Right content
                    </div>
                    <div style="margin-right:246px;text-align:right;">
                        Center<br />content<br />goes<br />right.<br />
                            Extra<br />words<br />are<br />added<br />
                            to<br />extend<br />the<br />content.
                    </div>
                </div>
            </div>
<!- ###### footer start ###### ->
            <div id="a5-footer"><span style="color:#ffffff;">Footer
                content</span></div>
<!- ###### footer end ###### ->
<!- ###### body content end ###### ->
        </div>
        </div>
    </div>
</div>
</body>
</html>
```

There are several things to note about the code in Listing 12.2:

- The `a5-header` row is the first structural element to be added. It is given relative positioning so it expands the full width of the page. It also is assigned a height of 117 pixels so the container collapses perfectly around the contents in all browsers. A horizontally repeating background is added to fill the space between the images and fill extra space if the design is changed to a liquid format.
- The `a5-column-left` rule floats the left column to the left side, under the header row. The width of the column is set to 181 pixels.

The border of the various containers is set to 1 for demonstration purposes for this step. They are reset to 0 in the final code.

- The `a5-body-content` is added under the header area to contain the center and right columns. It is given relative positioning to fill the width of the page. It is assigned a left margin of 181 pixels, so any content in it abuts the left column. One of the tricks to this design is to set the right margin of the center content at the local level. This ensures that the content does not cross over into the right column because it is nested inside this container. The right margin for the center area is set at 246 pixels. To position the content that will be added to this container, the top margin is set to 23 pixels, and the left is set to 20 pixels.

Technically, the right column is 250 pixels wide, so the right margin of the center content should be set to 250, instead of 246, to avoid overlapping. In this design, however, 246 pixels is acceptable.

- As mentioned in the previous note, the `a5-column-right` container is floated to the right inside the `a5-column-center` `<DIV>`. By floating it to the right and positioning the `bg-right-column.gif` image in the `a5-bg-right` container to the right, the background image of the column and the background of the image will always align with one another, whether the design is fixed or liquid. Because the center container is given a top margin of 23 pixels, the right column has the top margin set to –23 pixels, so it will be mortised with the header row. This is why the words "center content" and "right content" are set at different heights in Figure 12.8. The words also are not aligned vertically because the right column is set to 250 pixels, while the right margin of the center content is set to 246 pixels, as mentioned earlier.
- The `a5-footer` row is added outside the `a5-body-content` container, with the `clear` property set to both. This keeps the content in the `a5-left-column` and `a5-center-column` containers from crossing over the row.

Populating the Header, Footer, and Columns with Content

Once the framework of the design has been added, the designer need only populate the areas with the appropriate content. Because this styling is very similar to the previous three case studies, the discussion for Listing 12.3 is limited to unique aspects of this design. Figure 12.9 is the completed homepage design that is outlined in Listing 12.3.

 The newly added code is bold to differentiate it from the existing code that is being built upon in this example

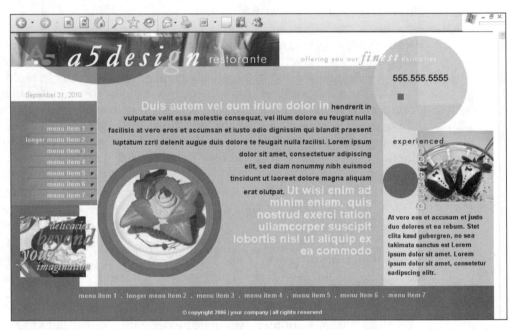

FIGURE 12.9   The completed design after the various containers have been populated and styled.

LISTING 12.3   Code for Figure 12.9

```
<!DOCTYPE html PUBLIC "-//W3C//DTD XHTML 1.0 Transitional//EN"
    "DTD/xhtml1-transitional.dtd">
<html xmlns="http://www.w3.org/1999/xhtml" xml:lang="en"
lang="en"><head><title>Design 131</title>
<meta http-equiv="Content-Type" content="text/html;
    charset=iso-8859-1" />
<style type="text/css">
/* ++++++++++ global general styles start ++++++++++*/
html, body {
```

```
        margin:0px;
        padding:0px;
        font: 12.8pt arial, helvetica, sans-serif;
        color:#000000;
        }
a:link { color:#D0FAFC; }
a:visited { color:#D0FAFC; }
a:active { color:#D0FAFC; }
a:hover { color:#000000; }

a.linklist1:link { text-decoration:none;color:#E9DF40;}
a.linklist1:visited { text-decoration:none;color:#E9DF40;}
a.linklist1:active { text-decoration:none;color:#E9DF40;}
a.linklist1:hover { text-decoration:underline;color:#ffffff;}

.color-1-text-98 {
    font-family:arial, helvetica, sans-serif;
    font-size:9.8pt;
    color: #16C7C1;
    }

.color-2-text-8 {
    font-family:arial, helvetica, sans-serif;
    font-size:8pt;
    color: #D0FAFC;
    }
.color-2-text-10 {
    font-family:arial, helvetica, sans-serif;
    font-size:10pt;
    color: #D0FAFC;
    }
.color-2-text-18 {
    font-family:arial, helvetica, sans-serif;
    font-size:18pt;
    color: #D0FAFC;
    }
.color-3-text-88 {
    font-family:arial, helvetica, sans-serif;
    font-size:8.8pt;
    color: #ffffff;
    }
/* ++++++++++ global general styles end ++++++++++*/
/* ++++++++++ global structure styles start ++++++++++*/
.a5-bg-left {
```

```
        width:100%;
        margin-bottom:-10px;
        background:url(images/bg-left-column.gif) repeat-y left top;
        }
    .a5-bg-right {
        width:100%;
        background:url(images/bg-right-column.gif) repeat-y right top;
        }
    #a5-body-center {
        text-align:left;
        }
    #a5-body {
        position: relative;
        width: 1000px; /* change this to a specific amount for a fixed
            design. E.g., 1000px. Or, it can be changed to a percentage,
            which will allow the design to be liquid */
/* remove these comment tags if the page is to be centered
        margin-left: auto;
        margin-right: auto;*/
        text-align:left;
        background:#7ED0D4 url(images/bg-right-column.gif) repeat-y right
            top;
        border:0px solid #000000;
        }
    #a5-header {
        position:relative;
        left:0px;
        top:0px;
        height:117px;
        background: url(images/bg-header.gif) repeat-x;
        border:0px solid #000000;
        }
        #a5-header-right {
            position:absolute;
            right:0px;
            top:0px;
            height:117px;
            border:0px solid #000000;
            }
    #a5-column-left {
        float:left;
        width:181px;
        border:0px solid #000000;
        }
```

```
        #a5-date {
            text-align:center;
            background:#ffffff;
            vertical-align:50%;
            line-height:26px;
            }
        #a5-menu {
            width:181px;
            padding:44px 0px 10px 0px;
            font:bold 12.8pt arial, helvetica, sans-serif;
            background: url(images/bg-menu.gif) repeat-y 0px 0px;
            }
        #a5-menu a {
            display:block;
            text-align:left;
            line-height:23px;
            vertical-align:50%;
            text-align:right;
            padding:0px 25px 0px 10px;
            text-decoration:none;
            background: url(images/bg-menu-off.jpg) no-repeat 0px 0px;
            color:#DEEFF0;
            }
        #a5-menu a:hover {
            background: url(images/bg-menu-on.jpg) no-repeat 0px 0px;
            color:#ffffff;
            }
        #a5-photo-bottom-left {
            margin:23px 0px 20px 0px;
            border:0px solid #000000;
            }
#a5-body-content {
    position:relative;
    margin-left:181px;
    border:0px solid #000000;
    }
    #a5-column-center {
        position:relative;
        left:0px;
        top:0px;
        margin:23px 0px 0px 20px;
        font: bold 10.8pt arial, helvetica, sans-serif;
        line-height:19pt;
        border:0px solid #000000;
        }
```

```
        #a5-column-right {
            float:right;
            width:250px;
            margin-top:-23px;
            text-align:left;
            border:0px solid #000000;
            }
        #a5-bottom-right-text {
            font: bold 12.8pt arial, helvetica, sans-serif;
            line-height:14pt;
            padding:0px 10px 10px 30px;
            }
#a5-footer {
    clear:both;
    text-align:center;
    line-height:35px;
    background:#4A7A7D;
    border:0px solid #000000;
    }
/* ++++++++++ global structure styles end ++++++++++*/
</style>
</head>
<body>
<div id="a5-body-center">
    <div id="a5-body">
        <div class="a5-bg-left">
        <div class="a5-bg-right">
<!-- ###### header start ###### -->
            <div id="a5-header">
                <div><img src="images/header-left.jpg" width="557"
                    height="117" alt="" border="0" /></div>
                <div id="a5-header-right"><a href="index.htm"><img
                    src="images/header-right.gif" width="403"
                    height="117" alt="" border="0" /></a></div>
            </div>
<!-- ###### header end ###### -->
<!-- ###### left column start ###### -->
            <div id="a5-column-left">
                <div id="a5-date" class="color-1-text-98">September
                    31, 2010</div>
                <div id="a5-menu">
                    <a href="index.htm">menu item 1</a>
                    <a href="menu-item-2.htm">longer menu item 2</a>
                    <a href="menu-item-3.htm">menu item 3</a>
```

```
                    <a href="index.htm">menu item 4</a>
                    <a href="index.htm">menu item 5</a>
                    <a href="index.htm">menu item 6</a>
                    <a href="index.htm">menu item 7</a>
            </div>
            <div id="a5-photo-bottom-left"><a href="index.htm">
                <img src="images/photo-bottom-left.jpg"
                width="180" height="125" alt="" border="0"
                /></a></div>
        </div>
<!— ###### left column end ###### —>
<!— ###### body content start ###### —>
        <div id="a5-body-content">
            <div id="a5-column-center">
                <div id="a5-column-right">
                    <div><img src="images/image-right-column-
                        top.gif" width="250" height="88" alt=""
                        border="0" /></div>
                    <div><img src="images/image-right-column-
                        middle.jpg" width="250" height="169"
                        alt="" border="0" /></div>
                    <div id="a5-bottom-right-text">
At vero eos et accusam et justo duo dolores et ea rebum. Stet clita
    kasd gubergren, no sea takimata sanctus est Lorem ipsum dolor sit
    amet. Lorem ipsum dolor sit amet, consetetur sadipscing elitr.
                    </div>
                </div>
                <div style="margin-right:246px;text-align:right;">
<span class="color-2-text-18">Duis autem vel eum iriure dolor in
    </span> hendrerit in vulputate velit esse molestie consequat, vel
    illum dolore eu feugiat nulla facilisis at vero eros et accumsan
    et iusto odio dignissim qui blandit praesent luptatum <span
    style="float:left;padding:10px 10px 10px 0px;margin-left:-20px;">
    <img src="images/photo-center-middle.jpg" width="256" height="256"
    alt="" border="0" /></span>zzril delenit augue duis dolore te
    feugait nulla facilisi. Lorem ipsum dolor sit amet, consectetuer
    adipiscing elit, sed diam nonummy nibh euismod tincidunt ut
    laoreet dolore magna aliquam erat olutpat. <span class="color-2-
    text-18">Ut wisi enim ad minim eniam, quis nostrud exerci tation
    ullamcorper suscipit lobortis nisl ut aliquip ex ea commodo</span>
                </div>
            </div>
        </div>
<!— ###### footer start ###### —>
```

```
              <div id="a5-footer"><div style="margin:0px 0px 10px 0px;
                 font-weight:bold;" class="color-2-text-10">
                    <a href="index.htm" class="linklist1">menu item 1
                       </a>  .  <a href="menu-
                       item-2.htm" class="linklist1">longer menu item
                       2</a>  .  <a href="menu-
                       item-3.htm" class="linklist1">menu item 3</a>
                         .  <a href="index.htm"
                       class="linklist1">menu item 4</a>  
                       .  <a href="index.htm" class=
                       "linklist1">menu item 5</a>  . 
                        <a href="index.htm" class="linklist1">
                       menu item 6</a>  .  <a
                       href="index.htm" class="linklist1">menu
                       item 7</a><br />
<span class="color-2-text-8">&copy; copyright 2006 | your company |
    all rights reserved</span></div></div>
<!- ###### footer end ###### ->
<!- ###### body content end ###### ->
        </div>
        </div>
    </div>
</div>
</body>
</html>
```

There are several things to note about the code in Listing 12.3:

- The linklist1 rules are added to style the second menu that runs horizontally in the footer. This is the same menu that is included in the left column. It is added to increase usability of the design by providing navigation at the bottom of the page so the user does not have to scroll back up the page.
- The a5-menu container is given a background image that is layered over the image that is repeated for the entire left column. Then each menu item is assigned yet another background image when an item is moused on and off. Not only is this layering seamless, but it requires less download time because all three images are of nominal file size. This layering of background images provides the design with more flexibility than with XHTML table-based designs because Netscape 4.7 always had difficulty with more than two nested background images.
- The a5-bottom-right-text container is assigned a left margin of 30 pixels to position the text to the right of the background color in the center column. Because this color is included in the right column background, which creates an overlapping effect, the text needs to be positioned differently if it is to remain over just the right two colors.

CONSTRUCTING SECOND-LEVEL PAGES

Similar to the previous three case studies, the homepage is reused and customized for secondary pages. The technique is the same, except for a couple of differences. One difference is that the 246-pixel right margin of the center column is removed so the text will run the full width of the content area. The second modification is that the `a5-bg-right` container is renamed `a5-bg-right-sl` for the full-page version, which is the Menu Item 3 page. Once it is renamed, the `a5-bg-right-sl` rule is added, which uses a background color, rather than an image, to populate the body of the page (see Figure 12.10).

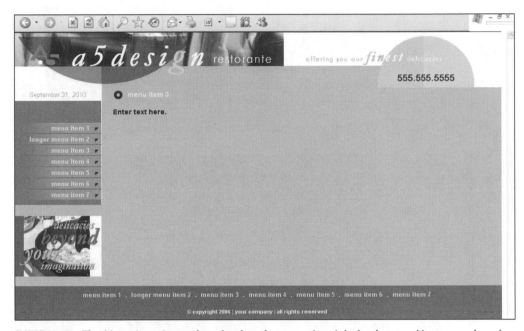

FIGURE 12.10   The Menu Item 3 template that has the repeating right background image replaced with a CSS-generated color that fills the page.

SUMMARY

The design explained in this case study is a succinct way to create one that has the background colors extended throughout all three columns. The coding is simple to understand and use, requiring no hacks or JavaScript. Not only are background images used to accomplish this technique, but the core structure of the design is written to allow for content that is scalable and will not run beyond the footer. As with other designs in this book, it allows for the page to be either a fixed-width or liquid design. Of all the design structures explained and included in this book, this one will, most likely, be the most widely used because of its flexibility and scalability.

13

CASE STUDY: BACKGROUND-BASED DESIGN

In This Chapter

- Understanding the Design's Structure
- Building the Structure
- Constructing Second-Level Pages

Another method that allows a designer to be creative is to base a design largely around a background image. With such a design, the majority of graphical elements are included with the image itself. The main con to such a design is that the background image can be a larger download size. The pro to this method is that the designer has more flexibility in terms of creating imagery and a layout that isn't limited as much by XHTML or CSS. Another advantage is that a designer can create designs that can have their look and feel easily modified by replacing only one image, whether on the homepage or second-level pages.

The design in this chapter is not only used to create a mood with the graphics, but the homepage image also provides for the boxes *in which* to place the content. The downside to this design is that the sections are not scalable. In other words, if the client wishes to expand the content, the imagery, along with the XHTML and CSS, would need to be modified so the text did not flow outside of the boxes. The upside is the boxes can look much more attractive because the designer isn't constricted as much by having to use various images, such as background or nested images, to create the look and feel.

This design structure isn't robust or flexible enough for many sites. There are, however, an increasing number of clients who request that their sites use large, powerful graphics to communicate, rather than relying just on text. For clients such as these, this type of design may very well satisfy their needs.

     The design explained in this chapter is design 141 on the CD-ROM (photos credits: www.ronsternimages.com and www.a5design.com).

Understanding the Design's Structure

Figure 13.1 represents the background-based design explained in this chapter. Unlike the previous case studies in this book, the homepage of this design not only uses a background image for the majority of the imagery of the design, but it also uses fixed boxes for the content. Because the boxes are not scalable, the text inside them has absolute positioning assigned to it. Normally, such positioning might be a problem because it does not adhere to document flow, which can change how the text in other areas relates to increased or decreased content.

The majority of the text is still provided as XHTML text so that search engines can read it. Because most elements of the imagery, including photos layered over photos and the larger text, are part of the background image, the user will not be able to click on them. This is why another design trick is employed. Spacer GIFs, friend of the table-based designer, are sized, positioned, and hyperlinked accordingly over the areas of the design that need to be clickable. It's similar to the older method of creating "hot spots" with image mapping.

FIGURE 13.1   The background-based design explained in this chapter.

Reasoning Behind Guides and the Creating of Slices in the Photoshop File

There is only one slice used for the homepage file of the design and two slices used for the secondary page design. Number 1 in Figure 13.2 illustrates the file that is used to provide the homepage images.

FIGURE 13.2   The only slice, identified by number 1, that is used to build the homepage design.

The goal of this design is to create a more graphically advanced design than with the designs in the previous case studies. To attain this for the current site, the design uses transparent images and curved corners coupled with various layered images. While much of this design could be accomplished using techniques explained previously in this book, a more simple design structure was used to provide the reader with another possibility.

The one thing to note about Figure 13.2, other than that there is only one slice, is that the bottom of the design uses a gradation that eventually turns into the color that is used for the background color of the design. This layout method allows the designer to simply set the background color of the page, identified by number 2 in Figure 13.3, to coincide with the color that is set just before the bottom of the slice is reached, identified by number 1 in the same figure.

FIGURE 13.3   The colors on both sides of the bottom of the slice, represented by numbers 1 and 2, are designed to be the same color, providing a seamless transition of images.

This method of blending colors of an image into the background color is also used for the secondary page. Figure 13.4 shows how the colors were blended into the black below the trees, number 1, with the background color of the page, number 2.

The other slice to note in the secondary-level page (see Figure 13.4) is just to the left of number 3. This slice is used as a background image for the page title <DIV>.

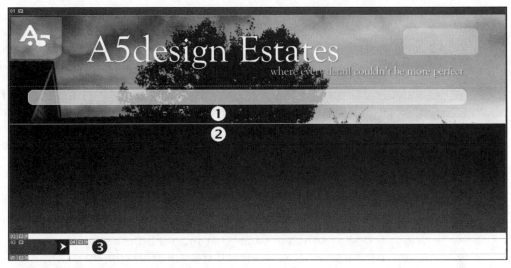

FIGURE 13.4   The blending technique used for the homepage in Figure 13.3 is employed exactly the same way for the second-level design.

Understanding the Placement of CSS Containers

There are 18 `<DIV>` tags that are used to create the homepage layout of this design. Many of them serve the same basic purpose for the structure of the site, as they do in the case study in Chapter 12. The thing to note about this design is that the majority of them are assigned absolute positioning.

Following are explanations of the 10 most useful containers, shown in Figure 13.5.

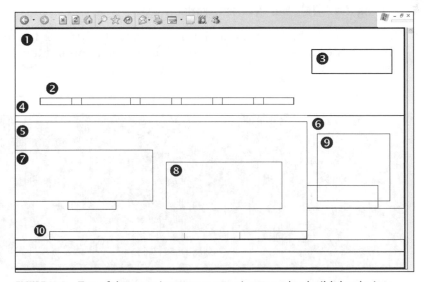

FIGURE 13.5   Ten of the most important containers used to build the design.

- The <DIV> tag to the top left of number 1 is used for centering the design in IE 5 and 5.5. It also represents the top left corner of the a5-body container that is used to control, among other things, the width of the design. Number 1 also points out where the "complete access" code is included for the top right portion of the design.
- Number 2 is placed right above the a5-menu-box <DIV> it represents. This container not only controls the absolute placement of the menu, but it also includes a <DIV>, a5-menu, that is nested inside it to provide style for each menu item.
- The top-right <DIV> tag, a5-header-right, is illustrated by the number 3. This is a fixed area that is used for the login area of the site.
- Number 4 represents the header <DIV>, which contains the <DIV> tags that are illustrated by numbers 2 and 3.
- The top-left corner of the left column begins at number 5.
- Number 6 represents the right column of the design.
- Number 7 shows the container that includes the hyperlinked spacer.gif and "winter & summer" text in the left column. This container, as well as the ones used for the center column content (represented by number 8) and the right column content (represented by number 9), are assigned absolute positioning.
- The bottom text area is positioned using the <DIV> to the right of number 10.

BUILDING THE STRUCTURE

Following are the steps to building the design. It is assumed the Photoshop file has already been created or customized and the designer needs only to position the images and text.

Creating the XHTML and CSS Framework

The first step in building the design is to create the XHTML framework and initial CSS containers. Listing 13.1 is the code that is used to output the page shown in Figure 13.6.

FIGURE 13.6   Basic XHTML and CSS framework for the design.

LISTING 13.1   Code for Figure 13.6

```
<!DOCTYPE html PUBLIC "-//W3C//DTD XHTML 1.0 Transitional//EN"
DTD/xhtml1-transitional.dtd">
<html xmlns="http://www.w3.org/1999/xhtml" xml:lang="en"
lang="en"><head><title></title>
<meta http-equiv="Content-Type" content="text/html; charset=iso-8859-1" />
<style type="text/css">
  /* ++++++++++ global general styles start ++++++++++*/
  html, body {
    margin:0px;
    padding:0px;
    font:10pt arial, helvetica, sans-serif;
    background:#000000;
    color:#ffffff;
    }
  /* ++++++++++ global general styles end ++++++++++*/
  /* ++++++++++ global structure styles start ++++++++++*/
  #a5-body-center {
    text-align:center;
    }
  #a5-body {
    position:relative;
    width:1000px;
    margin-left:auto;
    margin-right:auto;
    text-align:left;
    background:#6A4203 url(images/bg-body.jpg) no-repeat;
    border:0px solid #ffffff;
    }
  /* ++++++++++ global structure styles end ++++++++++*/
</style>
</head>
<body>
<div id="a5-body-center">
  <div id="a5-body">
  This is the main body area.
  </div>
</div>
</body>
</html>
```

There are several things to note about the code in Listing 13.1:

- The CSS style sheet is commented into two sections. The global general styles comment tags contain the general styles, such as the formatting of the <HTML>

and `<BODY>` tags, hyperlinks, and fonts. The `global structure styles` comment tags include the styles used to define the structure of the design and elements included in that structure.

- Several rules define the `<HTML>` and `<BODY>` tags. The `margin` and `padding` properties are used to ensure that the design is placed in the very top-left corner of the browser, with no space between the design and the edges. The default font style for the site is set using the shorthand `FONT` property. Defining the default font color is accomplished with the `COLOR` property. The background color also is assigned to ensure that all browsers display the same color, which is not always the case.

- How this design differs from the others is that the majority of graphical elements are created using the background image. This image, `bg-body.jpg`, is declared in the `a5-body` rule. Figure 13.7 illustrates that when more content is added to the design, this image will begin to appear. The background color of #6A4203 also is added to the rule. This is the color that is at the bottom of the `bg-body.jpg` image, which enables the two to blend into each other.

- The `a5-body-center` and `a5-body` rules are used to center the design in the browser window and to give it a fixed width of 1000 pixels. If the designer wants to fill the full width of the screen for higher resolutions, the value of `1000px` needs to be changed to `100%`. If, however, the designer wants to simply justify the design to the left, the value of the `text-align` property in the `a5-body-center` rule needs to be changed from `center` to `left`. The `margin-left` and `margin-right` properties in the `a5-body` rule ensure that the extra white space is split evenly on both sides.

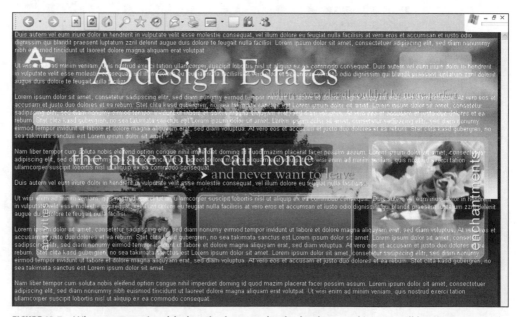

FIGURE 13.7   When content is added to the base code, the background image will begin to appear.

Adding the Header Area to the Framework

Depending on the design, the header area is usually the first primary area of content that needs to be added. This is certainly true for this case study. The header area not only contains the menu and the code for the login area, but it also takes up 220 pixels of vertical space with the design. Figure 13.8 shows the design with the header content, XHTML, and CSS added, which is included in Listing 13.2.

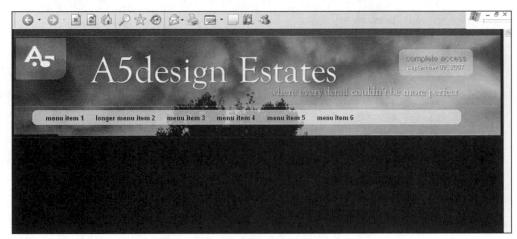

FIGURE 13.8   The design with the header content, XHTML, and CSS added.

LISTING 13.2   Code for Figure 13.8

```
<!DOCTYPE html PUBLIC "-//W3C//DTD XHTML 1.0 Transitional//EN" "DTD/xhtml1-
transitional.dtd">
<html xmlns="http://www.w3.org/1999/xhtml" xml:lang="en"
lang="en"><head><title></title>
<meta http-equiv="Content-Type" content="text/html; charset=iso-8859-1" />
<style type="text/css">
  /* ++++++++++ global general styles start ++++++++++*/
  html, body {
    margin:0px;
    padding:0px;
    font:10pt arial, helvetica, sans-serif;
    background:#000000;
    color:#ffffff;
    }
  a:link { text-decoration:none;color:#FF8037; }
  a:visited { text-decoration:none;color:#FF8037; }
  a:active { text-decoration:none;color:#FF8037; }
  a:hover { text-decoration:underline;color:#ffffff; }
```

```css
.color-1-text-10 {
  font: 10pt arial, helvetica, sans-serif;
  color: #ffffff;
  }
.color-1-text-10 {
  font: 10pt arial, helvetica, sans-serif;
  color: #ffffff;
  }
.color-1-text-13 {
  font: 13pt arial, helvetica, sans-serif;
  color: #ffffff;
  }
.color-2-text-10 {
  font: 10pt arial, helvetica, sans-serif;
  color: #92684B;
  }
.color-2-text-13 {
  font: 13pt arial, helvetica, sans-serif;
  color: #92684B;
  }
.color-3-text-8 {
  font: 8pt arial, helvetica, sans-serif;
  color: #A48B65;
  }
.color-4-text-12 {
  font: 12pt arial, helvetica, sans-serif;
  color: #000000;
  }
/* ++++++++++ global general styles end ++++++++++*/
/* ++++++++++ global structure styles start ++++++++++*/
#a5-body-center {
  text-align:center;
  }
#a5-body {
  position:relative;
  width:1000px;
  margin-left:auto;
  margin-right:auto;
  text-align:left;
  background:#6A4203 url(images/bg-body.jpg) no-repeat;
  border:0px solid #ffffff;
  }
```

```
#a5-header {
  position:relative;
  left:0px;
  top:0px;
  height:220px;
  border:0px solid #000000;
  }
  #a5-header-right {
    position:absolute;
    top:52px;
    right:30px;
    height:60px;
    width:200px;
    text-align:center;
    border:0px solid #000000;
    }
  #a5-header-right-bg {
    position:absolute;
    top:53px;
    right:29px;
    height:60px;
    width:200px;
    text-align:center;
    border:0px solid #000000;
    }
  #a5-menu-box {
    position:absolute;
    top:175px;
    left:65px;
    line-height:40px;
    vertical-align:50%;
    color:#ffffff;
    font:bold 10pt arial, helvetica, sans-serif;
    border:0px solid #000000;
    }
    #a5-menu a {
      display:inline;
      text-decoration:none;
      color:#030303;
      }
    #a5-menu a:hover {
      text-decoration:underline;
      color:#97370C;
      }
```

```
    /* ++++++++++ global structure styles end ++++++++++*/
</style>

</head>
<body>
<div id="a5-body-center">
  <div id="a5-body">
<!- ###### header start ###### ->
    <div id="a5-header">
      <div><a href="index.htm"><img src="images/spacer.gif"
width="770" height="157" alt="" border="0" /></a></div>
      <div id="a5-header-right-bg" class="color-3-text-13">complete
access<br /><span class="color-3-text-10">september 09, 2007</span></div>
      <div id="a5-header-right" class="color-1-text-13"><a
href="index.htm">complete access</a><br /><span class="color-1-text-
10">september 09, 2007</span></div>
<!- ###### menu start ###### ->
        <div id="a5-menu-box">
          <div id="a5-menu">
            <a href="index.htm">menu item 1</a>
                
            <a href="menu-item-2.htm">longer menu item 2</a>
                
            <a href="menu-item-3.htm">menu item 3</a>
                
            <a href="menu-item-4.htm">menu item 4</a>
                
            <a href="index.htm">menu item 5</a>
                
            <a href="index.htm">menu item 6</a>
          </div>
        </div>
<!- ###### menu end ###### ->
    </div>
<!- ###### header end ###### ->
  </div>
</div>
</body>
</html>
```

There are several things to note about the code in Listing 13.2:

- The basic hyperlink rules have been added to the design. These are used to style the "complete access" text in the top-right corner. They are also used to hyper-link the spacer.gif, which is the first of several such images that are layered over their respective visual elements in the background image. This method allows the designer to create more attractive and integrated graphics elements while also easily enabling them to be hyperlinked. Figure 13.9 shows the header area with the `spacer.gif` layered over the area. The border of the image has been turned on and set to `2px` to show how it's positioned in the code.

FIGURE 13.9   The header area with a `spacer.gif` layered over the title area, which enables the designer to hyperlink the area.

- The "complete access september 9, 2007" text and code in the top right corner is duplicated so it can be layered on top of itself. This enables the designer to create an XHTML-based drop shadow. This removes the need to create an image that not only takes more time to create and implement, but it also isn't search-engine and text-reader friendly. Both the `a5-header-right` and `a5-header-right-bg` styles that are used to create these duplicate styles are assigned absolute positioning. The latter moves the lower layer to the right and down 1 pixel. The important thing to note is the way that browsers position the `<DIV>` containers. The `a5-header-right-bg` container needs to come first in the XHTML code. This is because it is rendered, and then the layer than has a hyperlink assigned to it is rendered on top of it. If it is not positioned this way in the XHTML, the hyperlink will not work properly among the various browsers.
- The `a5-menu-box` selector uses absolute positioning to place the menu area. The `a5-menu a` rule is then applied to every hyperlinked menu item that is included in the container. The `display:inline;` property/value combination determines that the menu items will be output horizontally in a line. The `a5-menu a:hover;` property/value combination not only changes the color of the hyperlink when it is moused over, but it also turns on the underline below the link (see Figure 13.10).

FIGURE 13.10   The Longer Menu Item 2 link when it is moused over.

Adding the Body Content and Footer

The structure of this design's body content is not overly complicated compared to the previous designs. While it has left and center columns, they aren't used for the majority of the placement of items, unlike in the previous case studies. Rather, most of the content is positioned autonomously of other content because it is assigned absolute positioning. Listing 13.3 is all the code that is used to create the full design in Figure 13.11.

FIGURE 13.11   Design with the body content and footer added.

LISTING 13.3   Code for Figure 13.11

```
<!DOCTYPE html PUBLIC "-//W3C//DTD XHTML 1.0 Transitional//EN" "DTD/xhtml1-
transitional.dtd">
<html xmlns="http://www.w3.org/1999/xhtml" xml:lang="en"
lang="en"><head><title></title>
<meta http-equiv="Content-Type" content="text/html; charset=iso-8859-1" />
<style type="text/css">
/* ++++++++++ global general styles start ++++++++++*/
html, body {
  margin:0px;
  padding:0px;
  font: 10pt arial, helvetica, sans-serif;
  background:#000000;
  color:#ffffff;
  }
a:link { text-decoration:none;color:#FF8037; }
a:visited { text-decoration:none;color:#FF8037; }
a:active { text-decoration:none;color:#FF8037; }
a:hover { text-decoration:underline;color:#ffffff; }

a.a5-right-column:link { text-decoration:none;color:#ffffff;}
a.a5-right-column:visited { text-decoration:none;color:#ffffff;}
a.a5-right-column:active { text-decoration:none;color:#ffffff;}
a.a5-right-column:hover { text-decoration:none;color:#809ED6;}

a.a5-link-light:link { text-decoration:underline;color:#ffffff;}
a.a5-link-light:visited { text-decoration:underline;color:#ffffff;}
a.a5-link-light:active { text-decoration:underline;color:#ffffff;}
a.a5-link-light:hover { text-decoration:underline;color:#92684B;}

a.a5-link-dark:link { text-decoration:underline;color:#000000;}
a.a5-link-dark:visited { text-decoration:underline;color:#000000;}
a.a5-link-dark:active { text-decoration:underline;color:#000000;}
a.a5-link-dark:hover { text-decoration:underline;color:#92684B;}
.color-1-text-10 {
  font: 10pt arial, helvetica, sans-serif;
  color: #ffffff;
  }
.color-1-text-10 {
  font: 10pt arial, helvetica, sans-serif;
  color: #ffffff;
  }
.color-1-text-13 {
  font: 13pt arial, helvetica, sans-serif;
```

```
  color: #ffffff;
  }
.color-2-text-10 {
  font: 10pt arial, helvetica, sans-serif;
  color: #92684B;
  }
.color-2-text-13 {
  font: 13pt arial, helvetica, sans-serif;
  color: #92684B;
  }
.color-3-text-8 {
  font: 8pt arial, helvetica, sans-serif;
  color: #A48B65;
  }
.color-4-text-12 {
  font: 12pt arial, helvetica, sans-serif;
  color: #000000;
  }
/* ++++++++++ global general styles end ++++++++++*/
/* ++++++++++ global structure styles start ++++++++++*/
#a5-body-center {
  text-align:center;
  }
#a5-body {
  position: relative;
  width: 1000px;
  margin-left: auto;
  margin-right: auto;
  text-align:left;
  background:#6A4203 url(images/bg-body.jpg) no-repeat;
  border:0px solid #ffffff;
  }
#a5-header {
  position:relative;
  left:0px;
  top:0px;
  height:220px;
  border:0px solid #000000;
  }
  #a5-header-right {
    position:absolute;
    top:52px;
    right:30px;
    height:60px;
```

```
            width:200px;
            text-align:center;
            border:0px solid #000000;
            }
        #a5-header-right-bg {
            position:absolute;
            top:53px;
            right:29px;
            height:60px;
            width:200px;
            text-align:center;
            border:0px solid #000000;
            }
    #a5-menu-box {
        position:absolute;
        top:175px;
        left:65px;
        line-height:40px;
        vertical-align:50%;
        color:#ffffff;
        font:bold 10pt arial, helvetica, sans-serif;
        border:0px solid #000000;
        }
        #a5-menu a {
            display:inline;
            text-decoration:none;
            color:#030303;
            }
        #a5-menu a:hover {
            text-decoration:underline;
            color:#97370C;
            }
    #a5-left-middle-text {
        position:absolute;
        left:139px;
        top:443px;
        border:0px solid #ffffff;
        }
    #a5-left-middle-image {
        position:absolute;
        left:0px;
        top:311px;
        border:0px solid #ffffff;
        }
```

```
#a5-center-middle-text {
  position:absolute;
  left:390px;
  top:342px;
  width:297px;
  line-height:17px;
  color:#ffffff;
  border:0px solid #ffffff;
  }
#a5-right-middle-image {
  position:absolute;
  right:28px;
  top:225px;
  border:0px solid #ffffff;
  }
#a5-column-left {
  float:left;
  width:750px;
  margin:15px 0px 0px 0px;
  border:0px solid #ffffff;
  }
  #a5-column-left-text {
    margin:280px 0px 0px 90px;
    border:0px solid #000000;
    }
  #a5-column-center {
    position:relative;
    left:0px;
    top:0px;
    border:0px solid #000000;
    }
    #a5-column-center-text {
      margin:177px 65px 0px 730px;
      line-height:18px;
      border:0px solid #000000;
      }
#a5-footer-separator {
  clear:both;
  height:30px;
  }
#a5-footer {
  clear:both;
  padding:0px 30px 0px 0px;
```

```
  height:40px;
  line-height:40px;
  vertical-align:80%;
  text-align:right;
  border-top:1px solid #A48B65;
  background:#482C01;
  }
/* ++++++++++ global structure styles end ++++++++++*/
</style>
</head>
<body>
<div id="a5-body-center">
  <div id="a5-body">
<!- ###### header start ###### ->
      <div id="a5-header">
        <div><a href="index.htm"><img src="images/spacer.gif"
width="770" height="157" alt="" border="0" /></a></div>
        <div id="a5-header-right-bg" class="color-2-text-
13">complete access<br /><span class="color-2-text-10">september 09,
2007</span></div>
        <div id="a5-header-right" class="color-1-text-13"><a
href="index.htm">complete access</a><br /><span class="color-1-text-
10">september 09, 2007</span></div>
<!- ###### menu start ###### ->
        <div id="a5-menu-box">
          <div id="a5-menu">
            <a href="index.htm">menu item 1</a>
                
            <a href="menu-item-2.htm">longer menu item 2</a>
                
            <a href="menu-item-3.htm">menu item 3</a>
                
            <a href="menu-item-4.htm">menu item 4</a>
                
            <a href="index.htm">menu item 5</a>
                
            <a href="index.htm">menu item 6</a>
          </div>
        </div>
<!- ###### menu end ###### ->
      </div>
<!- ###### header end ###### ->
```

```
<!-- ###### left text box start ###### -->
      <div id="a5-left-middle-text" class="color-1-text-13"><a
href="x.htm" class="a5-link-dark">winter</a> &amp; <a href="x.htm"
class="a5-link-light">summer</a></div>

      <div id="a5-left-middle-image"><a href="x.htm"><img
src="images/spacer.gif" width="355" height="130" alt="" border="0"
/></a></div>
<!-- ###### left text box end ###### -->

<!-- ###### center text box start ###### -->
      <div id="a5-center-middle-text">Duis autem i vel eum iriure
dolor nwille hendrerit in vulputate alw d ays esse molestie consequat, vel
illum dolore eu feugiat loveukl facilisis at yvero eros et ayouccumsan et
iusto odio dignissim qui blandit praesent lumoreum zzril delenit aut duis
dolore te feugait nulla facilisi. Lorthan ipsum dyouolor sit
ametknowrae</div>

      <div id="a5-right-middle-image"><img src="images/spacer.gif"
width="231" height="161" alt="" border="0" style="border:1px solid #ffffff;"
/></div>
<!-- ###### center text box end ###### -->

<!-- ###### left column start ###### -->
      <div id="a5-column-left">
        <div id="a5-column-left-text" class="color-1-text-13">
          <a href="x.htm" class="a5-link-light">"why we were
sold from day one" testimonials</a>  <span
style="color:#AD8B28;">|</span>  <a href="x.htm" class="a5-link-
light">potential options</a>  <span
style="color:#AD8B28;">|</span>  <a href="x.htm" class="a5-link-
light">lifetime guarantee</a>
        </div>
      </div>
<!-- ###### left column end ###### -->

<!-- ###### center column start ###### -->
      <div id="a5-column-center">
        <div id="a5-column-center-text">
          <span class="color-4-text-12"><strong>Be forever
changed by
          "the heart of joans'" garden
          planted in 1979</strong></span>
        </div>
      </div>
<!-- ###### center column end ###### -->
```

```
<!--########## footer start ##########-->
    <div id="a5-footer-separator"> </div>
    <div id="a5-footer" class="color-3-text-8">© copyright
2007  |  your company  |  all rights
reserved</div>
<!--########## footer end ##########-->


  </div>
</div>


</body>
</html>
```

Following are things to note about the code in Listing 13.3:

- Several custom hyperlink rules (for example, `a.a5-right-column:link { text-decoration:none;color:#ffffff;}`), along with various text rules (for example, `color-4-text-12`), have been added to the style sheet to stylize the content throughout the page.

- The `a5-left-middle-text` and `a5-left-middle-image` `<DIV>` tags are added to create the box that appears in the left column, although the visual aspect of it is assigned in the code. The container is positioned 139 pixels from the left side and 443 pixels from the top. The Winter and Summer hyperlinks are then styled with the `a5-link-dark` and `a5-link-light` styles, respectively. Figure 13.12 illustrates what the design looks like with only the left column added and with the border turned on for the `spacer.gif` that is added to make that section clickable. Because the text is in an absolutely positioned container, it does not push the footer down until code is later added into the `a5-column-left` `<DIV>`—at least in IE 6.

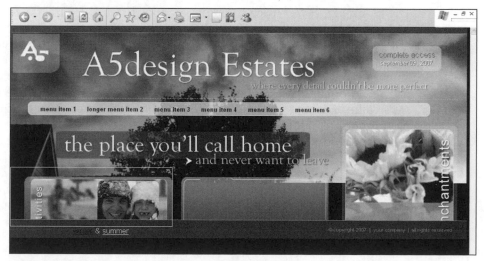

FIGURE 13.12   Design with the text for the left box added.

- Once the left box has been populated, the `a5-center-middle-text` container is added. This container is positioned 390 pixels from the left and 443 pixels from the top, similar to the container for the left box (that is, `a5-left-middle-text`). The width is set to 297 pixels to force the text to remain within the "visible" confines of the center box. The length of the text would need to be controlled by the designer, whether that means hand coding or controlling the number of output characters from a database. Figure 13.13 shows what the design looks like with the content added for the container.

FIGURE 13.13   Design with the text for the center box added.

- The `a5-right-middle-image` container is added to allow for the flowers area to be clickable. The "be forever changed" text on top of the flower image is added to the `a5-column-center-text` container, which is nested inside the `a5-column-center` <DIV>. The code that enables this can be found farther down the page. One advantage of adding this content, along with the '"why we were sold from day one testimonials | potential options | lifetime guarantee" text in the `a5-column-left` column, is that it populates the left and center columns, which forces the footer to its desired position.
- As mentioned in the previous bullet, the '"why we were sold from day one testimonials | potential options | lifetime guarantee" text is added to the `a5-column-left` container. The text is then nested inside the `a5-column-center-text` container. This nesting allows for the text area to have margins applied to the `a5-column-center-text` <DIV> without affecting the width of the `a5-column-left` container.
- The `a5-footer-separator` container is added to provide a margin between the bottom of the content and the top of the footer.

CONSTRUCTING SECOND-LEVEL PAGES

Similar to the previous three case studies, the homepage is reused and customized for secondary pages (see Figure 13.14). There are only a few changes that need to be made to create a modified version of the homepage:

- Once the homepage is saved as `menu-item-2.htm`, the containers that have absolute positioning added to them are removed. This is yet one more reason the left and center columns were included with the homepage design. They can now be easily used to their full potential by just adding content to them.
- The `a5-column-left-text` and `a5-column-center-text` containers are renamed to `a5-column-left-text-sl` and `a5-column-center-text-sl`, respectively. A rule for each is then added to the style sheet to modify the placement of the content that each contains.
- A second Photoshop file is created to provide a modified version of the background image. The `a5-body-sl` rule is then added to the style sheet that calls this new image, titled `bg-body-sl.jpg`.
- To provide a secondary page title, the `a5-sl-title` `<DIV>` is added at the top of the `a5-column-left-text-sl` container. A rule is then added to the style sheet to stylize the text in that `<DIV>`.

FIGURE 13.14   A second-level template that is created from the homepage design.

SUMMARY

The purpose of this design is to offer the designer the ability to create more graphical sites. Rather than providing a flexible, scalable design, the XHTML and CSS are used to place content over the background image, which provides the majority of graphical elements. The majority of items on the homepage are assigned absolute positioning. The secondary pages, however, provide a more traditional way of placing and stylizing content, considering they will need to be much more flexible. While this design is limited in its flexibility, it does provide an alternative for design that the other case studies cannot because this employs the graphics and content placement in entirely different ways.

14

CASE STUDY: A CSS FORM

In This Chapter

- Understanding the Form's Structure
- Explaining the Style Sheet Used for the Form
- Building the Form Row by Row

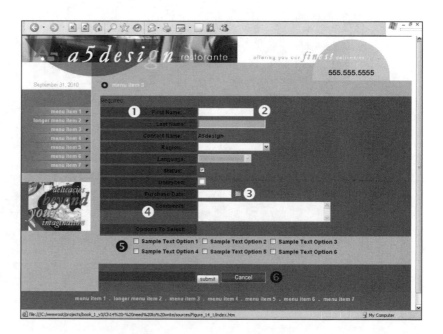

Building a CSS-based form is not overly difficult. While it's a completely new paradigm, compared with an XHTML table-based design, once the stylesheet rules have been created, the XHTML is very simple to employ. A form, in fact, is much easier to build because it reuses much of the CSS, making it more of a process of repeating and possibly tweaking the code.

As with web design, there are little tricks a designer should be aware of. The form in this chapter was built to show many of the challenges a designer may run into. Each row, in fact, illustrates a completely different element to consider.

The form is initially added to the design explained in Chapter 12 (see Figure 14.1) to provide a visual for how it would eventually look in a page. For the sake of simplicity, however, the form is later explained on its own. It could be added to any design, as long as it is not too wide for the allotted area on a page.

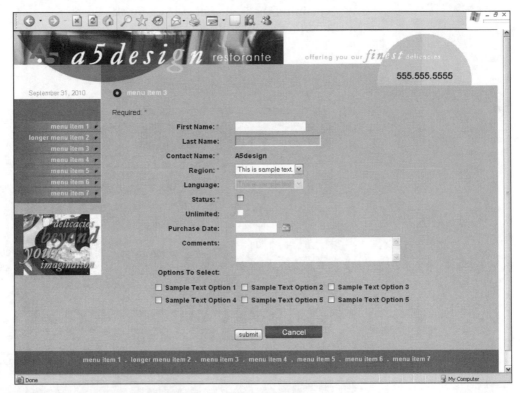

FIGURE 14.1   The sample form explained in this chapter.

UNDERSTANDING THE FORM'S STRUCTURE

The structure of this form is relatively simple. It is a two-column format nested inside opening and closing <FORM> tags. It is made into a two-column format by floating the form field's label, such as First Name, to the left of the actual form field. The background colors of the form elements are changed in Figure 14.2 to show the columns.

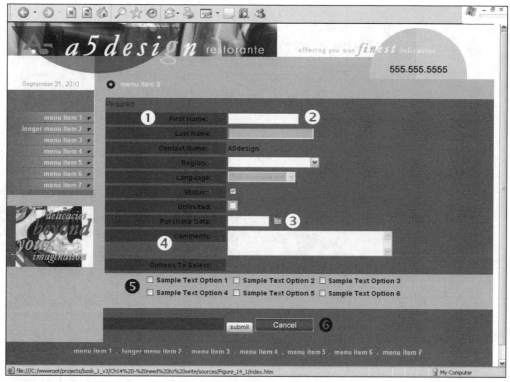

FIGURE 14.2   The background colors changed in the form to show how the two-column format is accomplished.

There are five things to note about the form's structure, shown in Figure 14.2:

1. The left column, shown by number 1, is set to 220 pixels wide. Because every label has the same width and is floated to the left, the entire column looks like it is the same width. If, however, the designer were to change the width of the label in one of the rows, it becomes apparent that each label is technically autonomous, unlike if the elements were to be structured in a traditional XHTML table layout (see Figure 14.3).

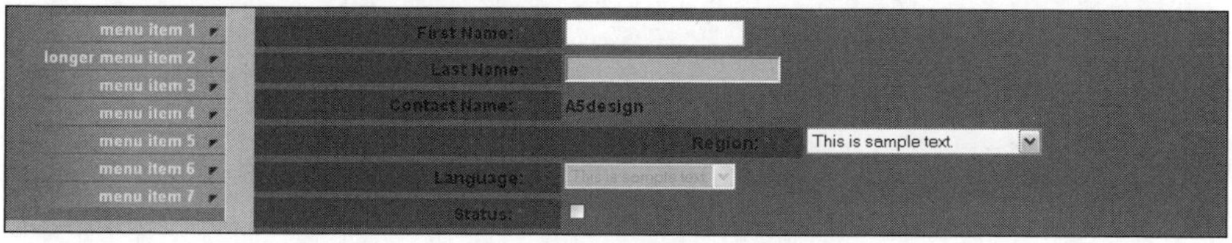

FIGURE 14.3   Example of how the width of each label is autonomous.

2. The right column is comprised of the form fields. As shown in Figure 14.3, if the width of the left label were widened, the form field in the right column would change accordingly, but only for that row.

3. The right column could be styled or modified however necessary, as long as the row has space to the right. Number 3 shows how a calendar image has been positioned to the right of the Purchase Date form field. The rule declaring the background color of the entire form has been changed to a different color, which would make the entire area look like one color if the color of the left column were not different. Figure 14.4 illustrates how the background color of the entire Last Name row could be changed if need be.

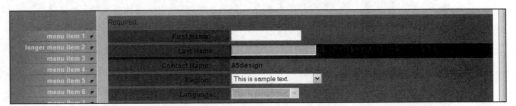

FIGURE 14.4   Example of how the background color of the Last Name row could be stylized separately from the other rows.

4. The height of the left column for each row is autonomous from the height of the right column because it is floated to the left, making it fall outside of the document flow. Number 4 represents how the height of the Comments label does not change when the height of the field in the right column increases the height of the row.

5. Because of the more involved layout of the row to the right of number 5, an XHTML table is used to position the form fields. The <DIV> the table nested inside is not assigned a class, which allows for the full width of the row to be used.

EXPLAINING THE STYLE SHEET USED FOR THE FORM

Because the global CSS rules are reused for nearly every form item, they are explained up front to give the reader a better overall understanding of what is happening. Listing 14.1 shows all the rules used in the style sheet.

LISTING 14.1   CSS Rules That Comprise the Stylesheet

```
.a5-form {
  margin:0px 0px 0px 0px;
  }
.a5-required-field {
  color:#D60000;
  }
```

```
.a5-disabled-field {
  background:#7ED0D4;
  }
.a5-disabled-checkbox {
  background:#7ED0D4;
  voice-family:"\"}\"";
  voice-family:inherit;
  }
  html>body .a5-disabled-checkbox {
    padding-top:3px;
  }
.a5-row-1 {
  height:30px;
  }
.a5-row-1 label {
  float: left;
  width: 220px;
  text-align: right;
  padding:0px 30px 0px 0px;
  }
```

There are several things to note about the styles used for the form. Following are explanations for each of the rules:

- **.a5-form**—Because browsers do not all apply the same default margin value for a form, the designer should declare it to provide consistency. One way this is accomplished is by setting the margins to 0.

- **.a5-required-field**—There are several ways to show a user which field is required. Creating an asterisk next to the form label is one of the most common. This rule simply makes the asterisk red.

- **.a5-disabled-field**—The form, when placed in the design (see Figure 14.1), has a background color behind it. Because of this, a background color for disabled fields is added to make the field look like it blends more into the background, visually representing the fact it's disabled. To complete this usability, or lack thereof, the designer must also include code in the XHTML to disable the field. This is explained later in the chapter.

- **.a5-disabled-checkbox**—This rule is added to consistently show the background color of a disabled checkbox in all browsers. Otherwise, some browsers render the background image entirely behind a checkbox or just partially behind it.

- **.a5-row-1**—This rule, along with the next, are the most commonly used in the form. This particular rule is added to set the default height of the row.

- **`.a5-row-1 label`**—This rule can be used to make the most sweeping changes in the form because it controls the default width of the left column. In this example, the width is set to 220 pixels. The rule also floats the column to the left side of the form, while forcing the label text to the right side of that column. A right padding value of 30 pixels is added to position the label text in from the right side, providing some visual space between the labels and the form fields.

BUILDING THE FORM ROW BY ROW

It is probably easiest to understand how to build the form if you see it built row by row. For demonstration purposes, the form is removed from the design and built separately. Following are explanations on how each row is built.

 The important thing to remember is to always test the form in various browsers. Sometimes there are more cross-browser anomalies that arise when building a form than when building a web page.

Adding the <FORM> Tag and Required Row

The first code to be added is the <FORM> tag. As with most forms, the main three attributes to add to the <FORM> tag are method, which tells the form to "post" or "get" the data; action, which in this case tells the form where to post the data; and the name attribute, which assigns a name to the form, uniquely identifying it. The final attribute added to this example is class, which calls the rule a5-form. This rule, declaring the default margin value as 0, defines the spacing outside the form tag, ensuring that all browsers display it the same rather than depending on their default values, which are not always the same.

The second section of code added is that which lays out the Required row. This row is added to let the user know the red asterisk included for certain rows indicates that row is required. This row has a local style added to create a top margin of 10 pixels to provide a little spacing between the form and the content it follows. Listing 14.2 displays this initial code added to the form.

LISTING 14.2   Initial XHTML and CSS Code Added to Form

```
<form action="menu-item-3.cfm" method="post" name="sample_form" class="a5-form">
<div class="a5-row-1" style="margin:10px 0px 0px 0px;">
  Required: <span class="a5-required-field">*</span>
</div>
</form>
```

Adding the First Name Row

The First Name row is the next item to be added to the form. Figure 14.5 illustrates how the form looks when the row is added to the form.

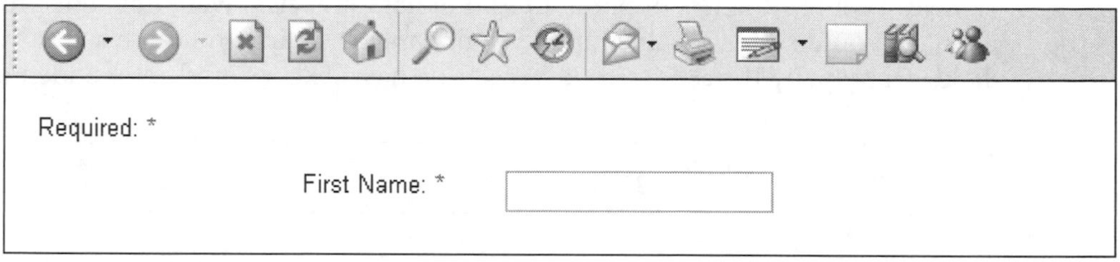

FIGURE 14.5   The form with the First Name row added to the form.

There are several things to note about this code:

- The row is created by the <DIV> that has an id value of a5-row-1 assigned to it. As stated earlier, this row is assigned a height of 30 pixels.
- The <LABEL> tag allows the designer the means to place a name next to the field it's identifying. While a <LABEL> tag is not necessary, doing so not only makes the content accessible, but it also allows the user to be able to click on that text, which will then make the field the focus of the cursor. In other words, if the user clicks on the text First Name, the cursor will appear blinking in the First Name field. The <LABEL> tag knows where to place the cursor because of the for attribute, which is assigned a value of first_name. The designer then adds the id value of first_name in the form field. So, when the <LABEL> text is clicked, the browser knows to match the for value of the tag with the same id value of whichever form field that has that value associated with it.
- The <LABEL> tag is styled by the a5-row-1 label rule in the style sheet. This rule assigns a width of 220 pixels to the tag, floating it to the left of the form field, aligning its text to the right, and creating 30 pixels of padding to the right.
- A <SPAN> tag, with the class a5-required-field assigned to it, is wrapped around an asterisk. The sole purpose of this style is to make the asterisk red to help it stand out visually.

Much of what is discussed with this example row is reused for many of the items in the form. Listing 14.3 shows the text that is added.

LISTING 14.3   XHTML Code for First Name Row

```
<div class="a5-row-1">
    <label title="First Name" for="first_name">First Name: <span class="a5-required-
field">*</span></label>
    <input type="text" name="first_name" id="first_name" />
</div>
```

Adding the Last Name Row

The Last Name row uses much of the same code as the First Name line. The main difference is this row is added to provide an example of a disabled row. Figure 14.6 shows how the disabled version appears when the `a5-disabled-field` class is added to the code in Listing 14.4. It is important to note that if the class were not added to the form field, it would still be disabled but it would appear nearly the same as the First Name field. This is why the `a5-disabled-field` rule has a background color added to it.

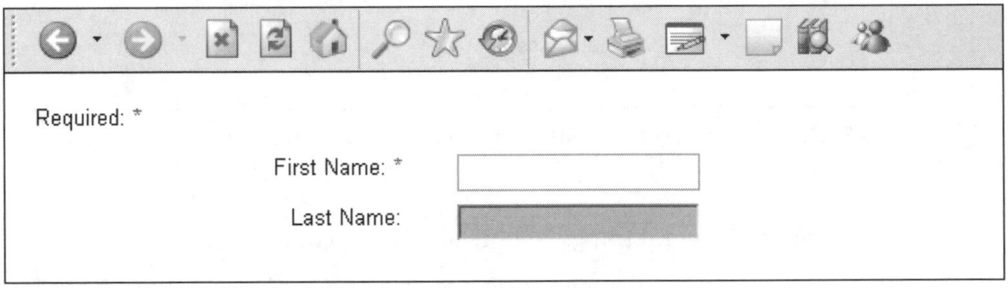

FIGURE 14.6   The form with the Last Name row added.

LISTING 14.4   XHTML Code for Last Name Row

```
<div class="a5-row-1">
    <label title="Last Name" for="last_name">Last Name:</label>
  <input type="text" name="last_name" id="last_name" disabled="disabled"
class="a5-
disabled-field" />
</div>
```

Adding the Contact Name Row

This row is added to show that text could be added in the right column instead of a form field (see Listing 14.5). This code is useful because dynamic forms many times output just text in spaces generally allocated for fields (see Figure 14.4), which, ultimately, are not submitted with the form, unless the data is also contained within a hidden form field. The code, however, also shows that the right column area provides a lot of flexibility for the designer. An image or instructional text, for instance, could be added, if need be.

LISTING 14.5   XHTML Code for Contact Name Row

```
<div class="a5-row-1">
    <label title="Contact Name">Contact Name: <span class="a5-required-
field">*</span></label>
    <strong>A5design</strong>
</div>
```

Adding the Region and Language Rows

The Region and Language rows are added to show how a dropdown menu would appear if it were added to a row. The Language element is different from the Region element in that it has been assigned the a5-disabled-field class. Similar to the Last Name field, it is assigned this class to change its background color to show it has been disabled. Unlike the <INPUT> tag, though, when the <SELECT> tag is disabled, it visually appears disabled by the way the browser renders it. Figure 14.7 shows how the four form elements appear when a background color is not assigned. Listing 14.6 shows the results of the code for the Region and Language rows.

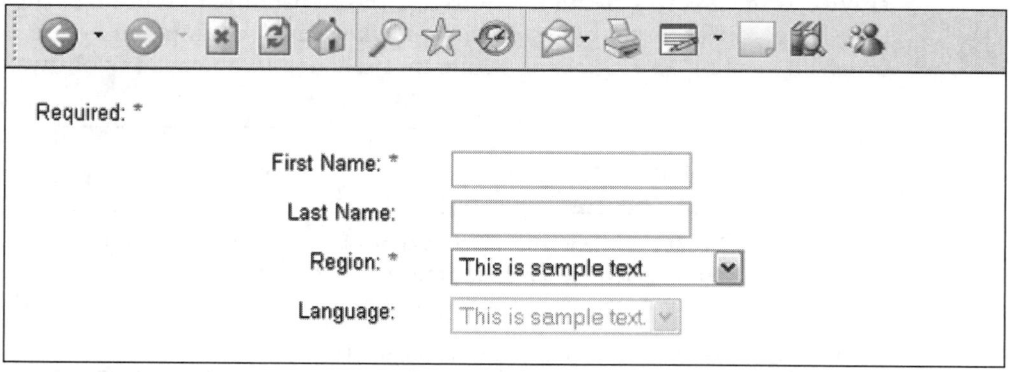

FIGURE 14.7   An example of how the <INPUT> and <SELECT> fields appear differently when they are enabled and disabled.

LISTING 14.6   XHTML Code for Region and Language Rows

```
<div class="a5-row-1">
    <label title="Region" for="region">Region: <span class="a5-required-
field">*</span></label>
  <select name="region" id="region">
    <option value="This is sample text">This is sample text.</option>
    <option>This is longer sample text</option>
  </select>
</div>
<div class="a5-row-1">
    <label title="Language" for="language">Language:</label>
  <select name="language" id="language" disabled="disabled">
    <option value="This is sample text">This is sample text.</option>
  </select>
</div>
```

Adding the Status and Unlimited Rows

Similar to the Region and Language rows, the Status and Unlimited rows are included to show how a different form element would look when it was enabled and disabled. The Unlimited checkbox is the same as the Status checkbox, except it has been disabled. The slight difference in this example, as with the Last Name and Language examples of disabled form elements, is that this type of form field employs a different disabled class (i.e., a5-disabled-checkbox). Figure 14.8 shows how the checkbox looks in different browsers if it is merely assigned a background color, as with the a5-disabled-field class. It illustrates how the background color does not make up a consistent height in the left and right examples. This is why the a5-disabled-field class was created. It adds 3 pixels of padding to the top of the checkbox field for compliant browsers, so it appears like the left example in Figure 14.8 for all browsers. Listing 14.7 shows the code that is added to build the two rows.

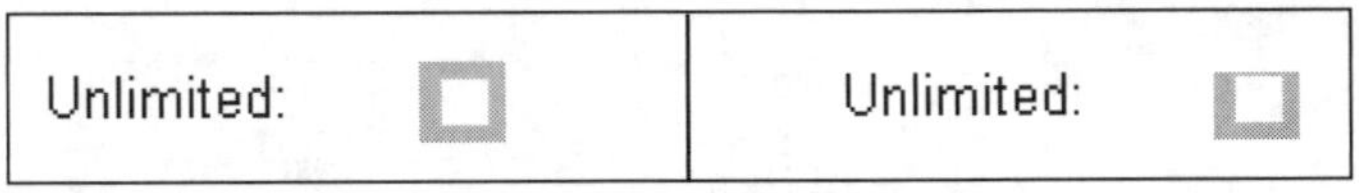

FIGURE 14.8 How the checkbox appears in different browsers if it is not assigned the a5-disabled-checkbox class.

LISTING 14.7 XHTML Code for Status and Unlimited Rows

```
<div class="a5-row-1">
    <label title="Unlimited" for="unlimited">Unlimited: </label>
  <input type="checkbox" name="status" id="status" />
</div>
<div class="a5-row-1">
    <label title="Unlimited" for="unlimited">Unlimited:</label>
  <span class="a5-disabled-checkbox"><input type="checkbox" name="unlimited"
id="unlimited" disabled="disabled" /></span>
</div>
```

Adding the Purchase Date Row

The Purchase Date row shows how an image can be included to the right of the form field. It is simply placed to the right of the field, as opposed to being floated to the right. If the designer were to get more technical, it could be assigned a few pixels of padding to the top so it is placed at the same height for all browsers. A <SPAN> container is wrapped around the image to provide 10 pixels of padding to the left. Listing 14.8 shows the code used to render the row.

LISTING 14.8   XHTML and CSS Code for Purchase Date Row

```
<div class="a5-row-1">
    <label title="Purchase Date" for="purchase_date">Purchase Date:</label>
  <input type="text" name="purchase_date" id="purchase_date" style="width:70px;"
/><span style="padding-left:10px;"><img src="images/icon-calendar.gif" width="16"
height="15" alt="" border="0" /></span>
</div>
```

Adding the Comments Row

The code required to produce the Comments row is almost identical to several of the other rows, barring one difference—the row includes the <TEXTAREA> tag, which does not force the height of the row for compliant browsers, such as Firefox. The designer, therefore, needs to force the height of the row. One way to do so is to add a local style to the parent <DIV>, shown in Listing 14.9. Without declaring the height of the row, the row would look like the right side of Figure 14.9. The left side illustrates what the row looks like if a height is defined.

FIGURE 14.9   The Comment row and how it will appear in compliant browsers when a height is and isn't defined when using the <TEXTAREA> tag.

LISTING 14.9   XHTML and CSS Code for Comments Row

```
<div class="a5-row-1" style="height:80px;">
    <label title="Comments" for="comments">Comments:</label>
  <textarea name="comments" id="comments" rows="3" cols="40"></textarea>
</div>
```

Adding the Options to Select Rows

The Options to Select rows add two more situations a designer may or may not come across. The first is to include only a section title and nothing more in a row. This is accomplished by merely not including a form field. The second is a little more involved. It requires two things: (1) define appropriate margins for positioning in the parent <DIV>, which, in this case, sets the bottom margin to 20 pixels and the left margin to 80 pixels; and (2) use a table to lay out the form fields in columns and rows. While the latter could be accomplished with CSS, the more simple and straightforward route is to use a table. The code in Listing 14.10 shows how simple the table needs to be.

LISTING 14.10 XHTML and CSS Code for Options to Select Row

```
<div class="a5-row-1">
    <label>Options To Select:</label>
</div>
<div style="margin:0px 0px 20px 80px;">
  <table cellspacing="0" cellpadding="3" border="0">
  <tr>
  <td>
     <input type="checkbox" name="sample_text_1" id="sample_text_1" />
     <label title="Sample Text Option 1" for="sample_text_1">Sample Text
Option 1</label>
    </td>
    <td>
     <input type="checkbox" name="sample_text_2" id="sample_text_2" />
     <label title="Sample Text Option 2" for="sample_text_2">Sample Text
Option 2</label>
    </td>
    <td>
     <input type="checkbox" name="sample_text_3" id="sample_text_3"
/>
     <label title="Sample Text Option 3" for="sample_text_3">Sample
Text Option 3</label>
    </td>
  </tr>
  <tr>
  <td>
     <input type="checkbox" name="sample_text_4" id="sample_text_4" />
     <label title="Sample Text Option 4" for="sample_text_4">Sample Text
Option 4</label>
    </td>
  <td>
     <input type="checkbox" name="sample_text_5" id="sample_text_5" />
     <label title="Sample Text Option 5" for="sample_text_5">Sample Text
Option 5</label>
    </td>
    <td>
     <input type="checkbox" name="sample_text_6" id="sample_text_6" />
     <label title="Sample Text Option 6" for="sample_text_6">Sample Text
Option 6</label>
    </td>
  </tr>
  </table>
</div>
```

Adding the Submit and Cancel Buttons

The final row is that which contains the Submit and Cancel buttons. There are several things to note about this section of code: (1) a local style is added to the <DIV> to provide 20 pixels of padding on the top and bottom, (2) the <LABEL> tag has   added so that all browsers recognize the tag and account for its width, and (3) the two buttons are placed side by side without any additional styling. The Cancel button calls an image, while the Submit button is generated with XHTML (see Listing 14.11).

LISTING 14.11   XHTML and CSS Code for Submit and Cancel Buttons

```
<div class="a5-row-1" style="padding:20px 0px 20px 0px;">
   <label> </label>
  <input type="submit" value="submit" />
  <input type="image" src="images/button-cancel.gif" />
</div>
```

The Final Product

When all the code and images are added, the final 13-row form only needs to have the back end functionality added to it. Figure 14.10 is the visual representation of the final code, which is shown in Listing 14.12.

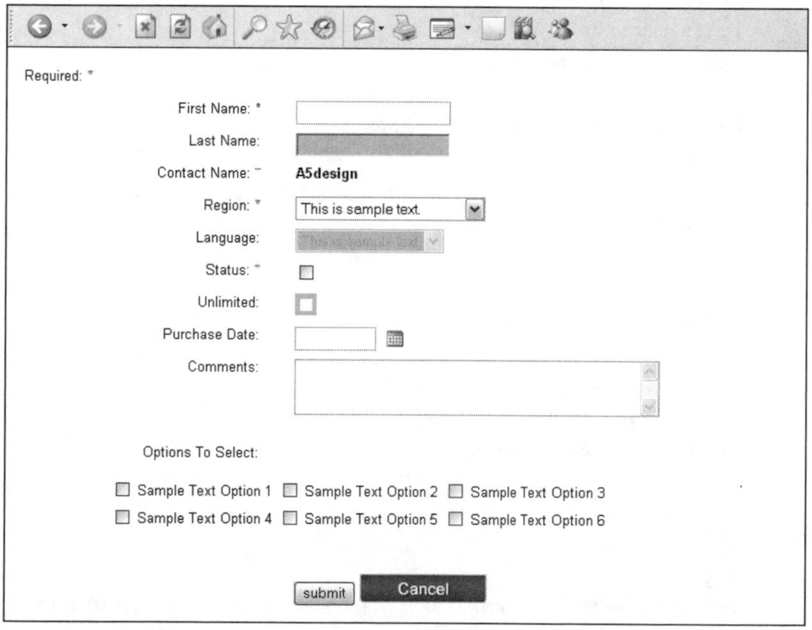

FIGURE 14.10   How the final form appears prior to being added to the design (see Figure 14.1).

LISTING 14.12   XHTML and CSS Code for Completed Form

```
<!DOCTYPE html PUBLIC "-//W3C//DTD XHTML 1.0 Transitional//EN" "DTD/xhtml1-
transitional.dtd">
<html xmlns="http://www.w3.org/1999/xhtml" xml:lang="en"
lang="en"><head><title></title>
<style type="text/css">
html, body {
  margin:0px;
  padding:10px;
  font: 9.8pt arial, helvetica, sans-serif;
  color:#000000;
  }
.a5-form {
  margin:0px 0px 0px 0px;
  }
.a5-required-field {
  color:#D60000;
  }
.a5-disabled-field {
  background:#7ED0D4;
  }
.a5-disabled-checkbox {
  background:#7ED0D4;
  voice-family:"\"}\"";
  voice-family:inherit;
  }
  html>body .a5-disabled-checkbox {
    padding-top:3px;
  }
.a5-row-1 {
  height:30px;
  }
.a5-row-1 label {
  float: left;
  width: 220px;
  text-align: right;
  padding:0px 30px 0px 0px;
  }
</style>
</head>
<body>
<form action="menu-item-3.cfm" method="post" name="sample_form" class="a5-form">
<div class="a5-row-1" style="margin:10px 0px 0px 0px;">
  Required: <span class="a5-required-field">*</span>
```

```
</div>
<div class="a5-row-1">
    <label title="First Name" for="first_name">First Name: <span class="a5-required-
field">*</span></label>
    <input type="text" name="first_name" id="first_name" />
</div>
<div class="a5-row-1">
    <label title="Last Name" for="last_name">Last Name:</label>
  <input type="text" name="last_name" id="last_name" disabled="disabled"
class="a5-
disabled-field" />
</div>
<div class="a5-row-1">
    <label title="Contact Name">Contact Name: <span class="a5-required-
field">*</span></label>
  <strong>A5design</strong>
</div>
<div class="a5-row-1">
    <label title="Region" for="region">Region: <span class="a5-required-
field">*</span></label>
  <select name="region" id="region">
    <option value="This is sample text">This is sample text.</option>
    <option>This is longer sample text</option>
  </select>
</div>
<div class="a5-row-1">
    <label title="Language" for="language">Language:</label>
  <select name="language" id="language" disabled="disabled" class="a5-disabled-
field">
    <option>This is sample text.</option>
  </select>
</div>
<div class="a5-row-1">
    <label title="Status" for="status">Status: <span class="a5-required-
field">*</span></label>
  <input type="checkbox" name="status" id="status" />
</div>
<div class="a5-row-1">
    <label title="Unlimited" for="unlimited">Unlimited:</label>
  <span class="a5-disabled-checkbox"><input type="checkbox" name="unlimited"
id="unlimited" disabled="disabled" /></span>
</div>
<div class="a5-row-1">
    <label title="Purchase Date" for="purchase_date">Purchase Date:</label>
```

```
    <input type="text" name="purchase_date" id="purchase_date" style="width:70px;"
/><span style="padding-left:10px;"><img src="images/icon-calendar.gif" width="16"
height="15" alt="" border="0" /></span>
</div>
<div class="a5-row-1" style="height:80px;">
    <label title="Comments" for="comments">Comments:</label>
   <textarea name="comments" id="comments" rows="3" cols="40"></textarea>
</div>
<div class="a5-row-1">
    <label>Options To Select:</label>
</div>
<div style="margin:0px 0px 20px 80px;">
  <table cellspacing="0" cellpadding="3" border="0">
  <tr>
  <td>
      <input type="checkbox" name="sample_text_1" id="sample_text_1" />
      <label title="Sample Text Option 1" for="sample_text_1">Sample Text
Option 1</label>
    </td>
    <td>
      <input type="checkbox" name="sample_text_2" id="sample_text_2" />
      <label title="Sample Text Option 2" for="sample_text_2">Sample Text
Option 2</label>
  </td>
  <td>
      <input type="checkbox" name="sample_text_3" id="sample_text_3" />
      <label title="Sample Text Option 3" for="sample_text_3">Sample Text
Option 3</label>
    </td>
  </tr>
  <tr>
  <td>
      <input type="checkbox" name="sample_text_4" id="sample_text_4" />
      <label title="Sample Text Option 4" for="sample_text_4">Sample Text
Option 4</label>
    </td>
  <td>
      <input type="checkbox" name="sample_text_5" id="sample_text_5" />
      <label title="Sample Text Option 5" for="sample_text_5">Sample Text
Option 5</label>
    </td>
  <td>
      <input type="checkbox" name="sample_text_6" id="sample_text_6"
 />
```

```
        <label title="Sample Text Option 6" for="sample_text_6">Sample
Text Option 6</label>
      </td>
    </tr>
    </table>
</div>
<div class="a5-row-1" style="padding:20px 0px 20px 0px;">
      <label> </label>
    <input type="submit" value="submit" />
    <input type="image" src="images/button-cancel.gif" />
</div>
</form>
</body>
</html>
```

SUMMARY

Creating a form with CSS is not difficult once the designer understands the basic structure of the layout. Once rules have been created for each row and the <LABEL> text, there are only a few nuances that need to be learned to control the form fields and the <DIV> tags that contain them. Once these are understood, it becomes much easier for the designer to satisfy the majority of form requests he will come across using the methods discussed in this chapter. Even if a form needs to be more involved, the basics that are explained will provide a strong foundation for such a request.

15

CASE STUDY: LOW-CONTENT XHTML TEMPLATE

In This Chapter

- Creating the Design for a Low Amount of Content
- Understanding the Strengths and Weaknesses of the Chosen Design
- Adding Guides and Slices
- Creating the Parent Table
- Creating and Linking the Style Sheet
- Creating the Menu Table
- Adding an Image to the Center Column
- Creating the Content (Right-Area) Table
- Creating the Footer Information

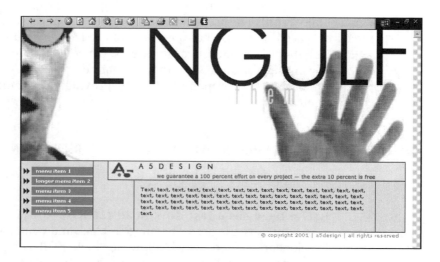

Although Web sites are no longer being built using nested XHTML tables, there are still uses for this design technique, the most frequent of which is creating e-mail templates. CSS is supported only sporadically among the many various e-mail programs and versions that continue to exist. Tables, however, are supported quite consistently, which is why this chapter is still included in this updated edition. Originally included to explain how to create a table-driven Web design, this chapter is now included to explain how to create XHTML table-driven e-mails. The fact of the matter is that many e-mail templates are nothing more than less-complicated versions of Web design layouts, so the crossover works quite well. Just for reference, the design explained in this chapter is the very first design in the first edition of the book—design 1.

 It is important that all hyperlinks and image source paths are assigned absolute paths. For example, instead of `src=" images/spacer.gif"`, *the designer should write the code as* `src=http://www.a5design.com/images/spacer.gif`. *This is also true for hyperlinks because without an absolute path, the hyperlink will look for the file on the user's computer, where it won't exist.*

CREATING THE DESIGN FOR A LOW AMOUNT OF CONTENT

Many times a client will simply want to create a design that doesn't have much content to display. Building such a site requires the designer to supplement the lack of content with graphics and HTML color.

Figure 15.1, the design used for this chapter, is an example of such a design. Because there is only one area of content used on the homepage, more than half of the vertical space is comprised of the photo of the face and hand, along with the words "ENGULF them." The menu has five items, which, many times, is a good number for a client wanting a small design. In an e-mail template, these menu items can easily be linked back to the company's Web site, providing yet another way for the user to get to their site.

UNDERSTANDING THE STRENGTHS AND WEAKNESSES OF THE CHOSEN DESIGN

As with any design, there are going to be strengths and weaknesses. Following is a list of the strengths of Figure 15.1:

1. **The page has a fast download (26 KB)**—This is because a large amount of white space is used, the image is black and white, and the number of solid colors are limited, which allows for higher GIF compression. Depending on the desired quality of the images, it is possible they could be compressed even more.
2. **Both the menu and content areas are flexible**—Despite more than half the design being made up of images, it is still flexible. If the client has only

three sections to include in the design, one menu item can be easily removed. (This makes up four items in the menu because of the Home link, represented by Menu Item 1 in Figure 15.1.) If, on the other hand, the client needs to add another section, this can also be easily accomplished. While the content area is limited in size, the area itself can be easily customized to accommodate different layouts.

3. **The overall layout of the design is not complicated**—Edits and revisions are simple.

4. **The parent table allows for the words "ENGULF them" and the hand to be edited separately from the face**—This could save the designer a lot of time if the homepage needs to be redesigned to accommodate more content.

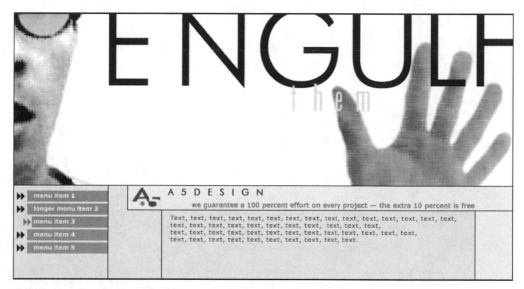

FIGURE 15.1   Site designed for a low amount of content.

Following is a list of weaknesses from Figure 15.1:

1. **The menu area does not allow for unlimited expansion without requiring the user to scroll**—While limited expansion (one menu item) can be easily and quickly accomplished, unless the menu area is redesigned so that the gray background areas take up less vertical space, adding two or more items to the menu may require the user to scroll down to view the entire menu.

2. **The header area takes up a lot of vertical real estate**—For e-mail templates, this is not so much of an issue as with Web designs because the header area does not need to be reused. The designer can also save text as an image, as opposed to XHTML text, because search engine optimization is

also not an issue. If the designer did want to provide for easily editable content, though, the image area would need to be redesigned for an image that was not as high, allowing for XHTML text.

3. **The design is too wide for an e-mail template.** Generally, e-mail templates are 500 to 650 pixels wide, so the designer would also need to decrease the width of the design. This chapter, however, is included to explain the process of creating such a design rather than provide a working example.

ADDING GUIDES AND SLICES

Creating guides and slices is the same for this chapter as with Chapters 9, 10, 11, 12, and 13. When adding such elements, though, there are several aspects of this design that should be taken into consideration:

1. The parent table contains three columns—the menu area on the left, the content area on the right, and a vertical line separating the two. Guide 1 in Figure 15.2 is two vertical guides one pixel apart, which creates these three columns.

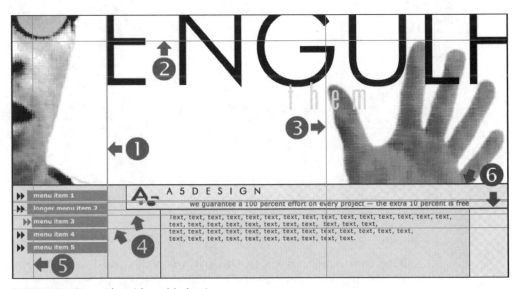

FIGURE 15.2   Site with guides added to it.

2. In the content area, the top half of the word "ENGULF" is all black and white, so it is sliced separately to maximize GIF compression. Guide 2 separates this image from the lower half of the word.

3. The lower half of the word "ENGULF" and the hand are saved as two different images. The left side is made up of only black, white, and yellow, which is why it is saved as a GIF, while the hand on the right side has many colors,

which is why it is saved as a JPG. Guide 3 separates these two images from one another.

4. Because the menu bullets are images, they must be saved as such. Guide 5, along with the two guides represented by guide 4, is used to outline the bullet in the On state. The guides above guide 4, along with guide 5, outline the bullet in the Off state.

Mouseovers are not included with e-mail templates because they require either JavaScript or CSS, both of which cannot be counted on to be supported. In some cases, the e-mail may even be rejected because of such coding.

5. The entire colored row to the right of guide 1, which includes the logo and title, is outlined by guide 6. Everything below the lower of the two guides and to the right of guide 1 will be HTML.
6. Once the guides are set in place, the slices are then added.

CREATING THE PARENT TABLE

Building the parent table is the first step toward bringing together all the images with text. To allow for the most flexibility with this design, the parent table has three columns: the left menu area (146 pixels), a center column (1 pixel), and the right content area (623 pixels). The entire table is 770 pixels wide, allowing it to fit on an 800 × 600–resolution screen without the horizontal scrollbar being activated.

Because the image of the face fills the left column (arrow 1 in Figure 15.3), a 1-pixel image fills the center column (arrow 2), and the title and logo image fills the right column. Adding a row at the bottom of the table for spacer GIFs forces the width of the columns.

If, for instance, the right column included images that were less than 623 pixels wide, the design would collapse in, thus requiring a row of spacer GIFs to be added at the bottom in order to force the width of the columns. Of course, until all the images are added in each column, the page will incorrectly stretch and collapse, depending on the images and text added. Therefore, it is wise to add a row with the spacer GIFs until the page is built. The row can always be deleted later. It can also be used as one of the lines in the footer area, which doubles its usefulness. Generally, it does not hurt to keep the spacer-GIF row in a design because it is not always known which content might change in size.

The reason the middle column was created (arrow 2 in Figure 15.3) was to provide a vertical line that stretched the height of the design. This way, if the menu on the left or content on the right stretches vertically, the line will also stretch because all three areas are columns in the same row. If the line, however, were part of the menu table, it would not stretch if the content on the right did. Figure 15.4 shows the parent table without any content in it.

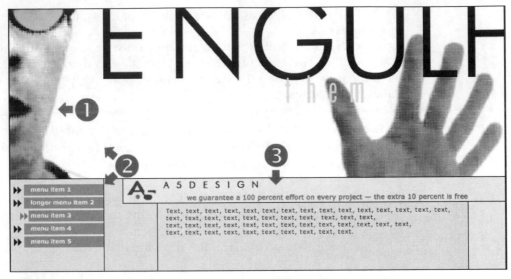

FIGURE 15.3   The design with arrows pointing to the different columns.

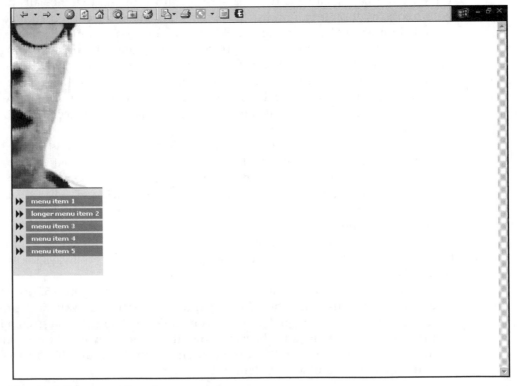

FIGURE 15.4   Parent table without content.

CREATING AND LINKING THE STYLE SHEET

Generally, a basic style sheet is created and linked to the homepage before content is added. More styles are then added as the site is built. For the design in this example, there really are only two styles that need to be added—one for the menu and one for the content text to the right.

 While it is usually prudent not to use linked style sheets in e-mail templates, inline styles are supported fairly well. In other words, the designer should always try to include style sheets locally in an e-mail template.

Listing 15.1 is the style sheet included with the code:

LISTING 15.1   Style Sheet Code

```
A:link { color: #AD4984 }
A:visited { color: #AD4984 }
A:active { color: #AD4984 }
A:hover { color: #000000 }

td {font-family: verdana, geneva, sans-serif; font-size: 7.8pt;}

.white78 {font-family: verdana, geneva, sans-serif; font-size: 7.8pt; color:
#ffffff;}
```

The `A:` properties determine the hyperlink colors of the site. To set the default style for all text inside the table cells, the `td` style was created. This way, style for the content in the right area will automatically be assigned to the table cell unless over-written for that specific instance. The `white78` style is used for the menu items.

CREATING THE MENU TABLE

The menu table in this design is actually the nested table for the entire left column. It not only includes the menu items, but it also includes the picture of the face. By including the face image in the same column, it can be reused in the second-level template, thus decreasing the download of other pages. Figure 15.5 shows the built menu table.

To better understand how the table is structured, Figure 15.6 shows the table with the images and text removed.

Using a two-column table is all that is needed to build the menu table. The face image is placed inside a table cell with `colspan="2"` (arrow 1 in Figure 15.6). Each bullet image is placed in a left cell (arrow 2), while the corresponding text menu items are placed in the right cell (arrow 3). Because the menu items in the right column cannot force the exact width of the column, a spacer-GIF row is added to the

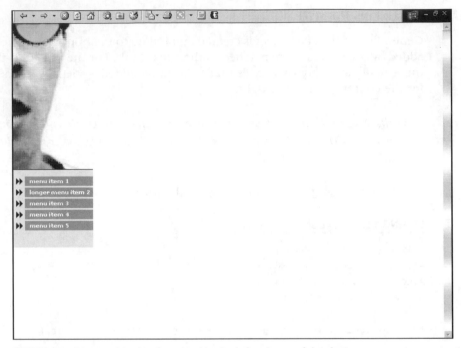

FIGURE 15.5 Menu table that is nested in the left column of the design.

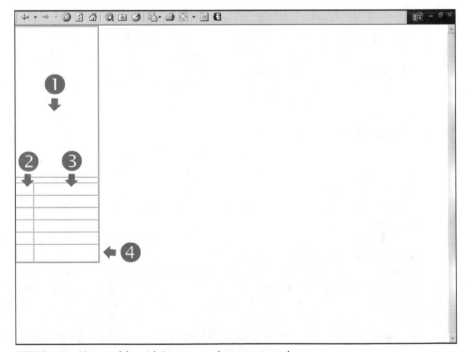

FIGURE 15.6 Menu table with images and text removed.

bottom of the table (arrow 4). Although the height of a spacer GIF is usually 1 pixel, the height of the left spacer GIF is set to 30 pixels. This ensures that the height of the menu table will fill the browser window. Listing 15.2 is the code for the menu table.

LISTING 15.2   Code for the Menu Table

```
<!- menu start ->

<table width="100%" cellspacing="0" cellpadding="0" border="2">
  <tr>
    <td colspan="2"><img src="http://www.a5design.com/images/spacer.gif"
width="146"
height="266" alt="Description goes here" border="0"></td>
  </tr>
  <tr>
    <td colspan="2"><img src="http://www.a5design.com/images/spacer.gif" width="1"
height="8"
alt="Description goes here" border="0"></td>
  </tr>
  <tr>
    <td><img src="http://www.a5design.com/images/spacer.gif" name="menu_item_1"
width="31"
height="20" alt="Description goes here" border="0"></td>
    <td class="white78"><a href="x.htm" style="text-decoration: none;
color: #ffffff"><b>menu item 1</b></a></td>
  </tr>
  <tr>
    <td><img src="http://www.a5design.com/images/spacer.gif" name="menu_item_2"
width="31"
height="20" alt="Description goes here" border="0"></td>
    <td class="white78"><a href="x.htm" style="text-decoration: none;
color: #ffffff"><b>longer menu item 2</b></a></td>
  </tr>
  <tr>
    <td><img src="http://www.a5design.com/images/spacer.gif" name="menu_item_3"
width="31"
height="20" alt="Description goes here" border="0"></td>
    <td class="white78"><a href="x.htm" style="text-decoration: none;
color: #ffffff"><b>menu item 3</b></a></td>
  </tr>
  <tr>
    <td><img src="http://www.a5design.com/images/spacer.gif" name="menu_item_4"
width="31"
```

```
height="20" alt="Description goes here" border="0"></td>
    <td class="white78"><a href="x.htm" style="text-decoration: none;
color: #ffffff"><b>menu item 4</b></a></td>
  </tr>
  <tr>
    <td><img src="http://www.a5design.com/images/spacer.gif" name="menu_item_5"
width="31"
height="20" alt="Description goes here" border="0"></td>
    <td class="white78"><a href="x.htm" style="color: #ffffff;"><b>menu item
5</b></a></td>
  </tr>
  <tr>
    <td><img src="http://www.a5design.com/images/spacer.gif" width="31"
height="1"
alt="Description goes here" border="0"></td>
    <td><img src="http://www.a5design.com/images/spacer.gif" width="115"
height="1"
alt="Description goes here" border="0"></td>
  </tr>
</table>
<!— menu end —>
```

There are a few things to note about the menu code:

1. The `cellpadding` and `cellspacing` attributes of the `<table>` tag are both set to 0. Were this not the case, the default in various browsers may not default to 0, which disallows the ability to mortise images.
2. A table cell with the `colspan="2"` is included right below the face image. Using a spacer GIF in this cell allows the designer to control how much space there is between the face image and the Menu Item 1 row.
3. A local style (boldfaced in the following example) is added to each menu item. When hyperlinking text, a color is applied to that text, despite the class of the table cell. (The class is `white78` for this menu.) To override this global setting, the following local style must be added to the `<a href>` tag. In this example, the color added to the menu items, using the `color` property, is white (#ffffff). The style, using the `text-decoration` property, also eliminates the underscore of the hyperlink.

```
<a href="x.htm" style="text-decoration: none; color: #ffffff"><b>menu item 5</b></a>.
```

ADDING AN IMAGE TO THE CENTER COLUMN

Although the center column is only 1 pixel wide, it offers considerable flexibility to the design. To have the column act as a line to the right of the menu (arrow 1 in Figure 15.7), the background color of the cell should be set to black.

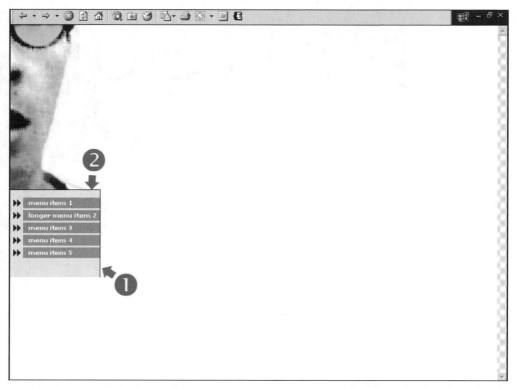

FIGURE 15.7   One-pixel column with `bgcolor="#000000"` serves as a black line added to the right of the menu.

Then, to make the line appear to run only as high as the yellow background part of the site (arrow 2 in Figure 15.7), a 1-pixel by 1-pixel white GIF need only be added to the cell. The height of the image needs to be 1 pixel less than the face image, and the `valign` attribute of the table cell should be set to `"top"`.

By building the column this way, the menu and content areas can expand vertically, while the center column will simply expand along with the area that requires the most vertical space. Another benefit to building the columns this way has to do with the flexibility of the second-level template.

CREATING THE CONTENT (RIGHT-AREA) TABLE

The content area of this design is relatively simple. There are only four images and one text area, which requires a two-column nested table. Building the area is accomplished in two steps. The first step is to build the parent table for this section and add the top three images (see Figure 15.8).

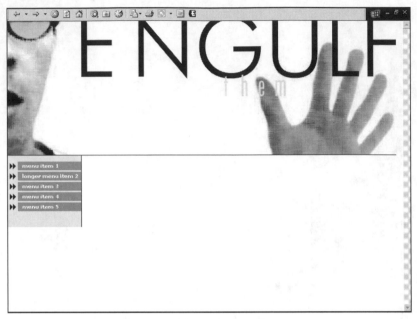

FIGURE 15.8 The first step in building the content area.

Figure 15.9 is the table structure without the images in the cells.

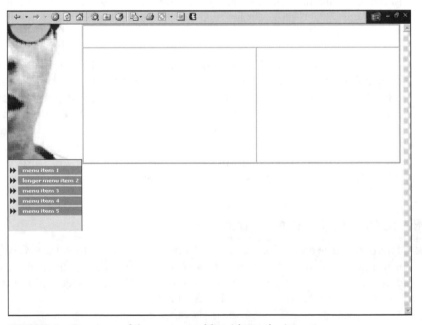

FIGURE 15.9 Structure of the content table without the images.

While the second step is nearly as simple, it does require nesting a table inside a cell of the content table. Doing so enables the nested table to be reused for the second-level template. Figure 15.10 shows the completed content area.

Figure 15.11 shows the nested table turned on with the images and text removed.

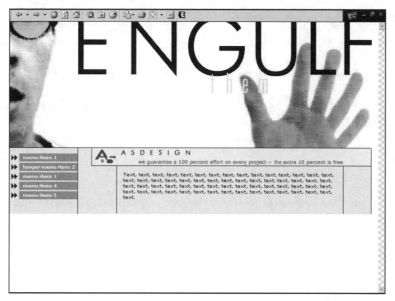

FIGURE 15.10   Content area completed with HTML, graphics, and CSS.

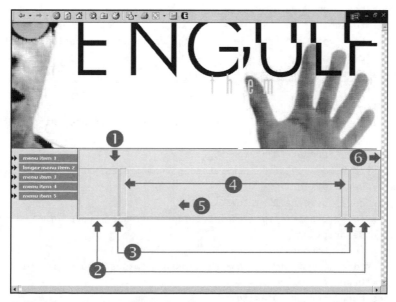

FIGURE 15.11   Content table with images and text removed and table border turned on and set to `"2"`.

The content table is eight table cells wide. All the color is generated by the background color of the cell the table is nested in. To keep the download to a minimum, the only image used in the entire table is the spacer GIF. Listing 15.3 is the code for building the content table:

LISTING 15.3   Code for Building the Content Table

```
<!- title and text start ->

<table width="100%" cellspacing="0" cellpadding="0" border="2">
  <tr>
    <td colspan="8"><img src="http://www.a5design.com/images/spacer.gif" width="623"
height="38"
alt="Description goes here" border="0"></td>
  </tr>
  <tr>
    <td> </td>
    <td><img src="http://www.a5design.com/images/spacer.gif" width="1" height="101"
alt=""
border="0"></td>
    <td> </td>
    <td valign="top"></td>
    <td> </td>
    <td><img src="http://www.a5design.com/images/spacer.gif" width="1" height="1"
alt="Description
goes here" border="0"></td>
    <td> </td>
    <td><img src="http://www.a5design.com/images/spacer.gif" width="1" height="1"
alt="Description
goes here" border="0"></td>
  </tr>
  <tr>
    <td><img src="http://www.a5design.com/images/spacer.gif" width="82" height="1"
alt="Description
goes here" border="0"></td>
    <td><img src="http://www.a5design.com/images/spacer.gif" width="1" height="1"
alt="Description
goes here" border="0"></td>
    <td><img src="http://www.a5design.com/images/spacer.gif" width="13" height="1"
alt="Description
goes here" border="0"></td>
    <td><img src="http://www.a5design.com/images/spacer.gif" width="455" height="1"
alt="Description
goes here" border="0"></td>
    <td><img src="http://www.a5design.com/images/spacer.gif" width="13" height="1"
```

```
alt="Description
goes here" border="0"></td>
    <td><img src="http://www.a5design.com/images/spacer.gif" width="1" height="1"
alt="Description
goes here" border="0"></td>
    <td><img src="http://www.a5design.com/images/spacer.gif" width="57" height="1"
alt="Description
goes here" border="0"></td>
    <td><img src="http://www.a5design.com/images/spacer.gif" width="1" height="1"
alt="Description
goes here" border="0"></td>
  </tr>
</table>

<!- title and text end ->
```

There are several important aspects to understand about the table:

1. The title and logo image are saved as one image that spans the full width of the table. Because the image uses few colors, it is possible to save it as a small GIF (arrow 1 in Figure 15.11).
2. The width of each of the cells is controlled by spacer GIFs in the bottom row.
3. The cells used for padding on both sides of the black lines (arrows 2 and 4) have only a blank character ( ) in the cells.

Cells that use a `bgcolor` attribute sometimes require that they have content in them, whether a blank character ( ) or a spacer GIF, for the color to appear. This used to be the case with Netscape 4.7.

4. Because a blank character is wider than 1 pixel, spacer GIFs are used in the cells that make up the black lines. The advantage of the lines being cells is that they will expand vertically as the text in the middle cell expands (arrow 5). One of the GIFs has its vertical height set to "101" to ensure that the content area does not shrink vertically if the content is not long enough. All it takes is one cell to set the vertical height of the entire row.
5. The cell on the far right (arrow 6) is also used to create a black line that stretches vertically.

CREATING THE FOOTER INFORMATION

As mentioned previously, the bottom row of the table with the spacer GIFs can also double as a line in the footer (see Figure 15.12). The cells only need a background color of black applied to them. Then all the designer needs to do is add another row to the parent table of the entire site; this row will contain the actual footer information. Listing 15.4 is the explained code.

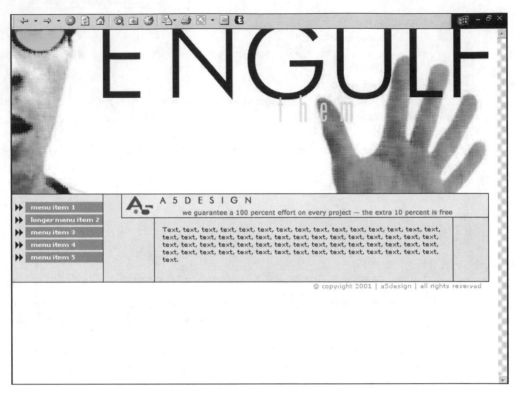

FIGURE 15.12   Complete design with footer added at bottom.

LISTING 15.4   Code for Figure 15.12

```
<!—this is a continuation of the already-opened table from above —>
  <tr>
    <td bgcolor="#000000"><img src="http://www.a5design.com/images/spacer.gif"
width="146" height="1"
alt="Description goes here" border="0"></td>
    <td bgcolor="#000000"><img src="http://www.a5design.com/images/spacer.gif"
width="1" height="1"
alt="Description goes here" border="0"></td>
    <td bgcolor="#000000"><img src="http://www.a5design.com/images/spacer.gif"
width="623" height="1"
alt="Description goes here" border="0"></td>
  </tr>
  <tr>
    <td colspan="3" align="right" style="color: #80838E">© copyright 2001 |
a5design | all rights reserved   </td>
  </tr>
```

```
</table>
</body>
</html>
```

 A spacer GIF with its color set as black could also be used to ensure the line is black. Sometimes this is the better choice because a row can become taller than 1 pixel, depending on the design of the table and amount of content.

SUMMARY

The design technique explained in this chapter used to be the standard for creating Web sites. With the advent of CSS design, this is no longer the case. This older technique of nesting XHTML tables, however, still has a use. Many designers now use it for creating e-mail templates because it's basically the same structure and functionality. This chapter explained how to use nested XHTML tables to create a more controllable, advanced layout.

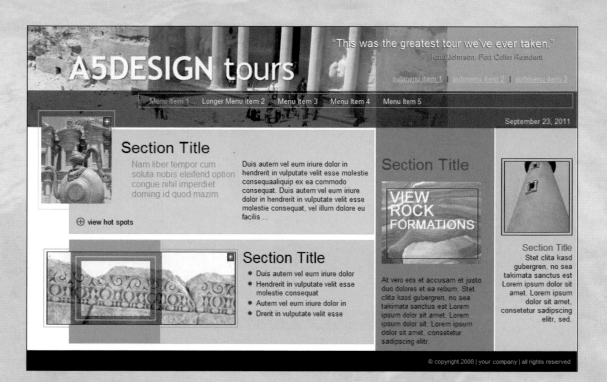

DESIGN 160 Homepage

DESIGN 159 Homepage

DESIGN 158   Homepage

DESIGN 157   Homepage

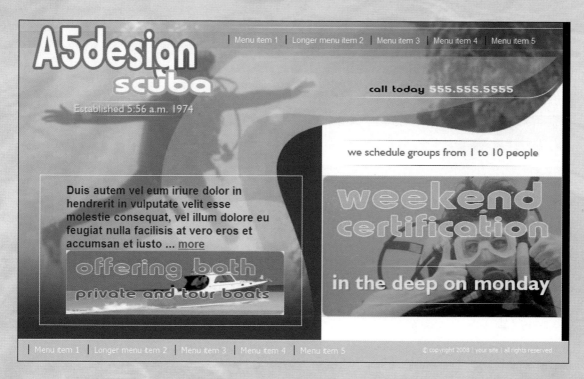

DESIGN 156 Homepage

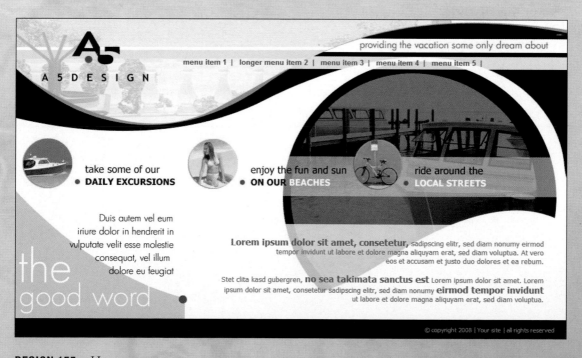

DESIGN 155 Homepage

DESIGN 154   Homepage

DESIGN 153   Homepage

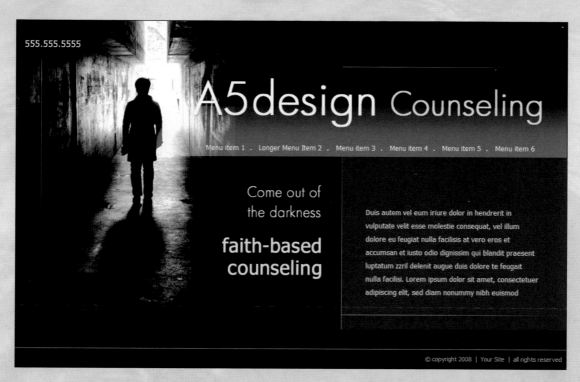

DESIGN 152   Homepage

DESIGN 151   Homepage

DESIGN 150 Homepage

DESIGN 149 Homepage

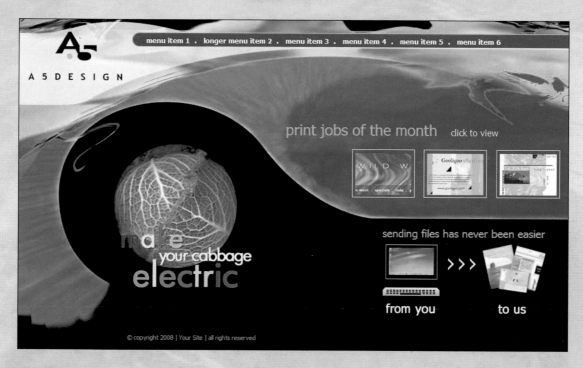

DESIGN 148   Homepage

DESIGN 147   Homepage

DESIGN 146   Homepage

DESIGN 145   Homepage

DESIGN 144 Homepage

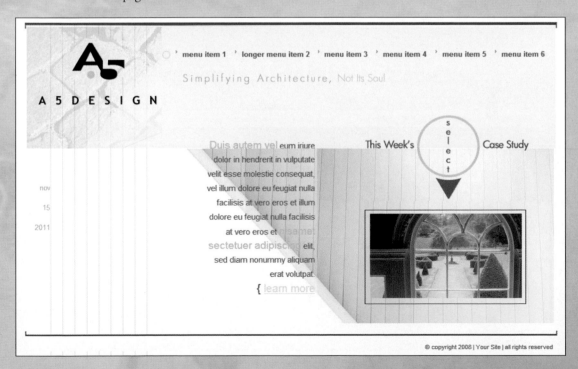

DESIGN 143 Homepage

DESIGN 142 Homepage

DESIGN 141 Homepage

DESIGN 140 Homepage

DESIGN 139 Homepage

DESIGN 138 Homepage

DESIGN 137 Homepage

DESIGN 136   Homepage

DESIGN 135   Homepage

DESIGN 134 Homepage

DESIGN 133 Homepage

DESIGN 132 Homepage

DESIGN 131 Homepage

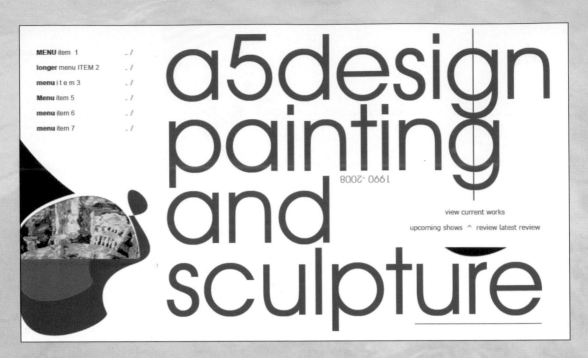

DESIGN 120   Photoshop Design

DESIGN 117   Photoshop Design

16

TIPS AND TECHNIQUES

In This Chapter

- Tantek or Box Model Hack
- Naming Rules and Properties Correctly
- Removing Body Margins and Padding
- Creating the Framework for a Fixed-Width CSS Design
- Taking Into Account Increasing and Decreasing Column Heights
- Centering a Fixed-Width Design
- Creating a Liquid Design
- Rendering the <HR /> Tag Consistently
- Creating a Line Without the <HR /> Tag
- Using Background Images as Design Elements
- Coding CSS Mouseovers
- Using JavaScript Dropdown Menus
- Remembering the Order of Margin and Padding Shortcuts
- Using the Border and Background Properties for Troubleshooting
- Commenting Out Code for Troubleshooting
- Using Unique Naming Conventions
- Controlling the Margins in <FORM> Tags
- Avoiding Horizontal Scrollbars
- Using CSS Shortcuts
- Understanding Font Units
- Using Globally Driven <SPAN> and <DIV> Tags for Printing Purposes
- Using Non-graphical Elements When Designing Rebrandable Sites
- Including Hidden <DIV> Tags for Future Use
- Positioning the line-height Property Correctly
- Testing Continually and Consistently
- Creating Source Image Files That Can Be Easily Customized and Resaved
- Breaking Out Sections of Source Image Files
- Creating Smart Navigation
- Reusing Images
- Indenting and Commenting Code
- Removing Spaces and Comments

When learning how to build Web sites, the most time-consuming aspect is not always creating the look and feel of the site in image editing software, such as Photoshop. Rather, more time is usually spent figuring out how to code the site. The tips and techniques included in this chapter will help the designer understand methods and workarounds that he will probably need to learn when creating sites. While not all the tips will be useful while building one site, many of them will eventually arise if the reader builds many sites over time.

TANTEK OR BOX MODEL HACK

If it were not for the Tantek hack, also referred to as the Celik or box model hack, creating more complex pure CSS designs for both compliant and noncompliant browsers would be considerably more difficult.

 It should be noted that the applicability of this hack has drastically decreased over the past couple of years with the decreased usage of IE 5.0 and 5.5. Plus, many purists do not approve of its use to begin with.

The main reason for the use of this hack is that versions of the IE 5 and 5.5 browsers treat the box model differently than other browsers. The way the box model is designed to work is that when the width property is assigned to a container, that width is supposed to represent only the width of the container. Borders, padding, and margin widths are not to be included in the total number of pixels. Thus if the width of the box is set to 200px, with the left and right padding properties set to 50px, which adds 50 pixels to both the left and right sides, the total width of the box would grow to 300 pixels (see Figure 16.1).

While newer browsers interpret the width property to W3C specifications, IE 5 and 5.5 do not. Rather than add the extra 100 pixels to the total, they include the extra pixels within the declared 200 pixels. This means the total width that is used for the content is reduced by the increased number of pixels. Thus in Figure 16.1, the total width of the content area has 100 pixels subtracted from the total 200 pixels.

Because of this bug, the designer needs to write code that works for two different environments. Some CSS purists feel style sheets should not include hacks. To accomplish this, a designer needs to resort to various workarounds, such as branching JavaScript. Many designers, however, use the Tantek hack, which feeds different values for IE 5 and 5.5, IE 6, and compliant browsers. The nontechnical way the hack functions is a three-step method:

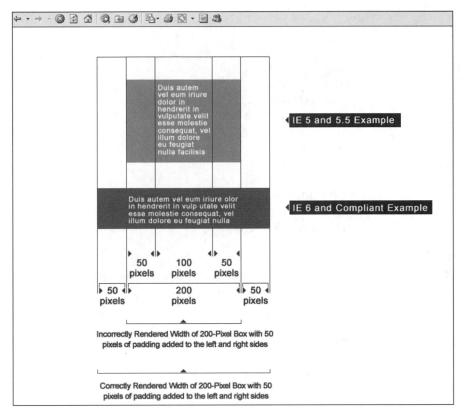

FIGURE 16.1   Example demonstrating how the box model is interpreted differently between IE 5 and 5.5 browsers and IE 6 and compliant browsers.

1. The CSS rule assigns the width, along with other styles, for the box element, from which all browsers read.

```
#tantek_hack_box {
position:relative;
background:#888787;
color:#ffffff;
padding-left:50px;
padding-right:50px;
width:200px; }
```

2. The hack is added, which first reassigns the width for the IE 6 browser.

```
#tantek_hack_box {
position:relative;
background:#888787;
color:#ffffff;
padding-left:50px;
padding-right:50px;
width:200px;
voice-family:"\"}\"";
voice-family:inherit;
    width:100px;
}
html>body #tantek_hack_box {
}
```

3. The hack then assigns the width that will be read by compliant browsers. In this step, the designer needs to add the same CSS selector to the new piece of code at the end.

```
#tantek_hack_box {
position:relative;
background:#888787;
color:#ffffff;
padding-left:50px;
padding-right:50px;
width:200px;
voice-family:"\"}\"";
voice-family:inherit;
    width:100px;
}
html>body #tantek_hack_box {
    width:100px;
}
```

Because there are other instances where various browsers treat CSS code differently, the Tantek hack can be used for other properties. A common use is to reposition elements that need to be altered when they have been nested inside other boxes and have inherited different values. The following code is used to position the two bottom-right columns of content in Figure 16.2 so that it appears the same in IE 5 and 5.5 and other major browsers.

```
#a5-featured-center {
    position:relative;
    left:-5px;
    top:-57px;
    color:#DF7A1B;
    border:0px solid #000000;
    margin:38px 124px 0px 208px;
    padding:19px 10px 0px 0px;
    voice-family:"\"}\"";
    voice-family:inherit;
        margin:140px 158px 0px 180px;
        left:27px;
        top:-159px;
    }
    html>body #a5-featured-center {
        margin:41px 130px 0px 207px;
        padding:19px 10px 0px 0px;
        left:0px;
        top:-60px;
    }
```

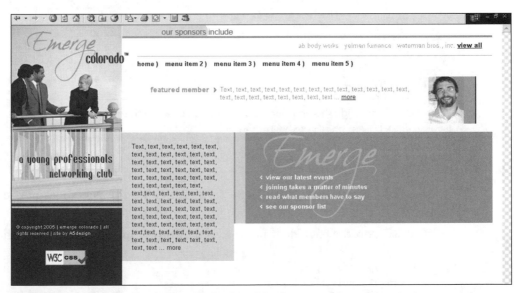

FIGURE 16.2   A design in IE 5.5 that uses the Tantek hack to correctly position the bottom-right columns of content in IE 5 and other major browsers. Copyright © 2006 Emerge Colorado. Used with permission.

When the hack is not applied, the site will look completely different in other browsers. Figure 16.3 shows how different the positioning would end up in IE 6, for example.

The Tantek hack is not always necessary. Sometimes the CSS code needs only to be cleaned up or reworked to accomplish the same look and feel.

While the Tantek hack is not considered pure form, the W3C CSS Validator will validate the code with only a warning. A good place to learn more about the hack is to go to http://tantek.com/CSS/Examples/boxmodelhack.html.

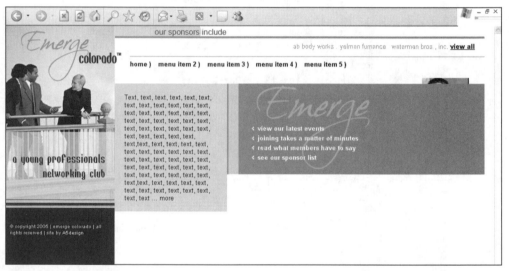

FIGURE 16.3   The design shown in Figure 16.2, viewed in IE 6 with the Tantek hack removed.

Copyright © 2006 Emerge Colorado. Used with permission.

NAMING RULES AND PROPERTIES CORRECTLY

Occasionally, the designer may add a style and either the page does not reflect the proper styling or the styling is incorrect. A few common errors can occur:

- The style on the page does not match the correct spelling in the style sheet.

```
<style type="text/css">
    #samplestyle {
    color:#ffffff;
    }
</style>
<div id="sample_style">
    This is sample text
</div>
```

Should read as

```
<style type="text/css">
    #samplestyle {
    color:#ffffff;
    }
</style>
<div id="samplestyle">
    This is sample text
</div>
```

- The style on the page may be referencing an ID selector when the selector in the style sheet is actually a class or vice versa.

```
<style type="text/css">
    .samplestyle {
    color:#ffffff;
    }
</style>
<div id="samplestyle">
    This is sample text
</div>
```

Should read as

```
<style type="text/css">
    .samplestyle {
    color:#ffffff;
    }
</style>
<div class="samplestyle">
    This is sample text
</div>
```

- The syntax of a style may not be correct. Missing semicolons are an occasional reason for this error.

```
<style type="text/css">
    #samplestyle {
    color:#ffffff;
    background:red
    }
</style>
```

Should read as

```
<style type="text/css">
    #samplestyle {
    color:#ffffff;
    background:red;
    }
</style>
```

Although it does not have anything to do with styling, another naming error a designer can make is to call the same ID class with two separate tags in the XHTML. While the page may still display correctly, the XHTML will not validate because an ID class can be referenced only once in a document.

Two other naming issues are more difficult to find. Sometimes, without removing code to test the problem, the designer will not find where the error is occurring.

- **Two rules could have the same selector name**—Because it is easy to copy a rule and simply modify it to serve as another rule, the designer can sometimes forget to rename the new rule. If a new rule has been added but its properties are not being applied in the browser, the problem could be that it has the same name as another rule.

```
<style type="text/css">
    #style1 {
    color:yellow;
    background:black;
    }
    #style2 {
    color:white;
    background:blue;
    }
    #style1 {
    color:green;
    background:purple;
    }
</style>
<div id="style1">
    This is sample text
</div>
<div id="style3">
    This is sample text
</div>
```

Should read as

```
<style type="text/css">
    #style1 {
    color:yellow;
    background:black;
    }
    #style2 {
    color:white;
    background:blue;
    }
    #style3 {
    color:green;
    background:purple;
    }
</style>
<div id="style1">
    This is sample text
</div>
<div id="style3">
    This is sample text
</div>
```

- **A rule applies correctly to IE browsers but not to compliant browsers—** This problem is hidden within the Tantek hack. The designer has to be sure the selector in the compliant-browser portion of the hack has the same name as the selector of the rule it is associated with.

```
#samplestyle {
position:relative;
background:#414141;
color:#ffffff;
padding-left:50px;
padding-right:50px;
padding-top:10px;
width:400px;
voice-family:"\"}\"";
voice-family:inherit;
    width:300px;
}
html>body #style2 {
    width:300px;
}
```

Should read as

```
#samplestyle {
position:relative;
background:#414141;
color:#ffffff;
padding-left:50px;
padding-right:50px;
padding-top:10px;
width:400px;
voice-family:"\"}\"";
voice-family:inherit;
    width:300px;
}
html>body #samplestyle {
    width:300px;
}
```

REMOVING BODY MARGINS AND PADDING

By default, browsers add top and left space between the browser window and the content that is output (see Figure 16.4). This space varies depending on the browser.

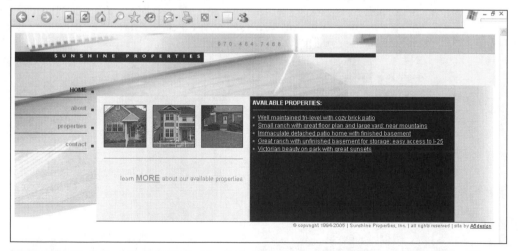

FIGURE 16.4 Web site with default margins that add space between the top and left edges of the Web window and the design.

Removing the space is easily accomplished. The designer needs only to assign the style to the HTML and BODY selectors in the main style sheet:

```
html, body {
    margin:0px;
    padding:0px;
    background:#ffffff;
    }
```

 For most browsers, setting the margin to 0px removes the spacing. Opera, however, requires the designer to set the padding setting to 0px.

Adding the margin and padding properties will make the page begin in the very top-left corner of the browser's window (see Figure 16.5). It is also always good form to define the background color.

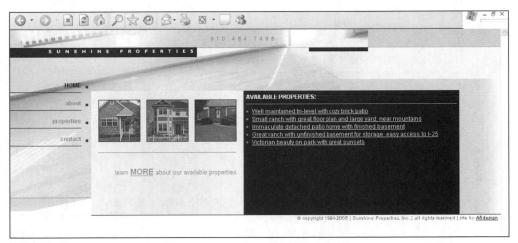

FIGURE 16.5   Page with the margin and padding properties for the <HTML> and <BODY> tags set to 0px.

CREATING THE FRAMEWORK FOR A FIXED-WIDTH CSS DESIGN

The four case studies in Chapters 9, 10, 11, 12, and 13 go into the specifics of creating fixed designs that can also be easily modified to be liquid layouts. This section explains the basics of creating the framework for such a design. Following are the various stages of creating such a design:

1. Add basic XHTML framework and initial style rule.

Things to note about the code in step 1:

- As with table-based designs, the code in Listing 16.1 provides the basic structure that contains the DocType, character encoding labeling, embedded or linked style sheet, and the code and content that are to be displayed on the page. A rule then defines the margins, padding, font, font color, and background color for the <HTML> and <BODY> tags.

LISTING 16.1   Code for Step 1

```
<!DOCTYPE html PUBLIC "-//W3C//DTD XHTML 1.0 Transitional//EN"
    "DTD/xhtml1-transitional.dtd">
<html><head><title>Fixed-Width Design</title>
<meta http-equiv="Content-Type" content="text/html;
    charset=iso-8859-1" />
<style type="text/css">
html, body {
    margin:0px;
    padding:0px;
    font: 13px Arial, Helvetica, sans-serif;
    color:#000000;
    background:#ffffff;
    }
</style>
</head>
<body>
</body>
</html>
```

2. Create body and header rules in the style sheet and add code to the XHTML body (see Figure 16.6).

FIGURE 16.6   Design with header area added, along with a tag that restrains the width of the design to 770 pixels.

Things to note about the code in step 2:

- The a5-body rule is used as a container to restrain the width of the entire page to 770 pixels. The advantage of being able to control the width is that if the designer wants the design to expand to the full width of the screen, the value of the width property simply needs to be set to 100%.

 <DIV> tags, by default, will stretch to 100% width of the screen when assigned relative positioning. If absolute positioning is assigned, the tag, by default, will expand only as wide as the content expands the container.

- The a5-header rule sets the basic properties of the <DIV> tag that will be assigned to the content inside the tag (see Listing 16.2).

LISTING 16.2   Code for Step 2

```
<!DOCTYPE html PUBLIC "-//W3C//DTD XHTML 1.0 Transitional//EN"
    "DTD/xhtml1-transitional.dtd">
<html><head><title>Fixed-Width Design</title>
<meta http-equiv="Content-Type" content="text/html;
    charset=iso-8859-1" />
<style type="text/css">
html, body {
    margin:0px;
    padding:0px;
    font: 13px Arial, Helvetica, sans-serif;
    color:#000000;
    background:#ffffff;
    }
#a5-body {
    position: absolute;
    left:0px;
    top:0px;
    width: 770px;
    text-align:left;
    }
#a5-header {
    position:absolute;
    left:0px;
    top:0px;
    text-align:center;
    color:#ffffff;
    width:100%;
    background:red;
    height:180px;
    }
```

```
    </style>
    </head>
    <body>
    <div id="a5-body">
        <div id="a5-header">
            Header content goes here.
        </div>
    </div>
    </body>
    </html>
```

3. Create rules in the style sheet that not only create the left and right columns but also the rule they are nested inside of. Then add the code to the XHTML body (see Figure 16.7).

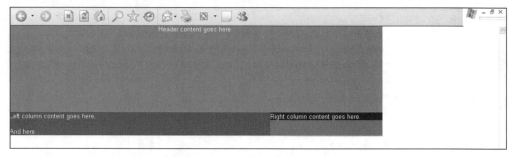

FIGURE 16.7   Design with the left and right columns added to a <DIV> tag that positions the content 180 pixels below the header <DIV>.

Things to note about the code in step 3:

- The a5-main-content rule is added to force the positioning of the left and right columns. It is positioned below the header, which is set to 180 pixels high. Therefore, the rule positions the <DIV> tag 180 pixels from the top. It also separates the nested left and right columns from the bottom footer area that will be added.
- The a5-column-left rule is created to force the <DIV> to the top-left corner of the a5-main-content <DIV> tag. The left property tells the <DIV> tag to position itself 0 pixels from the left side. The margin-right property of the rule restricts its positioning by telling it that it must end its width at 232 pixels from the right-hand side of the page or <DIV> tag in which it is nested.
- The a5-column-right rule is added to position the column on the right side of the page and force its width to 232 pixels. The right property tells the <DIV> tag that it is to be 0 pixels from the right side of the page.

Nesting <DIV> tags do not always function the same as nesting tables. Figure 16.7 shows that the background color of the right column does not stretch to the full height of the a5-main-content *tag in which it is nested. While the designer can force the height of the right column, if the left column grows, the right column will not change its height. This situation presents a problem when repeating a background color or image. The figure shows how the background of the* a5-main-content *extends vertically beyond the right column but not the left column because the left column is forcing the height. Unlike with table-based design, this changes the way a designer can control the look and feel of the site (see Listing 16.3).*

LISTING 16.3   Code for Step 3

```
<!DOCTYPE html PUBLIC "-//W3C//DTD XHTML 1.0 Transitional//EN"
    "DTD/xhtml1-transitional.dtd">
<html><head><title>Fixed-Width Design</title>
<meta http-equiv="Content-Type" content="text/html;
    charset=iso-8859-1" />
<style type="text/css">
html, body {
    margin:0px;
    padding:0px;
    font: 13px Arial, Helvetica, sans-serif;
    color:#000000;
    background:#ffffff;
    }
#a5-body {
    position: absolute;
    left:0px;
    top:0px;
    width:770px;
    text-align:left;
    }
#a5-header {
    position:absolute;
    left:0px;
    top:0px;
    text-align:center;
    color:#ffffff;
    width:100%;
    background:red;
    height:180px;
    }
```

```
#a5-main-content {
    position:absolute;
    left:0px;
    top:180px;
    color:#ffffff;
    width:100%;
    background:green;
    border:0px solid #ffffff;
    }
    #a5-column-left {
        position:relative;
        left:0px;
        top:0px;
        color:#ffffff;
        margin-right:232px;
        border:0px solid #ffffff;
        background:blue;
        }
    #a5-column-right {
        position:absolute;
        right:0px;
        top:0px;
        color:#ffffff;
        width:232px;
        background:black;
        border:0px solid #ffffff;
        }
</style>
</head>
<body>
<div id="a5-body">
    <div id="a5-header">
        Header content goes here.
    </div>
    <div id="a5-main-content">
        <div id="a5-column-left">
            Left column content goes here.<br /><br />And here.
        </div>
        <div id="a5-column-right">
            Right column content goes here.
        </div>
    </div>
</div>
</body>
</html>
```

4. Create a footer rule in the style sheet and add the code to the XHTML body (see Figure 16.8).

FIGURE 16.8   Design with the footer rule added.

Things to note about the code in step 4:

- The a5-footer rule is nested inside the a5-main-content tag. When the rule is assigned relative positioning, it is forced to the next line because the left and right columns fill the entire width of the page. If the a5-column-left rule were assigned absolute positioning without a width, the left and right columns together would not fill the entire width of the page, which would bump up the positioning of the a5-footer area, making the page look jumbled (see Figure 16.9).
- The a5-footer rule does not need a width assigned because it is assigned relative positioning, which makes it fill 100% of the width by default (see Listing 16.4).

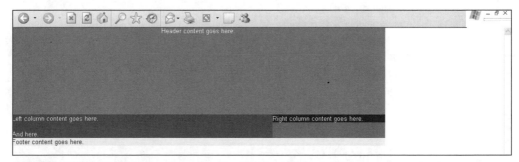

FIGURE 16.9   Completed framework of fixed-width design that includes two nested columns in a <DIV> tag that is positioned between the header and footer areas.

LISTING 16.4   Code for Step 4

```
<!DOCTYPE html PUBLIC "-//W3C//DTD XHTML 1.0 Transitional//EN"
    "DTD/xhtml1-transitional.dtd">
<html><head><title>Fixed-Width Design</title>
<meta http-equiv="Content-Type" content="text/html;
```

```
            charset=iso-8859-1" />
<style type="text/css">
html, body {
    margin:0px;
    padding:0px;
    font: 13px Arial, Helvetica, sans-serif;
    color:#000000;
    background:#ffffff;
    }
#a5-body {
    position: absolute;
    left:0px;
    top:0px;
    width:770px;
    text-align:left;
    }
#a5-header {
    position:absolute;
    left:0px;
    top:0px;
    text-align:center;
    color:#ffffff;
    width:100%;
    background:red;
    height:180px;
    }
#a5-main-content {
    position:absolute;
    left:0px;
    top:180px;
    color:#ffffff;
    width:100%;
    background:green;
    border:0px solid #ffffff;
    }
    #a5-column-left {
        position:absolute;
        left:0px;
        top:0px;
        color:#ffffff;
        margin-right:232px;
        border:0px solid #ffffff;
        background:blue;
        }
```

```
        #a5-column-right {
            position:absolute;
            right:0px;
            top:0px;
            color:#ffffff;
            width:232px;
            background:black;
            border:0px solid #ffffff;
            }
    #a5-footer {
        position:relative;
        left:0px;
        top:0px;
        color:#000000;
        background:yellow;
        border:0px solid #ffffff;
        }
    </style>
    </head>
    <body>
    <div id="a5-body">
        <div id="a5-header">
            Header content goes here.
        </div>
        <div id="a5-main-content">
            <div id="a5-column-left">
                Left column content goes here.<br /><br />And here.
            </div>
            <div id="a5-column-right">
                Right column content goes here.
            </div>
            <div id="a5-footer">
                Footer content goes here.
            </div>
        </div>
    </div>
    </body>
    </html>
```

Typically, the designer adds text, images, and additional code to the framework as it is being built. Figure 16.10 is a simplified example of how the page would look with content added and the style sheet modified to not only make the page more attractive but to also customize various <DIV> tags.

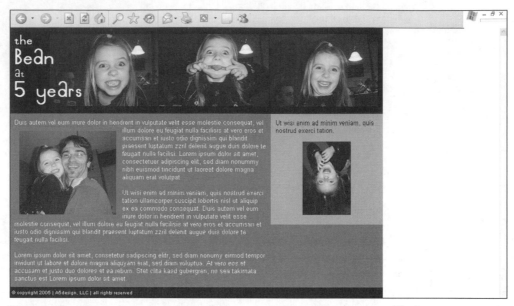

FIGURE 16.10   Sample content added to framework of the site, which was modified to accompany the content and to make it more attractive.

TAKING INTO ACCOUNT INCREASING AND DECREASING COLUMN HEIGHTS

Although it is nice to include the footer row at the bottom of the design in Figure 16.10, there are a couple of caveats to this layout, at least when including containers that use absolute positioning:

- Because the positioning of the right column is set to `absolute`, if the content in the column were to be increased, it would not only stretch lower than the left column, but because the footer also has relative positioning assigned to it, the right column would also flow above or below it, depending on the browser (see Figure 16.11).
- If the content in the left column were to be decreased, not only would the right column extend below both it and the footer `<DIV>`, but the footer `<DIV>` would move up past the `a5-main-content <DIV>` (see Figure 16.12).

Because the photo in the left column of Figure 16.12 is floated, it is not included in the document flow, meaning other elements could pass above and below it, as well as in front of and behind it.

If the amount of content is going to change dynamically, this design structure may not be the best solution. The designer may consider not including a footer area and assigning different positions to the `<DIV>` tags, or the designer may want to use the design technique in Chapter 12 or 13 that provides a solution to creating equal column designs.

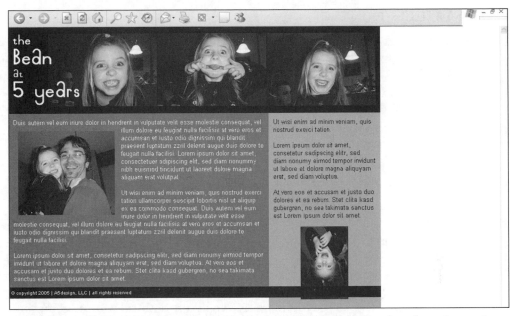

FIGURE 16.11   A problem with a container with absolute positioning (right column) running past a container with relative positioning (footer) that should, visually, remain below it.

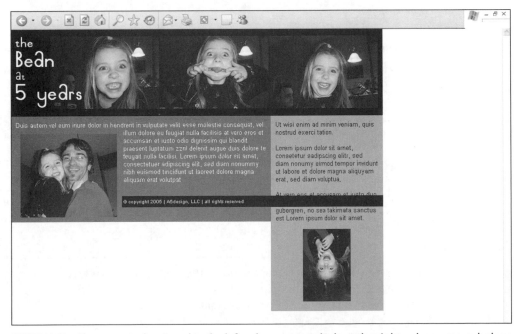

FIGURE 16.12   If content is decreased in the left column, not only does the right column move below the footer, but the footer moves up.

CENTERING A FIXED-WIDTH DESIGN

Depending on the requirements, some sites need to be designed with liquid layouts—that is, they fill the full width of the screen. Yet others require a fixed width. HTML and XHTML used to make the process simple, but with the varied browser support of CSS, the process is a little more involved. One way requires wrapping two different <DIV> tags around the body. Following are the steps to accomplish this task:

1. Add a rule to the style sheet that centers the fixed-width design, which is set at 770 pixels for this example. This rule centers the body for IE 5 and 5.5.

   ```
   #a5-body-center {
       text-align:center;
       }
   ```

2. Add a second rule that sets the text-align property to left, assigns the left and right margins to auto, and defines the positioning as relative. Setting the positioning to relative will allow the design to be positioned relative to the <DIV> tag in which it is nested. The auto value of the margins will tell the browser to set the margins evenly on both sides, thus centering the code. The text-align:left; code is added because the a5-body-center rule that was added centers not only the body, but also the text in that container, by inheritance.

   ```
   #a5-body-center {
       text-align:center;
       }
   #a5-body {
       position: absolute;
       left:0px;
       top:0px;
       width:770px;
       text-align:left;
       }
   ```

3. Add the two <DIV> tags around the code between the <BODY> tags in the XHTML page. Listing 16.5 is the code that was used to create Figure 16.10.

LISTING 16.5   Code for Figure 16.10

```
<!DOCTYPE html PUBLIC "-//W3C//DTD XHTML 1.0 Transitional//EN"
    "DTD/xhtml1-transitional.dtd">
<html><head><title>Fixed-Width Design</title>
<meta http-equiv="Content-Type" content="text/html;
    charset=iso-8859-1" />
<style type="text/css">
```

```
html, body {
    margin:0px;
    padding:0px;
    font: 13px Arial, Helvetica, sans-serif;
    color:#000000;
    background:#ffffff;
    }
#a5-body-center {
    text-align:center;
    }
#a5-body {
    position: relative;
    margin-left:auto;
    margin-right:auto;
    width:770px;
    text-align:left;
    }
#a5-header {
    text-align:center;
    color:#ffffff;
    width:100%;
    padding-top:15px;
    background:black;
    height:180px;
    }
#a5-main-content {
    position:absolute;
    left:0px;
    top:180px;
    color:#ffffff;
    width:100%;
    background:#89766F;
    border:0px solid #ffffff;
    }
    #a5-column-left {
        position:relative;
        left:0px;
        top:0px;
        color:#ffffff;
        padding:10px;
        margin-right:232px;
        background:#7A7878;
        border:0px solid #ffffff;
    }
```

```
            #a5-column-right {
                position:absolute;
                right:0px;
                top:0px;
                color:#000000;
                height:100%;
                width:232px;
                background:#B0ADAD;
                border:0px solid #ffffff;
                }
        #a5-footer {
            position:relative;
            left:0px;
            top:0px;
            font: 10px Arial, Helvetica, sans-serif;
            padding:5px;
            color:#ffffff;
            background:#000000;
            border:0px solid #ffffff;
            }
        </style>
        </head>
        <body>
        <div id="a5-body-center">
            <div id="a5-body">
                <div id="a5-header">
                        <div><img src="images/photo_beanie_faces.jpg"
                        width="750" height="150" alt="" border="0" /></div>
                </div>
                <div id="a5-main-content">
                    <div id="a5-column-left">
                        Duis autem vel eum iriure dolor in hendrerit in
                            vulputate velit esse <span  style="position:
                            relative;float:left;padding:10px;"><img
                            src="images/photo_beanie_daddy.jpg" width="200"
                            height="171" alt="" border="0" /></span>molestie
                            consequat, vel illum dolore eu feugiat nulla
                            facilisis at vero eros et accumsan et iusto odio
                            dignissim qui blandit praesent luptatum zzril
                            delenit augue duis dolore te feugait nulla
                            facilisi. Lorem ipsum dolor sit amet, consectetuer
```

```
                         adipiscing elit, sed diam nonummy nibh euismod
                         tincidunt ut laoreet dolore magna aliquam erat
                         volutpat
     <br /><br />
     Ut wisi enim ad minim veniam, quis nostrud exerci tation
         ullamcorper suscipit lobortis nisl ut aliquip ex ea commodo
         consequat. Duis autem vel eum iriure dolor in hendrerit in
         vulputate velit esse molestie consequat, vel illum dolore eu
         feugiat nulla facilisis at vero eros et accumsan et iusto
         odio dignissim qui blandit praesent luptatum zzril delenit
         augue duis dolore te feugait nulla facilisi.
     <br /><br />
     Lorem ipsum dolor sit amet, consetetur sadipscing elitr, sed diam
         nonumy eirmod tempor invidunt ut labore et dolore magna
         aliquyam erat, sed diam voluptua. At vero eos et accusam et
         justo duo dolores et ea rebum. Stet clita kasd gubergren, no
         sea takimata sanctus est Lorem ipsum dolor sit amet.
             </div>
             <div id="a5-column-right">
                 <div style="padding:10px;">
     Ut wisi enim ad minim veniam, quis nostrud exerci tation.
                     <br />
                     <div style="text-align:center;padding:15px 0px 10px
                         0px;"><img src="images/photo_beanie_right.jpg"
                         width="100" height="150" alt="" border="0"
                         /></div>
                 </div>
             </div>
             <div id="a5-footer">
                 © copyright 2005 | A5design, LLC | all rights
                     reserved  
             </div>
         </div>
     </div>
 </div>
 </body>
 </html>
```

When the page is rendered, it would look like Figure 16.13. Notice that there is an even amount of space on both sides of the design.

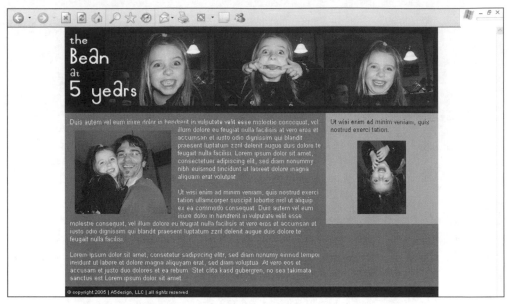

FIGURE 16.13   Fixed-width design that is centered using CSS.

CREATING A LIQUID DESIGN

Because of the way the fixed design was created, modifying it to be a liquid design is very simple. All the designer needs to do is change the 770px value of the a5-body rule to 100%. This is because the left column will always try to fill the screen because it is assigned relative positioning and it is included in a <DIV> tag, which together defaults to 100% width. There are two main reasons the design works the way it does:

- The left column has relative positioning assigned to it, so it can expand and contract, depending on the resolution and/or width of the screen.
- While the positioning will stretch to 100% by default, it can also be controlled with the margin property. In this case, the margin-right property is set to 232px, which means the column will stretch within 232 pixels of the right side of the screen but no further.

Figure 16.14 shows how the page shown in Figure 16.13 expands when the value of the a5-body rule is changed from 770px to 100%.

Chapters 9, 10, 11, 12, and 13 provide additional examples and explanations of how designs can be created to be liquid.

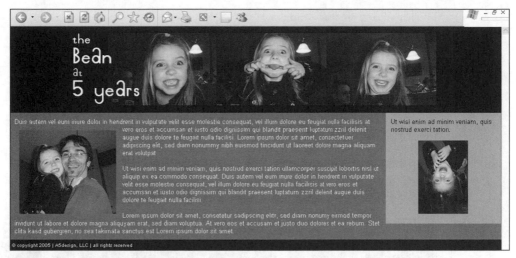

FIGURE 16.14   Liquid design that fills the full width of the screen.

RENDERING THE <HR /> TAG CONSISTENTLY

With XHTML table-based design, creating a line between content is very easy. The developer can either include the code <HR /> or add a table row with a one-pixel image (or whatever height the designer chooses) with a background color assigned to the table cell:

```
<tr>
    <td bgcolor="#000000"><img src="images/ spacer.gif" alt=" " width="1"
    height="1" border="0" /></td>
</tr>
```

CSS design, however, does not interpret the <HR /> tag consistently in all browsers. Figure 16.15 shows how the <HR /> tag is displayed in various browsers (see Listing 16.6).

LISTING 16.6   Code for Figure 16.15

```
<!DOCTYPE html PUBLIC "-//W3C//DTD XHTML 1.0 Transitional//EN"
    "http://www.w3.org/TR/xhtml1/DTD/xhtml1-transitional.dtd">
<html>
<head>
    <title>Untitled</title>
<style>
#samplebox {
    background:#000000;
    width:120px;
    height:50px;
```

```
        padding-bottom:15px;
        }
</style>
</head>
<body>
<div id="samplebox">
    <br />
        <hr />
    <br /><br />
</div>
</body>
</html>
```

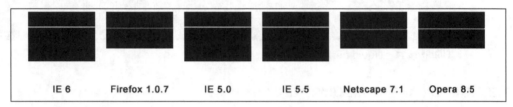

| IE 6 | Firefox 1.0.7 | IE 5.0 | IE 5.5 | Netscape 7.1 | Opera 8.5 |

FIGURE 16.15   Various ways the <HR /> tag, along with basic CSS formatting, will be displayed in different browsers.

There are a couple of items to notice about Figure 16.15:

- The <HR> line is not positioned at the same height in the browsers, which will affect pixel-specific placement of other elements.
- The default color of the <HR> line is not consistent.

This disparity in the rendering of the tag makes the designer have to use workaround code to maintain consistency among browsers. The code in Listing 16.7 can be used to provide a more consistent line in all six browsers tested for Figure 16.16.

LISTING 16.7   Code that Gives Line Consistency Across Browsers for Figure 16.16

```
<!DOCTYPE html PUBLIC "-//W3C//DTD XHTML 1.0 Transitional//EN"
    "http://www.w3.org/TR/xhtml1/DTD/xhtml1-transitional.dtd">
<html>
<head>
    <title>Untitled</title>
<style>
#samplebox {
    background:#000000;
    width:120px;
    height:50px;
    padding-bottom:15px;
```

```
    }
div.hrline {
    height:1px;
    background:url(images/sample-hr.gif) repeat-x scroll center;
}
div.hrline hr {
    display:none;
}
</style>
</head>
<body>
<div id="samplebox">
    <br />
    <div class="hrline"><hr /></div>
</div>
</body>
</html>
```

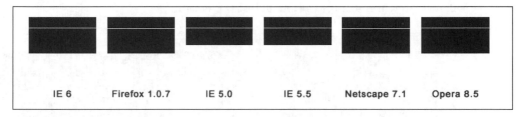

FIGURE 16.16   A more consistent rendering of CSS code that makes use of an image repeated as a line.

There are a couple of things to notice about Figure 16.16:

- Although it is impossible to tell with a black/white image, the color of the line is now consistent among all browsers.
- While the specific placement of the line is not at the exact same pixel height, the code renders the line in a more consistent manner in the different browsers.

CREATING A LINE WITHOUT THE <HR /> TAG

While it's possible to create the <HR /> tag consistently as in the previous section, a much easier way is to give either a top or bottom border of a <DIV> container a size of 1 and color of #000000, for example. Sometimes, though, the container may already have the border turned on for a reason or not be able to be turned on for a reason. In this case, a quick workaround is to add a <DIV> in the content flow. The spacing of the text above and below the <DIV> can be easily controlled by simply adding a top and bottom margin to the container (see Listing 16.8).

LISTING 16.8   Code that Creates a Line Using a <DIV> Tag

```
This would be the text in the top paragraph of the page.
<div style="border-bottom:1px solid #000000;margin:10px 0px 10px 0px;"></div>
This would be the text in the bottom paragraph of the page.
```

USING BACKGROUND IMAGES AS DESIGN ELEMENTS

One disadvantage of designing table-based sites is that once three or more tables are nested inside each other, some browsers, such as Netscape 4.7, will not properly render the images and portions of the table cells they do not fill up. CSS-based design allows for the full use of background images, which includes layering nested background images on top of one another. This change allows for more design possibilities. One example is to use a background image for the entire site. While this has always been available with XHTML table-based design, there is no longer concern for the designer of running into browser issues, as more and more background images are nested inside one another.

Figure 16.17 shows how background images can be used more extensively. There are three things to note about the design:

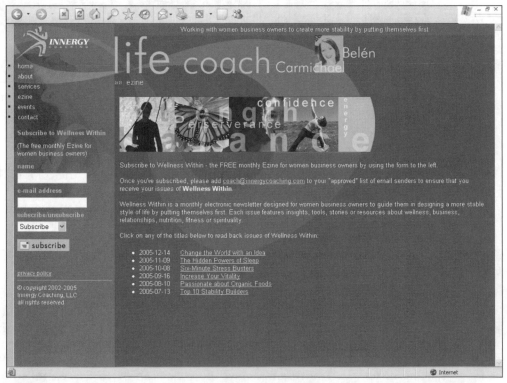

FIGURE 16.17   Design that uses background images as menu bullets, images for the left and right columns, and a repeating image for the entire page. Copyright © 2006 Innergy Coaching, LLC. Used with permission.

- The background in the right column (right side of the infinity loop) is broken up from the background in the left column (left side of the loop, along with the woman). This is because the right image is best saved as a GIF file, while the left image should be saved as a JPG.
- The entire left column of color is repeated as a background image in the page's <BODY> tag, so it will repeat endlessly down the left-hand side. It repeats underneath the background image of the left column. Because the bottom of the left background image looks exactly like the page background image, there is seamless repeating.
- Each menu item is assigned a background image to its left that serves as a bullet. The bullet changes when the menu item is moused over, which is explained in the next section.

CODING CSS MOUSEOVERS

Menu mouseovers used to require JavaScript to perform a simple image switch. Now, CSS allows the designer to simply replace the background image by assigning a different image when the user mouses over an item. The three-step process is as follows:

1. The designer creates a rule that will be used to display the menu item when it is not moused over. The two main properties to pay attention to in the following code are display and background. The display property, when assigned a block value, tells the browser to vertically stack each hyperlinked menu item when it is included inside the a5-menu container. The background property, with its values, determines what image will be used for the menu item, including how it will be positioned and whether it will be repeated. In this example, the image will not be repeated, and it will be positioned in the top-left corner of the block.

```
#a5-menu a {
    display: block;
    background: url(images/bg-menu-off.gif) no-repeat 0px 0px;
    text-decoration:none;
    color:#ffffff;
    font-weight:normal;
    padding: 3px 5px 2px 25px;
}
```

2. The designer then adds the hover element to the hyperlinks. When the user mouses over a link, the background image is changed from bg-menu-off.gif to bg-menu-on.gif, with the same positioning of the image. The font is turned bold, so not only the image, but also the changing text color, identifies the link.

```
#a5-menu a:hover {
        background: url(images/bg-menu-on.gif) no-repeat 0px 0px;
        font-weight:bold;
        color:#ffffff;
}
```

3. The menu items need to be added to a container with the ID value of a5-menu.

```
<div id="a5-menu">
        <a href="index.htm">home</a>
        <a href="about.htm">about</a>
        <a href="services.htm">services</a>
        <a href="ezine.htm">ezine</a>
        <a href="contact.htm">contact</a>
</div>
```

Figure 16.18 illustrates how the menu is displayed and how it appears when an item is moused over. Notice that the background image changes and the Services link becomes bold.

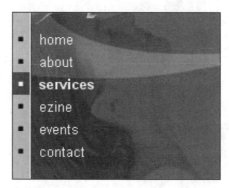

FIGURE 16.18   CSS-driven mouseover in the menu section of the site. Copyright © 2006 Innergy Coaching, LLC. Used with permission.

    A more complex CSS menu that provides dropdown menus is included on the CD. It allows for multi-level flyouts and customization possibilities.

USING JAVASCRIPT DROPDOWN MENUS

Often, a site requires more than a flat menu. Rather, it requires dropdown menus so the user can easily access the various levels of key pages by perusing the menu on one page. Figure 16.19 provides an example of such a menu.

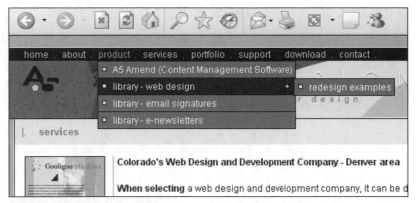

FIGURE 16.19   Example of a dropdown JavaScript menu.

Unless the designer or developer understands JavaScript, creating such a menu can be time-intensive. One solution is to purchase a system that will automatically create the menu. An example of such a system is EZ Menu, included on the CD-ROM that comes with this book. The software allows the designer to create a menu by using a simple user interface. Once the various attributes are assigned, the software builds the code for the designer.

ON THE CD

REMEMBERING THE ORDER OF MARGIN AND PADDING SHORTCUTS

Writing shorthand CSS properties and values makes designing and managing sites much easier. Sometimes remembering the order of the shorthand methods, however, is not always as easy. There is a visual reminder for the value order of the two most commonly used properties: `margin` and `padding`. Because the values are ordered in clockwise motion, they can be visualized as being positioned around a box, starting with the top border (see Figure 16.20).

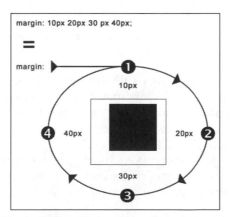

FIGURE 16.20   A visual reminder of how the values are ordered with the shorthand versions of the `margin` and `padding` properties.

USING THE BORDER AND BACKGROUND PROPERTIES FOR TROUBLESHOOTING

When developing CSS designs where containers of images and text are mortised together, it is important to know exactly where the boundaries of each box are. If this is not known, a simple process of adding a background color to a container can turn into a time-consuming task. Looking at Figure 16.21, it appears that the containers are properly positioned.

FIGURE 16.21   A page with three boxes laid out so no overlap or misplacement appears.

The truth, however, is while the text and images may be properly positioned, this does not mean the boxes that contain them are designed to be easily edited. Adding a background color to the top paragraph makes it readily apparent that the page's infrastructure is not as properly positioned as it may appear without the background color (see Figure 16.22).

Before a designer can correct such a problem with a design, it is necessary to understand where the boundaries are for the elements that are going to be modified. Two methods can be used to view the borders:

FIGURE 16.22   Results of adding a background color to the top container, which includes the text.

- **Turn on the border of the elements by setting it to at least one pixel (see Figure 16.23)** —The code to do so is `border:1px solid #000000;`. When the designer is done testing the container, the value of the border size can be set to 0, such as `border:0px solid #000000;`. Much of the code in this book contains such lines. Because the extra code takes up a nominal amount of file size, it is easier to turn the border off than to remove the code. One advantage to this is that the designer can view the shapes of the containers and what is layered behind them because, other than the borders, they are transparent.

- **Similar to the example in Figure 16.22, the background color can be set to contrast with the background of adjacent containers (see Figure 16.24)** —The code to do so is `background:red;`. The advantage of this method is that the designer understands the exact width a container will take up. If, on the other hand, a designer is trying to position two boxes to the exact pixel, turning on the borders of the boxes will be confusing because compliant browsers will add the extra width to the total width. Thus, if a box is 200 pixels wide, it will grow to 202 if the border is set to 1 because 1 pixel will be added to both the left and right sides.

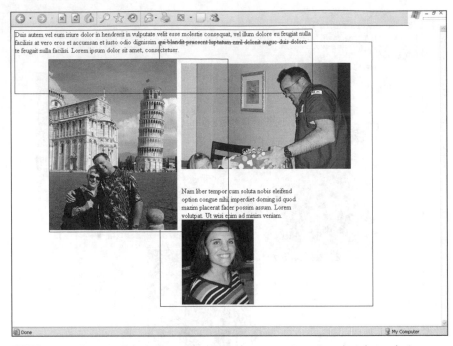

FIGURE 16.23   A page with the containers' borders set to 1 to view their boundaries.

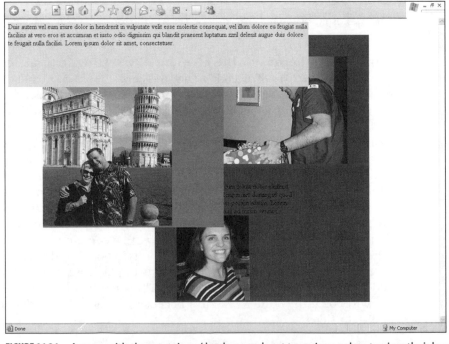

FIGURE 16.24   A page with the containers' backgrounds set to various colors to view their locations.

COMMENTING OUT CODE FOR TROUBLESHOOTING

Any novice designer or developer can create code. An experienced designer or developer, however, can fix things "under the hood." Being able to troubleshoot a page, whether it is XHTML, CSS, or a programming language, is a very useful skill to have. One helpful method for testing pages is to remove code to either see how a page will react in terms of layout or to see if the problem disappears when the code is removed.

While code can be cut and the page can be saved to perform such testing, the code can be lost if the computer crashes before the code can be reinserted and re-saved. A safer method is to comment out the code. This is accomplished by using comment tags. The tags tell the browser or server to either not display or interpret the code, depending on the method used. For most languages, comment tags work similarly to XHTML tags, where an opening tag is added to the beginning and a closing tag is added to the end of the code that is to be excluded. Comment tags vary depending on the language, and the following are three examples of commonly used tags:

- **XHTML**—The opening tag is <!– . The closing tag is –>. The second line of the following code would be output by the server but not displayed by the browser:

```
This is a sample line of text. <br />
<!– This is the line that would be commented out <br /> –>
This is the line of code the browser would begin displaying again.
```

An XHTML page will not validate if the comment tags do not have the correct syntax. If the developer, for instance, has too many hyphens in a comment tag, it will not validate.

- **CSS**—The opening tag is /*. The closing tag is */. The second property of the following rule would be interpreted by the browser:

```
#photo2 {
    position:absolute;

    /* width:90px; */
    height:80px;
    }
```

- **JavaScript**—This is one exception of using comment tags where the designer does not necessarily need to include a closing tag. The opening tag would merely be //. The second line of the following code would be output by the server but not interpreted by the browser:

```
bullet_text_on = new Image
// bullet_text_off = new Image
bullet_text_on.src = "http://www.a5design.com/images/
    bullet_text_on.gif"
```

If, however, the designer wanted to comment out the entire section of code, an opening /* could be used, along with a closing */. Following is how the code would look if it all were to be commented out:

```
/*
bullet_text_on = new Image
bullet_text_off = new Image
bullet_text_on.src = http://www.a5design.com/images/bullet_text_on.gif
*/
```

Comment tags apply to rows differently for different languages. Such tags for XHTML and CSS will turn off code on multiple lines. Comment tags for JavaScript, however, apply to only one row. While commenting out JavaScript code is more difficult, the advantage is that it doesn't require a closing tag.

USING UNIQUE NAMING CONVENTIONS

When designing and developing code, whether it is XHTML, CSS, or a programming language, it is usually a smart practice to come up with a unique naming convention because there will be times when one developer's code has to be integrated with another developer's code. If naming conventions conflict, then errors will occur that will require time to troubleshoot.

When creating ID and class selectors in CSS, for example, most of the rules in this book will begin with a5-, which is short for A5design. This helps prevent integrating a style sheet with another site's style sheet. If both style sheets contain a selector for the header, odds are that the other one will not be named a5-header. Instead, it may likely be header.

CONTROLLING THE MARGINS IN <FORM> TAGS

Depending on the browser, form tags come with a different default margin setting. If the form does not follow inline text, it will react similarly across most browsers. Figure 16.25, on the other hand, shows how the code in Listing 16.9 would be interpreted if it were to follow inline text.

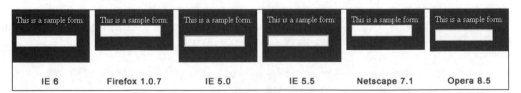

| IE 6 | Firefox 1.0.7 | IE 5.0 | IE 5.5 | Netscape 7.1 | Opera 8.5 |

FIGURE 16.25 How a <FORM> tag is interpreted differently in various browsers when it follows inline text.

LISTING 16.9   Code for Figure 16.25

```
<!DOCTYPE html PUBLIC "-//W3C//DTD XHTML 1.0 Transitional//EN"
    "http://www.w3.org/TR/xhtml1/DTD/xhtml1-transitional.dtd">
<html>
<head>
    <title>Untitled</title>
<style>
#a5-form {
    position:absolute;
    left:90px;
    top:80px;
    color:#ffffff;
    padding:10px;
    background:#000000;
    border:0px solid #000000;
    }
</style>
</head>
<body>
<div id="a5-form">
    This is a sample form:<br />
    <form action="test.cfm" method="post">
        <input type="text" size="15" name="test" />
    </form>
</div>
</body>
</html>
```

To make the margins consistent among the various tested browsers, the designer needs only to add the following style to the form: `style="margin: 0px;"`. Figure 16.26 demonstrates how consistently the form (see Listing 16.10) will be interpreted after using the `margin` property in Listing 16.10.

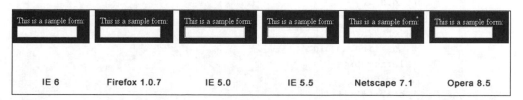

| IE 6 | Firefox 1.0.7 | IE 5.0 | IE 5.5 | Netscape 7.1 | Opera 8.5 |

FIGURE 16.26   The consistent manner in which a `<FORM>` tag will be displayed if a style is added that sets its margins to 0 pixels.

LISTING 16.10 Code for Figure 16.26

```
<!DOCTYPE html PUBLIC "-//W3C//DTD XHTML 1.0 Transitional//EN"
    "http://www.w3.org/TR/xhtml1/DTD/xhtml1-transitional.dtd">
<html>
<head>
    <title>Untitled</title>
<style>
#a5-form {
    position:absolute;
    left:90px;
    top:80px;
    color:#ffffff;
    padding:10px;
    background:#000000;
    border:0px solid #000000;
    }
</style>
</head>
<body>
<div id="a5-form">
    This is a sample form:<br />
    <form action="test.cfm" method="post" style="margin:0px;">
        <input type="text" size="15" name="test" />
    </form>
</div>
</body>
</html>
```

If desired, the designer could also place the style in a general <FORM> rule in the style sheet. If this is the case, the inline style does not need to be included in the XHTML <FORM> tag. The style sheet would then look like the following:

```
<style>
form {
margin:0px;
}
#a5-form {
    position:absolute;
    left:90px;
    top:80px;
    color:#ffffff;
    padding:10px;
    background:#000000;
    border:0px solid #000000;
    }
</style>
```

AVOIDING HORIZONTAL SCROLLBARS

When designing a page, it is usually best to avoid use of a horizontal scroll bar (see Figure 16.27). While some users already feel bothered to scroll vertically, scrolling horizontally, in many circles, is considered a cardinal sin. This is why a designer often wants to avoid making a page that is too wide, even if just by a few pixels, to make sure a design does not activate the horizontal bar.

The one exception to this rule is if the designer is creating a site for a higher resolution that some users will not have their monitors set to.

FIGURE 16.27   A page with the horizontal scrollbar activated because the page was made too wide.

While page width must obviously be taken into consideration, a more subtle consideration is the browser the site is being designed in. Compliant browsers do not include the right scroll bar until the height of the page requires it, unlike IE, which always includes it. This means that if the designer creates a page in a compliant browser, an extra 18 pixels will be added to the page, which means the designer has 18 pixels less horizontal space to work with. This is why it is a good practice to design sites initially in IE to ensure that the extra pixels are already included in the width. This avoids the need to test the page in compliant browsers because the extra width is already included in the screen real estate.

USING CSS SHORTCUTS

The goal of this book is not necessarily to produce the most efficient CSS coding possible. Rather, it is to make the examples as simple as possible, thus ensuring that the concepts are understood more easily. If the designer wanted to create more efficient code, one way is to use CSS shortcuts. One example of such a shortcut is using an abbreviated HEX number, such as `#fff` instead of `#ffffff`. This, however, is just the beginning of many options. More shortcuts can be easily found by using a search engine.

UNDERSTANDING FONT UNITS

There are many considerations when it comes to what type of unit to use when sizing fonts on the Web. The options include pixels, points, ems, and percentages. Following are some things to consider when selecting a font:

- Will the text be viewed in a browser, printed, or both?
- What type of operating system is the design primarily meant for?
- Do you want users to be able to resize the fonts using their browsers?

This subject requires thorough discussion, but it is being noted here for the designer to be aware of the various options for further possible investigation.

Using Globally Driven <span> and <div> Tags for Printing Purposes

Sometimes using local or inline styles can benefit the designer if an element on that page, for example, is the only item in the site that needs to be modified. For example, if a warning on a page needs to be colored red, such an inline style would work best. One disadvantage of using local or inline styles is if the designer wants to add a printing style sheet. Because a printing style sheet enables, and sometimes requires, a designer to be able to set the display property to none, if those styles cannot be controlled from one document, then the designer will have to modify each of those pages, which not only takes time, but also creates the unnecessary risk of possibly missing a style without thorough testing.

Using Non-graphical Elements When Designing Rebrandable Sites

Rebrandable sites many times require the designer to create elements that can be easily customizable for various clients. Figure 16.28 is an example of such a site.

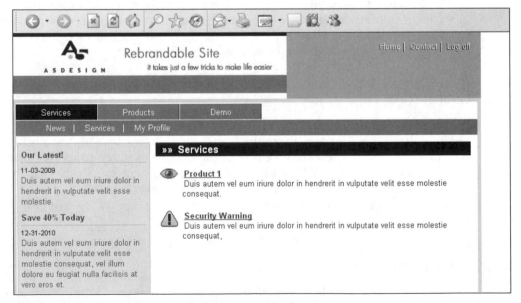

FIGURE 16.28 A rebrandable site with various reusable elements.

Following are four simple tricks being used to create more visual, reusable elements in Figure 16.28:

1. **Layered CSS text that could serve as a drop shadow**—By duplicating XHTML and CSS code, the designer can layer one element over the other. The CSS rule, of course, would need a unique name, but once it's renamed, it can be positioned under the other. This method is used for menu text in the top-right corner in Figure 16.28. The top layer of text is saved as white, while the lower layer is saved as black. The lower layer is simply moved one pixel to the right and one pixel down.

2. **Inline characters that are produced by XHTML code**—There are many XHTML characters that can be used in sites as bullets or other elements to provide easy visual recognition by the user. The arrows to the left of the Services page title are created by the following code: ».

3. **Icons that can be layered over any element, without the risk of anti-aliasing affecting their quality**—This element is not unique to Web design. Nearly all software uses it with its icons. The secret is to create clean edges that don't blend into the background (see Figure 16.29).

FIGURE 16.29 An icon that can stand on its own without requiring anti-aliasing.

By not blending into the background, the icon can be moved wherever on the page or have the background image changed without any consequences, other than the colors possibly not popping off the page. Figure 16.30 shows what the icon would look like on the page if its background were changed to black.

FIGURE 16.30 The same icon in Figure 16.29 with the background color changed to black.

4. **Using linear shapes**—With curves comes anti-aliasing, which makes it more difficult to change background colors of Web sites or portions of them. While curves are used in the icon, the designer is able to get away with that because the icon is small, making it more difficult to see the pixilation along the edges. This is why many sites use linear shapes that do not require any new images to be created. Instead, the background image is simply changed in the style sheet. All of the shapes in the header in Figure 16.28, barring the logo and the "Rebrandable Site" text, use CSS layered <DIV> tags to provide the design. It is a simple example but one that illustrates the possibilities if the designer were to get creative.

INCLUDING HIDDEN <DIV> TAGS FOR FUTURE USE

When creating rebrandable sites, it is necessary sometimes for the designer to prepare for content that may be added to the source code down the road. One way to do this is to create containers in the code. When the display property is set to none, the container will then be "invisible" until the property is removed. Figure 16.31 shows how Figure 16.28 would look if the following rule had its display property removed from the style sheet.

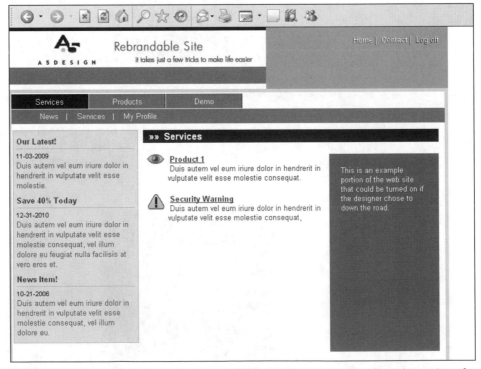

FIGURE 16.31   The same design as in Figure 16.28 but with a container in the right portion of the body made visible.

For a lot of sites, it is not overly difficult to go into the code to add elements after the site is live. Some sites, however, require more involved coding that may make it too time-consuming or difficult to add elements after the fact. This is a quick solution for sites with such future needs.

POSITIONING THE LINE-HEIGHT PROPERTY CORRECTLY

Using the `line-height` property allows the designer to not only play with a site's typography, but also have the ability to increase or decrease the height of a text area for structural purposes. To do this, the following code is all that needs to be added to a rule: `line-height:14px;`. This property, however, will not be read by browsers if it is positioned above the `font` property. Following is an example of the incorrect and correct placement of the `line-height` property:

Incorrectly positioned `line-height` property:

```
#a5-column-left-text {
  line-height:60px;
  ont: 10pt tahoma, arial, helvetica, sans-serif;
  }
```

Correctly positioned `line-height` property:

```
#a5-column-left-text {
  font: 10pt tahoma, arial, helvetica, sans-serif;
  line-height:60px;
  }
```

TESTING CONTINUALLY AND CONSISTENTLY

It is a good practice to continually test pages as they are being created, rather than waiting until the coding is completed because coding problems can quickly compound themselves. If a container, for example, is assigned the wrong width, padding, or margins, other related <DIV> or <SPAN> tags may also be incorrectly adjusted. Once the initial problem is discovered, any number of changes may need to be made to make the design flow correctly.

Testing should also be done consistently. One method of testing consistently is to always open the same browsers in the same order. The designer can then easily click on each browser and refresh it to see how the site appears. By using some method of consistency, the designer will recall more readily how each browser handles the nuances of CSS.

CREATING SOURCE IMAGE FILES THAT CAN BE EASILY CUSTOMIZED AND RESAVED

Most Web sites are in continual evolution. That is, they are constantly undergoing changes and revisions. While physically making changes to the source code of Web pages is not overly time-consuming, tweaking image files is an entirely different matter. There are two issues a designer should be aware of when editing images:

1. The quality of an image can only be maintained or degraded but not improved. Once an image is compressed, certain aspects of that file are permanently lost.
2. Images that are flattened (reduced to one layer) are difficult and sometimes impossible to edit, depending on the type of edits required.

For any designer who has had a client request that the "colors in an image or comp be replaced" or "this object be moved closer to that object," understanding the importance of sources files quickly becomes necessary. If the client wants these changes made to a flattened image, many times the task is difficult, if not impossible, without recreating the image.

This is why the designer should always save source files for the images created. They can be the original photos or images used to create images, the final images fully uncompressed, or layered Photoshop files that can be easily edited. Each of these options offers the designer the ability to easily resave or edit a file—and usually with very little effort.

Whenever a designer creates a Photoshop file for an image or design comp, that file should be saved in its original format without any flattening of the layers. If the designer needs to make revisions, then a new version of the file should be saved. While each Photoshop file for a Web page can easily reach 5 MB, the disk space used for each version is more than a fair trade-off when the designer needs to access an older version of the image; the stored original may be the only one that contains what the designer needs. For instance, what if the client asks that a file be cropped by 60 percent? Then, a day later, the client says the file was actually better the way it was. What then? If the original version of the file was not saved, the only option is to recreate the image. Take, for example, the comp shown in Figure 16.32. Considering that there are 64 layers in this image, reconstituting it could take hours.

BREAKING OUT SECTIONS OF SOURCE IMAGE FILES

Saving source image files provides flexibility and ease in editing Web site images down the road. Some pieces can even be saved separately from their original files for added convenience. Figure 16.33, for example, shows a screenshot of a second-level page that uses such images. In the site, nearly all second- and third-level pages use the oval image on the right. In this example, the U.S. Capitol building is included in the oval. Each section, however, has its own image.

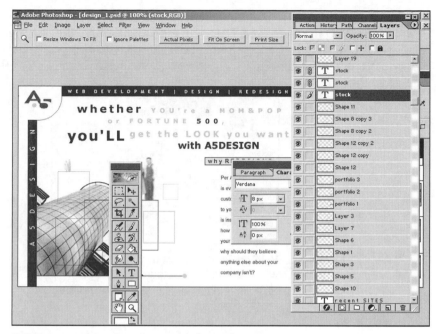

FIGURE 16.32   Photoshop design that has 64 layers.

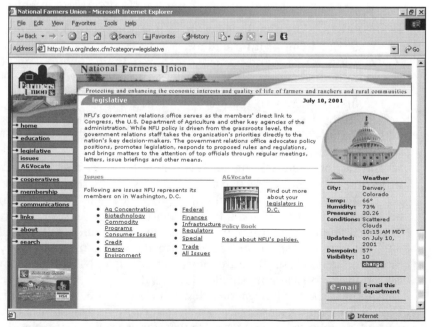

FIGURE 16.33   Site that uses a different photo in the right-hand oval for each section.

To make creating and editing these photos easier, the oval area was cropped from the source PSD file and saved as its own individual source file (see Figure 16.34). This allows the designer to apply that specific file to create or edit photos, rather than having to open the entire page and save the one desired image from that file.

FIGURE 16.34   Image used in Figure 16.33, which is saved from a source PSD file for all similar such images. Copyright © 2002 by National Farmers Union. All rights reserved.

CREATING SMART NAVIGATION

Navigation can and should, in most cases, satisfy two requirements:

1. Enhance the usability of a site so that a user can easily and consistently find desired items or information.
2. Allow for easy and efficient creation, editing, deletion, and downloading of individual menu items.

The first of these two requirements depends more on the architecture of a site than anything else. If the positioning, hierarchy, and naming conventions of sections and subsections of the site's architecture are intuitive, then the menu will only help capitalize on such planning and forethought.

The second requirement, however, is not always a given. It sometimes is less burdensome to create attractive menu items by saving them as images rather than as text. Doing so, though, limits the designer's flexibility when maintaining menus, and it increases the download. Editing menu items as text is not only simpler, but it helps facilitate easy maintenance of the site; source menu files need not be found, edited, and resaved. Text menu items also allow for a menu to be dynamically generated from a database. Because they are made up of XHTML text, such menu items also require a considerably smaller download.

Another aspect of navigation a designer must consider is whether to use horizontal or vertical menus. Each has its benefits. Horizontal navigation allows for the entire width of a screen to be used for a site that, for example, uses tables that require many columns of data. Vertical menus, though, offer the ease of unlimited growth. While horizontal menus eventually run out of space for items, adding more items to a vertical menu simply requires the user to scroll up and down, rather than forcing a redesign of the page. Horizontal menus, however, many times employ dropdown menus to allow for more menu items to be included.

REUSING IMAGES

Using browser caching is an easy way to decrease a site's download. The way it works is that once a browser downloads an image, it stores it in a temporary folder on the user's computer. That way, if the image is called again from another page or even on the same page, the browser uses the image stored on the computer, rather than downloading another copy.

Following are three instances where graphics can be reused:

1. **Framework graphics**—Graphics that are included in the homepage design can, many times, easily be reused in the framework of subsequent pages if the containers are built and mortised correctly.

Figure 16.35 is a site that reuses the left and top images for the second- and third-level templates, such as the second-level page shown in Figure 16.36.

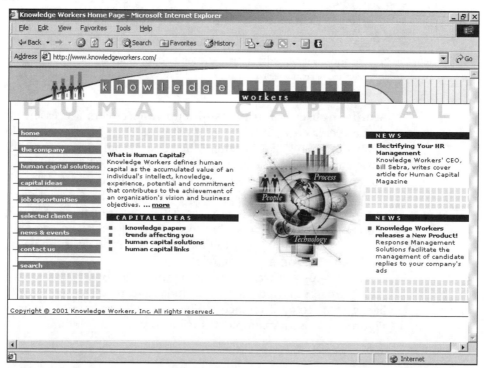

FIGURE 16.35   Site that reuses the left and top images on second- and third-level templates.

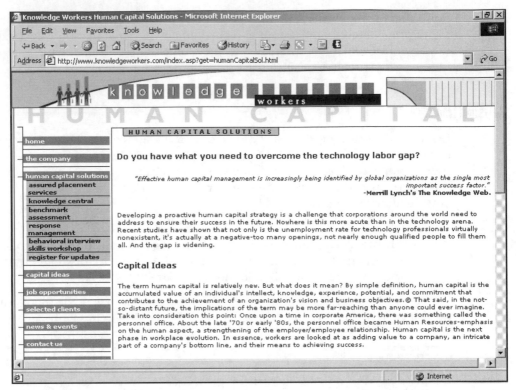

FIGURE 16.36   Second-level page that reuses the left and top graphics of Figure 16.35. Copyright © 2002 by Knowledge Workers, Inc. All rights reserved.

2. **Menu mouseover images**—Menu mouseovers are essential to designs that are created with the goal of high usability. Mouseovers allow a user to easily determine exactly where the cursor is pointing, something that is not always easy due to the shape or size of a cursor. Using images for the text is not a wise choice when XHTML text can be used as the menu item and two images less than 1 KB can each be reused as the On and Off states of the mouseovers. Figure 16.37 is a site that reuses two images for the mouseovers of its menus. The second menu item is in the On state with a single circle. All the other menu items are in the Off state with a circle layered and offset on a larger circle.

3. **Corners**—A good way of rounding the edges of a container is to use small corner images. While the rest of the area can be colored with the XHTML's background color, an image can be reused for as many corners as necessary. Figure 16.38 is an example of such a corner.

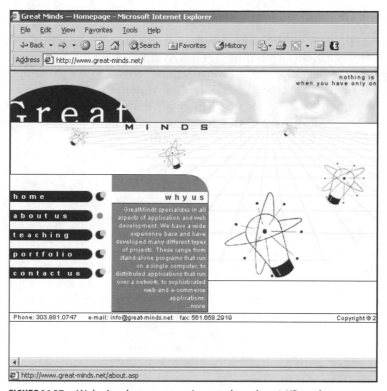

FIGURE 16.37   Web site that uses two images less than 1 KB each to serve as the mouseover images. Copyright © 2002 by Great Minds, Inc. All rights reserved.

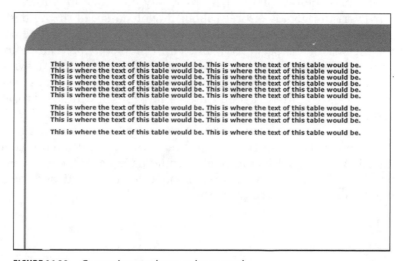

FIGURE 16.38   Corner image that can be reused.

INDENTING AND COMMENTING CODE

Sometimes it is difficult to tell which table is nested in which when building, editing, or troubleshooting complex mortised sites. Indenting and commenting code, however, can help alleviate this problem. Discovering the nesting order of containers is easier when the code for each nested container is indented farther to the right than the higher level (parent) containers. Comments also help a designer locate a single piece of code from within the entire page. Following is a sample of code that uses both indenting and comments to identify sections:

```
<!- ###### left column start ###### ->
  <div id="a5-column-left">
    <!-########## left column text start ##########->
    we create reasonably priced, highly professional web
designs, web sites, web applications, e-newsletters, and other visual, usable, and
functional work. while we create various custom designs for our clients, our best-
selling, internationally published designs are a good place to start to not only
understand our design skills but also to discover we're not a flash-in-the-pan
design firm. following are a few shortcuts to more commonly requested information:
    <!-########## left column text end ##########->
  </div>
<!- ###### left column end ###### ->
```

REMOVING SPACES AND COMMENTS

Sometimes the designer's goal is to easily find code for future editing. Sometimes, however, the goal is entirely about download speed. If the designer is more concerned about download, then removing extra spaces or comments will help decrease the file size of the page. XHTML compression software can be found on download sites, such as www.tucows.com and www.download.com, which automates this process. The only thing the designer needs to remember is to save the original source page for easy editing in the future. Otherwise, having to edit the compressed code could be quite cumbersome.

The code for the site shown in Figure 16.39 before removing the spaces and comments was nearly 18 KB. After removing the extraneous code, the size was reduced by nearly 2 KB. Although it could have been decreased even more by eliminating all the spaces, the text would have been jumbled, and the programming code would not have worked properly.

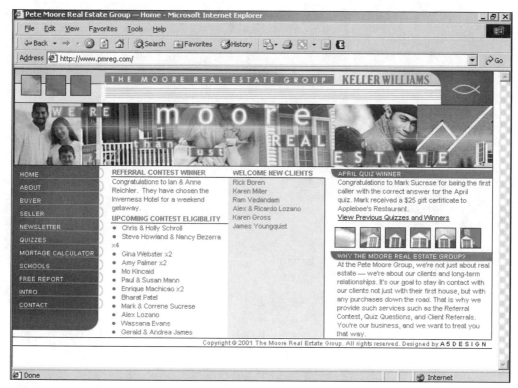

FIGURE 16.39   Site that could have nearly 2 KB trimmed by removing spaces and comments.

As mentioned in various examples in this book, while spacing in XHTML should not affect a CSS-driven design, it does in certain circumstances. In most all cases, though, removing spaces only makes the browser interpret the code more accurately.

SUMMARY

Understanding common roadblocks and issues with designing Web sites can make a designer or developer much more efficient. If a designer creates enough sites, she will run into most of the issues outlined and hopefully be able to easily work through them with the help of this chapter. Some of the tips and techniques in this chapter included explaining the Tantek hack to correctly render the box model bug, coding CSS mouseover menus, controlling content layout, using unique naming conventions, and learning basic testing tricks. If nothing else, the content in this chapter should help the designer imagine code in a more structured, forward-thinking way.

CUSTOMIZING THE DESIGNS INCLUDED IN THIS BOOK

In This Chapter

- Steps to Customizing a Template
- Photoshop Tutorials

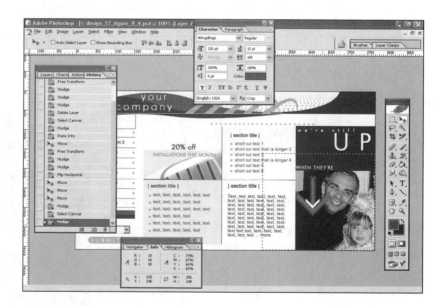

There are 210 templates included with this book, which contains both pure CSS and table-based XHTML Web designs: e-mail signatures, e-newsletters, and Photoshop designs that do not have code written for them. All the files are constructed in similar fashions, respectively, which makes understanding and customizing them a fairly consistent process. This chapter not only explains how to customize such templates, but it also provides basic Photoshop tips that can be used to quickly customize the templates.

STEPS TO CUSTOMIZING A TEMPLATE

There are six basic steps to customizing a template. The basic process involves customizing and saving a Photoshop file, which outputs GIF and JPG files that are then displayed, along with any text, by preprogrammed XHTML (HTML), Cascading Style Sheets, and, possibly, JavaScript files. Following are the six steps:

1. Open the main Photoshop file. The design used for this chapter is design 57 (see Figure 17.1).
2. Customize images and colors in the Photoshop file(s).
3. Optimize and save necessary images that will be used by precoded XHTML, CSS, and, possibly, JavaScript files.
4. Open XHTML, CSS, or JavaScript files with an HTML editor.
5. Customize text and any other code.
6. Test the design.

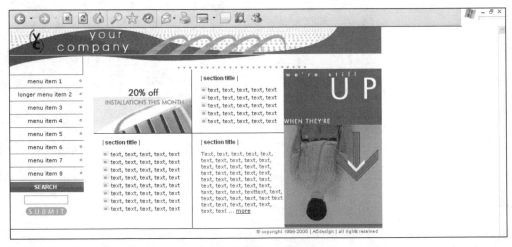

FIGURE 17.1   The design that is customized in this chapter.

Step 1: Open the Main Photoshop File

After copying the files from the CD-ROM and pasting them into a directory, the designer needs to locate and open the main design file (`design_57.psd`) in Photoshop (see Figure 17.2).

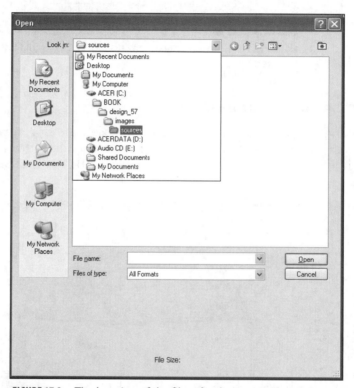

FIGURE 17.2   The location of the files after being saved to the hard drive.

Figure 17.2 represents one example of how the files would look on a hard drive after being saved from the CD. If the reader were looking at the files from the CD, the design_57 folder would appear under the CD drive (the E: drive in this case). This is all relative to the individual's system.

The templates included with this book are saved in Photoshop version 6 or higher. Adobe has continually changed how its software handles text, and the newer versions are no exception. When opening a file in a more recent version, Photoshop will ask if the reader wants to update the file (see Figure 17.3). Selecting Update will cause the vector-based text to have its positioning slightly readjusted.

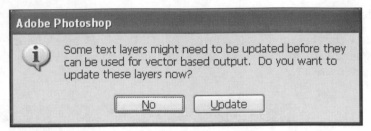

FIGURE 17.3   Photoshop dialog box asking if a file should have text updated.

Step 2: Customize Images and Colors

Making and saving changes in Photoshop (see Figure 17.4) will change all the images in a design and many of the colors, as well. Colors that are not changed when saving a Photoshop file can be changed in the XHTML or CSS files.

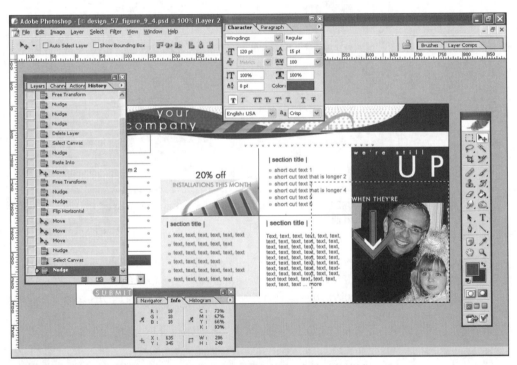

FIGURE 17.4   Design in Photoshop with customized colors and photos.

Step 3: Optimize and Save Necessary Images

Once changes have been made to the Photoshop file, the designer will need to save the file so that the necessary GIF and JPG images are saved from the sliced Photoshop file. Following are the steps to do so:

1. Select the Save For Web option from Photoshop's File menu(see Figure 17.5).

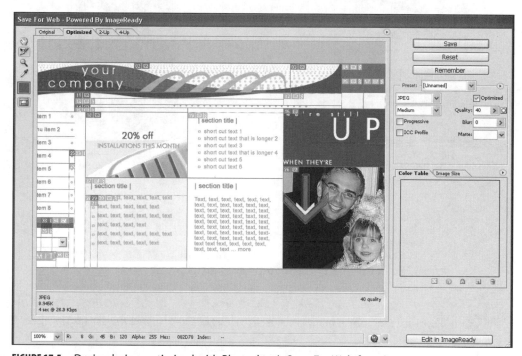

FIGURE 17.5   Design being optimized with Photoshop's Save For Web function.

2. Click on the Slice Select tool from the menu on the left (see Figure 17.6).
3. Select a slice to be optimized and select the compression on the right side of the window (see Figure 17.7).

If the designer changes the type of image a slice is saved as, such as GIF to JPG, the file extension must be changed in the CSS or XHTML template as well. For example, if `photo_middle_right` *is changed from a JPG file to a GIF file, all references to* `photo_middle_right.jpg` *in the template must be changed to* `photo_middle_right.gif`.

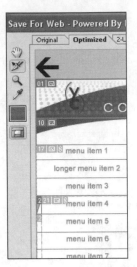

FIGURE 17.6   Slice Select tool in the Save For Web window.

FIGURE 17.7   The slice that has its file type and compression assigned in the Save For Web window.

4. Ensure that all changed slices of the template are still compressed to the best level possible.
5. Select Save in the top-right area of the Save For Web window.
6. Select Replace in the Replace Files window.

Once a user clicks on Replace, Photoshop will save all slices as either GIFs or JPGs from the file and place them in an Images subdirectory below where the design_57.html *file is saved.*

Step 4: Open an XHTML (HTML), CSS, and/or JavaScript File

All three file types can be opened in any HTML editor. In Figure 17.8 the sample file is opened in Adobe's ColdFusion Studio. This software is pretty much extinct in Web development; however, any quality software will be somewhat similar in style. It also shows that the designer does not need the latest and greatest software for such development. A reader, in fact, could even use basic text editing software, such as Notepad, which is included with Microsoft operating systems.

Step 5: Customize Text and Code

Once a template file has been opened in an HTML editor, it can be easily modified and saved however the designer may choose. Following are suggestions for customizing such files:

- Always save a backup to revert to or pull original pieces of code from, if necessary.
- Check pages in a browser frequently (refer to step 6).

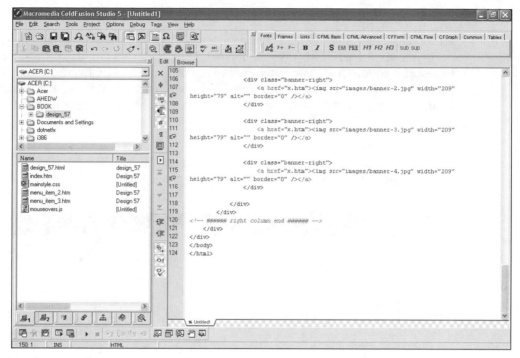

FIGURE 17.8   A file opened in Adobe's ColdFusion Studio HTML editing software.

- Switch the CSS or border value to 1 where code is being customized. This allows the designer to better understand how the design is constructed.
- Ensure that the location and image name for each menu item is consistent when working with XHTML templates that use mouseovers in the menu (see Listing 17.1). No two menu items can have the same location and image names.

LISTING 17.1   Unique JavaScript Names for Mouseover Code

```
<tr>
    <td valign="top"><img src="images/bullet_menu_off.gif" width="18"
        height="20" alt="" border="0" name="menu_item_1"></td>
    <td class="white2"><a href="index.htm" style="text-decoration:
        none; color: #ffffff" onmouseover="document.menu_item_1.src=
        bullet_menu_on.src;"
onmouseout="document.menu_item_1.src=bullet_menu_off.src"><b>menu
    item 1</b></a></td>
</tr>
```

This suggestion is only applicable to the table-based XHTML templates included with the book.

Step 6: Test the Design

As soon as a designer makes a change to a template, it should be opened in a browser or, better yet, in various browsers, depending on how thoroughly the designer wants to test the code. Then, as changes are made to the template from the HTML editor, the designer should continually refresh the browser(s) to ensure that the changes were made correctly. To open a design in IE, for example, the designer follows six steps:

1. Click the browser's File menu.
2. Click Open.
3. Click Browse.
4. Click on `index.htm`, which is the homepage for design in Figure 17.9.

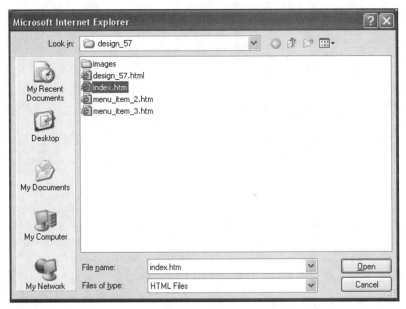

FIGURE 17.9   A locally saved `index.htm` file to be opened in IE 6.

5. Click on Open to open the file in a browser.
6. Click OK to confirm opening the file.

PHOTOSHOP TUTORIALS

This section includes tutorials on basic techniques a designer or developer will usually need to know how to customize a design. They include replacing photos, resizing photos, changing colors, and undoing or redoing actions.

Replacing Photos

Not all designs can have photos simply replaced in the code. With many mortised designs, the process of replacing a photo first begins with the Photoshop file, using masks. Following are instructions on replacing a photo in a Photoshop template, using the original photo as a mask.

1. Make sure the Layers panel is visible (see Figure 17.10).

FIGURE 17.10   The Layers panel in Photoshop where different layers may be selected.

2. Click on the Window menu in the top menu bar.
3. Click on the Layers option (see Figure 17.11).
4. Make sure the Layers tab is selected in the panel. If it is not, click on it (see Figure 17.11).
5. Open the image to be inserted into the existing image.
6. Select the entire image (Ctrl-A for Windows; Cmd-A for Macintosh) and then copy that image (Ctrl-C for Windows or Cmd-C for Macintosh; see Figure 17.12).
7. Select the layer of the photo in the design (in this example, it is the upside-down photo of the man) that is going to be replaced.

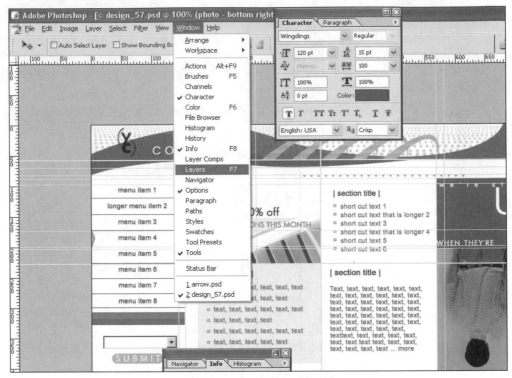

FIGURE 17.11 The Layers panel can be accessed from the Window menu.

FIGURE 17.12 The image selected that will be used in the design.

Windows users can right-click the photo to be replaced and then select the layer's name, which will send the user directly to that layer (see Figure 17.13). The user may have more than one option to select, so if they are not already named, it might be necessary to click on the various layers until the correct one is selected.

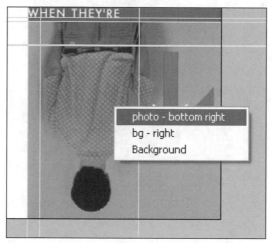

FIGURE 17.13   Possible layers to select if the user right-clicks on an image.

8. Click on the layer in the Layers panel. Once this layer has been selected, the content on the layer will be available for editing.

A layer can be made visible or invisible by clicking the eye icon on and off, located to the left of the layer name (see Figure 17.14). Toggling the eye on and off is a good way to test if the correct layer has been selected.

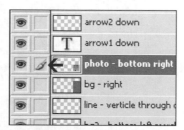

FIGURE 17.14   Toggling the eye icon on a layer will turn it off and on in the Photoshop file.

9. Activate the layer's image by selecting the entire layer area (Ctrl-A for Windows; Cmd-A for Macintosh) and move the layer up one pixel (one click) and down one pixel by using the up and down arrow keys (see Figure 17.15).

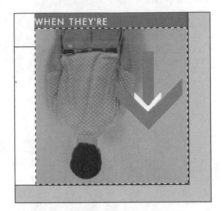

FIGURE 17.15 The image that will be used as a mask must first be selected.

The image is selected when the marching ants (moving dotted lines) are marching around that specific image or at least the part of the image that is viewable within the borders of the Photoshop file. Prior to moving the image up and down one pixel, ants will be marching around the border of the entire Photoshop file. If the marching ants are displayed in a square or rectangular shape that is larger than the image (see Figure 17.16), then the image is already set as a mask. If this occurs, the user must turn off the photo by turning off the eye for its layer and restarting this tutorial at step 3, this time selecting the correct layer (the square image that contains the actual photo).

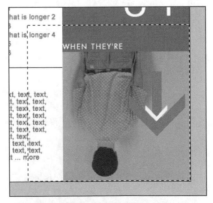

FIGURE 17.16 How the marching ants would appear if the image were already saved as a mask.

10. Insert the image already copied in step 2 (see Figure 17.12) by pressing Shift-Ctrl-V for Windows or Shift-Cmd-V for Macintosh. The image will then be placed inside the existing image (see Figure 17.17).

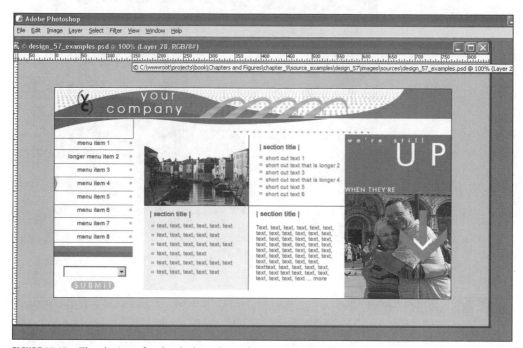

FIGURE 17.17   The design after both the selected image and the one in the center have been added into their respective masks.

Resizing Photos

Following are instructions for resizing a photo in Photoshop. Although this tutorial explains how to resize a photo in a mask, the same process occurs when resizing any photo or image on any layer.

1. Make sure the Layers panel is visible (refer to Figure 17.10).
2. Select the layer of the photo in the design (in this example, it is the couple hugging) that is going to be replaced (refer to Figure 17.13).
3. Click on the layer in the Layers panel. Once this layer has been selected, the content will be available for editing.
4. Activate the layer's image by selecting the entire layer area (Ctrl-A for Windows; Cmd-A for Macintosh) and move the layer up one pixel (one click) and down one pixel by using the up and down arrow keys (see Figure 17.18).

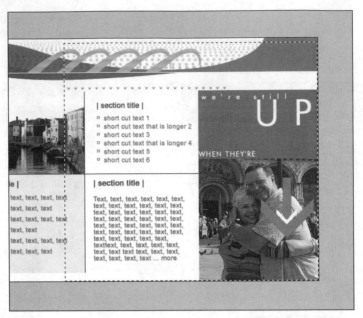

FIGURE 17.18   The photo after it has been activated in the window.

The image in Figure 17.18 extends below and to the right of the design. The marching ants, however, will remain inside the Photoshop file.

5. Activate the outer frame of the image by hitting Ctrl-T for Windows or Cmd-T for Macintosh. Once the outer frame is active, small square handles in the corners will appear (see Figure 17.19).
6. Resize the image by clicking and dragging any of the corners on the frame that turn the mouse into an up or down arrow.

Often the image will need to be resized proportionately. Holding the Shift key and the handles simultaneously while dragging will ensure that the image's proportions remain the same.

7. During the resizing process, the image can also be moved. To do so, select the Move tool (see Figure 17.20) in the toolbar and click and drag the image rather than the handles.
8. Deactivate the marching ants by hitting Ctrl-D for Windows or Cmd-D for Macintosh once the image has been resized and located correctly (see Figure 17.21). The border and corners will then disappear.

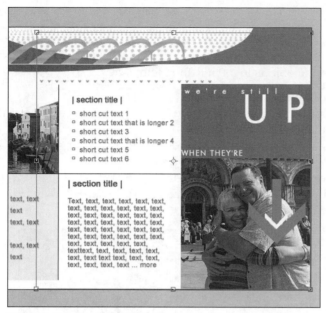

FIGURE 17.19   Small handles will appear when the image is ready to be resized.

FIGURE 17.20
The Move tool included in the menu bar.

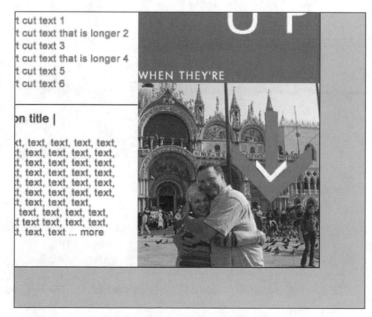

FIGURE 17.21   The photo after it has been resized and moved.

Changing Colors

Changing the colors of a design often begins with the Photoshop file because the colors are saved as images, rather than browser-generated colors. Following are instructions on changing colors of solid objects in a Photoshop template.

1. Make sure the Layers panel is visible.
2. Select the layer of the photo in the design (in this example, it is the couple hugging) that is going to be replaced.
3. Click on the layer in the Layers panel. Once this layer has been selected, content on the layer will be available for editing.
4. Select the layer of the photo in the design (in this example, the top-right corner) that is going to be changed (see Figure 17.22)

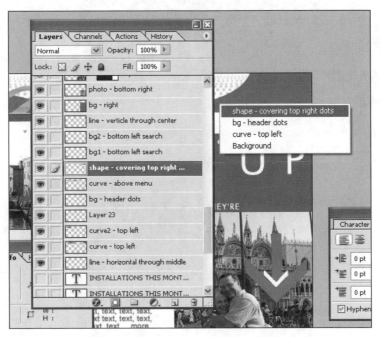

FIGURE 17.22   The layer, which represents the top-right curve of the design, to be recolored.

5. Click on the layer in the Layers panel. Once this layer has been selected, the content on the layer will be available for editing.
6. Activate the layer's image by selecting the entire layer area (Ctrl-A for Windows; Cmd-A for Macintosh) and move the layer up one pixel (one click) and down one pixel by using the up and down arrow keys (see Figure 17.23).

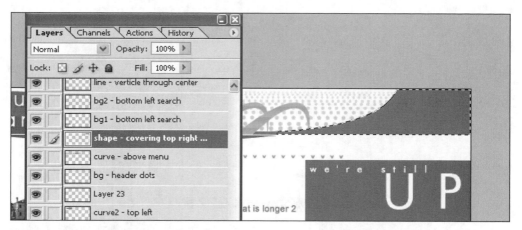

FIGURE 17.23   The image that will be recolored once it has been activated.

7. Click the Color Picker in the toolbar to open the Color Picker dialog box and select a replacement (see Figure 17.24).

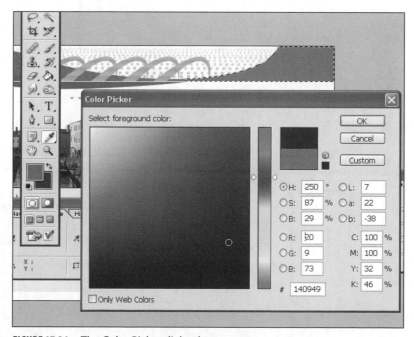

FIGURE 17.24   The Color Picker dialog box.

8. Click OK to close the Color Picker dialog once the replacement color has been selected.

9. Select Fill from the Edit menu (see Figure 17.25).

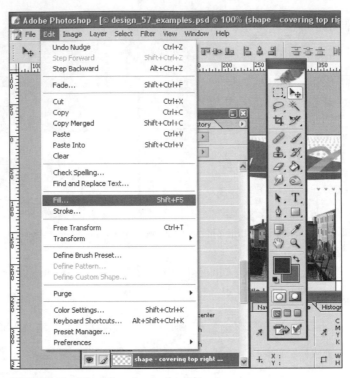

FIGURE 17.25   The Fill option in the Edit menu.

10. Click OK to confirm the fill (see Figure 17.26).

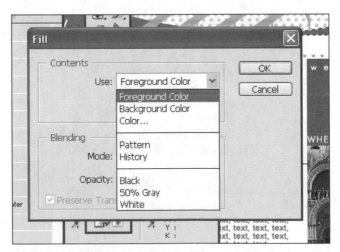

FIGURE 17.26   The Fill dialog box and the various possibilities the Use dropdown menu offers.

11. Deactivate the marching ants by hitting Ctrl-D for Windows or Cmd-D for Macintosh once the color has been replaced, or "filled." Figure 17.27 shows the design with many of the colors changed. Because it is a black-and-white image, the changes will appear mainly as tonal differences.

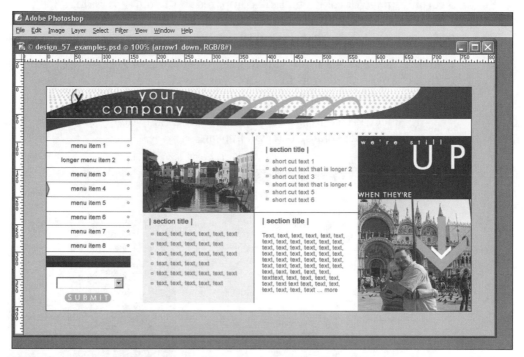

FIGURE 17.27   The design once many of the colors have been changed. Because the figure is black and white, the changes will appear only as tonal differences.

Undoing and Redoing Actions

The designer can undo and redo actions in Photoshop. This tutorial outlines the hot keys for undoing actions, but, more importantly, it shows how to configure Photoshop to allow for actions to be undone.

Undoing Actions

To undo an action using hot keys, the user needs to select Ctrl-Alt-Z for Windows or Cmd-Alt-Z for Macintosh. By holding down the Ctrl (or Cmd) and Alt keys, the user can repeatedly click the letter Z to undo however many actions the program has been configured to allow.

Redoing Actions

After undoing actions, the user can click Ctrl-Z for Windows and Cmd-Z for Macintosh to redo all the actions. By repeatedly hitting this key combination, the user can toggle between the two different states of change. This is useful when deciding how a certain image or color will look compared to the older version.

Configuring the Undo Actions (History States) Setting

Undoing actions has a limit with the default settings of Photoshop, so the user needs to first change the settings to ensure that it will allow a certain number of changes. Following are instructions on how to do so.

1. Select Preferences, General under the Edit menu (see Figure 17.28). The Preferences dialog box will appear.

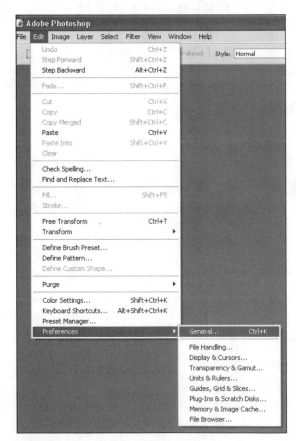

FIGURE 17.28 Selecting Preferences, General from the Edit menu.

2. Change the History States setting to the number of changes Photoshop should be able to revert back to. The number of changes in this example is 20 (see Figure 17.29).

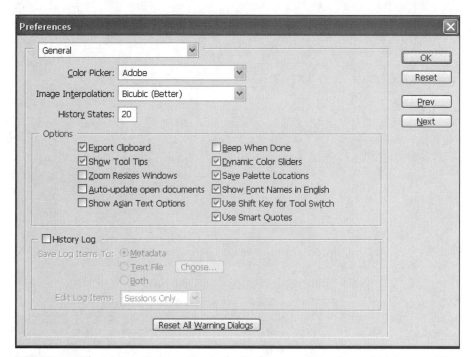

FIGURE 17.29   The History States option in the Preferences dialog box, which is set at 20.

    In some versions of Photoshop, the number of changes a designer can make is one less than what is stated in the History States. Therefore, to be safe, the user should increase the number by one.

3. Click OK to confirm the changes.

SUMMARY

Because all the designs included in this book are built similarly, whether they use an XHTML table- or CSS-based design, they also are customized in very much the same way. This chapter not only explains the steps for customizing a design, but it also provides brief Photoshop tutorials on how to make changes in the software. These tutorials include replacing photos, resizing photos, changing colors, and undoing and redoing actions. Filled with images, this chapter offers a quick read for fundamental Photoshop skills.

A

TEMPLATES INCLUDED ON THE CD

There are 210 designs included with this book. Because this book was first published in 2001, the designs have evolved graphically and technically over the years. Although designs become antiquated in terms of coding standards or hardware standards (for example, screen resolution), there are elements that can still be used, studied, or modified from older designs. This is why older templates are included with the newer ones.

Also important for the reader to keep in mind is that templates can and, in most cases should, be modified for specific projects. A5design's clients don't always realize that colors and images can be easily modified to turn a real estate template into a photography template or a wild magenta abstract template into a conservative blue business template. The layout of a design should be the driving force behind selecting it. Layout considerations include whether the title and logo are given the correct placement and prominence, the menu is horizontal or vertical, how many text sections are provided, and how scalable the design is for future functionality and growth.

The various types of designs on the CD include XHTML table-based templates, XHTML e-newsletter templates, XHTML signatures templates, Photoshop templates, and CSS-based templates. Barring the Photoshop templates, all designs include a source Photoshop file(s) along with the slices and code already completed. The Photoshop templates are the one exception because they do not have slices or code included.

The templates are broken up into two folders on the CD included with the book: Designs - First Edition and Designs - Third Edition. The 50 templates in the Designs - First Edition folder are XHTML-based and designed for 800 × 600 resolution with fixed widths. The 160 templates in the Designs - Third Edition folder are much more diverse. Some are XHTML-based designed for 800 × 600 resolution but with the ability to make the width liquid or relative; some are e-newsletters or e-mail templates; some are CSS-based designed for 800 × 600 resolution; some are pure Photoshop templates; and some are CSS-based designed for 1024 × 768 resolution. Following is a breakdown of the two folders and the templates included in them:

Designs – First Edition Folder

- **Designs 1–50:** XHTML table-based designs that were created for 800 × 600 resolution. They have fixed widths.

Designs – Third Edition Folder

- **Designs 51–80:** XHTML table-based designs that were originally created for 800 × 600 resolution but were also coded as liquid designs, which, if the designer chooses, allows for them to expand to greater widths.

- **Designs 81–90:** XHTML e-newsletters that can be either e-mailed from a browser or embedded into an e-mail and then e-mailed.

- **Designs 91–100:** XHTML signatures that can be embedded into e-mail messages, many times working in conjunction with a Web site and/or e-newsletter to provide consistent branding.

- **Designs 101–110:** Photoshop designs that were created for 800 × 600 resolution but could be easily modified for 1024 × 768 resolution. These designs have not been coded.

- **Designs 111–120:** Photoshop designs that were created for 1024 × 768 resolution. These designs have not been coded.

- **Designs 121–130:** CSS designs that were created for 800 × 600 resolution. Because the designs are liquid, they can be easily modified to fit higher resolutions or be centered within the browser in a fixed format.

- **Designs 131–160:** CSS designs that were created for 1024 × 768 resolution. Because the designs are liquid, they can be easily modified to fit higher resolutions or be centered within the browser in a fixed format.

There are a variety of ways of sending e-newsletters. One of the most simple ways is to upload the file to a server and in Internet Explorer, for example, select File, Send, Page by E-mail. The browser will then open the e-mail software, such as Microsoft Outlook, and embed the file into a new e-mail. The user then needs to send the e-mail as any other e-mail. It is important to note that all images included in such a file need to be stored on a server and given absolute addresses, such as `<img src="http://www.a5design.com/sample_ newsletter/header.gif">`, *rather than* `<img src="images/header.gif" >`. *If assigned a relative address, the e-mail will look for that image on the recipient's system, where the image will not exist.*

There are a variety of ways of sending e-mails with a signature file. One way is to save the XHTML file on the computer that contains the e-mail software the user sends e-mail with. Then in the software, such as Microsoft Outlook, go to Tools, Options, Mail Format and se-lect the file. The software will then embed the file into the e-mail. It is important to note that all images included in such a file need to be stored on a server and given absolute addresses, such as `<img src="http://www.a5design.com/sample_newsletter/header.gif">`, *rather than* `<img src="images/header.gif" >`. *If assigned a relative address, the e-mail will look for that image on the recipient's system where the image will not exist. To send an e-mail with a signature, the user should first read about how to do so with the e-mail soft-ware that is being used to send e-mail. Not all software offers the same functionality.*

Online color versions of all the designs included with this book can be found at www.a5design.com/a5-book-designs.

All designs have been validated by the W3C's CSS and XHTML validators.

DESIGNS – THIRD EDITION FOLDER

The designs in this folder decrease in numerical order. The most recent designs are shown first. These are CSS-based designs created for 1024 × 768 resolution. As the design numbers decrease, so does the resolution and coding method used. In other words, the resolution for which the designs are created eventually decreases to 800 × 600 resolution, and the coding method eventually becomes XHTML table-based designs, as opposed to CSS-based designs. The purpose of the older designs serves more as creative inspiration for readers to create their own designs or even to mod-ify more recent templates included with the book.

Design 160

Homepage design.

Second-level template for less content.

Second-level template for more content.

Photoshop source file names: Designs - Third Edition/121-160-css/design_160/ main.psd, bg-main.psd

XHTML pages: index.htm, menu-item-2.htm, menu-item-3.htm

Photo credits: ronsternimages.com

Design 159

Homepage design.

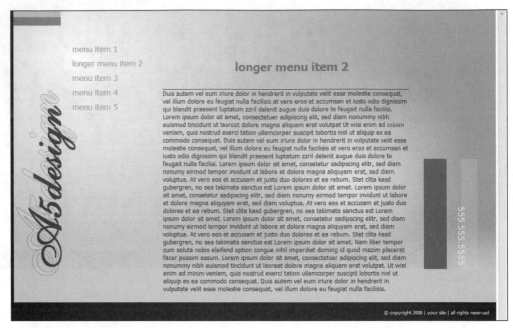

Second-level template for less content.

Photoshop source file names: Designs - Third Edition/121-160-css/design_159/ main.psd, bg-main.psd, bg-main-sl.psd

XHTML pages: index.htm, menu-item-2.htm

Design 158

Homepage design.

Second-level template for less content.

Second-level template for more content.

Photoshop source file names: Designs - Third Edition/121-160-css/design_158/ main.psd

XHTML pages: index.htm, menu-item-2.htm, menu-item-3.htm

Photo credits: ronsternimages.com

Design 157

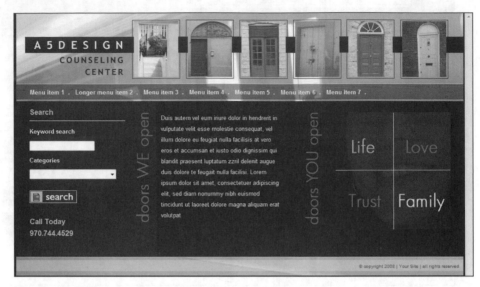

Homepage design.

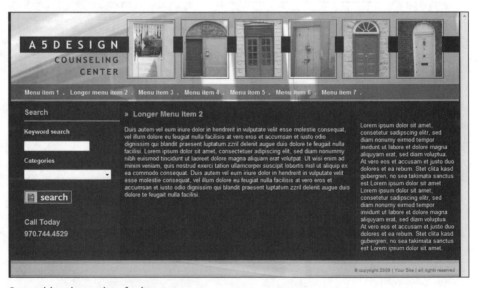

Second-level template for less content.

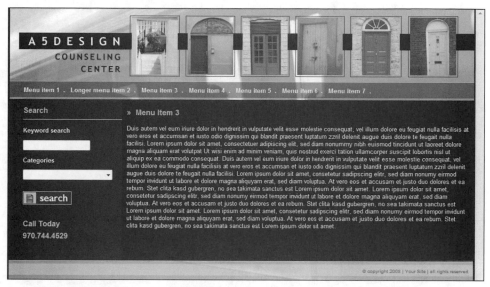

Second-level template for more content.

Photoshop source file names: Designs - Third Edition/121-160-css/design_157/ main.psd

XHTML pages: index.htm, menu-item-2.htm, menu-item-3.htm

Photo credits: ronsternimages.com

Design 156

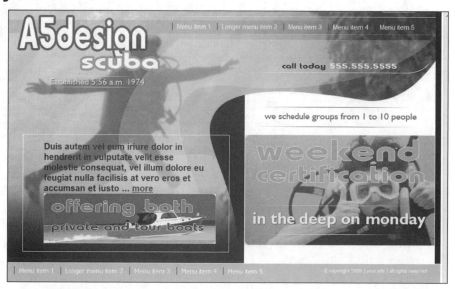

Homepage design.

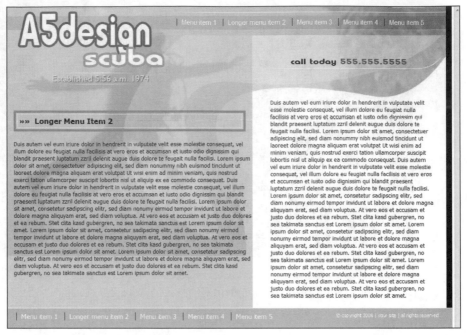

Second-level template for less content.

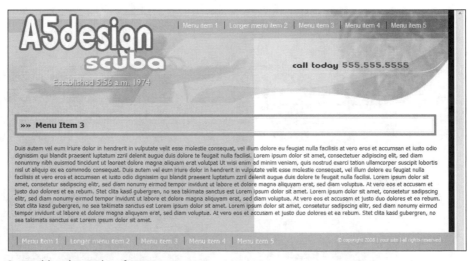

Second-level template for more content.

Photoshop source file names: Designs - Third Edition/121-160-css/design_156/ main.psd, main-sl.psd

XHTML pages: index.htm, menu-item-2.htm, menu-item-3.htm

Photo credits: ronsternimages.com, J&N Photography

Design 155

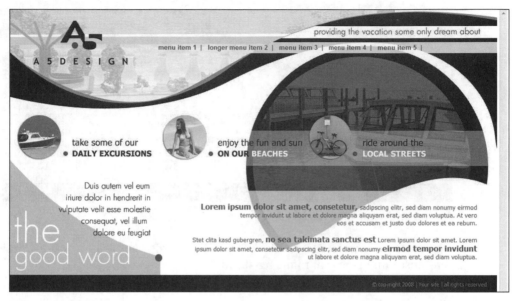

Homepage design.

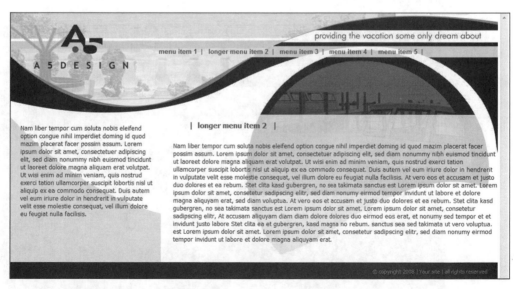

Second-level template for less content.

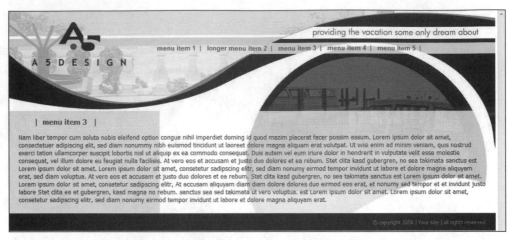

Second-level template for more content.

Photoshop source file names: Designs - Third Edition/121-160-css/design_155/ main.psd, main-bg.psd, main-bg-sl.psd

XHTML pages: index.htm, menu-item-2.htm, menu-item-3.htm

Photo credits: ronsternimages.com

Design 154

Homepage design.

Second-level template for less content.

Second-level template for more content.

Photoshop source file names: Designs - Third Edition/121-160-css/design_154/ main.psd

XHTML pages: index.htm, menu-item-2.htm, menu-item-3.htm

Photo credits: ronsternimages.com, A5design, onepartart.com

Design 153

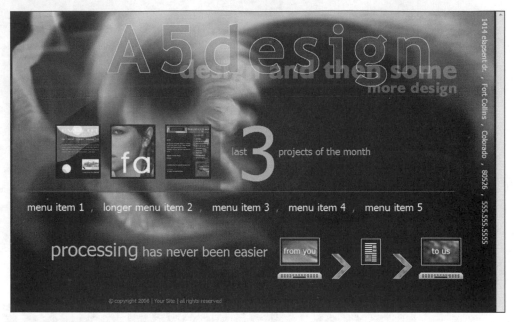

Homepage design.

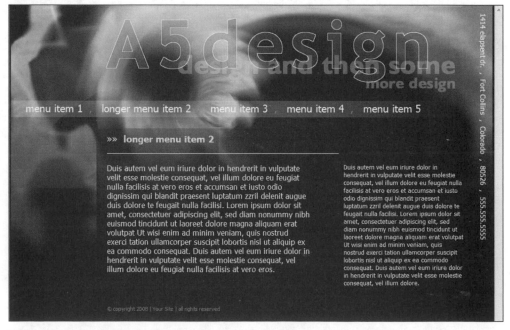

Second-level template for less content.

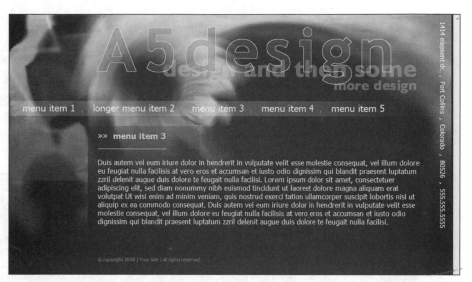

Second-level template for more content.

Photoshop source file names: Designs - Third Edition/121-160-css/design_153/ main.psd, bg-main.psd, bg-main-sl.psd

XHTML pages: index.htm, menu-item-2.htm, menu-item-3.htm

Photo credits: ronsternimages.com, A5design

Design 152

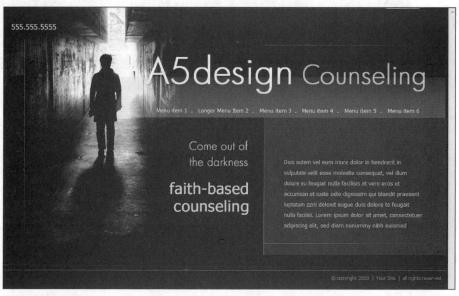

Homepage design.

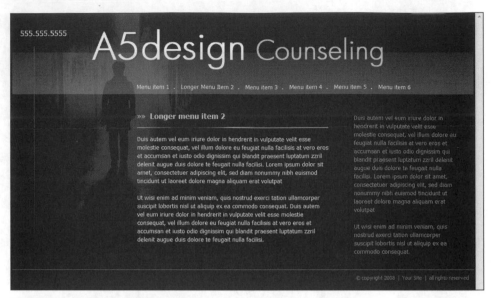

Second-level template for less content.

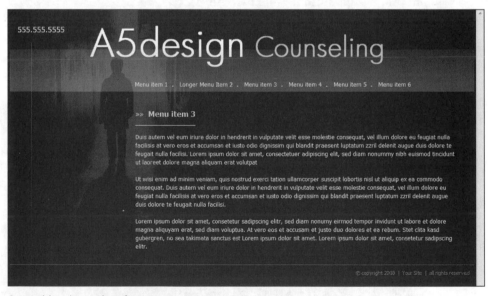

Second-level template for more content.

Photoshop source file names: Designs - Third Edition/121-160-css/design_152/ main.psd, main-bg.psd, main-bg-sl.psd

XHTML pages: index.htm, menu-item-2.htm, menu-item-3.htm

Photo credits: ronsternimages.com

Design 151

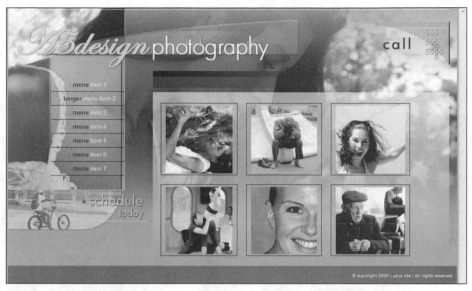

Homepage design.

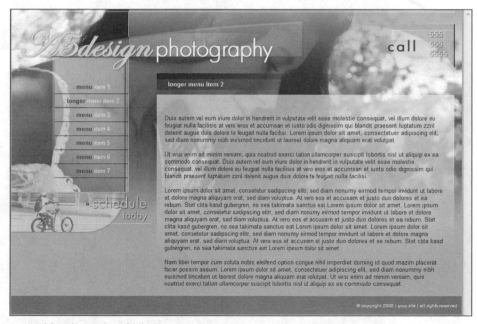

Second-level template for less content.

Photoshop source file names: Designs - Third Edition/121-160-css/design_151/main.psd, bg-main.psd

XHTML pages: index.htm, menu-item-2.htm

Photo credits: ronsternimages.com

Design 150

Homepage design.

Second-level template for less content.

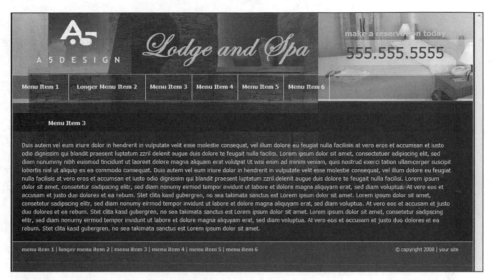

Second-level template for more content.

Photoshop source file names: Designs - Third Edition/121-160-css/design_150/ main.psd, bg-main.psd, bg-main-sl.psd

XHTML pages: index.htm, menu-item-2.htm, menu-item-3.htm

Photo credits: ronsternimages.com

Design 149

Homepage design.

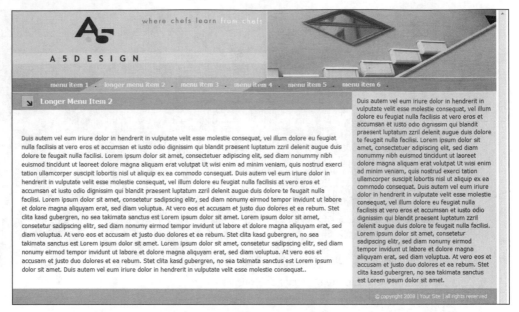

Second-level template for less content.

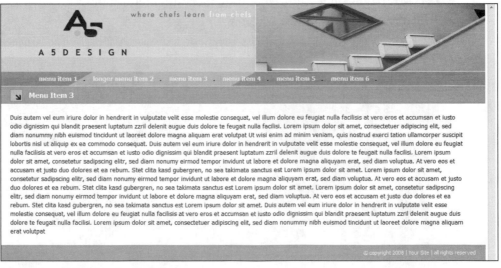

Second-level template for more content.

Photoshop source file names: Designs - Third Edition/121-160-css/design_149/ main.psd

XHTML pages: index.htm, menu-item-2.htm, menu-item-3.htm

Photo credits: ronsternimages.com

Design 148

Homepage design.

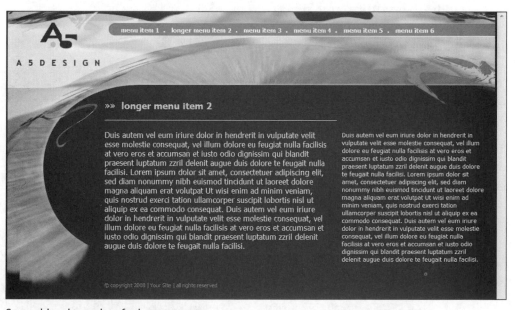

Second-level template for less content.

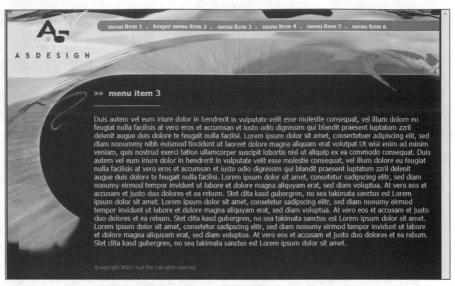

Second-level template for more content.

Photoshop source file names: Designs - Third Edition/121-160-css/design_148/ main.psd, bg-main.psd, bg-main-sl.psd

XHTML pages: index.htm, menu-item-2.htm, menu-item-3.htm

Photo credits: ronsternimages.com, A5design

Design 147

Homepage design.

Second-level template for less content.

Second-level template for more content.

Photoshop source file names: Designs - Third Edition/121-160-css/design_147/ main.psd

XHTML pages: index.htm, menu-item-2.htm, menu-item-3.htm

Photo credits: ronsternimages.com

Design 146

Homepage design.

Second-level template for less content.

Photoshop source file names: Designs - Third Edition/121-160-css/design_146/
main.psd, bg-main.psd, bg-main-sl.psd

XHTML pages: index.htm, menu-item-2.htm

Photo credits: ronsternimages.com

Design 145

Homepage design.

Second-level template for less content.

Second-level template for more content.

Second-level template for more content.

Photoshop source file names: Designs - Third Edition/121-160-css/design_145/ main.psd, main-sl.psd

XHTML pages: index.htm, menu-item-2.htm, menu-item-3.htm, menu-item-4.htm

Photo credits: ronsternimages.com

Design 144

Homepage design.

Second-level template for less content.

Photoshop source file names: Designs - Third Edition/121-160-css/design_144/ main.psd, main-sl.psd

XHTML pages: index.htm, menu-item-2.htm

Photo credits: ronsternimages.com

Design 143

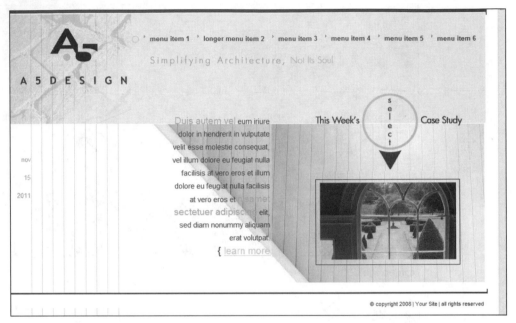

Homepage design.

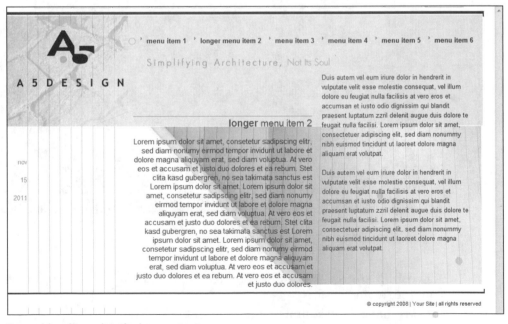

Second-level template for less content.

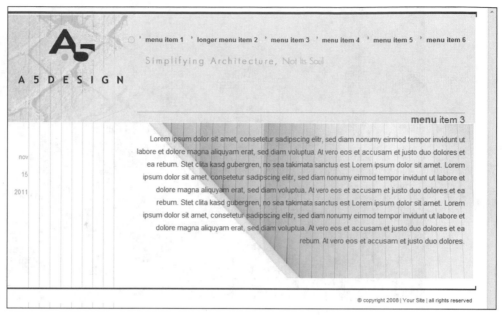

Second-level template for more content.

Photoshop source file names: Designs - Third Edition/121-160-css/design_143/ main.psd, bg-body.psd

XHTML pages: index.htm, menu-item-2.htm, menu-item-3.htm

Photo credits: ronsternimages.com, J&N Photography

Design 142

Homepage design.

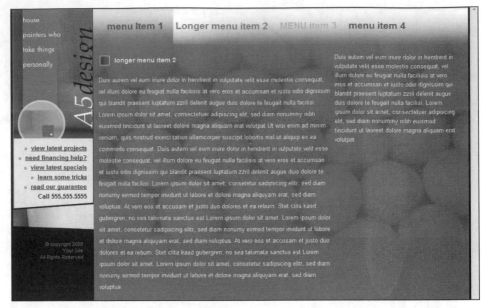

Second-level template for less content.

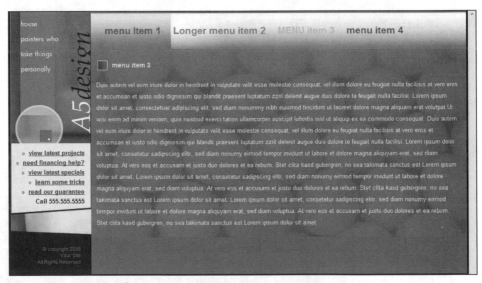

Second-level template for more content.

Photoshop source file names: Designs - Third Edition/121-160-css/design_142/ main.psd, main-sl.psd

XHTML pages: index.htm, menu-item-2.htm, menu-item-3.htm

Photo credits: ronsternimages.com

Design 141

Homepage design.

Second-level template for less content.

Second-level template for more content.

Photoshop source file names: Designs - Third Edition/121-160-css/design_141/
main.psd, main-bg-sl.psd

XHTML pages: index.htm, menu-item-2.htm, menu-item-3.htm

Photo credits: ronsternimages.com

Design 140

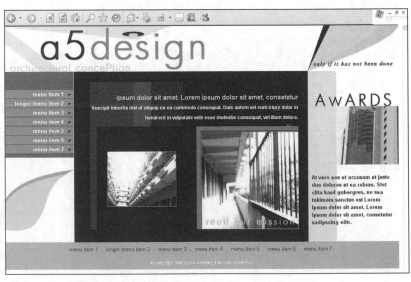

Homepage design.

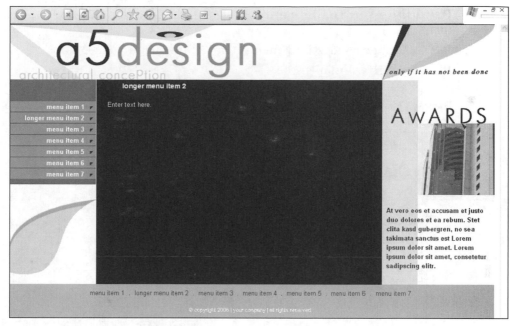

Second-level template for less content.

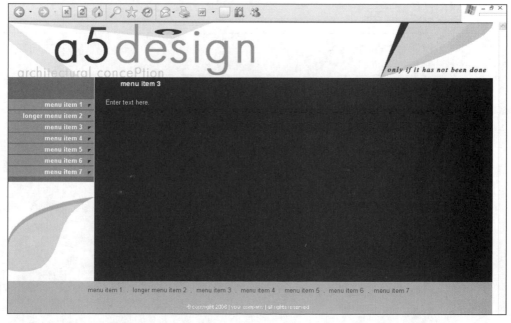

Second-level template for more content.

Photoshop source file names: Designs - Third Edition/121-160-css/design_140/ main.psd, main_sl.psd

XHTML pages: index.htm, menu_item_2.htm, menu_item_3.htm

Photo credits: Justin Discoe

Design 139

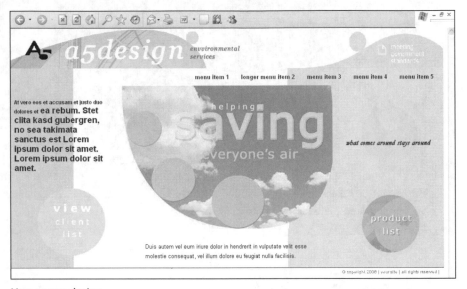

Homepage design.

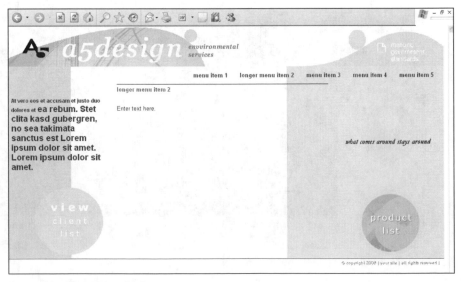

Second-level template for less content.

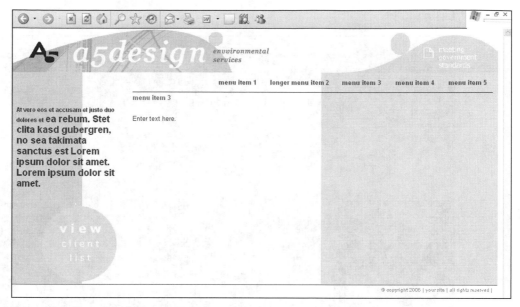

Second-level template for more content.

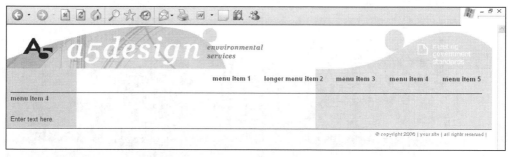

Second-level template for more content.

Photoshop source file names: Designs - Third Edition/121-160-css/design_139/design_139.psd

XHTML pages: index.htm, menu_item_2.htm, menu_item_3.htm, menu_item_4.htm

Photo credits: idlerphotography.com

Design 138

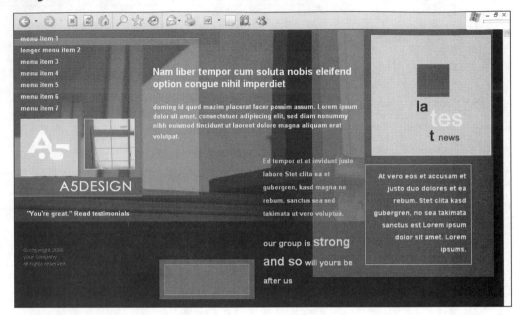

Homepage design.

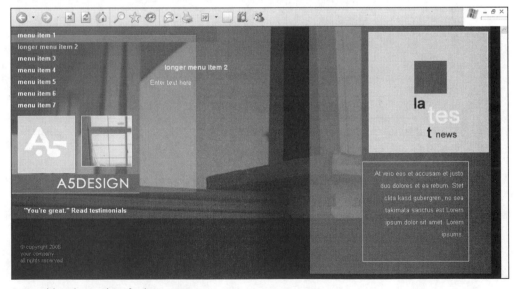

Second-level template for less content.

Second-level template for more content.

Photoshop source file names: Designs - Third Edition/121-160-css/design_138/ design_138.psd, bg_design_138.psd

XHTML pages: index.htm, menu_item_2.htm, menu_item_3.htm

Photo credits: idlerphotography.com

Design 137

Homepage design.

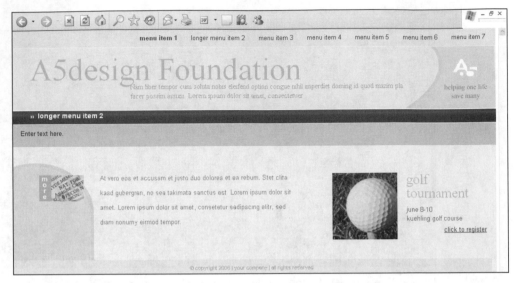

Second-level template for less content.

Second-level template for more content.

Photoshop source file names: Designs - Third Edition/121-160-css/design_137/design_137.psd

XHTML pages: index.htm, menu_item_2.htm, menu_item_3.htm

Photo credits: idlerphotography.com

Design 136

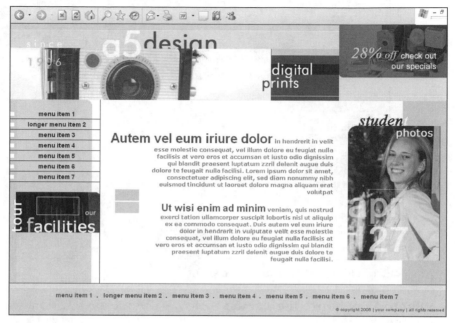

Homepage design.

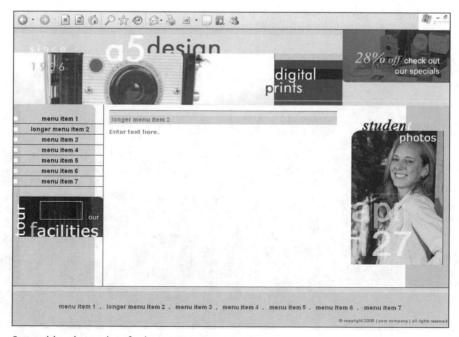

Second-level template for less content.

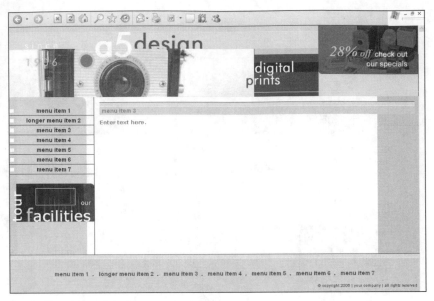

Second-level template for more content.

Photoshop source file names: Designs - Third Edition/121-160-css/design_136/ design_136.psd

XHTML pages: index.htm, menu_item_2.htm, menu_item_3.htm

Photo credits: idlerphotography.com

Design 135

Homepage design.

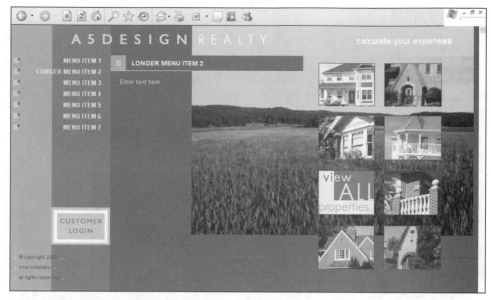

Second-level template for less content.

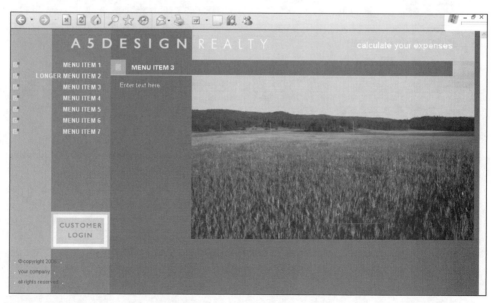

Second-level template for more content.

Photoshop source file names: Designs - Third Edition/121-160-css/design_135/ design_135.psd, bg_design_135.psd

XHTML pages: index.htm, menu_item_2.htm, menu_item_3.htm

Photo credits: idlerphotography.com

Design 134

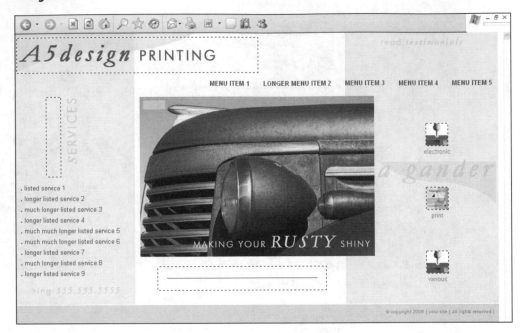

Homepage design.

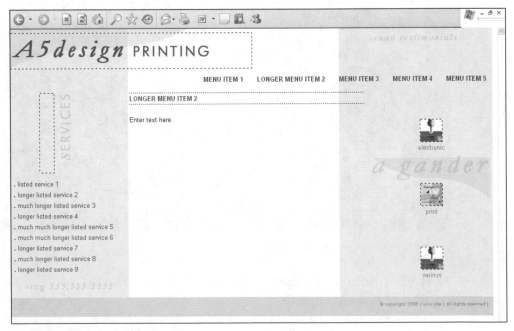

Second-level template for less content.

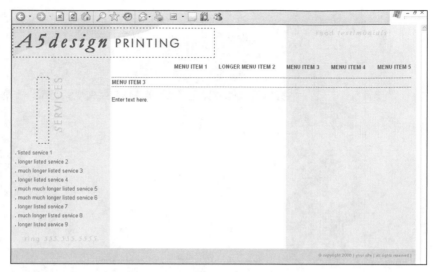

Second-level template for more content.

Photoshop source file names: Designs - Third Edition/121-160-css/design_134/design_134.psd

XHTML pages: index.htm, menu_item_2.htm, menu_item_3.htm

Photo credits: idlerphotography.com

Design 133

Homepage design.

Second-level template for less content.

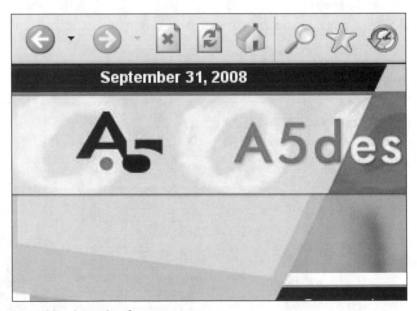

Second-level template for more content.

Photoshop source file names: Designs - Third Edition/121-160-css/design_133/ design_133.psd

XHTML pages: index.htm, menu_item_2.htm, menu_item_3.htm

Photo credits: idlerphotography.com

Design 132

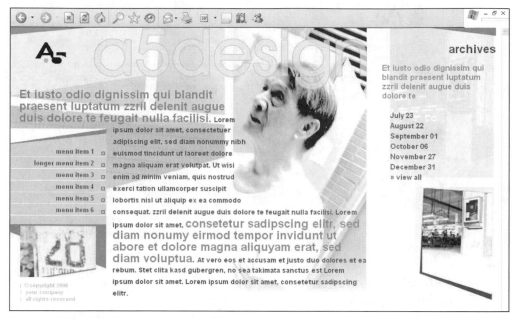

Homepage design.

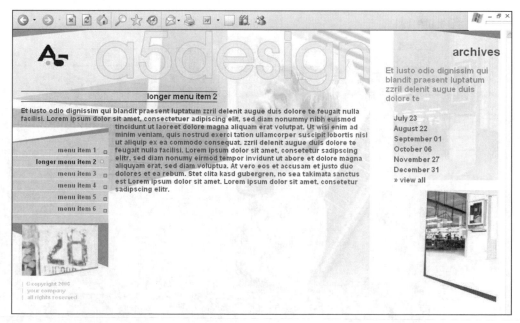

Second-level template for less content.

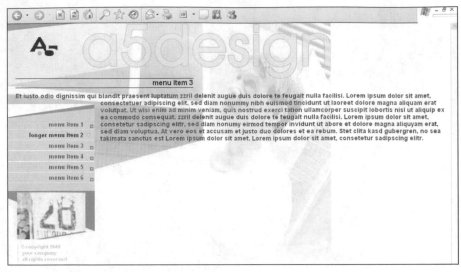

Second-level template for more content.

Photoshop source file names: Designs - Third Edition/121-160-css/design_132/ design_132.psd, bg_132.psd, bg_132_sl.psd

XHTML pages: index.htm, menu_item_2.htm, menu_item_3.htm

Photo credits: Justin Discoe

Design 131

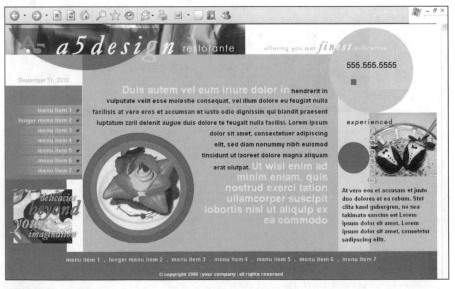

Homepage design.

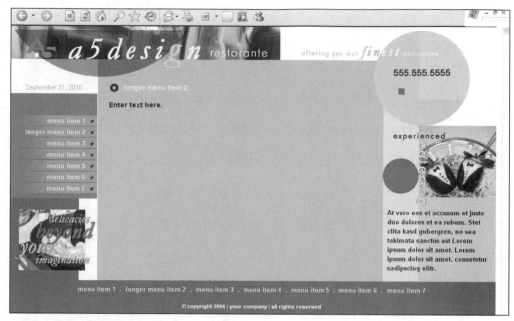

Second-level template for less content.

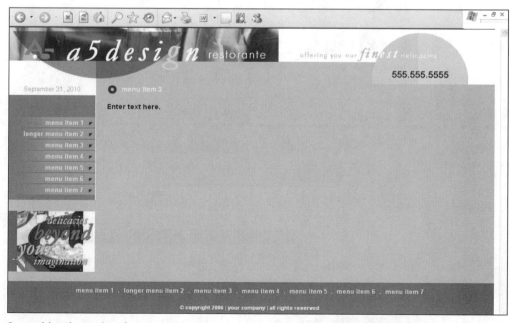

Second-level template for more content.

Photoshop source file names: Designs - Third Edition/121-160-css/design_131/ design_131.psd

XHTML pages: index.htm, menu_item_2.htm, menu_item_3.htm

Photo credits: idlerphotography.com

Design 130

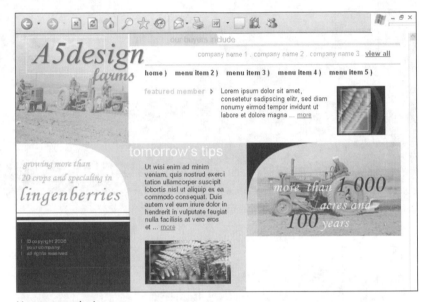

Homepage design.

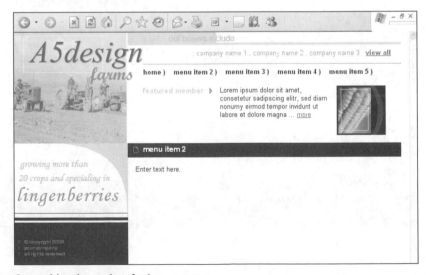

Second-level template for less content.

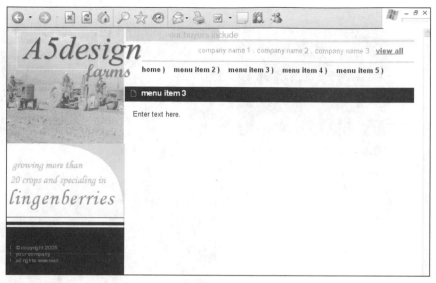

Second-level template for more content.

Photoshop source file names: Designs - Third Edition/121-160-css/design_130/design_130.psd

XHTML pages: index.htm, menu_item_2.htm, menu_item_3.htm

Photo credits: idlerphotography.com, Joe Eccher

Design 129

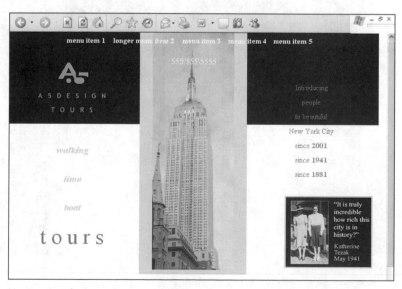

Homepage design.

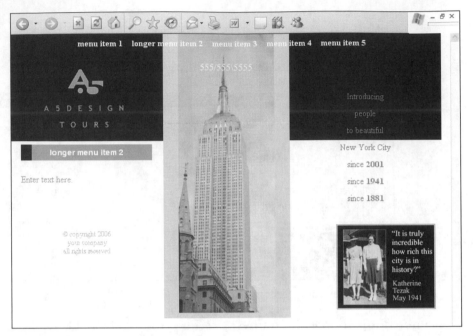

Second-level template for less content.

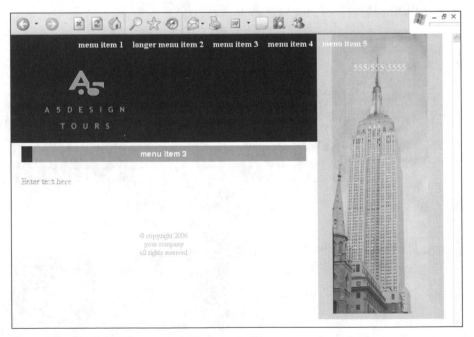

Second-level template for more content.

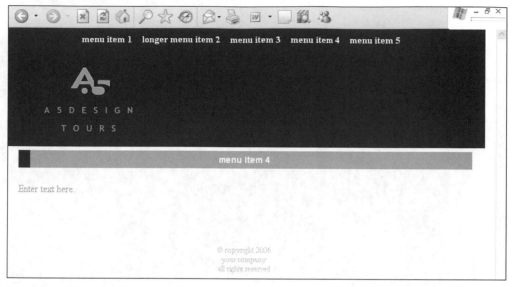

Second-level template for more content.

Photoshop source file names: Designs - Third Edition/121-160-css/design_129/ design_129.psd, bg_design_129.psd

XHTML pages: index.htm, menu_item_2.htm, menu_item_3.htm, menu_item_4.htm

Photo credits: Justin Discoe, Lori Discoe

Design 128

Homepage design.

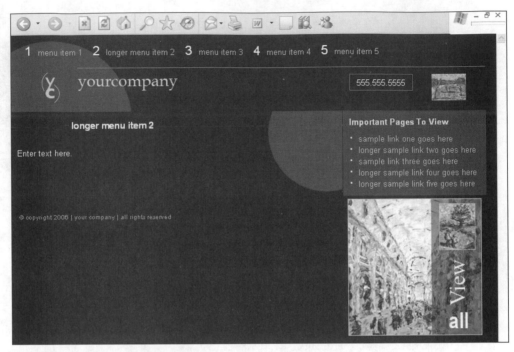

Second-level template for less content.

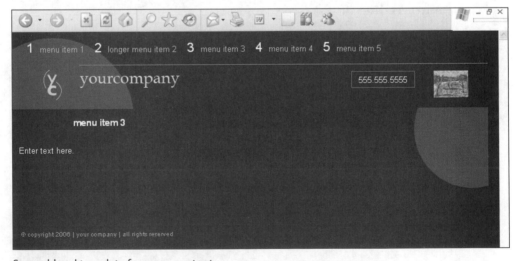

Second-level template for more content.

Photoshop source file names: Designs - Third Edition/121-160-css/design_128/design_128.psd

XHTML pages: index.htm, menu_item_2.htm, menu_item_3.htm

Photo credits: A5design

Design 127

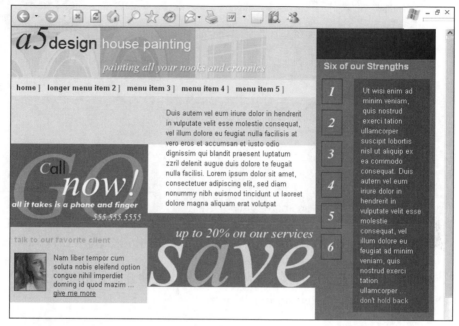

Homepage design.

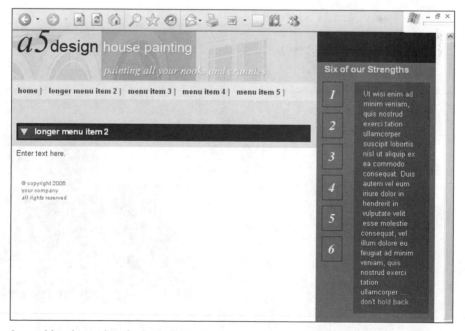

Second-level template for less content.

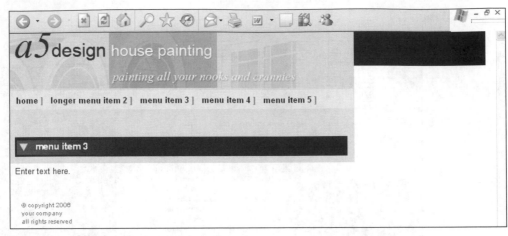

Second-level template for more content.

Photoshop source file names: Designs - Third Edition/121-160-css/design_127/ design_127.psd, bg_design_127.psd

XHTML pages: index.htm, menu_item_2.htm, menu_item_3.htm

Photo credits: idlerphotography.com

Design 126

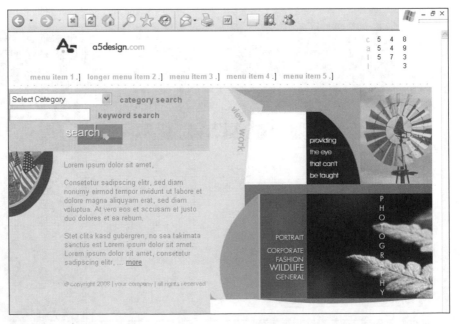

Homepage design.

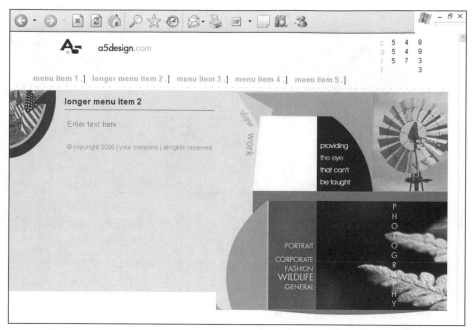

Second-level template for less content.

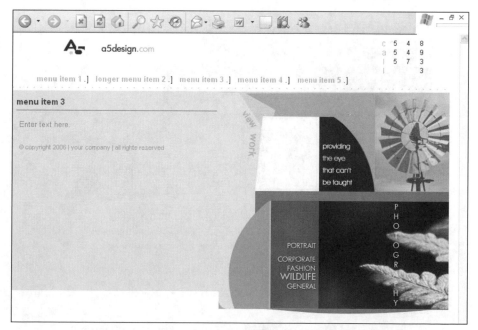

Second-level template for more content.

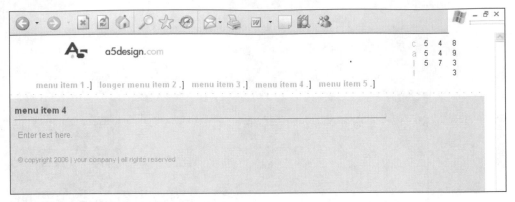

Second-level template for more content.

Photoshop source file names: Designs - Third Edition/121-160-css/design_126/design_126.psd

XHTML pages: index.htm, menu_item_2.htm, menu_item_3.htm, menu_item_4.htm

Photo credits: idlerphotography.com

Design 125

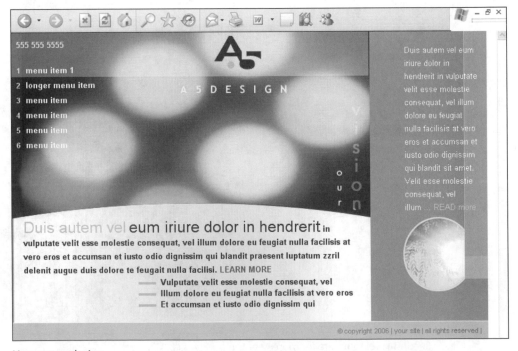

Homepage design.

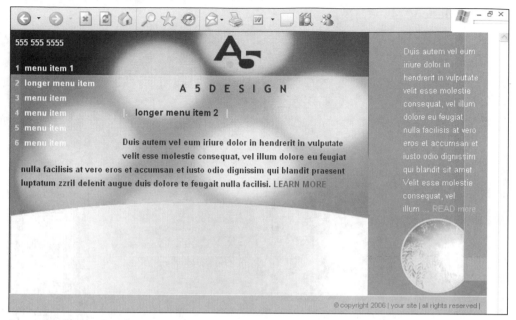

Second-level template for less content.

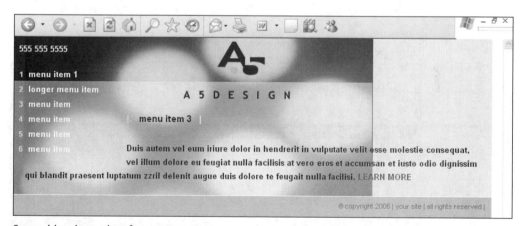

Second-level template for more content.

Photoshop source file names: Designs - Third Edition/121-160-css/design_125/ design_125.psd

XHTML pages: index.htm, menu_item_2.htm, menu_item_3.htm

Photo credits: A5design

Design 124

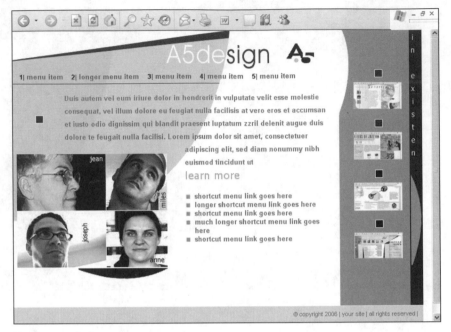

Homepage design.

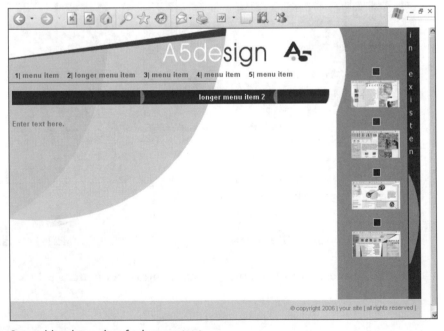

Second-level template for less content.

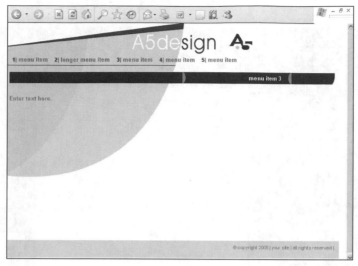

Second-level template for more content.

Photoshop source file names: Designs - Third Edition/121-160-css/design_124/ design_124.psd, bg_design_124.psd

XHTML pages: index.htm, menu_item_2.htm, menu_item_3.htm

Photo credits: Joe Eccher

Design 123

Homepage design.

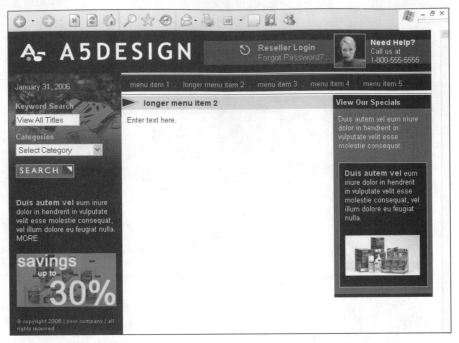

Second-level template for less content.

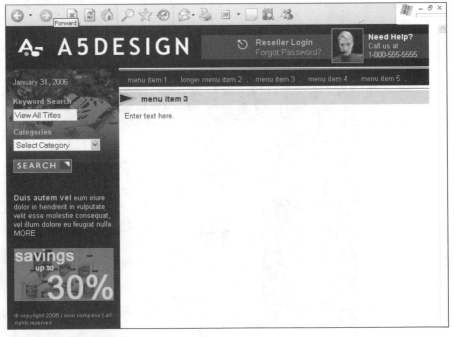

Second-level template for more content.

Photoshop source file names: Designs - Third Edition/121-160-css/design_123/ design_123.psd, bg-left-column.psd

XHTML pages: index.htm, menu_item_2.htm, menu_item_3.htm

Photo credits: idlerphotography.com

Design 122

Homepage design.

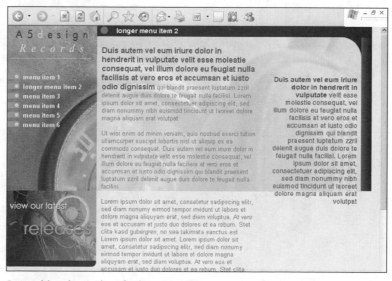

Second-level template for less content.

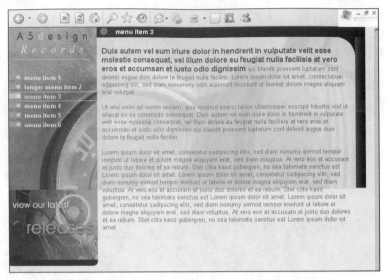

Second-level template for more content.

Photoshop source file names: Designs - Third Edition/121-160-css/design_122/ design_122.psd, design_122_sl.psd

XHTML pages: index.htm, menu_item_2.htm, menu_item_3.htm

Photo credits: idlerphotography.com

Design 121

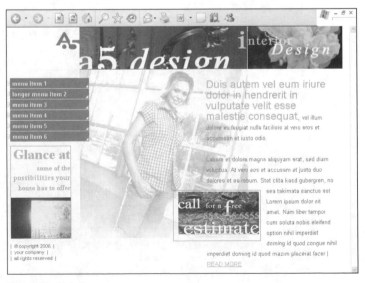

Homepage design.

Second-level template for less content.

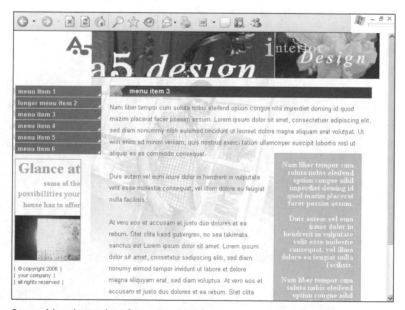

Second-level template for more content.

Photoshop source file names: Designs - Third Edition/121-160-css/design_121/ design_121.psd, design_121_sl.psd, bg_body_figure.psd

XHTML pages: index.htm, menu_item_2.htm, menu_item_3.htm

Photo credits: idlerphotography.com

Design 120

Homepage design (Photoshop only).

Photoshop source file names: Designs - Third Edition/101-120-photoshop/design_120/design_120.psd

Photo credits: A5design

Design 119

Homepage design (Photoshop only).

Photoshop source file names: Designs - Third Edition/101-120-photoshop/design_119/design_119.psd

Photo credits: idlerphotography.com

Design 118

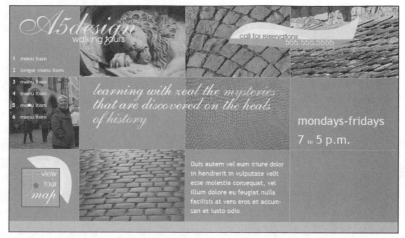

Homepage design (Photoshop only).

Photoshop source file names: Designs - Third Edition/101-120-photoshop/
design_118/design_118.psd

Photo credits: Joe Eccher

Design 117

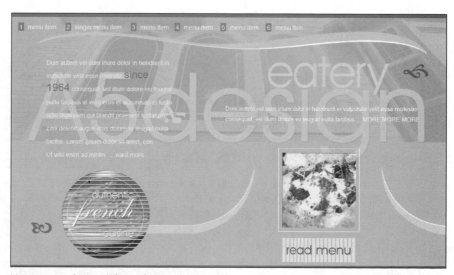

Homepage design (Photoshop only).

Photoshop source file names: Designs - Third Edition/101-120-photoshop/
design_117/design_117.psd

Photo credits: idlerphotography.com

Design 116

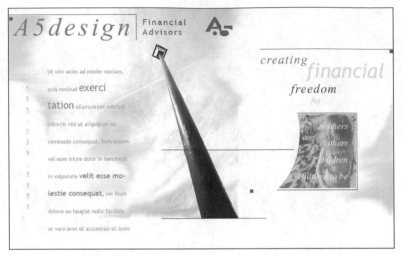

Homepage design (Photoshop only).

Photoshop source file names: Designs - Third Edition/101-120-photoshop/design_116/design_116.psd

Photo credits: idlerphotography.com, Joe Eccher

Design 115

Homepage design (Photoshop only).

Photoshop source file names: Designs - Third Edition/101-120-photoshop/design_115/design_115.psd

Photo credits: Joe Eccher

Design 114

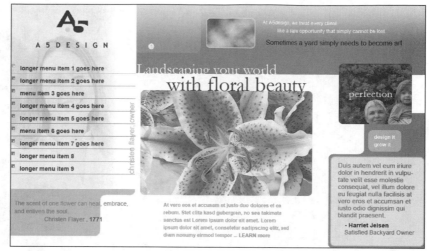

Homepage design (Photoshop only).

Photoshop source file names: Designs - Third Edition/101-120-photoshop/design_114/design_114.psd

Photo credits: idlerphotography.com, Joe Eccher

Design 113

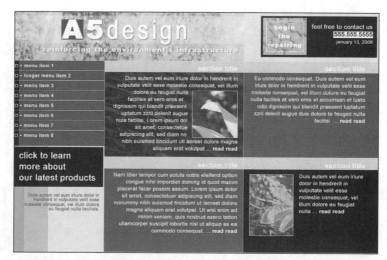

Homepage design (Photoshop only).

Photoshop source file names: Designs - Third Edition/101-120-photoshop/design_113/design_113.psd

Photo credits: Joe Eccher

Design 112

Homepage design (Photoshop only).

Photoshop source file names: Designs - Third Edition/101-120-photoshop/design_112/design_112.psd

Photo credits: idlerphotography.com

Design 111

Homepage design (Photoshop only).

Photoshop source file names: Designs - Third Edition/101-120-photoshop/design_111/design_111.psd

Photo credits: idlerphotography.com

Design 110

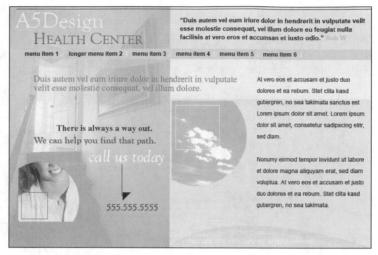

Homepage design (Photoshop only).

Photoshop source file names: Designs - Third Edition/101-120-photoshop/ design_110/design_110.psd

Photo credits: idlerphotography.com

Design 109

Homepage design (Photoshop only).

Photoshop source file names: Designs - Third Edition/101-120-photoshop/ design_109/design_109.psd

Photo credits: idlerphotography.com, Joe Eccher

Design 108

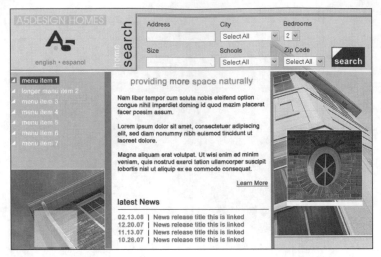

Homepage design (Photoshop only).

Photoshop source file names: Designs - Third Edition/101-120-photoshop/design_108/design_108.psd

Photo credits: idlerphotography.com

Design 107

Homepage design (Photoshop only).

Photoshop source file names: Designs - Third Edition/101-120-photoshop/design_107/design_107.psd

Photo credits: Lisa Murillo, Joe Eccher

Design 106

Homepage design (Photoshop only).

Photoshop source file names: Designs - Third Edition/101-120-photoshop/
design_106/design_106.psd

Photo credits: A5design

Design 105

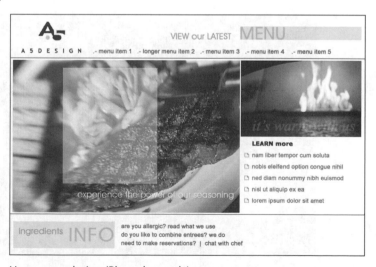

Homepage design (Photoshop only).

Photoshop source file names: Designs - Third Edition/101-120-photoshop/
design_105/design_105.psd

Photo credits: idlerphotography.com

Design 104

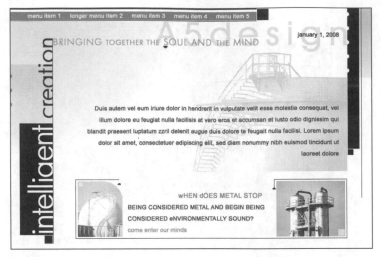

Homepage design (Photoshop only).

Photoshop source file names: Designs - Third Edition/101-120-photoshop/design_104/design_104.psd

Photo credits: idlerphotography.com

Design 103

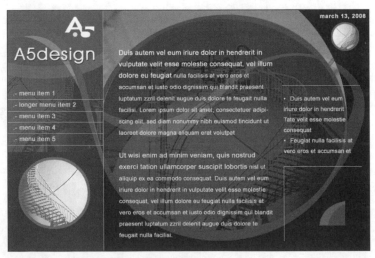

Homepage design (Photoshop only).

Photoshop source file names: Designs - Third Edition/101-120-photoshop/design_103/design_103.psd

Photo credits: idlerphotography.com

Design 102

Homepage design (Photoshop only).

Photoshop source file names: Designs - Third Edition/Designs - Third Edition/Designs - Third Edition/101-120-photoshop/design_102/design_102.psd

Photo credits: Joe Eccher, Justin Discoe

Design 101

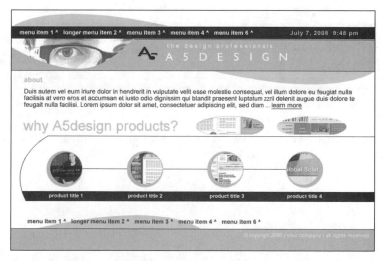

Homepage design (Photoshop only).

Photoshop source file names: 101-120-photoshop/design_101/design_101.psd

Photo credits: A5design

Design 100

Signature design.

Photoshop source file names: Designs - Third Edition/91-100-signatures/ design_100/design_100.psd

Photo credits: Joe Eccher

Design 99

Signature design.

Photoshop source file names: Designs - Third Edition/91-100-signatures/ design_99/design_99.psd

XHTML pages: index.htm

Photo credits: A5design

Design 98

Signature design.

Photoshop source file names: Designs - Third Edition/91-100-signatures/ design_98/design_98.psd

XHTML pages: index.htm

Photo credits: Lisa Murillo

Design 97

Signature design.

Photoshop source file names: Designs - Third Edition/91-100-signatures/ design_97/design_97.psd

XHTML pages: index.htm

Photo credits: Lisa Murillo, A5design

Design 96

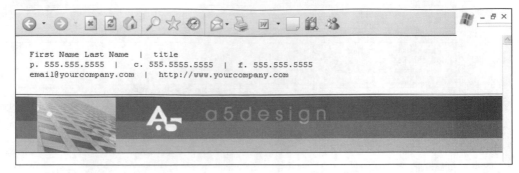

Signature design.

Photoshop source file names: Designs - Third Edition/91-100-signatures/ design_96/design_96.psd

XHTML pages: index.htm

Photo credits: Lisa Murillo

Design 95

Signature design.

Photoshop source file names: Designs - Third Edition/91-100-signatures/ design_95/design_95.psd

XHTML pages: index.htm

Photo credits: A5design

Design 94

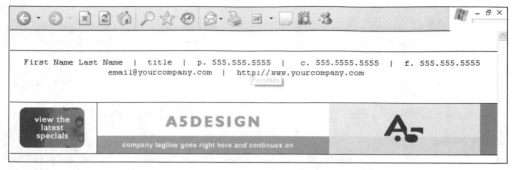

Signature design.

Photoshop source file names: Designs - Third Edition/91-100-signatures/design_94/design_94.psd

XHTML pages: index.htm

Photo credits: A5design

Design 93

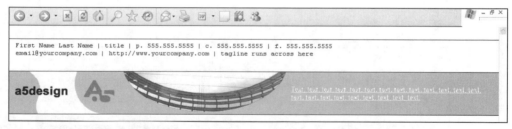

Signature design.

Photoshop source file names: Designs - Third Edition/91-100-signatures/design_93/design_93.psd

XHTML pages: index.htm

Photo credits: Lisa Murillo

Design 92

Signature design.

Photoshop source file names: Designs - Third Edition/91-100-signatures/ design_92/design_92.psd

XHTML pages: index.htm

Photo credits: Lori Discoe

Design 91

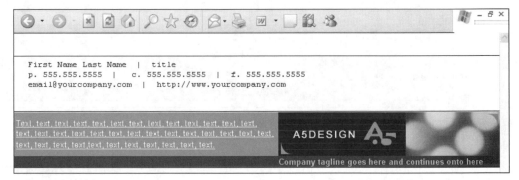

Signature design.

Photoshop source file names: Designs - Third Edition/91-100-signatures/ design_91/design_91.psd

XHTML pages: index.htm

Photo credits: A5design

Design 90

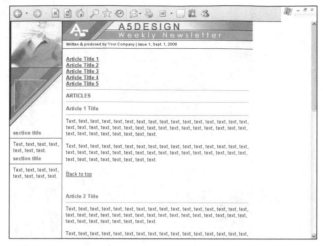

E-newsletter design.

Photoshop source file names: Designs - Third Edition/81-90-enewsletters/ design_90/design_90.psd

XHTML pages: index.htm

Photo credits: A5design

Design 89

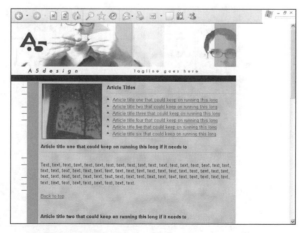

E-newsletter design.

Photoshop source file names: Designs - Third Edition/81-90-enewsletters/ design_89/design_89.psd

XHTML pages: index.htm

Photo credits: A5design

Design 88

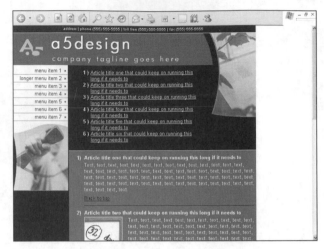

E-newsletter design.

Photoshop source file names: Designs - Third Edition/81-90-enewsletters/ design_88/design_88.psd

XHTML pages: index.htm

Photo credits: Lisa Murillo

Design 87

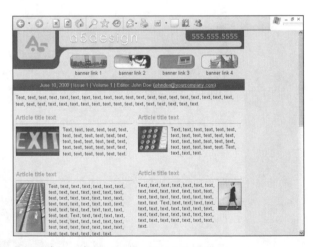

E-newsletter design

Photoshop source file names: Designs - Third Edition/81-90-enewsletters/ design_87/design_87.psd

XHTML pages: index.htm

Photo credits: Lisa Murillo, Joe Eccher, A5design

Design 86

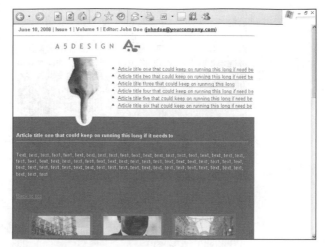

E-newsletter design.

Photoshop source file names: Designs - Third Edition/81-90-enewsletters/ design_86/design_86.psd

XHTML pages: index.htm

Photo credits: Lisa Murillo, A5design

Design 85

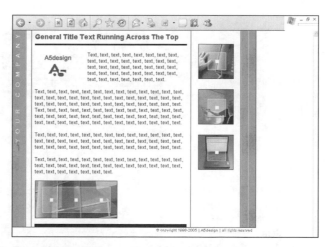

E-newsletter design.

Photoshop source file names: Designs - Third Edition/81-90-enewsletters/ design_85/design_85.psd

XHTML pages: index.htm

Photo credits: Lisa Murillo, A5design

Design 84

E-newsletter design.

Photoshop source file names: Designs - Third Edition/81-90-enewsletters/ design_84/design_84.psd

XHTML pages: index.htm

Photo credits: A5design

Design 83

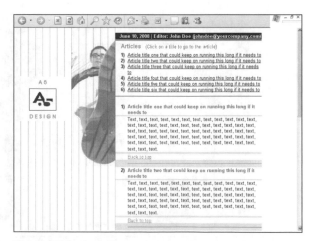

E-newsletter design.

Photoshop source file names: Designs - Third Edition/81-90-enewsletters/ design_83/design_83.psd

XHTML pages: index.htm

Photo credits: A5design

Design 82

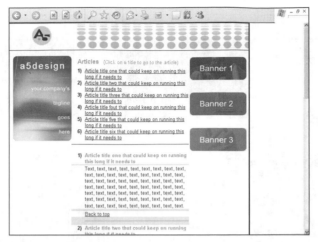

E-newsletter design.

Photoshop source file names: Designs - Third Edition/81-90-enewsletters/ design_82/design_82.psd

XHTML pages: index.htm

Photo credits: A5design

Design 81

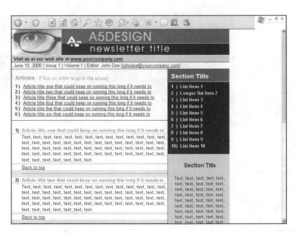

E-newsletter design.

Photoshop source file names: Designs - Third Edition/81-90-enewsletters/ design_81/design_81.psd

XHTML pages: index.htm

Photo credits: A5design

Design 80

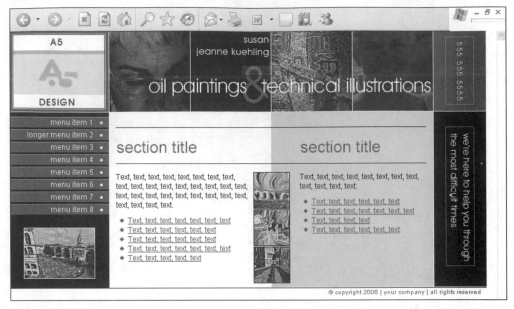

Homepage design.

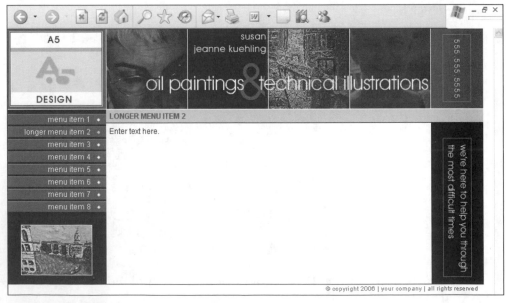

Second-level template for less content.

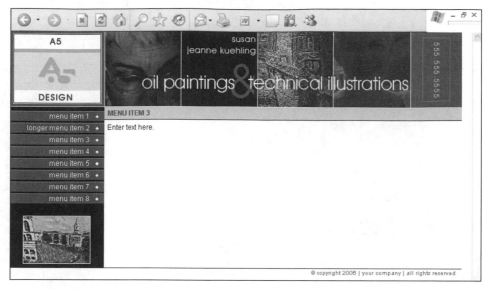

Second-level template for more content.

Photoshop source file names: Designs - Third Edition/1-80-xhtml/design_80/design_80.psd

XHTML pages: index.htm, menu_item_2.htm, menu_item_3.htm

Photo credits: A5design

Design 79

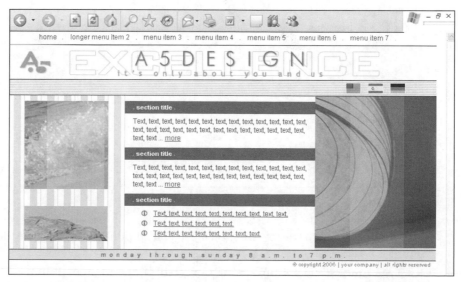

Homepage design.

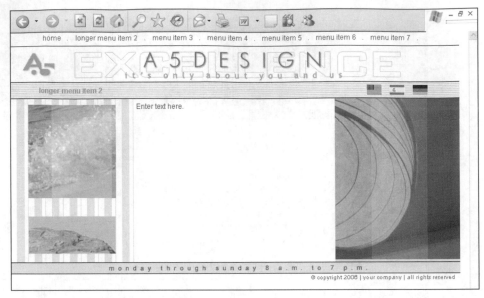

Second-level template for less content.

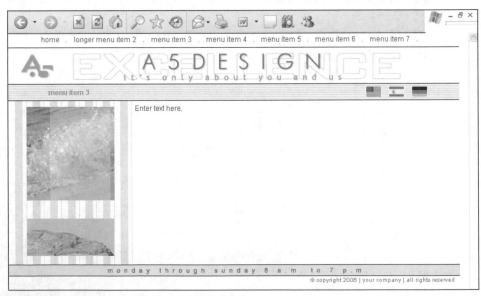

Second-level template for more content.

Photoshop source file names: Designs - Third Edition/1-80-xhtml/design_79/design_79.psd

XHTML pages: index.htm, menu_item_2.htm, menu_item_3.htm

Photo credits: Joe Eccher

Design 78

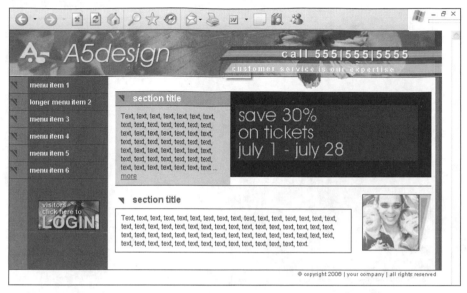

Homepage design.

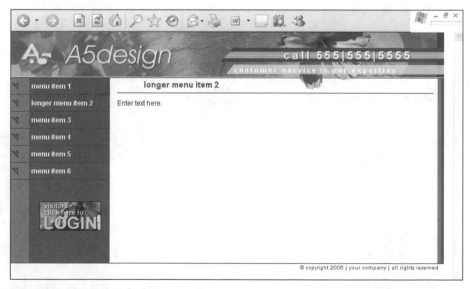

Second-level template for less content.

Photoshop source file names: Designs - Third Edition/1-80-xhtml/design_78/design_78.psd

XHTML pages: index.htm, menu_item_2.htm

Photo credits: Lori Discoe

Design 77

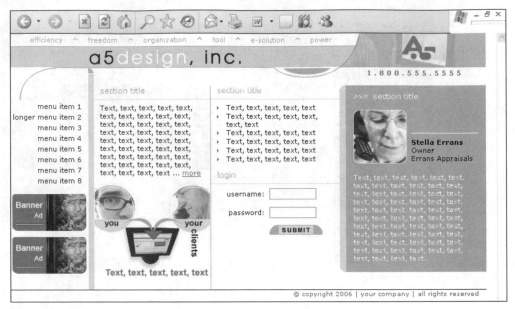

Homepage design.

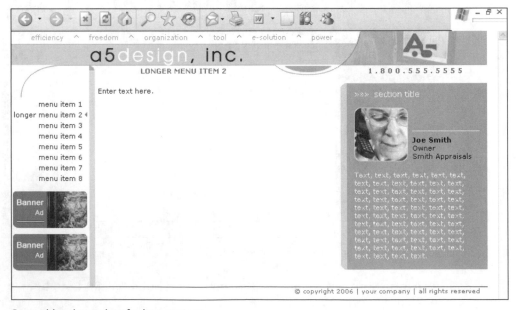

Second-level template for less content.

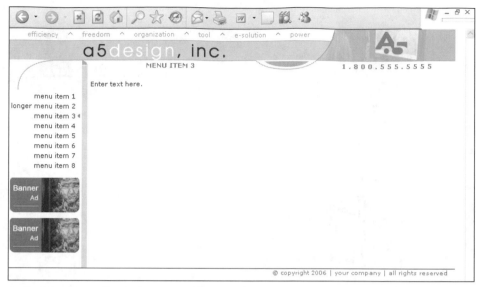

Second-level template for more content.

Photoshop source file names: Designs - Third Edition/1-80-xhtml/design_77/
design_77.psd

XHTML pages: index.htm, menu_item_2.htm, menu_item_3.htm

Photo credits: Joe Eccher, A5design

Design 76

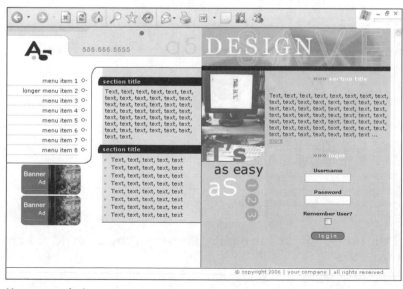

Homepage design.

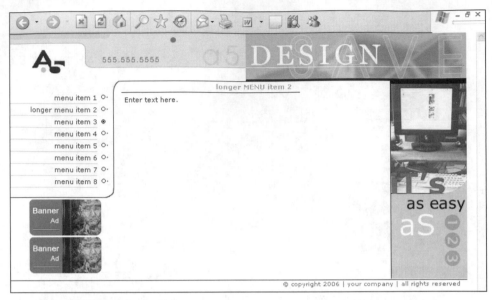

Second-level template for less content.

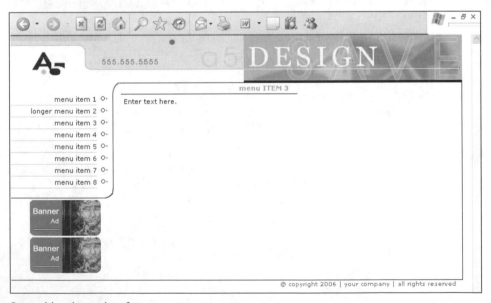

Second-level template for more content.

Photoshop source file names: Designs - Third Edition/1-80-xhtml/design_76/design_76.psd

XHTML pages: index.htm, menu_item_2.htm, menu_item_3.htm

Photo credits: A5design

Design 75

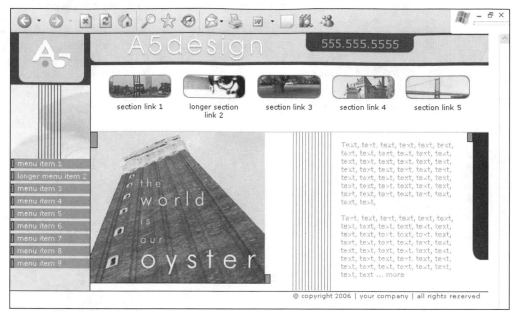

Homepage design.

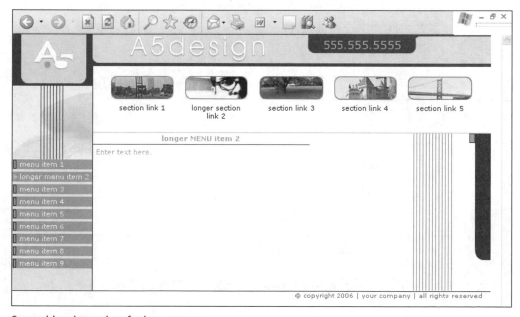

Second-level template for less content.

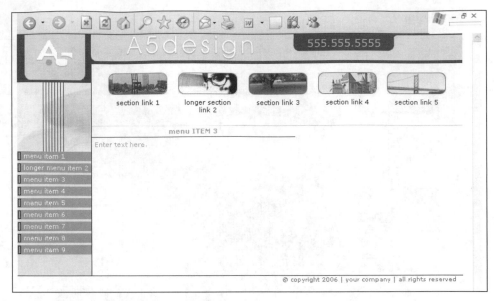

Second-level template for more content.

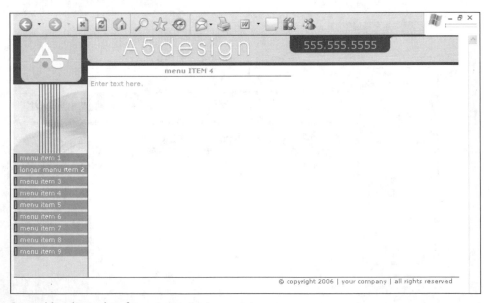

Second-level template for more content.

Photoshop source file names: Designs - Third Edition/1-80-xhtml/design_75/design_75.psd

XHTML pages: index.htm, menu_item_2.htm, menu_item_3.htm, menu_item_4.htm

Photo credits: Joe Eccher, A5design

Design 74

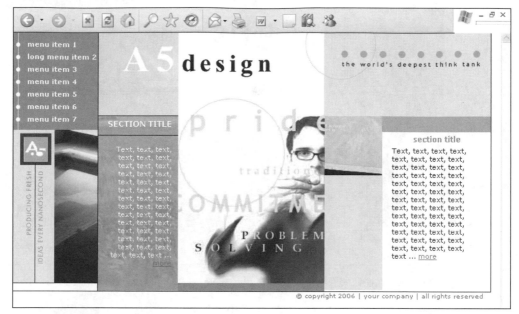

Homepage design.

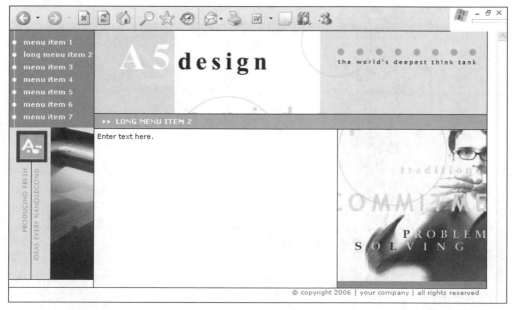

Second-level template for less content.

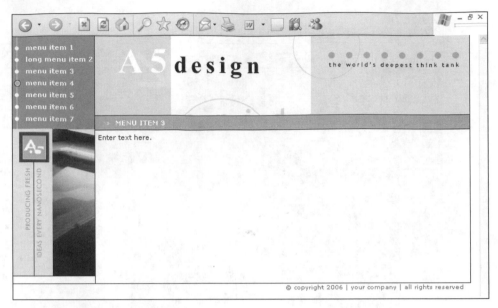

Second-level template for more content.

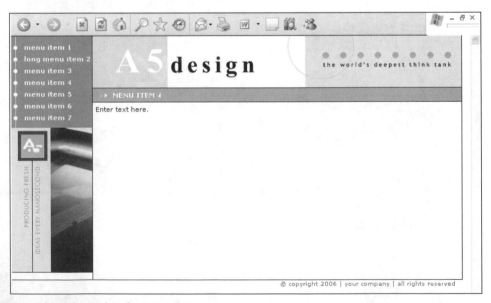

Second-level template for more content.

Photoshop source file names: Designs - Third Edition/1-80-xhtml/design_74/ design_74.psd, bg_images.psd

XHTML pages: index.htm, menu_item_2.htm, menu_item_3.htm, menu_item_4.htm

Photo credits: A5design

Design 73

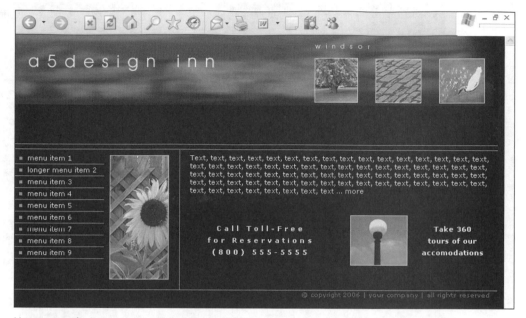

Homepage design.

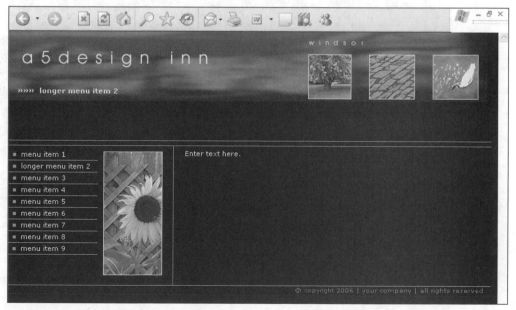

Second-level template for less content.

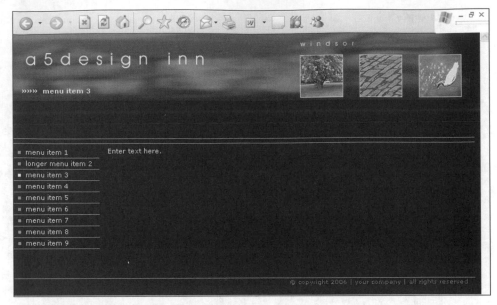

Second-level template for more content.

Second-level template for more content.

Photoshop source file names: Designs - Third Edition/1-80-xhtml/design_73/design_73.psd

XHTML pages: index.htm, menu_item_2.htm, menu_item_3.htm, menu_item_4.htm

Photo credits: A5design

Design 72

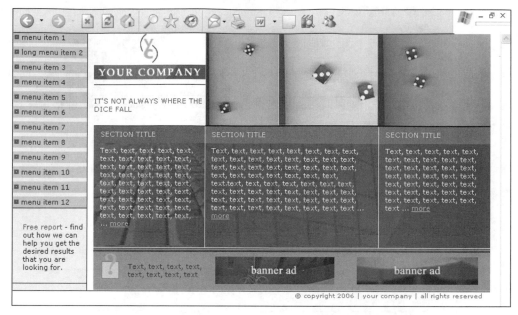

Homepage design.

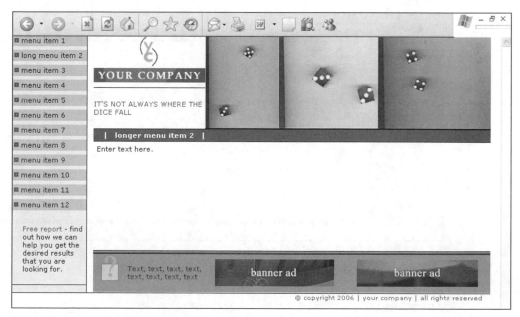

Second-level template for less content.

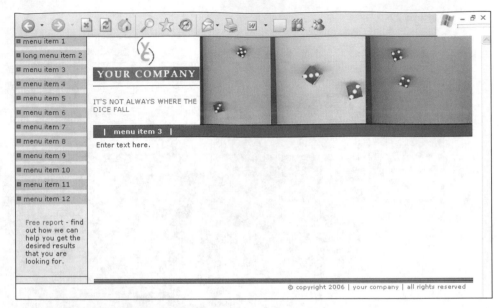

Second-level template for more content.

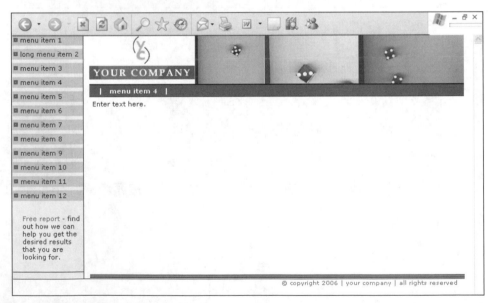

Second-level template for more content.

Photoshop source file names: Designs - Third Edition/1-80-xhtml/design_72/ esign_72.psd

XHTML pages: index.htm, menu_item_2.htm, menu_item_3.htm, menu_item_4.htm

Photo credits: A5design

Design 71

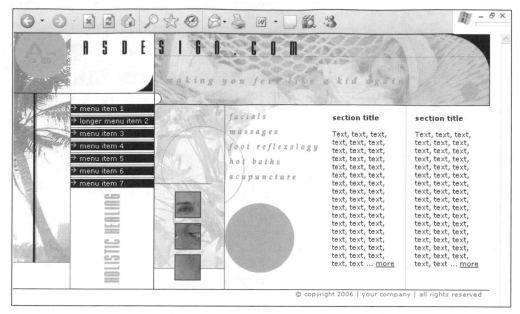

Homepage design.

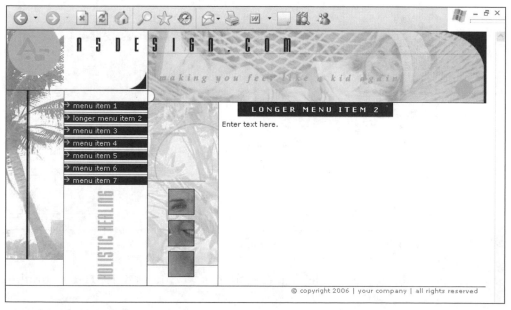

Second-level template for less content.

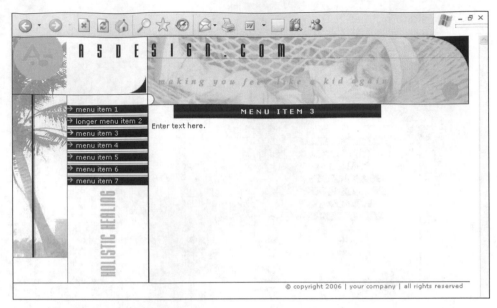

Second-level template for more content.

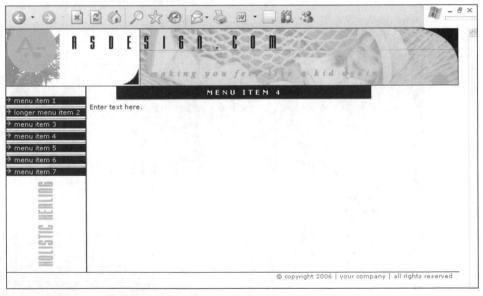

Second-level template for more content.

Photoshop source file names: Designs - Third Edition/1-80-xhtml/design_71/design_71.psd

XHTML pages: index.htm, menu_item_2.htm, menu_item_3.htm, menu_item_4.htm

Photo credits: Joe Eccher

Design 70

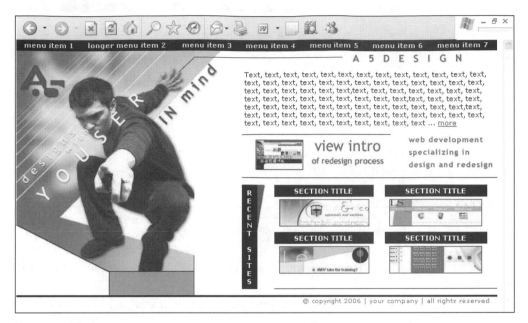

Homepage design.

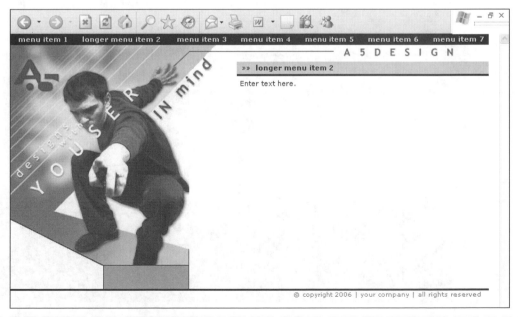

Second-level template for less content.

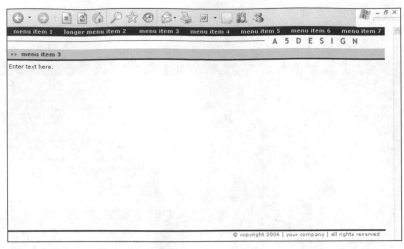

Second-level template for more content.

Photoshop source file names: Designs - Third Edition/1-80-xhtml/design_70/ design_70.psd

XHTML pages: index.htm, menu_item_2.htm, menu_item_3.htm

Photo credits: A5design

Design 69

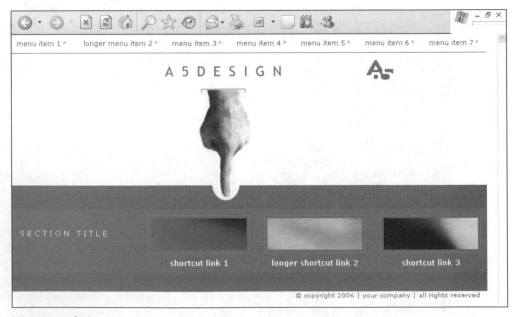

Homepage design.

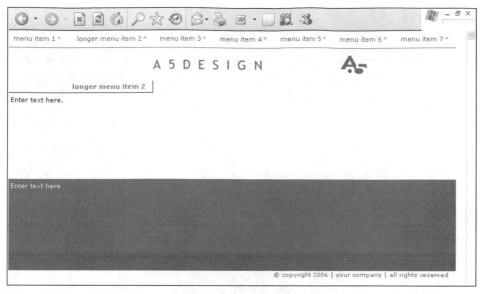

Second-level template for less content.

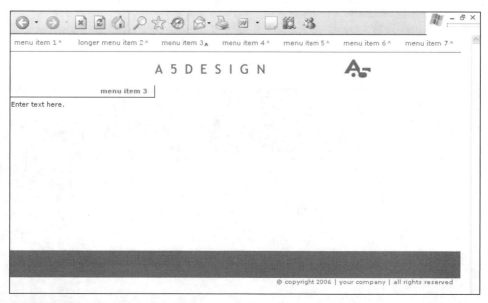

Second-level template for more content.

Photoshop source file names: Designs - Third Edition/1-80-xhtml/design_69/design_69.psd

XHTML pages: index.htm, menu_item_2.htm, menu_item_3.htm

Photo credits: A5design

Design 68

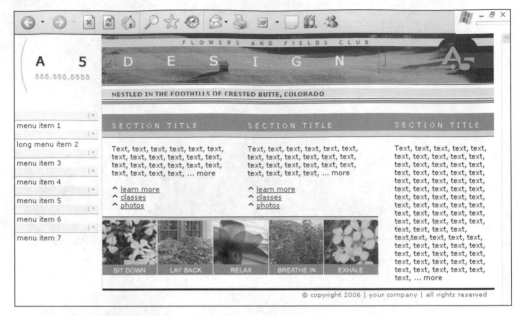

Homepage design.

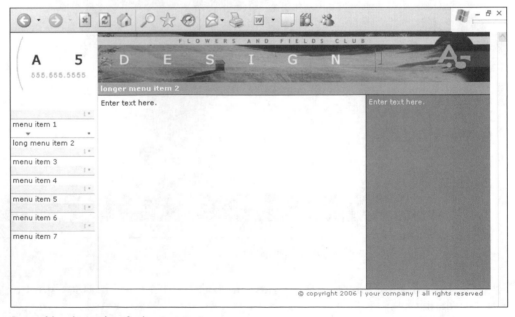

Second-level template for less content.

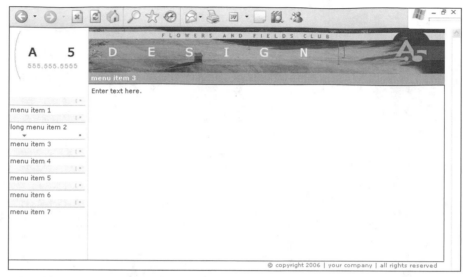

Second-level template for more content.

Photoshop source file names: Designs - Third Edition/1-80-xhtml/design_68/ design_68.psd

XHTML pages: index.htm, menu_item_2.htm, menu_item_3.htm

Photo credits: Joe Eccher

Design 67

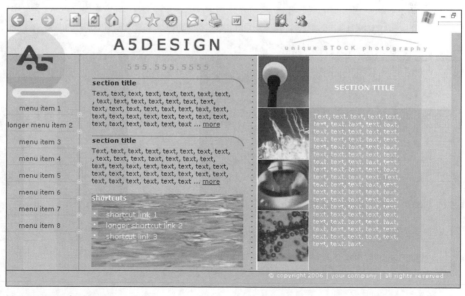

Homepage design.

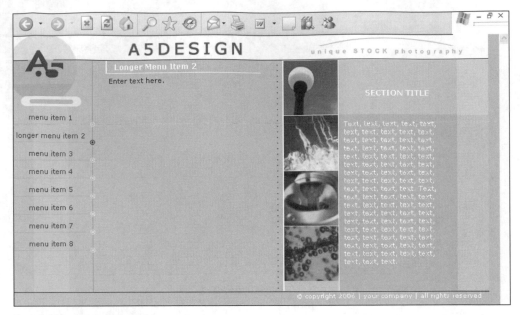

Second-level template for less content.

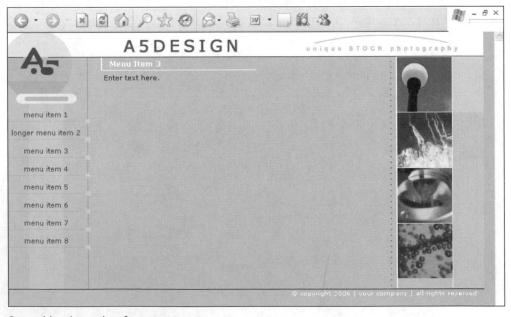

Second-level template for more content.

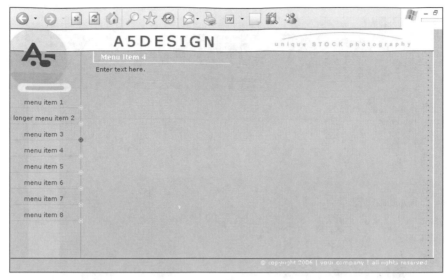

Second-level template for more content.

Photoshop source file names: Designs - Third Edition/1-80-xhtml/design_67/
design_67.psd, bg_images.psd

XHTML pages: index.htm, menu_item_2.htm, menu_item_3.htm, menu_item_4.htm

Photo credits: Lisa Murillo, A5design

Design 66

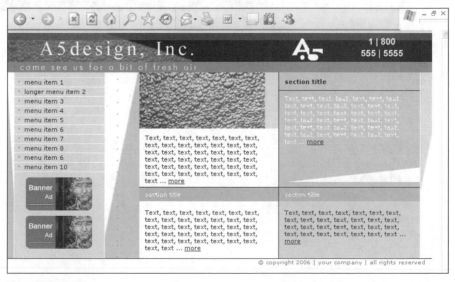

Homepage design.

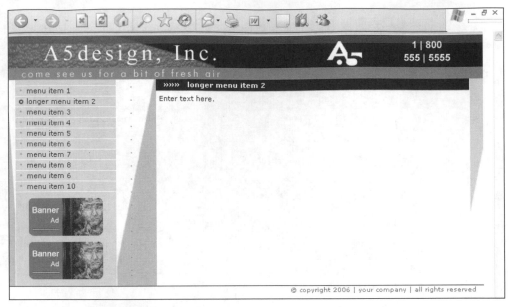

Second-level template for less content.

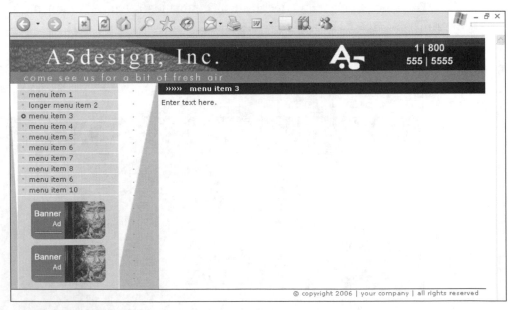

Second-level template for more content.

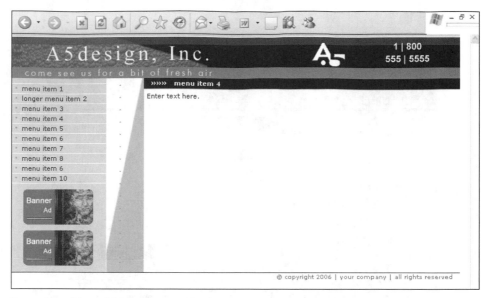

Second-level template for more content.

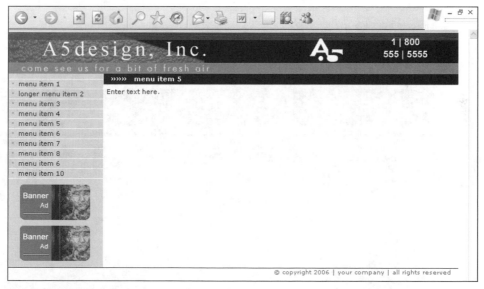

Second-level template for more content.

Photoshop source file names: Designs - Third Edition/1-80-xhtml/design_66/ design_66.psd

XHTML pages: index.htm, menu_item_2.htm, menu_item_3.htm, menu_item_4.htm, menu_item_5.htm

Photo credits: Joe Eccher

Design 65

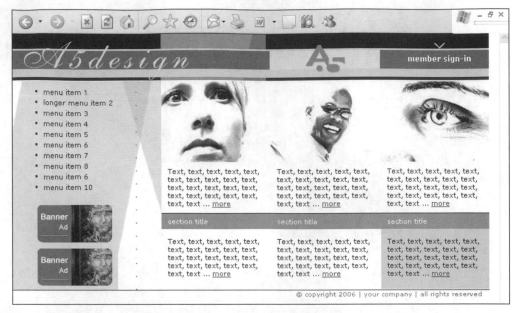

Homepage design.

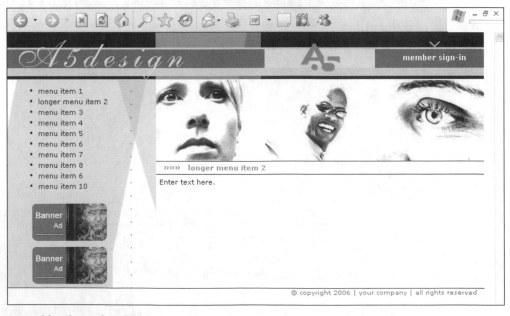

Second-level template for less content.

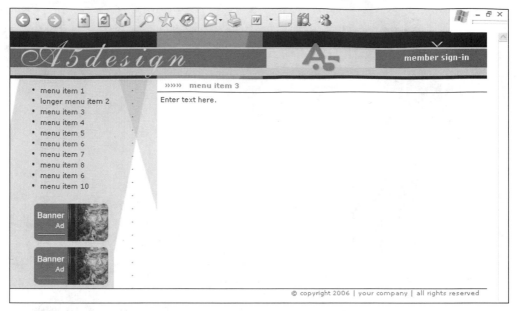

Second-level template for more content.

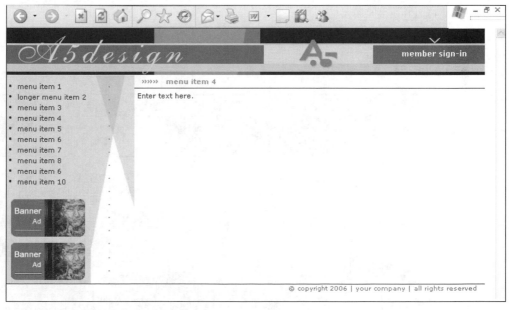

Second-level template for more content.

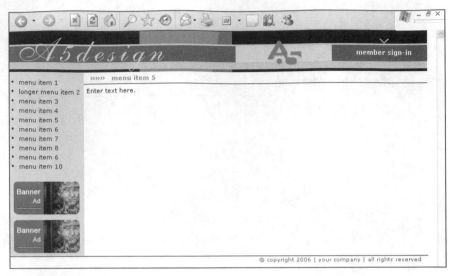

Second-level template for more content.

Photoshop source file names: Designs - Third Edition/1-80-xhtml/design_65/ design_65.psd

XHTML pages: index.htm, menu_item_2.htm, menu_item_3.htm, menu_item_4.htm, menu_item_5.htm

Photo credits: Lisa Murillo, A5design, Justin Discoe

Design 64

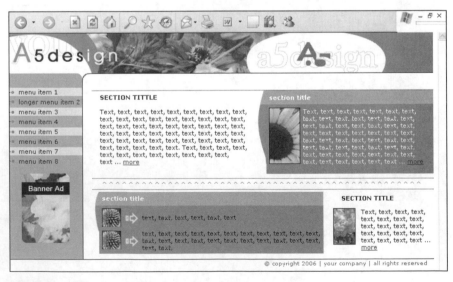

Homepage design.

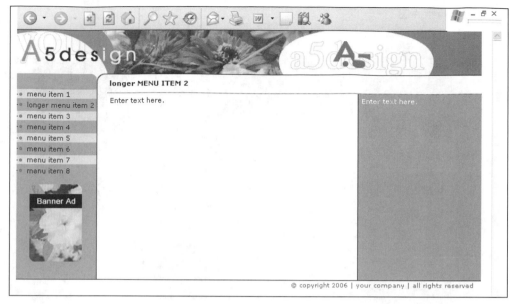

Second-level template for less content.

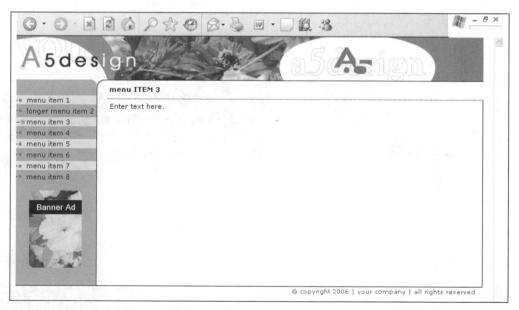

Second-level template for less content.

Photoshop source file names: Designs - Third Edition/1-80-xhtml/design_64/ design_64.psd

XHTML pages: index.htm, menu_item_2.htm, menu_item_3.htm

Photo credits: Joe Eccher

Design 63

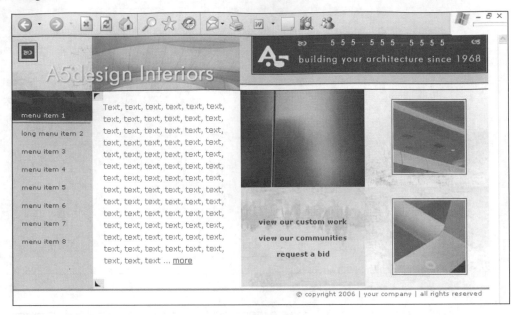

Homepage design.

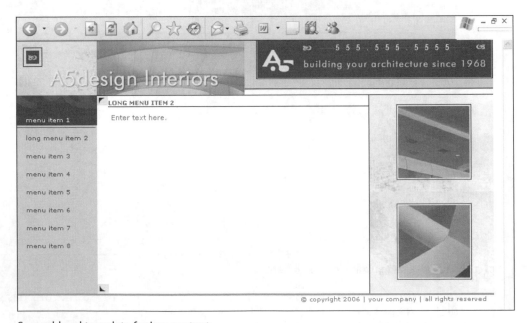

Second-level template for less content.

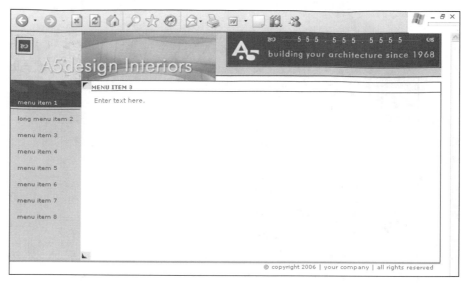

Second-level template for more content.

Photoshop source file names: Designs - Third Edition/1-80-xhtml/design_63/design_63.psd

XHTML pages: index.htm, menu_item_2.htm, menu_item_3.htm

Photo credits: Joe Eccher

Design 62

Homepage design.

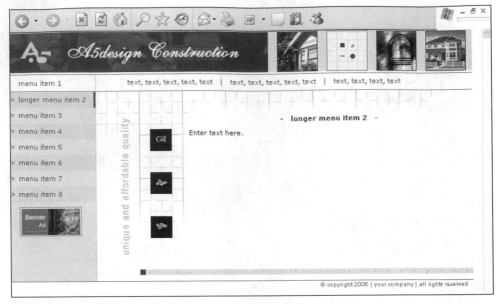

Second-level template for less content.

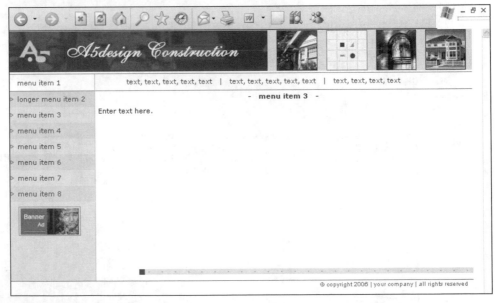

Second-level template for more content.

Photoshop source file names: Designs - Third Edition/1-80-xhtml/design_62/ design_62.psd

XHTML pages: index.htm, menu_item_2.htm, menu_item_3.htm

Photo credits: A5design

Design 61

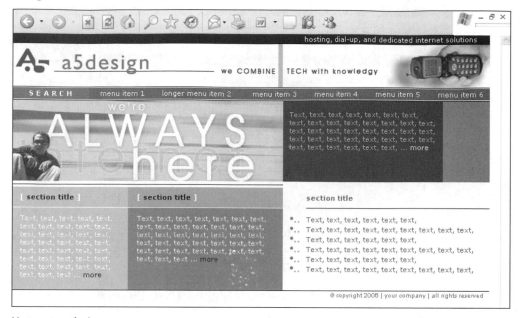

Homepage design.

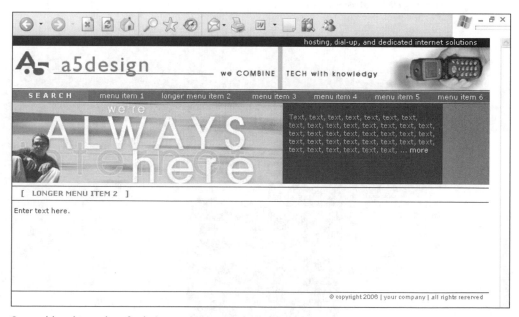

Second-level template for less content.

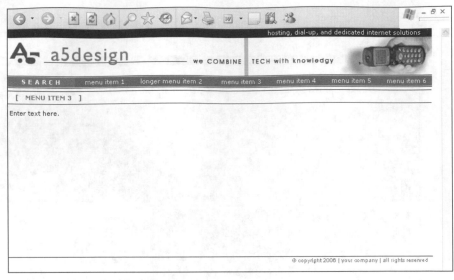

Second-level template for more content.

Photoshop source file names: Designs - Third Edition/1-80-xhtml/design_61/design_61.psd

XHTML pages: index.htm, menu_item_2.htm, menu_item_3.htm

Photo credits: A5design

Design 60

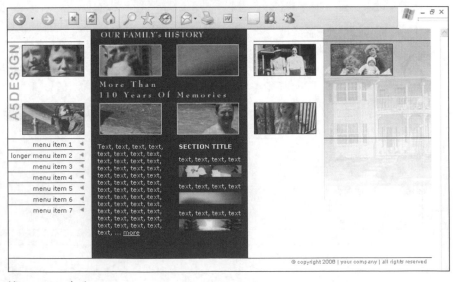

Homepage design.

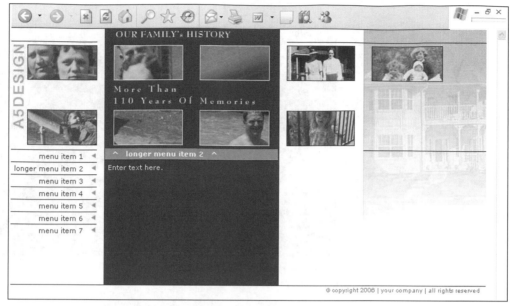

Second-level template for less content.

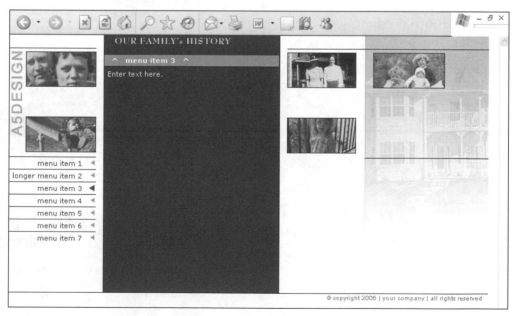

Second-level template for more content.

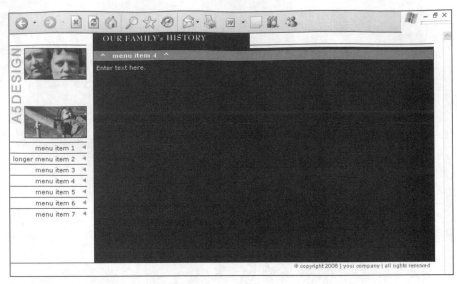

Second-level template for more content.

Photoshop source file names: Designs - Third Edition/1-80-xhtml/design_60/ design_60.psd

XHTML pages: index.htm, menu_item_2.htm, menu_item_3.htm, menu_item_4.htm

Photo credits: Joe Eccher, Lori Discoe, A5design

Design 59

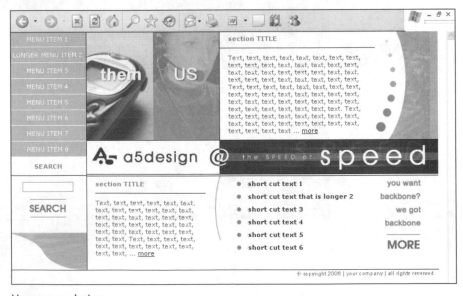

Homepage design.

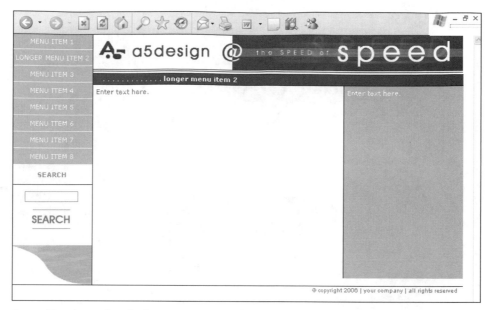

Second-level template for less content.

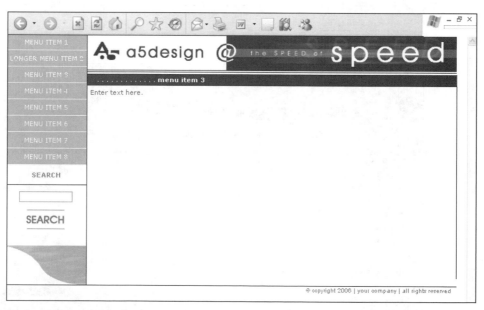

Second-level template for more content.

Photoshop source file names: Designs - Third Edition/1-80-xhtml/design_59/design_59.psd

XHTML pages: index.htm, menu_item_2.htm, menu_item_3.htm

Photo credits: A5design

Design 58

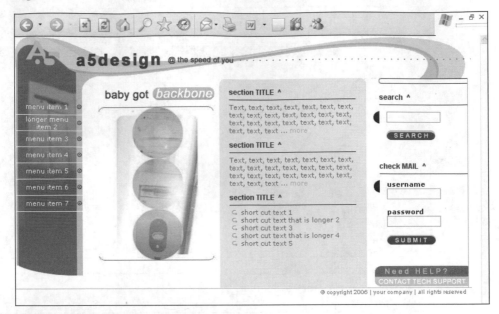

Homepage design.

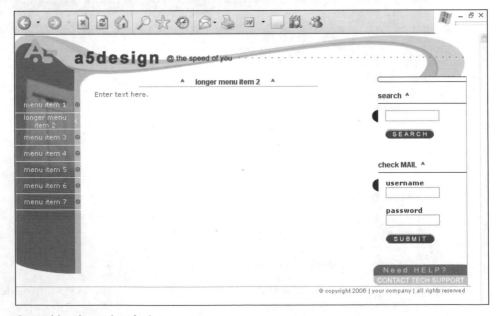

Second-level template for less content.

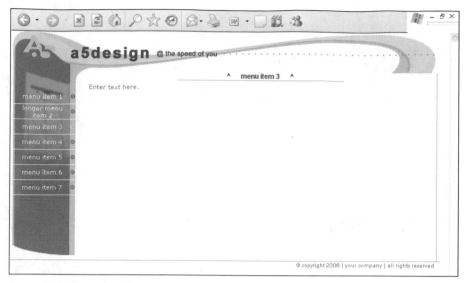

Second-level template for more content.

Photoshop source file names: Designs - Third Edition/1-80-xhtml/design_58/ design_58.psd, bg_images.psd

XHTML pages: index.htm, menu_item_2.htm, menu_item_3.htm

Photo credits: A5design

Design 57

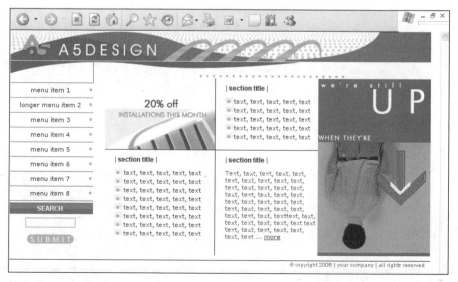

Homepage design.

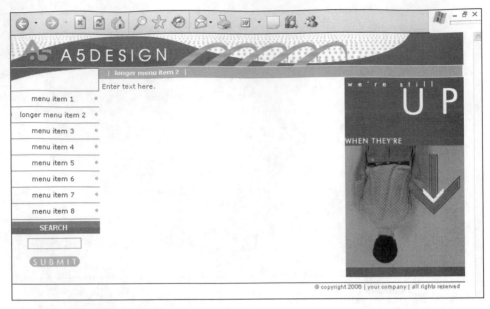

Second-level template for less content.

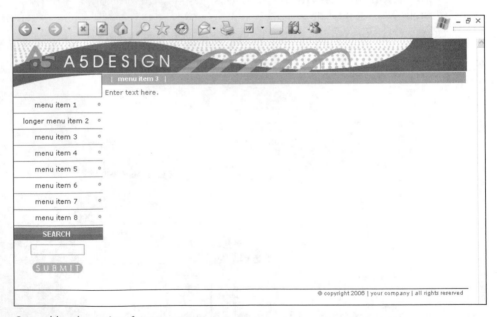

Second-level template for more content.

Photoshop source file names: Designs - Third Edition/1-80-xhtml/design_57/ design_57.psd

XHTML pages: index.htm, menu_item_2.htm, menu_item_3.htm

Photo credits: Lisa Murillo, A5design

Design 56

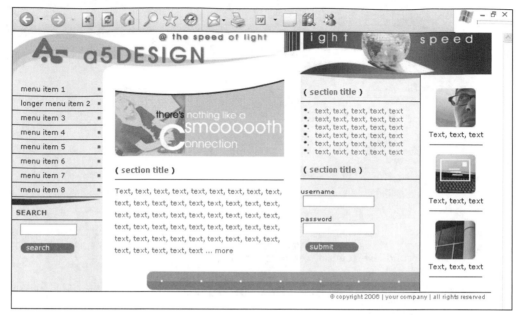

Homepage design.

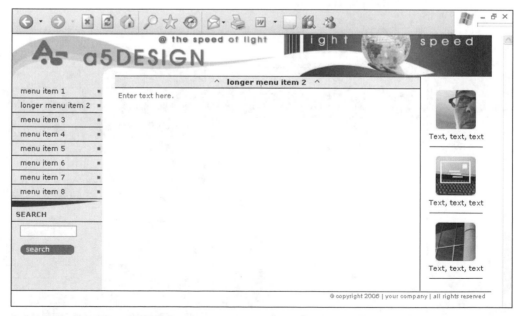

Second-level template for less content.

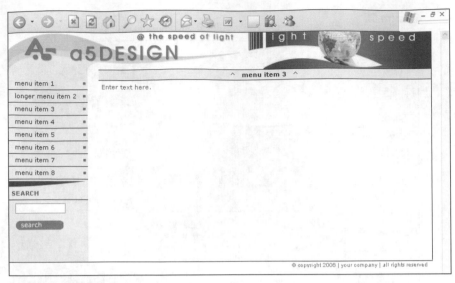

Second-level template for more content.

Photoshop source file names: Designs - Third Edition/1-80-xhtml/design_56/ design_56.psd

XHTML pages: index.htm, menu_item_2.htm, menu_item_3.htm

Photo credits: Lisa Murillo, A5design

Design 55

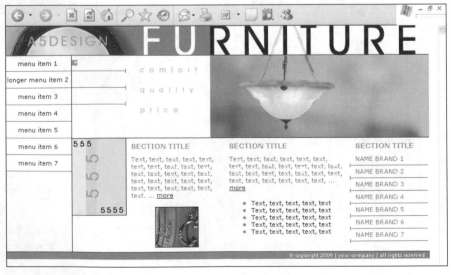

Homepage design.

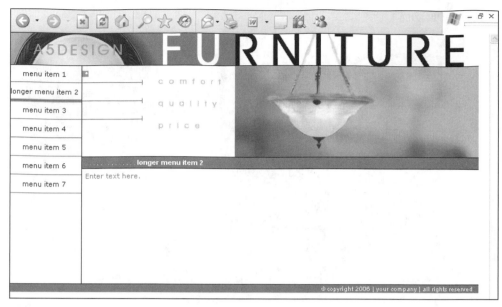

Second-level template for less content.

Second-level template for more content.

Photoshop source file names: Designs - Third Edition/1-80-xhtml/design_55/ design_55.psd

XHTML pages: index.htm, menu_item_2.htm, menu_item_3.htm

Photo credits: A5design

Design 54

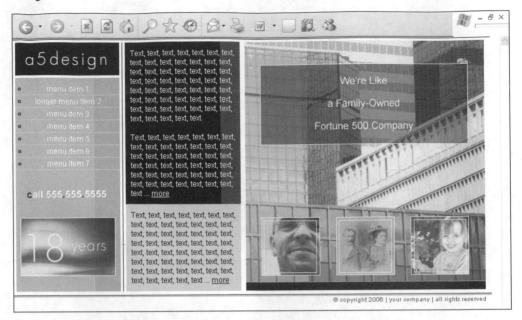

Homepage design.

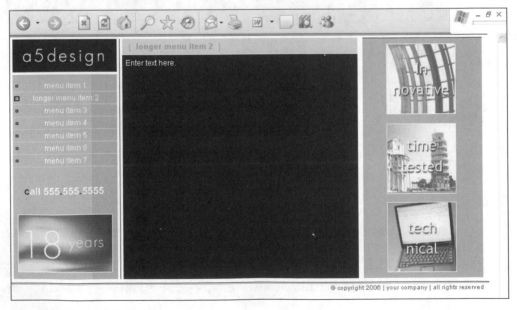

Second-level template for less content.

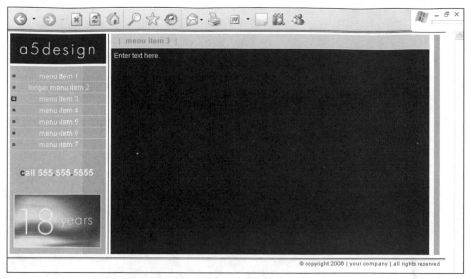

Second-level template for more content.

Photoshop source file names: Designs - Third Edition/1-80-xhtml/design_54/ design_54.psd, design_54_sl.psd

XHTML pages: index.htm, menu_item_2.htm, menu_item_3.htm

Photo credits: Joe Eccher, A5design

Design 53

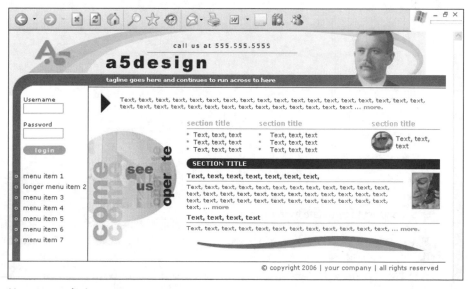

Homepage design.

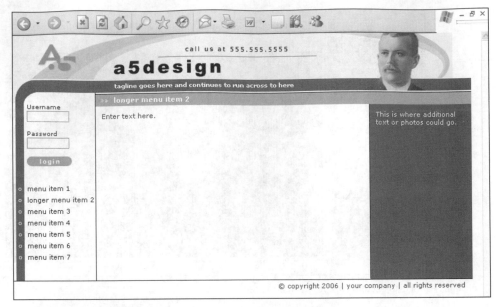

Second-level template for less content.

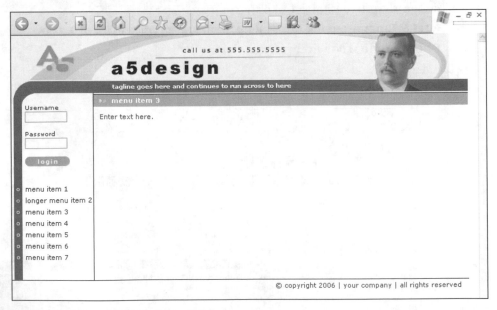

Second-level template for more content.

Photoshop source file names: Designs - Third Edition/1-80-xhtml/design_53/ design_53.psd

XHTML pages: index.htm, menu_item_2.htm, menu_item_3.htm

Photo credits: Lori Discoe

Design 52

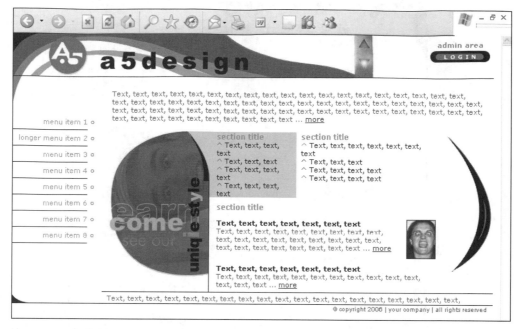

Homepage design.

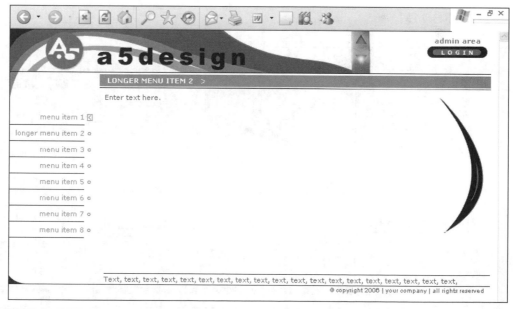

Second-level template for less content.

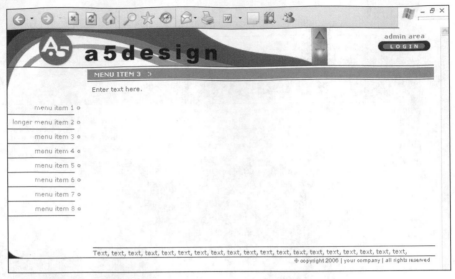

Second-level template for more content.

Photoshop source file names: Designs - Third Edition/1-80-xhtml/design_52/ design_52.psd

XHTML pages: index.htm, menu_item_2.htm, menu_item_3.htm

Photo credits: Justin Discoe, Lori Discoe

Design 51

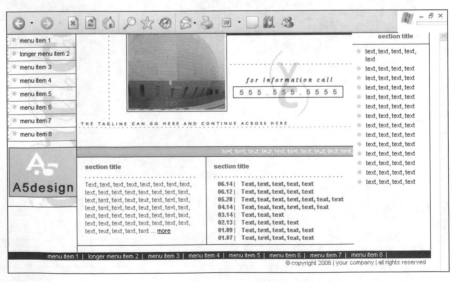

Homepage design.

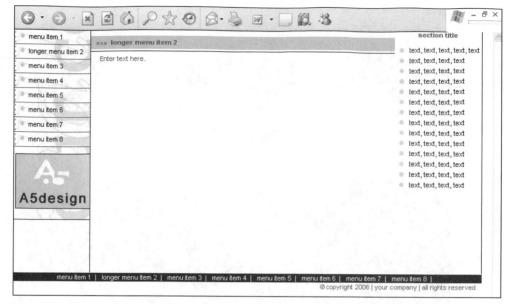

Second-level template for less content.

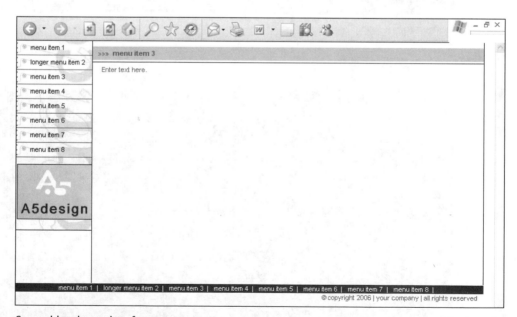

Second-level template for more content.

Photoshop source file names: Designs - Third Edition/1-80-xhtml/design_51/ design_51.psd, bg_images.psd

XHTML pages: index.htm, menu_item_2.htm, menu_item_3.htm

Photo credits: Joe Eccher

Design 50

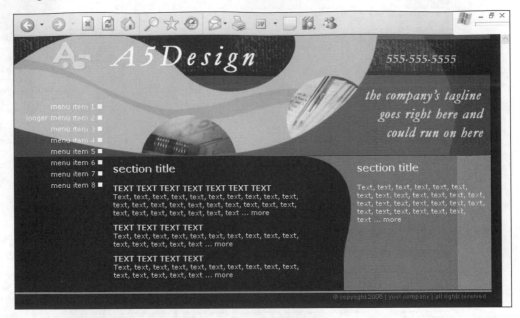

Homepage design.

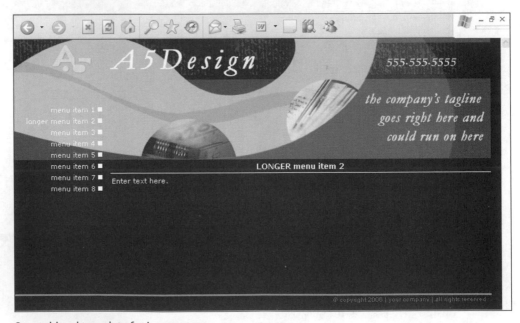

Second-level template for less content.

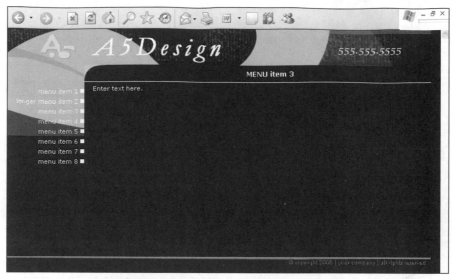

Second-level template for more content.

Photoshop source file names: Designs - Third Edition/1-80-xhtml/design_50/
design_50.psd, bg_images.psd

XHTML pages: index.htm, menu_item_2.htm, menu_item_3.htm

Photo credits: A5design

Design 49

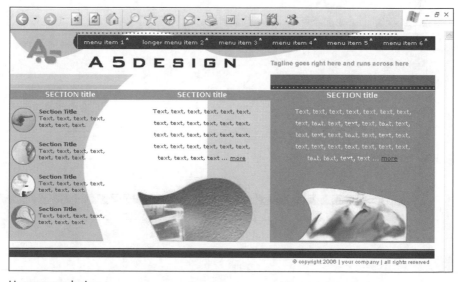

Homepage design.

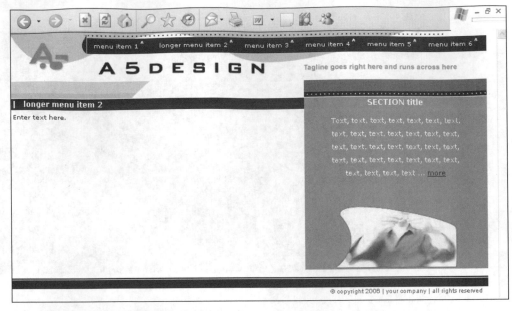

Second-level template for less content.

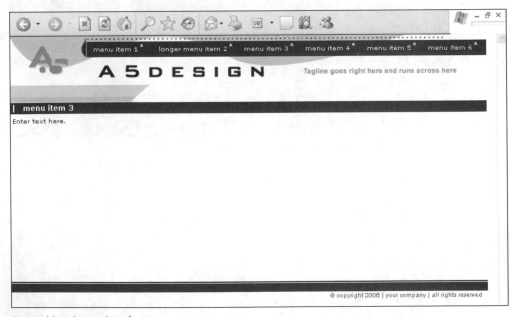

Second-level template for more content.

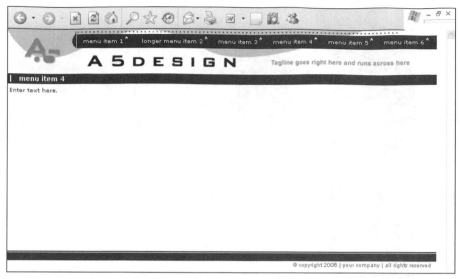

Second-level template for more content.

Photoshop source file names: Designs - Third Edition/1-80-xhtml/design_49/ design_49.psd, bg_images.psd

XHTML pages: index.htm, menu_item_2.htm, menu_item_3.htm, menu_item_4.htm

Photo credits: A5design

Design 48

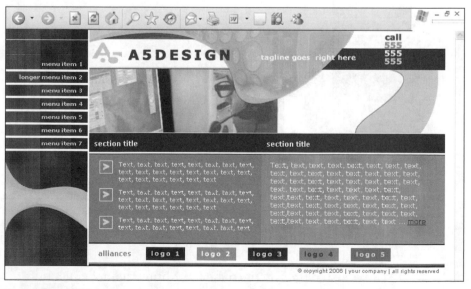

Homepage design.

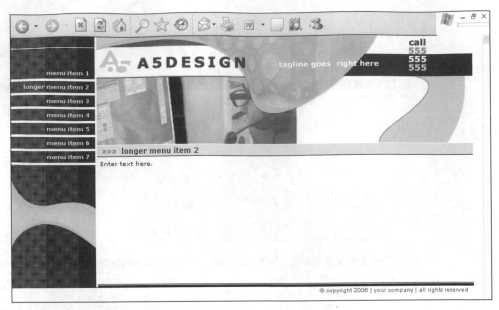

Second-level template for less content.

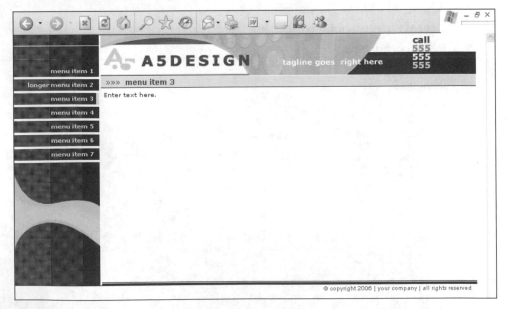

Second-level template for more content.

Photoshop source file names: Designs - Third Edition/1-80-xhtml/design_48/ design_48.psd

XHTML pages: index.htm, menu_item_2.htm, menu_item_3.htm

Photo credits: A5design

Design 47

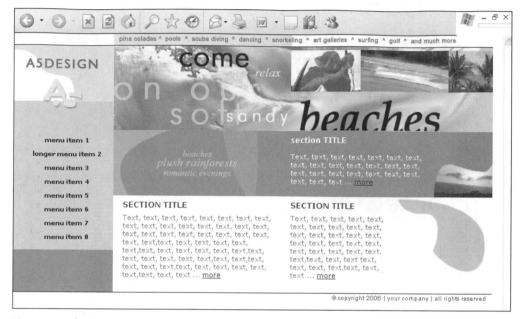

Homepage design.

Second-level template for less content.

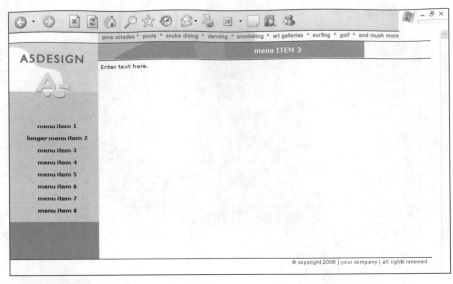

Second-level template for more content.

Photoshop source file names: Designs - Third Edition/1-80-xhtml/design_47/design_47.psd

XHTML pages: index.htm, menu_item_2.htm, menu_item_3.htm

Photo credits: Joe Eccher

Design 46

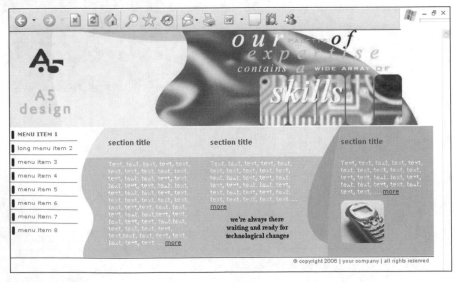

Homepage design.

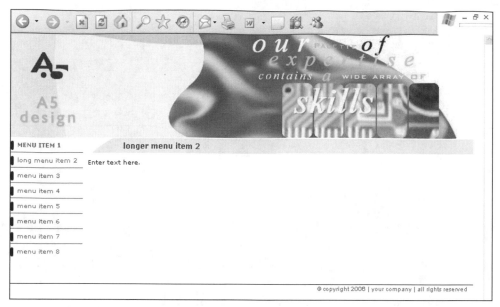

Second-level template for less content.

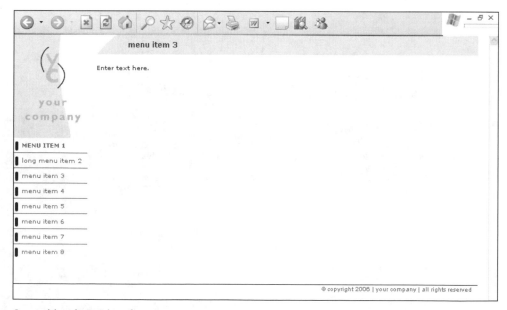

Second-level template for more content.

Photoshop source file names: Designs - Third Edition/1-80-xhtml/design_46/design_46.psd, sl_image.psd

XHTML pages: index.htm, menu_item_2.htm, menu_item_3.htm

Photo credits: Lisa Murillo, A5design

Design 45

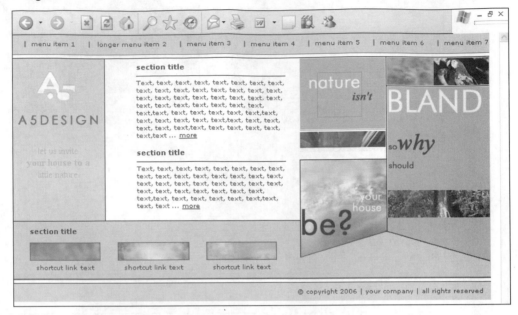

Homepage design.

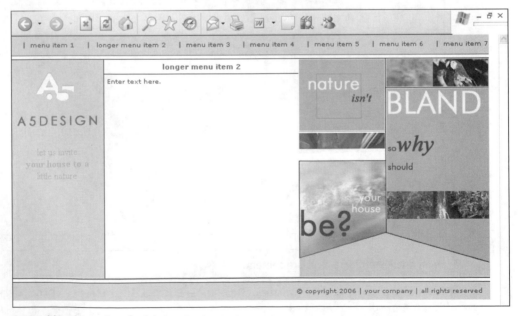

Second-level template for less content.

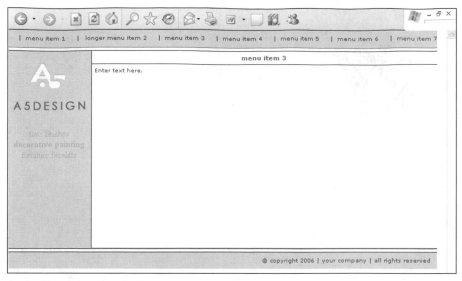

Second-level template for more content.

Photoshop source file names: Designs - Third Edition/1-80-xhtml/design_45/ design_45.psd

XHTML pages: index.htm, menu_item_2.htm, menu_item_3.htm

Photo credits: Joe Eccher, Lori Discoe

Design 44

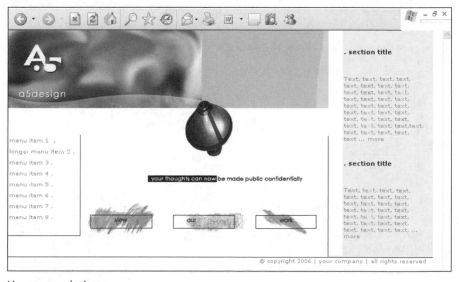

Homepage design.

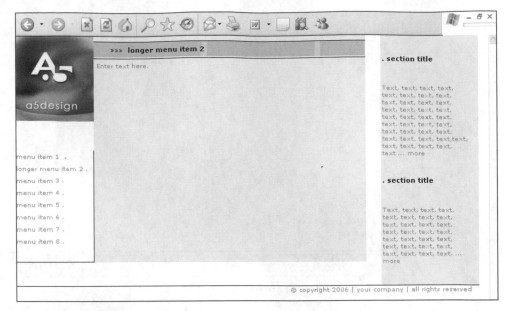

Second-level template for less content.

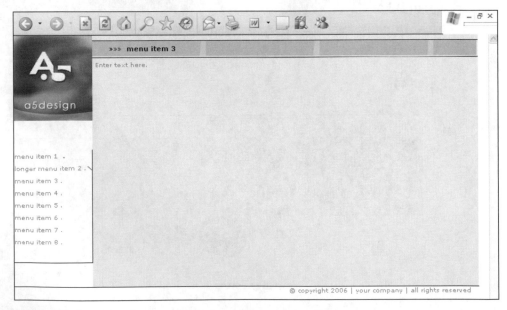

Second-level template for more content.

Photoshop source file names: Designs - Third Edition/1-80-xhtml/design_44/design_44.psd

XHTML pages: index.htm, menu_item_2.htm, menu_item_3.htm

Photo credits: A5design

Design 43

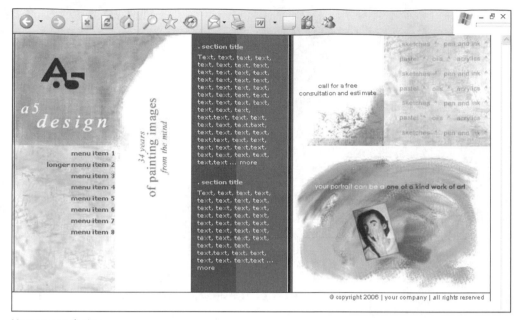

Homepage design.

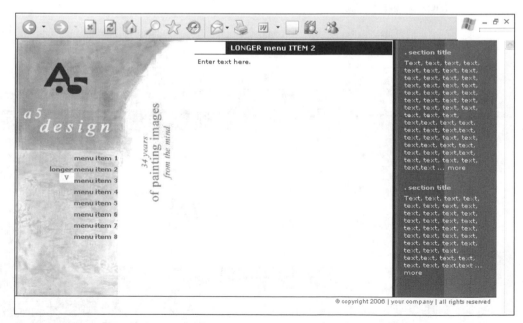

Second-level template for less content.

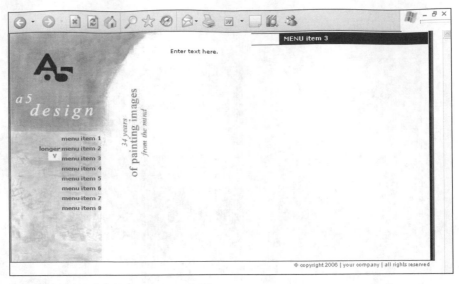

Second-level template for more content.

Photoshop source file names: Designs - Third Edition/1-80-xhtml/design_43/design_43.psd

XHTML pages: index.htm, menu_item_2.htm, menu_item_3.htm

Photo credits: Lori Discoe

Design 42

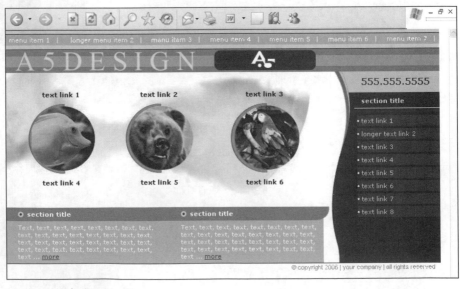

Homepage design.

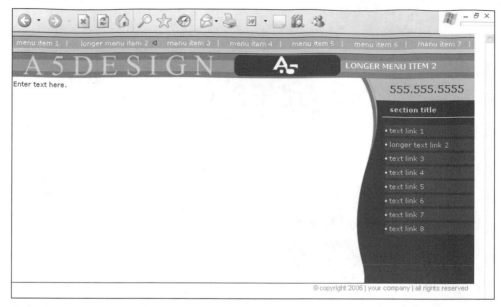

Second-level template for less content.

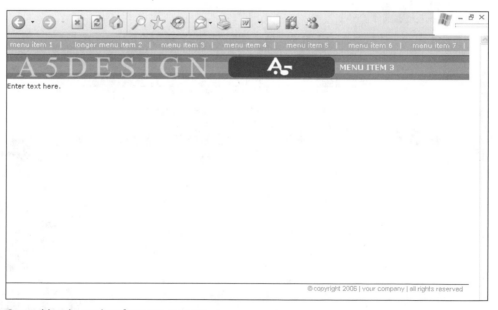

Second-level template for more content.

Photoshop source file names: Designs - Third Edition/1-80-xhtml/design_42/ design_42.psd

XHTML pages: index.htm, menu_item_2.htm, menu_item_3.htm

Photo credits: Lori Discoe

Design 41

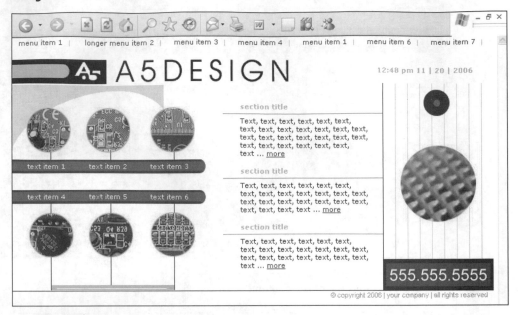

Homepage design.

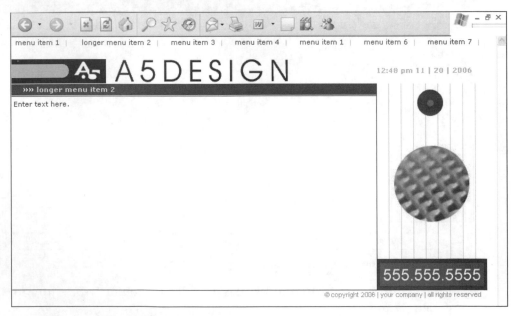

Second-level template for less content.

Second-level template for more content.

Photoshop source file names: Designs - Third Edition/1-80-xhtml/design_41/design_41.psd

XHTML pages: index.htm, menu_item_2.htm, menu_item_3.htm

Photo credits: Lisa Murillo

Design 40

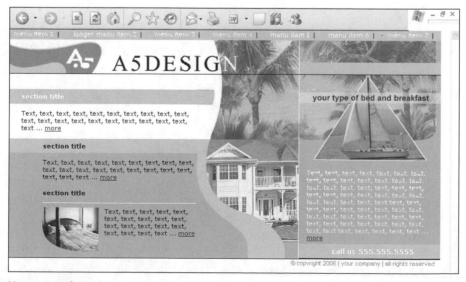

Homepage design.

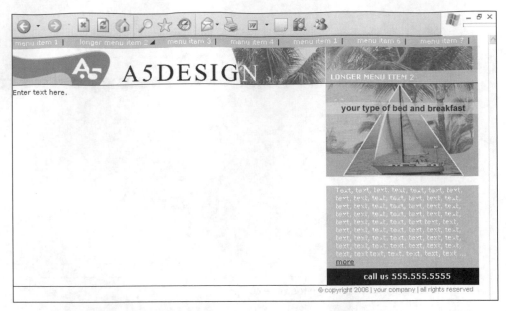

Second-level template for less content.

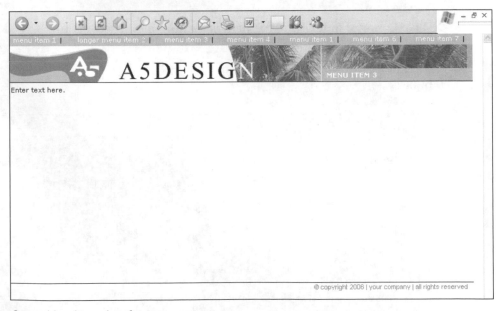

Second-level template for more content.

Photoshop source file names: Designs - Third Edition/1-80-xhtml/design_40/design_40.psd

XHTML pages: index.htm, menu_item_2.htm, menu_item_3.htm

Photo credits: A5design

Design 39

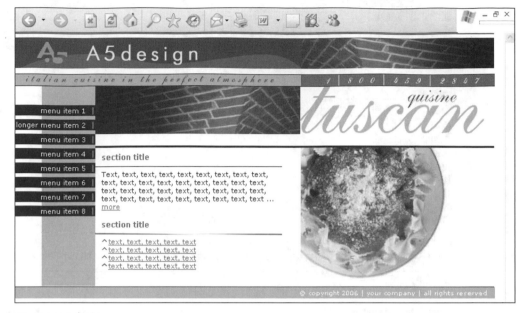

Homepage design.

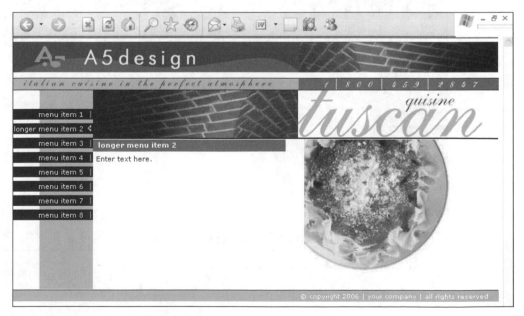

Second-level template for less content.

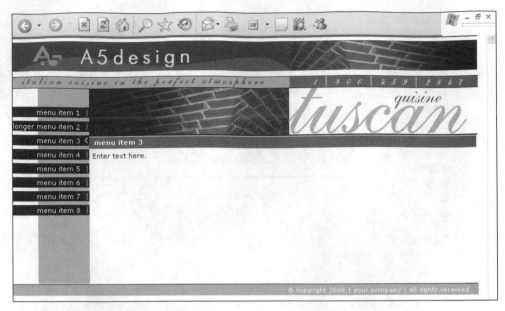

Second-level template for more content.

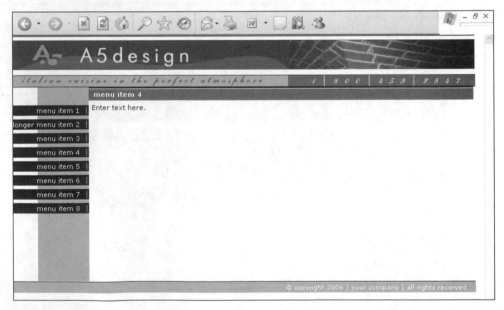

Second-level template for more content.

Photoshop source file names: Designs - Third Edition/1-80-xhtml/design_39/ design_39.psd

XHTML pages: index.htm, menu_item_2.htm, menu_item_3.htm, menu_item_4.htm

Photo credits: Lori Discoe

Design 38

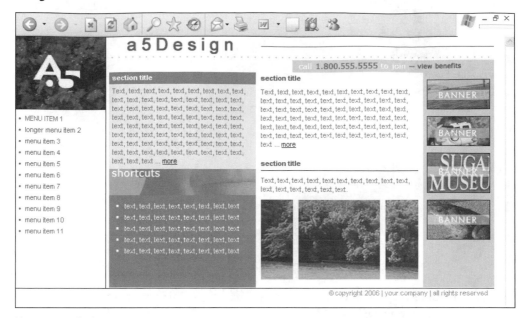

Homepage design.

Second-level template for less content.

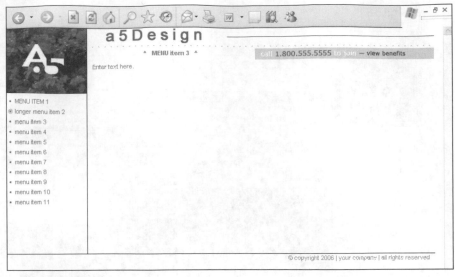

Second-level template for more content.

Photoshop source file names: Designs - Third Edition/1-80-xhtml/design_38/ design_38.psd

XHTML pages: index.htm, menu_item_2.htm, menu_item_3.htm

Photo credits: A5design

Design 37

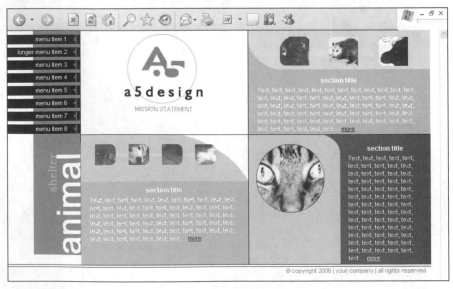

Homepage design.

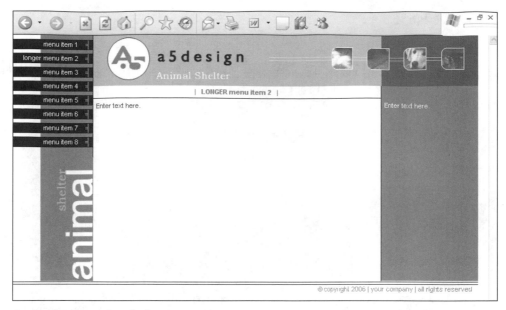

Second-level template for less content.

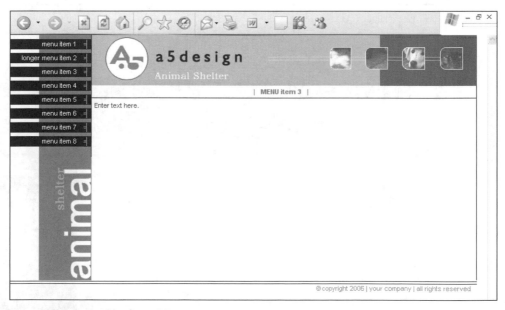

Second-level template for more content.

Photoshop source file names: Designs - Third Edition/1-80-xhtml/design_37/ design_37.psd, design_37_sl.psd

XHTML pages: index.htm, menu_item_2.htm, menu_item_3.htm

Photo credits: Lori Discoe

Design 36

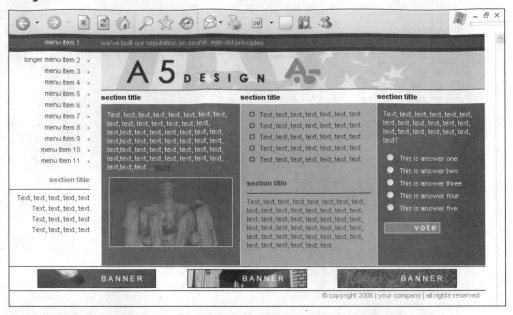

Homepage design.

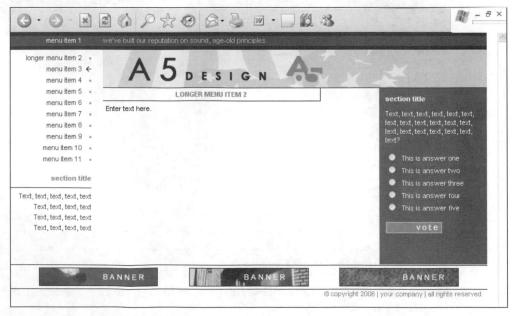

Second-level template for less content.

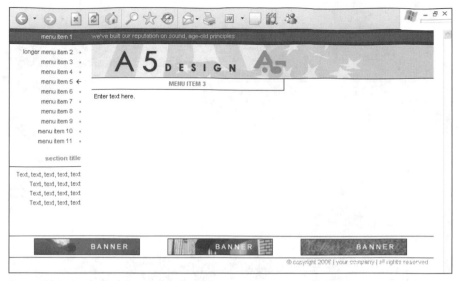

Second-level template for more content.

Photoshop source file names: Designs - Third Edition/1-80-xhtml/design_36/ design_36.psd, bg_images.psd

XHTML pages: index.htm, menu_item_2.htm, menu_item_3.htm

Photo credits: Justin Discoe, A5design

Design 35

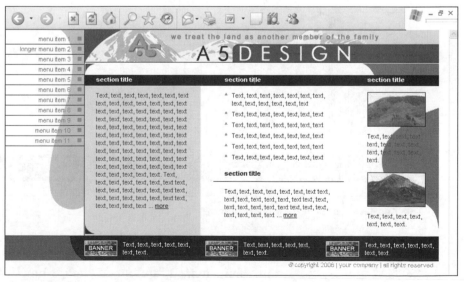

Homepage design.

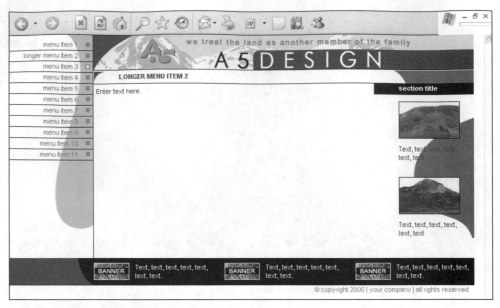

Second-level template for less content.

Second-level template for more content.

Photoshop source file names: Designs - Third Edition/1-80-xhtml/design_35/ design_35.psd, bg_images.psd

XHTML pages: index.htm, menu_item_2.htm, menu_item_3.htm

Photo credits: Joe Eccher

Design 34

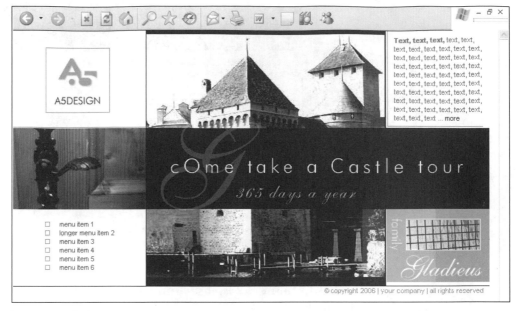

Homepage design.

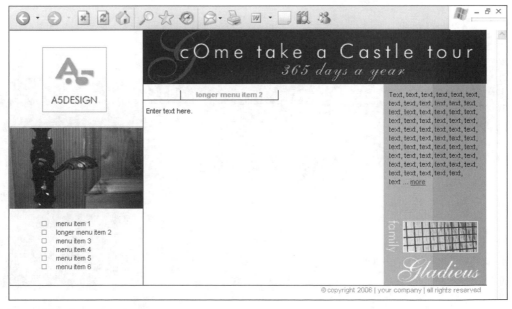

Second-level template for less content.

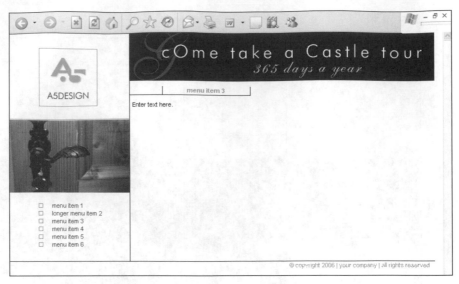

Second-level template for more content.

Photoshop source file names: Designs - Third Edition/1-80-xhtml/design_34/ design_34.psd, sl_header.psd

XHTML pages: index.htm, menu_item_2.htm, menu_item_3.htm

Photo credits: Joe Eccher

Design 33

Homepage design.

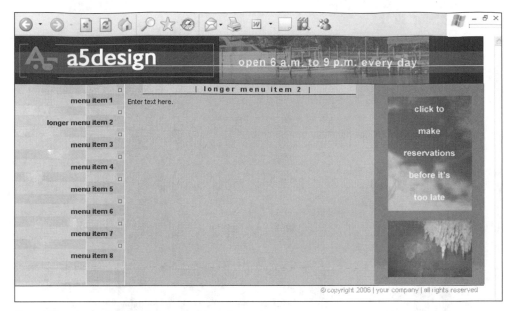

Second-level template for less content.

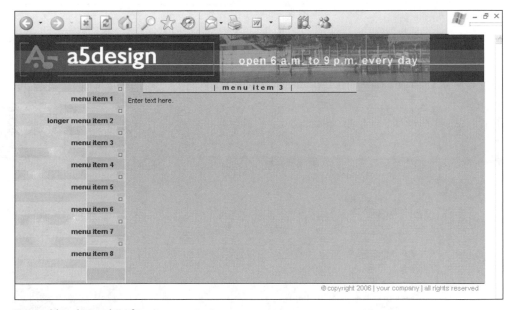

Second-level template for more content.

Photoshop source file names: Designs - Third Edition/1-80-xhtml/design_33/ design_33.psd, bg_images.psd

XHTML pages: index.htm, menu_item_2.htm, menu_item_3.htm

Photo credits: A5design

Design 32

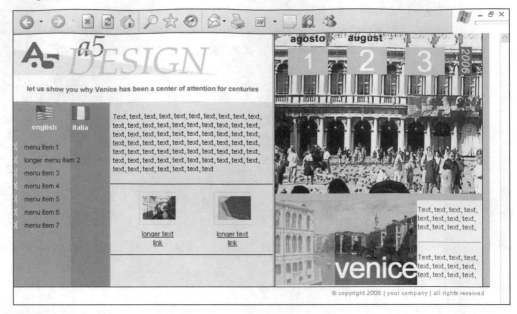

Homepage design.

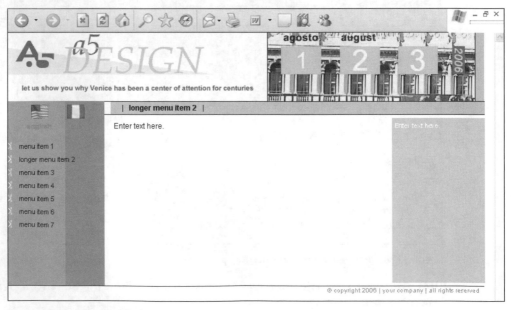

Second-level template for less content.

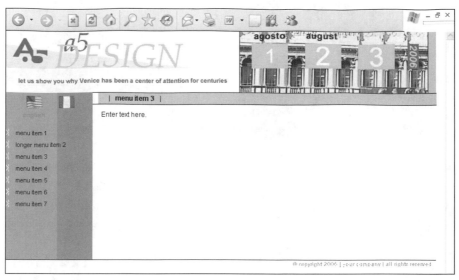

Second-level template for more content.

Photoshop source file names: Designs - Third Edition/1-80-xhtml/design_32/design_32.psd

XHTML pages: index.htm, menu_item_2.htm, menu_item_3.htm

Photo credits: A5design

Design 31

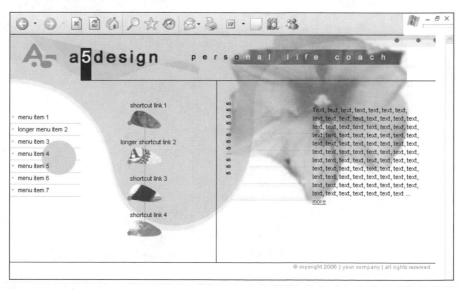

Homepage design.

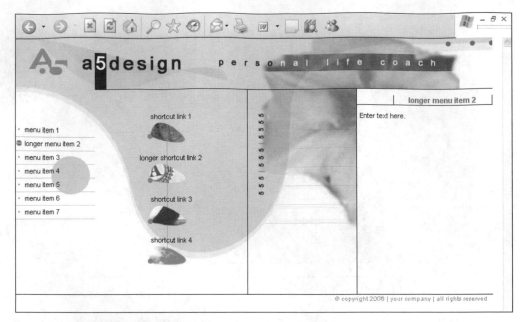

Second-level template for less content.

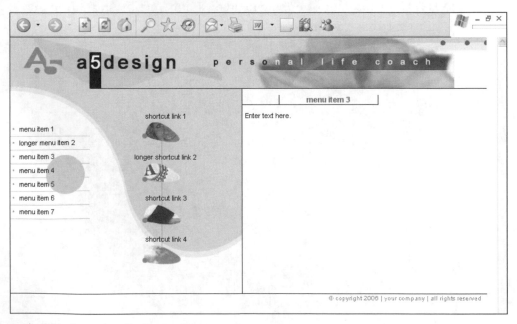

Second-level template for more content.

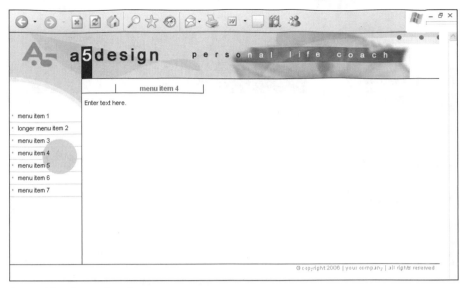

Second-level template for more content.

Photoshop source file names: Designs - Third Edition/1-80-xhtml/design_31/ design_31.psd, bg_images.psd

XHTML pages: index.htm, menu_item_2.htm, menu_item_3.htm, menu_item_4.htm

Photo credits: Joe Eccher, Justin Discoe

Design 30

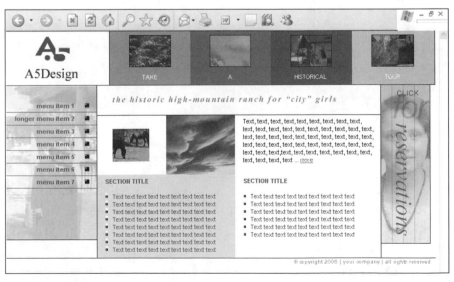

Homepage design.

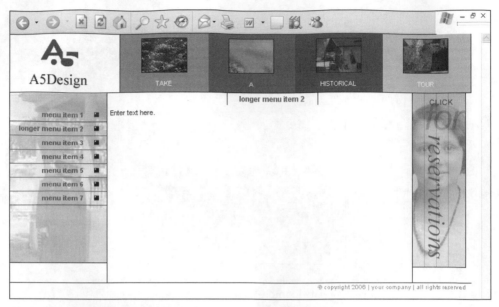

Second-level template for less content.

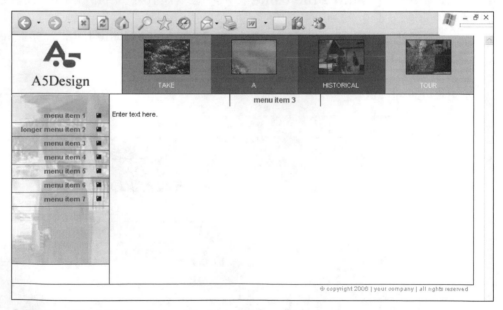

Second-level template for more content.

Photoshop source file names: Designs - Third Edition/1-80-xhtml/design_30/ design_30.psd, bg_menu.psd

XHTML pages: index.htm, menu_item_2.htm, menu_item_3.htm

Photo credits: Joe Eccher

Design 29

Homepage design.

Second-level template for less content.

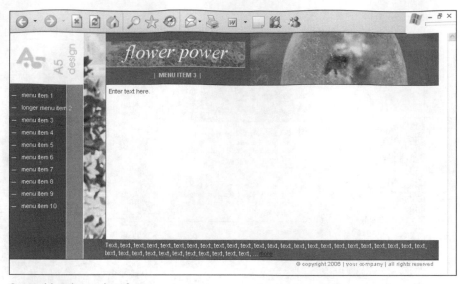

Second-level template for more content.

Photoshop source file names: Designs - Third Edition/1-80-xhtml/design_29/design_29.psd

XHTML pages: index.htm, menu_item_2.htm, menu_item_3.htm

Photo credits: Joe Eccher

Design 28

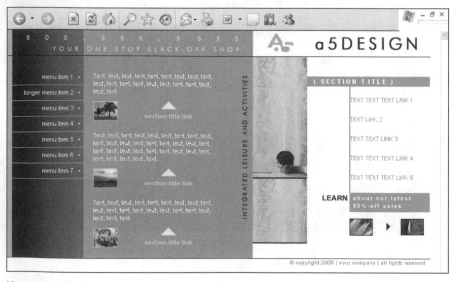

Homepage design.

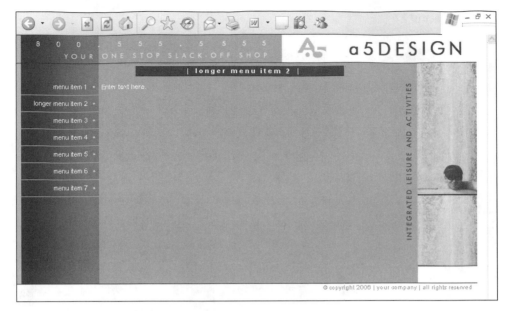

Second-level template for less content.

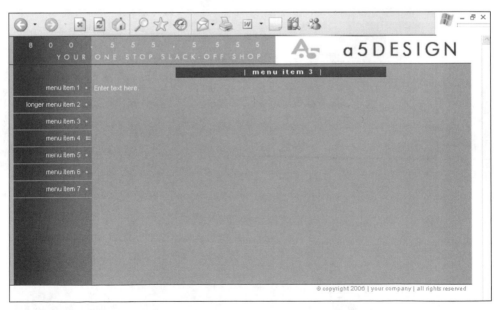

Second-level template for more content.

Photoshop source file names: Designs - Third Edition/1-80-xhtml/design_28/
design_28.psd

XHTML pages: index.htm, menu_item_2.htm, menu_item_3.htm

Photo credits: Joe Eccher

Design 27

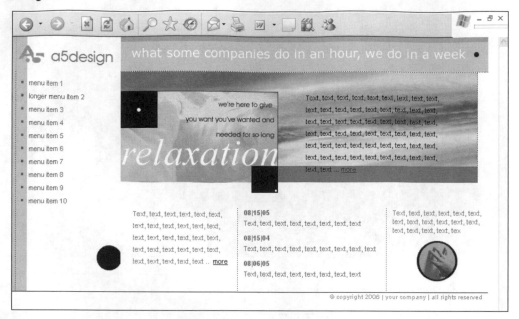

Homepage design.

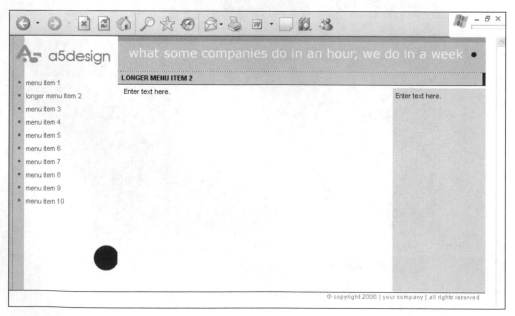

Second-level template for less content.

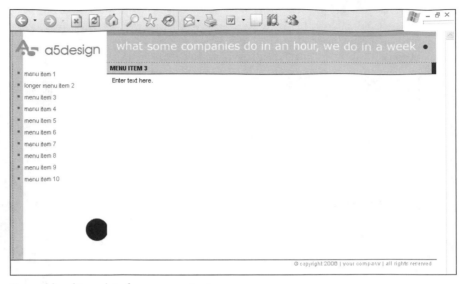

Second-level template for more content.

Photoshop source file names: Designs - Third Edition/1-80-xhtml/design_27/ design_27.psd

XHTML pages: index.htm, menu_item_2.htm, menu_item_3.htm

Photo credits: Joe Eccher, A5design

Design 26

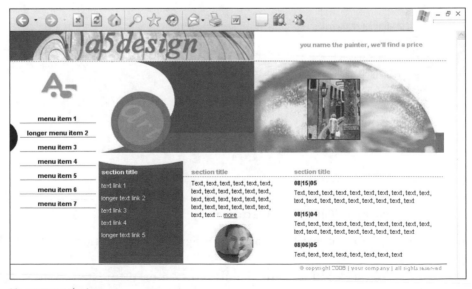

Homepage design.

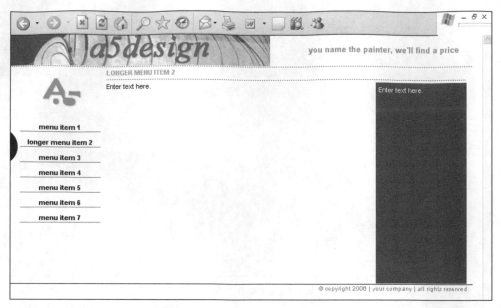

Second-level template for less content.

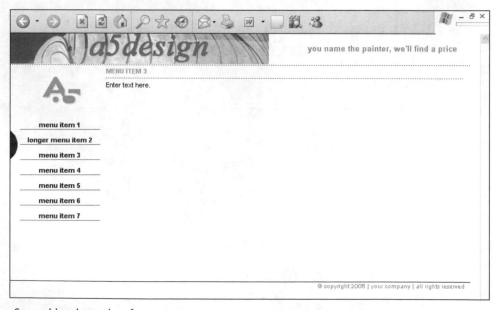

Second-level template for more content.

Photoshop source file names: Designs - Third Edition/1-80-xhtml/design_26/design_26.psd

XHTML pages: index.htm, menu_item_2.htm, menu_item_3.htm

Photo credits: Justin Discoe, A5design

Design 25

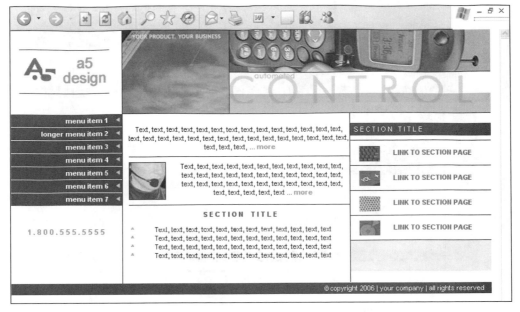

Homepage design.

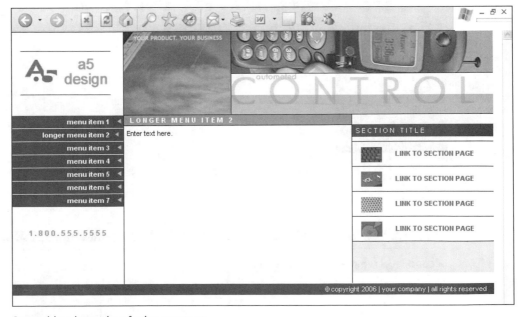

Second-level template for less content.

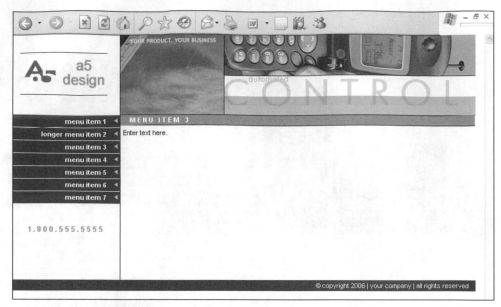

Second-level template for more content.

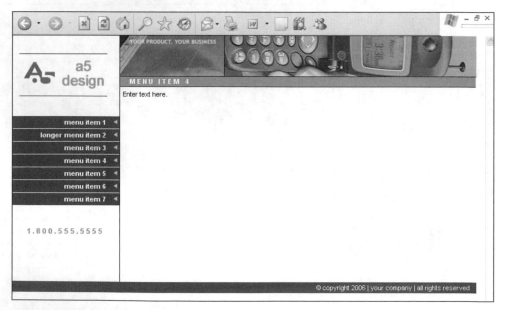

Second-level template for more content.

Photoshop source file names: Designs - Third Edition/1-80-xhtml/design_25/ design_25.psd

XHTML pages: index.htm, menu_item_2.htm, menu_item_3.htm, menu_item_4.htm

Photo credits: Lisa Murillo, A5design

Design 24

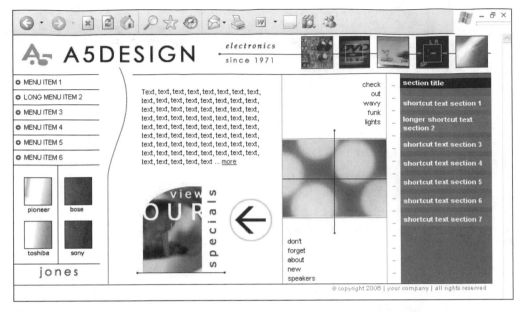

Homepage design.

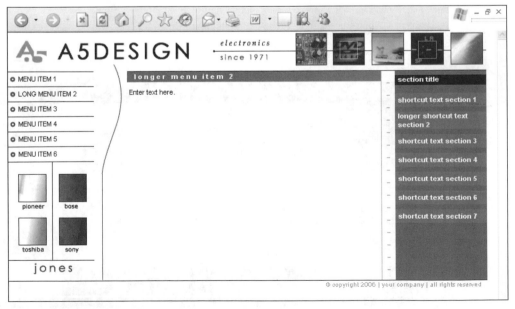

Second-level template for less content.

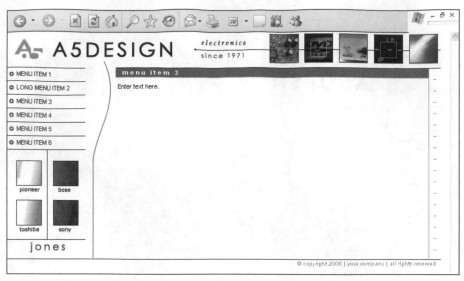

Second-level template for more content.

Photoshop source file names: Designs - Third Edition/1-80-xhtml/design_24/design_24.psd

XHTML pages: index.htm, menu_item_2.htm, menu_item_3.htm

Photo credits: Lisa Murillo, A5design

Design 23

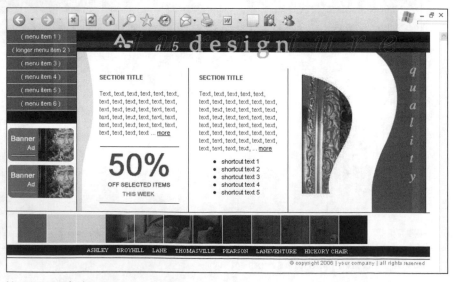

Homepage design.

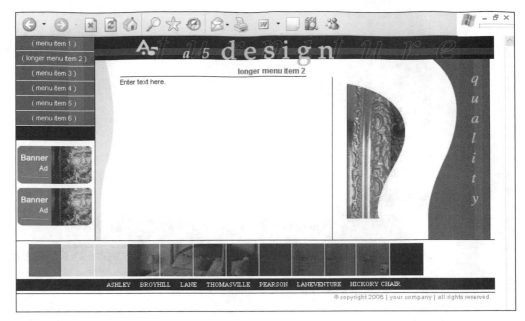

Second-level template for less content.

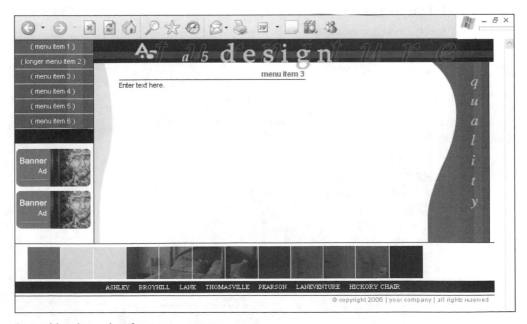

Second-level template for more content.

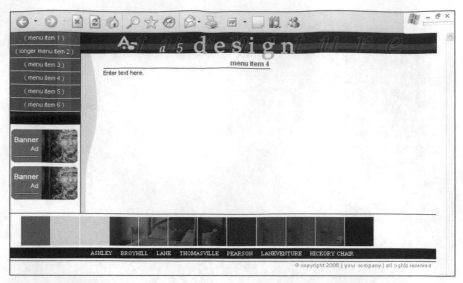

Second-level template for more content.

Photoshop source file names: Designs - Third Edition/1-80-xhtml/design_23/design_23.psd

XHTML pages: index.htm, menu_item_2.htm, menu_item_3.htm, menu_item_4.htm

Photo credits: A5design

Design 22

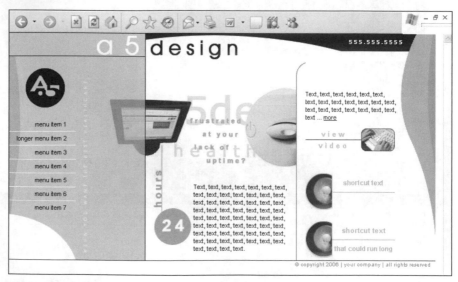

Homepage design.

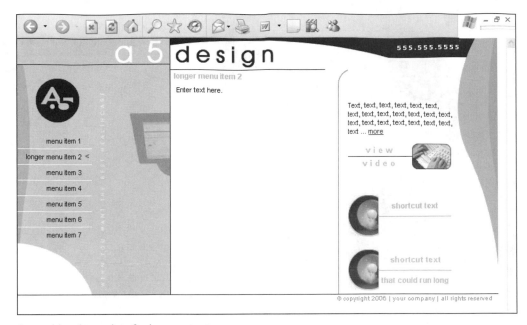

Second-level template for less content.

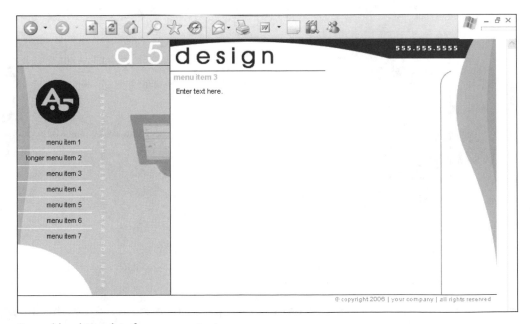

Second-level template for more content.

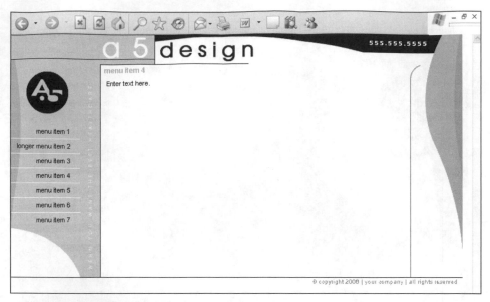

Second-level template for more content.

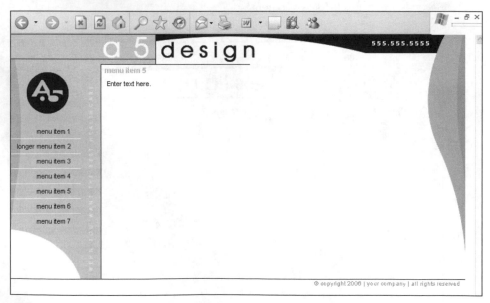

Second-level template for more content.

Photoshop source file names: Designs - Third Edition/1-80-xhtml/design_22/ design_22.psd, bg_menu.psd

XHTML pages: index.htm, menu_item_2.htm, menu_item_3.htm, menu_item_4.htm, menu_item_5.htm

Photo credits: A5design

Design 21

Homepage design.

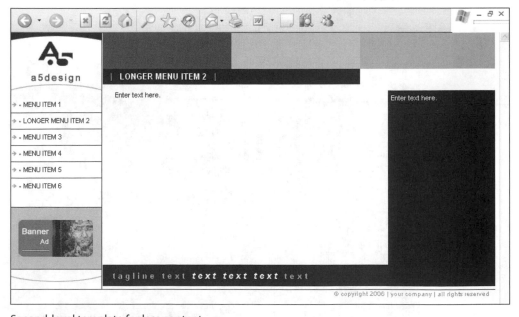

Second-level template for less content.

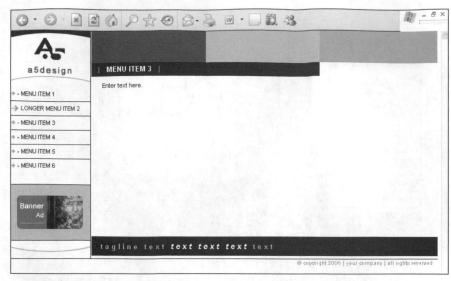

Second-level template for more content.

Photoshop source file names: Designs - Third Edition/1-80-xhtml/design_21/design_21.psd

XHTML pages: index.htm, menu_item_2.htm, menu_item_3.htm

Photo credits: Joe Eccher

Design 20

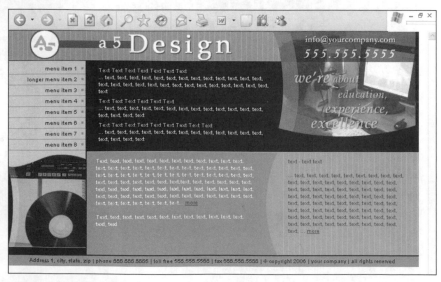

Homepage design.

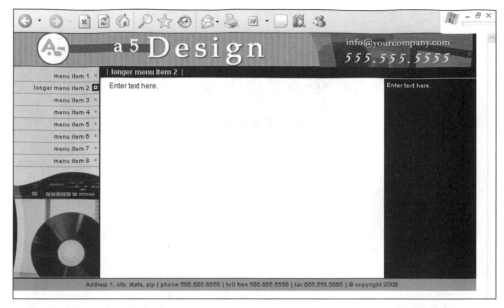

Second-level template for less content.

Second-level template for more content.

Photoshop source file names: Designs - Third Edition/1-80-xhtml/design_20/design_20.psd

XHTML pages: index.htm, menu_item_2.htm, menu_item_3.htm

Photo credits: A5design

Design 19

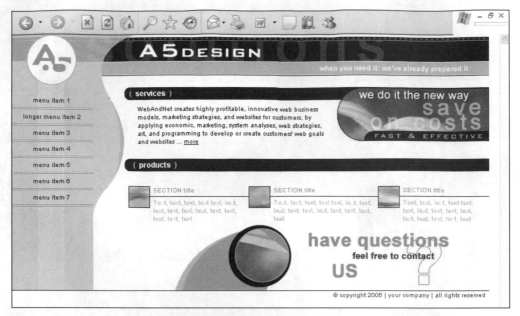

Homepage design.

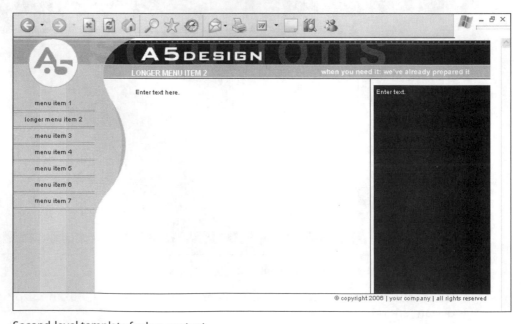

Second-level template for less content.

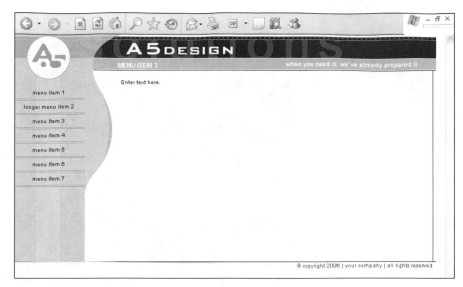

Second-level template for more content.

Photoshop source file names: Designs - Third Edition/1-80-xhtml/design_19/design_19.psd

XHTML pages: index.htm, menu_item_2.htm, menu_item_3.htm

Photo credits: A5design

Design 18

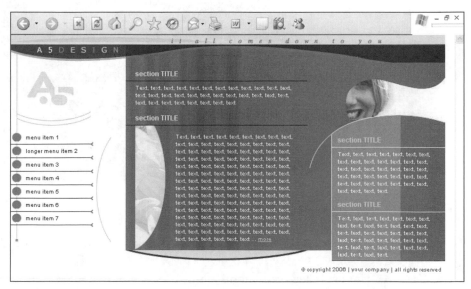

Homepage design.

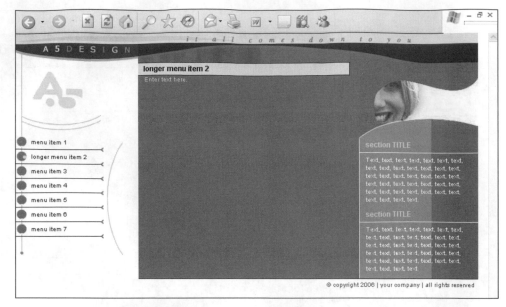

Second-level template for less content.

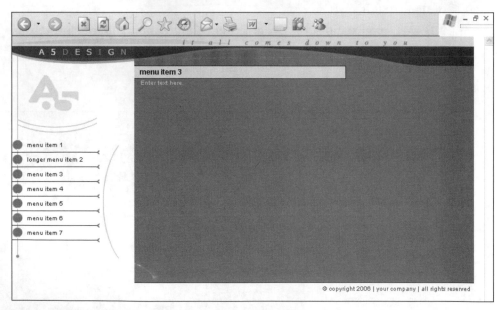

Second-level template for more content.

Photoshop source file names: Designs - Third Edition/1-80-xhtml/design_18/ design_18.psd, bg_left_column.psd

XHTML pages: index.htm, menu_item_2.htm, menu_item_3.htm

Photo credits: A5design

Design 17

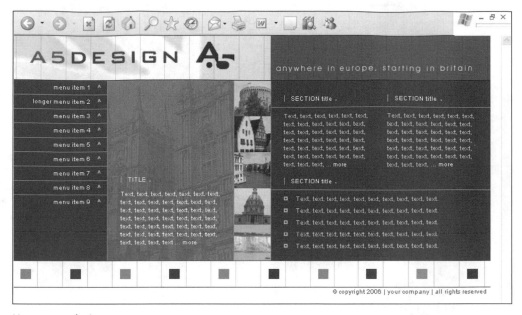

Homepage design.

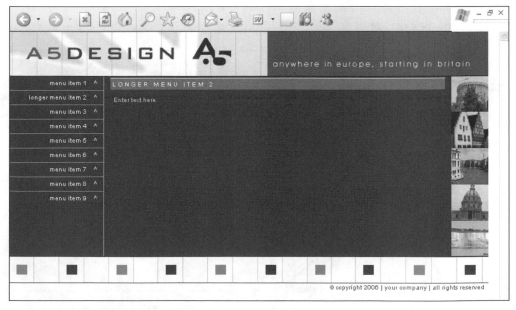

Second-level template for less content.

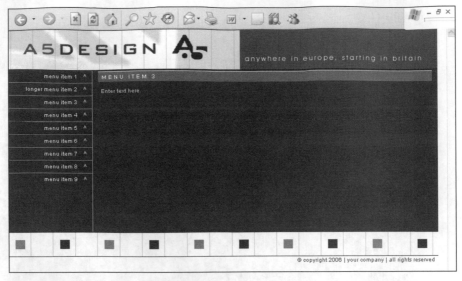

Second-level template for more content.

Photoshop source file names: Designs - Third Edition/1-80-xhtml/design_17/ design_17.psd

XHTML pages: index.htm, menu_item_2.htm, menu_item_3.htm

Photo credits: A5design

Design 16

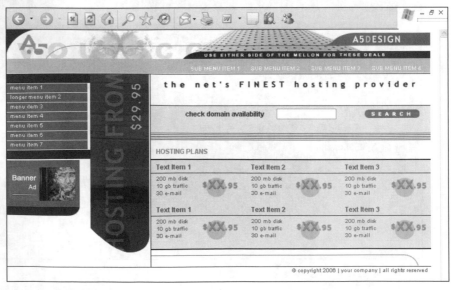

Homepage design.

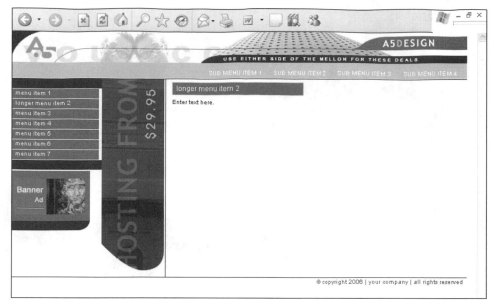

Second-level template for less content.

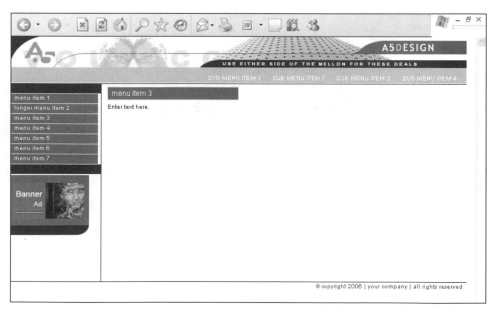

Second-level template for more content.

Photoshop source file names: Designs - Third Edition/1-80-xhtml/design_16/ design_16.psd

XHTML pages: index.htm, menu_item_2.htm, menu_item_3.htm

Photo credits: A5design

Design 15

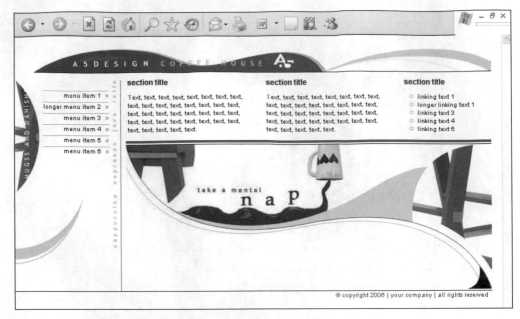

Homepage design.

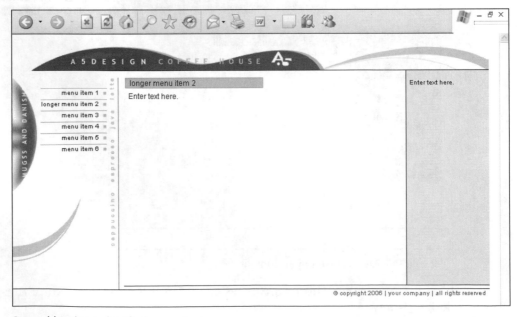

Second-level template for less content.

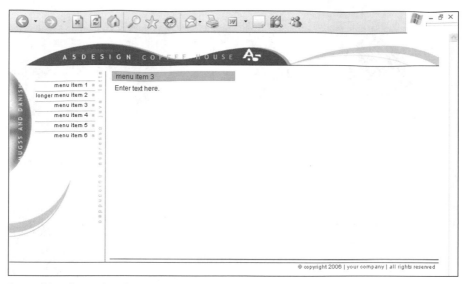

Second-level template for more content.

Photoshop source file names: Designs - Third Edition/1-80-xhtml/design_15/ design_15.psd

XHTML pages: index.htm, menu_item_2.htm, menu_item_3.htm

Photo credits: A5design

Design 14

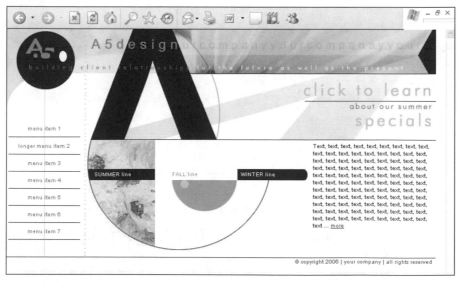

Homepage design.

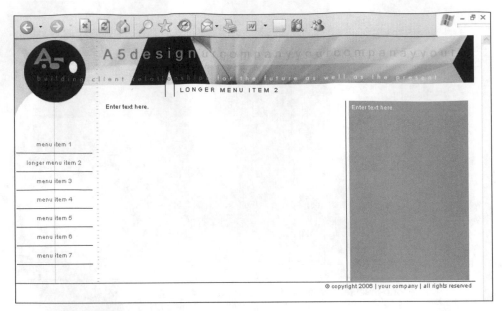

Second-level template for less content.

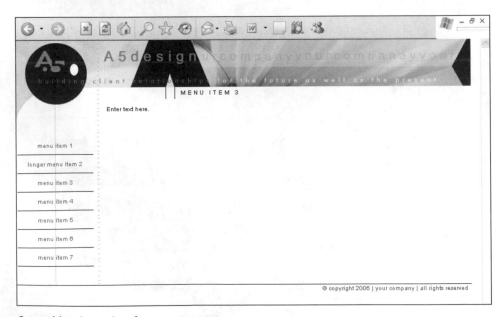

Second-level template for more content.

Photoshop source file names: Designs - Third Edition/1-80-xhtml/design_14/design_14.psd

XHTML pages: index.htm, menu_item_2.htm, menu_item_3.htm

Photo credits: A5design

Design 13

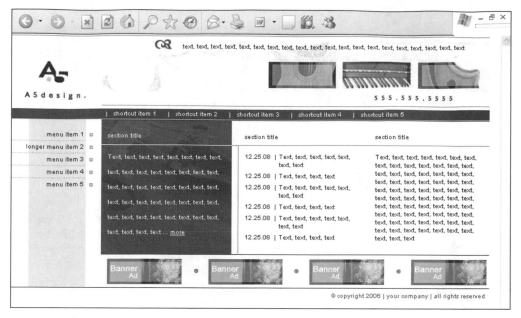

Homepage design.

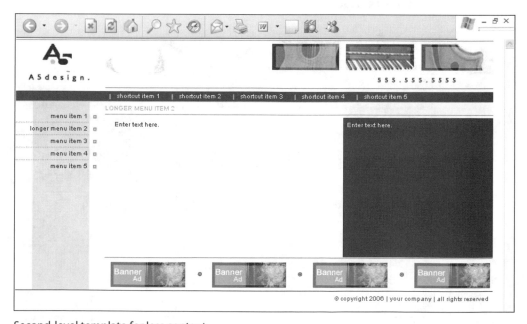

Second-level template for less content.

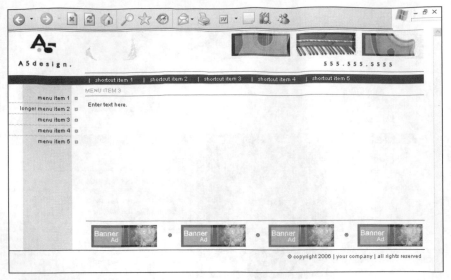

Second-level template for more content.

Photoshop source file names: Designs - Third Edition/1-80-xhtml/design_13/design_13.psd

XHTML pages: index.htm, menu_item_2.htm, menu_item_3.htm

Photo credits: A5design

Design 12

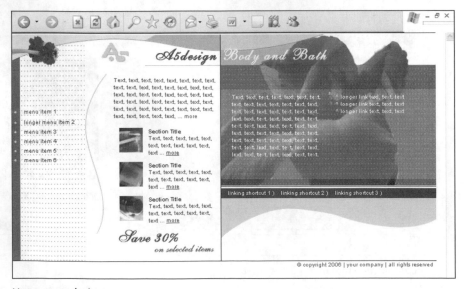

Homepage design.

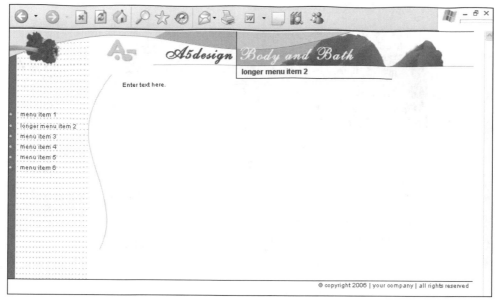

Second-level template for less content.

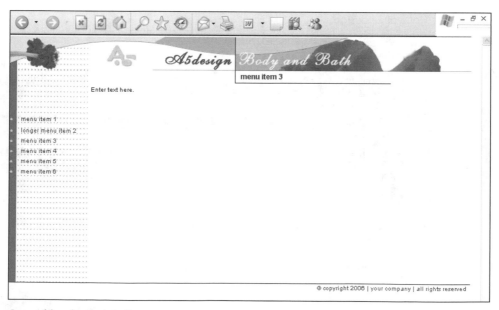

Second-level template for more content.

Photoshop source file names: Designs - Third Edition/1-80-xhtml/design_12/design_12.psd

XHTML pages: index.htm, menu_item_2.htm, menu_item_3.htm

Photo credits: Joe Eccher, A5design

Design 11

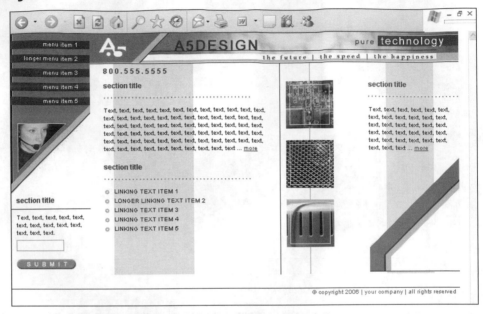

Homepage design.

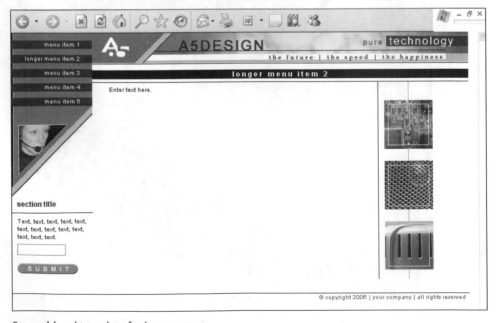

Second-level template for less content.

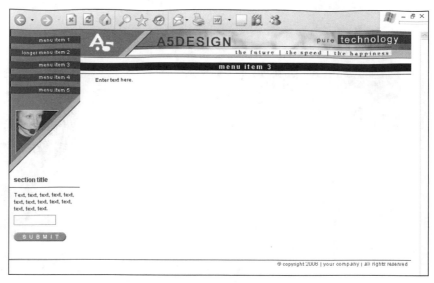

Second-level template for more content.

Photoshop source file names: Designs - Third Edition/1-80-xhtml/design_11/ design_18.psd

XHTML pages: index.htm, menu_item_2.htm, menu_item_3.htm

Photo credits: Lisa Murillo, A5design

Design 10

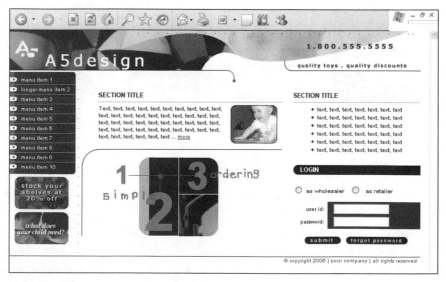

Homepage design.

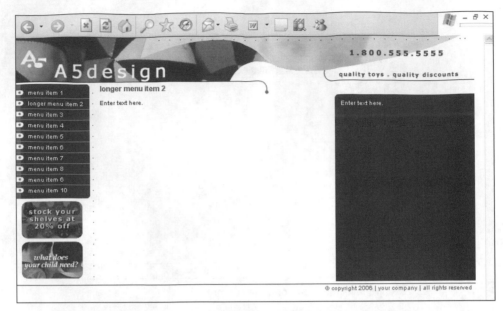

Second-level template for less content.

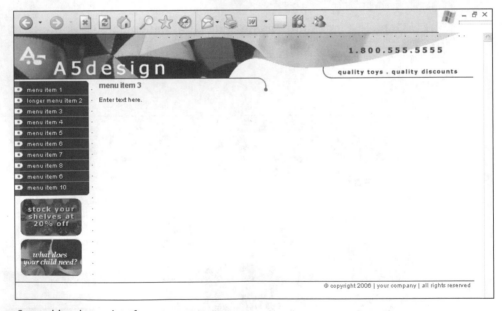

Second-level template for more content.

Photoshop source file names: Designs - Third Edition/1-80-xhtml/design_10/design_10.psd

XHTML pages: index.htm, menu_item_2.htm, menu_item_3.htm

Photo credits: Lisa Murillo, A5design

Design 9

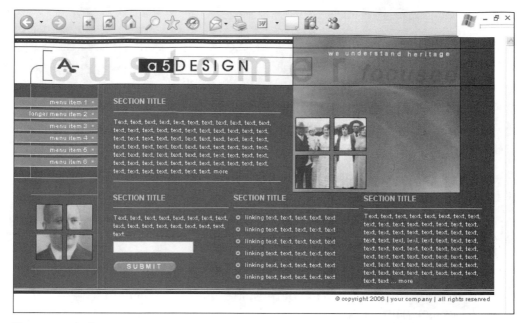

Homepage design.

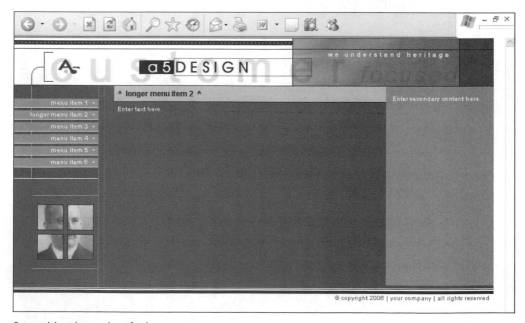

Second-level template for less content.

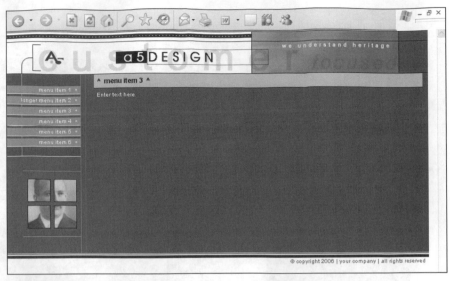

Second-level template for more content.

Photoshop source file names: Designs - Third Edition/1-80-xhtml/design_9/design_9.psd

XHTML pages: index.htm, menu_item_2.htm, menu_item_3.htm

Photo credits: Joe Eccher

Design 8

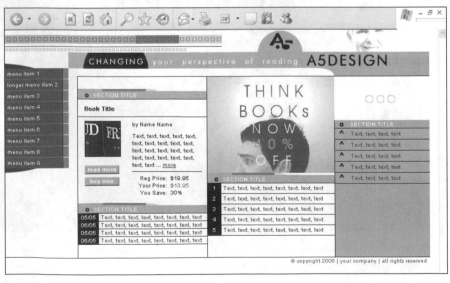

Homepage design.

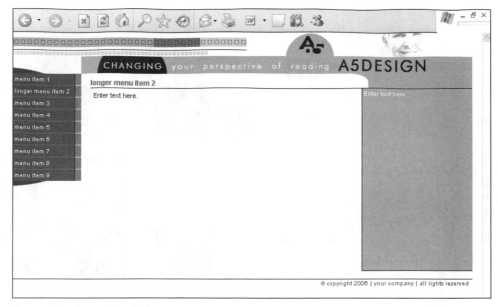

Second-level template for less content.

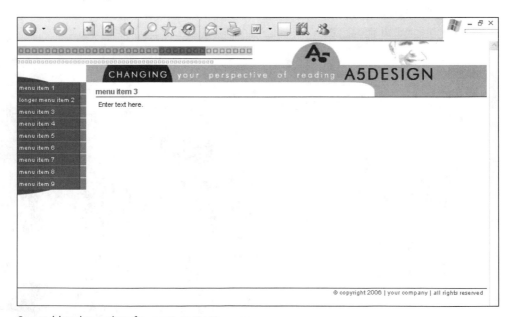

Second-level template for more content.

Photoshop source file names: Designs - Third Edition/1-80-xhtml/design_8/
design_8.psd

XHTML pages: index.htm, menu_item_2.htm, menu_item_3.htm

Photo credits: Lisa Murillo

Design 7

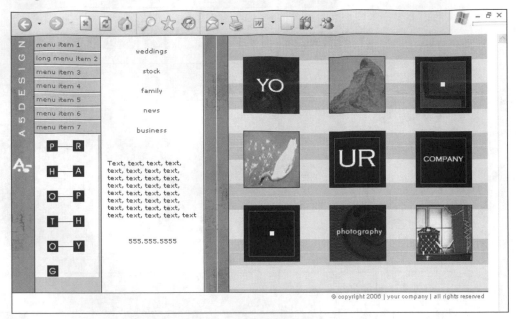

Homepage design.

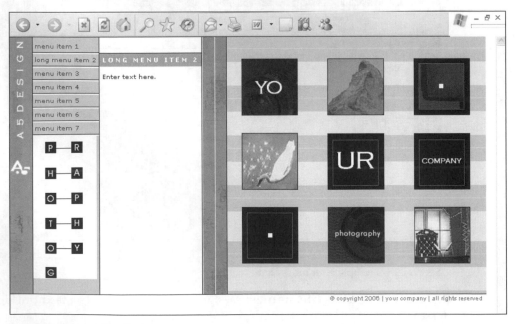

Second-level template for less content.

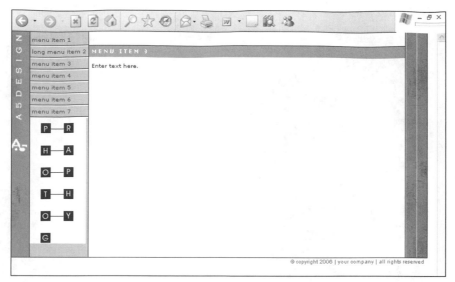

Second-level template for more content.

Photoshop source file names: Designs - Third Edition/1-80-xhtml/design_7/design_7.psd

XHTML pages: index.htm, menu_item_2.htm, menu_item_3.htm

Photo credits: Joe Eccher

Design 6

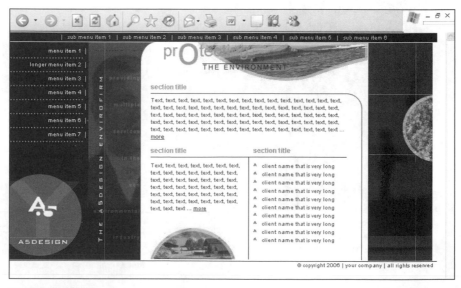

Homepage design.

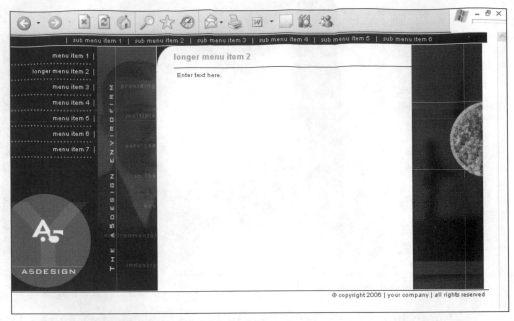

Second-level template for less content.

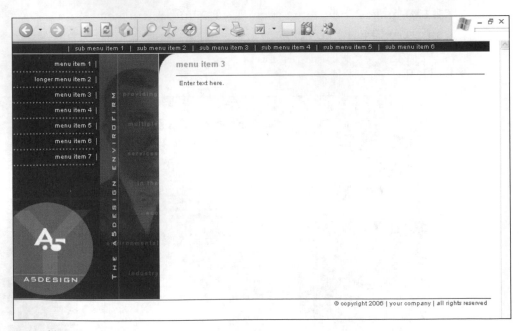

Second-level template for more content.

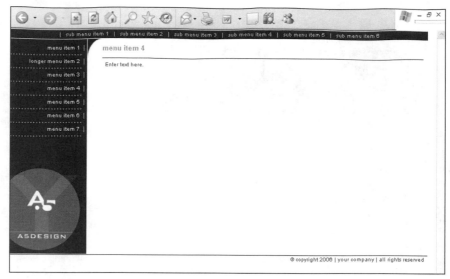

Second-level template for more content.

Photoshop source file names: Designs - Third Edition/1-80-xhtml/design_6/design_6.psd

XHTML pages: index.htm, menu_item_2.htm, menu_item_3.htm, menu_item_4.htm

Photo credits: Joe Eccher

Design 5

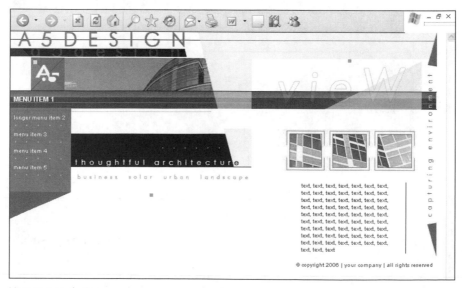

Homepage design.

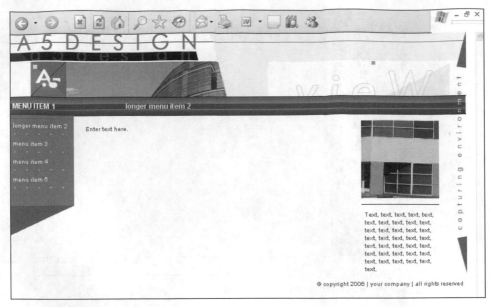

Second-level template for less content.

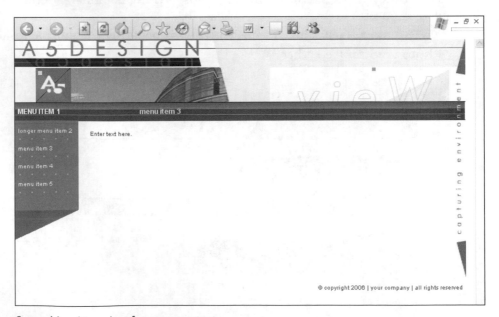

Second-level template for more content.

Photoshop source file names: Designs - Third Edition/1-80-xhtml/design_5/design_5.psd

XHTML pages: index.htm, menu_item_2.htm, menu_item_3.htm

Photo credits: A5design

Design 4

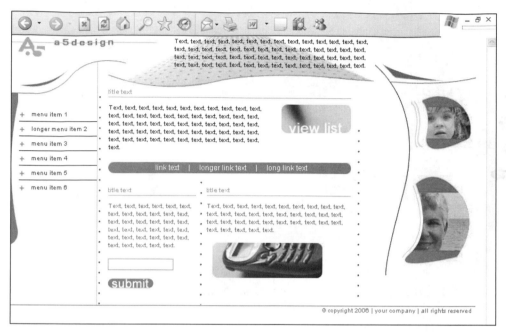

Homepage design.

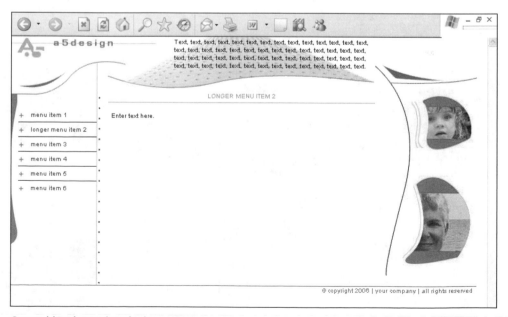

Second-level template for less content.

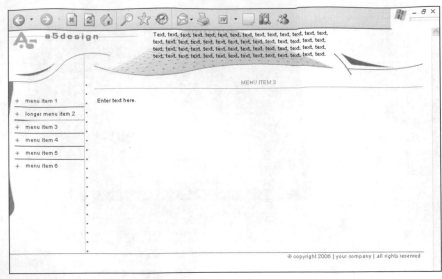

Second-level template for more content.

Photoshop source file names: Designs - Third Edition/1-80-xhtml/design_4/ design_4.psd, bg_top_photo.psd

XHTML pages: index.htm, menu_item_2.htm, menu_item_3.htm

Photo credits: A5design

Design 3

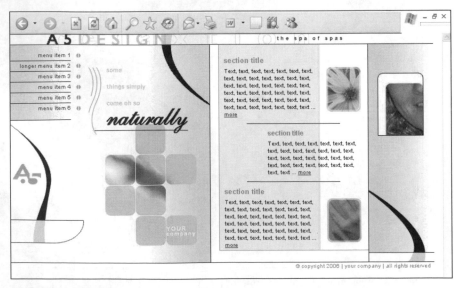

Homepage design.

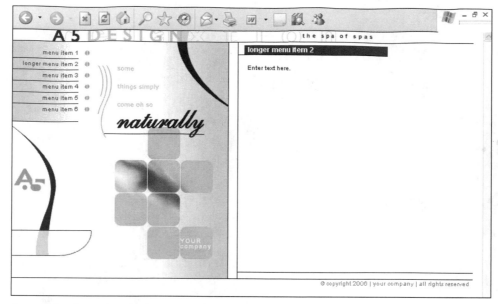

Second-level template for less content.

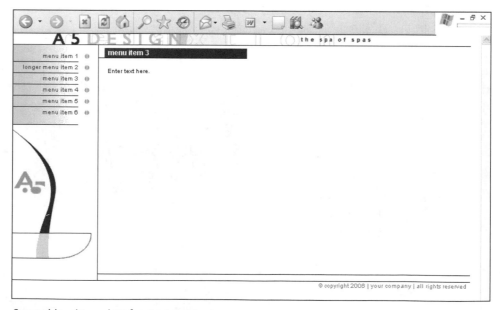

Second-level template for more content.

Photoshop source file names: Designs - Third Edition/1-80-xhtml/design_3/ design_3.psd, bg_center_column.psd

XHTML pages: index.htm, menu_item_2.htm, menu_item_3.htm

Photo credits: Justin Discoe

Design 2

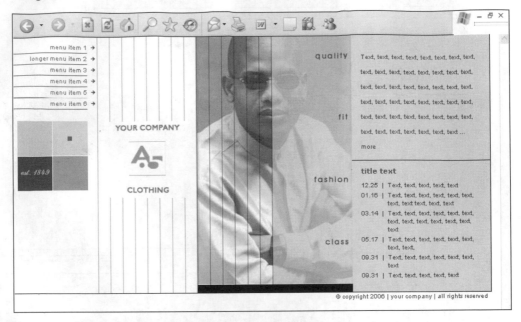

Homepage design.

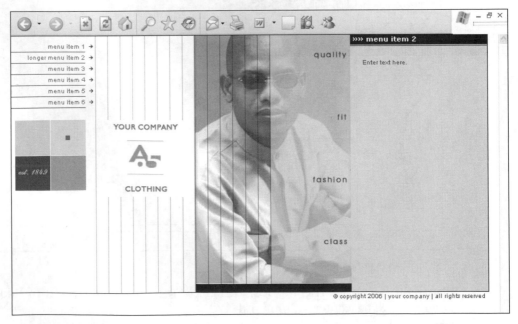

Second-level template for less content.

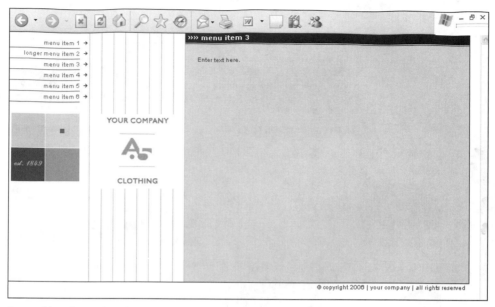

Second-level template for more content.

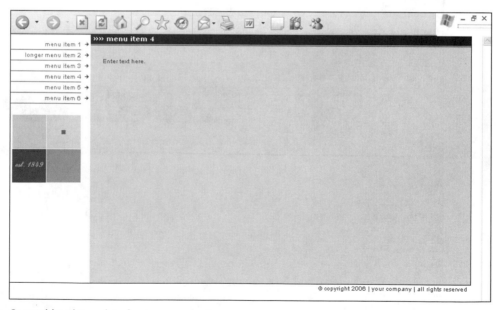

Second-level template for more content.

Photoshop source file names: Designs - Third Edition/1-80-xhtml/design_2/
design_2.psd

XHTML pages: index.htm, menu_item_2.htm, menu_item_3.htm, menu_item_4.htm

Photo credits: Lisa Murillo

Design 1

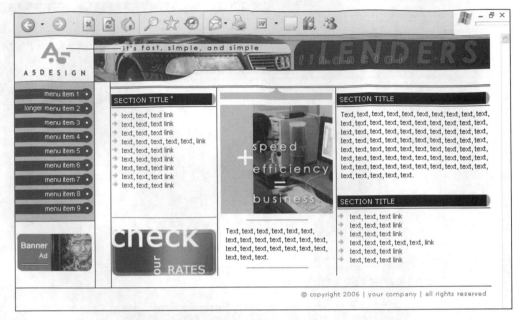

Homepage design.

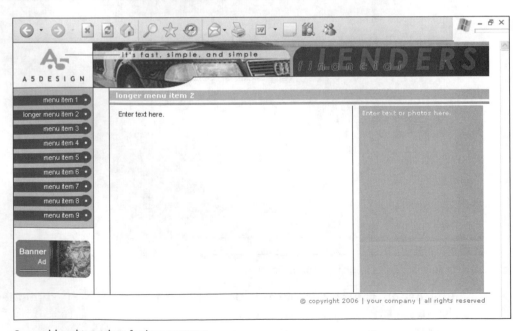

Second-level template for less content.

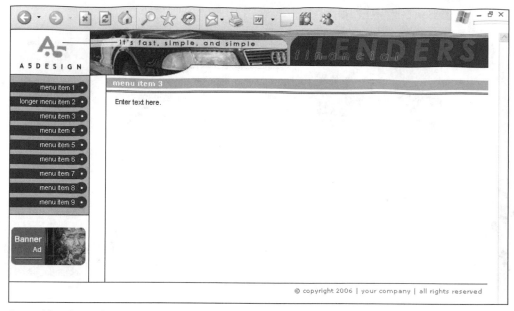

Second-level template for more content.

Photoshop source file names: Designs - Third Edition/1-80-xhtml/design_1/design_1.psd

XHTML pages: index.htm, menu_item_2.htm, menu_item_3.htm

Photo credits: A5design

DESIGNS – FIRST EDITION FOLDER

Following are the designs that were included with the first edition of this book. While the resolution and coding method are not appropriate for today's designer, the work can still be used for inspiration when creating a site.

Design 50 (First Edition)

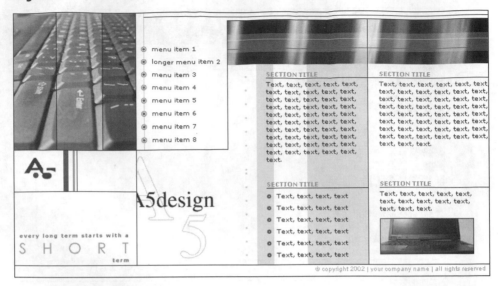

Homepage design.

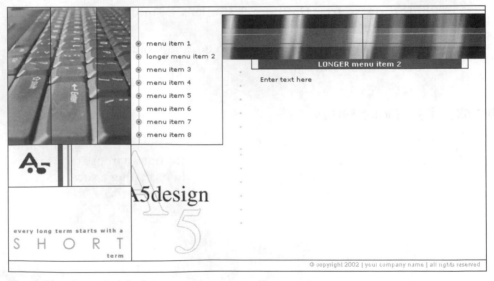

Second-level template for less content.

Photoshop source file names: Designs - First Edition/design_50/design_50.psd

HTML Pages: index.htm, menu_item_2.htm, menu_item_3.htm, menu_item_4.htm (second-level page for nearly full content)

Photo credits: A5design

Additional Designs Available on the CD

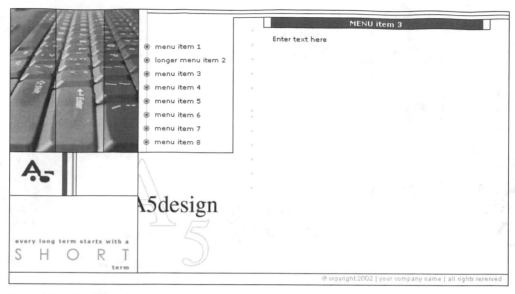

Second-level template for more content.

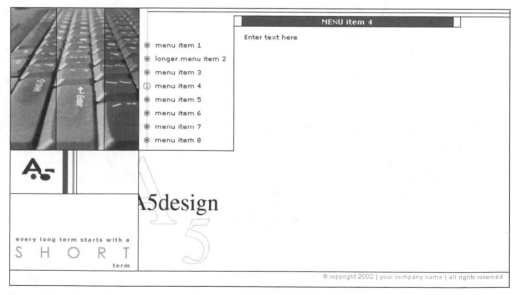

Second-level template for more content.

Design 49 (First Edition)

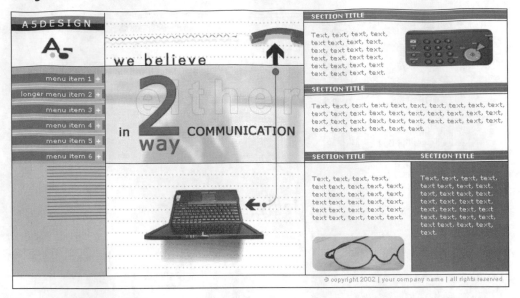

Homepage design.

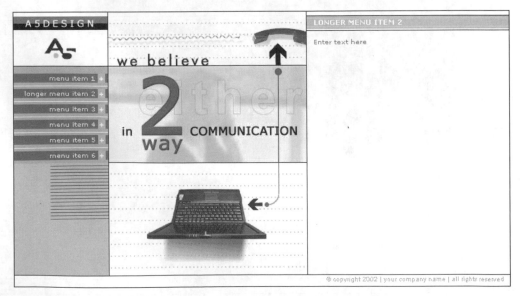

Second-level template for less content.

Photoshop source file names: Designs - First Edition/design_49/design_49.psd

HTML Pages: index.htm, menu_item_2.htm, menu_item_3.htm

Photo credits: Cameracaptured, A5design

Additional Designs Available on the CD

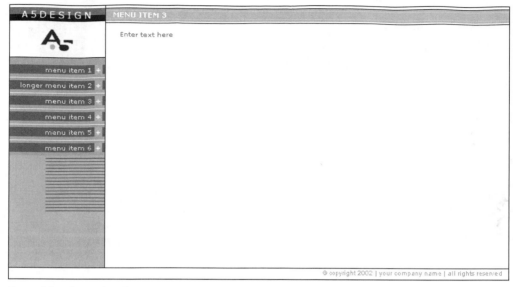

Second-level template for more content.

Design 48 (First Edition)

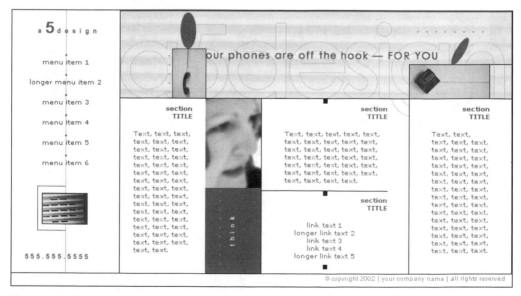

Homepage design.

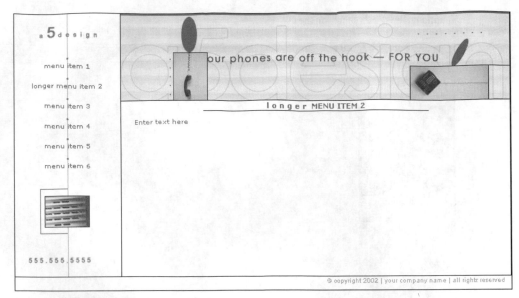

Second-level template for less content.

Photoshop source file names: Designs - First Edition/design_48/design_48.psd
HTML Pages: index.htm, menu_item_2.htm, menu_item_3.htm
Photo credits: Onepartart, Cameracaptured

Additional Designs Available on the CD

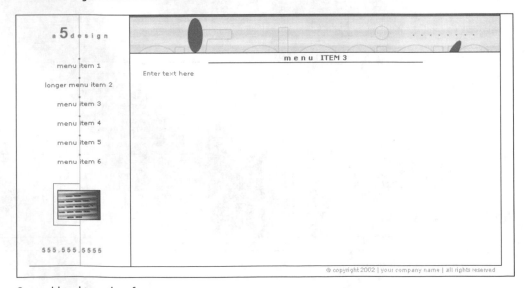

Second-level template for more content.

Design 47 (First Edition)

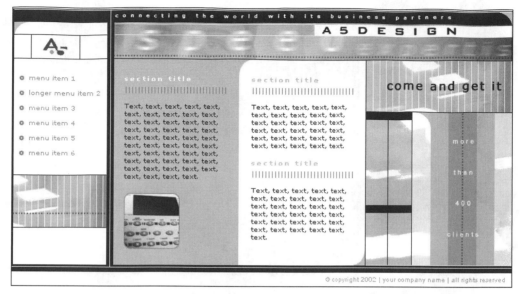

Homepage design.

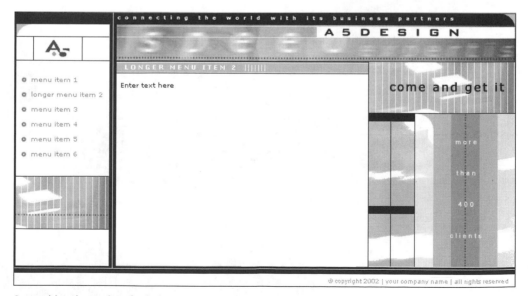

Second-level template for less content.

Photoshop source file names: Designs - First Edition/design_47/design_47.psd
HTML Pages: index.htm, menu_item_2.htm, menu_item_3.htm
Photo credits: Onepartart, Cameracaptured

Additional Designs Available on the CD

Second-level template for more content.

Design 46 (First Edition)

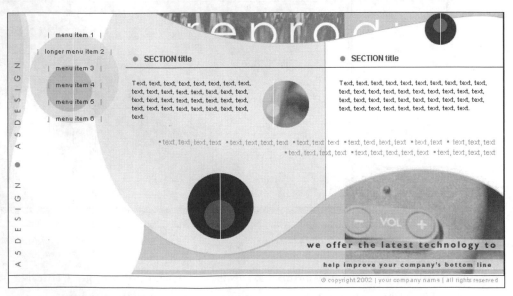

Homepage design.

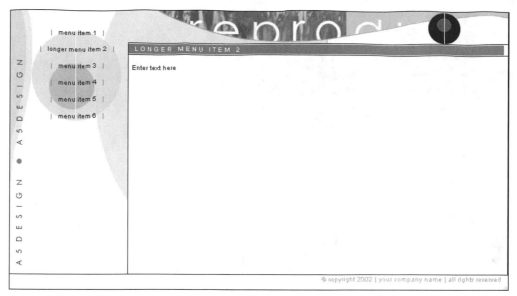

Second-level template.

Photoshop source file names: Designs - First Edition/design_46/design_46.psd
HTML Pages: index.htm, menu_item_2.htm
Photo credits: Cameracaptured, A5design

Design 45 (First Edition)

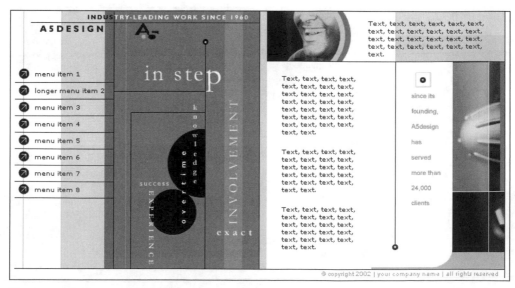

Homepage design.

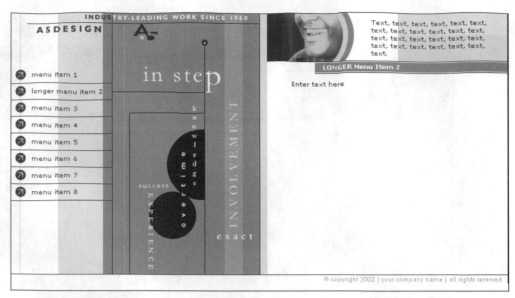

Second-level template for less content.

Photoshop source file names: Designs - First Edition/design_45/design_45.psd

HTML Pages: index.htm, menu_item_2.htm, menu_item_3.htm

Photo credits: Cameracaptured

Additional Designs Available on the CD

Second-level template for more content.

Design 44 (First Edition)

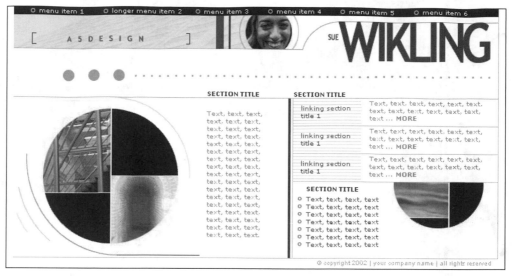

Homepage design.

Second-level template.

Photoshop source file names: Designs - First Edition/design_44/design_44.psd
HTML Pages: index.htm, menu_item_2.htm
Photo credits: Onepartart, A5design

Design 43 (First Edition)

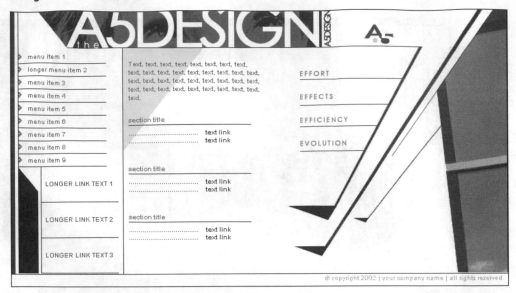

Homepage design.

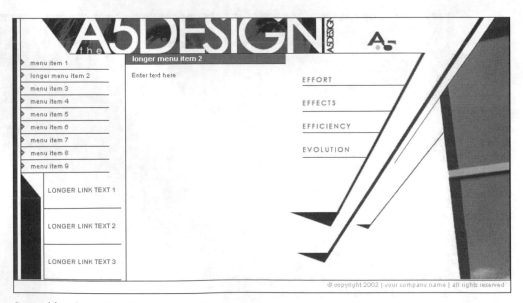

Second-level template for less content.

Photoshop source file names: Designs - First Edition/design_43/design_43.psd
HTML Pages: index.htm, menu_item_2.htm, menu_item_3.htm
Photo credits: A5design

Additional Designs Available on the CD

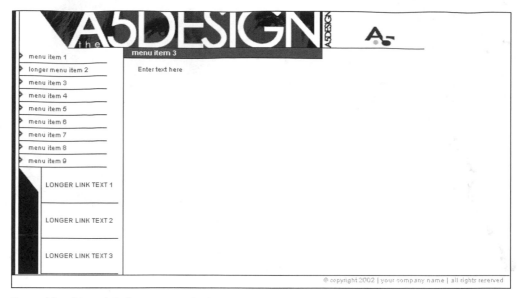

Second-level template for more content.

Design 42 (First Edition)

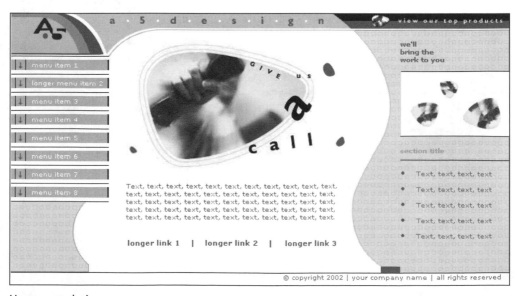

Homepage design.

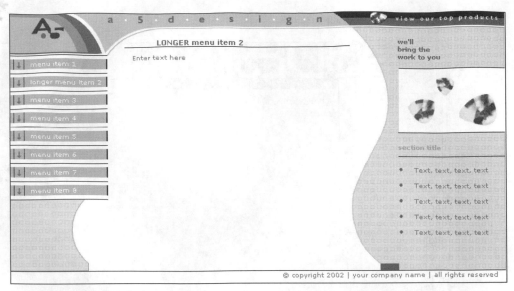

Second-level template for less content.

Photoshop source file names: Designs - First Edition/design_42/design_42.psd
HTML Pages: index.htm, menu_item_2.htm, menu_item_3.htm
Photo credits: Cameracaptured

Additional Designs Available on the CD

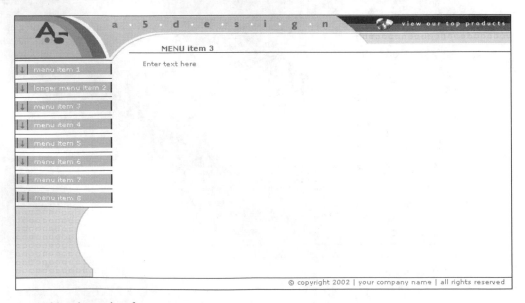

Second-level template for more content.

Design 41 (First Edition)

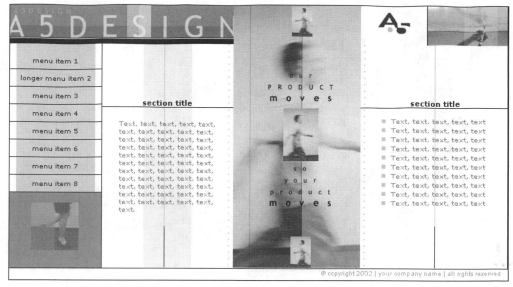

Homepage design.

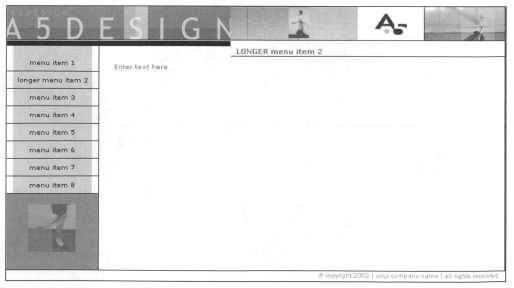

Second-level template.

Photoshop source file names: Designs - First Edition/design_41/design_41.psd
HTML Pages: index.htm, menu_item_2.htm
Photo credits: Cameracaptured

Design 40 (First Edition)

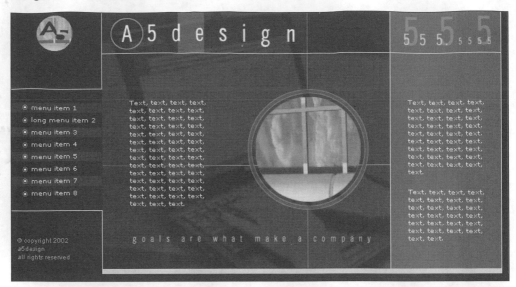

Homepage design.

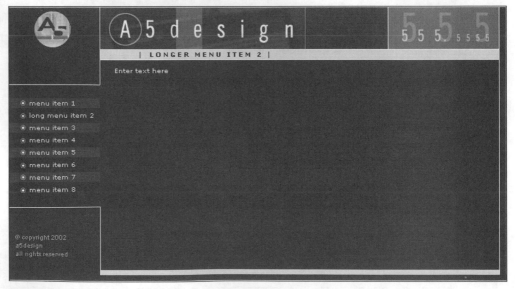

Second-level template.

Photoshop source file names: Designs - First Edition/design_40/design_40.psd
HTML Pages: index.htm, menu_item_2.htm
Photo credits: Cameracaptured, A5design

Design 39 (First Edition)

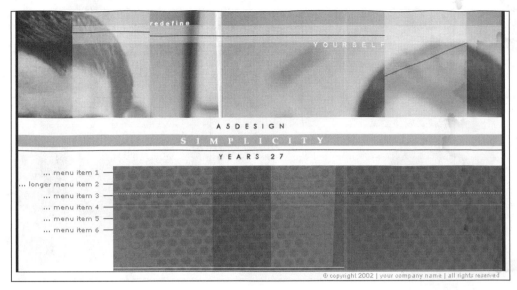

Homepage design.

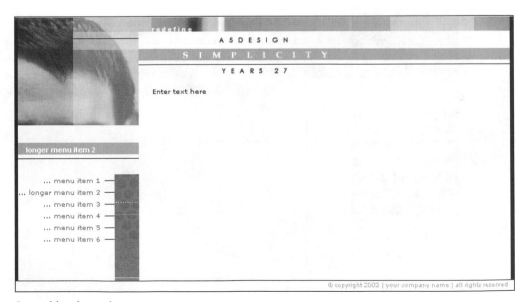

Second-level template.

Photoshop source file names: Designs - First Edition/design_39/design_39.psd

HTML Pages: index.htm, menu_item_2.htm

Photo credits: Cameracaptured

Design 38 (First Edition)

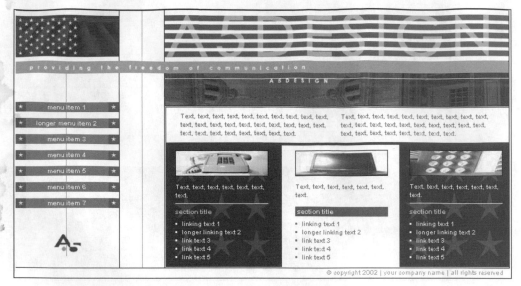

Homepage design.

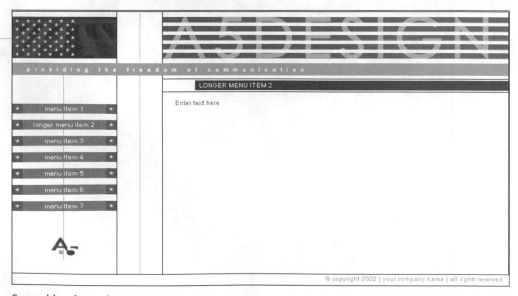

Second-level template.

Photoshop source file names: Designs - First Edition/design_38/design_38.psd
HTML Pages: index.htm, menu_item_2.htm
Photo credits: Cameracaptured, Onepartart, A5design

Design 37 (First Edition)

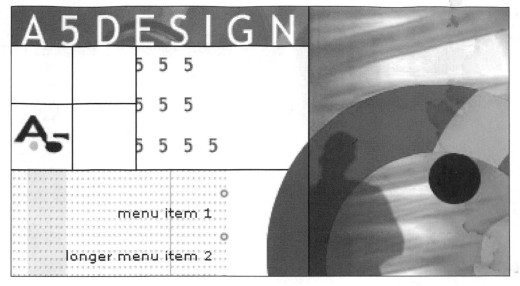

Homepage design.

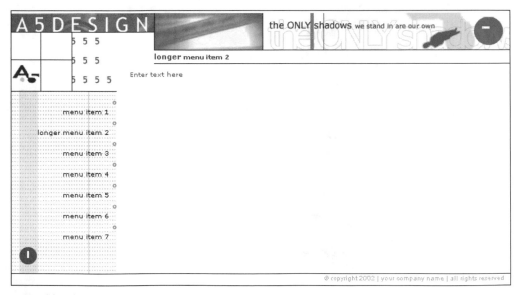

Second-level template.

Photoshop source file names: Designs - First Edition/design_37/design_37.psd

HTML Pages: index.htm, menu_item_2.htm

Photo credits: Cameracaptured, Onepartart

Design 36 (First Edition)

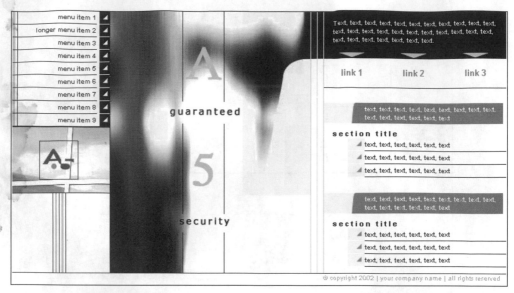

Homepage design.

Second-level template for less content.

Photoshop source file names: Designs - First Edition/design_36/design_36.psd

HTML Pages: index.htm, menu_item_2.htm, menu_item_3.htm, menu_item_4.htm (second-level page for nearly full content)

Photo credits: A5design

Additional Designs Available on the CD

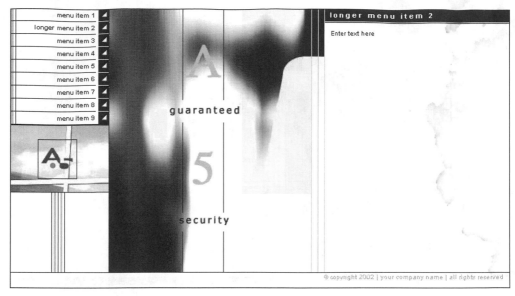

Second-level template for more content.

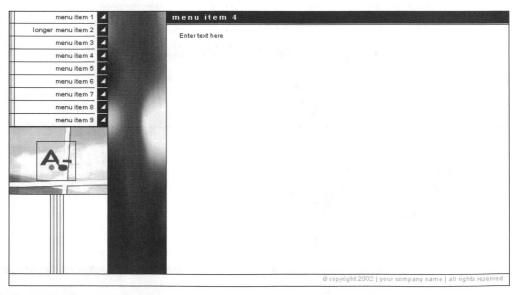

Second-level template for more content.

Design 35 (First Edition)

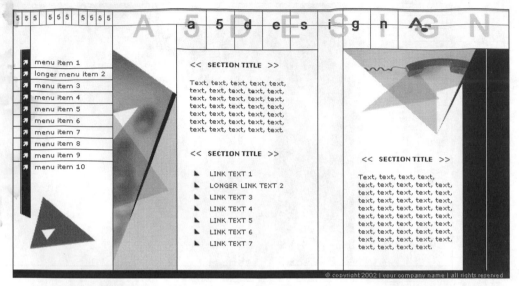

Homepage design.

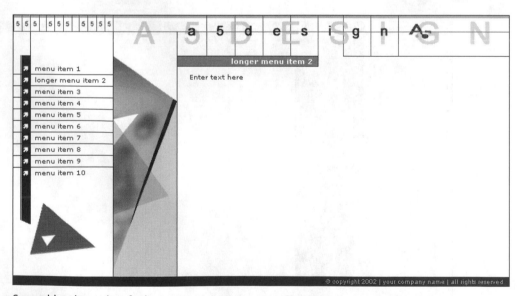

Second-level template for less content.

Photoshop source file names: Designs - First Edition/design_35/design_35.psd

HTML Pages: index.htm, menu_item_2.htm, menu_item_3.htm

Photo credits: A5design

Additional Designs Available on the CD

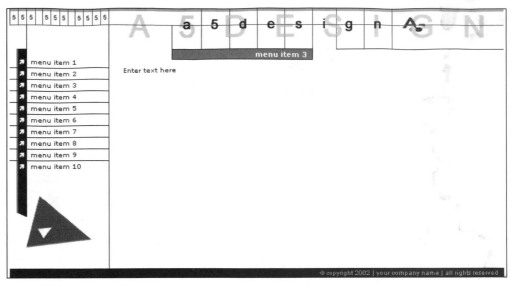

Second-level template for more content.

Design 34 (First Edition)

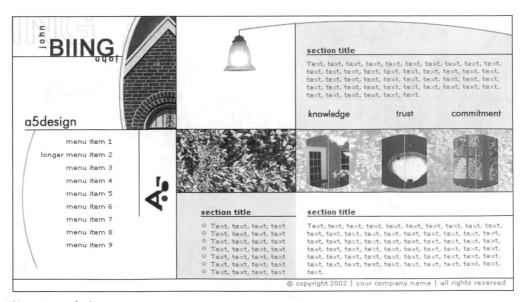

Homepage design.

Second-level template.

Photoshop source file names: Designs - First Edition/design_34/design_34.psd
HTML Pages: index.htm, menu_item_2.htm
Photo credits: A5design

Design 33 (First Edition)

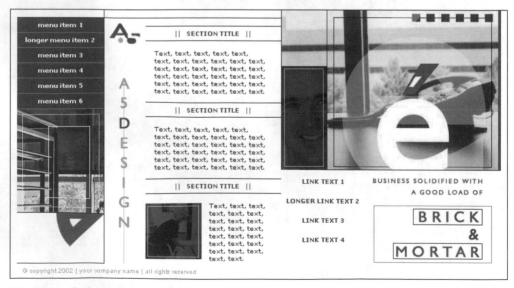

Homepage design.

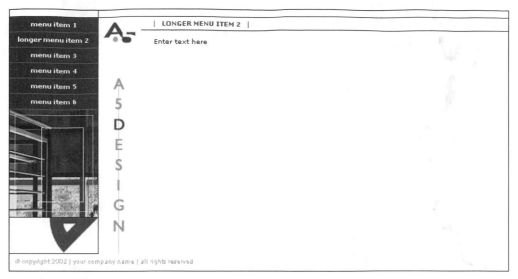

Second-level template.

Photoshop source file names: Designs - First Edition/design_33/design_33.psd
HTML Pages: index.htm, menu_item_2.htm
Photo credits: Cameracaptured, Onepartart, A5design

Design 32 (First Edition)

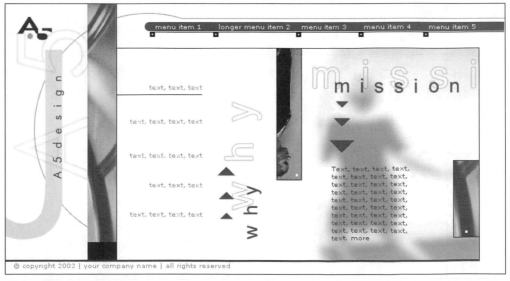

Homepage design.

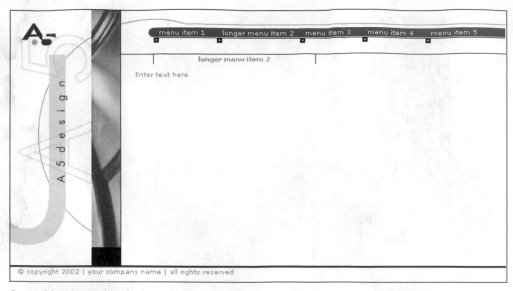

Second-level template for less content.

Photoshop source file names: Designs - First Edition/design_32/design_32.psd
HTML Pages: index.htm, menu_item_2.htm, menu_item_3.htm
Photo credits: Cameracaptured

Additional Designs Available on the CD

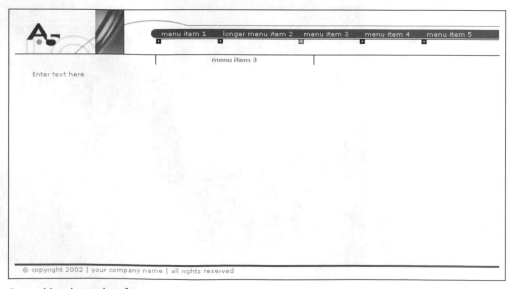

Second-level template for more content.

Design 31 (First Edition)

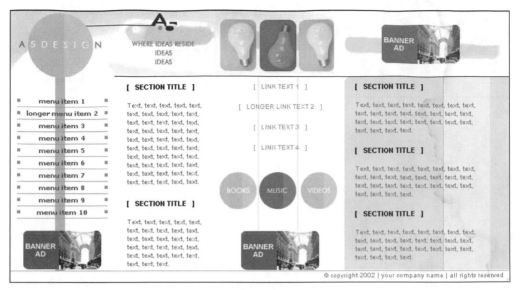

Homepage design.

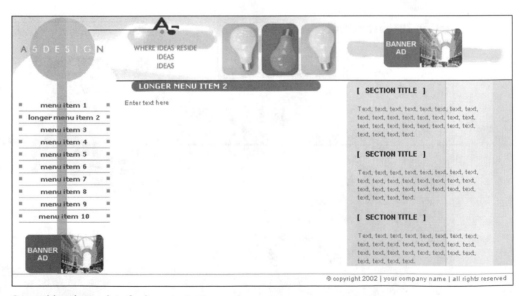

Second-level template for less content.

Photoshop source file names: Designs - First Edition/design_31/design_31.psd, title_curve.psd

HTML Pages: index.htm, menu_item_2.htm, menu_item_3.htm

Photo credits: Cameracaptured

Additional Designs Available on the CD

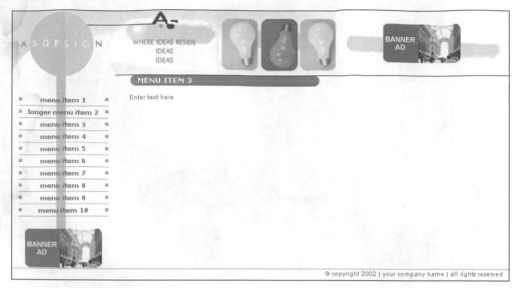

Second-level template for more content.

Design 30 (First Edition)

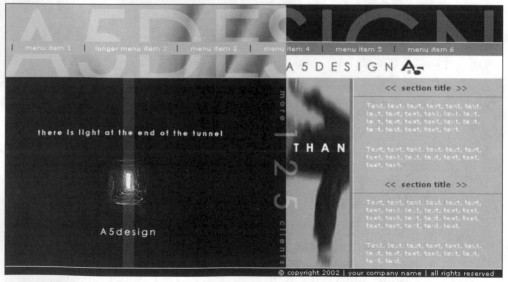

Homepage design.

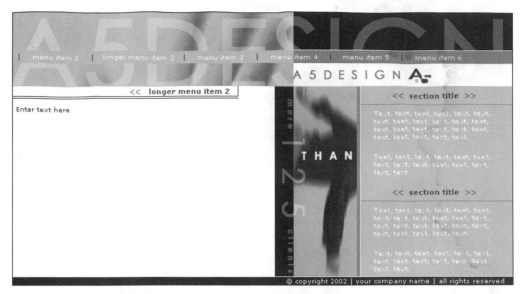

Second-level template for less content.

Photoshop source file names: Designs - First Edition/design_30/design_30.psd, bullets.psd, bg_menu.psd

HTML Pages: index.htm, menu_item_2.htm, menu_item_3.htm, menu_item_4.htm (second-level page for full content)

Photo credits: Cameracaptured, A5Design

Additional Designs Available on the CD

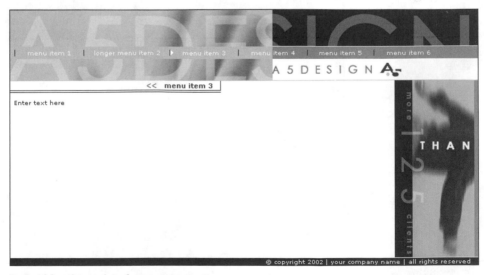

Second-level template for more content.

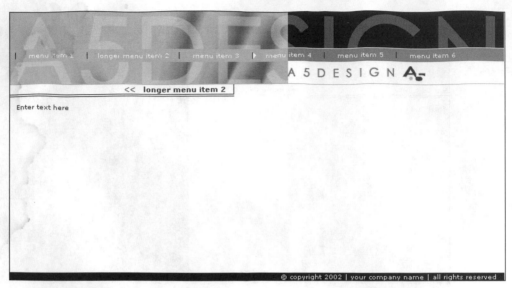

Second-level template for more content.

Design 29 (First Edition)

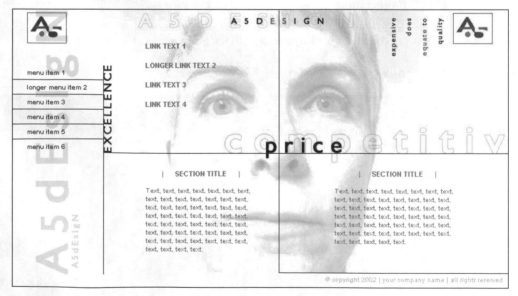

Homepage design.

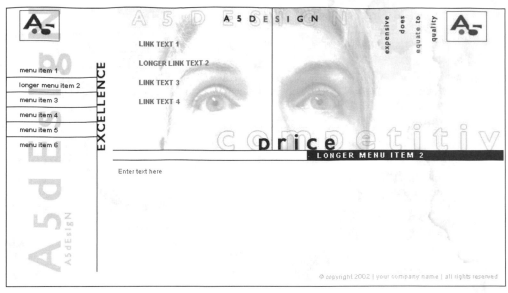

Second-level template for less content.

Photoshop source file names: Designs - First Edition/design_29/design_29.psd, design_29_sl.psd, bg_menu.psd

HTML Pages: index.htm, menu_item_2.htm, menu_item_3.htm

Photo credits: A5Design

Additional Designs Available on the CD

Second-level template for more content.

Design 28 (First Edition)

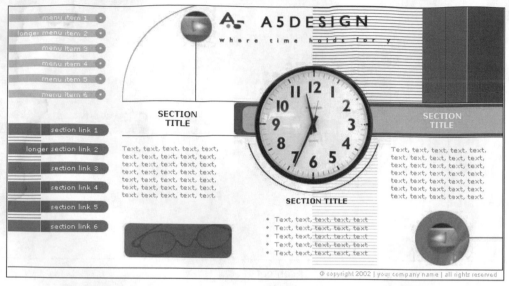

Homepage design.

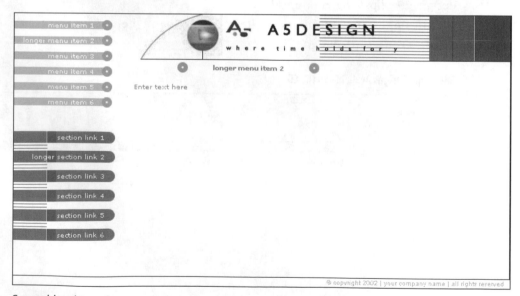

Second-level template.

Photoshop source file names: Designs - First Edition/design_28/design_28.psd
HTML Pages: index.htm, menu_item_2.htm
Photo credits: Onepartart

Design 27 (First Edition)

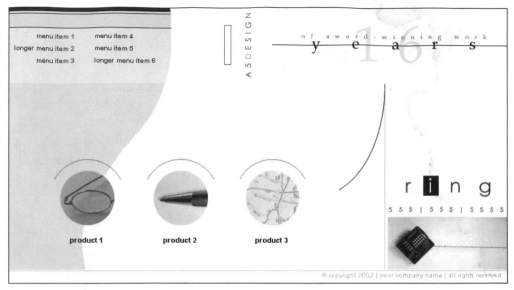

Homepage design.

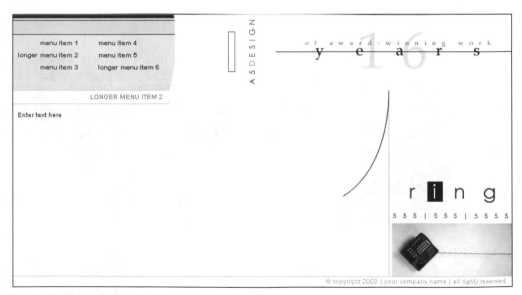

Second-level template for less content.

Photoshop source file names: Designs - First Edition/design_27/design_27.psd
HTML Pages: index.htm, menu_item_2.htm, menu_item_3.htm
Photo credits: Cameracaptured

Additional Designs Available on the CD

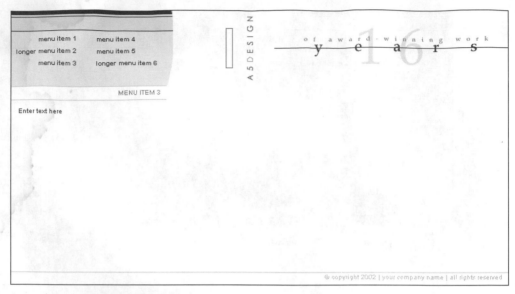

Second-level template for more content.

Design 26 (First Edition)

Homepage design.

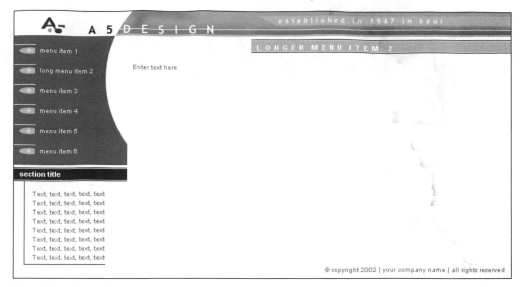

Second-level template.

Photoshop source file names: Designs - First Edition/design_26/design_26.psd
HTML Pages: index.htm, menu_item_2.htm
Photo credits: Cameracaptured

Design 25 (First Edition)

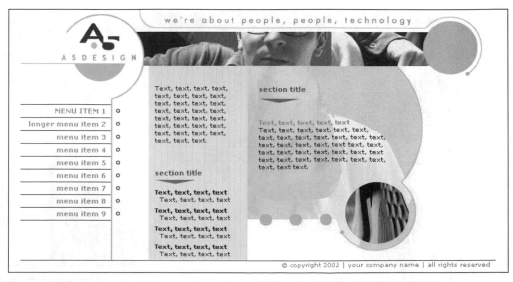

Homepage design.

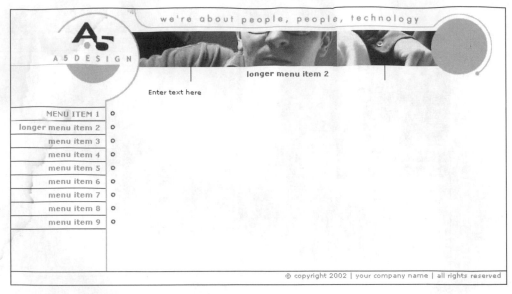

Second-level template.

Photoshop source file names: Designs - First Edition/design_25/design_25.psd
HTML Pages: index.htm, menu_item_2.htm
Photo credits: Cameracaptured, A5design

Design 24 (First Edition)

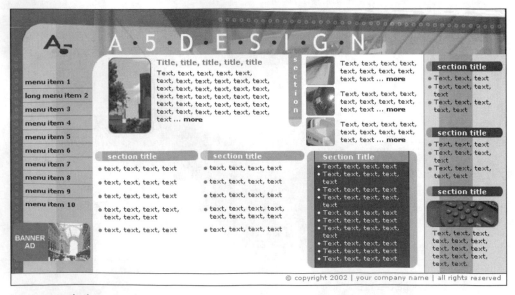

Homepage design.

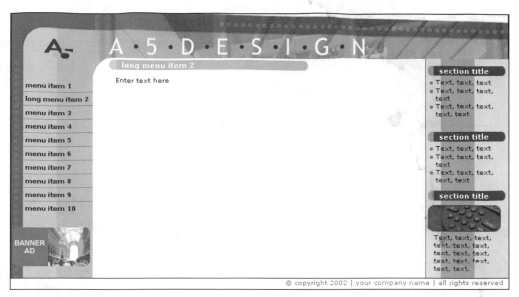

Second-level template for less content.

Photoshop source file names: Designs - First Edition/design_24/design_24.psd
HTML Pages: index.htm, menu_item_2.htm, menu_item_3.htm
Photo credits: Onepartart, Cameracaptured

Additional Designs Available on the CD

Second-level template for more content.

Design 23 (First Edition)

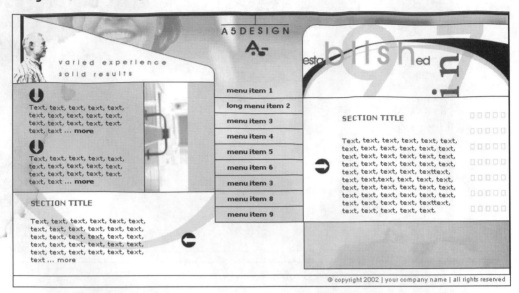

Homepage design.

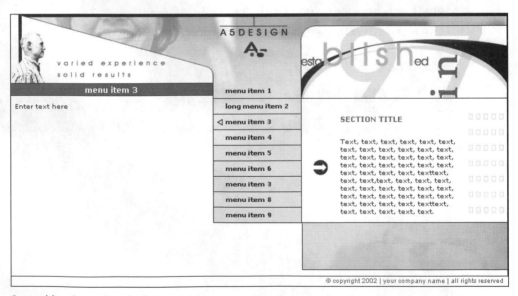

Second-level template for less content.

Photoshop source file names: Designs - First Edition/design_23/design_23.psd
HTML Pages: index.htm, menu_item_2.htm, menu_item_3.htm
Photo credits: A5design

Additional Designs Available on the CD

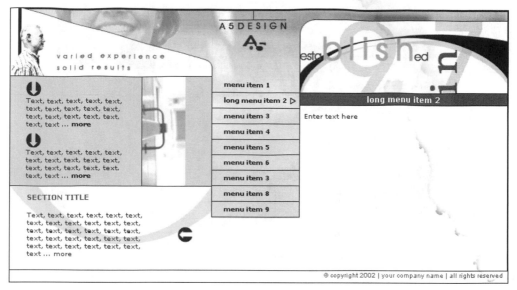

Second-level template for more content.

Design 22 (First Edition)

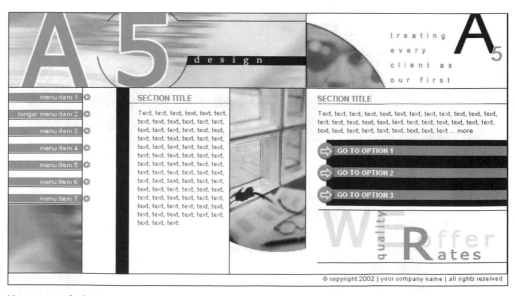

Homepage design.

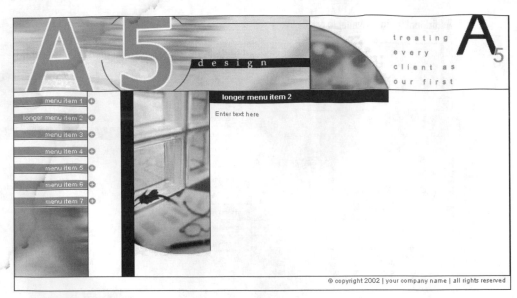

Second-level template for less content.

Photoshop source file names: Designs - First Edition/design_22/design_22.psd
HTML Pages: index.htm, menu_item_2.htm, menu_item_3.htm
Photo credits: Cameracaptured

Additional Designs Available on the CD

Second-level template for more content.

Design 21 (First Edition)

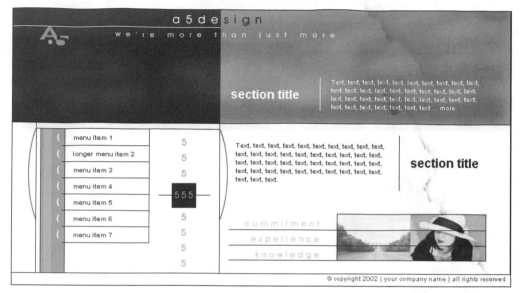

Homepage design.

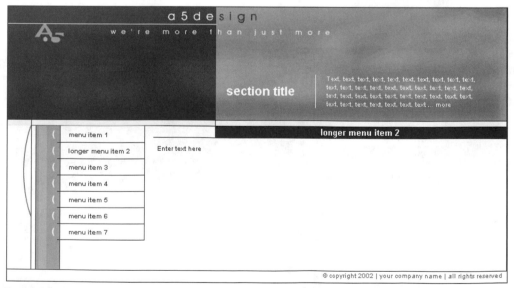

Second-level template for less content.

Photoshop source file names: Designs - First Edition/design_21/design_21.psd
HTML Pages: index.htm, menu_item_2.htm, menu_item_3.htm
Photo credits: Cameracaptured, A5design

Additional Designs Available on the CD

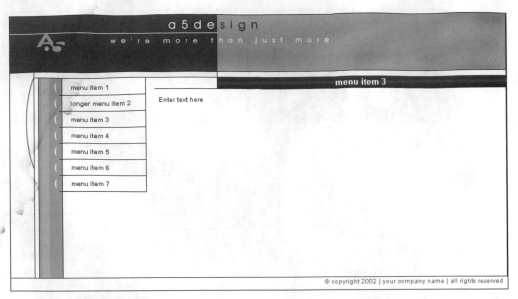

Second-level template for more content.

Design 20 (First Edition)

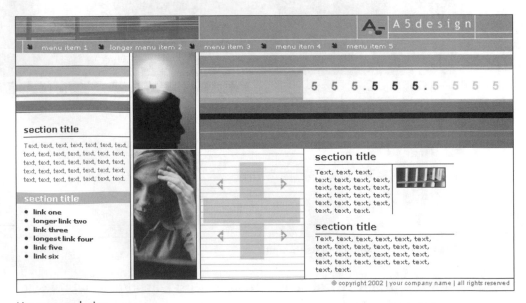

Homepage design.

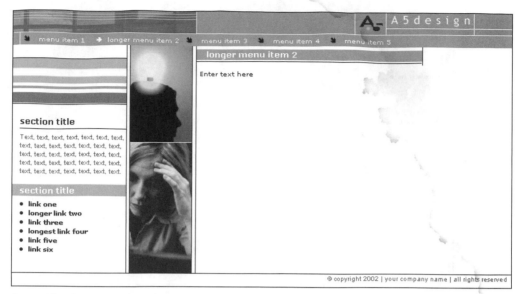

Second-level template for less content.

Photoshop source file names: Designs - First Edition/design_20/design_20.psd

HTML Pages: index.htm, menu_item_2.htm, menu_item_3.htm, menu_item_4.htm (second-level page for full content)

Additional Designs Available on the CD

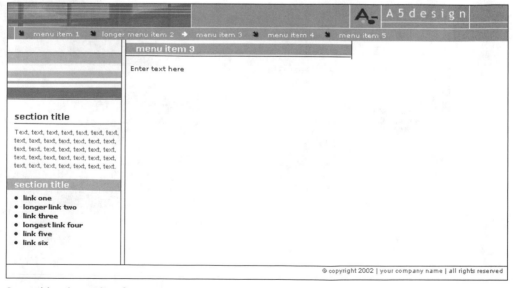

Second-level template for more content.

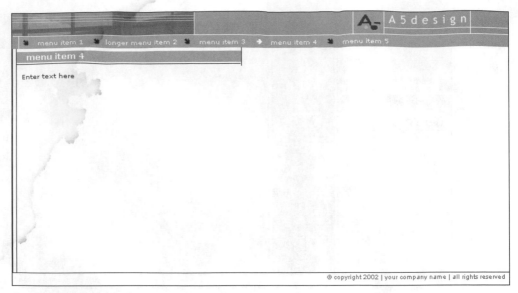

Second-level template for more content.

Design 19 (First Edition)

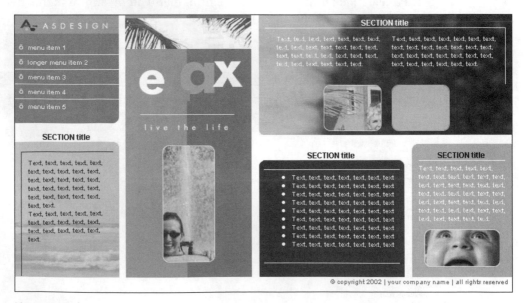

Homepage design.

Second-level template for less content.

Photoshop source file names: Designs - First Edition/design_19/design_19.psd
HTML Pages: indcx.htm, menu_item_2.htm, menu_item_3.htm
Photo credits: J&N Photography

Additional Designs Available on the CD

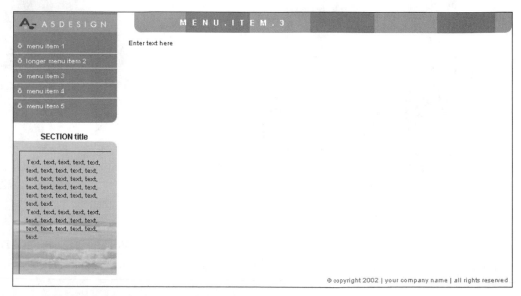

Second-level template for more content.

Design 18 (First Edition)

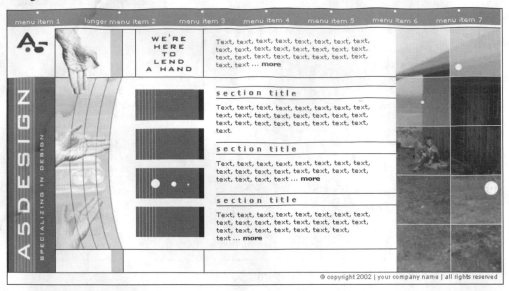

Homepage design.

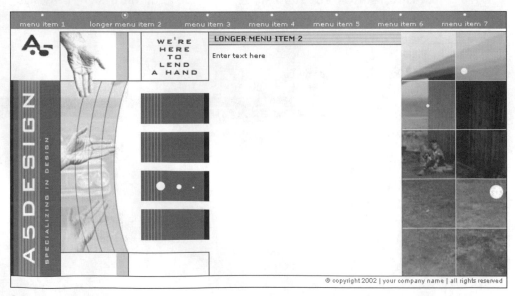

Second-level template for less content.

Photoshop source file names: Designs - First Edition/design_18/design_18.psd

HTML Pages: index.htm, menu_item_2.htm, menu_item_3.htm, menu_item_4.htm (second-level page for full content)

Photo credits: J&N Photography

Additional Designs Available on the CD

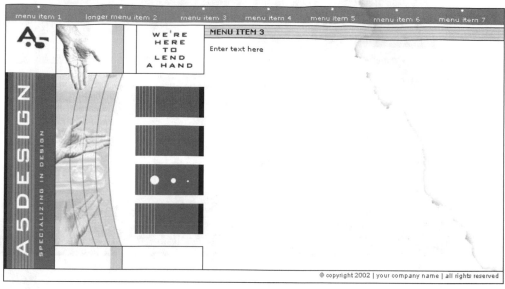

Second-level template for more content.

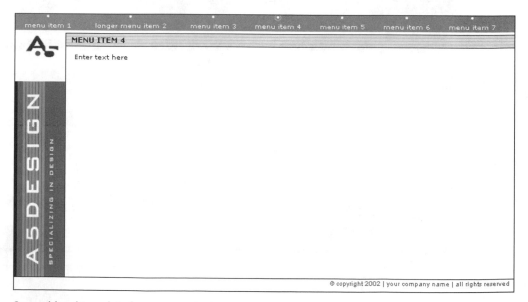

Second-level template for more content.

Design 17 (First Edition)

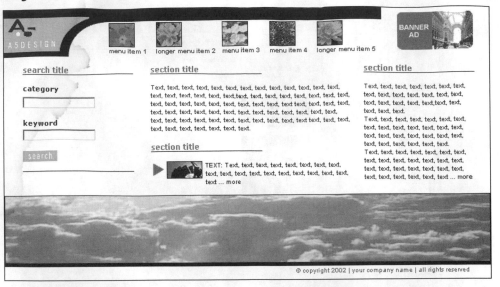

Homepage design.

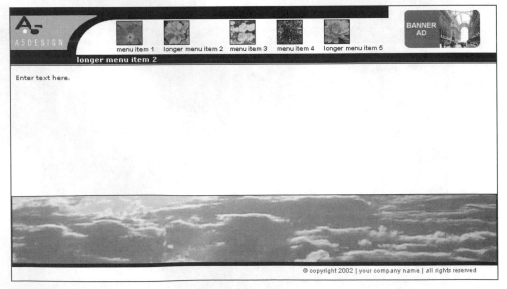

Second-level template.

Photoshop source file names: Designs - First Edition/design_17/design_17.psd, menu_item_text.psd

HTML Pages: index.htm, menu_item_2.htm

Photo credits: J&N Photography

Design 16 (First Edition)

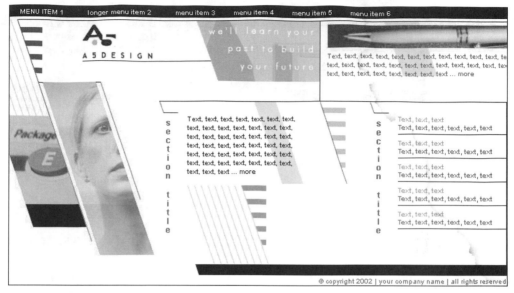

Homepage design.

Second-level template for less content.

Photoshop source file names: Designs - First Edition/design_16/design_16.psd
HTML Pages: index.htm, menu_item_2.htm, menu_item_3.htm
Photo credits: Cameracaptured

Additional Designs Available on the CD

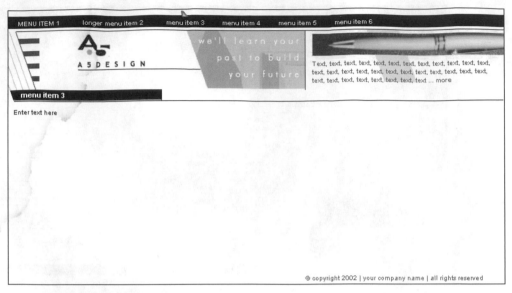

Second-level template for more content.

Design 15 (First Edition)

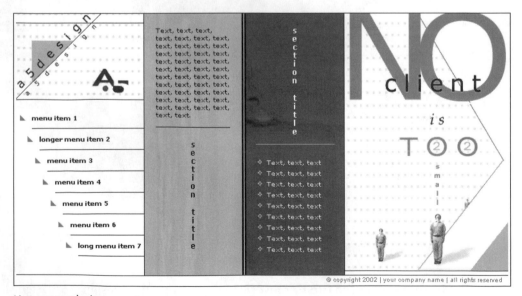

Homepage design.

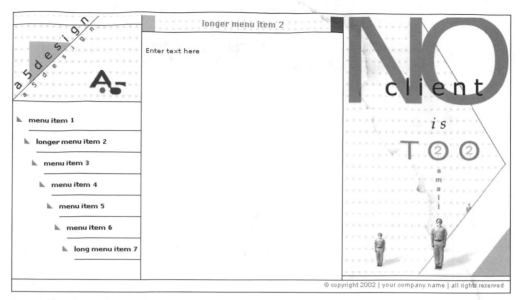

Second-level template for less content.

Photoshop source file names: Designs - First Edition/design_15/design_15.psd
HTML Pages: index.htm, menu_item_2.htm, menu_item_3.htm
Photo credits: A5design

Additional Designs Available on the CD

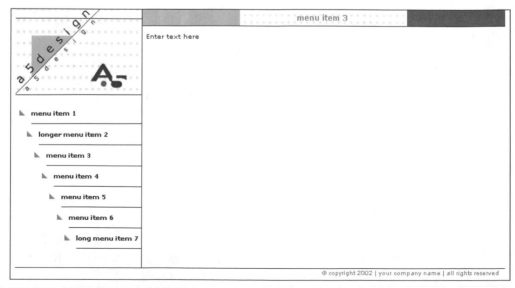

Second-level template for more content.

Design 14 (First Edition)

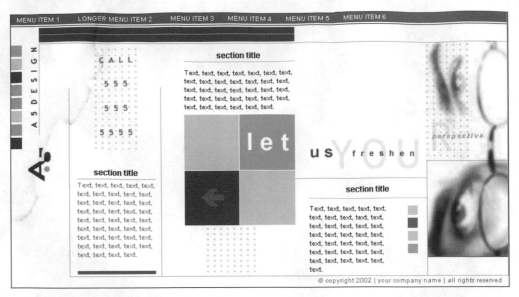

Homepage design.

Second-level template for less content.

Photoshop source file names: Designs - First Edition/design_14/design_14.psd

HTML Pages: index.htm, menu_item_2.htm, menu_item_3.htm

Photo credits: A5design

Additional Designs Available on the CD

Second-level template for more content.

Design 13 (First Edition)

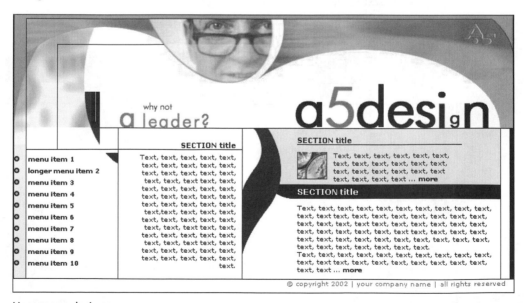

Homepage design.

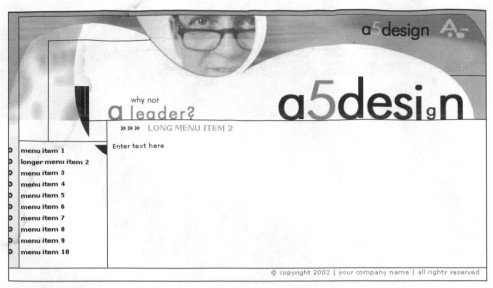

Second-level template for less content.

Photoshop source file names: Designs - First Edition/design_13/design_13.psd, design_13_sl.psd

HTML Pages: index.htm, menu_item_2.htm, menu_item_3.htm

Photo credits: Cameracaptured, A5design

Additional Designs Available on the CD

Second-level template for more content.

Design 12 (First Edition)

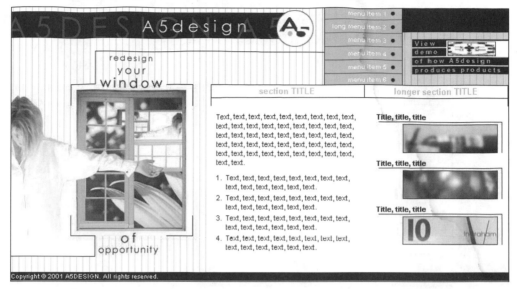

Homepage design.

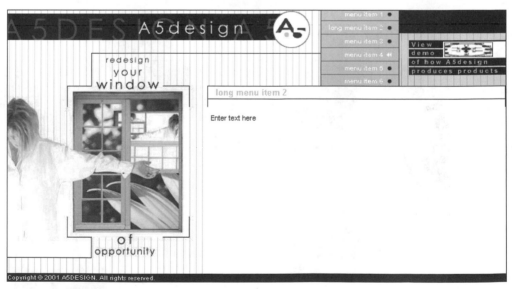

Second-level template for less content.

Photoshop source file names: Designs - First Edition/design_12/design_12.psd, design_12_sl.psd, photo_on.psd

HTML Pages: index.htm, menu_item_2.htm, menu_item_3.htm

Photo credits: J&N Photography, Onepartart, A5design

Additional Designs Available on the CD

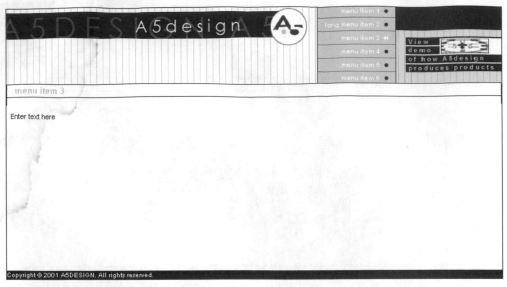

Second-level template for more content.

Design 11 (First Edition)

Homepage design.

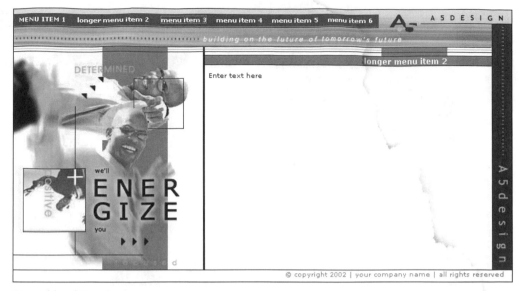

Second-level template.

Photoshop source file names: Designs - First Edition/design_11/design_11.psd
HTML Pages: index.htm, menu_item_2.htm
Photo credits: Cameracaptured

Design 10 (First Edition)

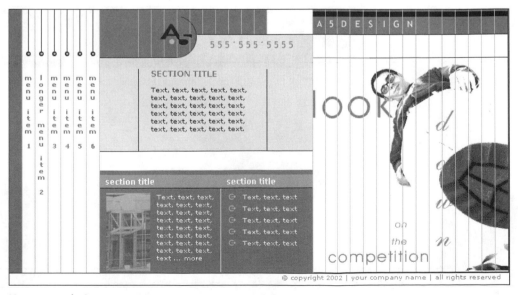

Homepage design.

Second-level template for less content.

Photoshop source file names: Designs - First Edition/design_10/design_10.psd
HTML Pages: index.htm, menu_item_2.htm, menu_item_3.htm
Photo credits: Onepartart

Additional Designs Available on the CD

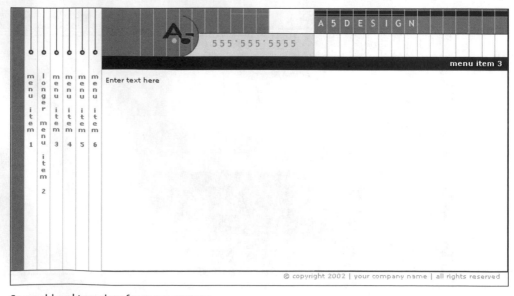

Second-level template for more content.

Design 9 (First Edition)

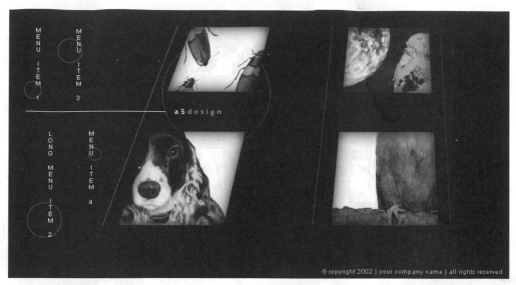

Homepage design.

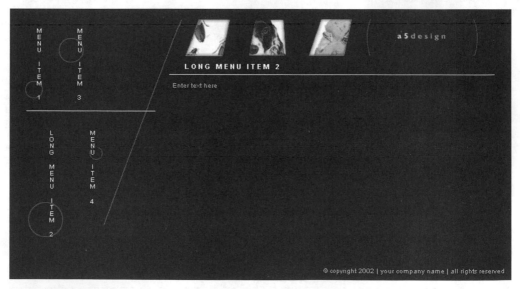

Second-level template.

Photoshop source file names: Designs - First Edition/design_9/design_9.psd, design_9_sl.psd

HTML Pages: index.htm, menu_item_2.htm

Photo credits: Onepartart

Design 8 (First Edition)

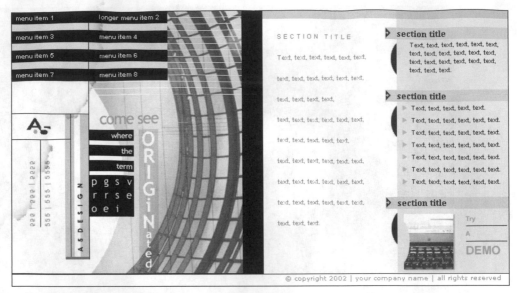

Homepage design.

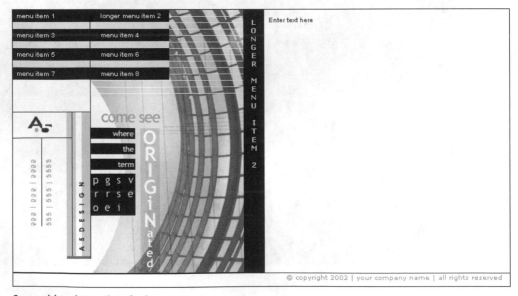

Second-level template for less content.

Photoshop source file names: Designs - First Edition/design_8/design_8.psd

HTML Pages: index.htm, menu_item_2.htm, menu_item_3.htm

Photo credits: Cameracaptured

Additional Designs Available on the CD

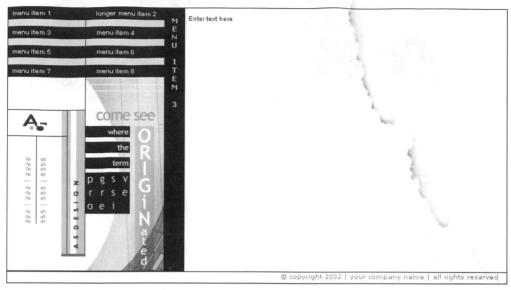

Second-level template for more content.

Design 7 (First Edition)

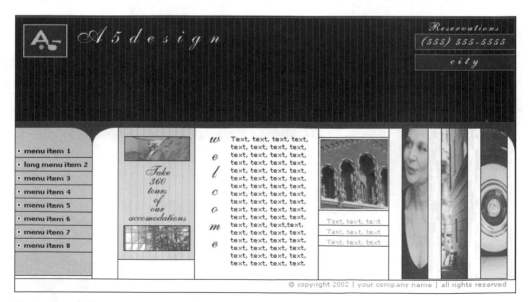

Homepage design.

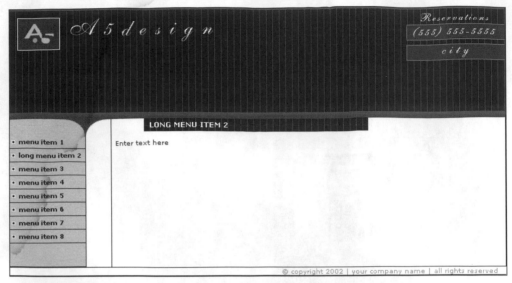

Second-level template for less content.

Photoshop source file names: Designs - First Edition/design_7/design_7.psd
HTML Pages: index.htm, menu_item_2.htm, menu_item_3.htm
Photo credits: Cameracaptured, A5design

Additional Designs Available on the CD

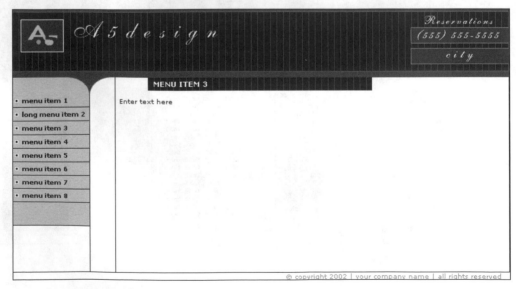

Second-level template for more content.

Design 6 (First Edition)

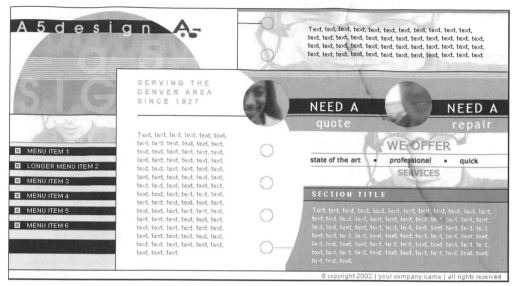

Homepage design.

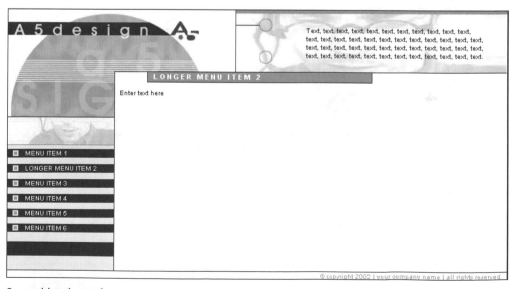

Second-level template.

Photoshop source file names: Designs - First Edition/design_6/design_6.psd
HTML Pages: index.htm, menu_item_2.htm
Photo credits: Onepartart, A5design

Design 5 (First Edition)

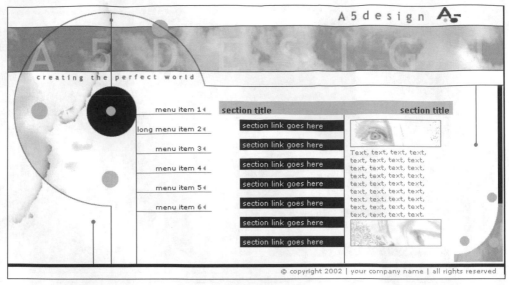

Homepage design.

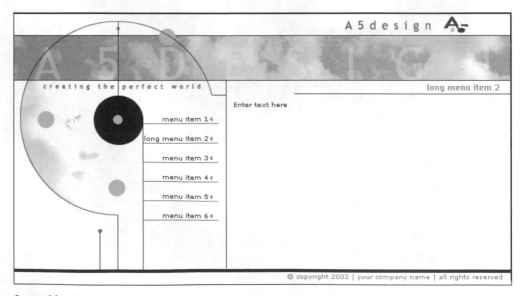

Second-level template for less content.

Photoshop source file names: Designs - First Edition/design_5/design_5.psd
HTML Pages: index.htm, menu_item_2.htm, menu_item_3.htm
Photo credits: A5design

Additional Designs Available on the CD

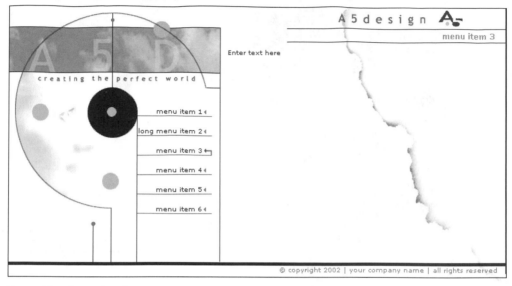

Second-level template for more content.

Design 4 (First Edition)

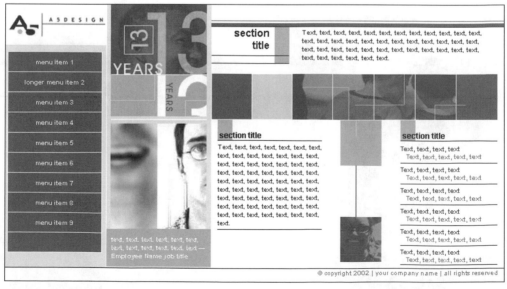

Homepage design.

Second-level template for less content.

Photoshop source file names: Designs - First Edition/design_4/design_4.psd
HTML Pages: index.htm, menu_item_2.htm, menu_item_3.htm
Photo credits: Cameracaptured, A5design

Additional Designs Available on the CD

Second-level template for more content.

Design 3 (First Edition)

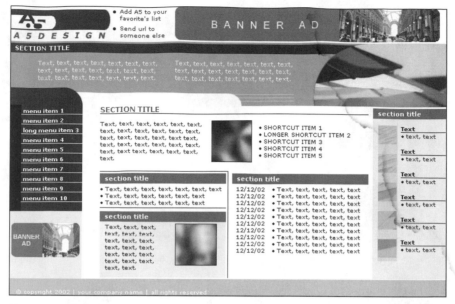

Homepage design.

Second-level template for less content.

Photoshop source file names: Designs - First Edition/design_3/design_3.psd

HTML Pages: index.htm, menu_item_2.htm, menu_item_3.htm

Photo credits: Cameracaptured

Additional Designs Available on the CD

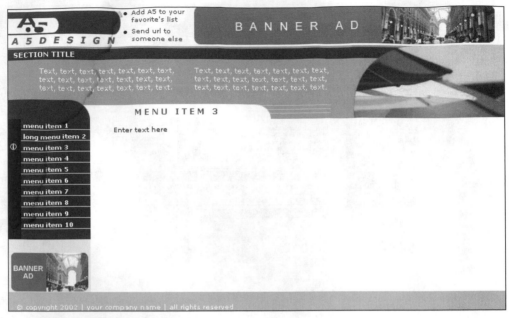

Second-level template for more content.

Design 2 (First Edition)

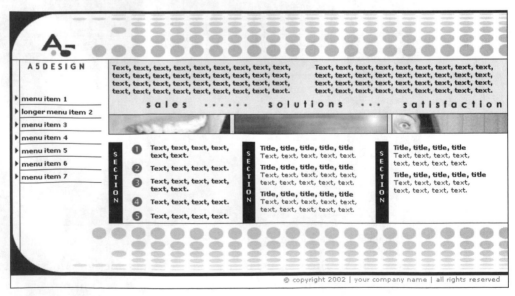

Homepage design.

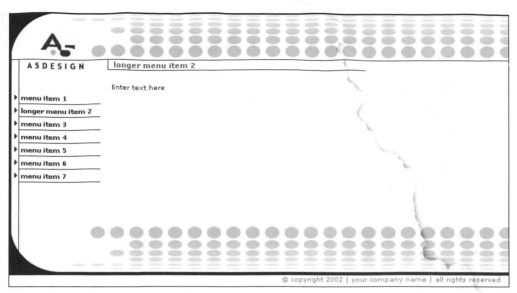

Second-level template.

Photoshop source file names: Designs - First Edition/design_2/design_2.psd
HTML Pages: index.htm, menu_item_2.htm
Photo credits: Onepartart, A5design

Design 1 (First Edition)

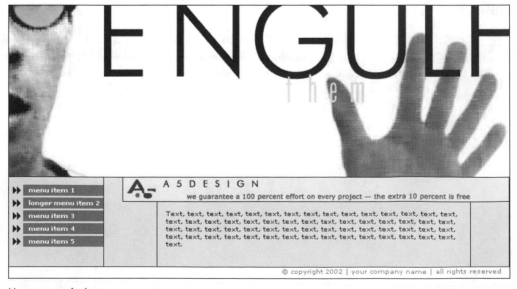

Homepage design.

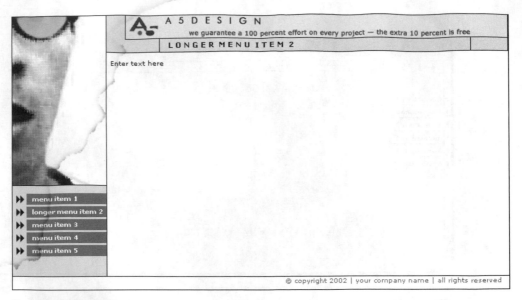

Second-level template.

Photoshop source file names: Designs - First Edition/design_1/design_1.psd
HTML Pages: index.htm, menu_item_2.htm
Photo credits: A5design

SUMMARY

The designs included on the CD with this book offer a variety of options for the reader. The types of designs include XHTML table-based coded Web sites, e-newsletters, signatures, Photoshop-only designs, and CSS-coded designs. This not only offers the reader a variety of designs that can be quickly customized and used, but they can be used for inspiration, as well.

INDEX

0px setting, 379

A

absolute positioning
    with box model, 150–154
    in high-content design, 266
    in medium-content design, 207
    in mortised sites, 94–95
accessibility
    designing for, 70
    in usability philosophy, 8
action items in site, 40
Adobe. *See also* ColdFusion; Flash;
    Photoshop
    Dreamweaver, 13
advertisements in headers, 64
aesthetics, 7
    and comps, 78
    and mortised sites, 13
A5design's site, 45–47
alternatives to client, offering, 87
animated GIFs, 114
    large animated GIFs, saving, 132
anti-aliasing, 113
    icons, layering, 411
    linear shapes and, 412
AOL (America OnLine) bandwidth
    issues, 44
Apache HTTP Server (SHTML) include
    files, 109
architecture
    cascading architecture, 62–63
    clicking, limits on, 61
    flat architecture, 62–63
    linking user out of section, 61–62
    naming conventions, consistency
        in, 61
    simplifying, 60–63
artistic issues, 3
assumptions about site, 40
audience
    and bandwidth, 44
    and color selection, 82–83

B

back-end programming, 3
background images, 28–32
    as design elements, 398–399
    mortising with, 97
    repeating, 30–32, 398–399
    transparent backgrounds, 160
background properties
    with box model, 152
    contrasting colors, setting, 403–404
    for forms, 335–336
    for full-height three-column layout,
        294–295
    in low-content design, 176
    in medium-content design, 207
    troubleshooting, using for,
        402–404
background-based design, 309–322
    containers, placement of, 313–314
    content, adding, 322–330
    <DIV> tag in, 313–314
    footers, adding, 322–330
    framework, creating, 314–316
    guides in, 311–313
    header area, adding, 317–322
    second-level pages, constructing,
        331
    slices in, 311–313
    structure of, 310–314
banding, 116
bandwidth, 23–25
    requirements, 38, 43–45
bgcolor attribute, 365
bitmap images, 112–114. *See also*
    Photoshop
    BMP format, 131–132
    multimedia sites and, 12
    rasterizing text, 86
blending colors in background-based
    design, 312
block-level tags, 105–106
BMP format, 131–132
body of page, positioning, 65

<BODY> tag
 in background-based design,
  316
 for full-height three-column
  layout, 294
 in high-content design, 244
 in low-content design,
  164–165
 in medium-content design,
  203
bookmarking sites, 26
borders
 and a5-body rules, 165
 in CSS site, 140
 for full-height three-column
  layout, 299
 in high-content design, 244
 in medium-content design,
  203
 troubleshooting, border
  properties for, 402–404
 turning on/off, 403–404
box model, 149–154
 absolute positioning with,
  150–154
 code for site using, 150
 relative positioning with,
  150–154
box model hack. *See* Tantek
 hack
brain processes, 9
branching pages, 22–23
bread crumbs technique, 61
broadband, 23
browsers. *See also* Firefox; Internet Explorer
 CSS and, 137
 issues of, 18–20
 line consistency across,
  396–397
 non-Microsoft browsers,
  downloading, 156
 and philosophy of, 12
 spacing, removing, 379
 testing designs in, 155–156
 usage statistics and, 20–22
bugs. *See* troubleshooting
bullets
 background images as, 398
 XHTML characters as, 411
bundled stock collections, 81–82

C
carriage returns and <DIV> tag,
 168–169
cascading architecture, 62–63.
 See also CSS (Cascading Style
 Sheets)
CD, templates included on,
 445–726
Celik hack. *See* Tantek hack
circular flow in site, 61–62
clicking, limits on, 61
client contacts, site including,
 39
code
 indenting code, 420
 templates, customizing code
  in, 428–429
ColdFusion, 2
 include files, 109
 mortised sites and, 15
 and multimedia software, 12
color blindness, 83
color depth, 51–53
color palettes and GIF format,
 114
colors, 4–5. *See also* GIF format
 alternatives, offering, 87
 comps, selecting for, 82–83
 leading eye with, 10
 in low-content design,
  164–165
 in medium-content design,
  208
 Photoshop tutorial for
  changing design colors,
  438–441
 templates, customizing colors
  in, 426
 uncontrolled colors, 33
columns and rows. *See also*
 high-content design; low-
 content design; medium-
 content design
 full-height three-column
  layout, adding columns
  and rows to, 295–299
comments. *See also* global general styles
 in high-content design, 265,
  276
 identifying sections with, 420

removing, 420–421
 troubleshooting, commenting out code for, 405–406
compression. *See also* GIF format; JPG format
 over-compressing images,
  129–131
 software, 132–133, 420
 uncompressed images, 33–34
comps, 41, 74
 colors, selecting, 82–83
 creating, 78–86
 decisions on, 87–88
 editing, 87–88
 folder system for, 79–80
 layers, developing, 84–86
 layout decisions, 83–84
 masks in, 86
 source directory, creating,
  79–80
comstock.com, 82
consistency
 of menus, 66
 in naming conventions, 61
 in navigation, 66
 in usability philosophy, 8
containers. *See also* floating
 containers
 background-based design,
  placement in, 313–314
 corner images, rounding
  container edges with,
  418–419
 CSS containers, placement
  of, 162–163
 for full-height three-column
  layout, 291
 in high-content design,
  241–242
 medium-content design,
  placement in, 200–201
content
 background-based design,
  adding in, 322–330
 bandwidth and, 44
 designing for, 70–72
 flexibility of design and,
  56–57
 in headers, 65
 in low-content XHTML
  template, 352–353

positioning of, 64–65
requirements, 38
resolution and, 47–48
corbis.com, 82
corner images, rounding container edges with, 418–419
corporate audience, 44
costs of multimedia sites, 12
Creating Killer Web Sites (Siegel), 13
crossover experience, 6
CSS (Cascading Style Sheets), 2. *See also* box model; fixed-width CSS design; full-height three-column layout; high-content design; low-content design; medium-content design; mortised sites; mouseovers
  background images, use of, 28
  basics of design, 137–149
  code compared to XHTML, 147–149
  comment tags, troubleshooting with, 405
  containers, placement of, 162–163
  drop shadows, CSS code for, 411
  expandability of site and, 54
  HTML editor, opening files in, 428
  importing style sheets, 106
  list of properties, 104–105
  menus, 69–70
  shortcomings of, 136–137
  shortcuts, using, 409
  Status row, adding, 342
  terminology of, 102–103
  testing designs in browsers, 155–156
  understanding, 101–105
  Unlimited row, adding, 342
  validating code, 154–155
  XHTML compared, 136–149
CSS form design, 333–349
  back end functionality, adding, 345–349
  Cancel button, adding, 345
  changes to forms, making, 338
  Comments row, adding, 343
  Contact Name row, adding, 340

disabled fields, 337
final form, appearance of, 345–349
First Name row, adding, 339
<FORM> tag, 334–335, 338
Language row, adding, 341
Last Name row, adding, 340
margins in, 337
Options to Select row, adding, 343–344
Purchase Date row, adding, 342–343
Region row, adding, 341
required fields in, 337
required row, adding, 338
structure of form, 334–336
style sheets for, 336–338
Submit button, adding, 345
width of labels, 335
CSS Validation Service, 155
CSS Validator, 155

D
dates, site including, 39
declarations with DocType Declaration (DTD), 106
defining Web design, 2–5
dependencies of site, 40
directory of sources, creating, 79–80
disabled fields in forms, 337
disabled users. *See* accessibility
discretion in multimedia sites, 12
dithering, 116
<DIV> tag, 90, 94–95, 105–106. *See also* medium-content design; wrapping <DIV> tags
  in background-based design, 313–314
  in box model, 149–150
  containers, placement of, 241–242
  CSS sites using, 138
  in fixed-width CSS design, 380–388
  for forms, 339
  for full-height three-column layout, 291
  for header content, 168
  hidden tags, including, 412–413
  line consistency with, 397–398

in medium-content design, 198–201
  navigation rules, replacing, 107
  nesting, 383
    left and right columns, 169–170
  placement of, 162–163
  printing, globally driven tags for, 410
  spaces affecting, 168–169
DocType Declaration (DTD), 106
documentation of client communications, 87
DOM (Document Object Model), 22
download.com, 420
downloading
  bandwidth and, 23–25
  image buttons and, 27–28
  low-content XHTML design, 352
  non-Microsoft browsers, 156
  uncompressed images and, 33–34
  in usability philosophy, 8
Dreamweaver, 13
drop shadows, 117
  CSS code for, 411
dropdown menus, using, 400–401
DSL (digital subscriber line), 23

E
editable sites, 54
editing comps, 87–88
e-mail. *See also* low-content XHTML template
  signature file, sending e-mails with, 447
ems, 409–410
e-newsletters, 447
EPS format, 132
exceptions in Web design, 6
executive summary, 40
extremetracking.com, 22
EZ Menu, 401

F
feel requirements, 38
files. *See also* specific formats
  include files, 109
  mortising and formats, 93

Firefox, 18
usage statistics and, 20–22
fixed sites, designing, 49–51
fixed-width CSS design,
379–388
centering design, 390–394
heights of columns, adjust-
ing, 388–389
liquid design, creating,
394–395
wrapping <DIV> tags in, 390
Flash, 5. *See also* mortised sites
menus, 68
multimedia sites, 11–12
flat architecture, 62–63
flexible design, 55–58
and comps, 87
layout and, 57–58
floating containers
bugs with, 195
for full-height three-column
layout, 299
low-content design, adding
in, 189–195
flowcharts for site, 42–43
folders for source directory, 80
fonts
in low-content design,
164–165
style sheets and, 107
units, understanding,
409–410
footers
background-based design,
adding footers in,
322–330
low-content XHTML tem-
plate, creating footer
information in, 365–367
<FORM> tag, 334–335, 338. *See
also* CSS form design
controlling margins in,
406–408
forms. *See also* CSS form design;
mortised sites
building form row by row,
338–349
in high-content design, 254
framed sites, 25–26
framework graphics, 417–418
front-end requirements, 41–42
gathering, 75
full-height three-column layout, 287–307

background properties for,
294–295
columns and rows, adding,
295–299
containers, placement of,
291
content, populating areas
with, 300–306
<DIV> tag for, 291
framework in XHTML and
CSS, creating, 292–295
guides, creating, 288–290
horizontally repeating background, adding, 299
populating areas with content, 300–306
second-level pages,
constructing, 307
slices, creating, 288–290
structure for, 288–291
functionality, 7. *See also* mortised sites
bandwidth and, 44
graphic technology and, 10
of image buttons, 27–28
future site considerations, 40

G
gathering requirements,
74–78
getty-images.com, 82
GIF format, 122–123. *See also*
animated GIFS
color depth and, 52
for line drawings, 117
mixing GIF and JPG formats,
128–129
multimedia sites and, 12
original color, maintenance
of, 115–119
over-compressing images,
130–131
photo as GIF, saving, 127
PNG format and, 114
small graphics saved in, 119
for thumbnails, 118–119
uncompressed images as,
33–34
understanding GIF compression, 120–121
using GIFs, 114–119
global general styles
in background-based design,
315–316

for full-height three-column
layout, 294
in low-content design, 164
in medium-content design,
203
global structure styles in low-
content design, 164
gradations
in background-based design,
312
saving images with, 121–123
graphics, 4, 101. *See also* bitmap
images; images; mortised
sites
functionality and, 10
leading eye with, 10
software, understanding,
132–133
in usability philosophy, 9
vector images, 112–114
guides
in background-based design,
311–313
for full-height three-column
layout, 288–290
in high-content design,
239–241
in low-content design,
159–161
low-content XHTML tem-
plate, adding in, 354–355
in medium-content design,
199–200

H
headers
background-based design,
adding header area to,
317–322
height of, 84
high-content design, adding
in, 245–249
low-content design , adding
in, 165–169
in low-content XHTML tem-
plate, 353–354
positioning of, 64–65
height
fixed-width design, columns
in, 388–389
of headers, 84
line-height property, 413
high-content design, 72,
237–286

center column, adding, 255–267
comment tags, using, 265, 276
containers, placement of, 241–242
framework in XHTML and CSS, building, 242–245
header row, adding, 245–249
left column, creating, 249–255
second-level pages
three columns, constructing page with, 267–277
two columns, constructing page with, 277–286
structure of design, 238–239
three columns, constructing page with, 267–277
two columns, constructing page with, 277–286
Holly hack, 195
homepages
duplicating source file for, 159–161
framework graphics, 417–418
mortised XHTML homepage, 137–138
horizontal layout, 83–84
horizontal scrollbars, adding, 409
horizontally-structured menus, 67–68
hot spots, 310
<HR> tag
creating lines without, 397–398
rendering, 395–397
HTML editor, opening files in, 428
HTML (Hypertext Markup Language), 2. *See also* mouseovers
<HTML> tag
in background-based design, 315–316
for full-height three-column layout, 294
in high-content design, 244
in low-content design, 164–165
in medium-content design, 203
hyperlinks. *See* links

I
icons, layering, 411
ID class, calling, 376
ideograms, 9–10
IFrames, 25–27
image buttons, 27–28
image-mapping, 300
for menus, 68
images. *See also* background images; compression; mouseovers; source image files; stock images
corner images, rounding container edges with, 418–419
framework graphics, 417–418
image buttons, 27–28
misusing formats, 126–132
reusing images, 417–419
templates, customizing images in, 426
thumbnails, 34–35
uncompressed images, 33–34
saving, 126–127
images folder, 80
importing/exporting CSS style sheets, 106
include files, 54–55, 109
indenting code, 420
inline-level tags, 105–106
Internet Explorer, 18
box model, interpretation of, 154
branching and, 22–23
e-newsletters, sending, 447
Tantek hack and, 370–374
usage statistics and, 20–22
Intranet sites, bandwidth of, 44
ISP usage and bandwidth, 44
istockphoto.com, 82

J
Java applet menus, 68
JavaScript. *See also* mortised sites
browsers supporting, 20–22
comment tags, troubleshooting with, 405–406
dropdown menus, using, 400–401
HTML editor, opening files in, 428

menus, 68
mouseover code, names for, 429
JavaServer Pages. *See* JSP (JavaServer Pages)
JPG format, 24–25
color depth and, 52
gradations, saving images with, 121–123
increasing/decreasing compression, 133
mixing GIF and JPG formats, 128–129
over-compressing images, 129–130
solid colors as JPG, saving, 127–128
top of photo, saving text on, 123–125
uncompressed images, 33–34
saving, 126–127
using JPGs, 121–125
JSP (JavaServer Pages), 2
include files, 109
mortised sites and, 15
and multimedia software, 12
judging Web design, 6

L
<LABEL> tag for forms, 339
layers
and comps, 84–86
merging, 86
layout
for comps, 83–84
content, positioning, 64–65
creating, 63–65
flexible design and, 57–58
for low-content XHTML template, 353
mortising and, 93
scrolling, pros and cons of, 64
line drawings, GIF format for, 117
linear shapes, using, 412
line-height property, 413
linklist style, 247–248
for full-height three-column layout, 306
links
in background-based design, 320–321

CSS style sheets, 106
in headers, 64–65
in high-content design,
247–248
hover links, 208
low-content XHTML tem-
plate, linking style sheets
for, 357
print style sheets, 106–108
liquid design, 138
fixed-width CSS design,
creating from, 394–395
in medium-content design,
214, 222
logos
in headers, 64–65
in high-content design, 248
in medium-content design,
207
look requirements, 38
low-content design, 70–71,
157–196
center (right) column,
adding, 176–182
floating containers, adding,
189–195
framework in XHTML and
CSS, creating, 163–165
header content, adding,
165–169
left column, creating,
170–176
nesting left and right
columns in, 169–170
second-level pages,
constructing, 182–188
low-content XHTML template,
351–367
bgcolor attribute, 365
center column, adding image
to, 360–361
content table, creating,
361–365
design, creating, 352
expansion requirements, 353
footer information, creating,
365–367
guides, adding, 354–355
headers in, 353–354
linking style sheets, 357
menu table, creating,
357–360
mouseovers in, 355

parent table, creating,
355–356
slices, adding, 354–355
strengths and weakness of
design, 352–354
style sheets, creating, 357
width of design, 354

M
Macromedia Flash. *See* Flash
margins
<FORM> tag, controlling
margins in, 406–408
for forms, 337
full-height three-column
layout, properties for, 294
in low-content design, 165
margin:0px property, 152
order of shortcuts, remembering, 401
removing body margins,
378–379
masks
comps using, 86
for replacing photos,
431–435
medium-content design, 70–71,
197–235
bottom content area, adding,
216–224
center content area, adding,
216–224
containers, placement of,
200–201
framework in XHTML and
CSS, creating, 202–204
guides in, 199–200
left column, adding, 204–209
liquid design, using, 214,
222
nesting center and right
columns with <DIV> tag,
209–210
right content area, adding,
216–224
second-level pages
three columns, construct-
ing page with, 224–230
two columns, construct-
ing page with, 230–235
slices in, 199–200
structure of design, 198–201
style sheets for, 229

three columns, constructing
page with, 224–230
top-right images, adding,
210–216
two columns, constructing
page with, 230–235
wrapping <DIV> tags in,
215
menus. *See also* mouseovers;
navigation
background images for, 30
consistency in, 66
flexibility of design and, 56
in high-content design,
264–265
horizontally-structured
menus, 67–68
JavaScript dropdown menus,
using, 400–401
in low-content design, 175
in low-content XHTML
template, 352–353
in medium-content design,
208
number of menus, limiting,
66
positioning of, 64
text for items in, 66
types of, 68–70
vertically-structured menus,
67–68
width of, 68, 84
merging layers, 86
Microsoft. *See also* Internet
Explorer; .NET
PowerPoint flowcharts,
creating, 42
SharePoint Designer, 13
Visio flowcharts, creating,
42–43
modular sites, 54
include files, using, 54–55
monitors. *See also* resolution
color depth, 51–53
mortised sites. *See also* CSS
(Cascading Style Sheets)
absolute positioning in,
94–95
advantages of, 93–94
background images,
mortising, 97
concept of, 90–99
modularity of, 15

nested mortised containers, 90

philosophy of, 13–15

pros and cons of, 14–15

relative positioning in, 94–95

seamlessly pieced-together images, 91–93

steps in building, 90

tags for building, 100–101

XHTML, 13

homepage, 137–138

mouseovers, 27

coding for, 399–400

in e-mail templates, 355

JavaScript mouseover code, names for, 429

in low-content design, 175

for menus, 69

reusing images for, 418

multimedia sites, 11–12

N

naming/renaming

consistency in conventions, 61

JavaScript mouseover code, names for, 429

rules and properties, 374–378

site/client name, 39

unique conventions, using, 406

navigation. *See also* menus

consistency in, 66

developing, 65–70

flexibility of design and, 56

smart navigation, creating, 416–417

and usability, 8, 65–70, 416

nesting. *See also* <DIV> tag

mortised containers, 90

.NET, 2

include files, 109

mortised sites and, 15

and multimedia software, 12

Netscape, 398

branching and, 22–23

newsletters, sending, 447

Nicholls, Stuart, 69

novelty and technology, 5

O

objectives of site, 40

online applications, usage statistics from, 22

Opera, spacing in, 379

optimizing images in templates, 427–428

over-compressing images, 129–131

P

padding, 254

for full-height three-column layout, 294

order of shortcuts, remembering, 401

padding:0px property, 152

removing, 378–379

PDAs (personal data assistants), 18

Peek-a-boo bug, 195

percentages, 409–410

philosophies of Web design, 7

phone lines, condition of, 44

photographs. *See also* JPG format

GIF, saving photo as, 127

Photoshop. *See also* full-height three-column layout; guides; mortised sites; slices; source image files; templates

building designs in, 159

Color Picker, 208, 439–440

colors of design, tutorial for changing, 438–441

for comps, 78–79

History States setting, configuring, 442–443

layers, developing, 85–86

Layers panel, working with, 432–434

marching ants, displaying, 434

redoing actions in, 442

replacing photos, tutorial for, 431–435

resizing photos, tutorial for, 435–437

tutorials, 430–443

Undo Actions setting, configuring, 442–443

undoing actions in, 441

PHP format

include files, 109

mortised sites and, 15

pixels, 409–410

PNG format, 114

points, 409–410

PowerPoint flowcharts, creating, 42

preparation information, 39

Print Preview mode, 107–108

printing

globally driven <SPAN> and <DIV> tags for, 410

style sheets, 106–108

project name folder, 80

properties. *See also* background properties

in CSS, 102

naming, 374–378

proposed solutions, 40

PSD files. *See* Photoshop

R

rasterizing text, 86

rebrandable sites

hidden tags, including, 412–413

non-graphical elements for, 410–412

redoing actions in Photoshop, 442

relative absolute positioning in mortised sites, 94–95

relative positioning

for box model, 150–154

of headers, 167–168

relative sites, designing, 49–51

repeating background images, 30–32, 398–399

replacing photos, Photoshop tutorial for, 431–435

required fields in forms, 337

requirements. *See* site requirements

resizing photos, Photoshop tutorial for, 435–437

resolution

critical mass determination, 47

fixed sites, designing, 49–51

menu structure and, 67

relative sites, designing, 49–51

requirements, 38, 45–49

resources

for color theory, 83

for stock images, 82

reusable elements for rebrandable sites, 410–412

rounded edges/corners, use of, 84
rounding container images, 418–419
royalties and stock images, 81
RSS (really simple syndication), 40
rules
  in CSS (Cascading Style Sheets), 103
  naming, 374–378
  of Web design, 5–6

S
saving. *See also* GIF format; JPG format
  gradations, saving images with, 121–123
  templates, saving images in, 427–428
  transparent backgrounds, 160
  uncompressed images, 126–127
  versions, saving documents in different, 41
scalability
  designing for, 54–58
  flexible design, creating, 55–58
  include files, using, 54–55
  requirements, 38
Scalable Vector Graphics (SVG), 113
scope creep, 38
scroll bars, 26
  horizontal scrollbars, adding, 409
  pros and cons of scrolling, 64
search engines
  and framed sites, 26
  of image buttons, 27
second-level pages. *See also* high-content design; medium-content design
  background-based design, constructing pages in, 331
  full-height three-column layout, constructing in, 307
  guides and slices for, 160–161
  low-content design, constructing in, 182–188
selectors in CSS, 102

semicolons, missing, 375
shadows. *See* drop shadows
shapes, using, 412
SharePoint Designer, 13
shortcuts
  CSS shortcuts, using, 409
  margin order, remembering, 401
  padding order, remembering, 401
shorthand properties in CSS, 102
Siegel, David, 13
signature file, sending e-mails with, 447
sign-offs, 40
  on site requirements, 41
site maps, 60
site requirements
  collecting, 39–41
  documentation of, 41
  flowcharts, 42–43
  front-end requirements, 41–42
  gathering requirements, 74–78
  using, 38–39
slices
  in background-based design, 311–313
  for full-height three-column layout, 288–290
  in high-content design, 239–241
  in low-content design, 159–161
  low-content XHTML template, adding in, 354–355
  in medium-content design, 199–200
smart navigation, creating, 416–417
SmarterStats, 21–22
software
  compression software, understanding, 132–133, 400
  multimedia software, 12
  Web logs, analysis of, 21–22
source directory, creating, 79–80
source image files
  breaking out sections of, 414–416

creating, 414
sources folder, 80
spacer GIFs, 310. *See also* low-content XHTML template
spaces
  <DIV> tag and, 168–169
  removing, 378–379, 420–421
<SPAN> tag, 90, 92, 105–106
  in box model, 149
  CSS sites using, 138
  for forms, 339
  navigation rules, replacing, 107
  printing, globally driven tags for, 410
specifications, dealing with, 6
speed and bandwidth, 23–25
standards
  bandwidth standards, 23
  for browsers, 18
  working with, 6
stock images
  collecting/documenting, 80–82
  folder for, 80
  resources for, 82
style sheets. *See also* CSS (Cascading Style Sheets)
  for forms, 336–338
  for low-content XHTML template, 357
  in medium-content design, 229
  naming rules and properties, 374–378
  print style sheets, 106–108

T
<TABLE> tag, 360
tables. *See also* low-content XHTML template; XHTML (Extensible Hypertext Markup Language)
  CSS, including XHTML tables in, 154–155
taglines in headers, 65
Tantek hack, 102–103, 370–374
  in high-content design, 254
  in low-content design, 195
  rules, naming, 377–378
targeting frames, 26
technical standards, 3
templates. *See also* low-content XHTML template

CD, templates included on, 445–726
code, customizing, 428–429
colors, customizing, 426
HTML editor, opening files in, 428
images, customizing, 426
main Photoshop file, opening, 425–426
optimizing images, 427–428
saving images in, 427–428
steps to customizing, 424–430
testing design, 430
text, customizing, 428–429
testing
  CSS designs in browsers, 155–156
  template design, 430
  tips for, 413
  in usability philosophy, 8
text. *See also* GIF format; JPG format; mortised sites
  brain and processing of, 9–10
  for menu items, 66
  rasterizing, 86
  templates, customizing text in, 428–429
<TEXTAREA> tag, 343
thumbnails, 34–35
  GIF format for, 118–119
TIF format, 132
times, site including, 39
title areas, design of, 57–58
transparency. *See also*
  background-based design
  of backgrounds, 160
  GIF format and, 114
troubleshooting
  background properties for, 402–404
  border properties for, 402–404
  commenting out code for, 405–406
  floating containers, bugs with, 195

tucows.com, 420
tutorials in Photoshop, 430–443

U
uncompressed images. *See* images; JPG format
undoing actions in Photoshop, 441
usability, 7–11. *See also* accessibility
  architecture and, 60–63
  and content, 70–72
  of headers, 64–65
  layout and, 63–65
  navigation and, 8, 65–70, 416
users
  browsers and, 20–22
  judging Web design, 6

V
validating code, 154–155
values in CSS, 102
vector images, 112–114
  multimedia sites and, 12
versions
  of requirement document, 40
  resolutions, differing, 51
  saving documents in different versions, 41
vertical layout, 83–84
vertically-structured menus, 67–68
vischeck.com, 83
Visio flowcharts, creating, 42–43

W
Web logs and browsers, 20–22
Web resources. *See* resources
WebTrends, 21
weight of page, 23–24
width. *See also* fixed-width CSS design
  CSS form design, labels in, 335

and low-content XHTML design, 354
menu requirements, 68, 84
  Tantek hack and, 370–374
wrapping <DIV> tags
  in fixed-width CSS design, 390
  in medium-content design, 215
writing in usability philosophy, 8
W3C Schools, statistics from, 156
W3C validating code, 154–155
WYSIWYG and mortised sites, 13

X
XHTML (Extensible Hypertext Markup Language), 2. *See also* full-height three-column layout; high-content design; low-content design; medium-content design; mortised sites
  basic tags in, 100–101
  browsers and, 18–20
  code compared to CSS, 140–147
  comment tags, troubleshooting with, 405
  compression software, 420
  CSS-based design compared, 136–149
  HTML editor, opening files in, 428
  inline characters produced by, 411
  low-content XHTML template, 351–367
  nesting tables in, 138
  understanding, 99–101
  using XHTML tables, 154–155
  validating code, 154–155
XHTML Markup Validation Service, 155

License Agreement/Notice of Limited Warranty